John Steuart Curry
INVENTING THE MIDDLE WEST

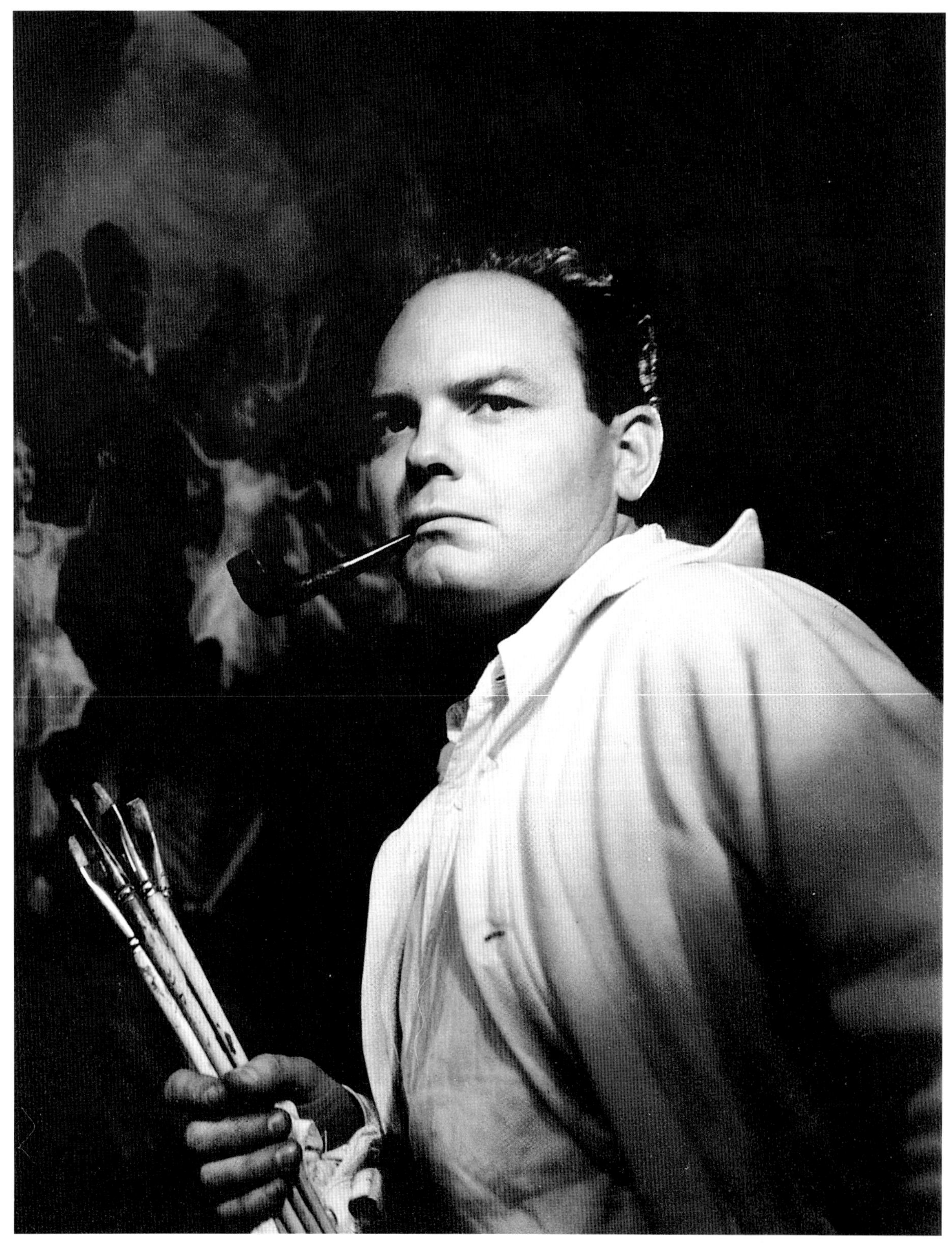

John Steuart Curry
INVENTING THE MIDDLE WEST

PATRICIA JUNKER

With contributions by

HENRY ADAMS

CHARLES C. ELDREDGE

ROBERT L. GAMBONE

M. SUE KENDALL

LUCY J. MATHIAK

THEODORE F. WOLFF

HUDSON HILLS PRESS NEW YORK

In association with the Elvehjem Museum of Art, University of Wisconsin–Madison

First Edition

Published in the United States by Hudson Hills Press, Inc., Suite 1308, 230 Fifth Avenue, New York, NY 10001-7704.

Distributed in the United States, its territories and possessions, and Canada by National Book Network.

Distributed in the United Kingdom, Eire, and Europe by Art Books International Ltd.

Editor and Publisher: **Paul Anbinder**

Assistant Editor and Proofreader: **Faye Chiu**

Copy Editor: **Phil Freshman**

Indexer: **Karla J. Knight**

Designer: **Martin Lubin**

Composition: **Angela Taormina**

Manufactured in Japan by Dai Nippon Printing Company.

Library of Congress Cataloguing-in-Publication Data

Junker, Patricia A.
John Steuart Curry : inventing the Middle West / Patricia Junker ; with contributions by Henry Adams . . . [et al.]. — 1st ed.
p. cm.
Catalogue of an exhibition held at the Elvehjem Museum of Art, University of Wisconsin–Madison, Mar. 7–May 17, 1998, the Fine Arts Museums of San Francisco, June 13–Aug. 30, 1998, and the Nelson-Atkins Museum of Art, Kansas City, Mo., Oct. 11, 1998–Jan. 3, 1999.
Includes bibliographical references and index.
ISBN 1-55595-139-2 (cloth : alk. paper).
1. Curry, John Steuart, 1897–1946—Exhibitions. 2. Regionalism in art—United States—Exhibitions. 3. Middle West—In art—Exhibitions. I. Curry, John Steuart, 1897–1946. II. Adams, Henry, 1949– . III. Elvehjem Museum of Art. IV. Fine Arts Museums of San Francisco. V. Nelson-Atkins Museum of Art. VI. Title.
ND237.C88A4 1998 97-49621
759.13—dc21 CIP

This book is published on the occasion of the exhibition *John Steuart Curry: Inventing the Middle West,* organized by Patricia Junker in association with the Elvehjem Museum of Art.

SCHEDULE OF THE EXHIBITION

Elvehjem Museum of Art, University of Wisconsin–Madison
March 7–May 17, 1998

Fine Arts Museums of San Francisco
June 13–August 30, 1998

Nelson-Atkins Museum of Art
Kansas City, Missouri
October 11, 1998–January 3, 1999

Funding for *John Steuart Curry: Inventing the Middle West* has been provided by The Henry Luce Foundation, Inc.; the National Endowment for the Humanities, a federal agency; the National Endowment for the Arts, a federal agency; the Anonymous Fund, Brittingham Fund, Inc., Evjue Foundation, Inc./The Capital Times; Walter and Dorothy Frautschi; Wisconsin Sesquicentennial Commission with funds from individual and corporate contributors and the State of Wisconsin; Dane County Cultural Affairs Commission with additional support from the Madison Community Foundation; the Wisconsin Humanities Council and the National Endowment for the Humanities; and the Wisconsin Arts Board with funds from the State of Wisconsin.

At the Fine Arts Museums of San Francisco, the exhibition has been made possible by the Ednah Root Foundation.

Frontispiece: John Steuart Curry in his Westport, Connecticut, studio with the oil *Gospel Train,* 1929. Photograph courtesy Mrs. John Steuart Curry.

CONTENTS

DIRECTOR'S FOREWORD

It is highly appropriate that the Elvehjem Museum of Art of the University of Wisconsin–Madison undertake a new assessment of John Steuart Curry and his place in American art. Curry came to Madison in 1936 as the country's first university artist-in-residence. His appointment to this position at the College of Agriculture came under the broad aegis of the Wisconsin Idea. This progressive plan was first formulated in the 1920s to promote the economic, social, intellectual, and moral development of the people of the state. The Wisconsin Idea led to the creation of the Elvehjem in 1970, and it continues to be central to the university's mission. Like the experiment that brought Curry and his art to rural Wisconsin, the museum's purpose is to make art available and serve as an educational resource to the state.

The present exhibition does not attempt to be a comprehensive retrospective; rather, it brings together a selection of Curry's finest work. Many of the paintings included have not been on public view for more than twenty-five years. Furthermore, the authors of this catalogue have drawn extensively on a good deal of archival material in public and private collections that has never been subject to scholarly examination. As well, several of the authors have conducted interviews with Curry's family members, friends, associates, and fellow artists that have yielded important facts and anecdotes. Research for this exhibition and book was greatly facilitated by Mrs. John Steuart Curry, the artist's close friend William McCloy, and Curry's son-in-law, the late Dr. Daniel Schuster. These three provided unprecedented access to Curry's personal papers, library, and the artworks remaining in his estate. Their openness and generosity, combined with the hard work of exhibition curator Patricia Junker and her coauthors, have helped produce the most thorough assessment of the artist's career and milieu to date.

An encompassing array of Curry's art has been selected for the exhibition and catalogue from public and private collections around the country. Collectively, the works displayed provide both a broad overview and an intimate insight into a rich oeuvre whose influence is still felt among artists today. The exhibition travels to the Fine Arts Museums of San Francisco and to the Nelson-Atkins Museum of Art in Kansas City, Missouri. I wish to thank the directors of those institutions, Harry S. Parker III and Marc Wilson, respectively, for their cooperation.

I also thank Patricia Junker for her durable enthusiasm for John Steuart Curry, for diligently working out the concept of the project, and for putting together the sterling roster of catalogue contributors: Henry Adams, Charles C. Eldredge, Robert L. Gambone, M. Sue Kendall, Lucy J. Mathiak, and Theodore F. Wolff. Patricia herself wrote two essays and compiled the extensive annotated chronology, which vitally enhances our understanding of the artist. From the time of the initial project-planning meeting in November 1994, the writers have evinced strong commitment to this undertaking and have, by their involvement, made a lasting contribution to American art-historical scholarship. We thank Walter Frautschi for underwriting the meetings that set the plans for this book and exhibition in motion.

The expertise and support of our museum staff were essential to mounting the exhibition and preparing this book. I especially want to recognize Patricia Powell, the museum's editor, for securing the many photographs that accompany the essays and chronology and for helping to move the publication along. Thanks go as well to Preparator Jerl Richmond for his innovative installation at the Elvehjem and Registrar Pam Richardson for superintending the shipping and crating of the artworks.

I also want to acknowledge the public and private lenders to the exhibition, listed on page 245. Without their cooperation, *John Steuart Curry: Inventing the Middle West* would not have had the depth and comprehensiveness that so clearly distinguish it.

Finally, it gives me great pleasure to thank our major sponsors: funding for *John Steuart Curry: Inventing the Middle West* has been provided by The Henry Luce Foundation, Inc.; the National Endowment for the Humanities, a federal agency; the National Endowment for the Arts, a federal agency; the Anonymous Fund, Brittingham Fund, Inc., Evjue Foundation, Inc./The Capital Times; Walter and Dorothy Frautschi; Wisconsin Sesquicentennial Commission with funds from individual and corporate contributors and the State of Wisconsin; Dane County Cultural Affairs Commission with additional support from the Madison Community Foundation; the Wisconsin Humanities Council and the National Endowment for the Humanities; and the Wisconsin Arts Board with funds from the State of Wisconsin. Taken together, their support truly made this landmark project feasible.

Russell Panczenko
Director
Elvehjem Museum of Art
University of Wisconsin–Madison

CURATOR'S ACKNOWLEDGMENTS

John Steuart Curry wanted nothing so much as to bring his art to a wide audience, and this exhibition and book continue to make that possible. Gathering the present large group of pictures and so much new material on Curry's life and career has required the work of many dedicated people. I am pleased to be able to acknowledge their help here.

This project was conceived at the Elvehjem Museum of Art, University of Wisconsin–Madison, and the staff of that institution has carried it through to completion. I owe special thanks to Director Russell Panczenko for his unflagging enthusiasm, even when we were forced into a long-distance collaboration by my move to San Francisco in 1992. Registrar Pam Richardson has carried out complex shipping and crating plans with great facility. Assistant Director for Administration Corinne Magnoni oversaw planning and funding details, while Development Specialists Rebecca Olson Garrity and Kathy Paul helped prepare grant proposals. Curator of Prints and Drawings Andrew Stevens and Curator of Education Anne Lambert have helped with numerous aspects of presentation, and Preparator Jerl Richmond has overseen installation of the exhibition. Editor Pat Powell assisted with editing the manuscript and gathered illustrations.

To Paul Anbinder of Hudson Hills Press I offer especially warm thanks for his masterly production of this book. I also wish to thank copy editor Phil Freshman for his careful reading and shaping of the manuscript. Thomas O'Sullivan and Susan Curvin Jones offered Mr. Freshman editorial counsel.

At the Nelson-Atkins Museum of Art, the project won early support from Director Marc Wilson and especially from Margaret Conrads, the Samuel Sosland Curator of American Art.

My colleagues at the Fine Arts Museums of San Francisco have honored my effort by sharing in this exhibition. Director Harry S. Parker III and Associate Director and Chief Curator Steven A. Nash followed the progress of my work for several years and welcomed the show in San Francisco. Those responsible for mounting the exhibition at my home institution include Exhibitions Designer Bill White, Coordinator of Exhibitions Kathe Hodgson, Registrar Therese Chen, Director of Media Relations Pamela Forbes, Director of Marketing Paula March, Director of Development Barbara Boucke, paintings conservators Ulrich Birkmeier, Carl Grimm, Patricia O'Regan, and Tony Rockwell, and Lighting Engineer William Huggins. Marion Hitchcock proved an invaluable assistant as a summer intern in 1997.

I wish to extend special thanks to Mr. and Mrs. J. Burgess Jamieson, whose gift made possible the acquisition of Curry's extraordinary 1937 *Self-Portrait* for the Fine Arts Museums. That painting has been an important catalyst to this project.

The Ednah Root Foundation, which supports all of the Fine Arts Museums' programs in American art, has generously underwritten presentation of the exhibition in San Francisco.

Access to the rich resources of the American Art Study Center, housed in the M. H. de Young Memorial Museum, greatly facilitated my work on the catalogue essays and chronology. The study center is a public facility combining the holdings of the Bothin Library of books and periodicals and the microfilmed collections of the Smithsonian Institution's Archives of American Art. Having this wealth of material available just beyond my office door enabled me to dig deeply into primary sources. I wish to thank secretary Jane Glover for her research assistance in the study center and Librarian Allison Pennell. My colleagues Renée Dreyfus, curator of ancient art, and Marion Stewart, associate curator of European paintings, also aided my research.

A great many people at institutions across the country assisted with research as well. They include: Emily Clark, associate librarian, Chicago Historical Society; Fred Dahlinger, Jr., director, Robert L. Parkinson Library and Research Center, Circus World Museum, Baraboo, Wisconsin; Mollie Donovan, John Steuart Curry Fresco Restoration Committee, Westport, Connecticut; Abigail Booth Gerdts; Professor William H. Gerdts, Graduate School and University Center, City University of New York; Edward Alan Gokey, Syracuse University; Professor Constance Cain Hungerford, Swarthmore College, Swarthmore, Pennsylvania; Don Lambert, Topeka, Kansas; Scott Shields, University of Kansas, Lawrence; Professor Gary Smith, Hartnell College, Salinas, California; and the staff of the Archives of American Art, especially New England Regional Director Bob Brown and Chief of Reference Services Judy Throm.

Throughout this project, I have had the great pleasure of a warm working relationship with the artist's family and friends. I am deeply grateful to Kathleen Curry, who welcomed me into her home and, over the years, shared her thoughts and insights in long, wonderful letters. Her own efforts to preserve and exhibit her husband's paintings since his death in 1946 have been extraordinary. We are extremely fortunate that she made the 1937 *Self-Portrait* available to the Fine Arts Museums. I cannot thank her enough for her generosity and help. Professor William McCloy, Curry's close friend and painting assistant—and a gifted painter in his own right—helped by sharing his knowledge of Curry's painting technique and by tracking down photographs and other materials. The delightful John Van Koert, a celebrated silversmith and longtime friend of the Currys, shared reminiscences as well. There are no words to convey the affection and appreciation that I feel for the late Dr. Daniel Schuster, the artist's son-in-law. It was he who first proposed this project, followed its progress daily, and gave to it his vast storehouse of knowledge and his great enthusiasm. He died without seeing the fruits of his labors, but his touch is everywhere in this book and exhibition.

To locate Curry paintings held in private collections, I relied heavily upon the assistance of several dealers. I wish to thank: John Driscoll, Babcock Galleries, New York; Martha Fleischman, Kennedy Galleries, Inc., New York; Gregory Hedberg, Hirschl and Adler Galleries, Inc., New York; Vivien Kiechel, Lincoln, Nebraska; Peter Rathbone, Sotheby's, New York; Andrew Schoelkopf, Christie's, New York; David Henry and D. Wigmore, D. Wigmore Fine Art, Inc., New York; and Rudolf Wunderlich, Mongerson Wunderlich Galleries, Chicago.

The lenders to this exhibition, listed at the back of this book, are most generous stewards of John Steuart Curry's paintings. I am pleased to thank, too, my fellow authors, all eminent authorities in the field of American art, whose collaboration has been a source of pride and inspiration for me.

I owe a debt of gratitude to my husband, David, for his careful reading of much of this text, for his patience, and for his many kindnesses. And, finally, I wish to dedicate this book to the memory of my mother, Lois Laurene Floyd.

Patricia Junker
San Francisco

Color Plates

Note to the reader

All works are by John Steuart Curry. Whenever possible, titles are given as assigned by the artist when each work was first exhibited. The artist's alternate or later titles appear in parentheses. Works marked with an asterisk are *not* included in the exhibition.

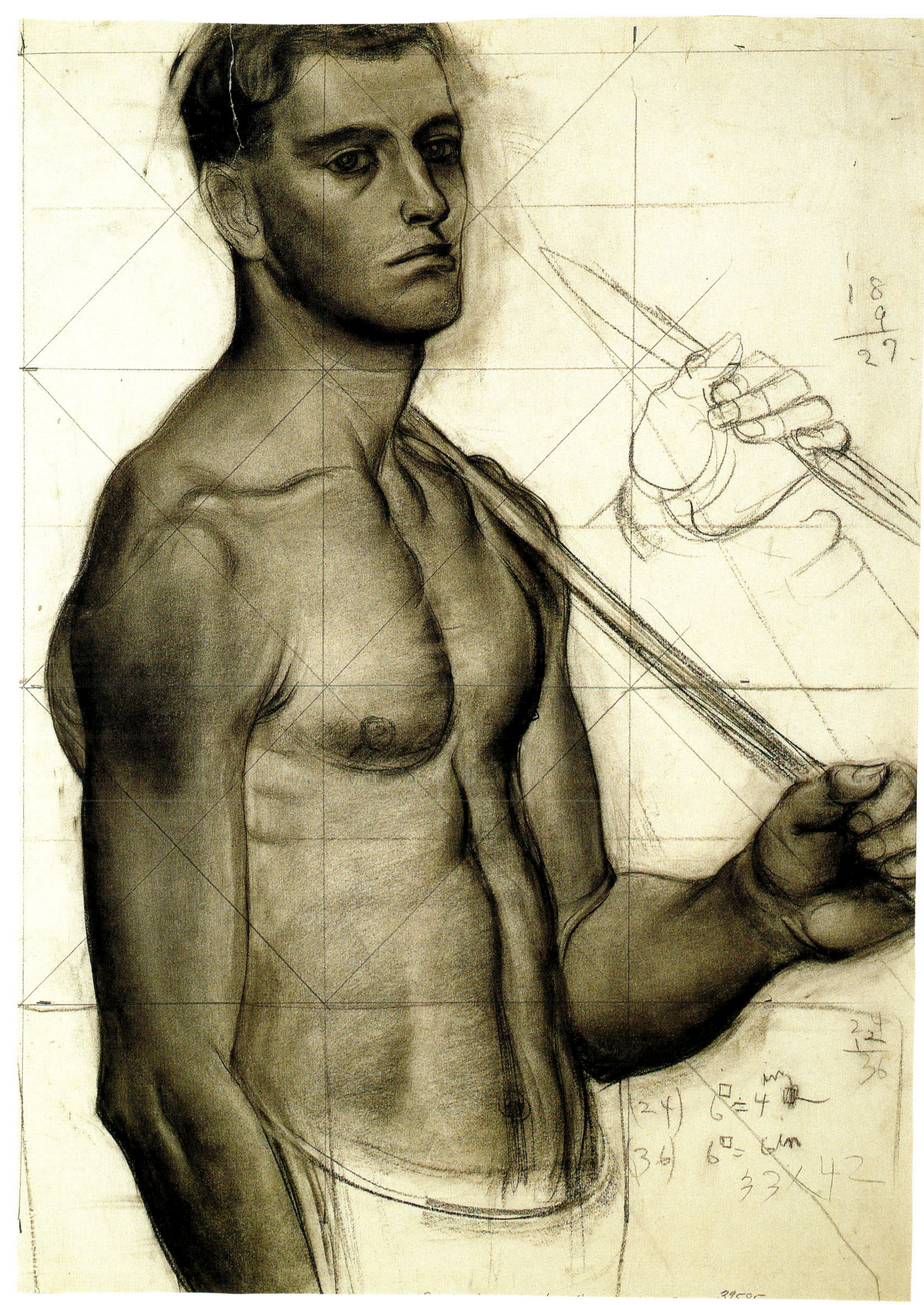

***PLATE 1**

Figure Study: Man with Staff,
1926–27

Charcoal on paper
24½ × 18½ in.
Estate of the artist. Courtesy Mongerson Wunderlich Gallery, Chicago.

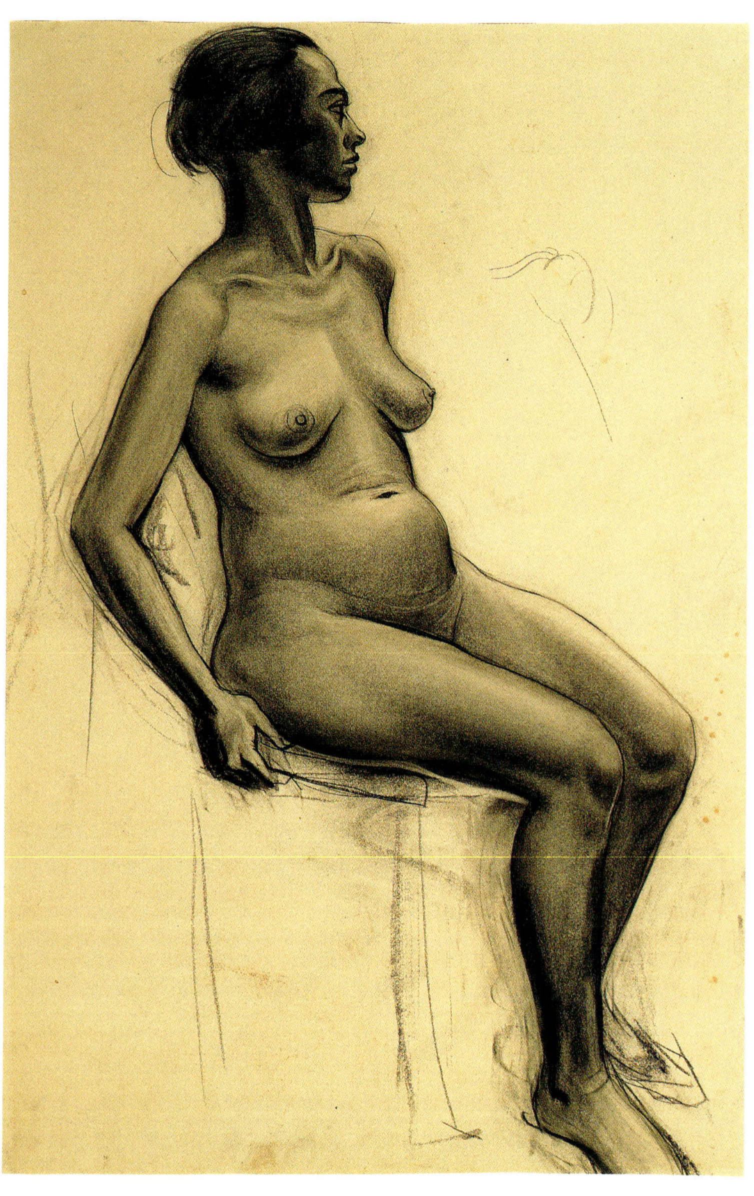

PLATE 2

Figure Study: Seated Female Nude, 1926–27
Charcoal on paper
24¼ × 16 in.
Estate of the artist. Courtesy Mongerson Wunderlich Gallery, Chicago.

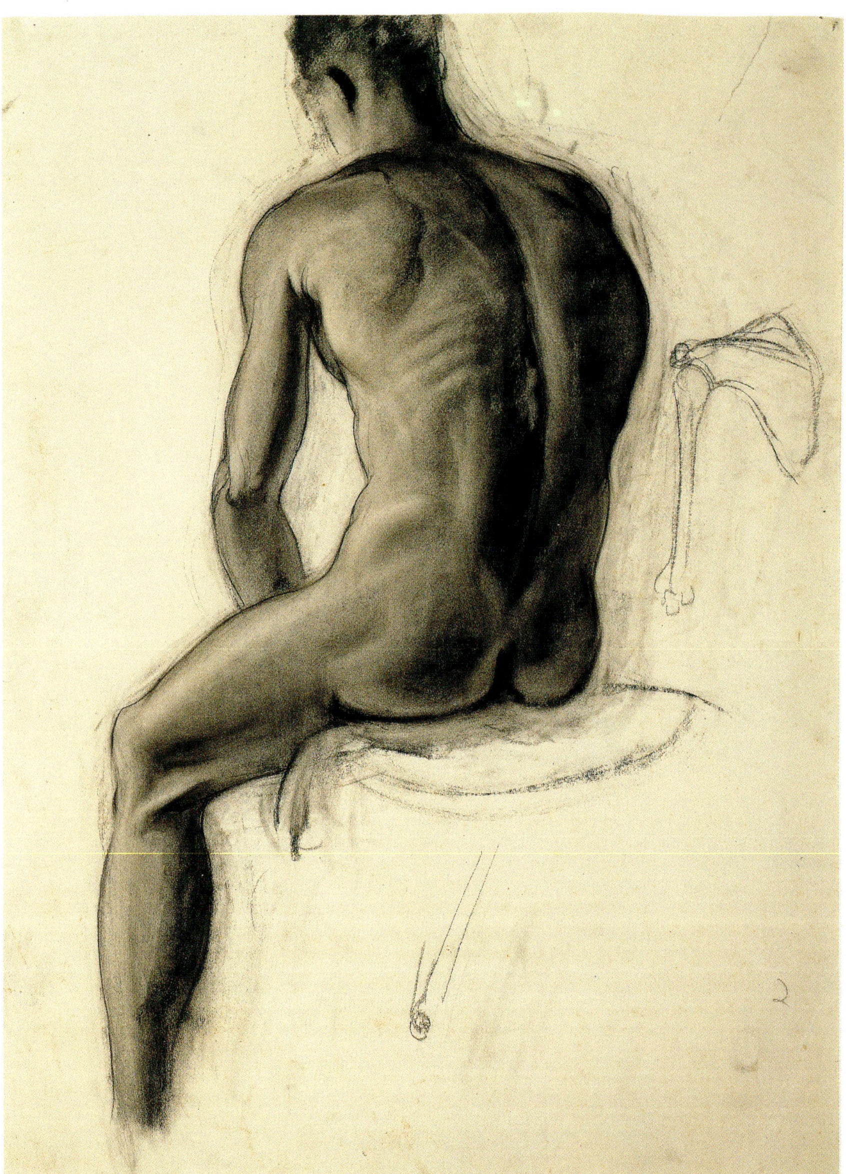

PLATE 3

Figure Study: Seated Male Nude, 1926–27
Charcoal on paper
25¼ × 19¼ in.
Estate of the artist. Courtesy Mongerson Wunderlich Gallery, Chicago.

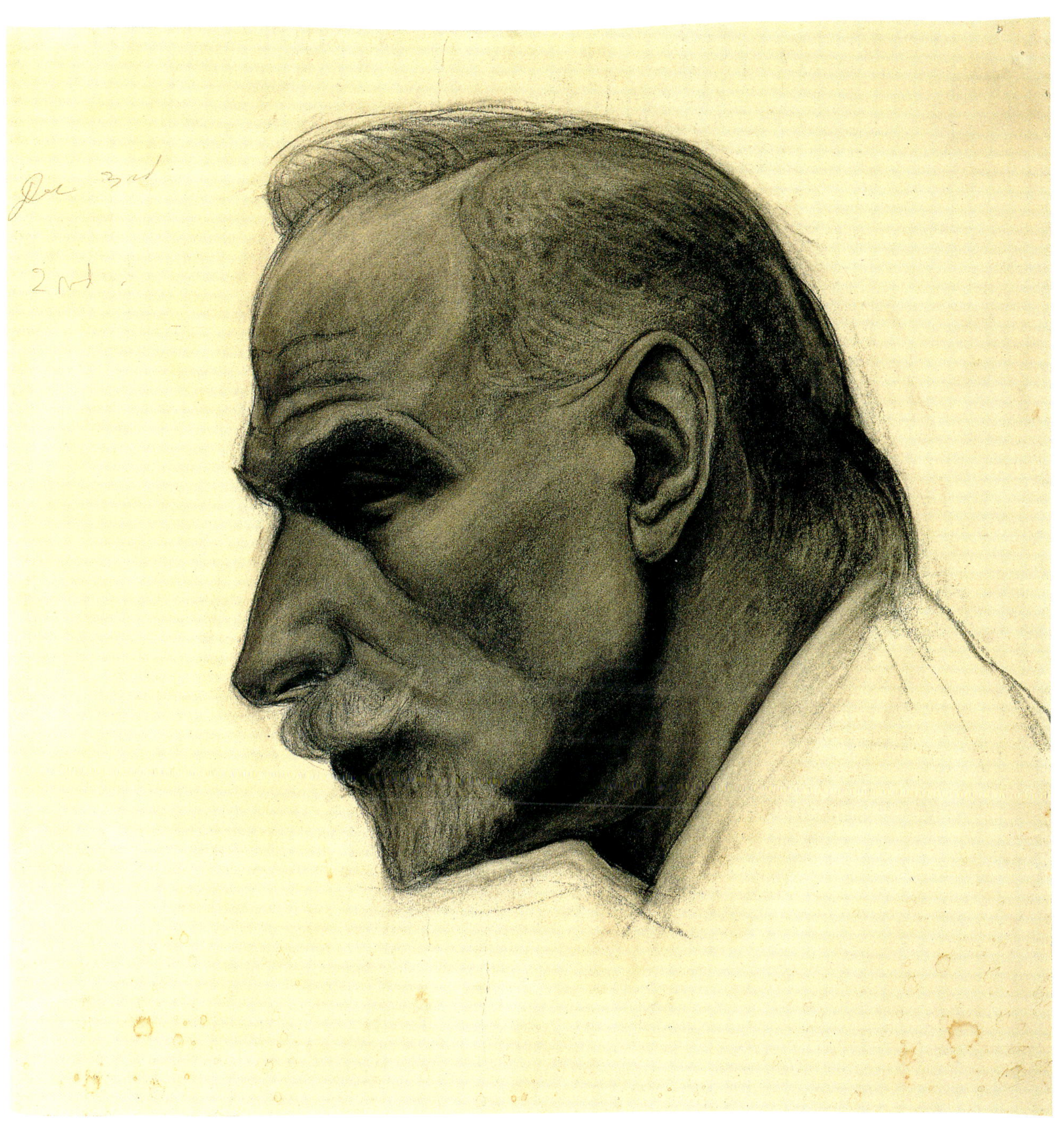

PLATE 4

Study of a Head: Man, 1926–27
Charcoal on paper
24 × 17 in.
Estate of the artist. Courtesy Mongerson Wunderlich Gallery, Chicago.

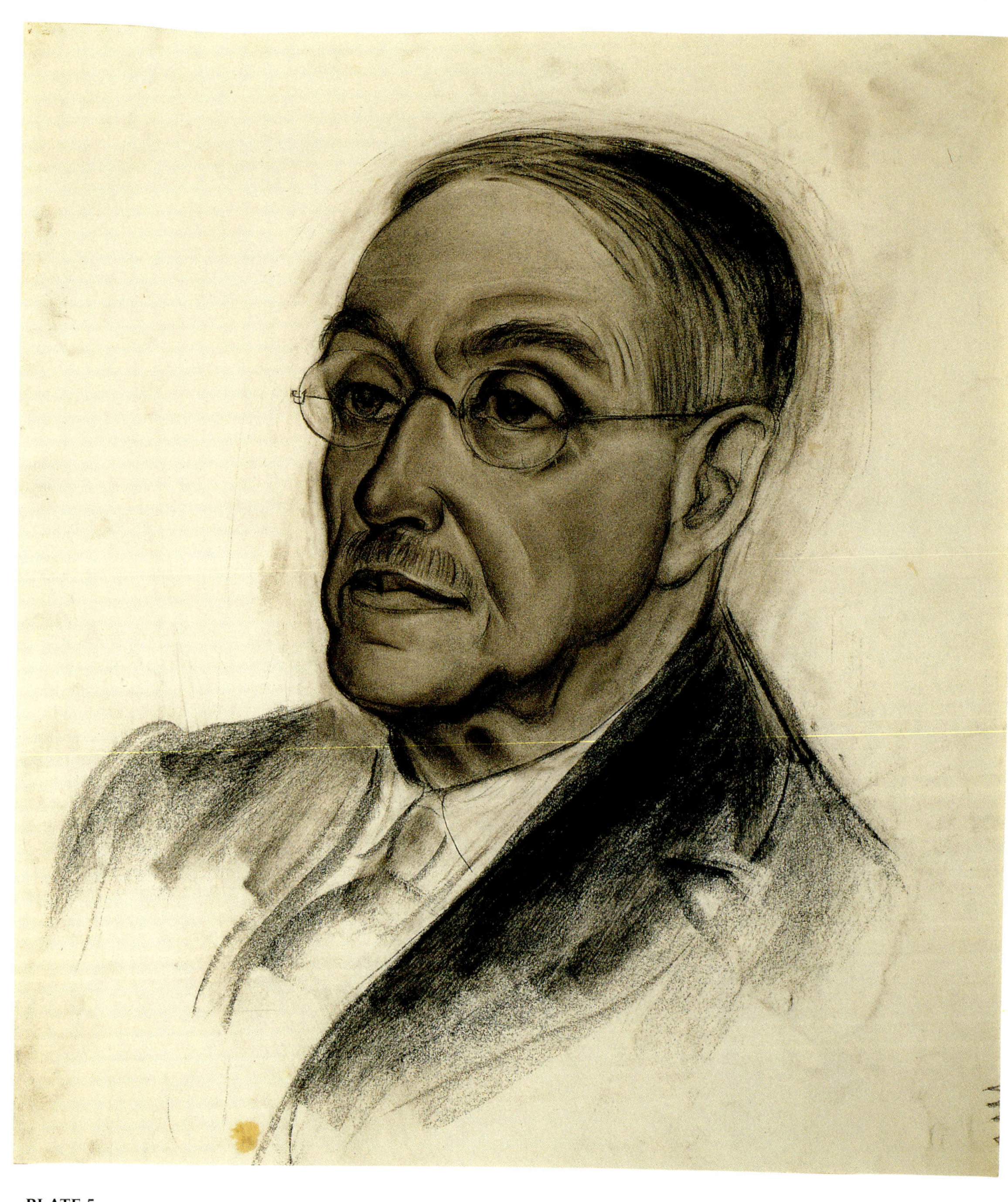

PLATE 5

Study of a Head: Man with Glasses, 1926–27
Charcoal on paper
25½ × 19¼ in.
Estate of the artist. Courtesy Mongerson Wunderlich Gallery, Chicago.

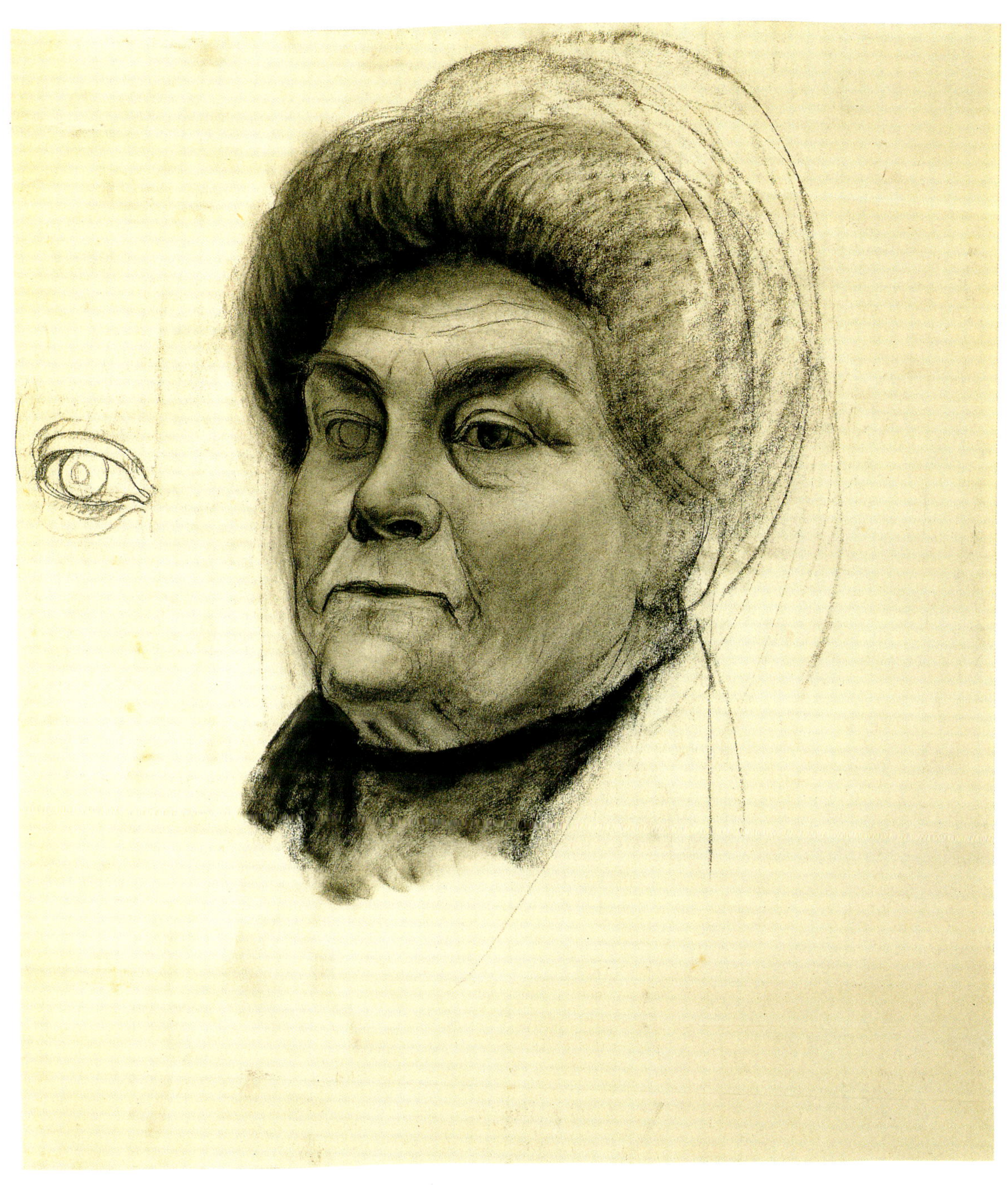

PLATE 6

Study of a Head: Woman, 1926–27
Charcoal on paper
19¼ × 17¼ in.
Estate of the artist. Courtesy Mongerson Wunderlich Gallery, Chicago.

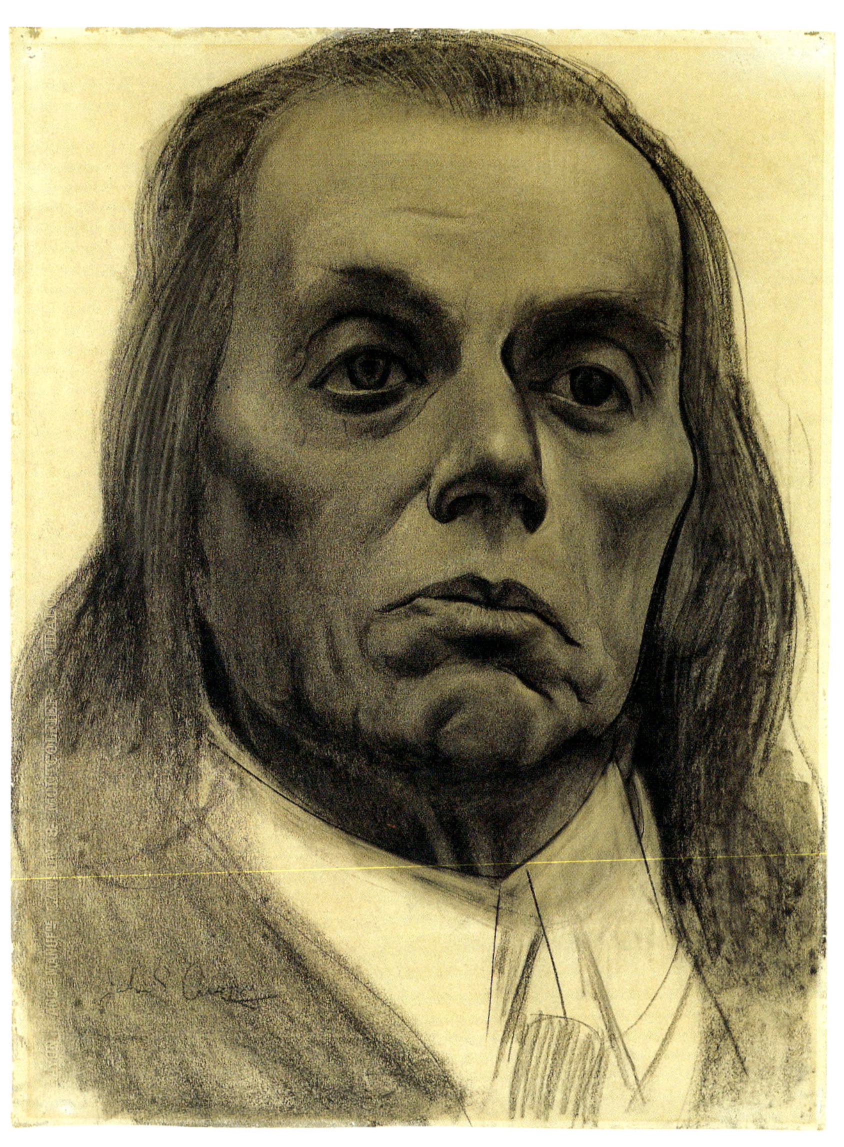

PLATE 7

Study of a Head: Italian Man, 1927
Charcoal on paper
24½ × 18½ in.
Signed lower left: *John S. Curry*
Elvehjem Museum of Art, University of Wisconsin–Madison.
University Fund purchase.

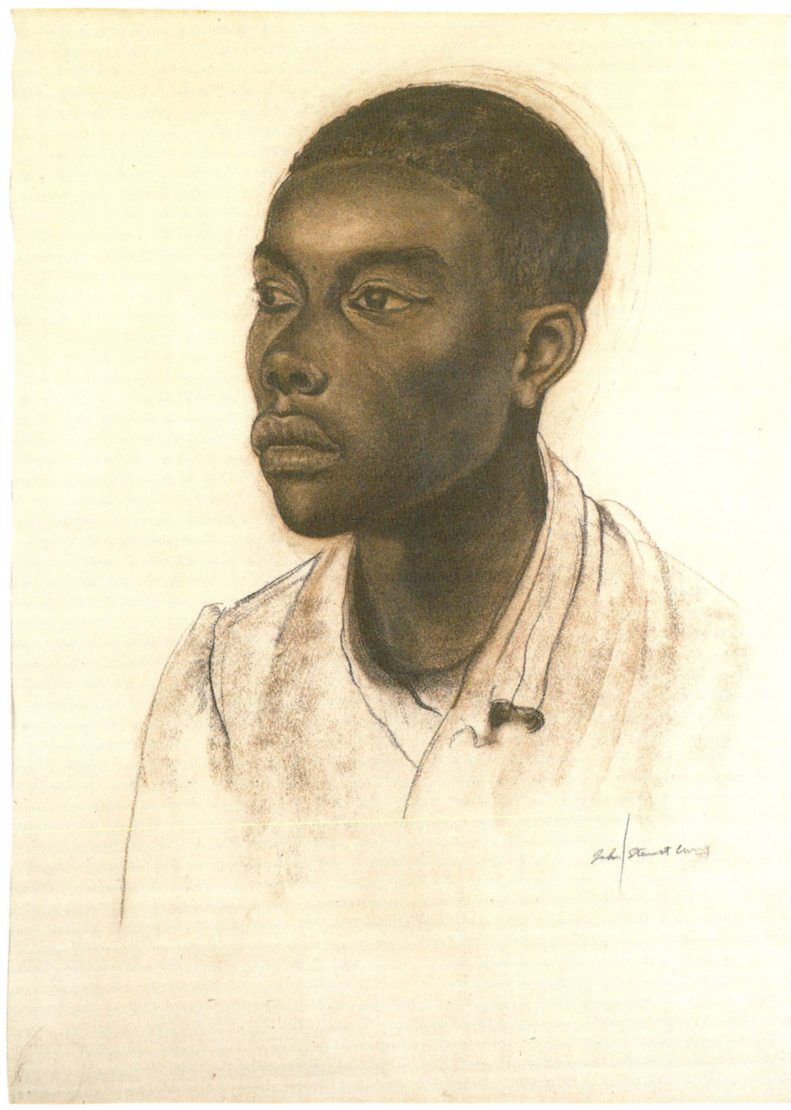

PLATE 8

Study of a Head: African American Youth, 1927
Conté on paper
20¾ × 15¾ in. (sight)
Signed lower right: *John Steuart Curry*
Mrs. John Steuart Curry.

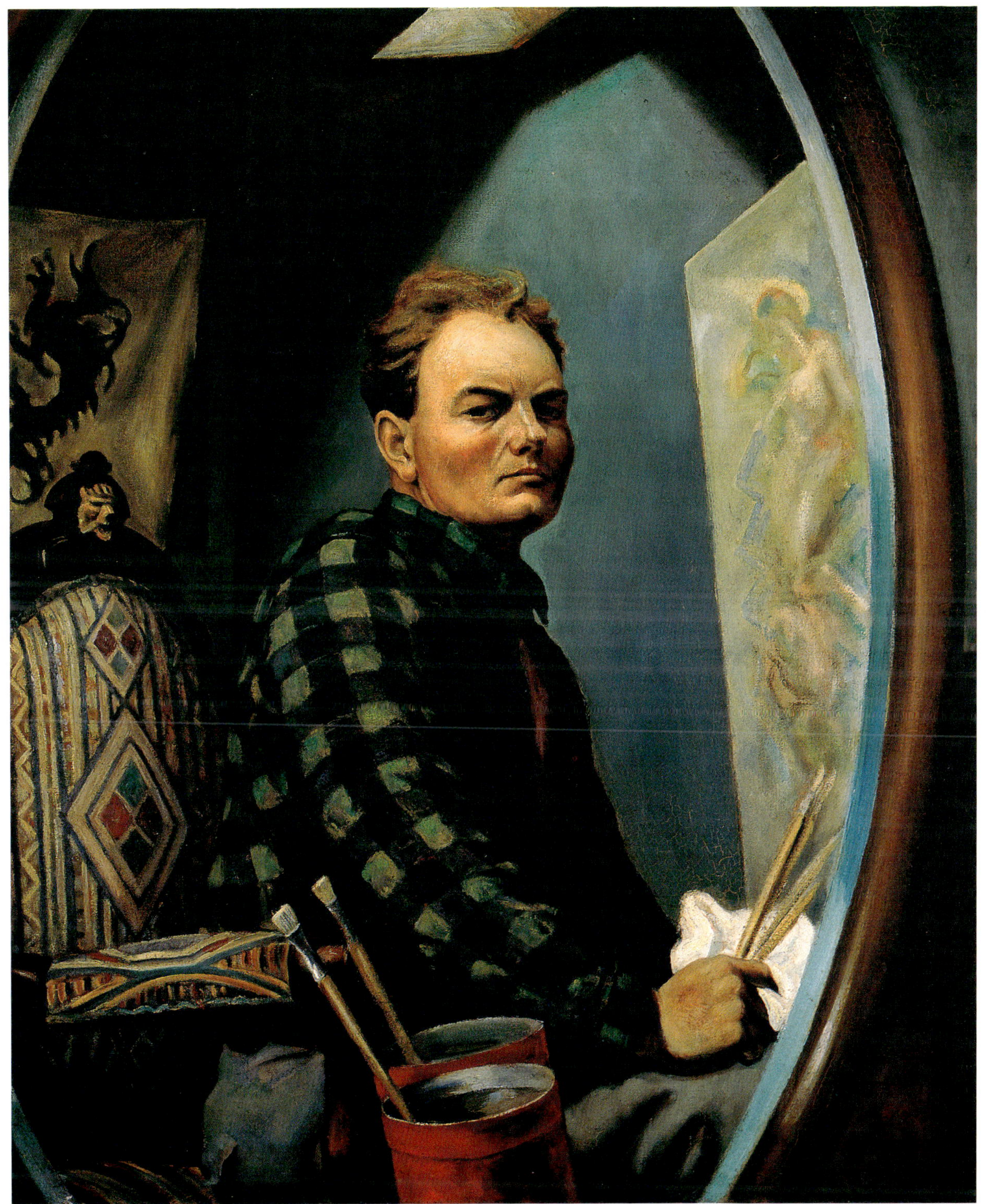

PLATE 9

Self-Portrait, 1927–29
Oil on canvas
30 × 24 in.
Signed lower right: *JOHN STEUART CURRY*
Spencer Museum of Art, University of Kansas, Lawrence. Gift of the Friends of the Art Museum, the Students of the University of Kansas, the Price R. and Flora A. Reid Foundation, Maupintour, Inc., Margaret and Darwin Daicoff, Mr. and Mrs. Robert C. Braden, Mr. and Mrs. Richard Barber, and Mr. Stan E. Wisdom.

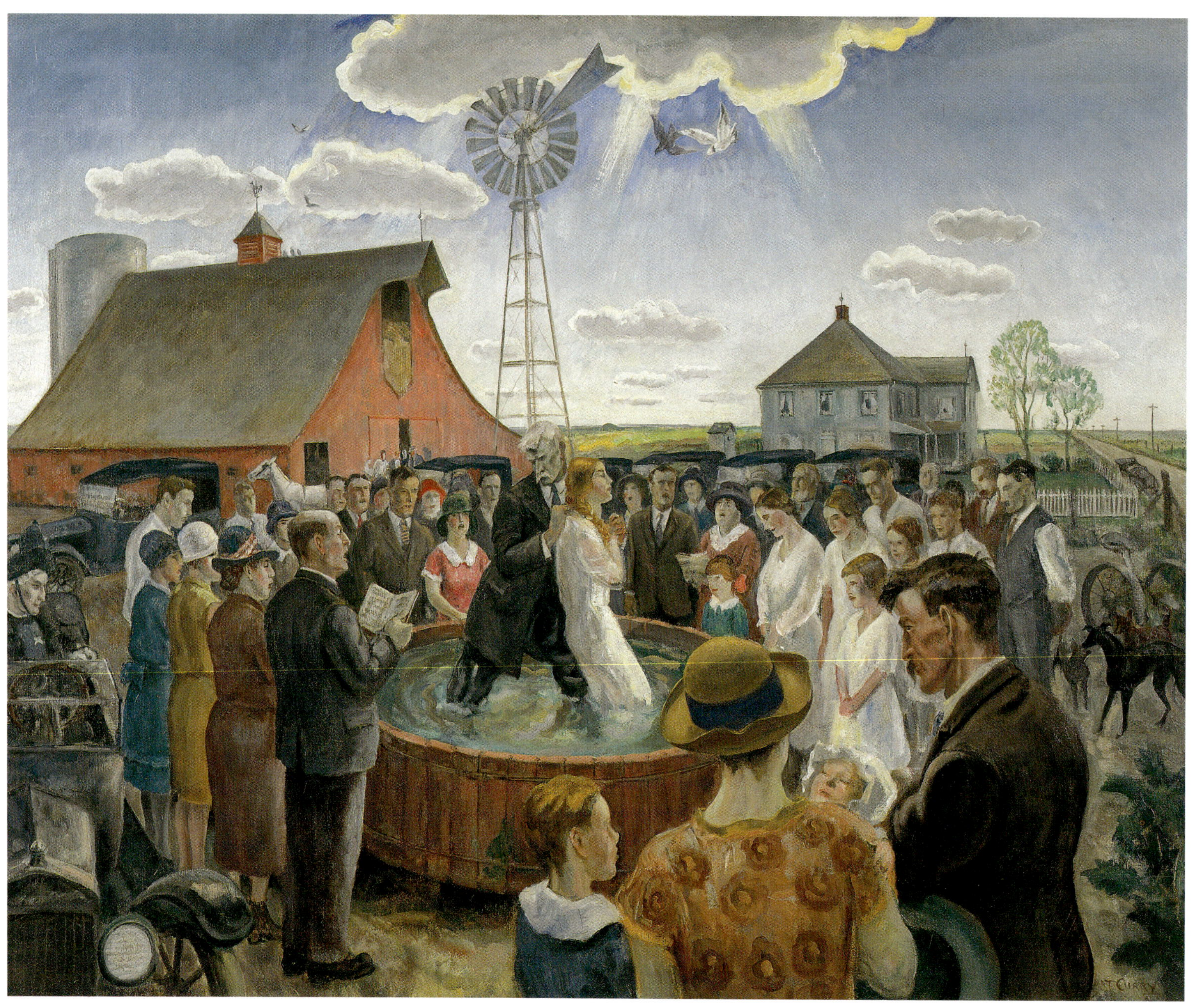

PLATE 10

Baptism in Kansas, 1928
Oil on canvas
40 × 50 in.
Signed lower right: *JOHN STEUART CURRY*
Collection of Whitney Museum of American Art, New York. Gift of Gertrude Vanderbilt Whitney.
Photograph © 1996: Whitney Museum of American Art

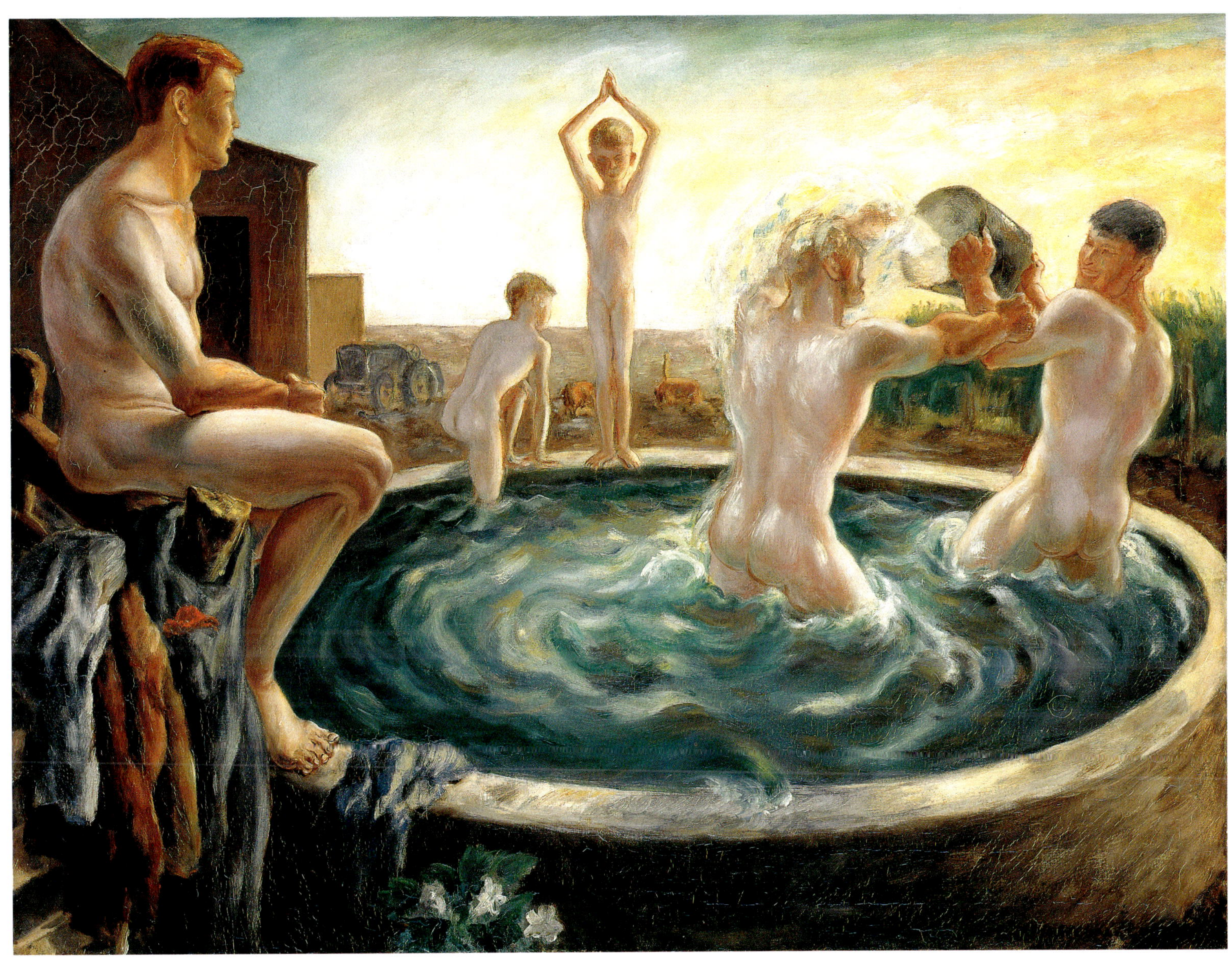

PLATE 11

Bathers, 1928
Oil on canvas
40 × 50 in.
Signed lower right: *JOHN STEUART CURRY*
John Steuart Curry Foundation.

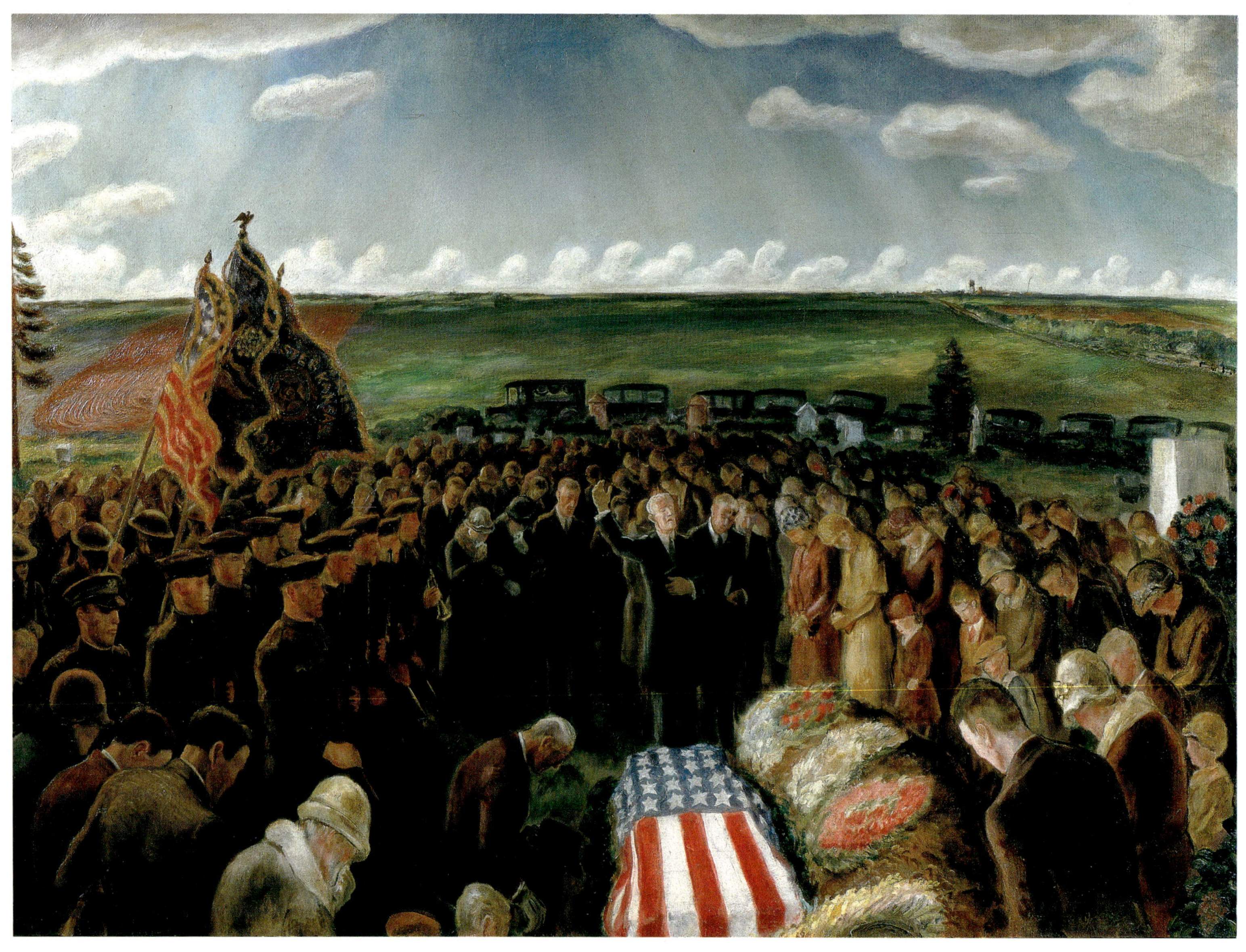

PLATE 12

The Return of Private Davis from the Argonne, 1928–40
Oil on canvas
38 × 52 in.
The Warner Collection of Gulf States Paper Corporation, Tuscaloosa, Alabama.

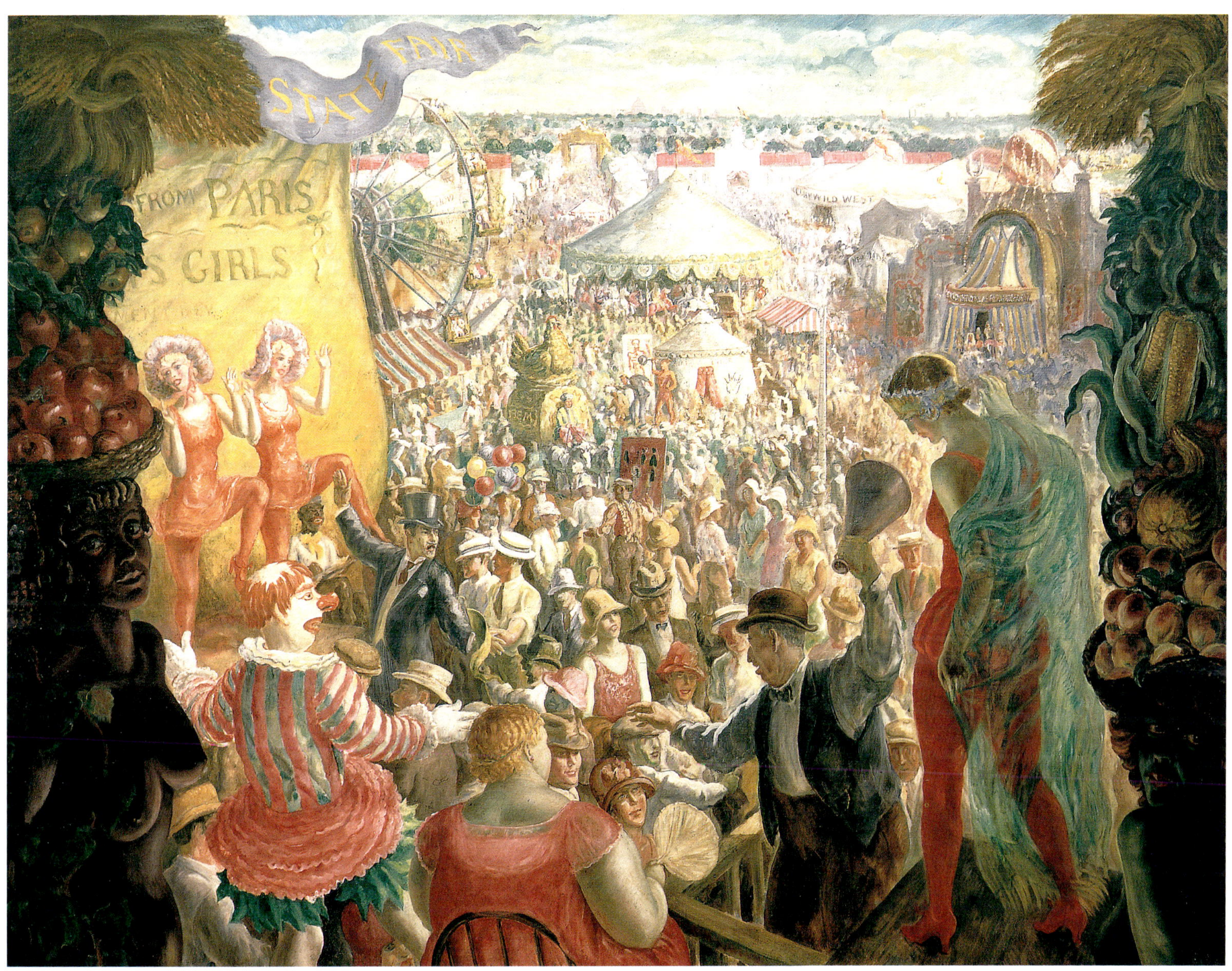

PLATE 13

State Fair, 1928

Oil on canvas

69 × 91½ in.

The Virginia Steele Scott Collection, Huntington Library, Art Collections, and Botanical Gardens, San Marino, California.

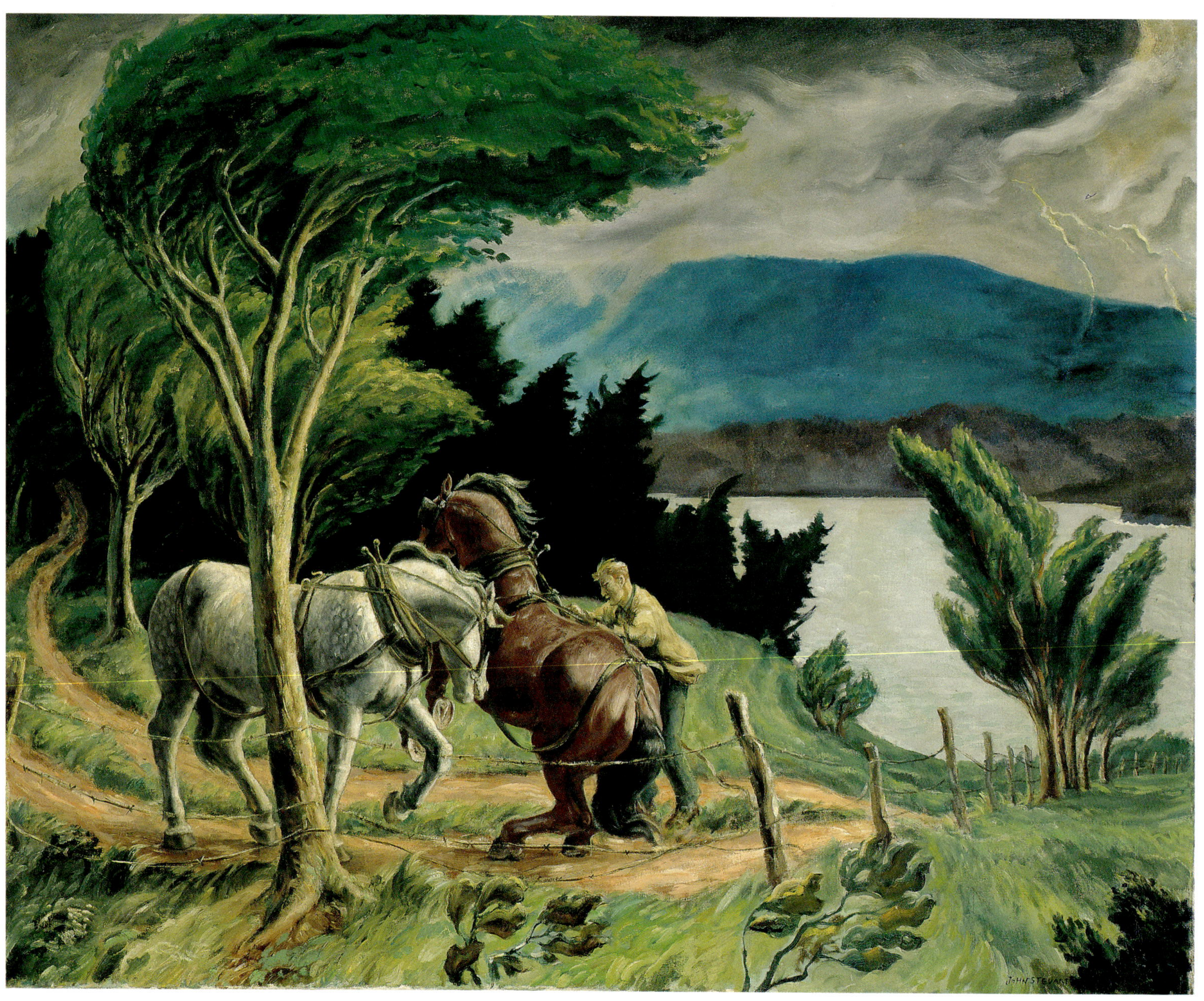

PLATE 14

Storm Breaking over Lake Otsego, 1928
Oil on canvas
40⅛ × 50¼ in.
Signed lower right: *JOHN STEUART CURRY*
Museum of Fine Arts, Boston. Gift of Mr. and Mrs. Donald C. Starr.

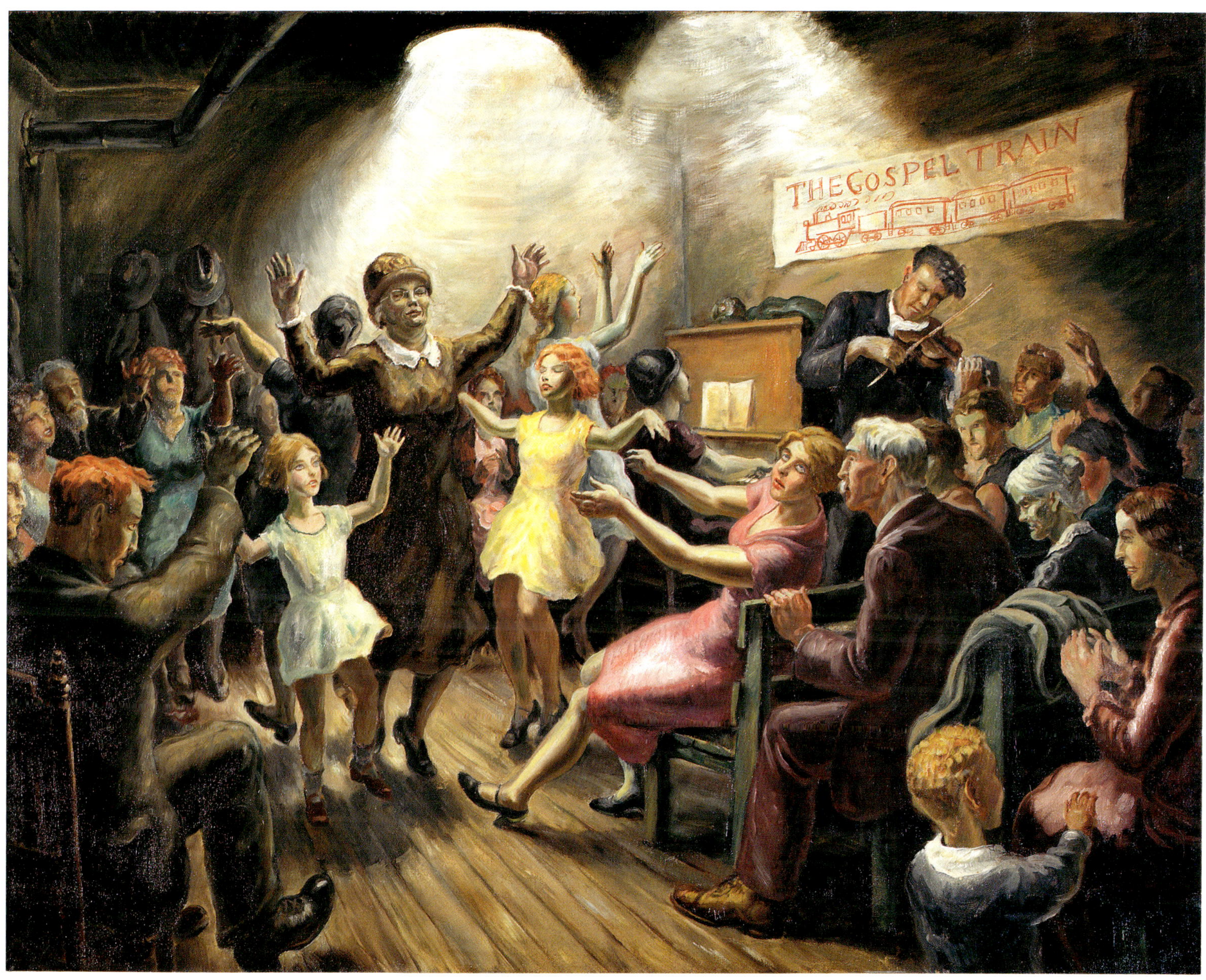

PLATE 15

Gospel Train, 1929
Oil on canvas
40 × 52 in.
Signed lower left: *JOHN STEUART CURRY*
Courtesy Syracuse University Art Collection, Syracuse, New York.

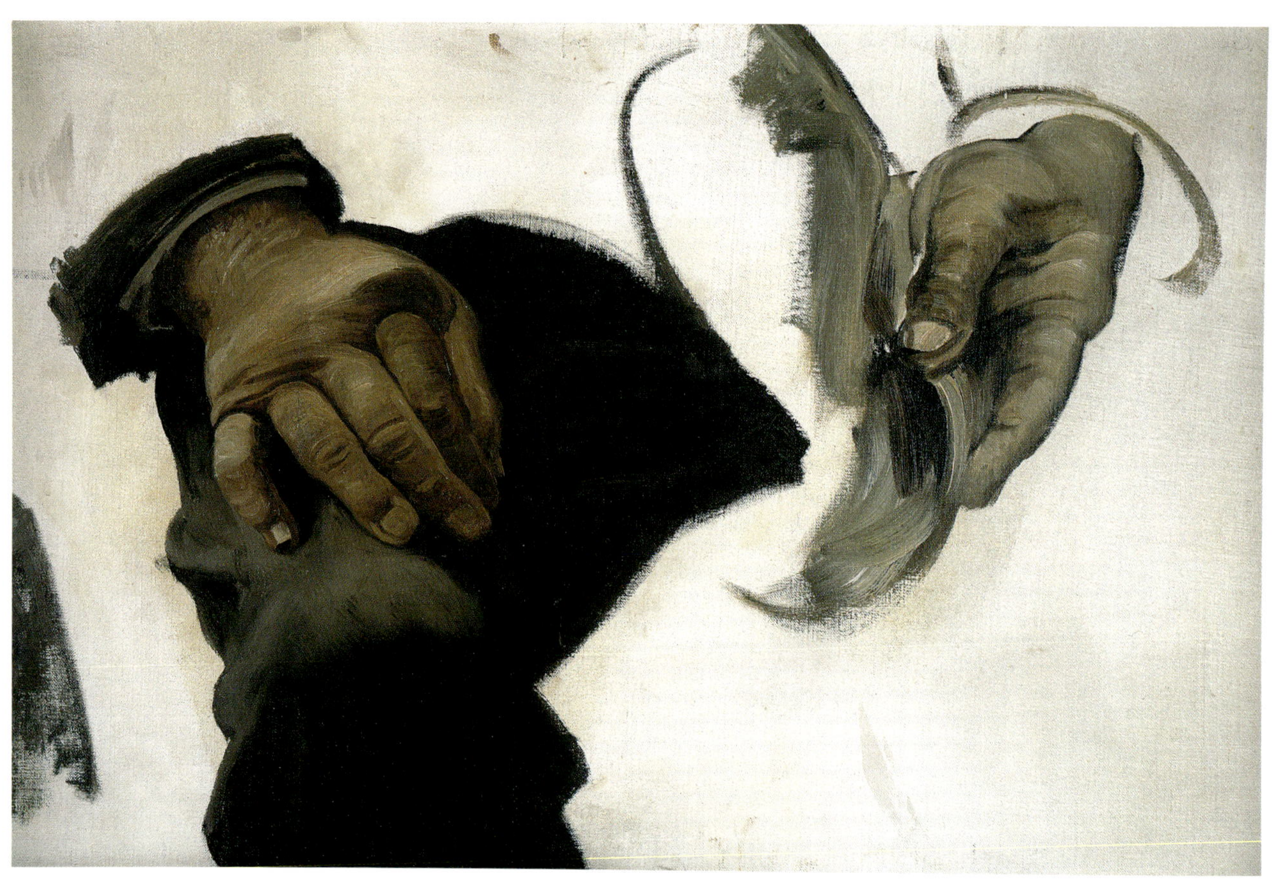

PLATE 16

My Father's Hands, 1929
Oil on canvas
20¼ × 29 in.
Collection of Beth and John Cartland.

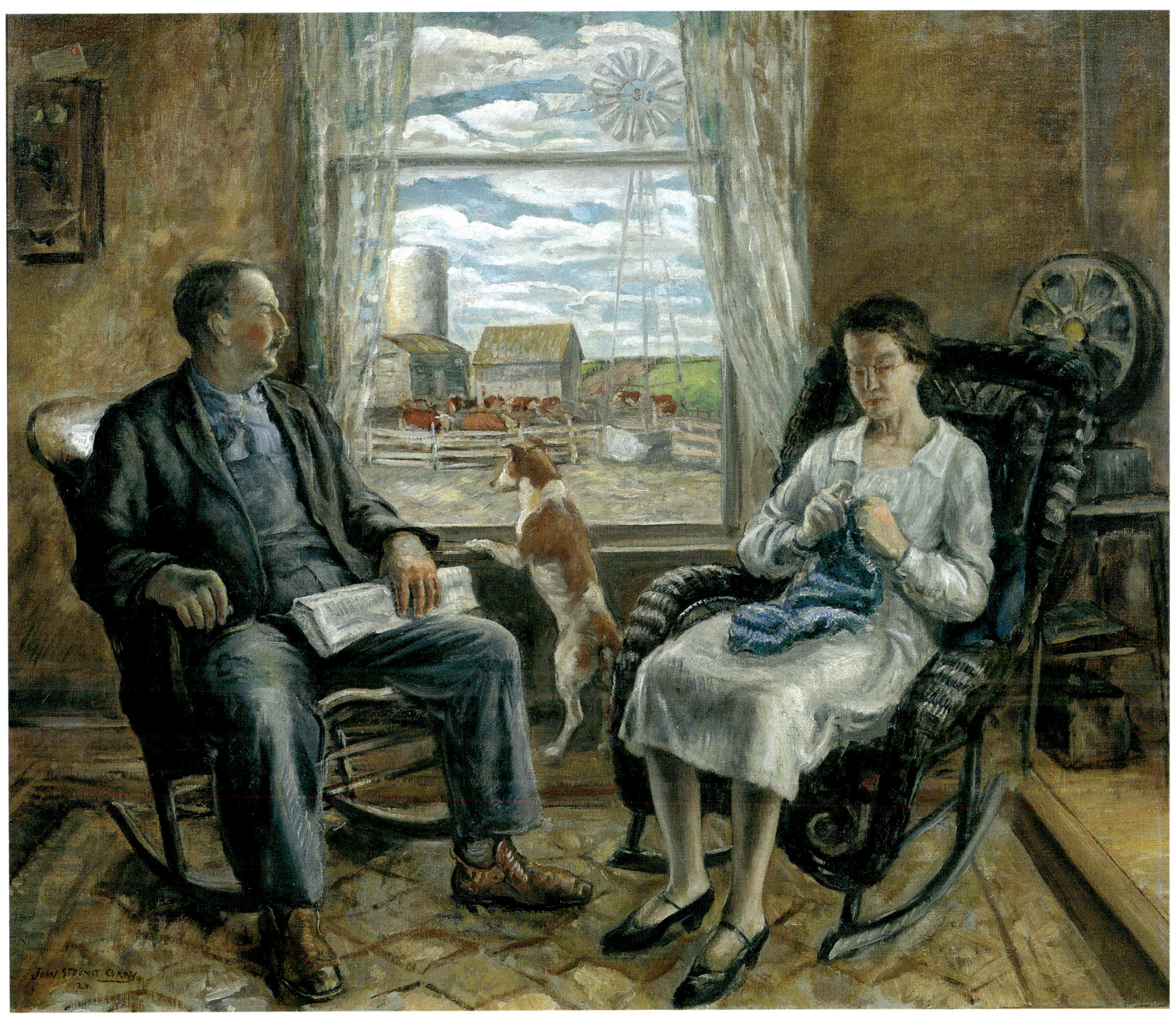

PLATE 17

The Old Folks (Mother and Father), 1929
Oil on canvas
30 × 36 in.
Signed and dated lower left: *JOHN STEUART CURRY/29*
Courtesy D. Wigmore Fine Art, Inc., New York.

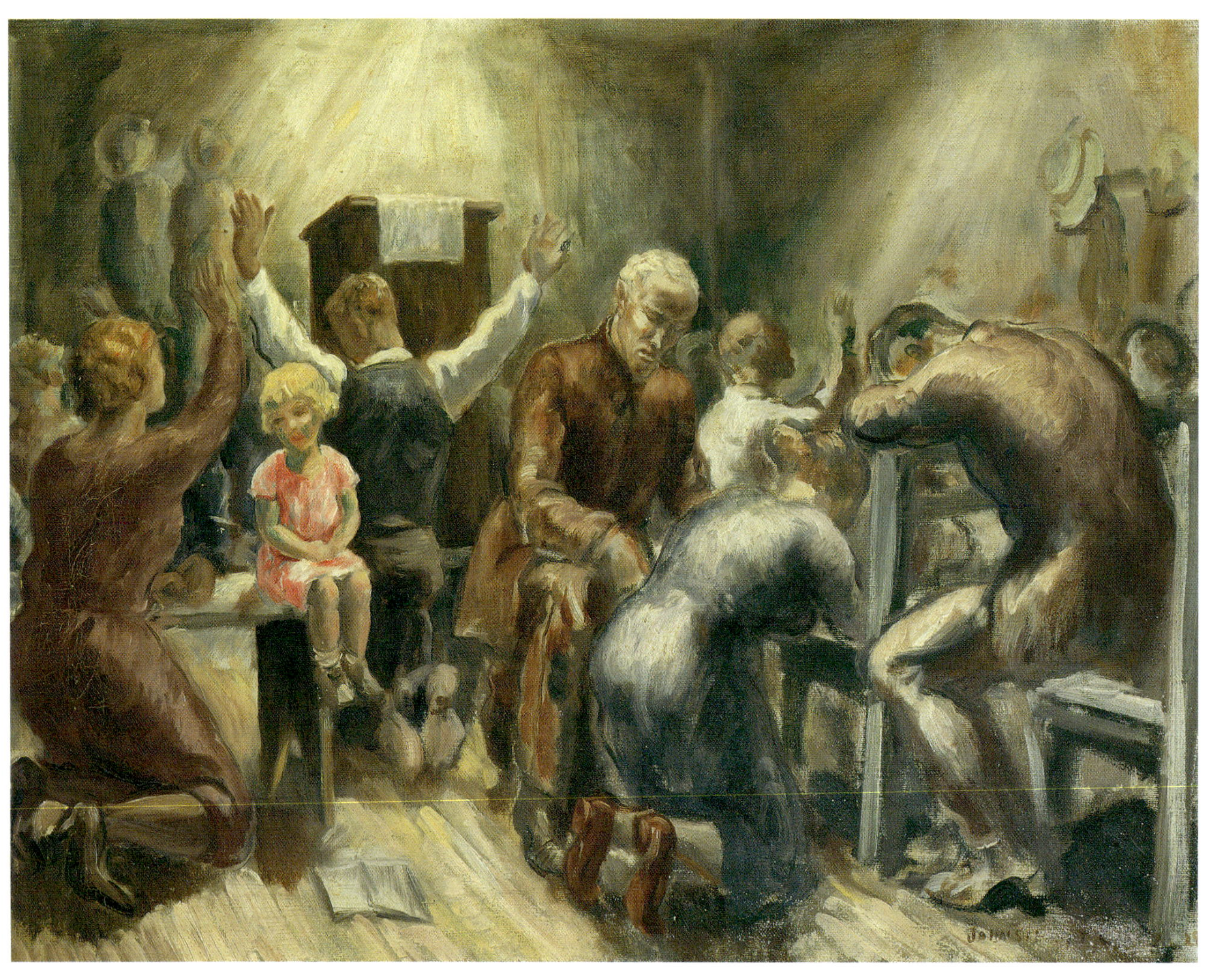

PLATE 18

Prayer for Grace, 1929
Oil on canvas
20 × 26 in.
Signed and dated lower right: *JOHN STEUART CURRY 29*
Jean Chapman Born.

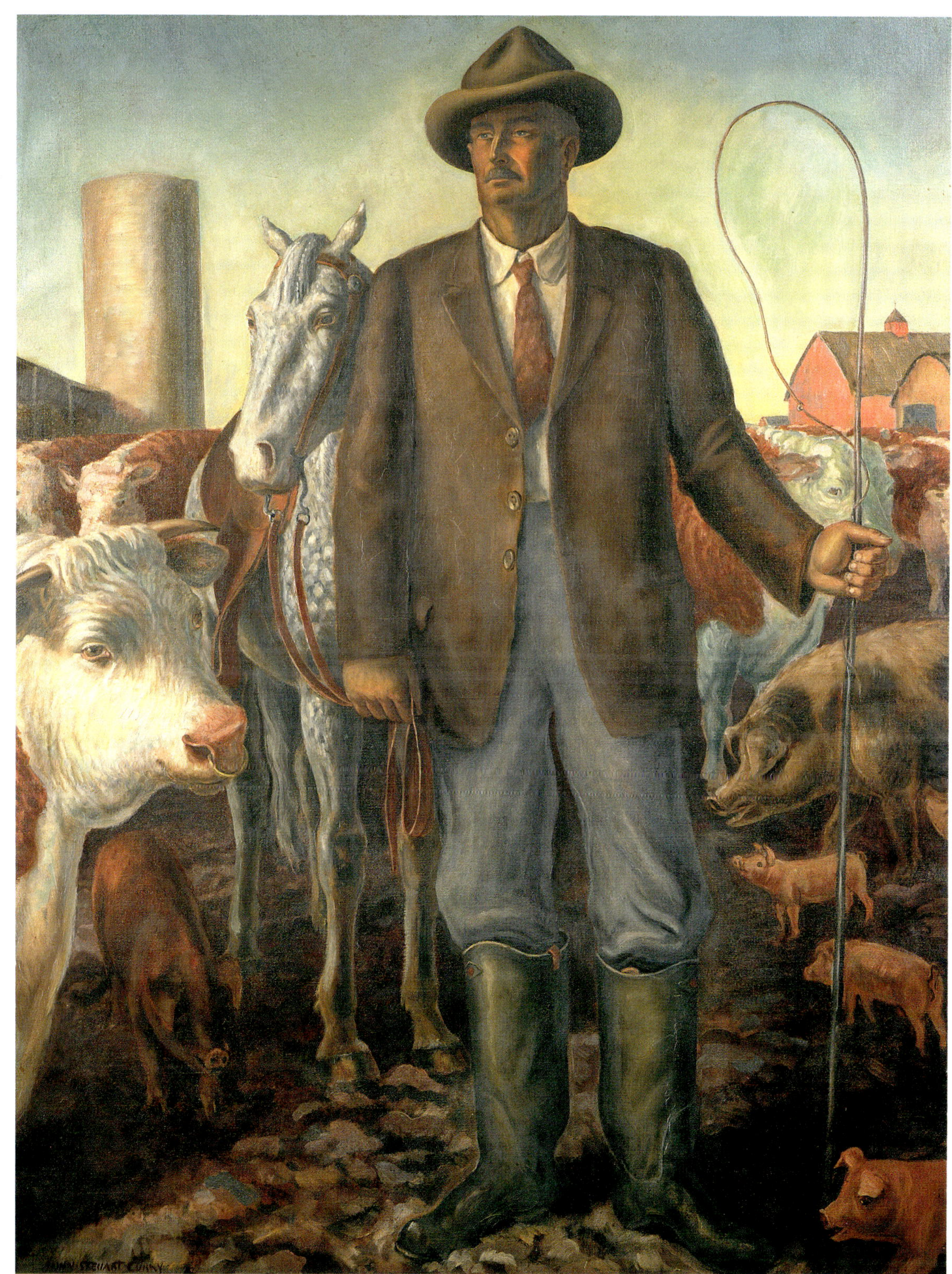

PLATE 19

The Stockman, 1929
Oil on canvas
52 × 40 in.
Signed lower left: *JOHN STEUART CURRY*
Collection of Whitney Museum of American Art, New York. Purchase.
Photograph © 1997: Whitney Museum of American Art

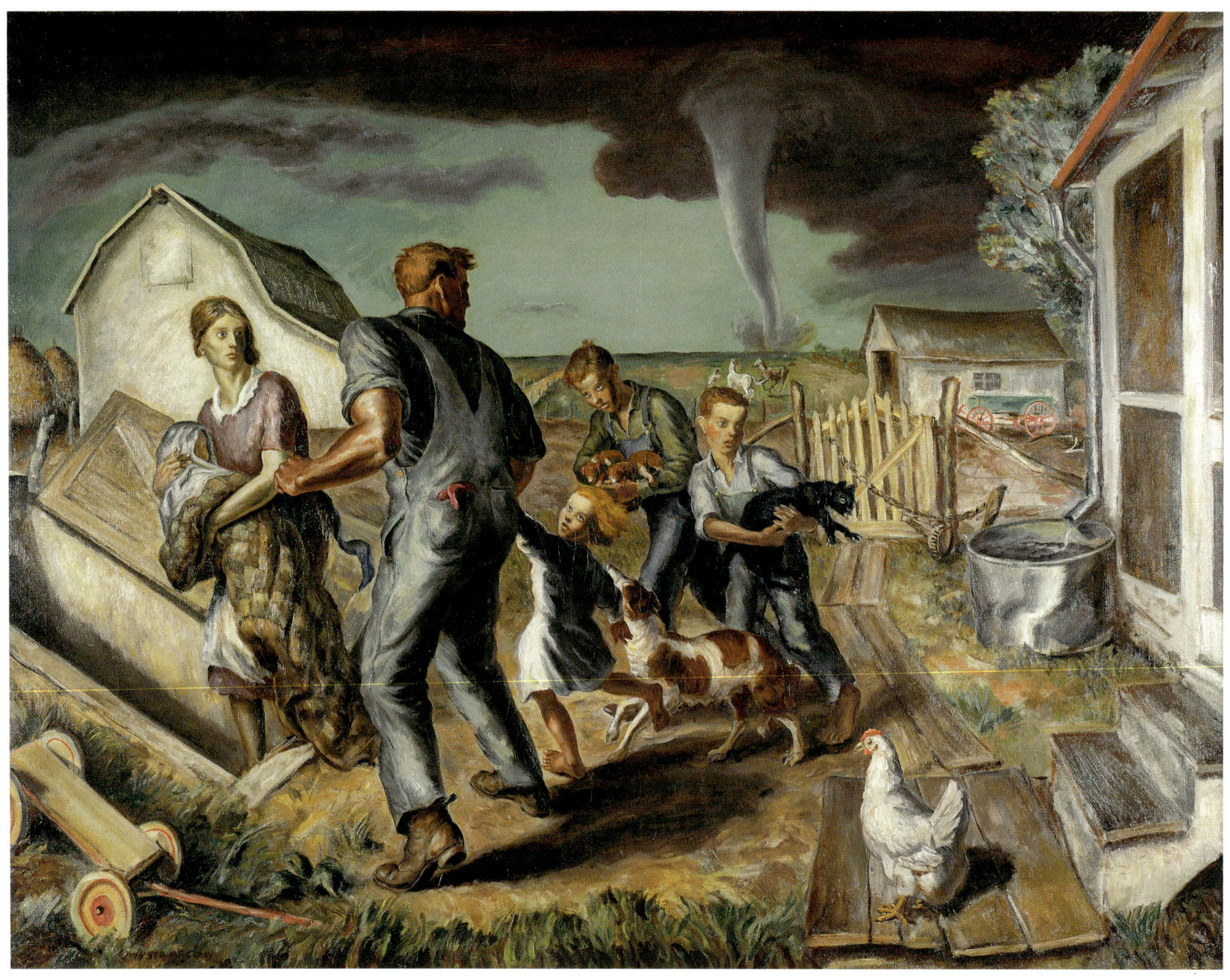

PLATE 20

Tornado, 1929
Oil on canvas
46¼ × 60½ in.
Signed lower left: *JOHN STEUART CURRY*
Muskegon Museum of Art, Muskegon, Michigan. Hackley Picture Fund purchase.

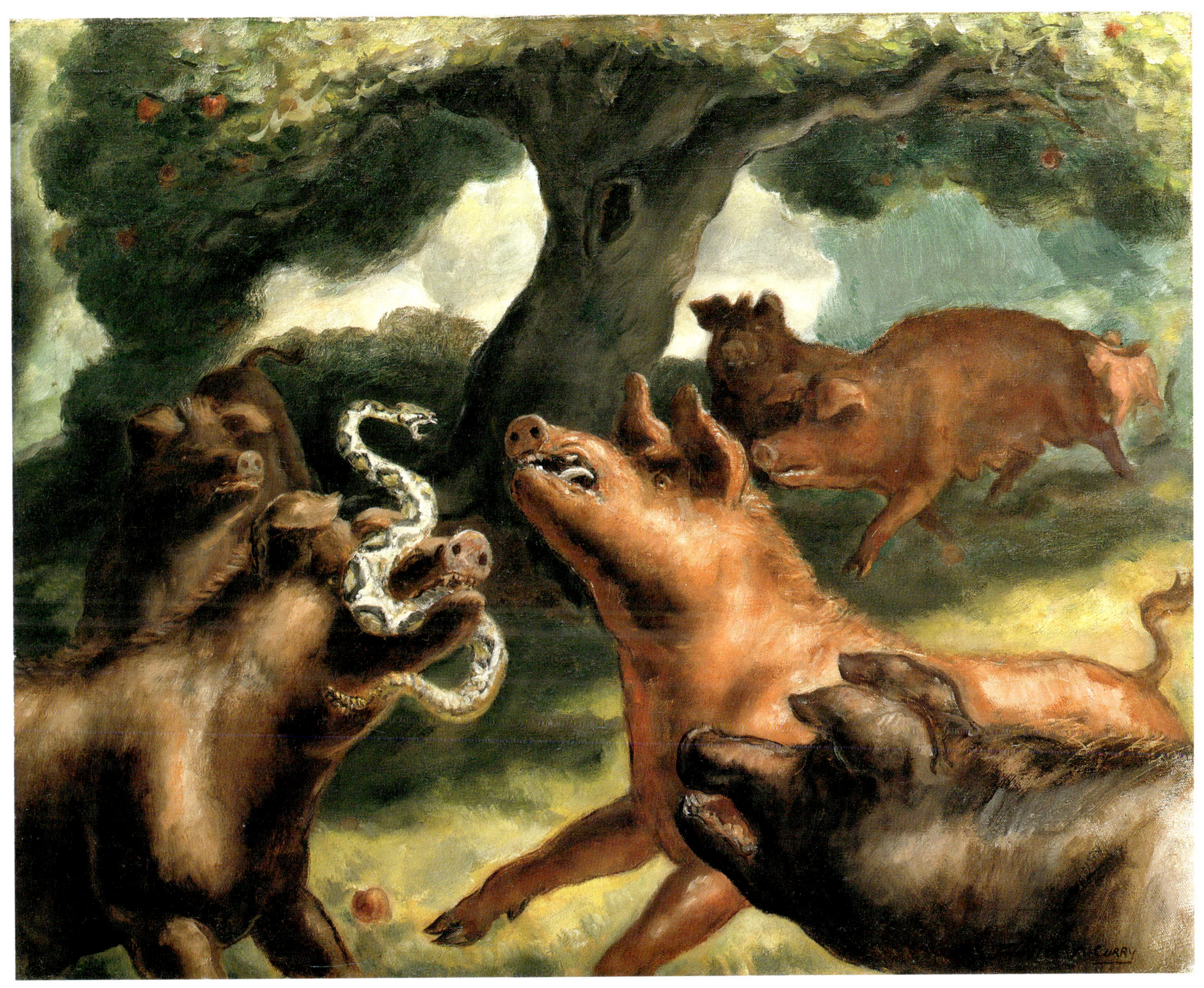

PLATE 21

Hogs Killing a Snake (Hogs Killing a Rattlesnake), 1930
Oil on canvas
$30\frac{3}{8} \times 38\frac{3}{8}$ in.
Signed lower right: *JOHN STEUART CURRY*
The Art Institute of Chicago. Gift of an anonymous donor.
Photograph © 1997: The Art Institute of Chicago

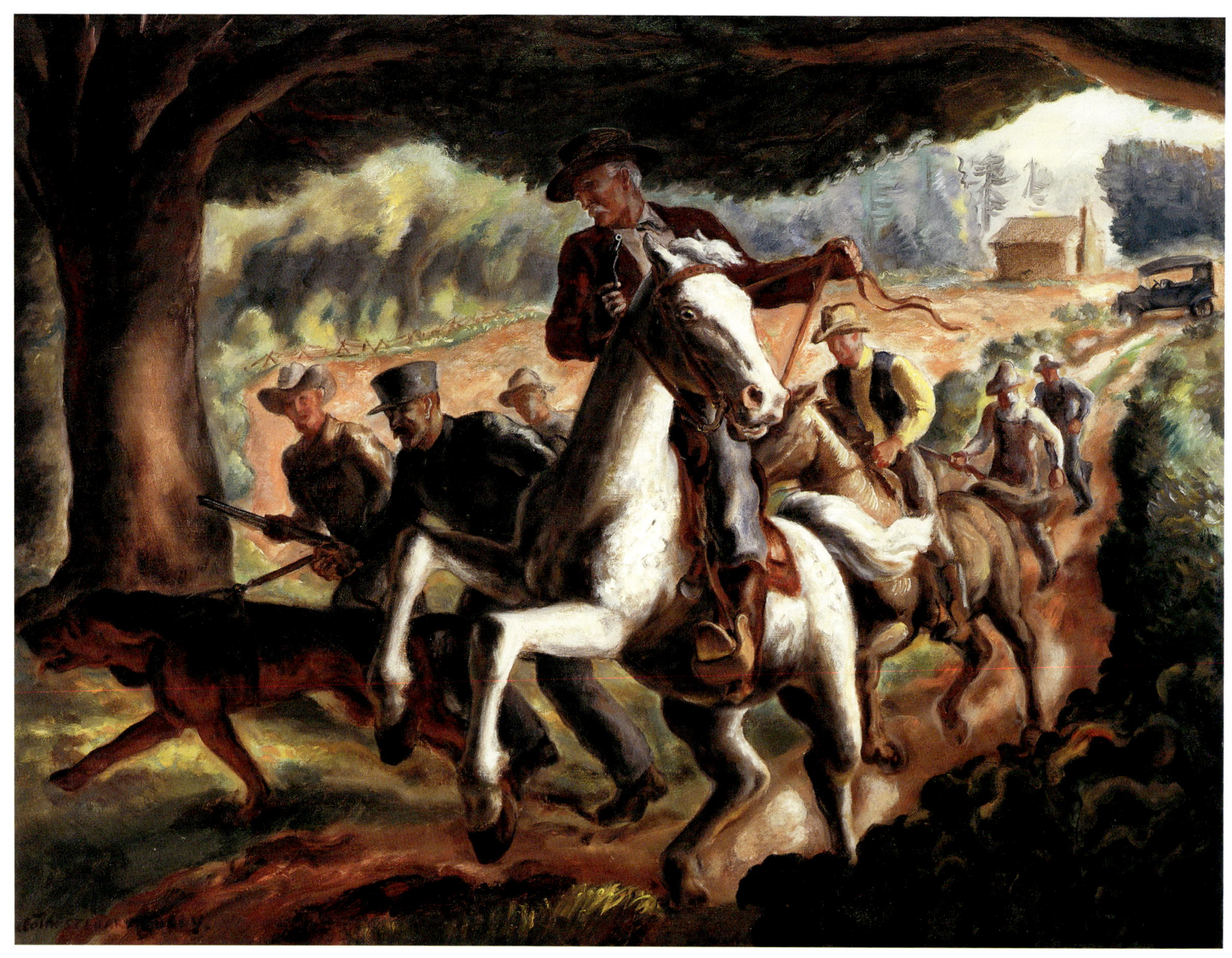

PLATE 22

Manhunt, 1931
Oil on canvas
30 × 40 in.
Signed lower left: *JOHN STEUART CURRY*
Joslyn Art Museum, Omaha, Nebraska.

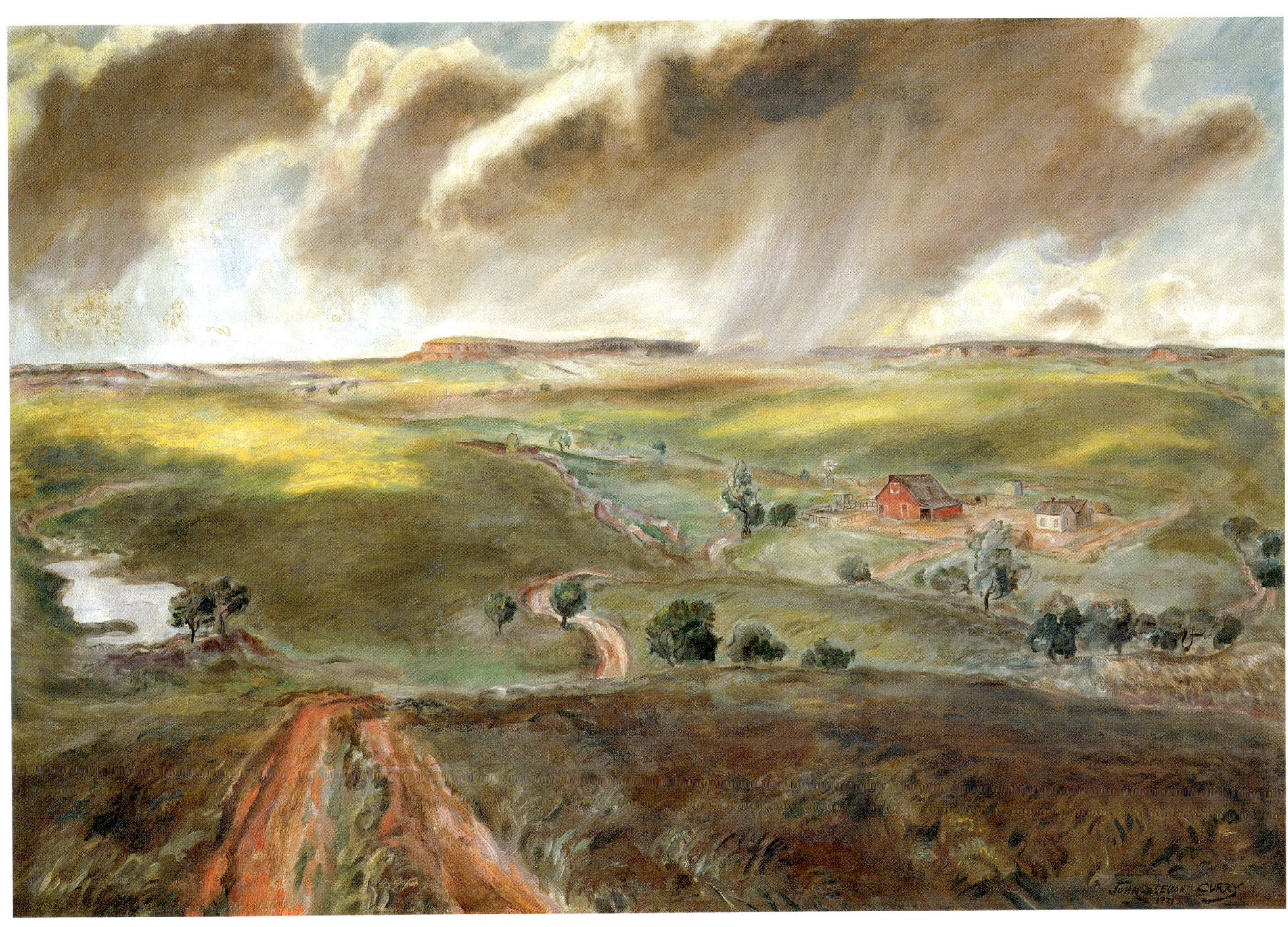

PLATE 23

Spring Shower, 1931

Oil on canvas

$29\frac{7}{8} \times 43\frac{7}{8}$ in.

Signed and dated lower right: *JOHN STEUART CURRY/1931*

The Metropolitan Museum of Art, New York. Arthur Hoppock Hearn Fund, 1932.

PLATE 24

Elephants (Circus Elephants), 1932

Oil on canvas
25¼ × 36 in.
Signed and dated lower right:
JOHN STEUART CURRY/1932
National Gallery of Art, Washington, D.C. Gift of Admiral Neill Phillips in memory of Grace Hendrick Phillips. Photograph © 1997: Board of Trustees, National Gallery of Art

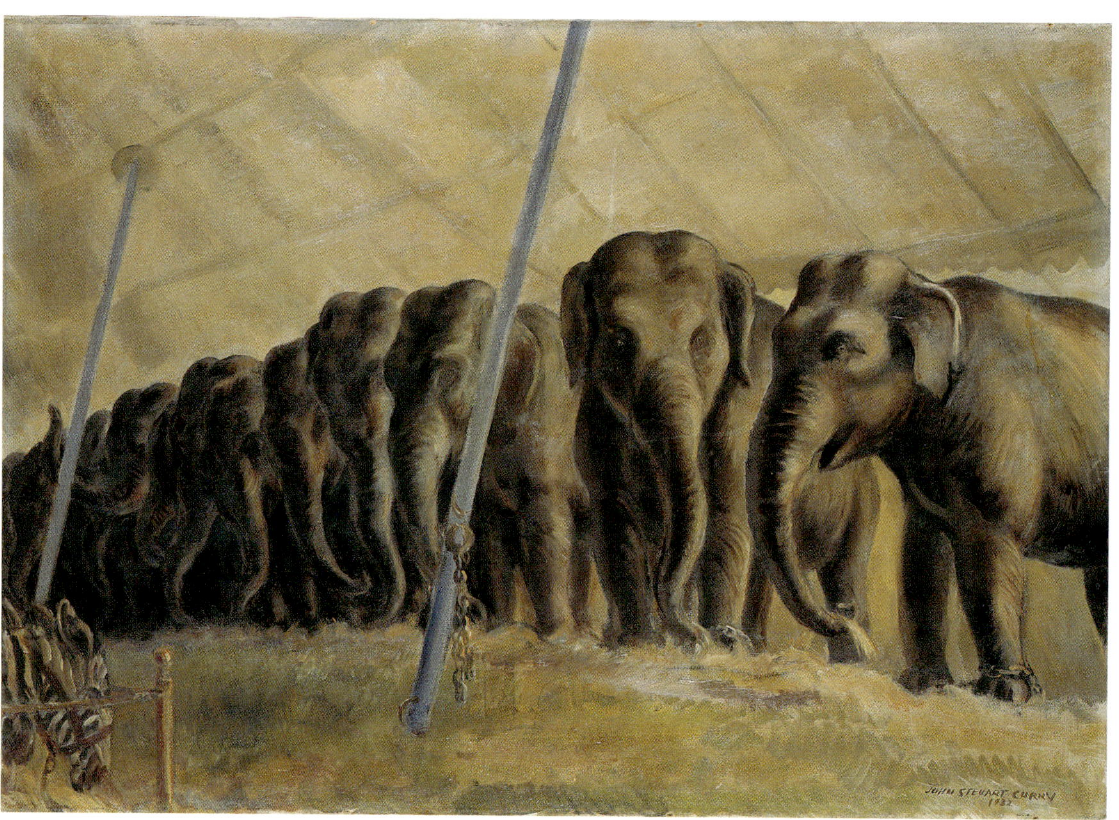

PLATE 26

The Runway, 1932

Oil on Masonite-process fiber building board
30 × 39⅞ in.
Signed and dated lower right:
JOHN STEUART CURRY/1932
Swarthmore College Art Collection, Swarthmore, Pennsylvania.

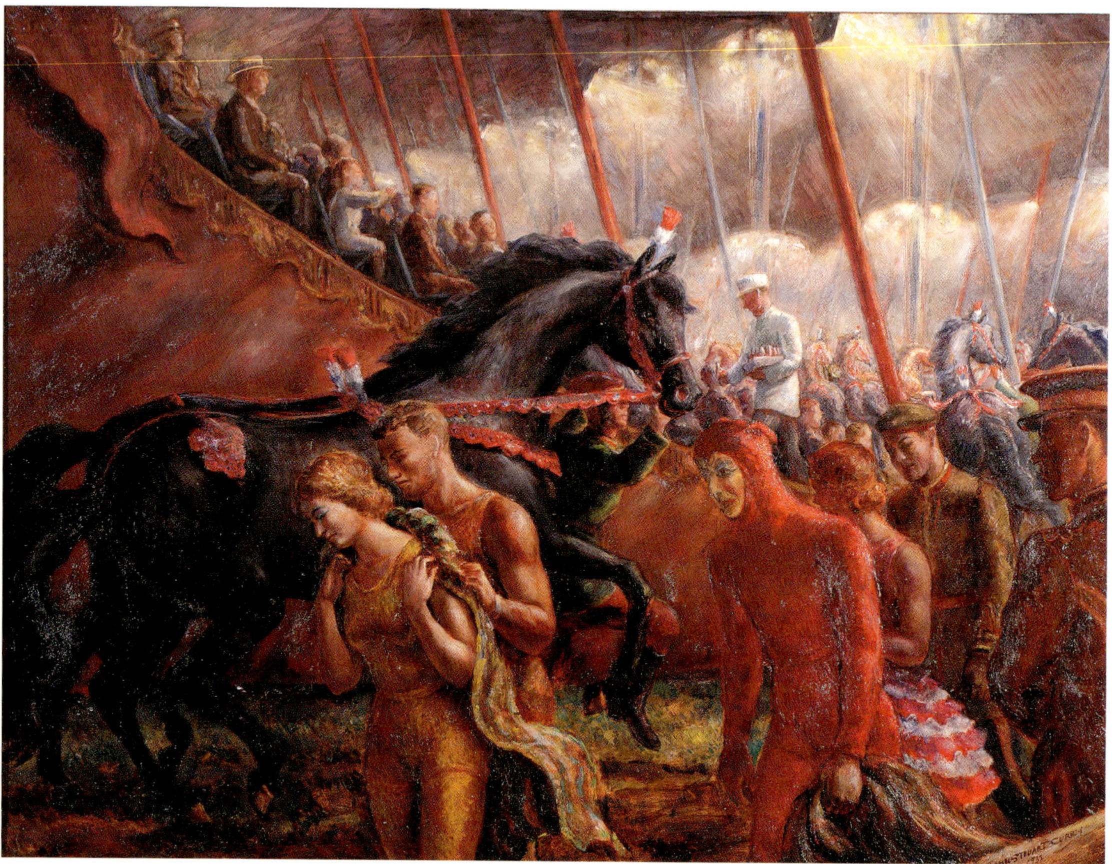

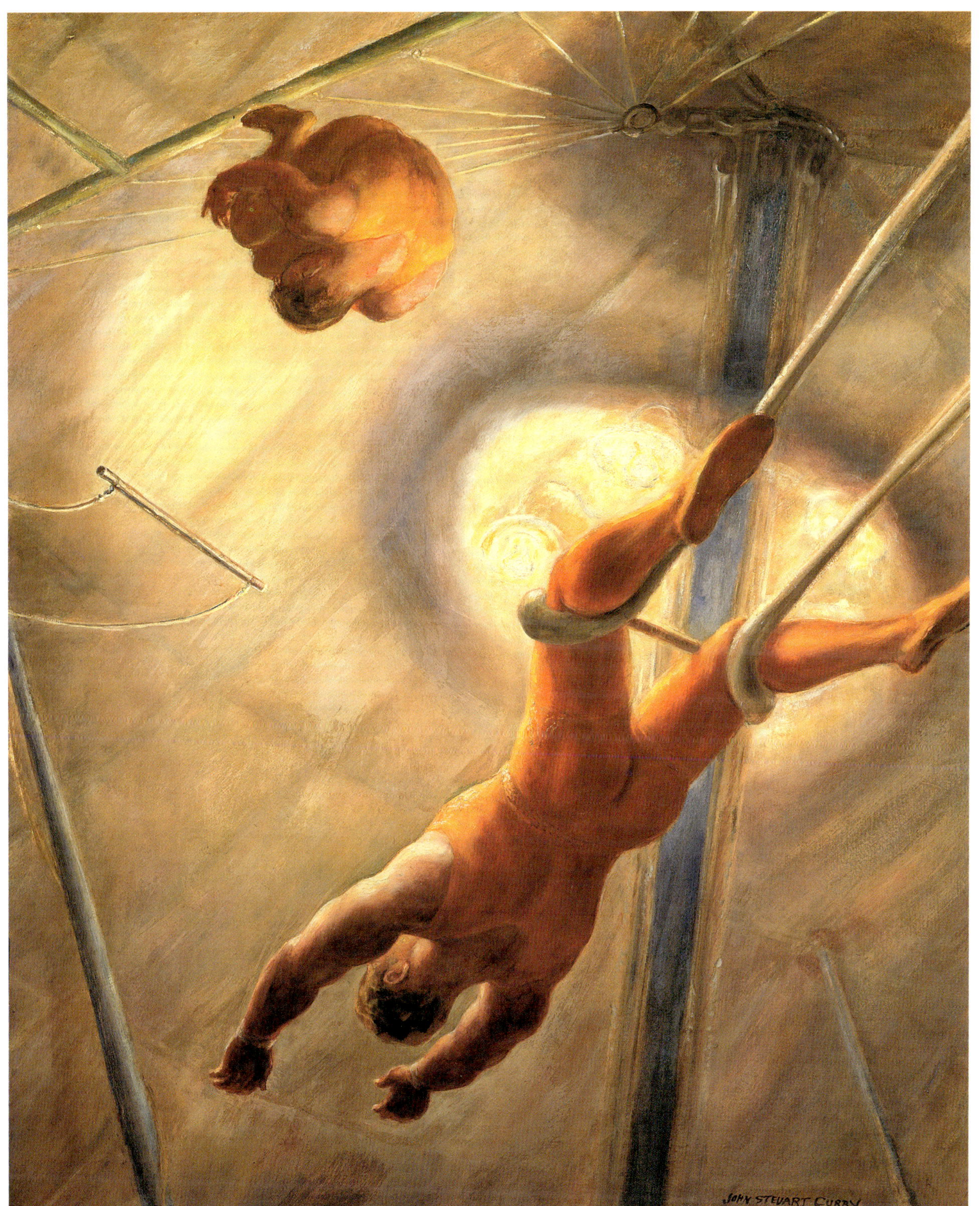

***PLATE 25**

The Flying Codonas, 1932
Tempera and oil on composition board
36 × 30 in.
Signed lower right:
JOHN STEUART CURRY
Collection of Whitney Museum of American Art, New York. Purchase.
Photograph © 1997: Whitney Museum of American Art

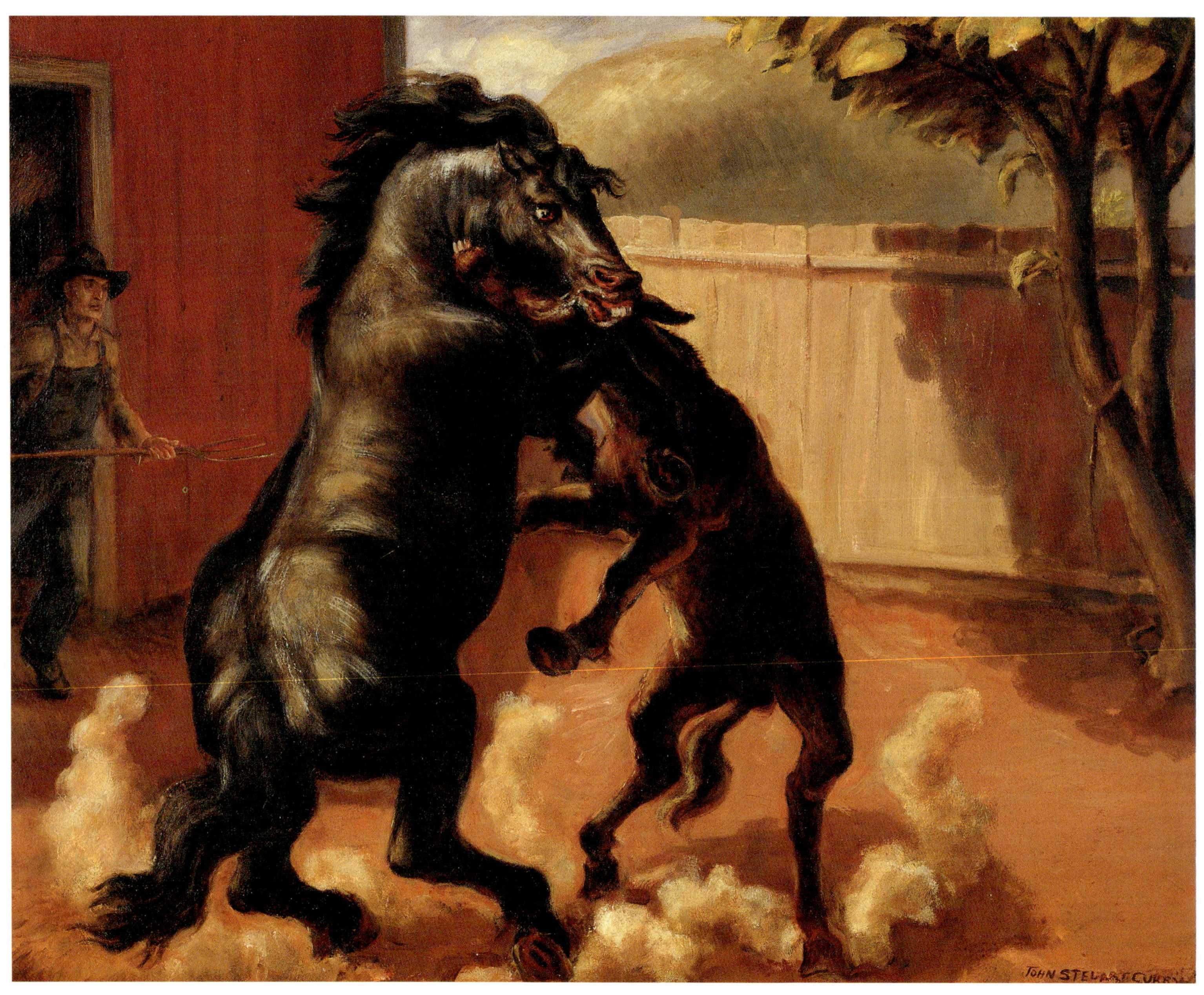

PLATE 27

Stallion and Jack Fighting, 1932

Oil on canvas
24 × 30 in.
Signed and dated lower right: *JOHN STEUART CURRY/1932*
The Minnesota Museum of American Art, St. Paul. Katharine Ordway Fund purchase.

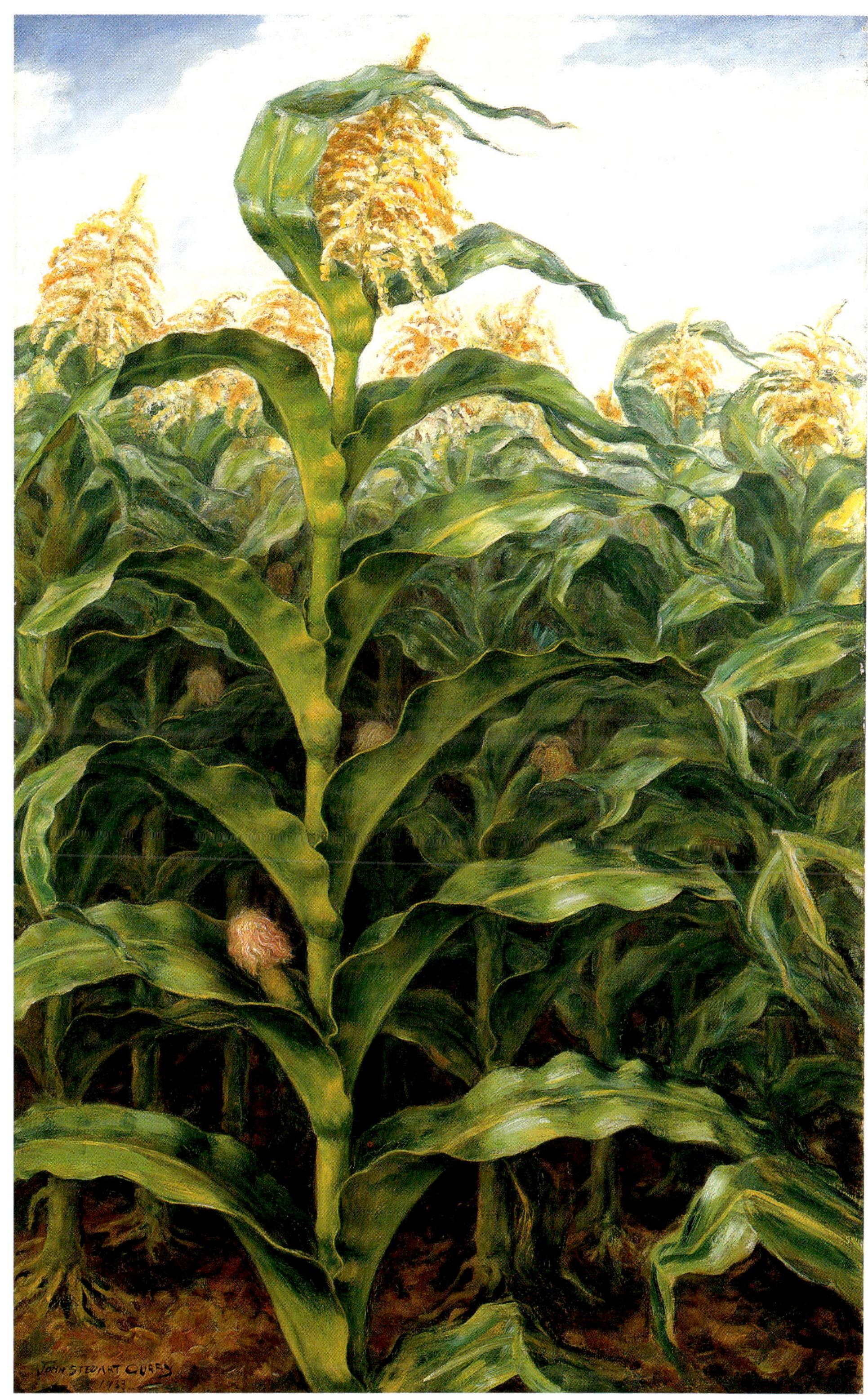

***PLATE 28**

Kansas Cornfield, 1933
Oil on canvas
60 × 38¼ in.
Signed and dated lower left: *JOHN STEUART CURRY/1933*
The Roland P. Murdock Collection, Wichita Art Museum, Wichita, Kansas.
Photograph © 1997: Wichita Art Museum

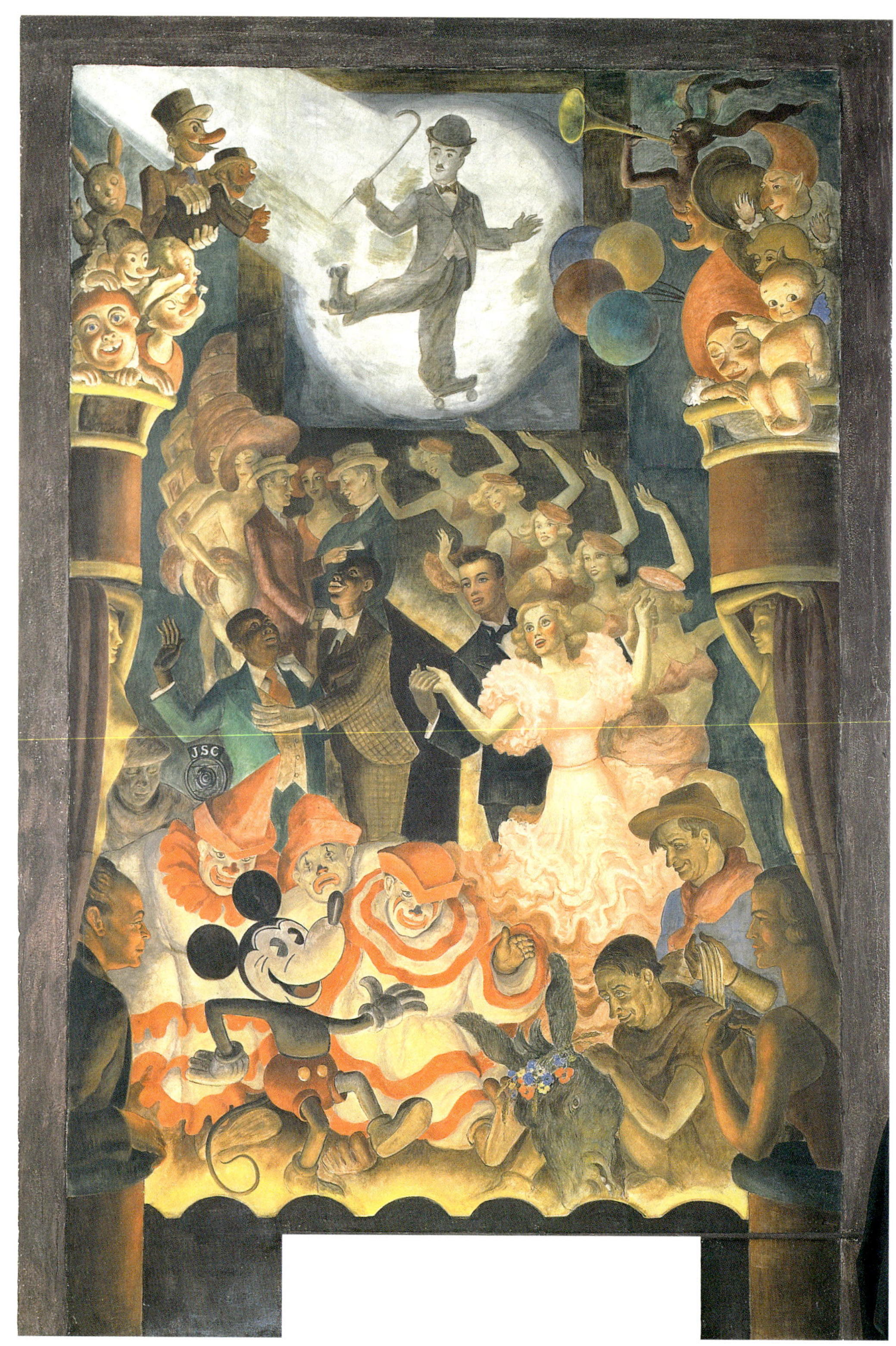

*PLATE 29

Comedy, 1934
Mural for Bedford Junior High School (now Kings Highway School), Westport, Connecticut
Fresco
15 × 8 ft.
Photograph courtesy Cunningham-Adams Painting Conservation, Sandy Hook, Connecticut

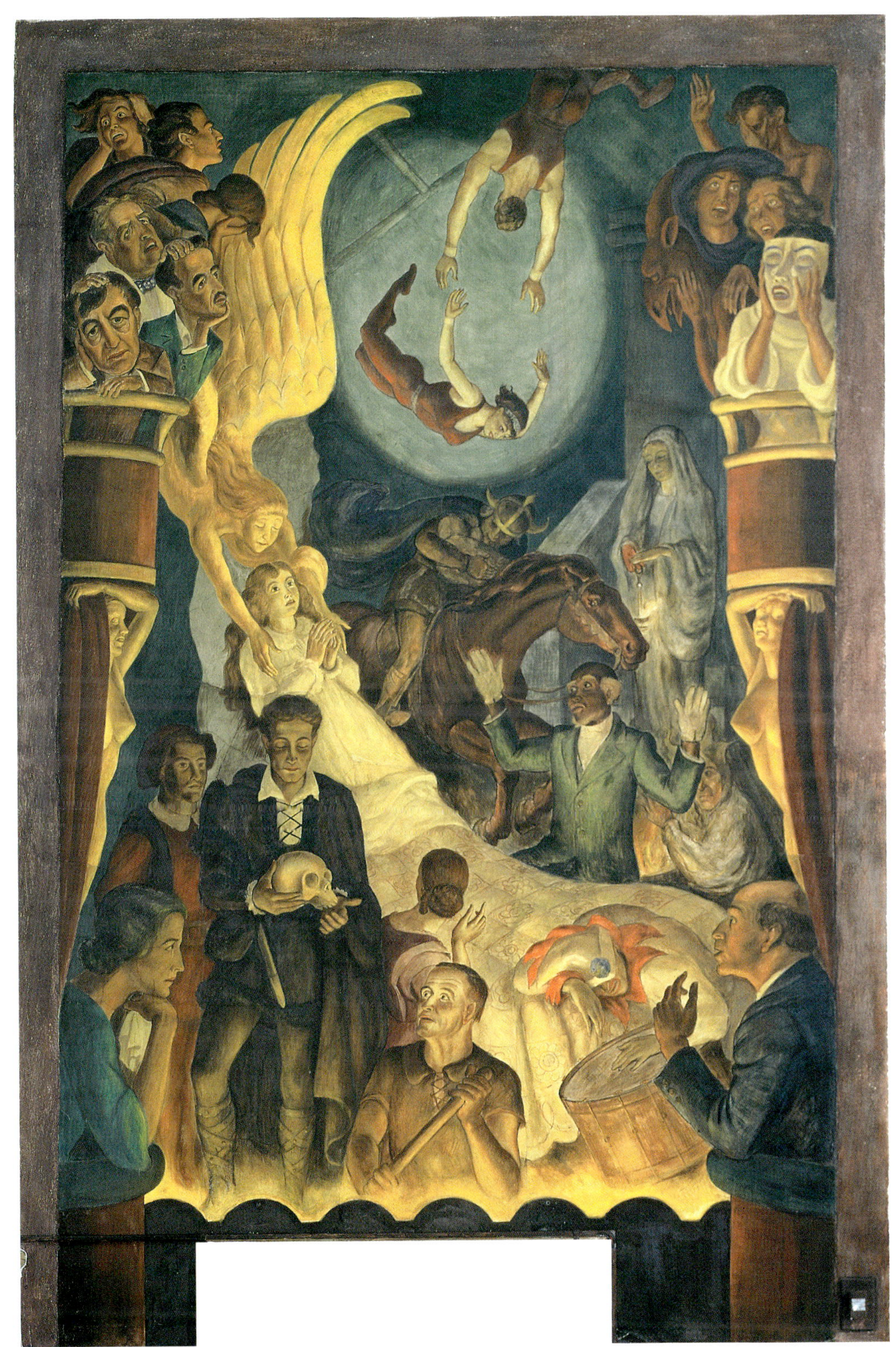

***PLATE 30**

Tragedy, 1934
Mural for Bedford Junior High School (now Kings Highway School), Westport, Connecticut
Fresco
15 × 8 ft.
Photograph courtesy Cunningham-Adams Painting Conservation, Sandy Hook, Connecticut

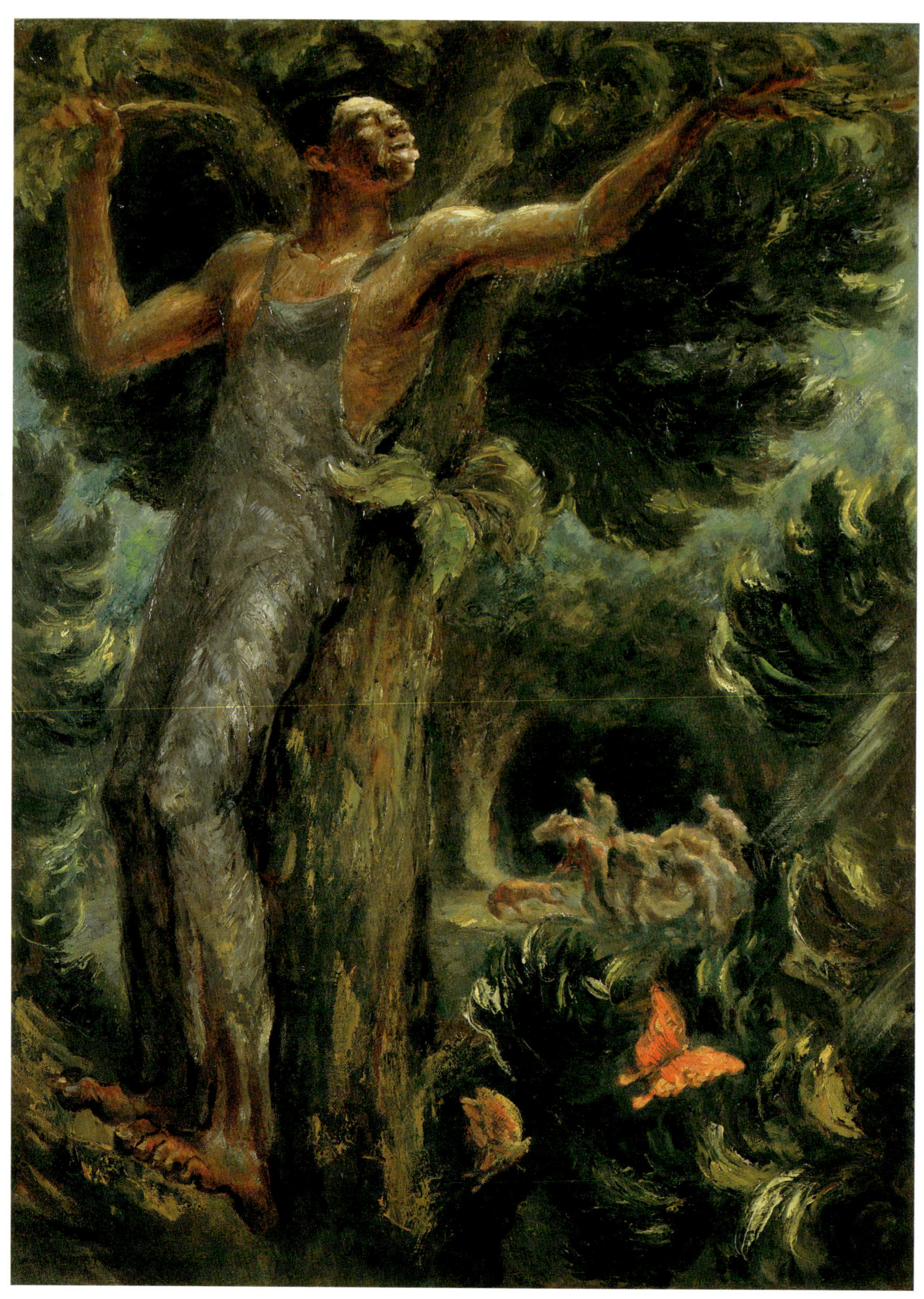

*PLATE 31

The Fugitive, 1934–36
Oil on canvas
38 × 36 in.
Private collection.
Photograph courtesy Kennedy
Galleries, Inc., New York

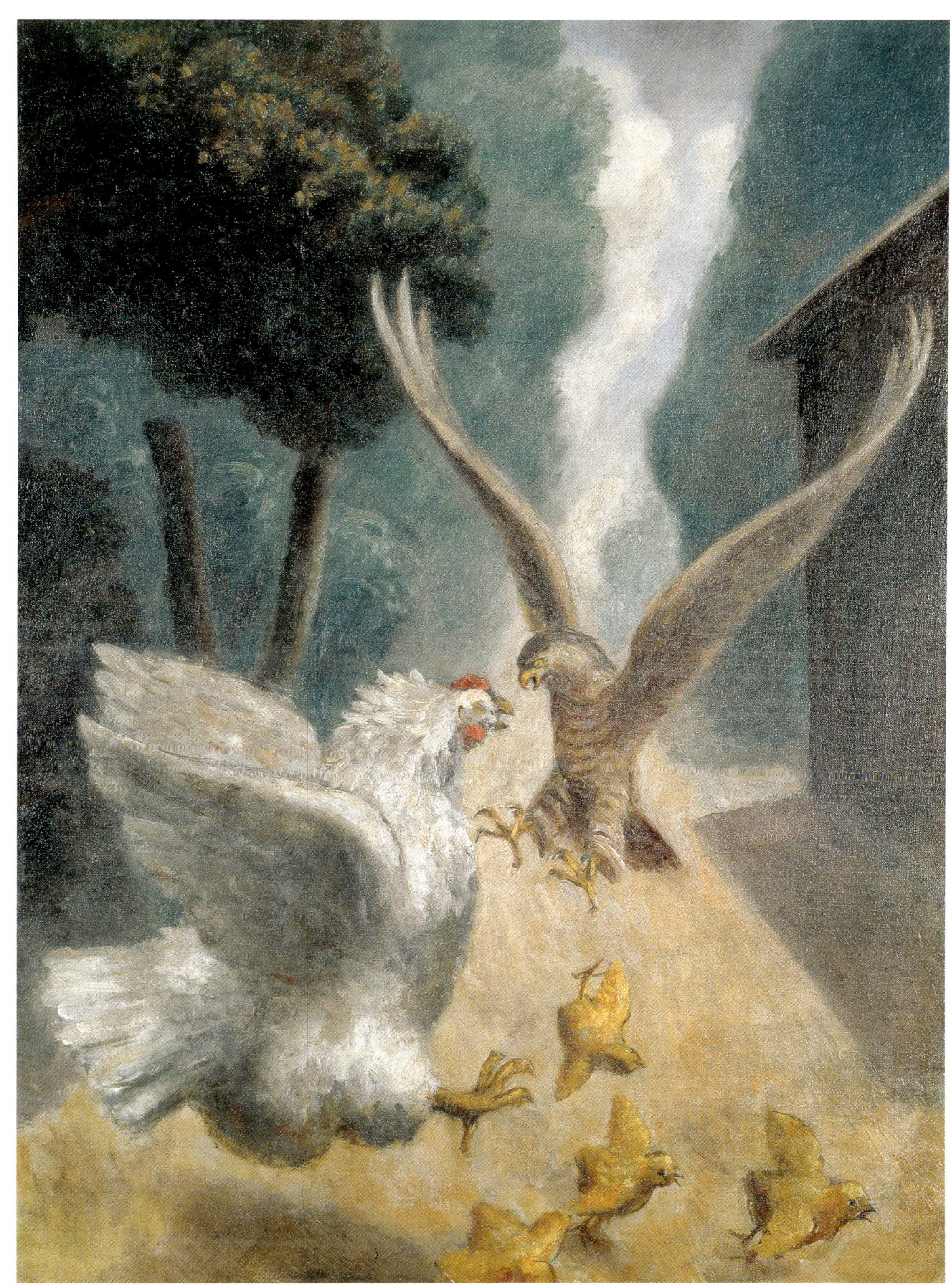

PLATE 32

Hen and the Hawk, 1934
Oil on canvas
$26\frac{1}{4} \times 20\frac{1}{4}$ in.
Signed and dated upper left:
JOHN STEUART CURRY/1934
Memphis Brooks Museum of
Art, Memphis, Tennessee.
Bequest of Mrs. C. M. Gooch.

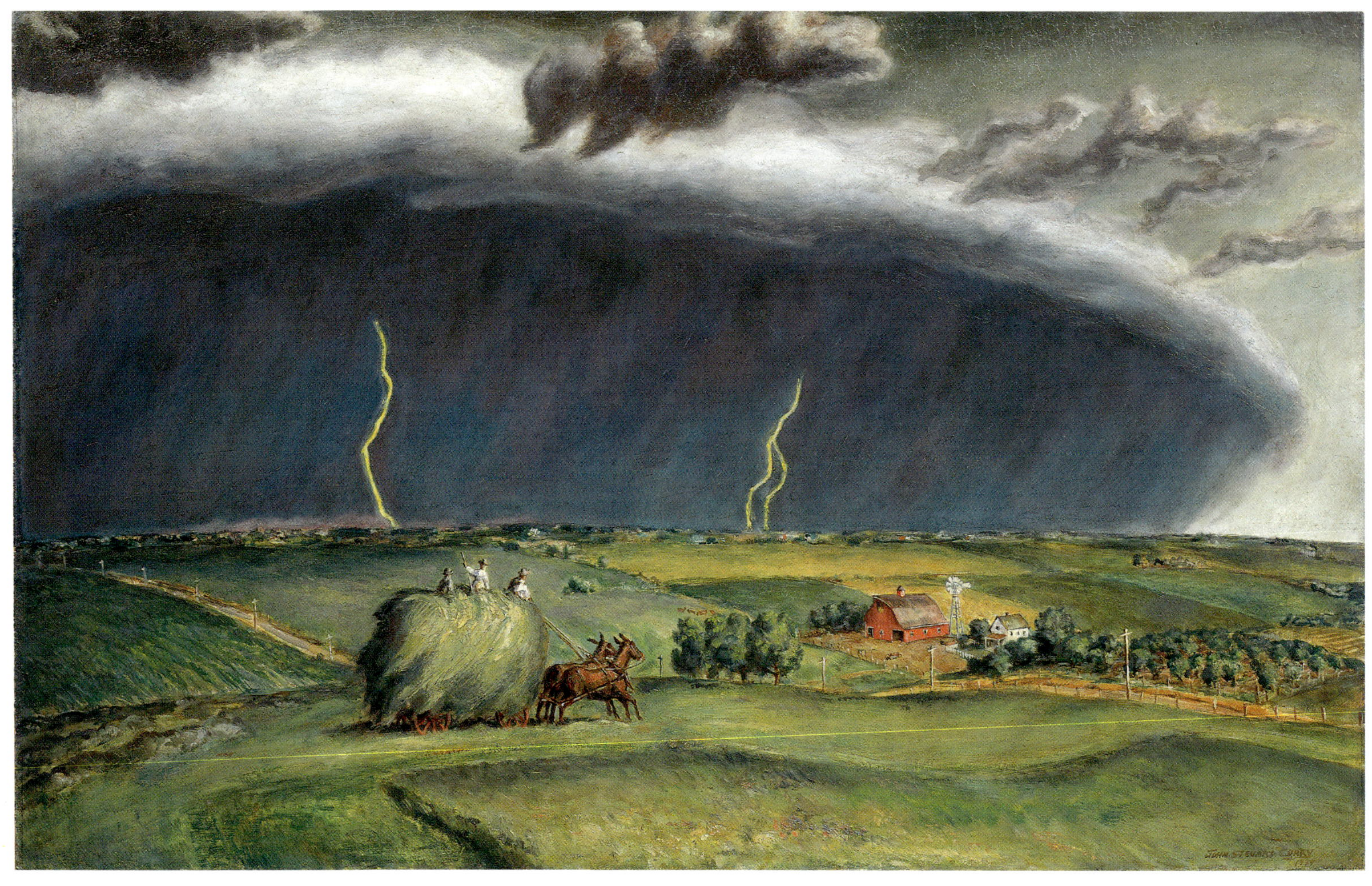

PLATE 33

Line Storm, 1934
Oil and tempera on panel
36 × 48 in.
Signed and dated lower right: *JOHN STEUART CURRY/1934*
Babcock Galleries, New York.

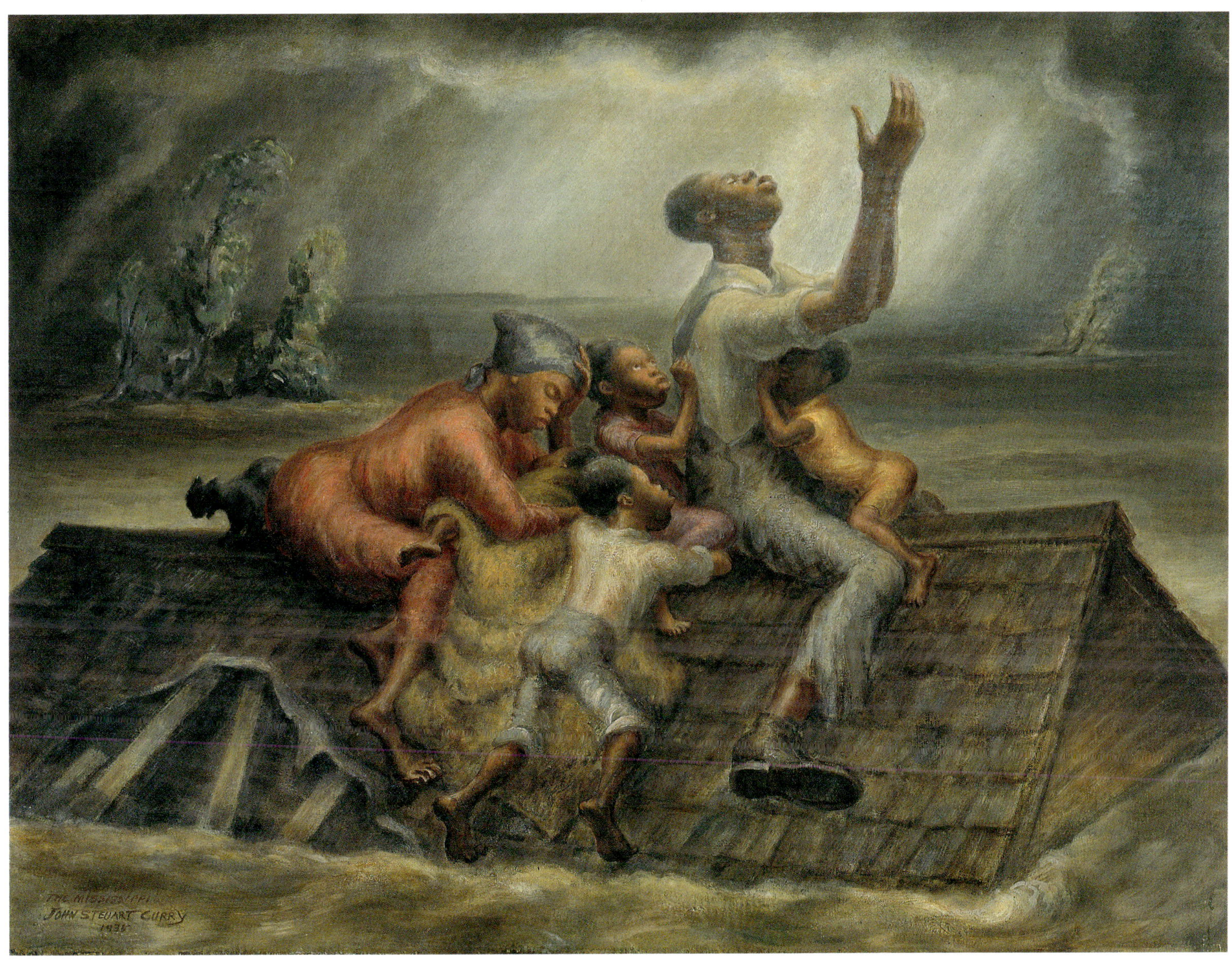

PLATE 34

The Mississippi, 1935
Oil and tempera on panel
36 × 47½ in.
Signed, dated, and inscribed lower left:
THE MISSISSIPPI 1935/JOHN STEUART CURRY/1935
The Saint Louis Art Museum. Purchase.

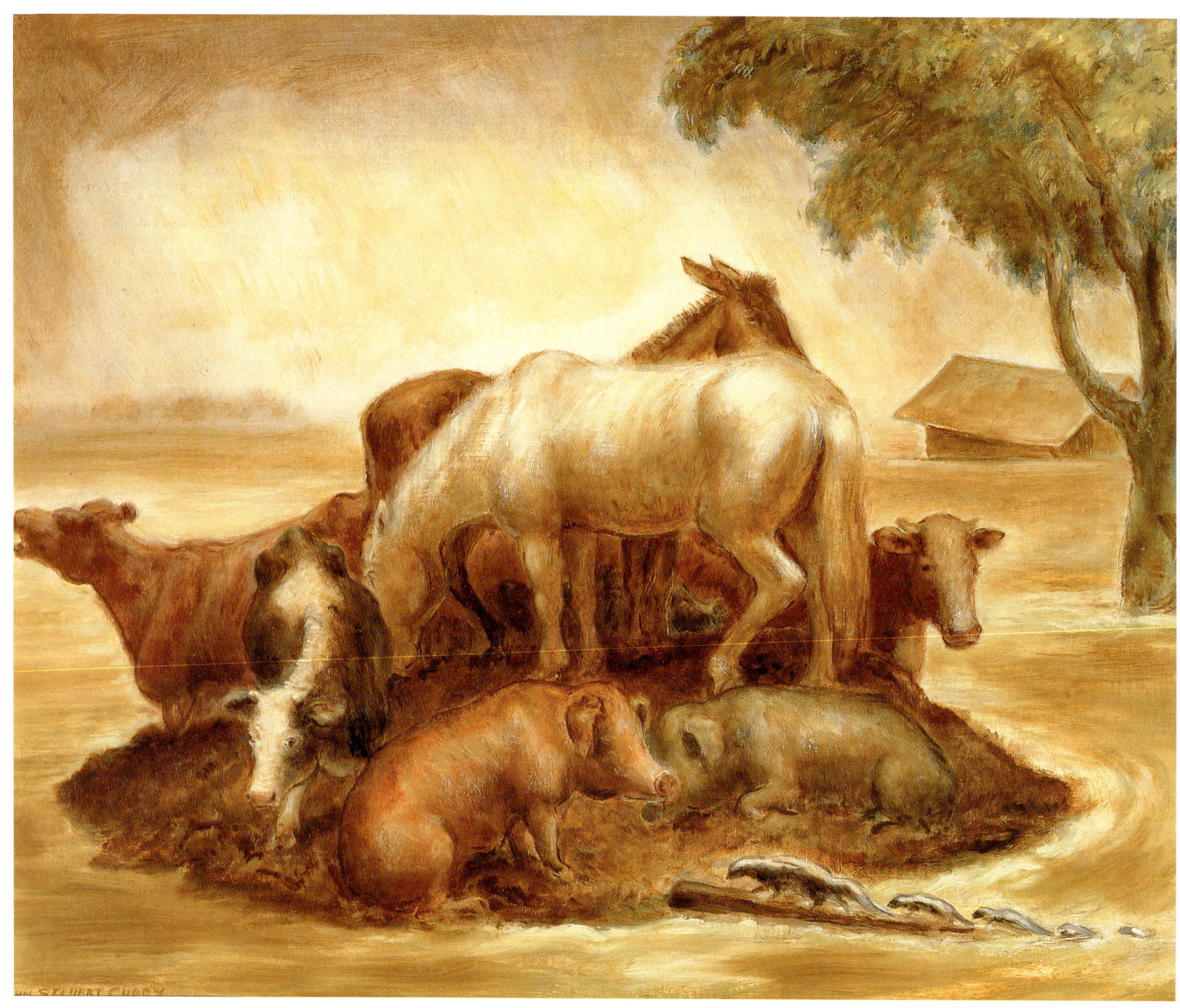

PLATE 35

Sanctuary, 1935
Oil on canvas (now mounted on Masonite)
24⅛ × 30½ in.
Signed lower left: *JOHN STEUART CURRY*
Museum of American Art of the Pennsylvania Academy of the Fine Arts, Philadelphia. Collections Fund.

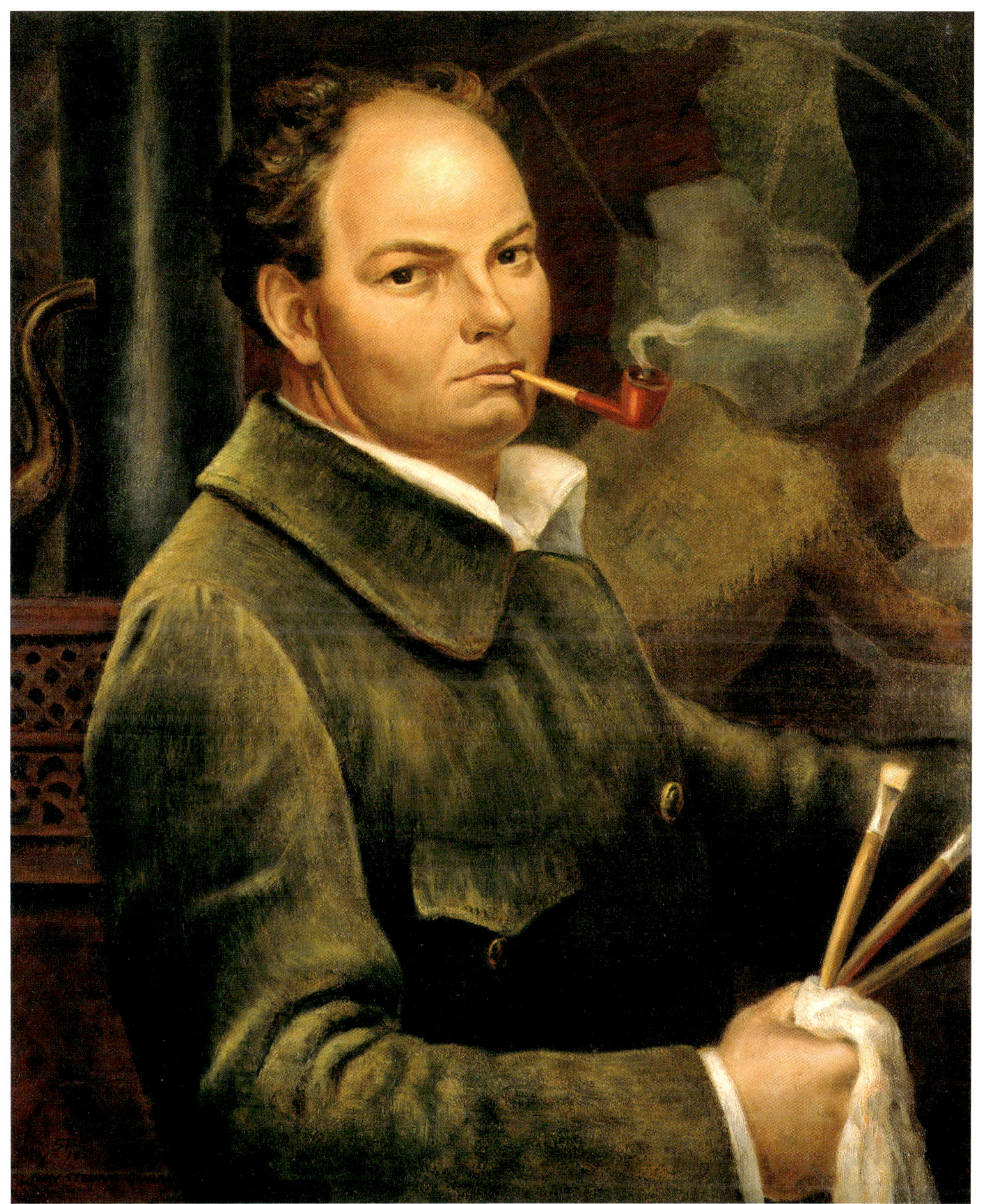

PLATE 36

Self-Portrait, 1935
Oil and tempera on canvas
30¼ × 25⅛ in.
Signed, dated, and inscribed lower left: *SELF/1935/JOHN STEUART CURRY*
Curtis Galleries, Inc., Minneapolis.

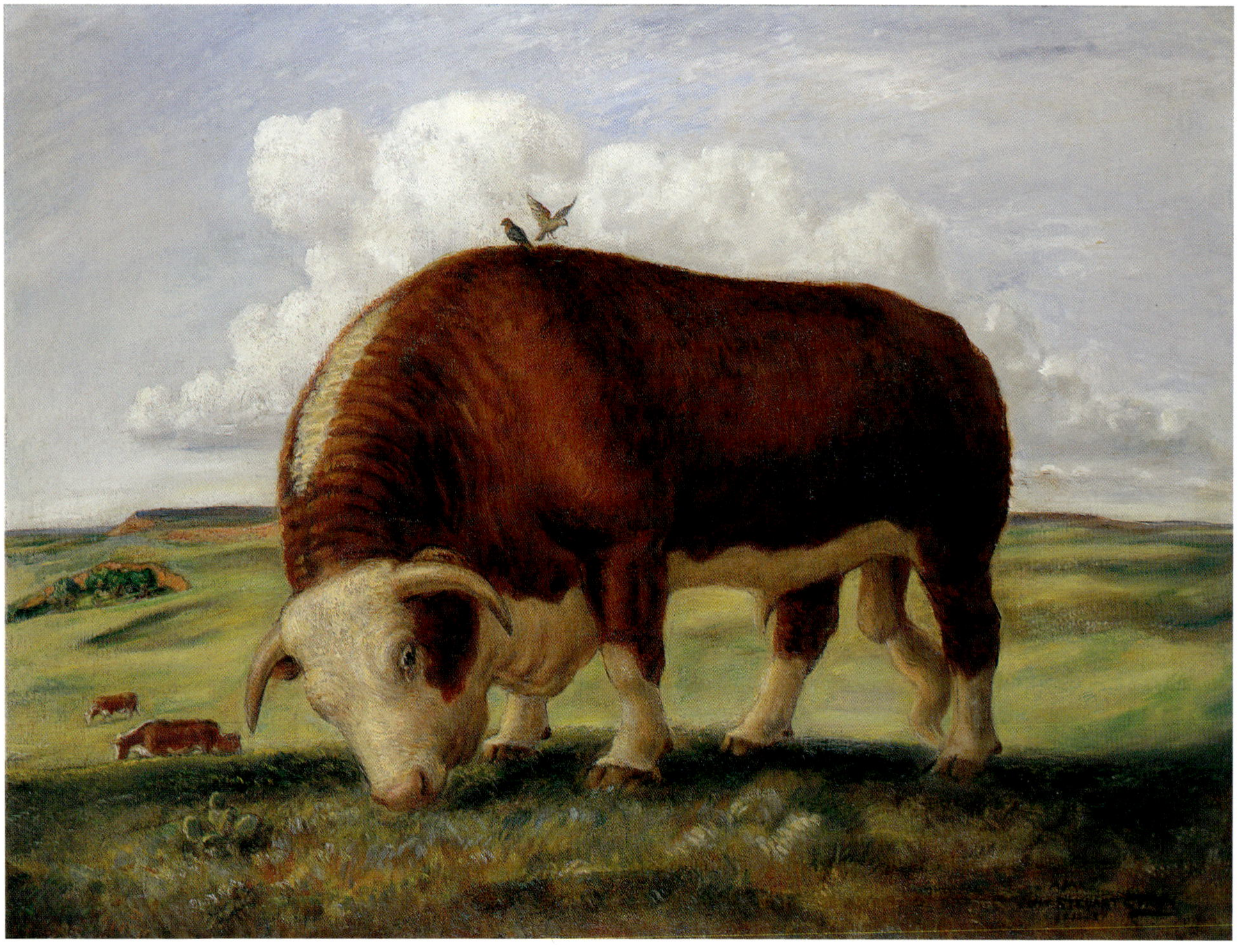

PLATE 37

Ajax, 1936–37

Oil on canvas
36¼ × 48¾ in.
Signed, dated, and inscribed lower right:
AJAX/JOHN STEUART CURRY/1936–37
The FORBES Magazine Collection, New York.

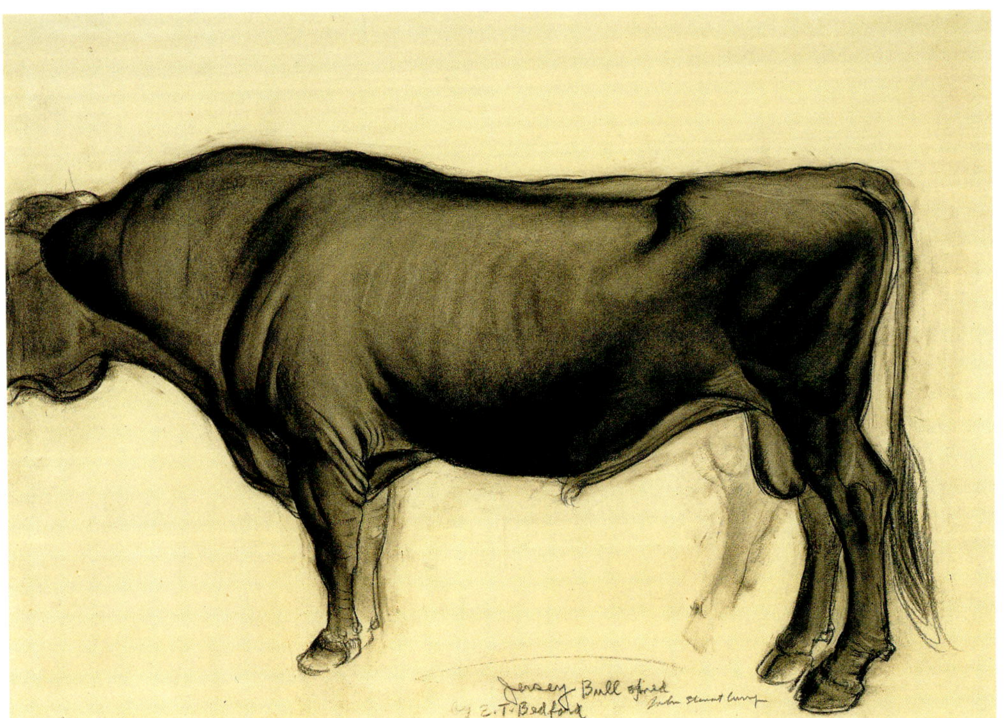

PLATE 39

Jersey Bull Sired by E. T. Bedford, ca. 1936–40

Charcoal on paper
25 × 18¼ in.
Estate of the artist. Courtesy Mongerson Wunderlich Gallery, Chicago.

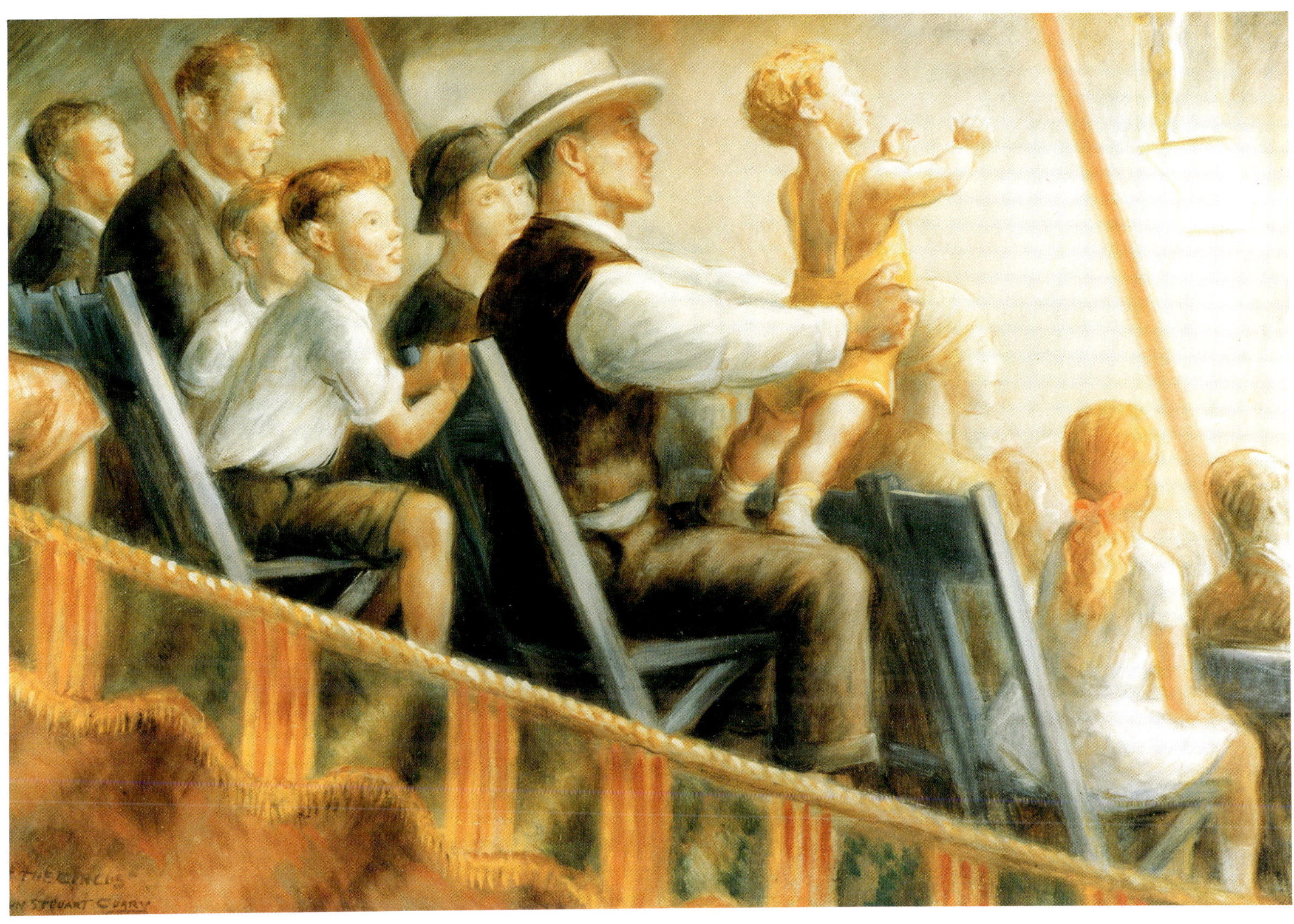

PLATE 38

At the Circus, 1936
Oil on canvas
21 × 30½ in.
Signed, dated, and inscribed lower left: *AT THE CIRCUS/JOHN STEUART CURRY/1936*
Private collection.
Photograph courtesy Guggenheim, Asher Associates, Inc., New York
(EXHIBITED IN SAN FRANCISCO ONLY)

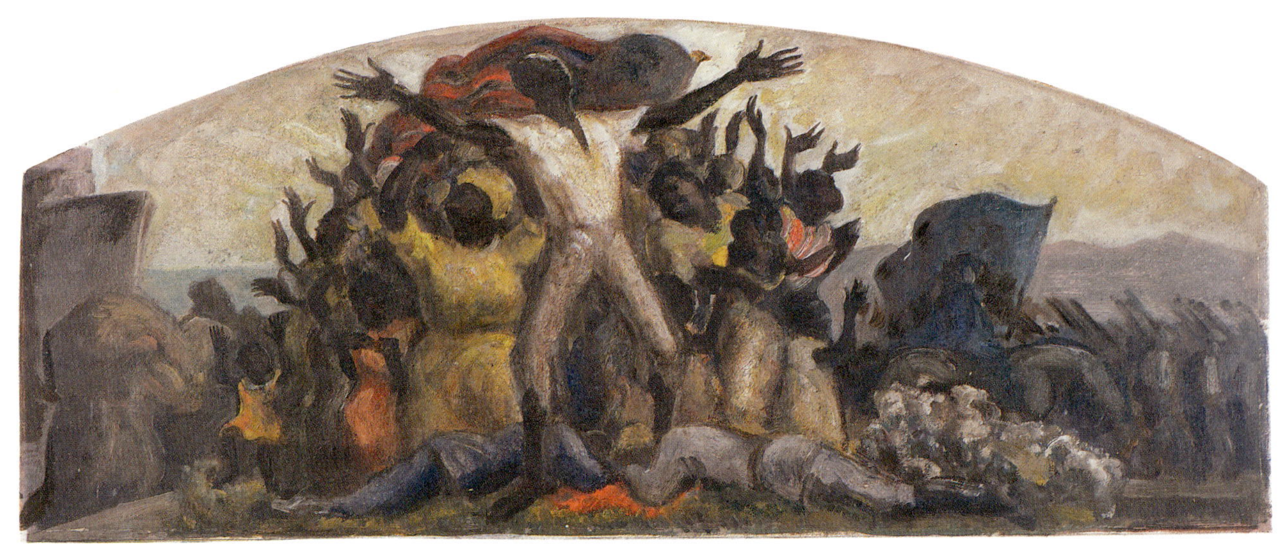

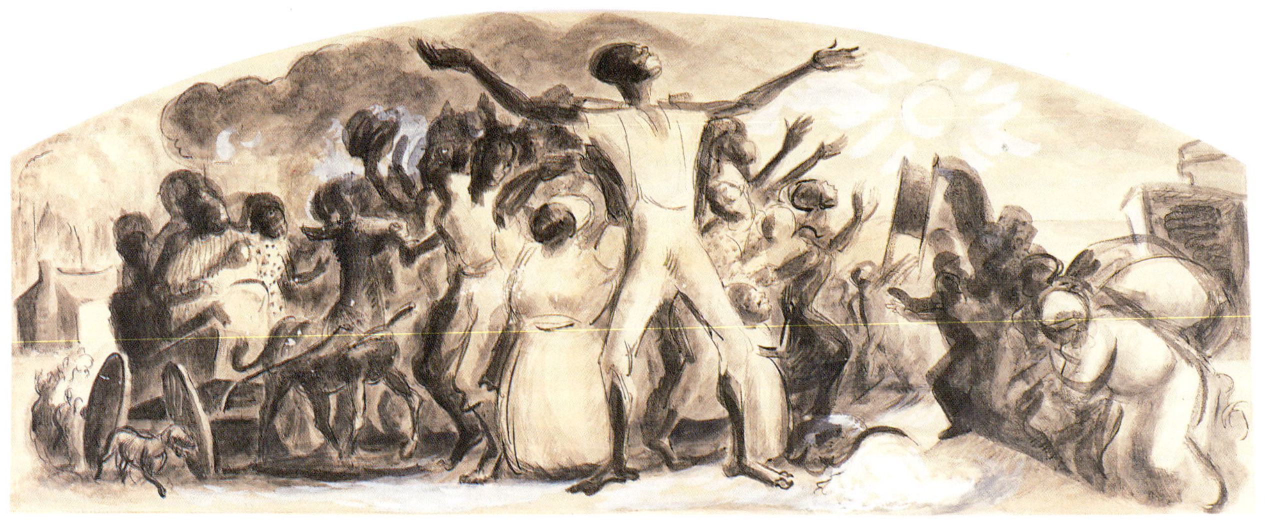

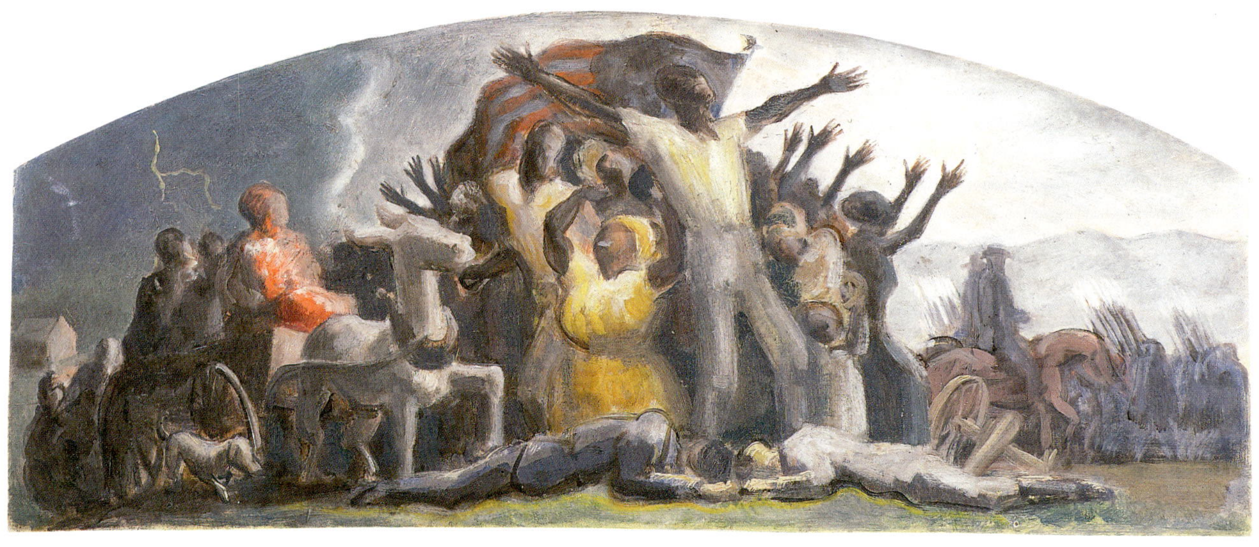

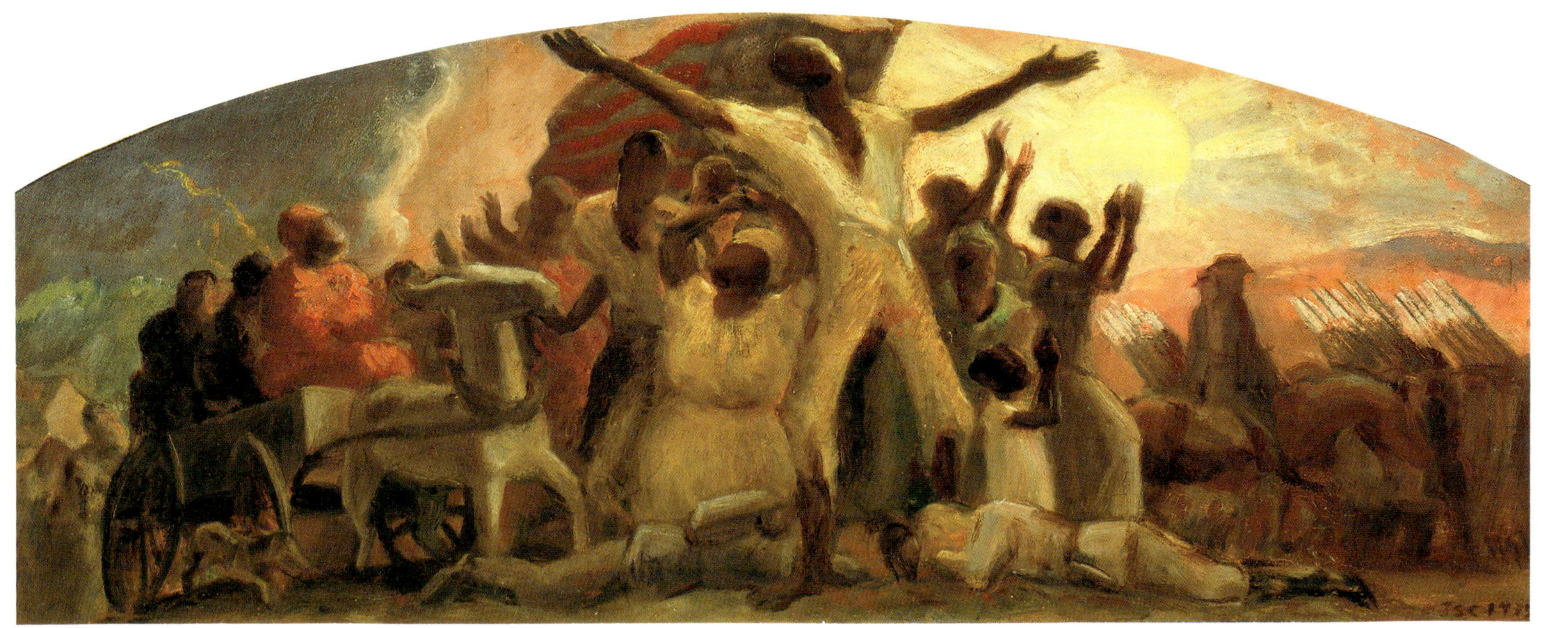

PLATE 43

Freeing of the Slaves, 1936
Mural study, U.S. Department of Justice building, Washington, D.C.
Oil on paperboard (now mounted on board)
14½ × 33¼ in.
Greendyke Fine Art, Pittsford, New York.

PLATE 40 *(facing page, top)*

Freeing of the Slaves, 1936
Mural study, U.S. Department of Justice building, Washington, D.C.
Oil on paperboard
8½ × 20½ in.
Mrs. John Steuart Curry.

PLATE 41 *(facing page, middle)*

Freeing of the Slaves, 1936
Mural study, U.S. Department of Justice building, Washington, D.C.
Gouache on paperboard
8½ × 20½ in.
Mrs. John Steuart Curry.

PLATE 42 *(facing page, bottom)*

Freeing of the Slaves, 1936
Mural study, U.S. Department of Justice building, Washington, D.C.
Gouache on paperboard
8½ × 20½ in.
Mrs. John Steuart Curry.

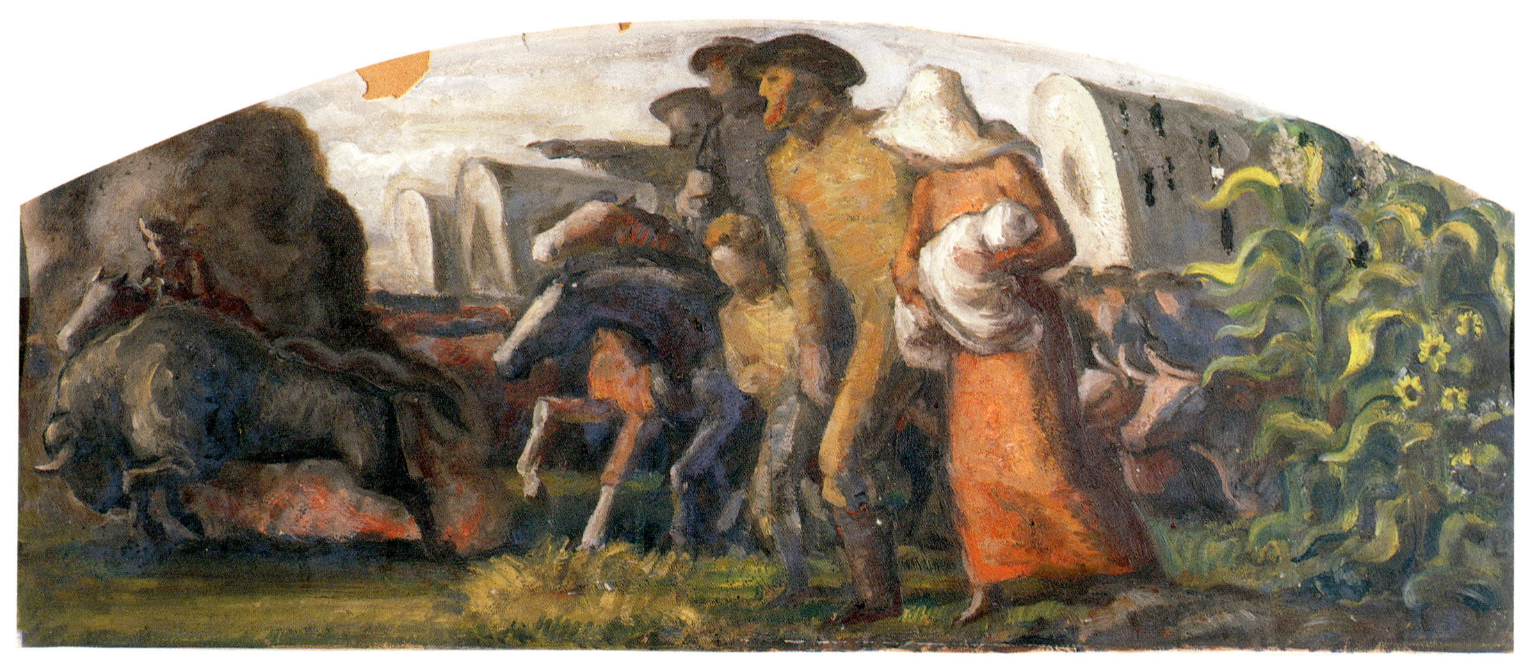

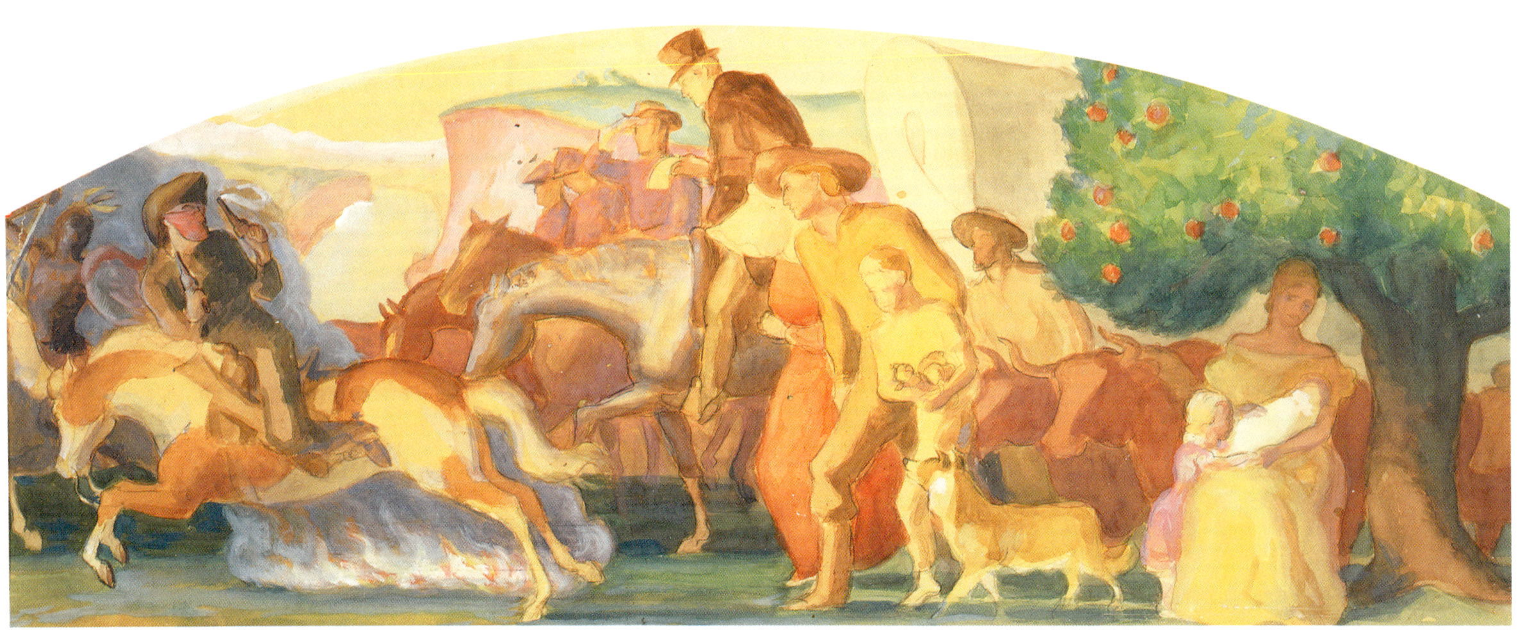

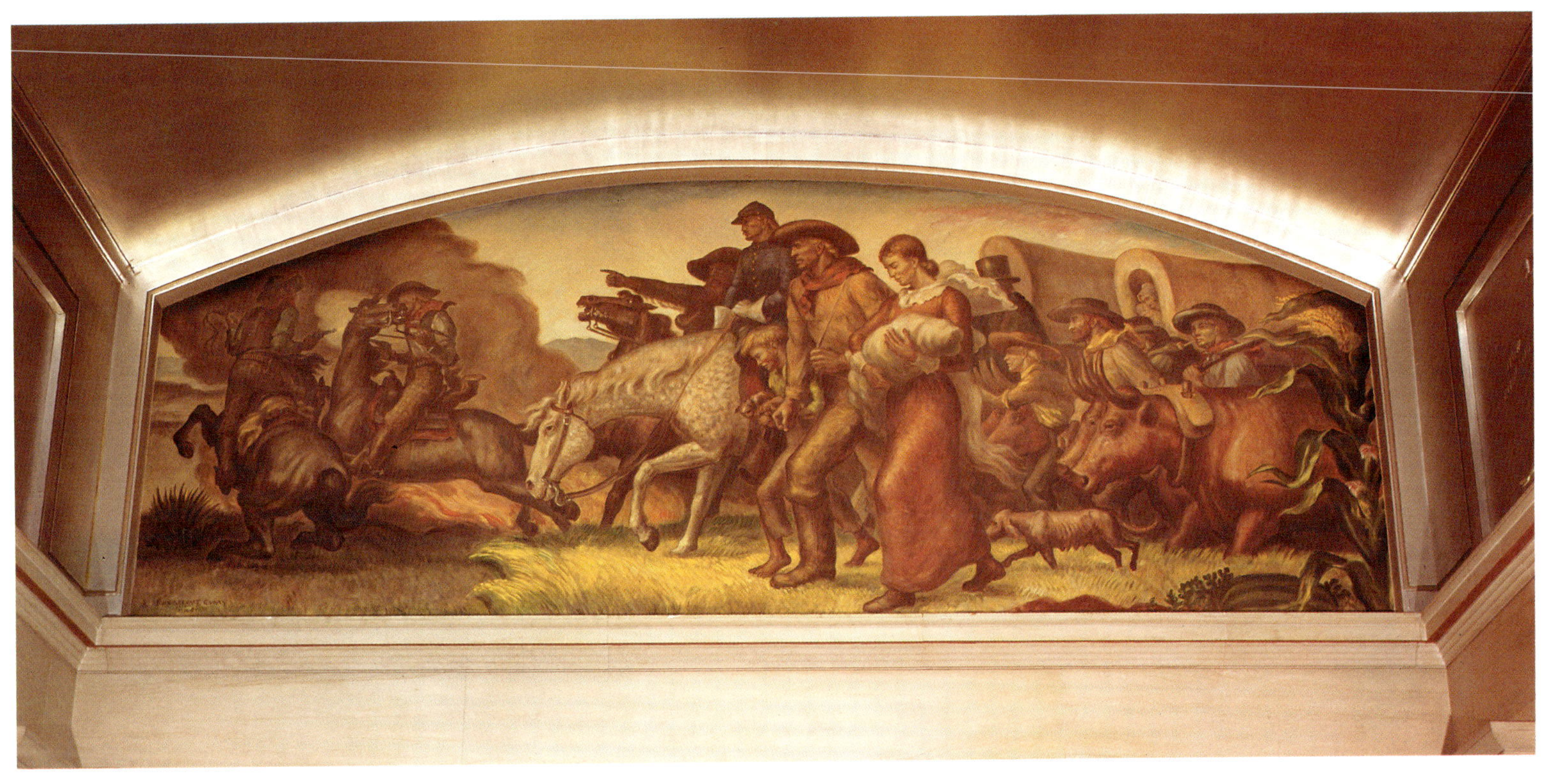

*PLATE 46

Westward Movement: Justice of the Plains, 1937
Mural, U.S. Department of Justice building, Washington, D.C.
Oil and tempera on canvas
8 ft., 6 in. × 20 ft., 6 in.
Photograph courtesy Fine Arts Program, Public Buildings Service, United States General Services Administration, Washington, D.C.

PLATE 44 *(facing page, top)*

Westward Movement: Justice of the Plains, 1936
Mural study, U.S. Department of Justice building, Washington, D.C.
Oil on paperboard
12¼ × 30¾ in.
Mrs. John Steuart Curry.

PLATE 45 *(facing page, bottom)*

Westward Movement: Justice of the Plains, 1936
Mural study, U.S. Department of Justice building, Washington, D.C.
Tempera on paper
12¼ × 30¾ in.
Estate of the artist. Courtesy Mongerson Wunderlich Gallery, Chicago.

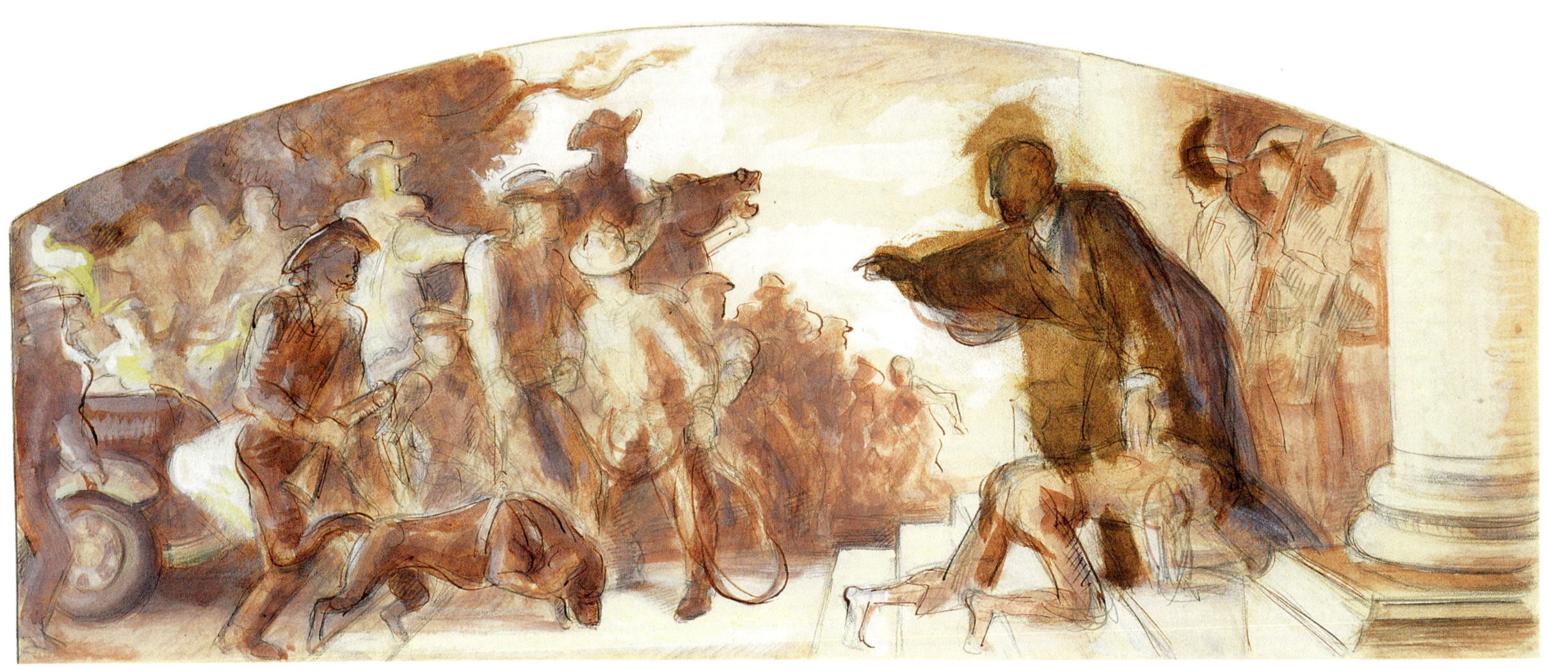

PLATE 47

Law versus Mob Rule, 1937
Mural study, U.S. Department of Justice building, Washington, D.C.
Tempera, watercolor, and ink on paperboard
8½ × 20½ in.
Estate of the artist. Courtesy Mongerson Wunderlich Gallery, Chicago.

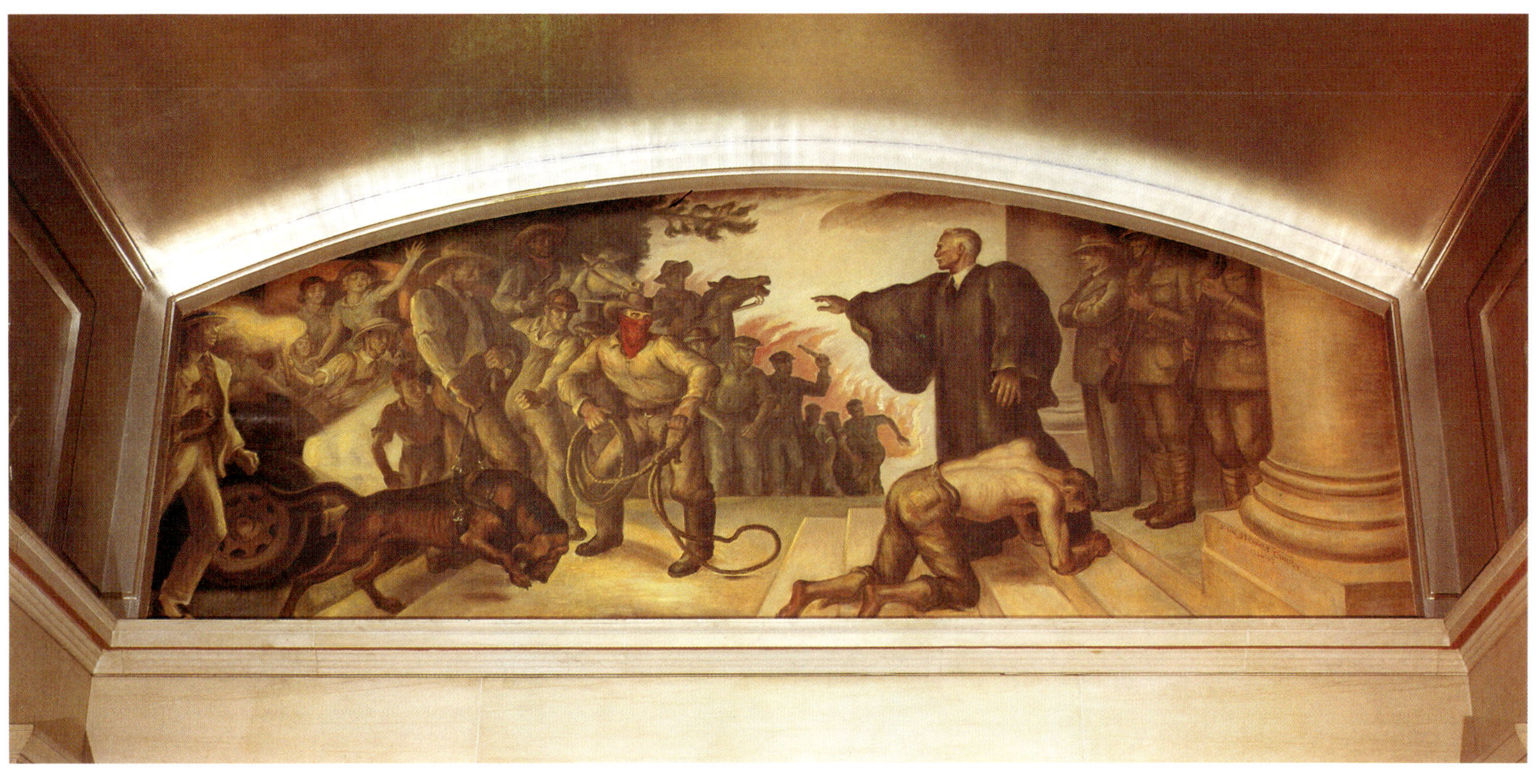

***PLATE 48**

Law versus Mob Rule, 1937
Mural, U.S. Department of Justice building, Washington, D.C.
Oil and tempera on canvas
8 ft., 6 in. × 20 ft., 6 in.
Photograph courtesy Fine Arts Program, Public Buildings Service, United States General Services Administration, Washington, D.C.

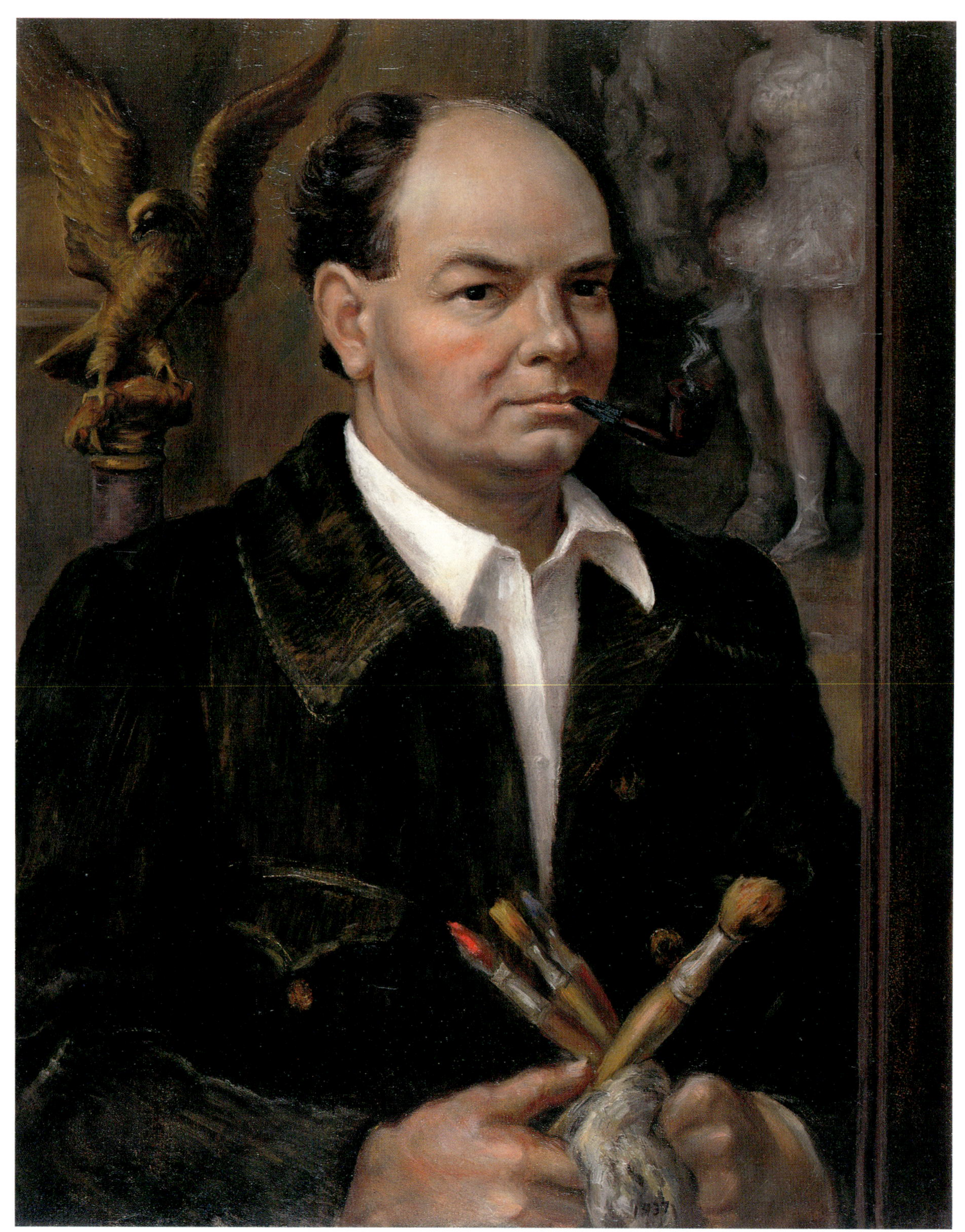

PLATE 49

Self-Portrait, 1937
Oil and tempera on canvas
30 × 24 in.
Dated bottom center: *1937*
Fine Arts Museums of San Francisco. Gift of Mr. and Mrs. J. Burgess Jamieson.

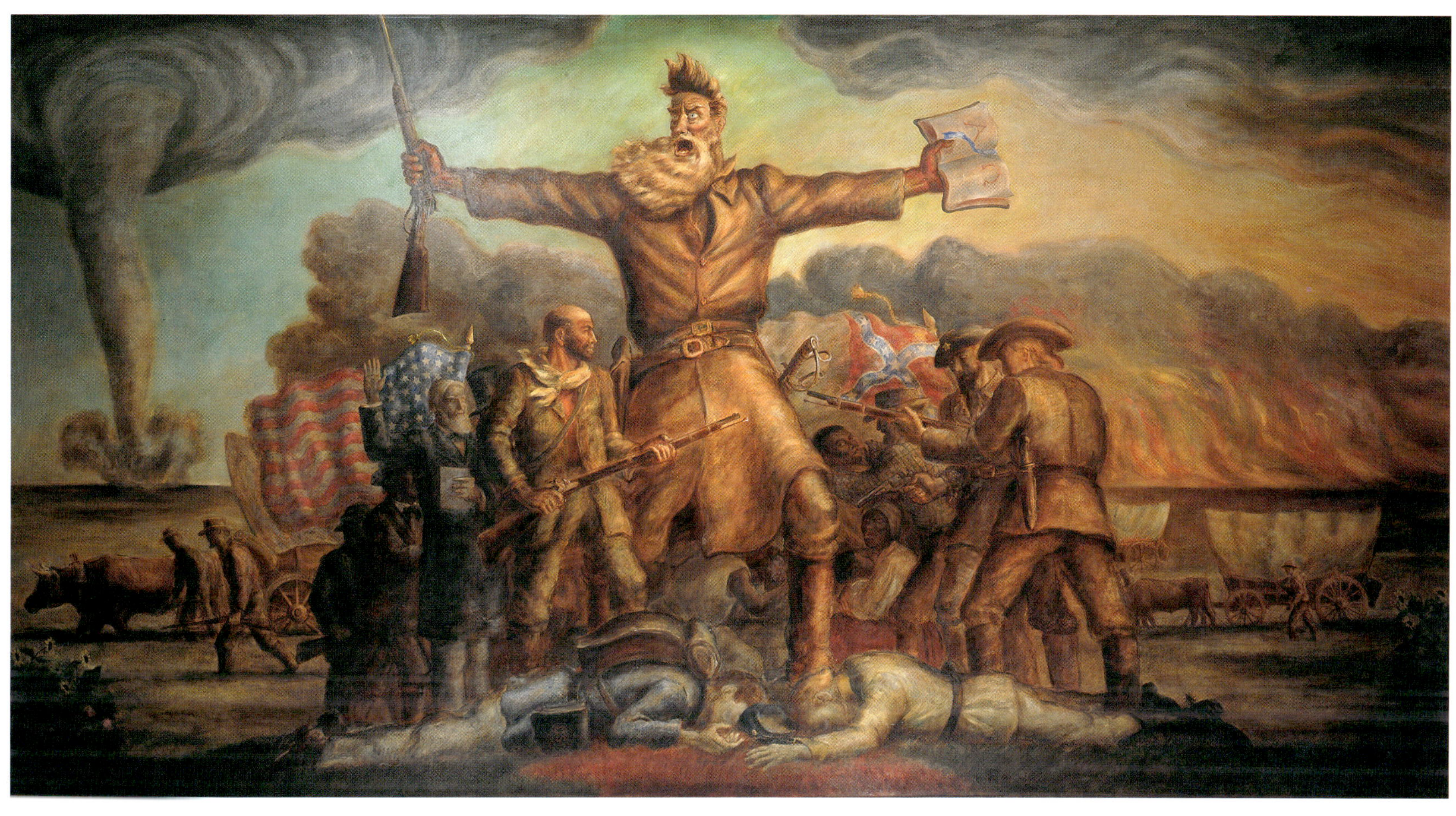

*PLATE 50

Tragic Prelude—John Brown, 1937–42
Mural, Kansas Statehouse, Topeka
Oil and tempera on canvas
11 ft., 6 in. × 31 ft. (overall)
Photograph courtesy Nathan Ham, Topeka, Kansas

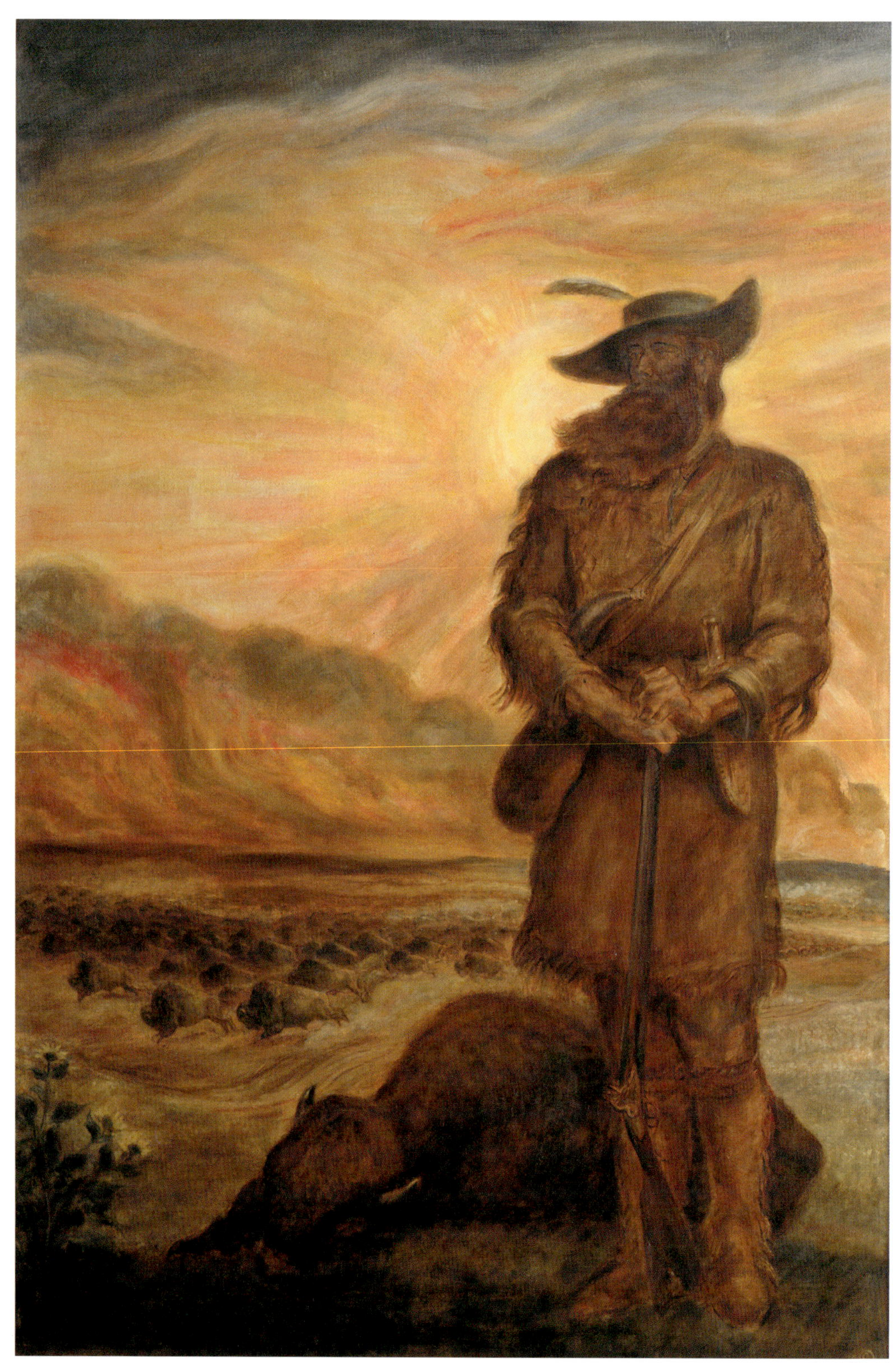

*PLATE 51

Tragic Prelude—The Plainsman, 1937–42
Mural, Kansas Statehouse, Topeka
Oil and tempera on canvas
11 ft., 6 in. × 22 ft. (overall)
Photograph courtesy Nathan Ham, Topeka, Kansas

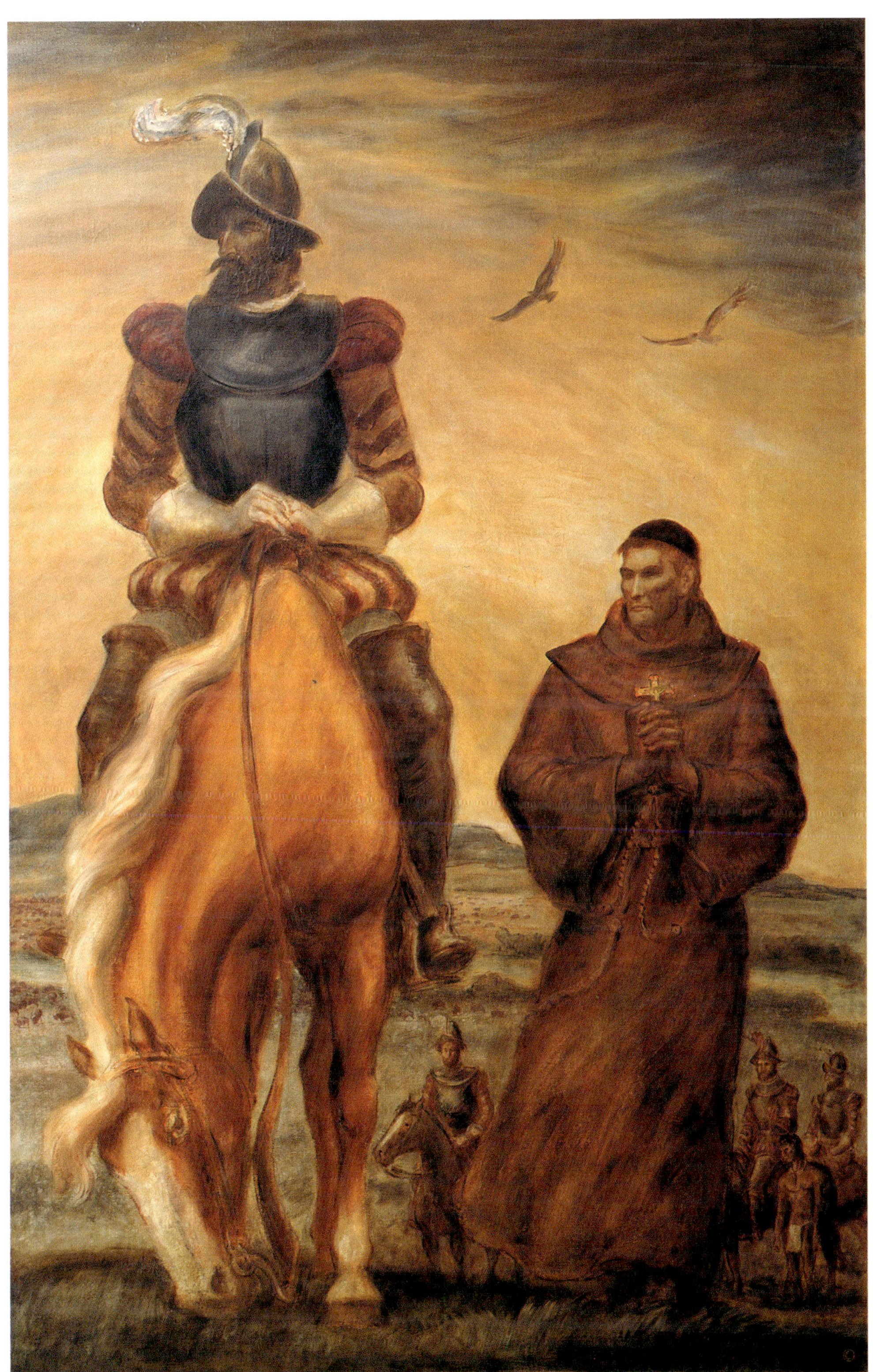

***PLATE 52**

Tragic Prelude—Coronado and Padre Padilla, 1937–42
Mural, Kansas Statehouse, Topeka
Oil and tempera on canvas
11 ft., 6 in. × 22 ft. (overall)
Photograph courtesy Nathan Ham, Topeka, Kansas

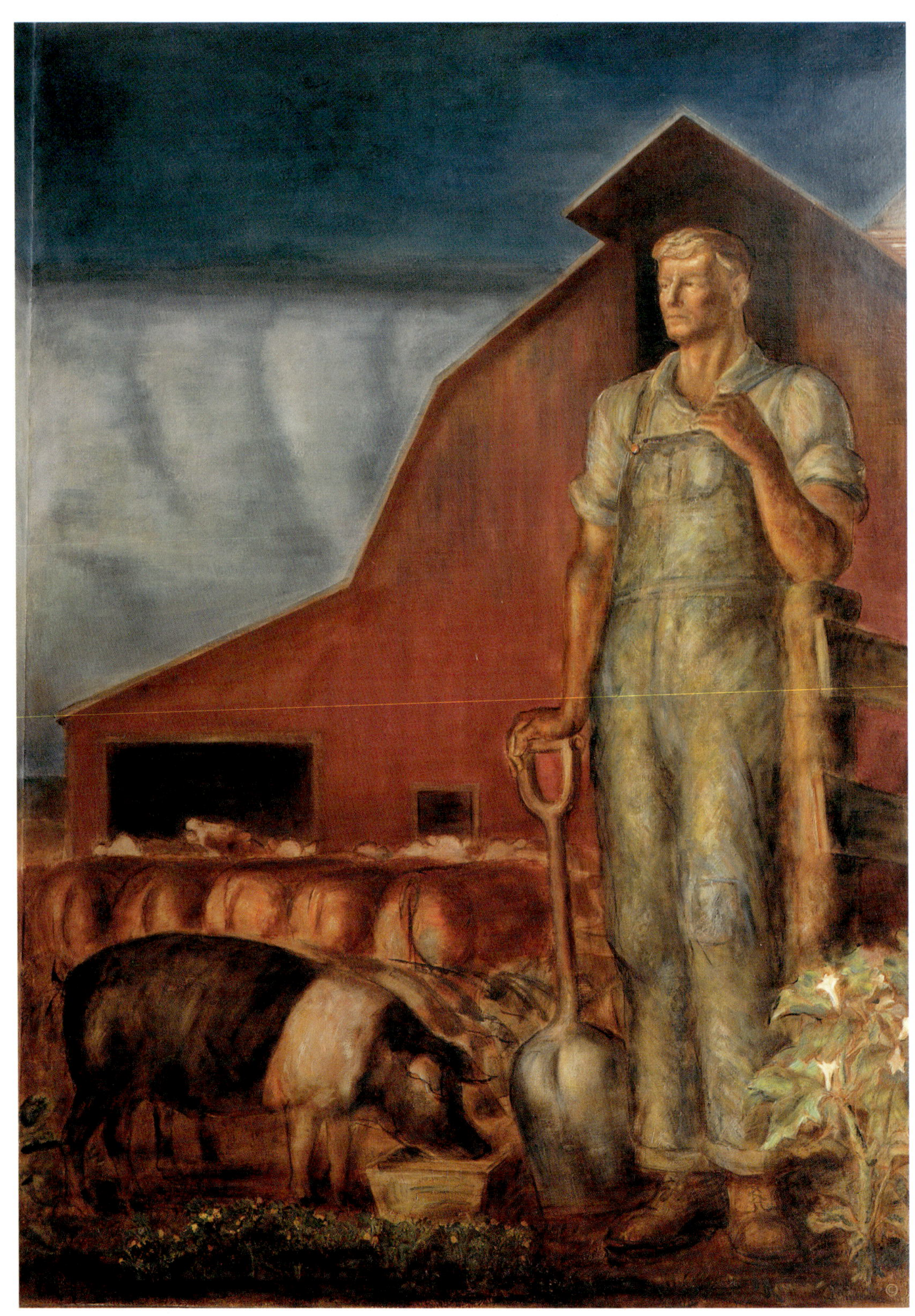

*PLATE 54

Kansas Pastoral—Farmer and Livestock, 1937–42
Mural, Kansas Statehouse, Topeka
Oil and tempera on canvas
11 ft., 6 in. × 22 ft. (overall)
Photograph courtesy Nathan Ham, Topeka, Kansas

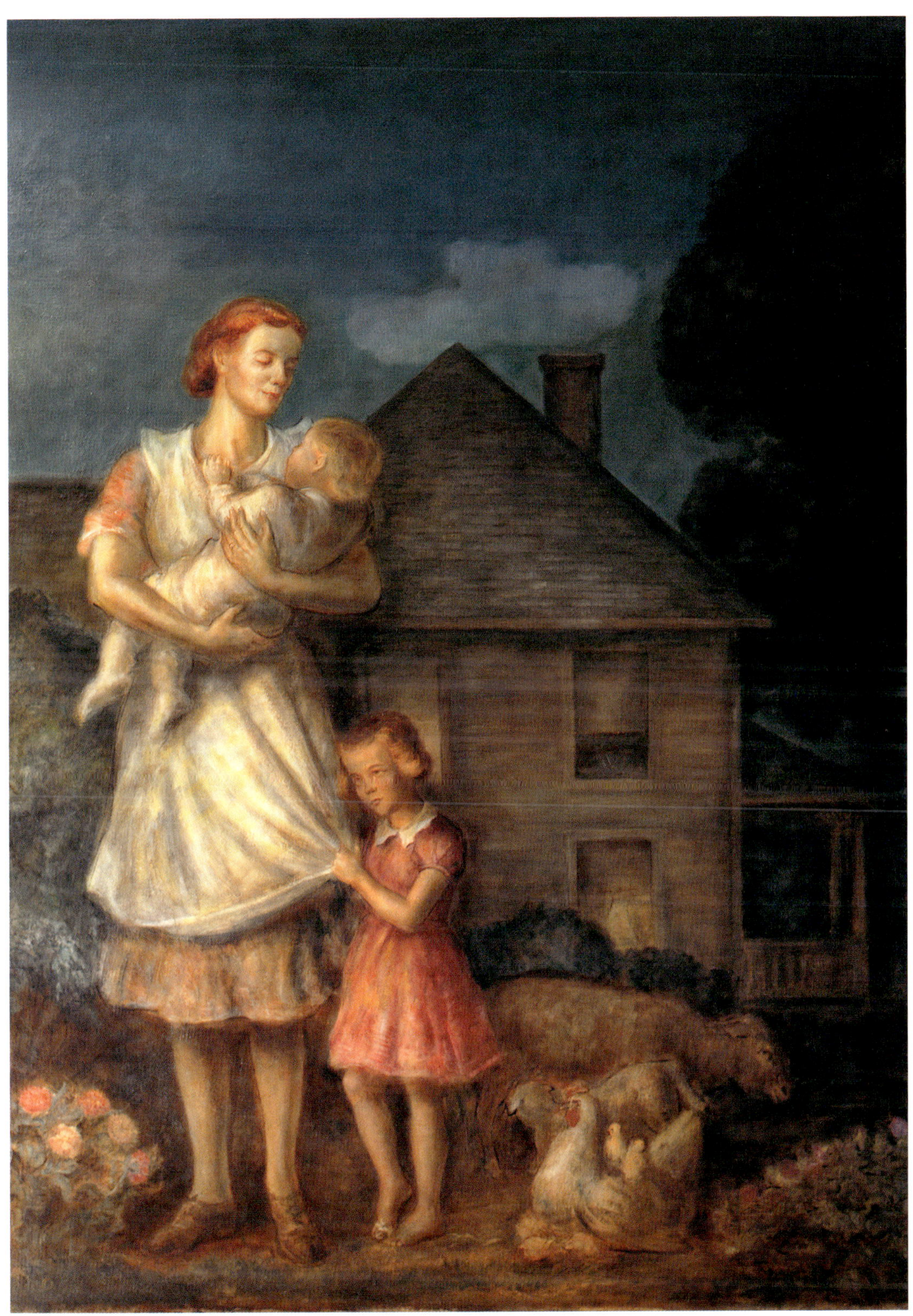

*PLATE 55

Kansas Pastoral—Farmer's Family, 1937–42
Mural, Kansas Statehouse, Topeka
Oil and tempera on canvas
11 ft., 6 in. × 22 ft. (overall)
Photograph courtesy Nathan Ham, Topeka, Kansas

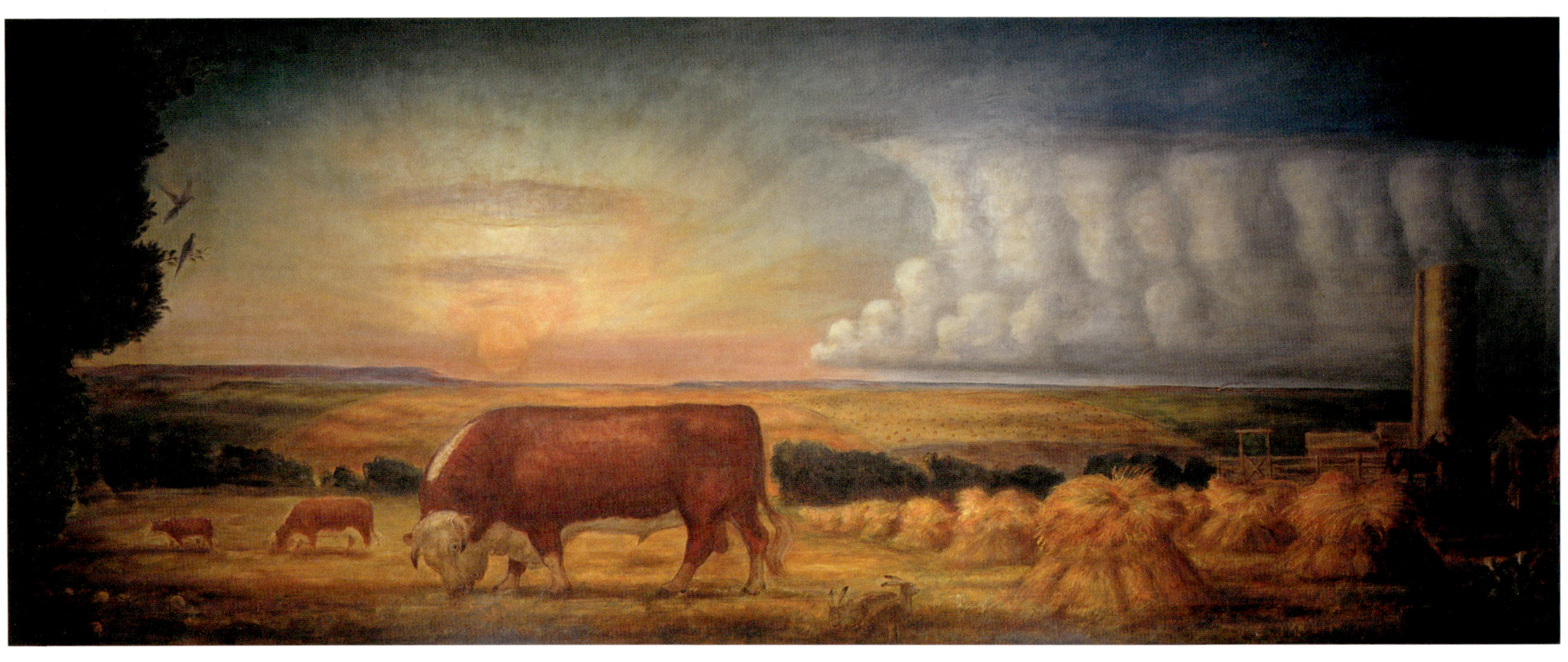

***PLATE 53**

Kansas Pastoral—The Unmortgaged Farm, 1937–42
Mural, Kansas Statehouse, Topeka
Oil and tempera on canvas
11 ft., 6 in. × 29 ft. (overall)
Photograph courtesy Nathan Ham, Topeka, Kansas

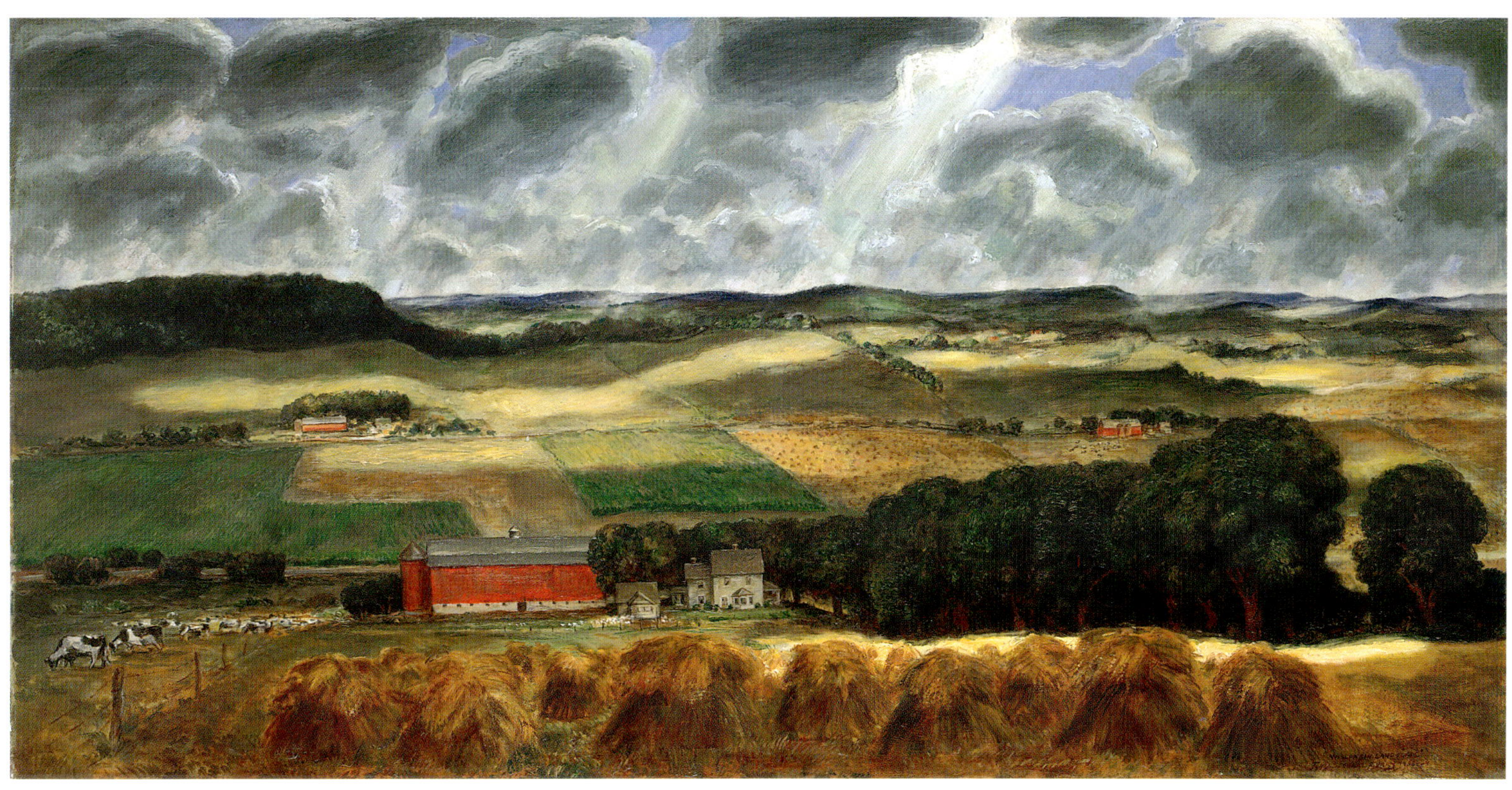

PLATE 56

Wisconsin Landscape, 1937–39

Oil on canvas

42 × 84 in.

Signed, dated, and inscribed lower right: *WISCONSIN LANDSCAPE/JOHN STEUART CURRY/1938–39*

The Metropolitan Museum of Art, New York. George A. Hearn Fund, 1942. Photograph © 1981: The Metropolitan Museum of Art

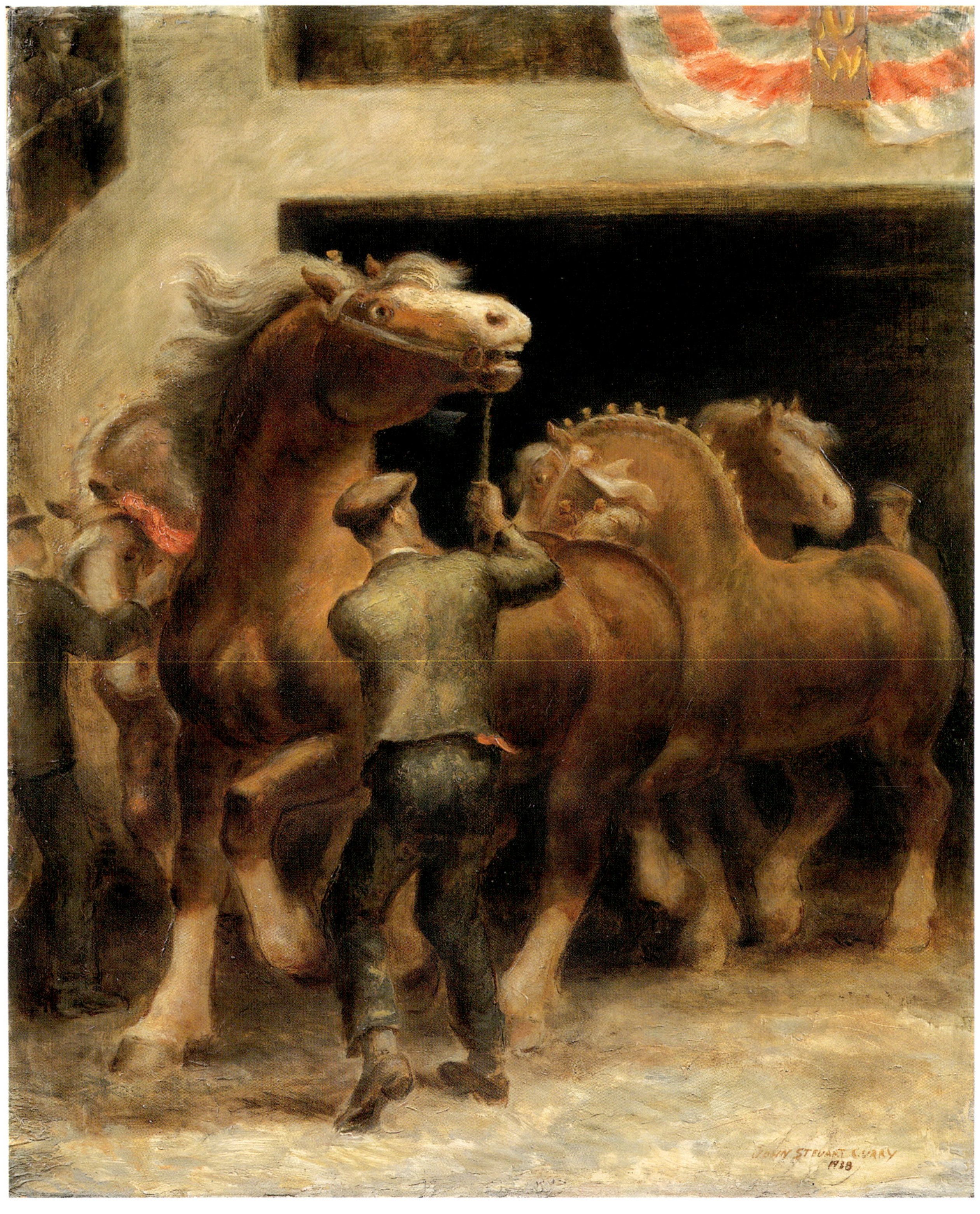
JOHN STEUART CURRY
1938

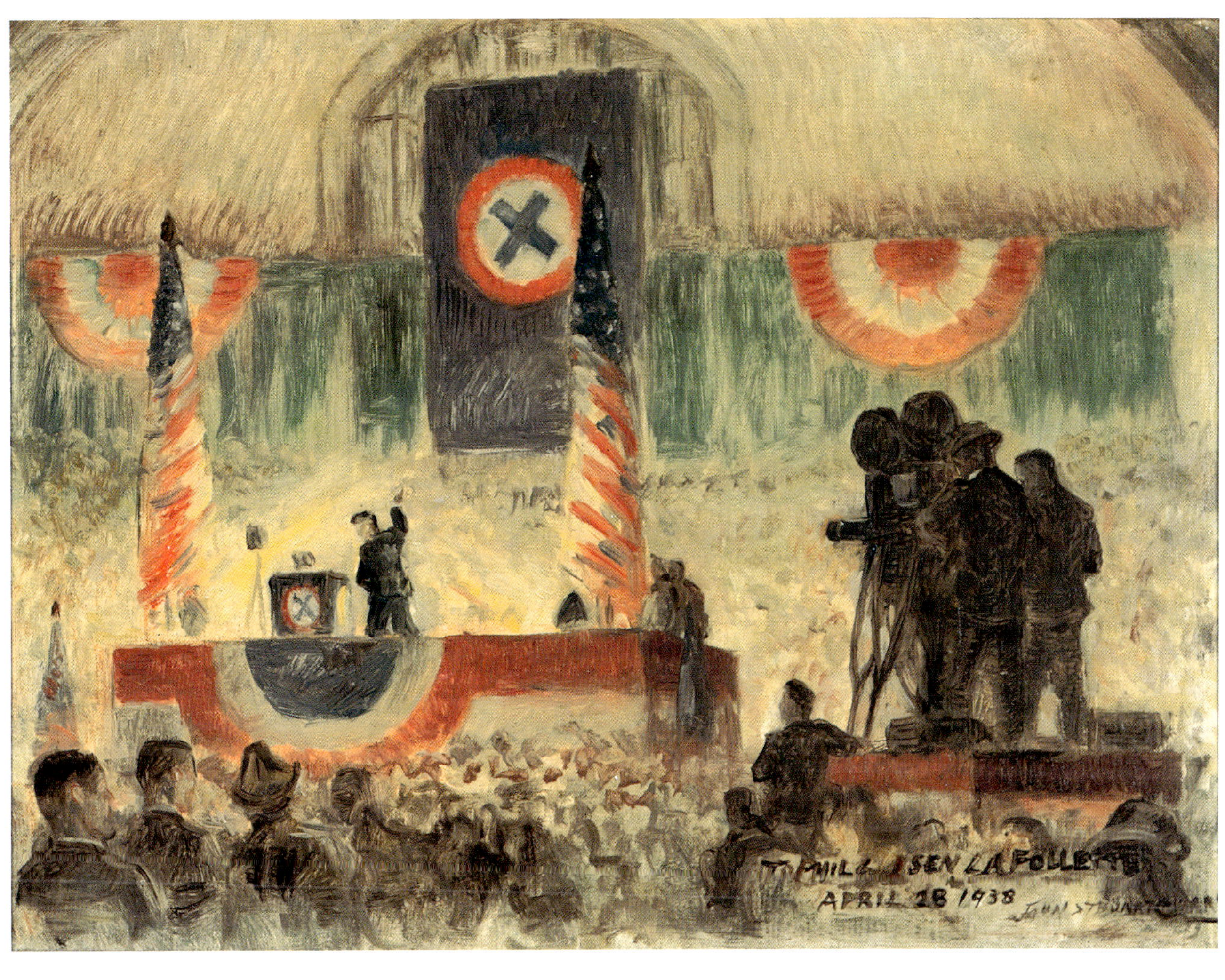

PLATE 58

First Rally of the National Progressive Party, Madison, Wisconsin, April 28, 1938, 1938
Oil on canvas
$11\frac{1}{2} \times 15\frac{1}{2}$ in.
Signed, dated, and inscribed lower right: *TO PHIL SEN LA FOLLETTE/APRIL 28TH 1938/JOHN STEUART CURRY*
Madison Art Center, Madison, Wisconsin. Gift of the family of Philip and Isabel La Follette in their memory.

PLATE 57

Belgian Stallions (Wisconsin Belgians), 1938
Oil on panel
30 × 25 in.
Signed and dated lower right: *JOHN STEUART CURRY/1938*
National Academy of Design, New York.

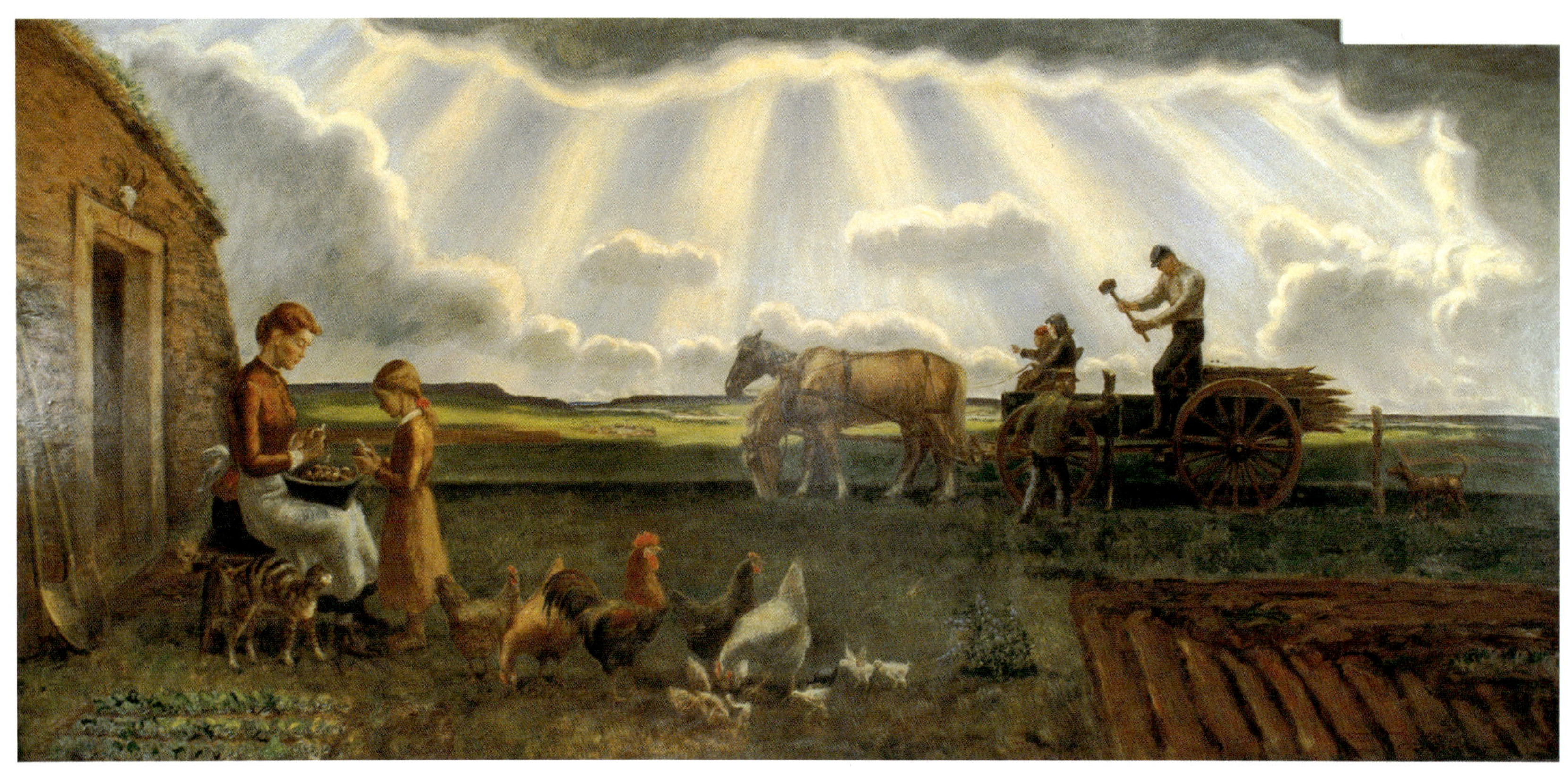

PLATE 59

The Homestead, 1938
Mural, U.S. Department of the Interior building, Washington, D.C.
Oil and tempera on canvas
9 ft. × 19 ft., 8 in.
Photograph courtesy Cunningham-Adams Painting Conservation, Sandy Hook, Connecticut

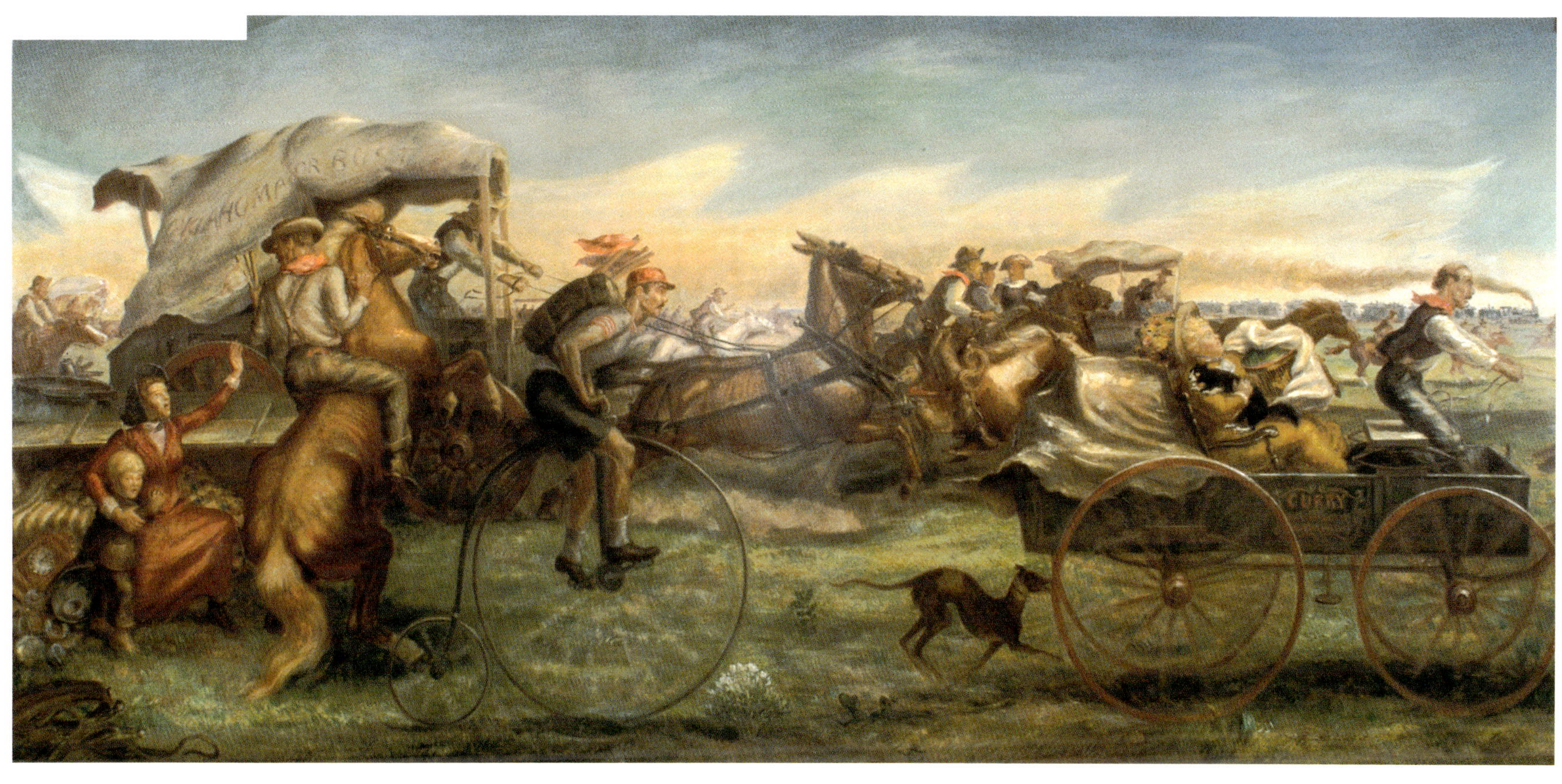

***PLATE 60**

The Oklahoma Land Rush, 1938
Mural, U.S. Department of the Interior building, Washington, D.C.
Oil and tempera on canvas
9 ft., 2 in. × 19 ft., 8 in.
Photograph courtesy Cunningham-Adams Painting Conservation, Sandy Hook, Connecticut

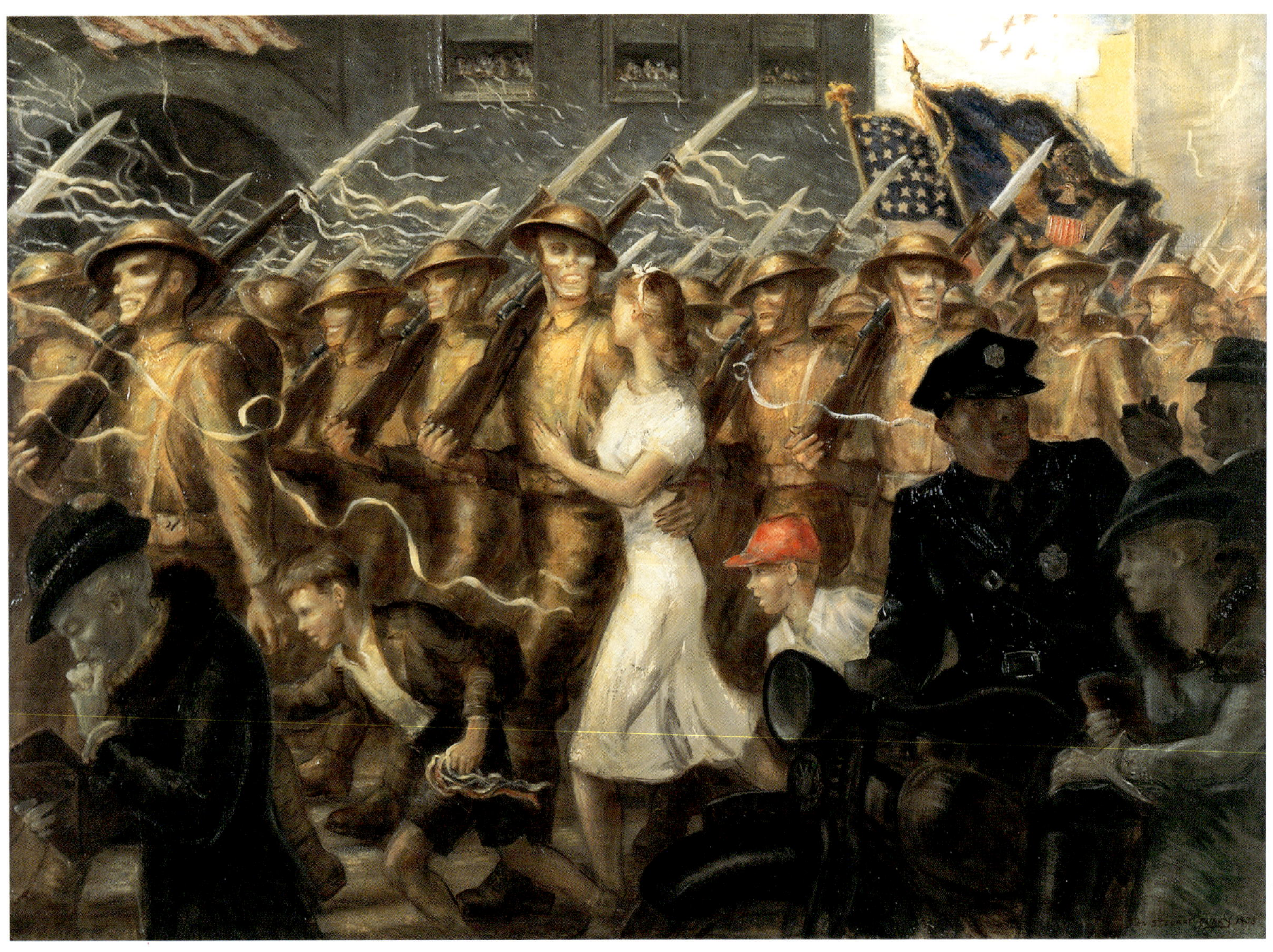

PLATE 61

Parade to War, 1938
Oil on canvas
40½ × 56 in.
Signed and dated lower right: *JOHN STEUART CURRY 1938*
The Cummer Museum of Art and Gardens, Jacksonville, Florida. Gift of Barnett Banks, Inc.

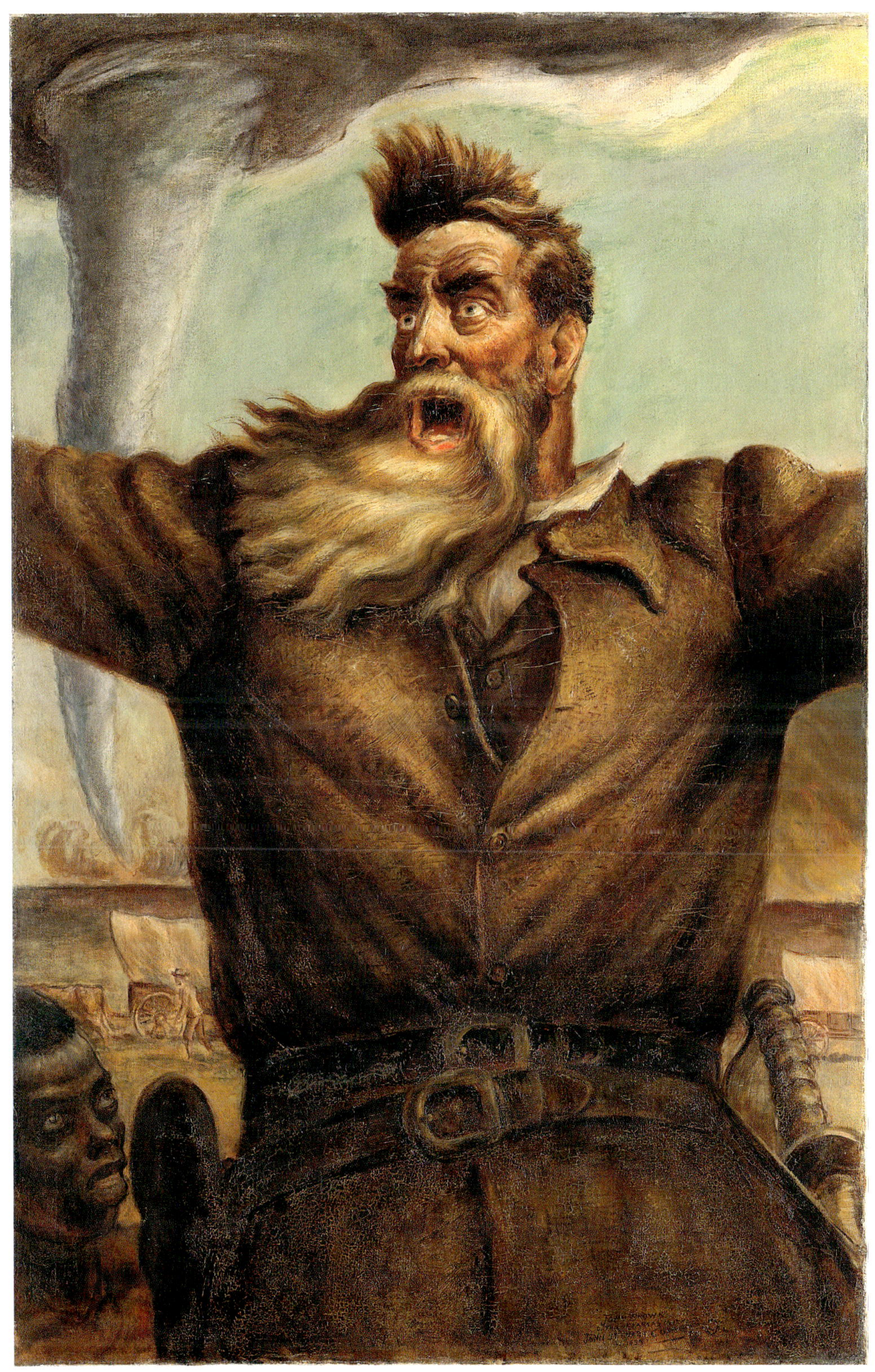

PLATE 62

John Brown, 1939
Oil and tempera on canvas
69 × 45 in.
Signed, dated, and inscribed lower right:
"JOHN BROWN"/DETAIL OF KANSAS MURAL/ JOHN STEUART CURRY/1939
The Metropolitan Museum of Art, New York.
Arthur Hoppock Hearn Fund, 1950.

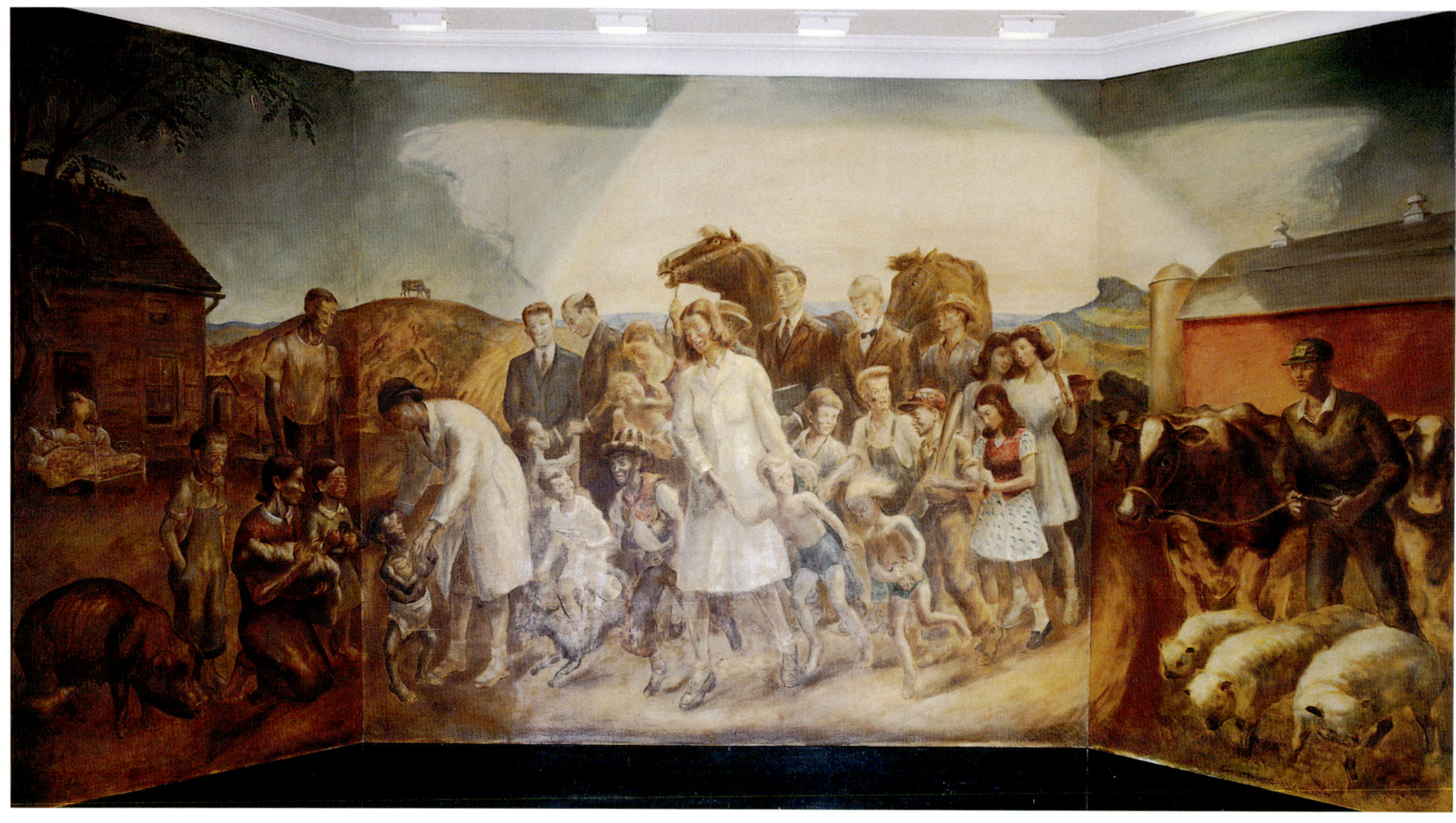

***PLATE 64**

The Social Benefits of Biochemical Research, 1941–43
Mural, biochemistry building, University of Wisconsin, Madison
Oil and tempera on canvas
9 ft. × 14 ft., 4 in.
Photograph courtesy University of Wisconsin–Madison

***PLATE 65** *(facing page, left)*

The Social Benefits of Biochemical Research—Farm Stock, 1941–43
Mural, biochemistry building, University of Wisconsin, Madison
Oil and tempera on canvas
9 ft. × 4 ft., 7 in.
Photograph courtesy University of Wisconsin–Madison

***PLATE 66** *(facing page, right)*

The Social Benefits of Biochemical Research—Corn and Tobacco, 1941–43
Mural, biochemistry building, University of Wisconsin, Madison
Oil and tempera on canvas
9 ft. × 4 ft., 7 in.
Photograph courtesy University of Wisconsin–Madison

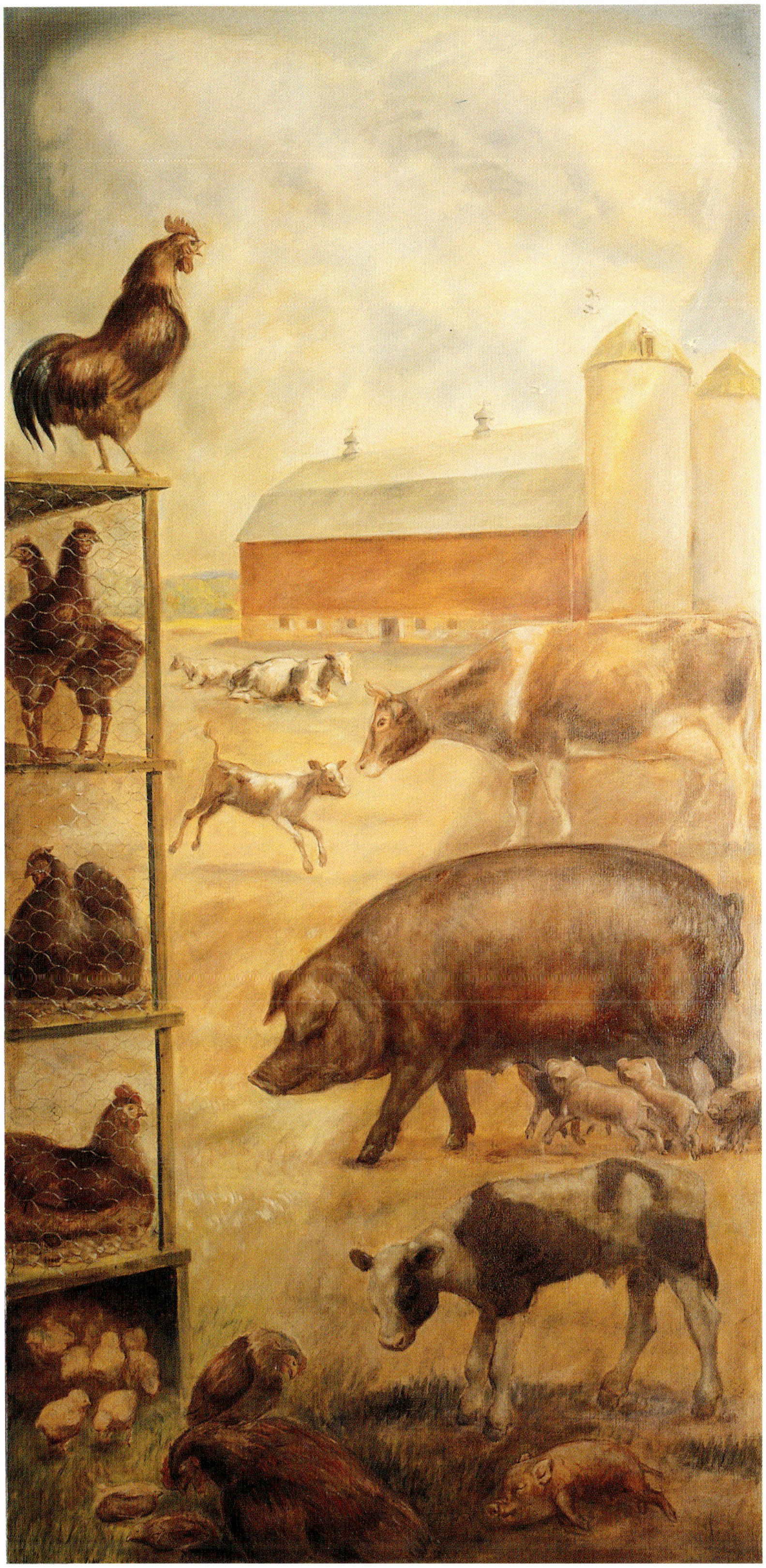

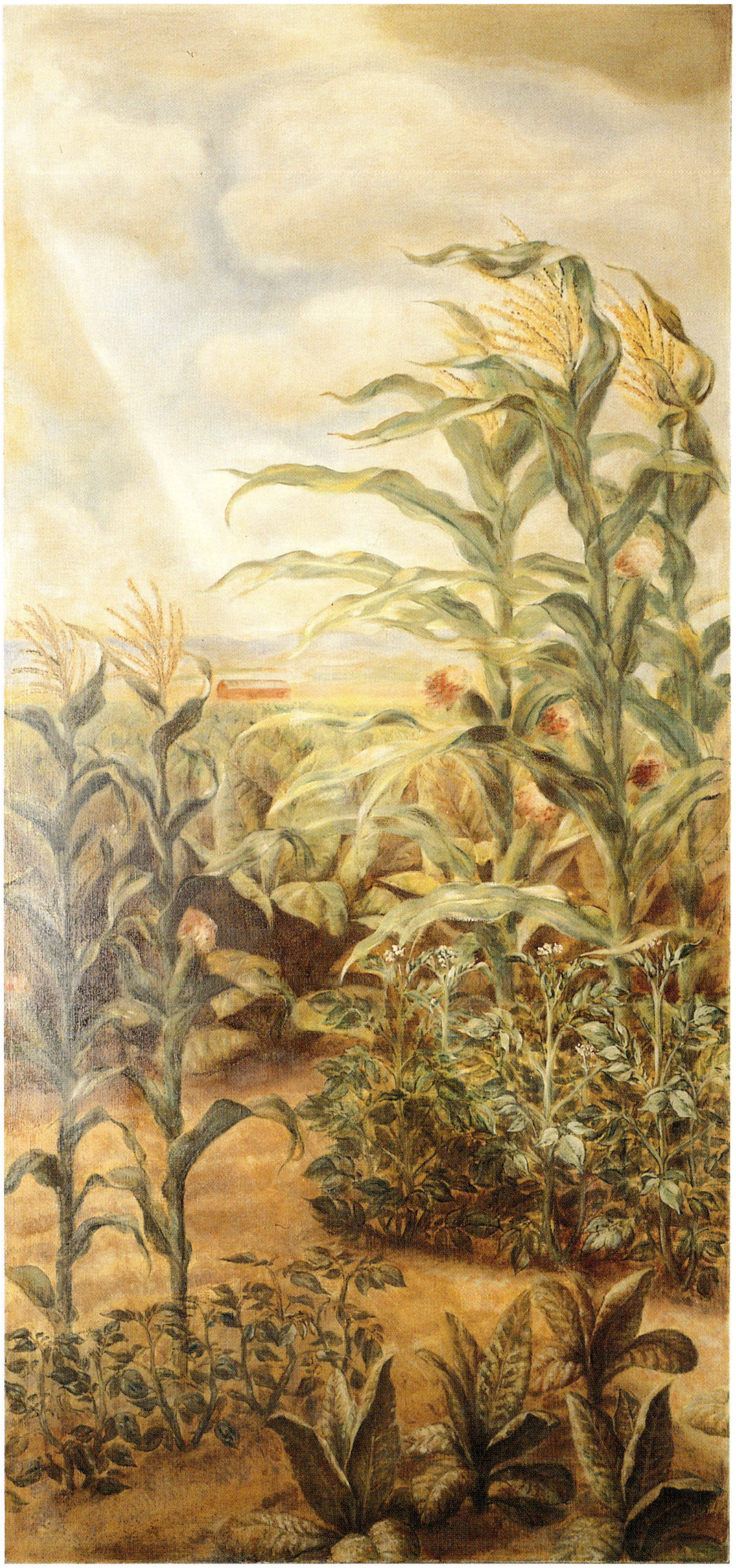

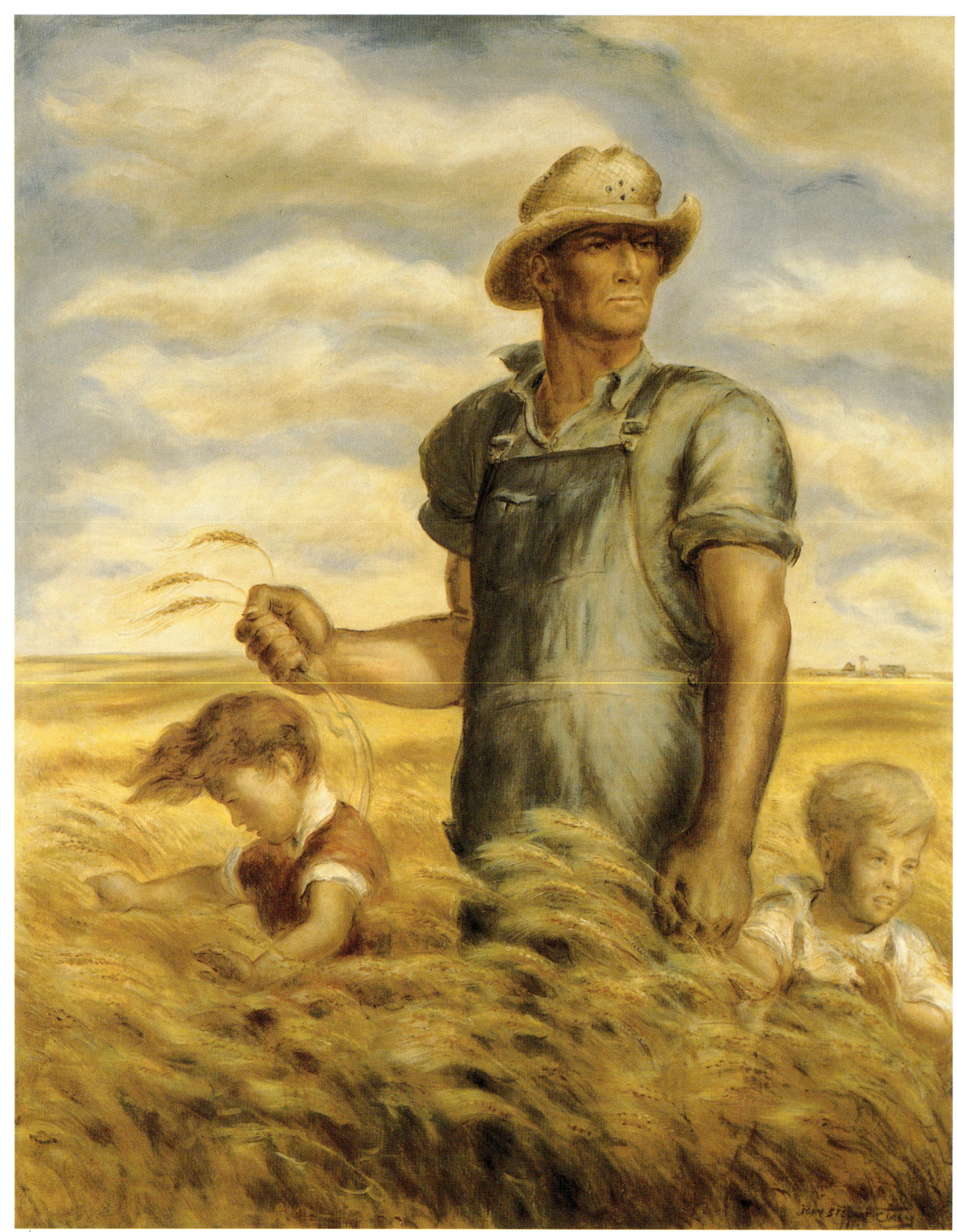

PLATE 63

Our Good Earth,
1940–41

Oil and tempera on canvas
52 × 40 in.
Signed and dated lower right: *JOHN STEUART CURRY/1941*
College of Agricultural and Life Sciences, University of Wisconsin–Madison.

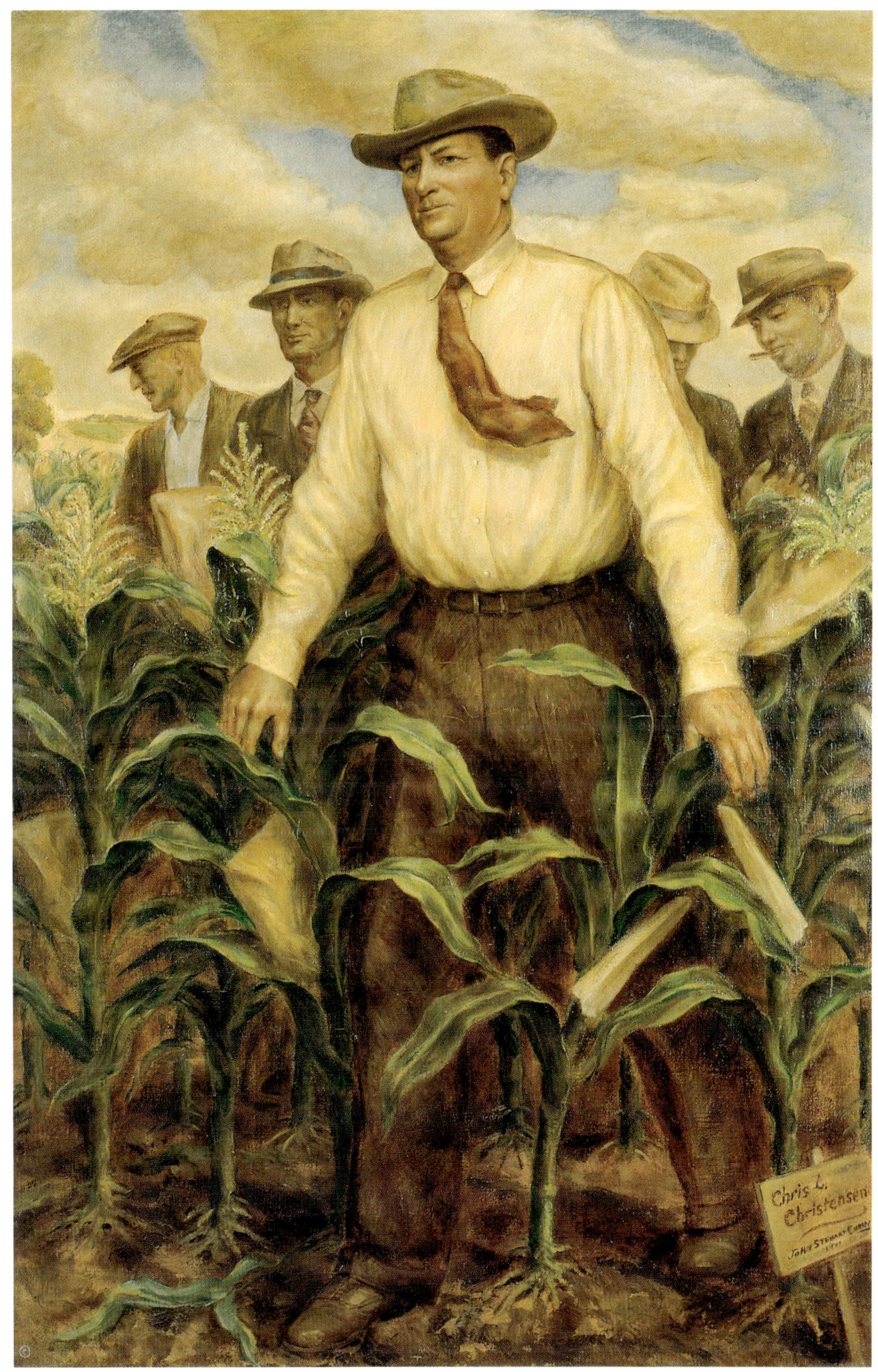

PLATE 67

Chris L. Christensen, 1941
Oil and tempera on canvas
59 × 42 in.
Signed and inscribed lower right: *CHRIS L. CHRISTENSEN/JOHN STEUART CURRY*
College of Agricultural and Life Sciences, University of Wisconsin–Madison.

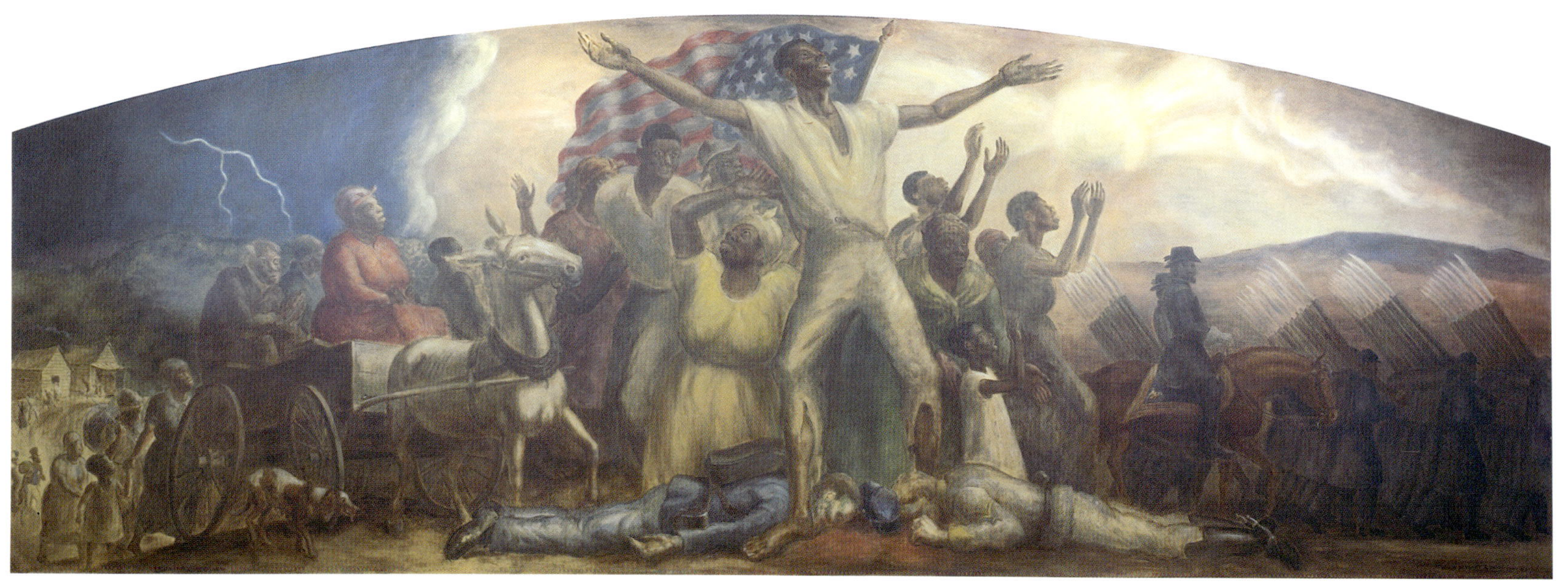

*PLATE 68

Freeing of the Slaves, 1942
Mural, Law School library, University of Wisconsin, Madison
Oil and tempera on canvas
14 × 37 ft.
Photograph courtesy University of Wisconsin–Madison

John Curry

THOMAS H. BENTON

I met John Curry in 1926 at an Architectural League exhibition in New York where I was showing my first American History Panels.[1] I told him that most of the artists and critics thought the panels were all wrong. He said he knew that. But he also said that he didn't believe it. So we became friends.

That meeting was before either of us had figured in the public press. It was before Grant Wood was known, before he was known to us also. There was no American school of painters. The influence of the Henri, Bellows, Sloan group and of Ryder and Eakins had been smashed by the famous Armoury Show of 1913, and painting in and around New York was a scrambling imitation of the new schools of Paris. Everybody was trying to swallow the "modernism" of the boulevards.

I found that John was as dissatisfied with that as I had come to be. I had been subjected to ten years of Parisian influence, directly and derivatively, but the war years of 1917 and 1918 had cleared it away and a rising feeling of American things had come to me. I found that John's Middle Western Americanism coincided with my own outlook. He was offended by the satellite condition of American painting and by the denial of value to the particularities of American experience and expression which followed therefrom. We agreed that unless American Art came back to dealing with things about which American artists knew something it would accomplish nothing.

Neither John nor I objected to the school of Paris itself. We vastly admired its father genius, Paul Cézanne, and other painters also who were a part of it and to whom we were indebted for many suggestions as to method. But we did object to its American imitations. We objected also to the outrageous rationalizations by which artists and critics defended their total capitulation to an exotic culture, to the nonsensical jargon which explained why they had sold themselves out.

We admired the new Mexican school rising then into public notice. Its indigenous flavor made us jealous for our own land. We did not relish, however, all its political overtones. We found ourselves sharing a suspicion about the new Russian phase of man's ancient utopian dream some of the Mexicans advocated and which was also much agitated among left-wing artists in New York. John, good son of Kansas, was an old fashioned, Lincoln-inspired Republican. I, as Missourian, though a long time expatriate, was a Jacksonian Democrat. We were not altogether in political harmony, but we united over a fear that dictatorships of any kind, once enthroned, could never be removed except by violent revolutionary action. Because of the inevitable fluxes and changes of life, we saw in the Russian brand of Communism only a series of revolutions. Knowing through our family histories and the histories of our native states how bloody American violence could be, we wanted none of a system which seemed to us to promise little else. Though not satisfied with American social conditions (John was something of a Single Taxer as well as a Kansas Republican), he wanted American solutions for these—solutions more in harmony with American ways of thought. Like a farmer John was a slow and clumsy talker. It took a good many months to know him and understand what was in his mind. But in the end I found we were united in all our basic ideas. Our friendship stuck.

I was nine years older than John. I was nine years older in experience with the Art World and knew its propensity for seeking out and knifing the weak spots of artists who did not fit within its accepted patterns. There were certain things I had learned it was better never to show. First among these was self doubt. This was a profound part of John Curry's character and I lectured him on the matter. He listened to me and to Rita, my wife, who was very fond of him and attached to his interests; but he never learned to cover himself, and in the years to follow, as his reputation grew, he suffered much from the stings of critical assault. His humility was public and it laid him wide open to the shafts of little and jealous men.

Every true artist lives close to the demon of self criticism. John lived closer than any artist I ever knew. Nothing he did satisfied him. When the critics yapped, "He can't paint," John went by himself and wept. "It's true," he said, "I can't." There was no use telling him, as I did and as Grant Wood did later, that most judgments about painting were based on fragile and fleeting standards of the moment and were of no consequence. He transferred the validity of his own self-criticism to any fool's language.

John had profound standards within himself, profounder than any momentary or passing vogue. It always seemed to him that his critics were judging him by these. It was as if he believed they saw through him and gauged him by how much he missed what his vision called for.

John's vision of Art was unusual. It was very much bound up with spectator response. He saw his work instrumentally. His Art must move others. It must live by and through what others felt about it, by the sympathetic responses of those who faced it. The key to his character lies in this submergence of his personal ego in a concept of social function. The artist is nothing in himself. He becomes something only as the world finds meaning in his creations. That is, of course, profoundly true of

---

Thomas Hart Benton's essay, "John Curry," originally appeared in the *University of Kansas City Review,* Volume 13, number 2 (Winter 1946). It is reprinted here with the permission of *New Letters* (formerly *The University of Kansas City Review*) and the Curators of the University of Missouri–Kansas City.

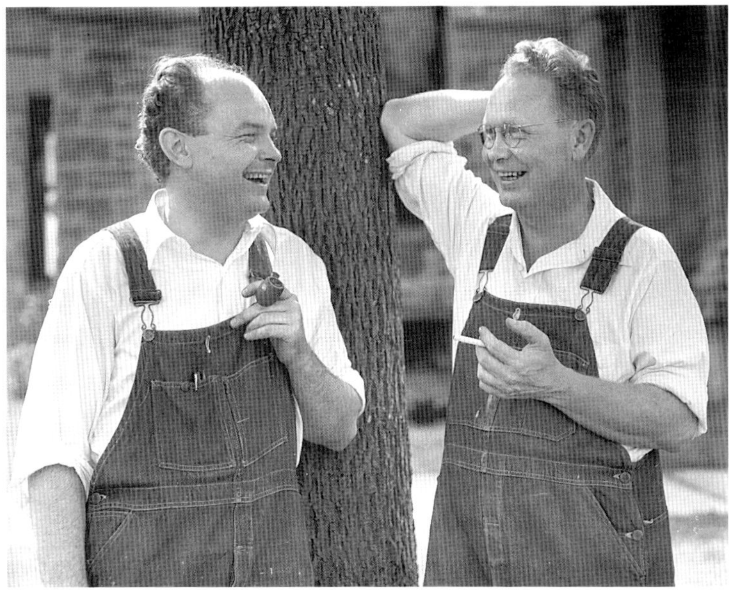

FIGURE 1
Curry and Grant Wood in a publicity photograph taken at the Stone City Colony and Art School, Stone City, Iowa, in July 1933. The picture appeared in the 24 December 1934 issue of *Time* magazine, accompanying a cover story on the new midwestern regionalist movement. Photograph by John Barry, Jr., Cedar Rapids, Iowa. Courtesy John W. Barry.

all artists, though few make the humble obeisance to the fact that John Curry did. Few also search so persistently as he searched for symbols which would carry meaning to common men—few at least in our day.

John Curry never forgot that he came off a Kansas farm, that his folks were plain Kansas folks whose lives were spent with the plain, simple, elemental things of the earth and sky. His Art and the meanings of his Art were never cut loose from this background. To the end his ideal audience was a Kansas audience. Dealing with what that audience experienced and knew about, John wanted its appreciation more than anything else. He didn't get it.

The mural he made for Kansas was never finished. A few slabs of imported marble meant more to the Kansas legislature than the work of her greatest son. The art societies of the state wanted fancier goods than those John delivered, businessmen did not like to be reminded of tornadoes, polite society of shouting baptism, university men of the too common realities of their culture. So John, who envisaged his final triumph in and through the mural which was to express the true values of his birth land found instead that he was criticized on all sides. The people he had finally counted on to vindicate his long struggle for simple meanings and unpretentious poetry failed him. The sympathetic response which was bound up with his art, which was an essential part of its functioning, a part even, to his mind, of the validity of its form, was not to be had.

But though the world failed him on this count, the philosophy which included it did not. Because of his feeling that the world, the world of man outside himself, was a part of his creative process, because sympathetic spectator response was fundamental to his work, he himself gave out sympathy. He gave out what he always expected to get. He could weep because of the stings that came to him, weep literally and to deep sadness, but he continually gave out love. It is in his pictures.

Love is in the simple poetry of a turtle dove on her nest in an osage orange thicket. It is in the great mural, *Freeing of the Slaves,* in the University [law] library at Madison, Wisconsin [color plate 68]. In this latter painting, which is to my mind the greatest single picture of modern times, human love and sympathy reach to the sublime. No technical virtuosities, no pyrotechnics of design, no labored universalities stand in the way of its humanity. It is a simple and plain representation of people realizing a dream of freedom. It has an overtone of the sadness which follows from the fact that the realization was mostly illusory.

It is presumptuous to talk of *Freeing of the Slaves* in the jargon of aesthetic technicalities. The work, however, in spite of its obvious and deliberate use of associative factors, has a magnificent formal organization. The sequential flow of its lines, the massive sculptural quality of its three dimensional anatomy, the loose ease of its execution, all attest to the master craft behind it. When art criticism passes through the fog of idiocy which now envelops it these things will be seen along with the humanity they enclose and *Freeing of the Slaves* will get the fame it deserves.

John Curry was not always up to himself. The inner cry for sympathy which made him great sometimes gave his work a touch of vulgarity and cheapness. He fell occasionally into the syrupy conventions of the American advertising business. The illustrations he so much loved to do were sometimes hackneyed. Straining to envelop the feelings of his customers, his portraits were often less than they might have been and his smaller decorations often exhibited a banal prettiness. John was cursed like all other American artists by the pressures of a society which goes in for vulgarity, fake sentimentality, and cheapness on a pretty large scale. The human realities, the real and substantial values of American life, are sometimes hard to find in the fogs of commercially motivated pretense which lie over them.

No artist can wholly escape the ugly stuff of his environment. John, with a philosophy of sympathetic interpenetration at the base of his aesthetic, was bound to be warped. Perhaps he could not have found so much that was real in America without also finding that which was false. All considered, however, John Curry comes off well. He never deliberately sold himself out. His failures were failures of time and place and his successes will outweigh them in the end.

Grant Wood is dead and John Curry is dead. They were closer to me in basic attitude of mind, in their social and aesthetic philosophies, than all other artists. Together we stood for things which most artists do not much believe in. We stood for an art whose forms and meanings would have direct and easily comprehended relevance to the American culture of which we were by blood and daily life a part. In spite of the deficiencies of that culture and of our inclusion of some of these in our arts, we did not believe this stand separated us from the world family of artists. It was our belief, in fact, that it would best enable us to join them. We hoped to build our "universals" out of the particularities of our own times and our own places, out of the substances of our actual lives as most of the great artists of the world's past have done.

It is not for me, yet standing, to judge our success as a whole. But I will risk this—whatever may be said of Grant Wood and me, it will surely be said of John Curry that he was the most simply human artist of his day. Maybe in the end that will make him the greatest.

NOTE

1. Now in the University of Kansas City.

John Steuart Curry

A CRITICAL ASSESSMENT

THEODORE F. WOLFF

John Steuart Curry presents a particularly challenging problem for anyone writing about him today. Although he was highly regarded during his lifetime as one of Midwest regionalism's three leading artists, his reputation, since his death in 1946, has declined to the point where he now all too frequently is perceived as a talented and effective but somewhat naive exponent of a romantically parochial vision of American life (color plate 9, fig. 1).

His fellow regionalists have fared somewhat better, although Thomas Hart Benton and Grant Wood have also received their share of criticism for the highly personal, even idiosyncratic, manner in which they gave form to their vision of a culturally self-contained America free of any and all European ties. Of course, both artists had certain advantages. Benton's long life and talent for self-promotion kept him and his art in the public eye well beyond his death in 1975. Wood had the good fortune to produce several remarkably popular paintings, one of which, *American Gothic* (1930; Art Institute of Chicago), became a national icon almost immediately after its completion.

Curry was less fortunate. While few art professionals today would deny that he painted a number of powerful works or claim that his niche in twentieth-century American art history is undeserved, the fact remains that for the past five decades, Curry's paintings have received neither the critical nor curatorial attention accorded those of his two closest colleagues.

Some of this is due to the greater fame and popularity of Benton's and Wood's works, factors that made it easier for their reputations to weather the dramatic and far-reaching upheavals American painting underwent during the post–World War II period.

Equally important, these artists seemed more sophisticated in their formal approach. Younger postwar critics and curators, many with extensive backgrounds in modernist theory, could dismiss Benton's and Wood's regionalist ideas and sentiments out-of-hand but still find something to admire in the formal clarity with which they designed their works. To their eyes, Benton's and Wood's precisely ordered canvases appeared both more discriminating and contemporary than Curry's traditionally structured and apparently rather casually executed compositions and thus more worthy to be taken seriously within a twentieth-century modernist context. Even so, Benton's and Wood's critical acceptance as major twentieth-century American creative figures remained marginal until well into the 1980s, when their importance was reaffirmed by two multimuseum retrospective exhibitions detailing their accomplishments.

Curry currently is undergoing a similar reevaluation. From a position of relative obscurity, he once again is gaining recognition as a significant twentieth-century American painter. Museums and galleries are again exhibiting his paintings, and collectors of mid-twentieth-century American art are competing for representative examples of his work. This vindication should come as no surprise. As this essay will demonstrate, no other American artist of his time set higher or more challenging goals for himself, and none succeeded more often or more dramatically in realizing his objectives.

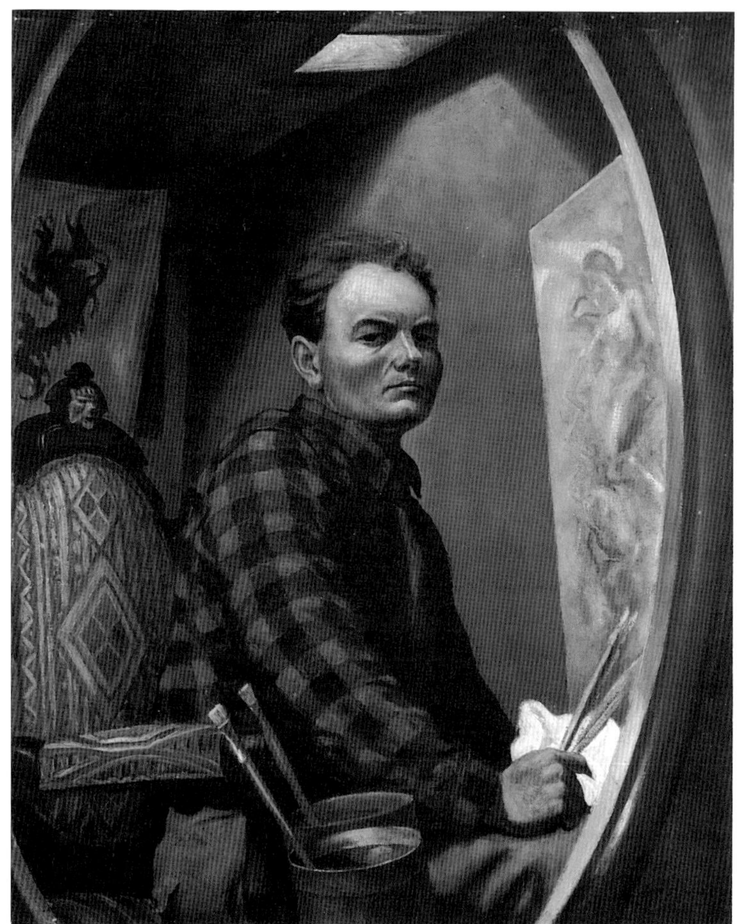

FIGURE 1

John Steuart Curry
Self-Portrait, 1927–29
Oil on canvas
36 × 30 in.
Spencer Museum of Art, University of Kansas, Lawrence. Gift of the Friends of the Art Museum, the Students of the University of Kansas, the Price R. and Flora A. Reid Foundation, Maupintour, Inc., Margaret and Darwin Daicoff, Mr. and Mrs. Robert C. Braden, Mr. and Mrs. Richard Barber, and Mr. Stan E. Wisdom.

As a boy on his parents' farm near Dunavant, Kansas, where he was born on 14 November 1897, Curry had learned to accept responsibility. "I was raised on hard work," he told his biographer, Laurence Schmeckebier. "We were up at 4 o'clock the year 'round, feeding the cattle, planting and plowing corn, cutting hay and wheat, and in the school months doing half a day's work before we rode to town on horseback to our lessons. But we didn't mind. It was the only life we knew—and I had a strong constitution.[1]

No matter how busy he was with chores or school, young Curry always found time to draw. Very little escaped his pencil, from the newspaper illustrations of Indians, railroad engines, and cowboys that he copied to the farm animals he sketched after first carefully tying them up beside the barn.

When Curry was twelve, his mother made arrangements for him to take art lessons from Mrs. Alice Worswick in nearby Oskaloosa. Although his association with her lasted only one summer, Mrs. Worswick not only managed to teach him basic skills with charcoal and watercolor but also encouraged his growing desire to be an artist.

Armed with his mother's support and his father's acceptance of his career choice, Curry left high school at the end of his junior year to enroll in the Kansas City Art Institute. He lasted exactly one month but only because he felt out of place in what appeared to him too sophisticated an atmosphere. His next step, the School of the Art Institute of Chicago, obviously suited him better because he stayed there for two years, supporting himself with odd jobs.

In 1919, aged twenty-two and having spent a fruitless year at Geneva College in Beaver Falls, Pennsylvania, Curry decided to devote all his energies to illustration. For his teacher he chose the well-known illustrator Harvey Dunn, then living in Tenafly, New Jersey. Under the latter's guidance, Curry quickly mastered the fundamentals of his new profession, and by 1921, he was illustrating stories in *Boy's Life, Country Gentleman,* the *Saturday Evening Post,* and other Curtis publications. Most of these illustrations were of outdoor or western action scenes and generally consisted of dramatic renderings of men and animals battling the elements or each other.

In 1923 he felt sufficiently certain of his future to ask Clara Derrick, the daughter of the head of the New Jersey State Home for Boys, to marry him. She accepted his proposal, and after their wedding they moved first to New York City's Greenwich Village and then to their own house in Westport, Connecticut.

By 1925 Curry's commitment to illustration had become tenuous. Not only was he receiving fewer commissions, those he did receive seldom permitted him to develop his ideas beyond the point defined by the commercial demands of his clients. The harder he tried to adapt, the more he was informed by his editors that his images were beginning to look too much like paintings. Finally, toward the end of the year, he decided to leave the field for good and to strike off on his own as a serious creative artist.

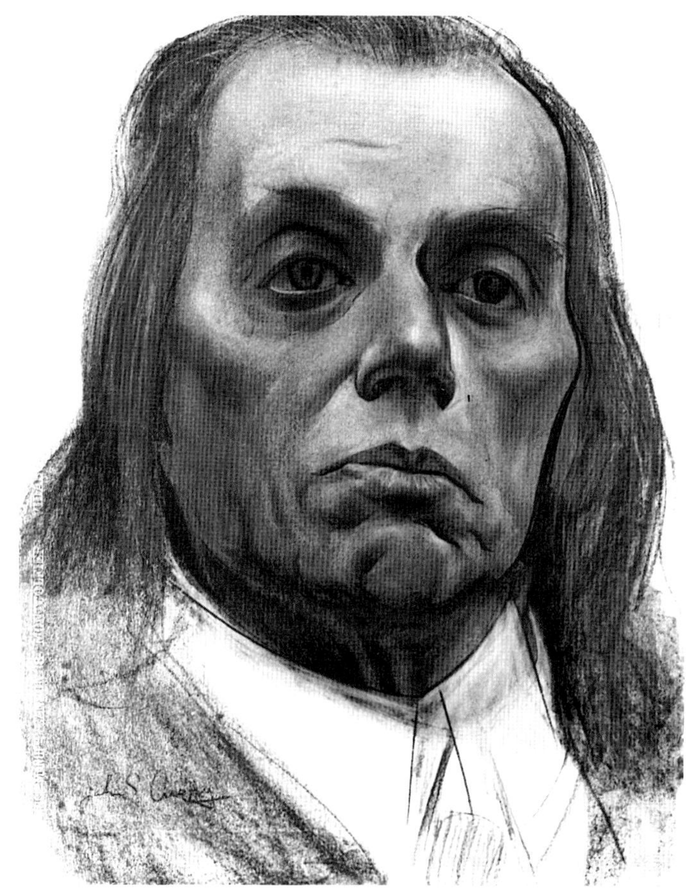

FIGURE 2

John Steuart Curry

Study of a Head: Italian Man, 1927

Charcoal on paper

24½ × 18½ in.

Elvehjem Museum of Art, University of Wisconsin–Madison. University Fund purchase.

He soon ran into financial difficulties. Although he had made several attempts during his years as an illustrator to produce paintings of museum quality—and had even exhibited one of his canvases, *The Fence Builders* (1924), at New York's National Academy of Design in 1924—none had garnered even a hint of critical approval. And worse still, none had sold.

Faced with the harsh reality of his situation, but as determined as ever to succeed as an artist, Curry and his wife traveled to Paris in 1926 with $1,500 borrowed from the art patron Seward Prosser so that John could study drawing with the Russian academician Basil Schoukhaieff. Their stay lasted only eight months, but it produced positive results (color plate 7, fig. 2). Curry's draftsmanship improved and, equally as impor-

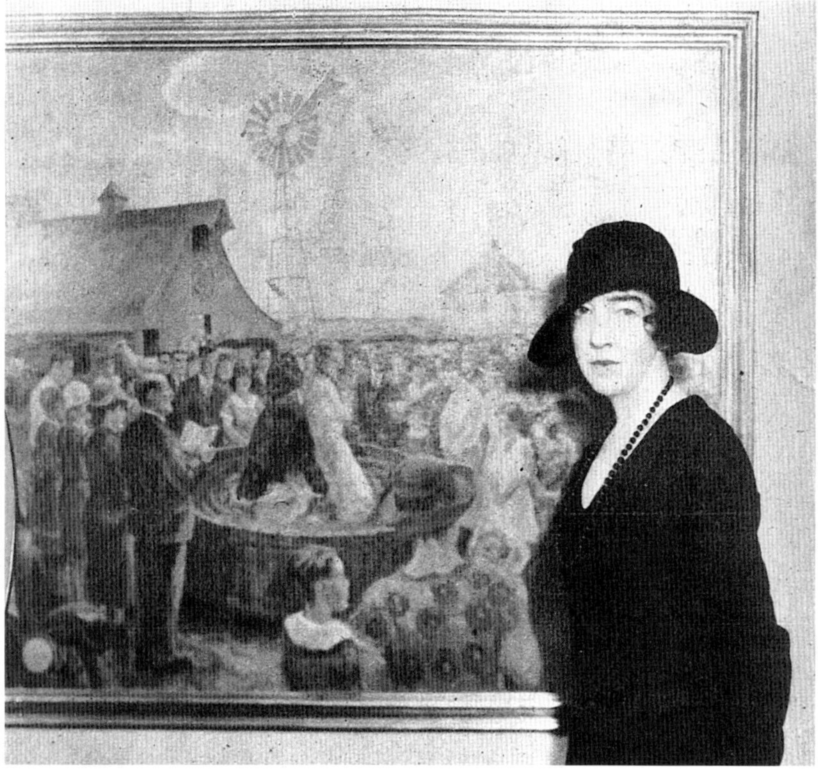

FIGURE 3

Gertrude Vanderbilt Whitney with Curry's *Baptism in Kansas,* acquired for the new Whitney Museum of American Art. Photograph from the *New York Times,* 22 November 1931. Courtesy Maynard Walker Papers, Archives of American Art, Smithsonian Institution, Washington, D.C. Gift of Maynard Walker.

tant, his study of the Old Masters at the Louvre, especially Rembrandt and Rubens, gave him a clearer insight into what it meant to be an artist.

All this was put to good use when the Currys returned to Westport in June 1927. Back at work, Curry borrowed more money and redoubled his efforts in the studio. By the summer of 1928 he had finished his first major painting, *Baptism in Kansas* (color plate 10). This large and impressive canvas broke the ice. When it was shown later that year in the Corcoran Gallery of Art's prestigious *Eleventh Biennial Exhibition of Contemporary American Oil Paintings* in Washington, D.C., it was singled out by the *New York Times* art critic Edward Alden Jewell for special praise. Jewell was not alone in his appreciation. The public and other art professionals took notice of it as well. Probably best of all, the financially strapped Currys were notified that Gertrude Vanderbilt Whitney was granting John a stipend of $200 per month for one year so that he could work with greater freedom.

Curry took full advantage of his improved financial condition. Within a year he had completed several of his most important paintings, including *Tornado* (1929, color plate 20), which would win second prize in the Carnegie Institute's *Thirty-first Annual International Exhibition of Paintings* in the fall of 1933. In January 1930, the Whitney Studio Galleries gave him his first one-man show, which turned out to be a smashing success. That year also marked the beginning of museum interest in his work. *Baptism in Kansas,* two other oils, and some watercolors were bought by the Whitney Museum of American Art (fig. 3). This was followed by another Whitney Museum purchase and the sale of the landscape *Spring Shower* (1931, color plate 23) to the Metropolitan Museum of Art.

After the death of his wife in July 1932, Curry worked harder than ever. With additional time on his hands, he accepted temporary teaching positions at both the Cooper Union and the Art Students League in New York City.

His marriage to Kathleen Gould Shepherd in June 1934, followed by commissions for murals in two public schools in Westport and Norwalk, Connecticut, raised his spirits dramatically. News of the successful completion of the murals reached officials in Washington, D.C., and in June 1935 he was asked by the recently formed Federal Arts Project to paint a mural for the new U.S. Department of Justice building in the nation's capital.

Curry was appointed artist-in-residence at the University of Wisconsin in Madison the next year. This meant creative independence as well as financial security. The university did not require him to teach, lecture, or even mingle with the students, although he did so to a great extent. He *was* expected to paint, and he more than fulfilled that obligation by producing a large number of canvases on a wide variety of subjects as well as an impressive group of murals for state and federal agencies.

Fame and controversy were Curry's lot during the last decade of his life. The high regard many had for his art was tempered by criticism from a growing number of art professionals for what they perceived as his inflexibly parochial, even regressive, approach to painting at a time when modernism was successfully challenging America's traditional views on art. To no one's surprise, he stuck to his guns and in the process produced several of his most significant and challenging works.

Curry's sudden death of a heart attack on 29 August 1946, while in the midst of preparations for a retrospective exhibition of his paintings at the Milwaukee Art Institute, took most who knew him by surprise. Although he had been in failing health for some time, the abruptness of his passing came as a shock. Nevertheless, the retrospective opened as scheduled on September 5. A memorial service was held in Madison, after which his body was returned to Winchester, Kansas, for burial.

Curry's death, coming four years after that of Wood and at the beginning of the rise to international prominence of a handful of aggressive American modernists soon to be known as abstract expressionists, marked the end, in every sense, of Midwest regionalism. Thomas Hart Benton remained, of course, but less as an exponent of a collective vision of rural and small-town America than as a powerful but highly idiosyncratic painter whose primary virtue, in the eyes of many, was that his teaching and example had a significant impact on the creative evolution of Jackson Pollock, abstract expressionism's original golden boy.

Regionalism's demise was not unexpected. It would, in fact, have ended much sooner had World War II not occurred. With so many young artists in uniform, and few, if any, new ideas arriving from Europe, American art, during the war years, remained largely on hold. By 1945 that had begun to change, and by 1948 the majority of the nation's talented younger artists were solidly in the modernist camp and openly contemptuous of the kind of painting produced by Benton, Curry, and Wood.

No one looking ahead during regionalism's heyday could have anticipated this backlash, least of all the conservative art critic Thomas Craven, its most ardent and controversial champion (fig. 4). He had claimed a decisive victory for a purely American art in 1939 when he wrote:

A battle has been waged and won. . . . Today, save for . . . a handful of defeated purists who believe with Picasso that art is a species of vacuous dabbling removed from the pressures of time and place, there is not a self-respecting artist in this country who is not eager to contribute to a movement which has gained the sympathies and support of the American public. . . . Never before has French pictorial stock stood so low; the succession of fancy cults emanating from the studios of Paris is dead and, for the most part, forgotten.[2]

Preposterous as this pronouncement sounds today, Craven was right about one thing: The American public of his time, when it concerned itself about contemporary art at all, was overwhelmingly on the side of homegrown, mildly romanticized depictions of American life and derisively opposed to any form of what it perceived to be imported modernist nonsense.

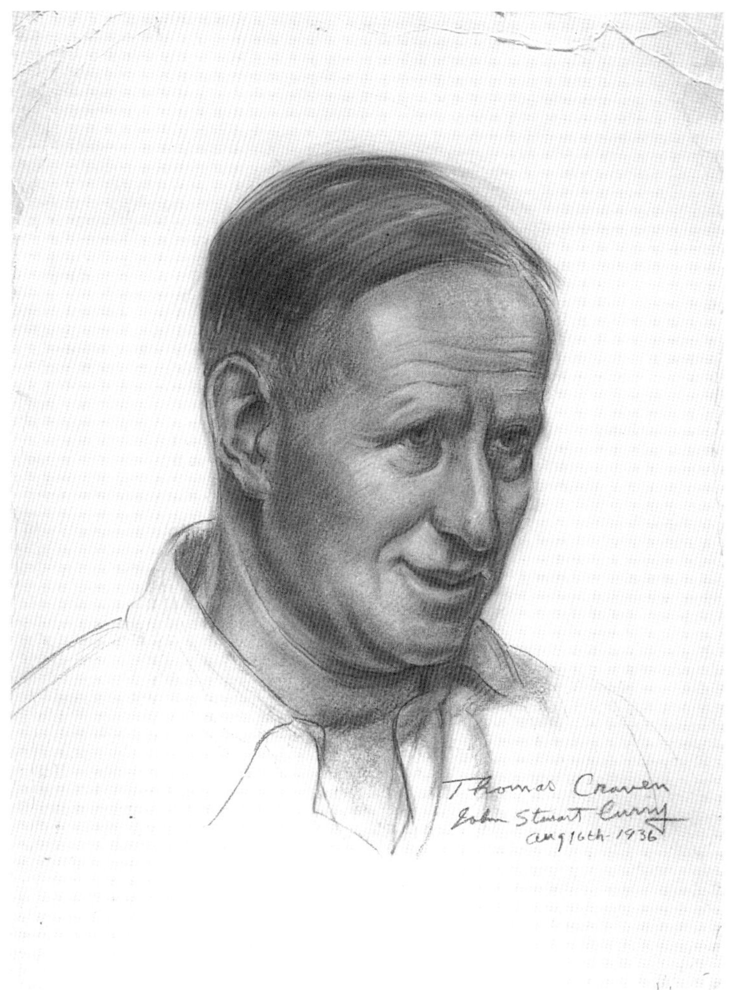

FIGURE 4

John Steuart Curry
Thomas Craven, 1936
Red crayon on paper
24 × 19 in.
Location unknown
Photograph courtesy Curry Papers, Archives of American Art, Smithsonian Institution, Washington, D.C.

Of course, it was Craven himself, thanks largely to his zeal and to the wide distribution of his writings, who had helped shape the notion that art in the United States had become a matter of Them or Us, of foreign modernist decadence versus native American wholesomeness. This antimodernist stance struck a sympathetic chord with an increasingly isolationist American public less willing than ever, after the Great Depression began in 1929, to answer Europe's cries for help or tolerate its more farfetched cultural exports.

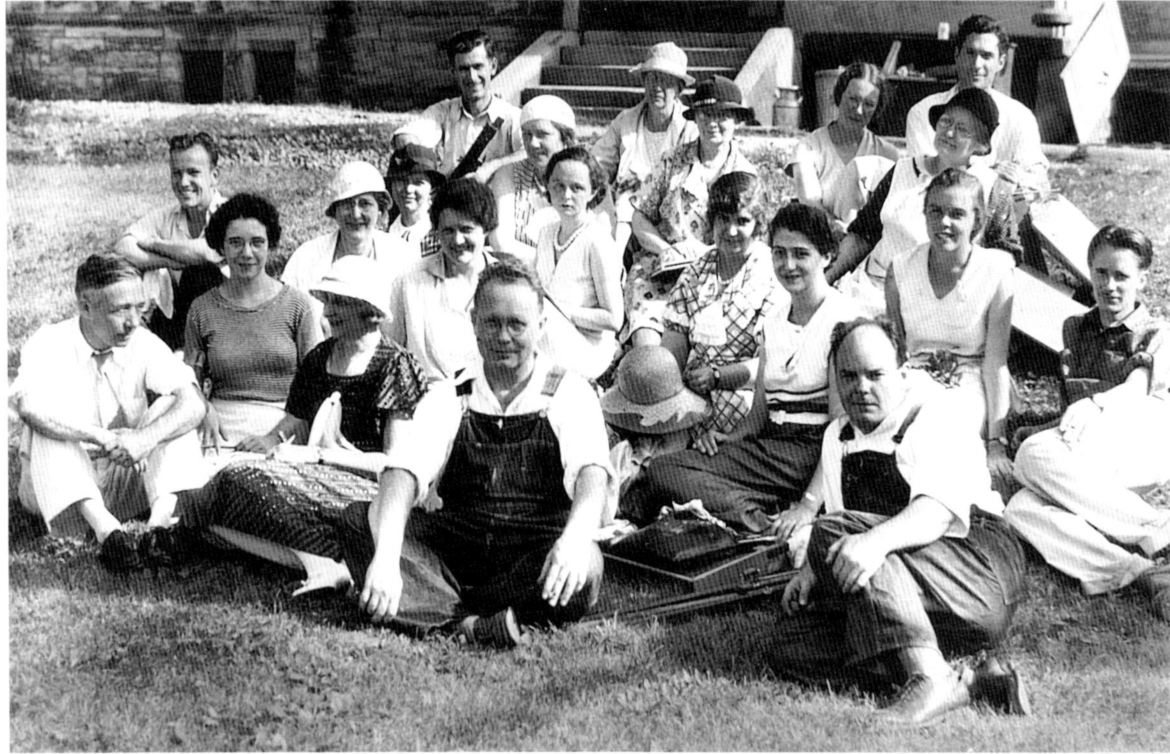

FIGURE 5
Curry and Grant Wood with students at Stone City Colony and Art School, Stone City, Iowa, July 1933. Photograph by John Barry, Jr., Cedar Rapids, Iowa. Courtesy Mrs. John Steuart Curry.

Craven's call for an indigenous American art coincided with the rise to prominence throughout the United States of several exceptionally gifted artists, all of whom had arrived independently at their decisions to paint strictly American subjects in as straightforwardly nonmodern a manner as possible. Charles Burchfield, Edward Hopper, Reginald Marsh, and Charles Sheeler, as well as Benton, Curry, and Wood, to name only a few, had struck off on their own and had begun receiving serious critical attention. Craven took note and wrote respectfully about many of them. But it was the work of the three midwestern regionalists that impressed him the most, not only because he recognized their quality but also because they best represented the new American painting he saw emerging. The fact that Benton, Curry, and Wood barely knew one another, and worked in dramatically different styles, mattered less to him than that each depicted American life honestly and convincingly, without reference to modernist ideas or forms.

Craven proved to be a persistent and persuasive—if also, at times, an embarrassingly strident—spokesman for regionalism and its artists. Indeed, without his unceasing and ultimately prejudicial advocacy, midwestern regionalism probably would not have acquired quite the militantly antimodernist reputation it did; and Benton, Curry, and Wood might be less stigmatized today as the leading exponents of parochialism in twentieth-century American art.

Which is not to say that, individually, the three did not believe wholeheartedly in a native American art. Benton's pronouncements in this area were as colorful, and frequently as pointed, as Craven's. And Wood, whom *Time* magazine characterized in 1934 as the nation's most "fervid believer in developing regional art," even went so far as to establish a colony in Stone City, Iowa, where artists could be taught to "paint the 'U.S. scene [fig. 5].'"[3]

Curry, whose commitment to American themes was as great but whose involvement with regionalism occurred largely by chance, clarified his position in a talk delivered shortly after his arrival in Madison to become artist-in-residence at the university: "I learned that I belonged to the regional school of art long after I had done the work as I pleased, without giving a thought as to what 'school' it might fit." To which he added, "There is a great deal of nonsense in the critics' attempts to classify artists and their work."[4]

Curry also differed from his colleagues in that he made no attempt to create a distinctive painting style. Unlike Benton, who developed a remarkably effective, rhythmically mannered mode for his ideas, and Wood, who found his expressive voice through extreme stylization, Curry saw no advantage in fashioning a formal method that called as much attention to itself as to what he wanted to communicate about his subjects.

This unwillingness to compromise the integrity of his ideas by placing a greater emphasis on style or manner weighed both in his favor and against it. Early in his career, when the frankness of his paintings had taken everyone by surprise, his direct, no-frills narrative approach won him accolades. Later, however, when regionalism began faltering and formal innovation once again took precedence over subject matter, that very directness of manner and emphasis on narration caused many in the art world to reconsider their original, favorable opinions of his work.

But while a growing number of art professionals may have begun questioning Curry's vision and work, most interested Americans did not follow suit. They liked and admired the breadth and power of his canvases and murals. They felt comfortable with paintings that celebrated the land and its people and were quite willing to accept the declarations of *Life, Time,* and other national magazines and newspapers that Curry was one of the country's most important artists.

The many honors and important commissions that Curry received justified the good opinions of his admirers. These ranged from prestigious awards presented by the Carnegie Institute in 1933 and the Metropolitan Museum of Art in 1942 to requests for murals in the Department of Justice and the Department of the Interior buildings in Washington, D.C., between 1936 and 1938 and the Kansas State Capitol in Topeka in 1937.

Even without such confirmation, however, the public, especially in the Midwest after his move to Madison in 1936, was fully aware of the nature and quality of this work. While some Kansans might have preferred more sanitized depictions of their state, most midwesterners appreciated his commitment to their region. Furthermore, he made it clear that he wanted no special treatment. He was accessible and available—much as he might have preferred not to be interrupted at work, or to be asked to give speeches, judge local art exhibitions, or answer questions about his art.

Curry was particularly effective with the art students and amateur painters he advised and encouraged throughout the state as part of the University of Wisconsin's Rural Art Program. This writer, for one, remembers with gratitude Curry's detailed and helpful response, first by letter and then in person, to his request for advice about whether and where to study art.

Although Curry was remarkably open during that particular conversation, Don Anderson, former publisher of the *Wisconsin State Journal* and a close friend of the artist during his Madison years, saw another side of him:

It was not easy to become friends with John Curry. A gentle and soft-spoken man, he would not seek favor or acceptance in dishonest agreement of opinion, even little polite white lies. Easy conversation was not his forte, and even friendly talks with him tended to become two-sided monologues rather than dialogue. But once contact was established, there was no more delightful man to be with.[5]

The traits that characterized Curry the man also characterized Curry the artist. Both were rooted in the realities and attitudes of early-twentieth-century American rural life: love of the land, self-reliance, and respect for hard work and common sense, and plain speaking in one's dealings with the outside world.

The United States, in fact, has produced few artists as thoroughly defined by rural values and ideals as Curry. Unlike the majority of his predecessors and peers who bypassed the nation's farmlands in favor of more dramatic or picturesque locations, he not only made farms and farmers the primary subjects of his art but also depicted them as only an insider familiar with every aspect of their existence could.

To do so he developed a manner of working—one could hardly call it a style—that enabled him to portray the people, places, and events he knew best simply and directly and without sacrificing either their character or the formal integrity of his art. The paintings that resulted were straightforward and descriptive, and they combined unadorned representationalism, a slightly romanticized narrative approach (which, at its weakest, could be described as illustrational), and a formal agenda derived largely from Renaissance and baroque compositional ideals.

With these elements and an effective but unsophisticated drawing style, Curry produced a body of work unique in its empathetic and keenly observed depiction of American rural life. More than any of his contemporaries, he caught the spirit and character of the Midwest shortly before and during the Depression years. Benton's Midwest, after all, was just that, *Benton's* Midwest, fascinating and brilliantly presented throughout but always stamped with, and dominated by, his stylistic mannerisms. And Wood, whose involvement with the region was as deep as Curry's, all too often permitted his distinctive stylizations to detract from some of the deeper and more substantive aspects of his subjects.

That is not to say Curry was the best artist of the lot. Indeed, from the vantage point of the 1990s, the three now appear roughly equal in accomplishment, if not, perhaps, in native ability. Each had his strengths and weaknesses, although they differed in kind and degree, and they all learned early in their careers how best to deal with them—Benton by highlighting his remarkable compositional skill, Wood by inventing an iconic, starkly stylized formal manner, and Curry by applying the narrative skills he had learned as an illustrator to give a dramatic edge to his images.

Curry's greatest strength lay not in his talents and skills but in the clarity and persistence of his vision of a truly indigenous, grandiloquent American art. He believed in artistic grandeur, in an expansive view of human capabilities. He had seen both in the works of art he admired most: the paintings of Rembrandt and Rubens as well as those by the nineteenth-century European romantics and a handful of other creative individuals scattered throughout the history of art. He himself was a romantic. Nature in its various manifestations, but especially at its most violent and awesome, fascinated him. And when it came to history, he invariably favored peak moments in mankind's struggle for freedom and progress.

Always, his objective was to paint the "big picture," to create art as powerful and heroic as possible without descending into melodrama. To accomplish this, he felt that an empathetic bond had to exist between himself and his subjects. As he wrote in his 1935 essay "Curry's View": "The artist must paint the thing that is most alive to him. . . . There must first be a lively interest in the subject; then comes the step of designing the form so that the feeling and underlying motive that comes through will be sharpened and given its full dramatic power. . . . If you feel the significance of the life, the design builds itself."[6]

Perhaps. But Curry was not one to relinquish control over the creative process, least of all in matters of design or composition. He had learned, as an illustrator, how to organize pictorial components for maximum narrative and dramatic effect, and he put that knowledge to good use in his canvases and murals. This ability to heighten the drama of any situation, whether as simple as a hawk attacking a chicken (color plate 32, fig. 6) or as complex as a farm family seeking refuge from a tornado (color plate 20), proved to be another of his major strengths, one that enabled him to produce images of extraordinary visual impact and authority.

Every element in *Wisconsin Landscape* (1937–39, color plate 56), for instance, falls into place neatly and irrevocably to fashion not only the perfect "portrait" of a southern Wisconsin farm and its surrounding acres and rolling hills but also what may well be the finest American landscape of the mid–twentieth century. Yet this canvas is not unique in his body of work. The organizational skills that help make it so outstanding also contribute to the thematic clarity of almost everything else he produced.

Of course, Curry was not only a pictorial storyteller and occasional mythmaker; he was a professional illustrator as well. *What* he painted mattered most. *How* he painted it depended

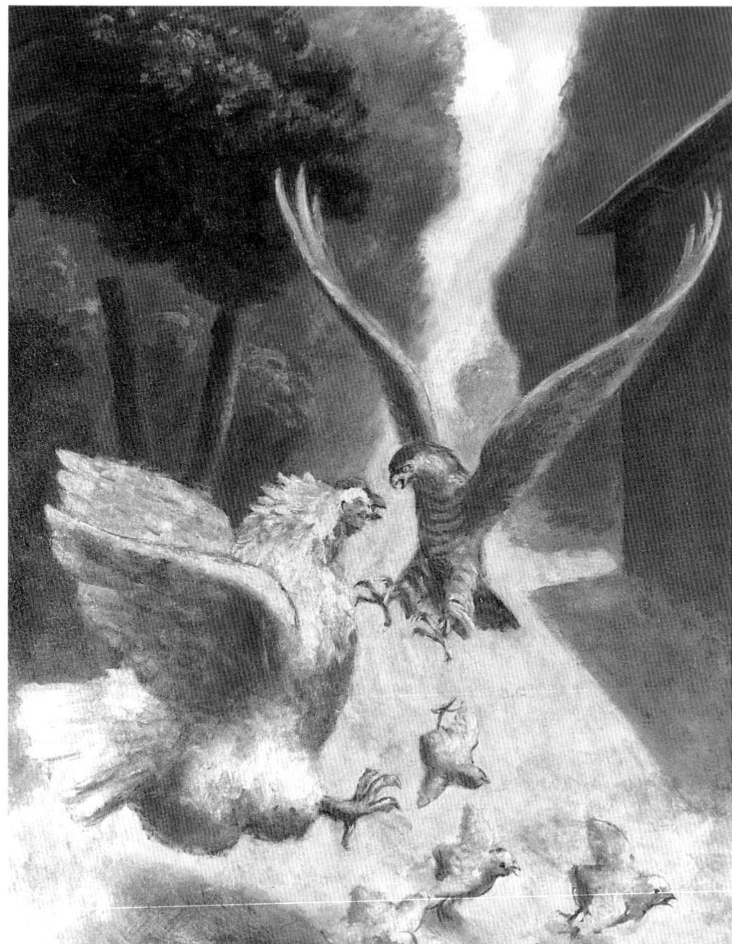

FIGURE 6
John Steuart Curry
Hen and the Hawk, 1934
Oil on canvas
26¼ × 20¼ in.
Memphis Brooks Museum of Art, Memphis, Tennessee. Bequest of Mrs. C. M. Gooch.

entirely on the manner in which he could best communicate his subject's identity and significance to others. One of the marvels of Curry's career is the skillful way he accomplished that task, even with subjects as complex and demanding as any painted in America at that time, and with a formal background in art as limited as his. Equally amazing is the fact that he did so with talents that were wide-ranging but modest and technical skills that were always sufficient for his needs but not particularly remarkable in themselves.

How, then, did Curry accomplish what he did? How did this moderately talented artist from Kansas, with only a rudimentary education in art, several years' experience as a magazine illustrator, and an eight-month stint in Paris studying drawing, manage to produce a number of the most provocative and powerful American paintings of the pre–World War II period?

The answer lies in his larger-than-life vision of art, his total commitment to the realities and values of the American Midwest, and his determination to push his talents and skills to their limits in order to produce art that embodied and celebrated these qualities. Curry had lofty ideas about art, a subject he passionately desired to communicate, and the skill required to express what he felt and believed in a manner sufficiently grand to stand comparison with the art he most admired.

Add to that his knack for capturing subtle nuances of character and mood; his ability to give epic, even mythic, dimensions to ordinary people, places, and events; and his flair for the dramatic—and one begins to understand why Curry could be as effective as he was.

Seen in this light, it hardly matters that his draftsmanship was generally uninspired, his color unimaginative, and his painterly touch somewhat heavy-handed. What *does* matter is that Curry brought all elements of his art together to produce a whole that was considerably greater than the sum of its parts.

This passion for the whole was already apparent in his 1928 *Baptism in Kansas.* Even after seventy years, the painting remains impressive and moving. Yet if one examines it carefully, there is not one square inch in this forty-by-fifty-inch canvas that legitimately can be described as sensitively drawn or beautifully painted. Every element in it, whether technical or thematic, exists entirely for the realistic depiction of an unusual event occurring in a midwestern farmyard among farm animals, automobiles, a water tank, a barn, and numerous spectators, set against a typically flat Kansas landscape.

As much as anything else, this unadorned, technically unsophisticated narrative approach, in which everything is kept subordinate to his various subjects' identities and the ideas they represent, sets Curry apart from his more self-consciously "artistic" contemporaries and makes it somewhat difficult to appreciate him even today.

To Curry's detractors, his insistence on giving precedence to subject matter over more purely formal considerations was nothing short of heresy. Had he paid greater attention to the stylistic and technical niceties, as had Benton and Wood, he might have been partially forgiven. But his priorities prevented it. Only the obvious sincerity and power of a few major works, including *Tornado, Spring Shower, The Flying Codonas* (1932, color plate 25), *Line Storm* (1934, color plate 33), *Wisconsin Landscape,* and *John Brown* (1939, color plate 62), gave these critics pause and caused a few to acknowledge that Curry was indeed a major figure in mid-twentieth-century American art.

Curry understood his critics' objections and did his best to weaken their legitimacy by enhancing and enriching his formal means. For instance, when comparing *Baptism in Kansas* and *Wisconsin Landscape,* paintings separated by a decade, one finds a world of difference in his handling of paint and in his compositional control. Similar changes occurred in his draftsmanship, which grew increasingly more economical and incisive during the 1930s.

When it came to his primary creative objectives, however, he would not and could not change. After all, he had written: "I believe in subject matter. The artist ought to paint people doing things. . . . The use of life as an excuse for clever arrangements of color or other pictorial elements ends where it begins."[7]

The closest he ever came to modifying these opinions was in *Wisconsin Still Life* (1940, fig. 7), which exists largely as a demonstration of painterly sumptuousness in the tradition of late-nineteenth-century French still-life painting, most notably the canvases of Pierre Auguste Renoir. Even here he remained dependent on his subject, choosing the colorful plumage of two dead pheasants as justification for departing from his usual greens and browns.

It is ironic, considering the profoundly serious, socially oriented nature of Curry's creative ambitions, that it would be his simpler and less thematically ambitious paintings, such as *Spring Shower, Wisconsin Still Life,* and *Wisconsin Landscape,* that are now leading the way toward a more sympathetic reappraisal of his qualities and importance. Certainly, *Wisconsin Landscape,* which the Metropolitan Museum of Art featured prominently on two separate occasions over the past several years in its Twentieth Century Galleries, and which appeared on the cover of the catalogue accompanying its 1991 exhibition *The Landscape in Twentieth-Century American Art,* has regained much of the popularity and critical acclaim it acquired when first shown at that museum in 1942.

The same is true, in varying degrees, of Curry's circus paintings featuring aerialists and performing animals, his still lifes, his depictions of farming activities, and a number of his smaller Wisconsin and Kansas landscapes. These were so keenly observed and sensitively rendered that they are of interest today for social and historical reasons as well as for more purely aesthetic ones.

Curry's monumental undertakings, however, especially his epic canvases and murals devoted to dramatic historical, political, and social events, have not as yet regained the same level of acceptance as his more informal works. The reason for this is not difficult to ascertain. Confronted by the towering passions of *John Brown,* the unabashed patriotism of *The Return of Private Davis from the Argonne* (1928–40, color plate 12), the social ide-

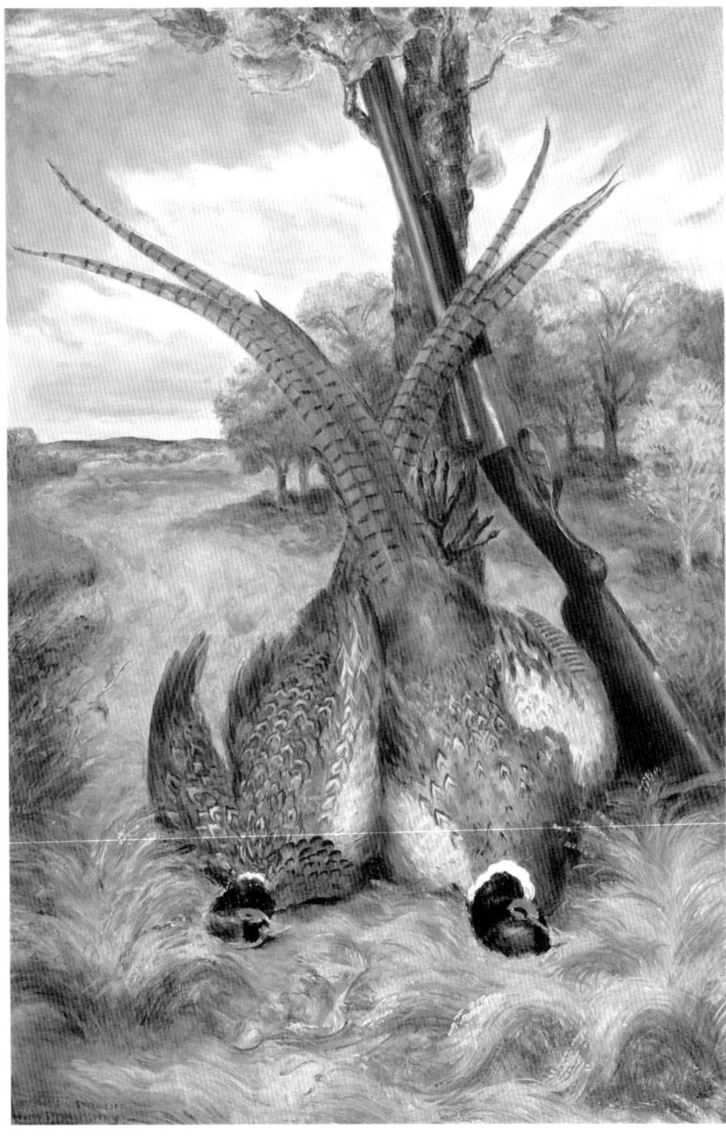

FIGURE 7

John Steuart Curry
Wisconsin Still Life, 1940
Oil and tempera on canvas
45 × 36 in.
Estate of the artist.
Photograph courtesy Mongerson Wunderlich Gallery, Chicago.

alism of *Law versus Mob Rule* (1937, color plates 47 and 48), or the blatantly antiwar sentiments of *Parade to War* (1938, color plate 61), the typical art lover of the 1990s is as likely to feel embarrassed at what appears to be Curry's romanticized and simplistic perceptions of American life as to feel respect for his accomplishments as an artist.

Still, with the exception of *Wisconsin Landscape* and two or three other panoramic views of the midwestern countryside, Curry's major achievements are to be found among the grandly conceived and executed paintings and murals that more fully represent his vision both of art and of a greater and more socially and technologically progressive America. Today, with our greater cynicism and disenchantment with notions of inevitable progress, we may have difficulties with Curry's more optimistic view of the nation's future. Furthermore, we tend to judge Curry and his colleagues from the vantage point of a victorious modernism that successfully resisted any and all attacks mounted against it by the regionalists and their supporters, and that now exacts, if not revenge, then at least a reappraisal of their accomplishments more in line with modernist objectives.

This should not deter us, however, from attempting to evaluate Curry's contributions as objectively as possible. The attempt is more than worth it, for Curry is and will remain one of mid-twentieth-century America's most interesting and valuable artists.

To begin with, he caught the spirit of an especially trying and challenging period of American history in images that embodied not only many of that period's harsher realities but some of its most deeply rooted and persistent values and ideals as well.

In addition, because of his familiarity with farms and farming, his insistence that every element in his compositions be identifiably authentic, and his ability to dignify even the most commonplace subjects without recourse to exaggeration or distortion, he brought increased weight and dimension, as well as a new level of authority, to depictions of rural life.

Most important, Curry increasingly came to believe that, as an artist with a wide audience, he had a creative and moral obligation to use his art to help clarify, and perhaps even to help resolve, the crucial issues of his time and place. This belief strengthened after his appointment in 1936 as artist-in-residence at the University of Wisconsin. It was very much on his mind, in fact, during his 1942 conversation with this writer, who remembers very clearly Curry's insistence that an artist in his position was as much a responsible public figure as any elected official. Indeed, this writer, the son and grandson of missionaries, was struck by the quiet fervor with which the artist spoke of social injustice, the insanity of war, political corruption, and the difficulties endured by the poor, the victims of drought and flood, and the racially disenfranchised. John Brown, Curry said, was not merely a pre–Civil War antislavery crusader but a living symbol of mankind's need to fight oppression.

If one takes this belief into account and then factors in Curry's profound admiration for the powerful, highly energized paintings of Rembrandt, Rubens, and the baroque masters in general, it should come as no surprise that his ambition for his own art would lead him toward epic pictorial statements pertaining to social and moral issues and ideals.

A less committed individual envisioning an art of such magnitude, and fully aware of his own limitations as a painter, would almost certainly have adjusted his creative ambitions downward. Curry, however, did not. No matter how modest his talents—and he knew the nature and extent of his abilities quite well—he felt compelled to do the very best he could with what he had.

To that end, he studied the Old Masters and turned them upside down and inside out in order to discover the secrets of their effectiveness. He probed into matters of technique, composition, color, and draftsmanship with an intensity seldom seen in one so famous as he. Fame, in fact, meant little to him. He was as willing to ask totally unknown painters with skills he admired for technical advice as he was happy to share whatever "secrets" he had learned with anyone, student or professional, who asked how he had a achieved a particular effect.

What mattered was the final result, the dramatic, larger-than-life images that depicted John Brown thundering out against slavery, a black-robed Judge defying a lynch mob *(Law versus Mob Rule)*, or rows of skull-faced soldiers marching off to war *(Parade to War)*.

Not all of these efforts were entirely successful. Some were flawed in conception or execution. Others ended up more as oversized illustrations than as works of art. But the majority scored extraordinarily well, and several fused theme, context, form, and vision so effectively, and in so carefully crafted and authentic a manner, that they rose above being merely outstanding examples of regionalist art to take their place among the most interesting and valuable paintings produced in America between the two world wars.

NOTES

1. Quoted in Laurence E. Schmeckebier, *John Steuart Curry's Pageant of America* (New York: American Artists Group, 1943), 8.

2. Thomas Craven, Introduction, *A Treasury of American Prints* (New York: Simon and Schuster, 1939), unpaginated.

3. "U.S. Scene," *Time* 24, no. 6 (24 December 1934): 26.

4. Schmeckebier, *Pageant,* 70.

5. *John Steuart Curry, 1897–1946,* exh. cat. (Madison, Wis.: Madison Art Center, 1969), unpaginated.

6. John Steuart Curry, "Curry's View," *Art Digest* 9, no. 20 (September 1935): 29.

7. Ibid.

Prairie Prodigal

JOHN STEUART CURRY AND KANSAS

CHARLES C. ELDREDGE

Kansas schoolchildren of John Steuart Curry's generation learned lessons of good behavior and responsible citizenship along with their three R's. For instance, one history primer, part of the Twentieth-Century Classics and School Readings series popular while Curry was growing up, instructed that "to herself Kansas has always tied her children with an attachment which amounts to devotion." In a community and an economy that were still largely agrarian, parents and pupils alike would respond positively to the message that "the land always had a fascination for men of talent, learning, genius" (color plate 17, fig. 1).[1] Whether Curry learned from that particular volume is unknown, but its typical message of patriotic virtue and regional pride surely bore fruit in the work of the Kansas farmboy-turned-artist.

The Midwest has long exercised its peculiar spell. "What would American art do without the Midwest, so averse to artifice or embellishment in its manners and morals?" a critic in the *New York Times* recently asked. Modern American literature was distinguished by the contributions of artists from the Midwest—from Willa Cather to Langston Hughes, with F. Scott Fitzgerald, Ernest Hemingway, T. S. Eliot, and Marianne Moore in between—"writers who transformed the stern and plain into the rich and strange. They were looking for the route that ties the spare to the ecstatic, and reserve to passionate intensity."[2] Midwestern painters were similarly moved to invention, extracting from the spare and reserved the stuff of pictorial drama and regional fealty.

Hamlin Garland, author and Midwest booster, was among the earliest to proclaim the region's artistic possibilities. He urged attention to the local, in lieu of travel to Europe or eastern art colonies. Garland proposed that the midwestern artist, "being denied certain picturesque aspects of seashore and mountainside, has a rare chance to develop unhackneyed themes in sky and plain."[3]

As Garland had done a generation earlier, Curry also delighted in the pictorial possibilities of midwestern life and urged his neighbors to recognize the same; he wanted them to realize

that there is art right here . . . in our rolling green hills, dotted with the white of farm houses and the red of barns. We have art in the new life constantly springing up on the farm. . . . We have art, also, in the shine of brown earth as it rolls from the plowshare, in the swing of the fork as the hired man scatters hay-cocks after an untimely rain, and in the healthy gusto with which threshers eat their food.[4]

Such were the sights that informed Curry's vision during his childhood on a Kansas farm. And such were the subjects that vaulted him to prominence in the American art scene of the

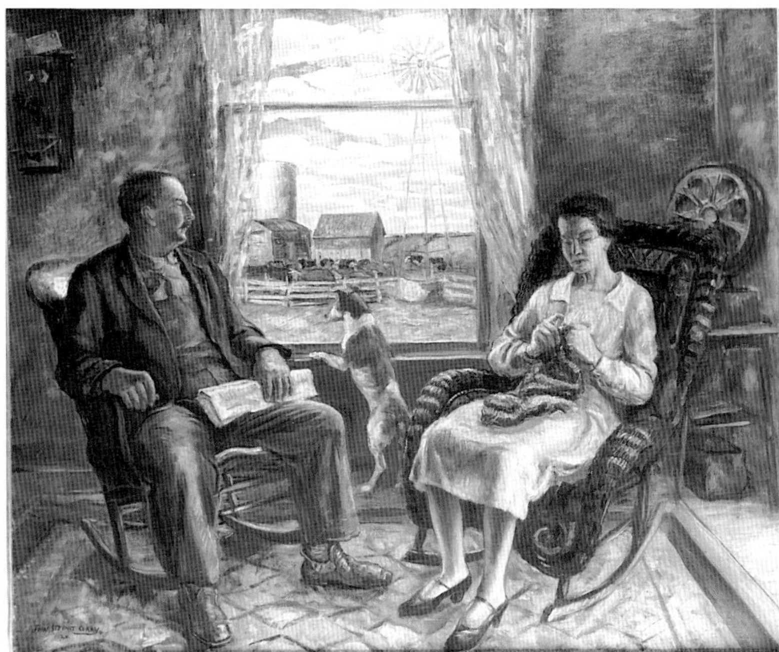

FIGURE 1
John Steuart Curry
The Old Folks (Mother and Father), 1929
Oil on canvas
30 × 36 in.
Courtesy D. Wigmore Fine Art, Inc., New York.

late 1920s, when the Midwest became, as one painter explained, "the great reservoir of the American Idea. As the East grows more effete and European, the middle-west will retain the thing Europe calls America. It's the old swimming hole, the shack in the woods, and the Fourth-of-July oration down in the town square."[5]

Bathers in a farm tank, a farm on the prairie, baptisms in Kansas: This was the iconography of Curry's early scenes that captured the imagination of critics and collectors in the "effete and European" East. At last, proclaimed the *New York Times,* "Kansas has found her Homer."[6] America rediscovered its fundamental verities, depicted anew in the unlikely setting of a midwestern barnyard.

Hamlin Garland and the *New York Times* notwithstanding, rural Kansas still appeared to some an unlikely incubator for artists. In 1883 Edgar Howe, longtime Atchison editor, had published *The Story of a Country Town,* a dyspeptic novel about small-town Kansas that eastern critics greeted as "so curious a product of Western life. . . . A more dreary waste than the country town . . . could not well be imagined," complained the *Atlantic Monthly.* Kansas appeared to have "no traditions, even of beauty, and certainly no anticipations of hope." Howe's town was "degraded spiritually and mentally," a place where "nature is as cheerless as human life."[7]

The novel's protagonist, describing "the rough but honest ways of us farmers," tried to explain the local circumstance. "Those of us who live in the country, and earn our bread in the sweat of our brow . . . cannot be particular. . . . We may have our ambitions like other men, but they are dwarfed and bent by holding the plow, and pitching the hay. . . . We have no time for the fine arts, you may be certain."[8] That attitude persisted into Curry's own time. His contemporary and compatriot Kenneth Adams recalled that when he started taking private painting lessons in his native Topeka, "I was looked upon as perhaps just a little odd. That women painted, and painted china and that sort of thing [was acceptable], but it was not a masculine occupation, painting."[9] Well into the 1920s poets lamented, "There's no time to be spent by a farmer's son / Dreaming, dreaming, dreaming."[10]

Around the Curry farm, the sentiment was shared, at least by T. Smith Curry, the artist's father. Curry's friend and biographer, Laurence Schmeckebier, related that while the elder Curry did not overtly oppose his wife's support of John's artistic interests, "at times he found it rather trying to see his husky twelve-year-old son drawing pictures on white paper when there were farm chores to be done."[11] The father recalled that John "was always drawing. . . . [H]e was a good worker on the farm, when we could get him away from his drawing."[12] Like many sons, the younger Curry's recollection differs from his father's; in later years he occasionally embroidered the childhood tale for dramatic effect, as when he told one journalist that he was "up at 4 o'clock the year round, doing half a day's work before we rode to town on horseback to our lessons."[13]

Whatever the physical exertions, life on the Winchester farm did afford the boy a variety of sensory experiences that left their impress on the artist. In later years he remembered fondly: "My whole life was made up of sensations. I used to go out in the garden and pull tomato vines to pieces so that I could smell them. I used to go out into the pasture to the mudholes where the doves had gathered so that I could see them fly up against the sky. . . . I loved the smell of wet dust."[14] When his Kansas farm subjects first drew wide attention in the late 1920s, they were praised in similar terms, for "savor[ing] so splendidly of the soil."[15] And later, when he was drawn to the University of Wisconsin as artist-in-residence in the College of Agriculture, it was, university President Glenn Frank announced, with the intention of introducing him to that state's rich farmlands, so that Curry "may come to think in terms of the roots and soil of Wisconsin, just as he has of his native Kansas."[16]

The loamy metaphors that proliferated around Curry's work are typical of the critical and popular rhetoric of the day. After the upheavals of World War I and the frenetic migrations of the Lost Generation, many Americans rejoiced in homecoming and were newly content to return to familiar locales, to root in native soil, to be, socially and organically, *of* a place. *On Native Grounds,* the title Alfred Kazin chose in 1942 for his classic study of modern American literature, might also have served as the rubric for any of Curry's exhibitions in the early 1930s.

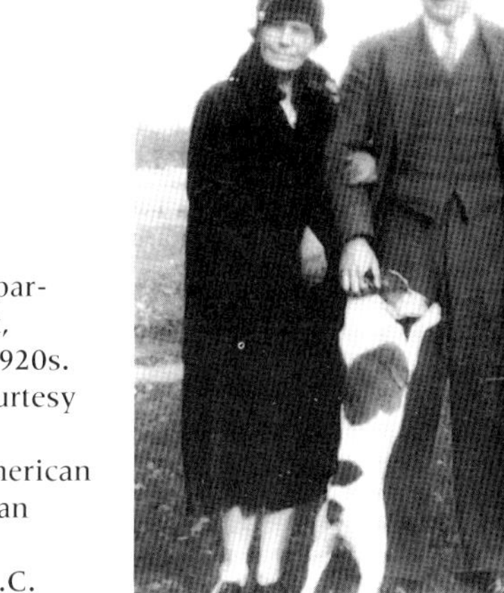

FIGURE 2
Curry and his parents, Dunavant, Kansas, early 1920s. Photograph courtesy Curry Papers, Archives of American Art, Smithsonian Institution, Washington, D.C.

The rural environment that prompted such imagery in Curry's mature art was the subject of ambivalence during his adolescence. In 1917, from Chicago, where he was studying at the School of the Art Institute, he wrote longingly to his mother: "O, I wish I was in the country. I sometimes feel like coming home and hauling manure."[17] He was frustrated by his lack of progress and envious of his roommate's success with commercial art work, while "all I seem to know is the art of manure hauling."[18] Finally, however, artistic aspirations triumphed over agricultural ones, and Curry confessed: "I would rather draw a picture of myself shoveling manure than do it."[19]

The "Self-Portrait with Manure" does not exist today, and likely it never did. But in numerous other Kansas images—portraits, genre scenes, and landscapes—Curry immortalized the beauties and occasional terrors in the hardscrabble life of the midwestern farm.

To some critics it appeared ironic that such memorable paintings of the Kansas scene were, by the late 1920s, the product of Curry's studio in Westport, Connecticut, remote from the subjects and inspirations of his youth. The artist took exception to what one friend called "the aimless carpings of the metropolitan scribes who know nothing about America save from hearsay."[20] For, unlike them, Curry often made the pilgrimage back to Kansas to visit family, to sketch the landscape and the locals, and generally to recharge himself, like some agricultural Antaeus returning to touch native ground (fig. 2). This orbit

FIGURE 3 *(right)*

Thomas Hart Benton (American, 1889–1975)
Prodigal Son, ca. 1939–41
Oil and tempera on panel
26⅛ × 30½ in.
Courtesy Dallas Museum of Art, Dallas, Texas. Photograph ©1997 T. H. Benton and R. P. Benton Testamentary Trusts/Licensed by VAGA, New York, N.Y.

FIGURE 4 *(right, below)*

John Steuart Curry
Prodigal Son, 1929
Watercolor on paper
Location unknown
Photograph courtesy National Museum of American Art, Smithsonian Institution, Washington, D.C., Peter A. Juley and Son Collection.

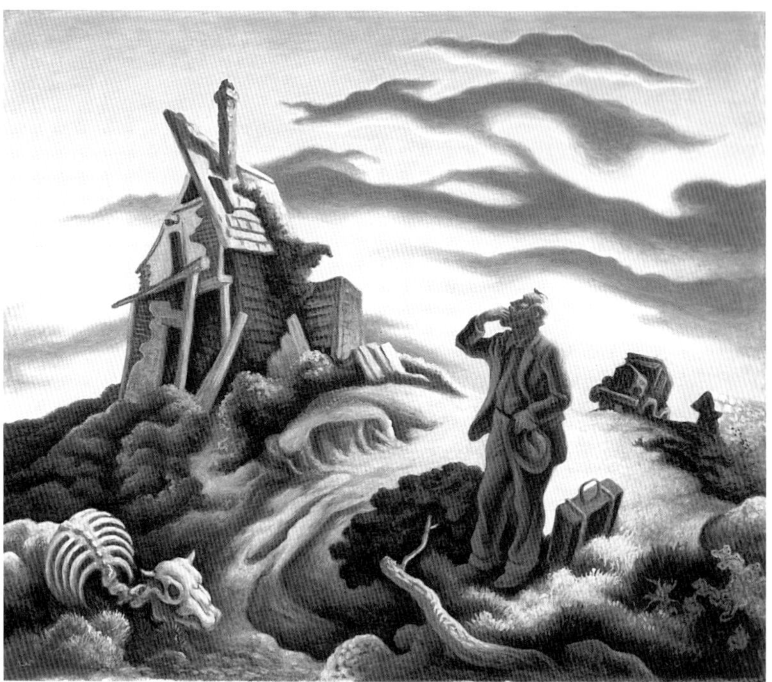

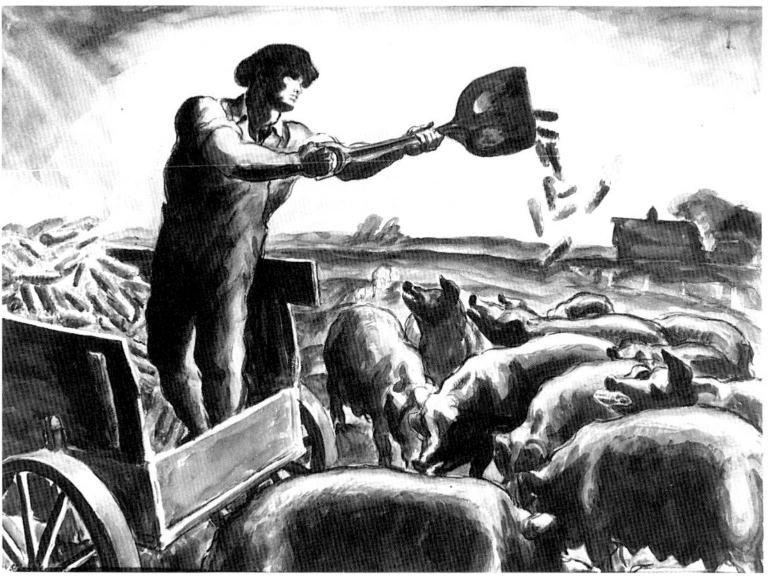

was foretold by earlier Kansas artists, such as Topeka's George Stone, of whom one commentator wrote that "when one is in love with Kansas not even gay and fascinating Paris can alienate his affections."[21]

The passage outward from midwestern farms and villages to urban training grounds, to Europe, and then back homeward, was traced by many of Curry's contemporaries, including his principal regionalist allies, Thomas Hart Benton and Grant Wood. Each of them responded to the experience of repatriation in his art. Wood's *Return from Bohemia* (1935; Regis Collection, Minneapolis) presents an enigmatic tableau of the artist surrounded by members of his Iowa community, to which he returned after his extended European sojourns. Benton's *Prodigal Son* (ca. 1939–41, fig. 3) shows the returnee confronting the ruined homestead and landscape of his youth, an image likely inspired by the dreary wartime circumstances of its creation, agricultural and military calamity.

Curry's two interpretations of *The Prodigal Son* were created during his first fervid period of Kansas imagery. One, from 1929, features the dungareed young man feeding hogs before a barn seen in the distance in what Curry years later called "one of the best water colors I have ever done" (fig. 4).[22] The other, a work in oil from the late 1920s that is more awkwardly composed and drawn, depicts the herdsman in coarse shirt, posed before his swinish charges in a generalized landscape (fig. 5). Curry was aware of the pictorial precedents for his motif, most notably Rembrandt's early etching of the prodigal's return and Dürer's engraving of the same subject. The latter he especially admired for the manner in which the artist "puts the biblical character into the actual setting which he and his people knew as something real so that this is not only a good interpretation of the repentant prodigal, but it is also a good account of a farm scene in Germany in 1495."[23] Curry, too, seems ultimately to have preferred the watercolor depiction of Kansas actualities in 1929 to the timeless biblical subject essayed in oils.

Some eastern reviewers thought that Curry "paint[ed] life 'out there' in rural Kansas with a homesick brush."[24] Laurence Schmeckebier also found personal meaning and autobiograph-

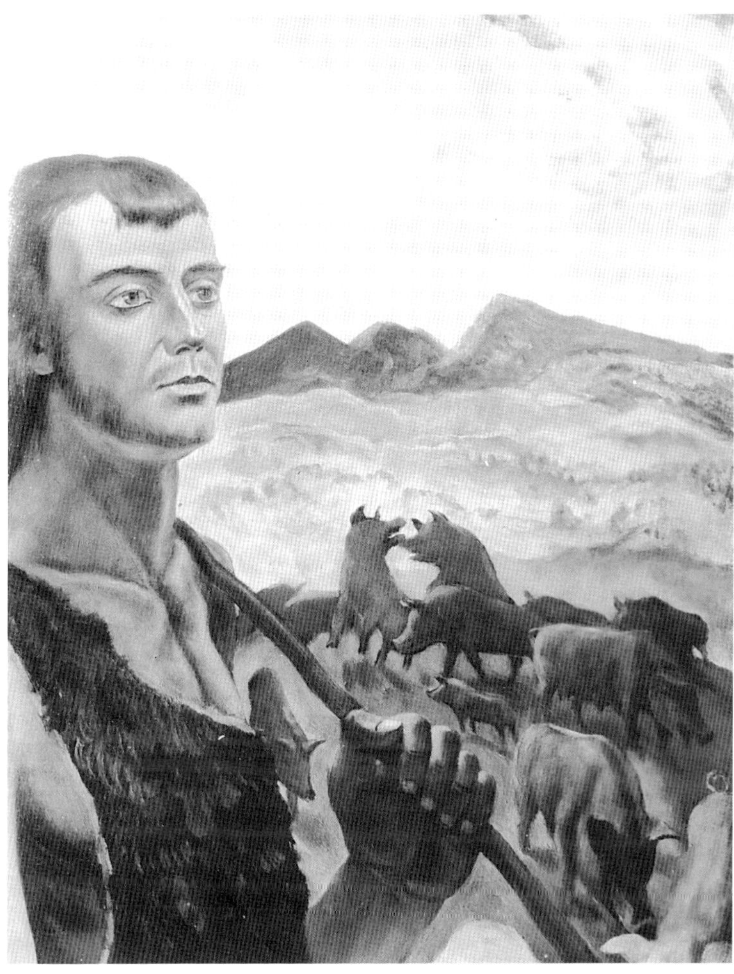

FIGURE 5

John Steuart Curry

Prodigal Son, late 1920s

Oil

Location unknown

Photograph courtesy Curry Papers, Archives of American Art, Smithsonian Institution, Washington, D.C.

ical sentiment in Curry's work, especially the prodigal's story. He noted that during the artist's period of despondency in Connecticut, Smith Curry had offered his son land and stock to start life over again in Kansas.[25] For this and other acts the son voiced pride in his "remarkable" father, whose prosperity and worldliness he recounted to the *New York Herald Tribune.*[26] (Smith Curry had astonished his neighbors when he took his bride on a European honeymoon at a time when, by one account, for most Kansans, "a journey to Topeka was their 'trip abroad.'"[27])

Yet elsewhere, the son's words and images about farm and family, and particularly father, suggest some filial ambivalence. This is perhaps the inevitable lot of the prodigal, as acknowledged by at least one urban writer who confessed: "It's not the smoke in the atmosphere, nor the taste for 'life' that brought me here. . . . [N]o fear of toil or love of dress is driving off the farmer lads, but just the methods of their dads!" [28] Curry's father made a decent living from his eighty-five-acre farm, sufficient to support John during his art training in Chicago and to assist in the early years of his career, while also maintaining his wife and four other children. Because his wife encouraged their eldest son's interests, Smith Curry tolerated the art lessons, the distractions, and the expense. In a candid moment the artist once admitted: "I turned out to be a great satisfaction to him, and also a great surprise. I think that for some years he about gave up hope that I would ever be anything but a liability financially."[29] Despite his mother's encouragement, Curry maintained that "My family had no leanings in that [art] direction." His father he described simply as "a farmer, a fattener of livestock," who fed Herefords for market until they were so large that "the rain set in the middle of their backs."[30] In the eyes of the son, the father's only artistic pride was directed to "the construction of concrete water tanks," which, unlike the Herefords, "didn't hold water."[31]

The yeoman farmer who, from Thomas Jefferson's day forward, had comprised the backbone of the American democracy and the strength of the republic, was invoked anew by Curry's biographer in a paean to paternity. Since Curry was himself the product of farm life, Schmeckebier described the artist as resolute in the belief that "the American farmer is no 'peasant.' As a proud individual the farmer claims the right to own his farm unmortgaged, pay his taxes, raise and market the vital crops, educate his children, and above all to live and act as a free and independent citizen. That is what Curry saw in his father and idealized in *The Stockman.*"[32]

Painted in 1929 and included in the artist's first solo exhibition in New York the following year, *The Stockman* (color plate 19, fig. 6) poses Smith Curry amid and looming over his prized livestock. A masterly figure of stern, unsmiling demeanor, he maintains order with strong body and personality, as well as with whip. His rectitude is echoed in the upright concrete silo behind him, a priapic monument to paternity and a marker of prosperity.[33] *The Stockman*—not "My Father," nor even "Portrait of Smith Curry"—stands as an emblem of good breeding, suggesting a preoccupation with bloodlines more than sentimental ties.

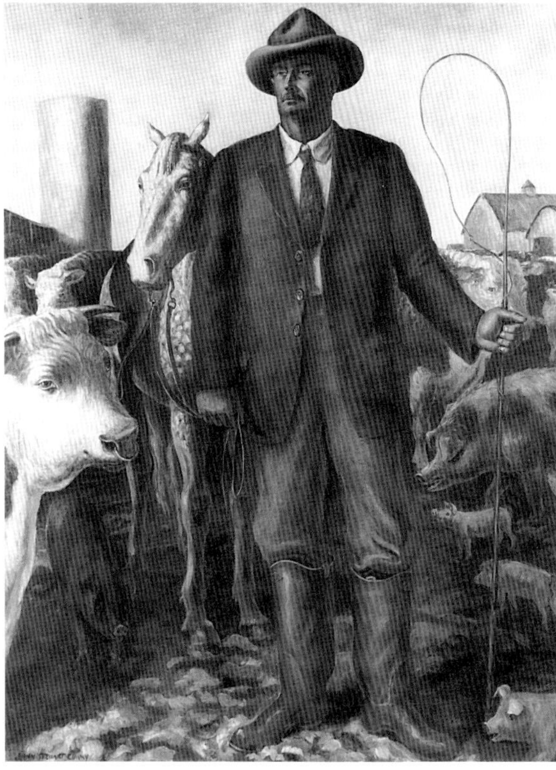

FIGURE 6

John Steuart Curry
The Stockman, 1929
Oil on canvas
52 × 40 in.
Collection of Whitney Museum of American Art, New York. Purchase.
Photograph ©1997: Whitney Museum of American Art

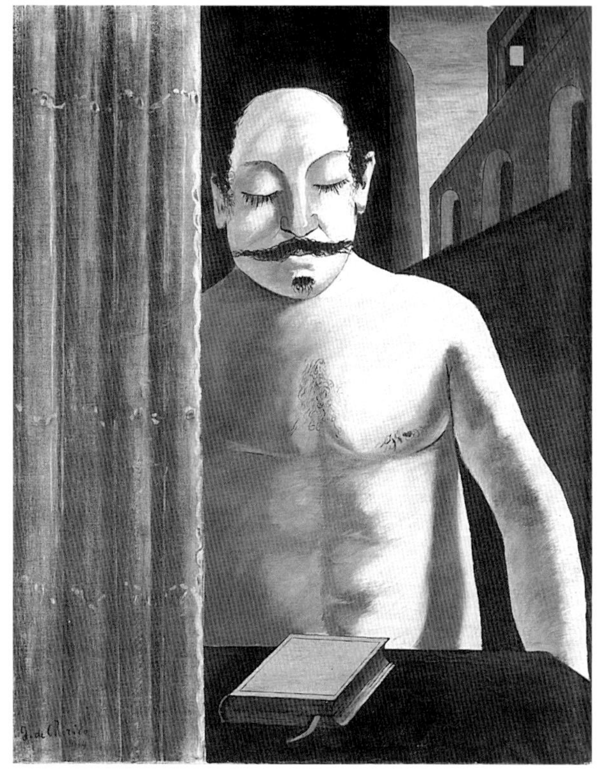

FIGURE 7

Giorgio di Chirico (Italian, 1888–1978)
Child's Brain, 1914
Oil on canvas
31½ × 24¾ in.
Courtesy Moderna Museet, Stockholm.

The father stands with booted feet squarely planted in the mire, his figure controlled by firm outline and darkened shading. He sternly dominates the composition, superior to son and viewer, an imposing, even intimidating figure of authority, like some barnyard Pantokrator. Other parental portraits provide striking parallels, for instance, those by the St. Louis painter Joe Jones, who literally could not face his father and painted him from the rear *(Portrait of the Artist's Father,* 1932; Munson-Williams-Proctor Institute Museum of Art, Utica, New York), or the Italian modern Giorgio di Chirico, whose *Child's Brain* (1914, fig. 7) imagines a young child's disturbing vision of masculine power. The stockman's prominence amid his flock was recalled in later Curry compositions, such as *Our Good Earth* (1940–41, color plate 63), where he looms over wheat and children, a symbol of the fecund prairie that Kansans revered as "the land that grows the best grain and the choicest fruit and the finest stock, and, most of all, grows *men* and *women*."[34] And the pose appeared most famously in Curry's Kansas Statehouse murals, in which John Brown unfurls his might over a crowded landscape of fire and storm.

When their son's commission for the Statehouse murals was announced—the greatest assignment imaginable for any Kansas artist—Mr. and Mrs. Curry were absent from the press conference honoring the painter. According to newspaper reports, they remained at home on the farm, he preferring to thresh, she to busy herself with housework.[35] When Curry painted his parents' portrait, the parlor certainly looked tidy and the distant fields well-threshed! The paired parents were depicted twice, in 1929 (fig. 1) and again in *Father and Mother* of 1933 (fig. 8).

The Kansas newspaper editor William Allen White once cautioned his distant, urban readers that "because we live in country towns, where the only car-gongs we hear are on the baker's

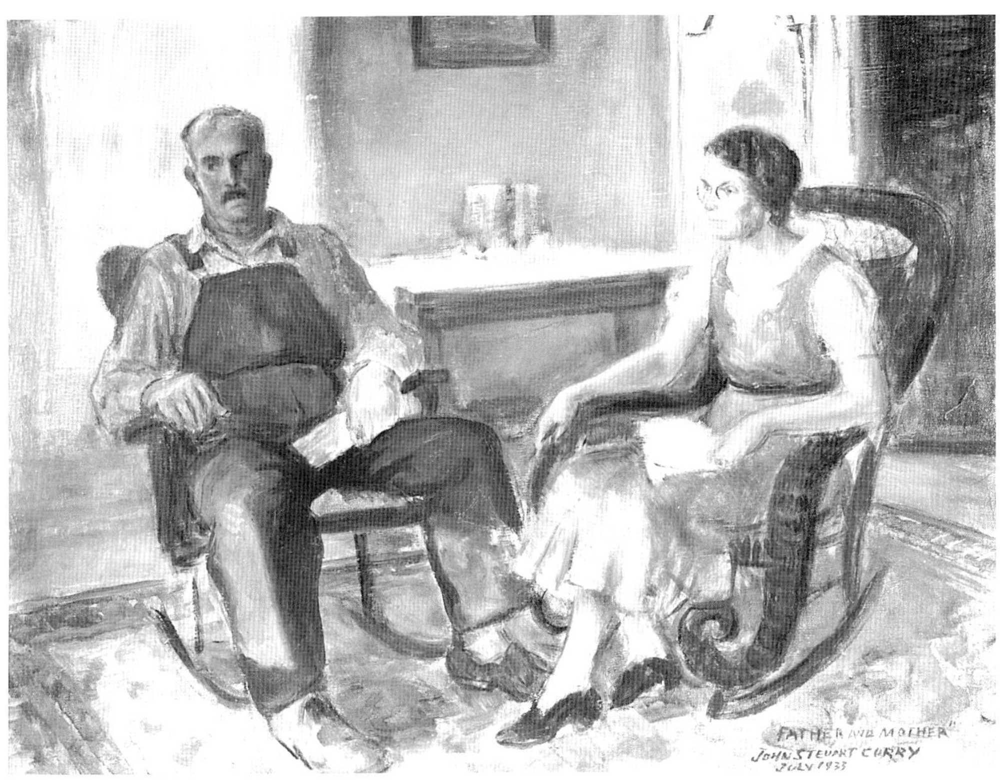

FIGURE 8

John Steuart Curry
Father and Mother, 1933
Oil on canvas
18⅛ × 24⅛ in.
Courtesy Wichita Art Museum, Wichita, Kansas.
On loan from Wichita Public Schools.

wagon, . . . is no reason why city dwellers should assume that we are natives . . . you will find that all the things advertised in the backs of magazines are in our houses."[36] So it was on the Curry farm, where everything was up-to-date, including telephones, electric fans, and other modern conveniences advertised in magazines and the *Kansas City Star.* (Curry remembered his father reading that metropolitan newspaper; it is likely the one Mr. Curry holds in the 1929 portrait.[37]) Rural Kansans followed trends in decorating with the same interest as their contemporaries in Kansas City or beyond. In *Sod and Stubble* (1936), his classic novel of Kansas farm life, John Ise described a widow whose daughters urged her "to have the parlor carpet torn up, the floor planed and polished, and a rug put down—town people were treating their floors in that way."[38] So, too, was Mother Curry a follower of fashion, to judge from her son's painting. Margaret Curry illustrated the claim of one rural sociologist that "the farm house is a symbol that expresses the thinking of the people who live in it,"[39] in her case indicating a cosmopolitan aspiration to life's finer things. In the 1933 portrait, a framed artwork on the wall between the parents suggests another departure from the traditions of country folk. Years later, Curry recalled his mother's use of these art prints, souvenirs of her remarkable European honeymoon: "Instead of grain and feed calendars in our house as the only art we had Rubens, Bellini and Millet. That was unusual and had a great deal to do with forming my future."[40]

In the earlier parental portrait, a telephone hangs on the wall behind Smith Curry, an instrument that was then still a rarity in many Kansas farm homes. Starting in his school days, however, Curry had occasionally included electric and telephone lines and poles in his landscape sketches, indicative of the early date by which power came to Jefferson County, well before the establishment of the Rural Electrification Administration in 1935.[41] With electrification came myriad conveniences. To some, like the prim figure in Grant Wood's well-known *Victorian Survival* (1931; private collection), the telephone might appear as a rude intrusion, its jangling note disturbing the quiet of generations. For most, however, the instrument dramatically changed lives, broadening the world beyond the confines of one's immediate family and neighbors and redefining community, now linked telephonically. Rural Kansans delighted in the telephone line in the landscape, which

Like a fishing net of a single strand
. . . reaches out into the wide ocean of the air
And gathers in a harvest of messages:
Market reports and recipes, sermons and solos,
The weather, bedtime stories, and music,
Music from Los Angeles, Hawaii, and Edgewater Beach.[42]

For all its modern touches, the Curry household was still deeply traditional in the values and rituals it sheltered. In 1929 the father gazes through the window upon the barns, pastures, and livestock, the basis for prosperity hard won with coarse and calloused hands; the property is characteristic of successful Kansas farms, whose structures were described by one visitor as giving "evidence of thrift and comfort."[43] By contrast, the mother looks inward, literally and figuratively, absorbed in the feminine task of knitting. Her delicate wicker rocker is all frills and curlicues, while his manly seat is plain, sturdy, and oaken.

Curry's penchant for selecting subjects symbolic of universal experience was the basis for his popularity, then and now. That his themes were familiar from his Kansas upbringing was "but incidental," wrote one of his partisans, for "these are great experiences of life that are universal, and the power of John Steuart Curry's paintings transcend [*sic*] all scenic localisms."[44] One writer described Curry's painting of his parents as an "idea-portrait of the folks at home," a concept that could evolve into other domestic vignettes. These range from various genre subjects to large murals, such as the U.S. Department of Justice building motif of a homesteading family (1937) and the *Kansas Pastoral* of farmer and wife on their unmortgaged farm, which concludes the Statehouse suite in Topeka (1937–42, color plate 53).[45] The farm theme might also exemplify an ideogram for American agricultural life and traditions that were under considerable pressure in the 1930s. Charles Burchfield, like Curry a son of the Middle West, in 1932 painted *Evening* (Newark Museum, Newark, New Jersey), a design of three elderly folks resting in rocking chairs before an old farmhouse. He described the picture as "evening of a certain phase of farm life in America. The old farms are going and a new conception is coming in."[46] In Curry's Kansas, as in Burchfield's country, the times were changing.

Curry called his 1929 depiction of parents and the family farm "rare Americana."[47] The painting was first exhibited with the title *The Old Folks,* a generalized concept like Burchfield's "Evening" and less specific than "My Parents." Shortly after its completion, *The Old Folks* was several times reproduced with that title, on one occasion bearing the additional caption "A touch of New England under a western sky."[48]

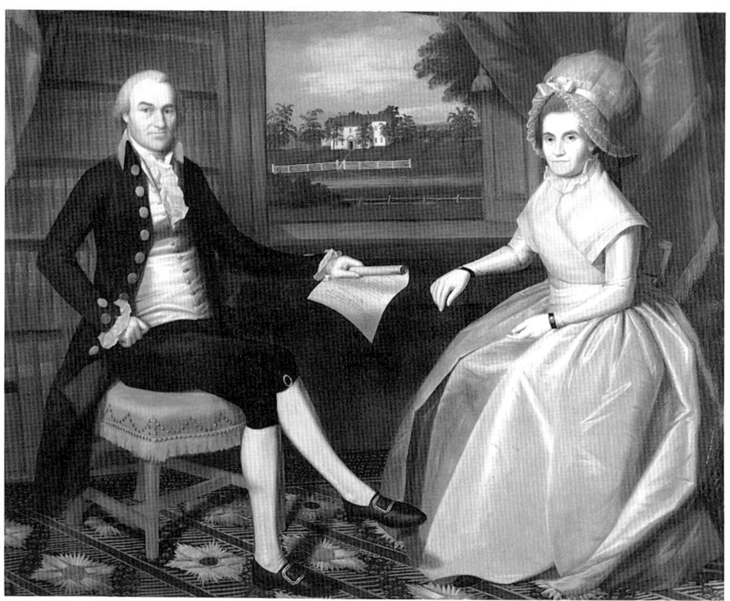

FIGURE 9
Ralph Earl (American, 1751–1801)
Oliver Ellsworth and Abigail Wolcott Ellsworth, 1792
Oil on canvas
76 × 86¾ in.
Courtesy Wadsworth Atheneum, Hartford, Connecticut. Gift of the Ellsworth Heirs.

This curious geographical reference, as well as mentions of Americana and "old folks," suggests that Curry's iconic image of a Kansas farm couple might be infused with significance beyond its connotations of region and family. This portrait of a modern farmer and wife also looks backward to pictorial traditions as old as the nation, specifically to paintings from New England that were being newly appreciated in the years after World War I. Among the reputations rescued from near oblivion was that of the Connecticut painter Ralph Earl, whose late masterwork, a double portrait of Oliver Ellsworth and Abigail Wolcott Ellsworth (1792, fig. 9), is among the treasures of the Wadsworth Atheneum in Hartford. Acquired in 1903, Earl's painting has routinely been on display since at Connecticut's largest art museum. Curry certainly knew the collections in Hartford, an easy drive from his Westport home, and appears to have borrowed the composition of his parents' double portrait from the Ellsworth precedent. Like the Kansas couple, the colonial patriot and his wife are seated flanking a window that opens onto a view of their home and expansive property. The interest in Earl was part of a general vogue for colonial Americana that was fueled by the nation's sesquicentennial in 1926. In Connecticut, as in the other original colonies, that celebration was marked by numerous events that collectively sparked an outpouring of neocolonial enthusiasm evident in nearly all aspects of American life and provided Curry's inspiration for the painting of his "old folks."[49] Near the end of his life, Judge Ellsworth claimed with pride that he lived in the pleasantest place in the pleasantest town in the best state of the Union.[50] To Smith Curry on his Kansas farm in 1929, that sentiment would have been as familiar as it would be unfamiliar to his wandering son.

Beyond their indications of practices in modern farm decor or neocolonial enthusiasm, Curry's parental portraits provide a barometer of the artist's relations with the subjects. Unlike the colonial Connecticut couple, who are united in their poses of attention to the artist, Mr. and Mrs. Curry of 1929 scarcely relate to each other; he gazes away from wife and viewer, while she stares downward, lost in thought and handiwork. The window and the farm property it frames seem to divide rather than unite the couple. In the 1933 painting, the figures and space are rearranged, so that each is posed against the light of a separate window but with gazes both directed offstage to the left, apparently in response to the same stimulus. Moreover, in the later work there is something of a sense of intimacy between the two figures, whose feet meet even if their eyes and hands do not. Jane Comstock, a student of Curry's work, suggests that the mother's greater support of her son's artistic aspirations perhaps accounts for her serene appearance in the later work, in which her husband seems uneasy. Comstock also reminds us that the two paintings coincide approximately with a tumultuous period in Curry's life. In 1929 he was torn between public acclaim for his art and private concerns over his marriage, strains that eventually led to the artist's drinking problem and to separation from his wife, Clara; in July 1932, while he was escaping his professional and personal responsibilities to travel with a circus troupe, his wife died of heart disease.[51] In 1933 it was the widowed son who returned to Kansas to visit his parents, perhaps sharing with them word of his new friendship with Kathleen Gould Shepherd, who the following year would become his second wife. "Considering its strategic position in Curry's life," Comstock concludes (apropos the 1933 example but also pertinent to the earlier painting), this domestic scene may be the artist's personal reverie on "the complexities of marriage."[52]

If the transition from the portrait of 1929 to that of 1933 was from distance to intimacy, a third variation on the theme, painted in watercolor in 1938, presents yet another view of domestic relations. *The Folks at Home* (1938, fig. 10) poses a generalized mother and father—no longer a portrait of the senior Currys—seated back to back in a corner room, each comforting a child from the lightning and storm that rage outside. Now the home has become a refuge from the world's travails, and Curry, who had adopted Kathleen's daughter, Ellen, seemingly projects himself into the role of caring father.

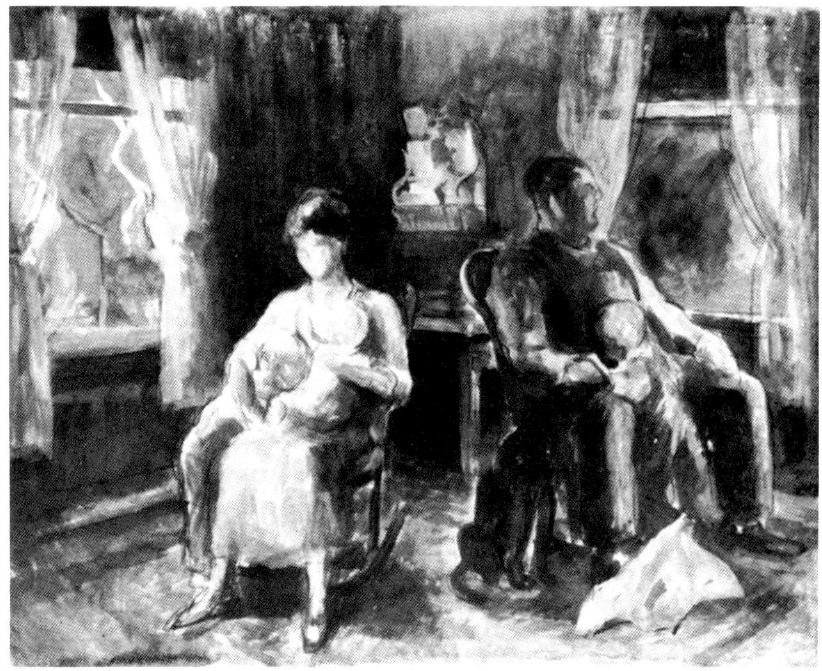

FIGURE 10
John Steuart Curry
The Folks at Home, 1938
Location unknown
As reproduced in Laurence E. Schmeckebier, *John Steuart Curry's Pageant of America* (New York: American Artists Group, 1943). Photograph courtesy State Historical Society of Wisconsin.

These human dramas took place not only indoors but also at large, on the farm and in the landscape beyond. When he returned from the East to visit his parents in 1929 and subsequent summers, Curry's landscape interests extended beyond the familiar terrain of northeastern Kansas, the rolling prairie near the family's farm; he traveled as well to the south-central part of the state, to Barber County on the Oklahoma line southwest of Wichita, there to vacation and sketch on the Heart Ranch.

The oil, watercolor, and pencil studies he made that summer and on a return visit the following year served him well during the decade to come, providing the basis for his distinctive views of the Kansas landscape by which a generation of eastern connoisseurs came to know the lay of the heartland.

The ranch country of Barber County was wilder than the farmlands of Jefferson County and the Kaw River valley. The rolling emptiness of the western, red-earth country pulled the eye to distant horizons and, with it, the imagination. In *Spring Shower* (1931, color plate 23), *Sunrise (over Kansas)* (1935–37; Kistler Beach Museum, Kansas State University, Manhattan), and other early views based on the Heart Ranch studies, Curry described a landscape more rugged than the cultivated acres of his native precinct. The ranch country's land and climate are hostile to cultivation of the sort practiced in the northeastern quadrant of the state. Curry's intent was not, like some earlier Kansas artists, to advertise the fertility of the land or the bountiful harvests. The emptiness of Barber County's Gypsum Hills seemed productive primarily of mood, a haunting drama in the sweeping expanse that is marked but not managed by human intervention. Laurence Schmeckebier noted that "in his landscapes, in particular, Curry uses space to express moods that vary from the utter physical abandon . . . to a quiet spiritual, almost romantic dreaming or even yearning."[53] To native son William Allen White, these wide expanses, reminiscent of the Russian steppes, seemed "a vast, mystical terrain where sky and earth unite."[54]

Mystical. Romantic and spiritual. Physical abandonment. For some, the high plains clearly had the capacity to stir the emotions, even if they lacked any of the conventional attributes of landscape scenery. The playwright William Inge used to delight in recounting the beauties of his native state, boasting that in Kansas there were no mountains in the way. Kansas poets wondered, "Who would choose a small land / Where the hills / Steadily asserting / Granite wills, / Narrow all horizons, / Stand apart?"[55] In this landscape wide and airy, the sky dominated in a manner unfamiliar to outsiders. Visitors gape at the vastness: "It's amazing here! The sky is like a person yawned and never stopped!"[56] To explain the peculiar effect required a long familiarity, such as Willa Cather's: "Elsewhere the sky is the roof of the world," she wrote, "but here the earth was the floor of the sky. The landscape one longed for when one was far away, the thing all about one, the world one actually lived in, was the sky, the sky!"[57]

The space of the great plains elicited strong reactions from visitors and natives alike. In recent years, the writer Ian Frazier responded exuberantly to Curry's country; after visiting the prairie of central Kansas, he concluded, "Joy seems to me a product of the geography, just as deserts can produce mystical ecstasy and English moors produce gloom. Once happiness gets rolling in this open place, not much stops it."[58]

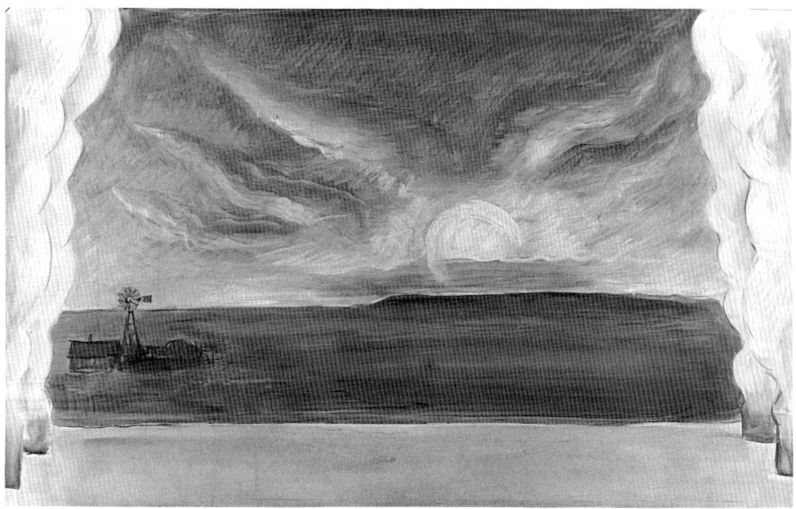

FIGURE 11

John Steuart Curry

Set design for the ballet *Pagan Poem*, 1941–42

Gouache on illustration board

20 × 30 in.

Courtesy Spencer Museum of Art, University of Kansas. Gift of Daniel Bradley Schuster in memory of Ellen Curry Schuster.

In the mid-1930s Curry returned to the Heart Ranch studies for a new series of landscape paintings. His sunrise images mark a new motif in his work and a new release in his life. To his friend Schmeckebier he admitted that his youthful interest in powerful midwestern cataclysms—tornados, floods, and the like—correlated with the turmoil in his own mind, occasioned by uncertainties relating to career, marriage, and finance as well as to the more general social upheavals of the period. After the protracted difficulties of 1928–32, Curry's sunrise motifs might be seen as bringing the promise of New Deal prosperity to the nation at large. ("Happy days are here again.") On a more personal level, Schmeckebier argued, "the happiness he experienced during 1933 and 1934 as a result of the friendship and subsequent marriage with Kathleen Gould may have had much to do with the boyish enthusiasm of the sunrise pictures." He even went so far as to propose that "the sunrise theme is another form of artistic self-portrait," noting the artist's practice from the mid-1930s of adding a sunrise sketch to his autograph.[59]

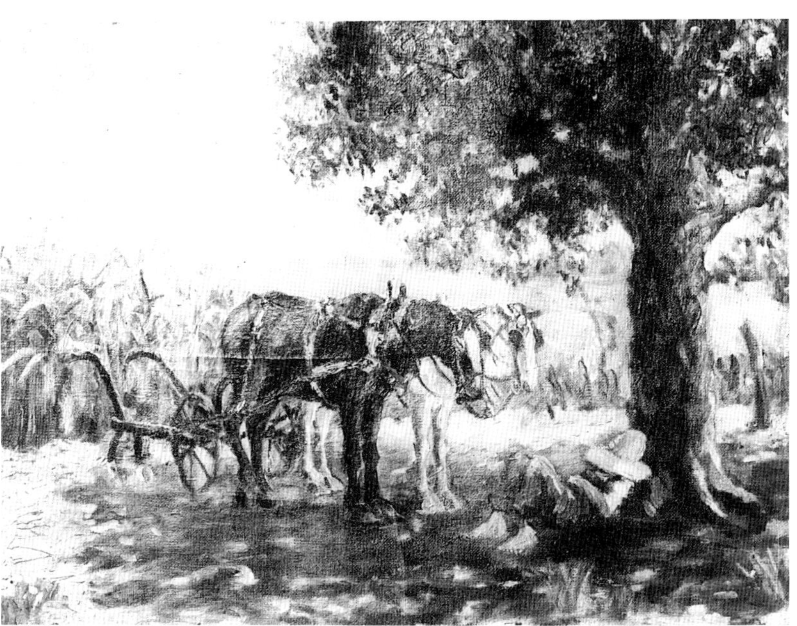

FIGURE 12
John Steuart Curry
The Corn Plower, 1917
Oil on canvas
18 × 23½ in.
Location unknown
Photograph courtesy Archives of American Art, Smithsonian Institution, Washington, D.C., Curry Papers.

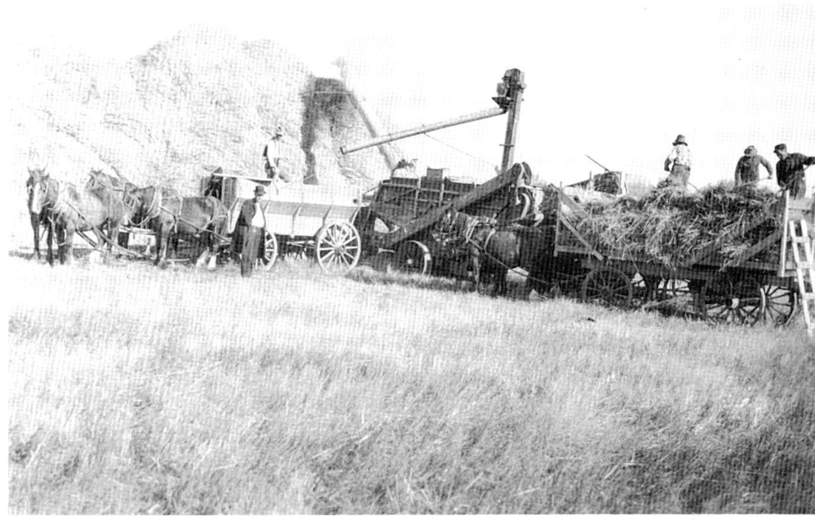

FIGURE 13
Photograph inscribed *Threshing in Kansas: Where the Money Comes From,* early 1920s. Courtesy Curry Papers, Archives of American Art, Smithsonian Institution, Washington, D.C.

Curry's identification with Kansas began early in his career, even while a student at the School of the Art Institute of Chicago, where, as he proudly reported to his mother, he was known as "Jack Kansas."[60] If he identified with the Kansas landscape, with the plains country and its joyous skies, others identified the landscape with its depictor. Typical was one writer who, while driving in the state, spied a large cloud "lying round and roseate on the horizon, like the head of a Middle-Western painter claiming possession. Like the head of John Steuart Curry."[61]

The drama of the Kansas skies, of clouds and sunrises, was sometimes viewed panoramically across the wide and uncontained land; at other times it was glimpsed from between the eroded prairie's rust red mesas, which framed the view like stage wings. The sun rises above the land like an enormous stage curtain, lending a theatrical air to the matinal events. Curry recalled this years later when designing a set for the ballet *Pagan Poem* (1941–42, fig. 11). The sense of the Kansas landscape as a stage set there became actual, providing a backdrop against which universal human dramas could be played out.

The landscape arena—the pastures and prairie beyond the barnyard—had supplied Curry with inspiration from early in his career, even when he was away from it. One of his earliest oil paintings, *The Corn Plower* (1917, fig. 12), shows a field hand, daydreaming in the shade of a tree while the rich cornfield rests untended. The agrarian landscape here prompts reverie and thoughts about a harvest of paintings, not produce. Such scenes of indolence amid cultivation are rare in Curry's work, however. Characteristically, he depicted rural types as pious and industrious, explaining that "it is the iron in these farmers . . . that I would like to bring out in my paintings."[62] The plowboy's crop, albeit untilled, suggests an awareness of the farm and its agricultural landscape as an economic unit. As a reminder of that—and as if to rebut more romantic notions of the pastoral life—a photograph in the artist's family album depicting threshing on the Kansas farm is inscribed on its verso, "Where the Money Comes From" (fig. 13).[63] Only rarely, however, do Curry's best-known images show actual labor in the landscape, at planting or harvest time—perhaps because for much of his life Curry managed to live far away from that seasonal grind.

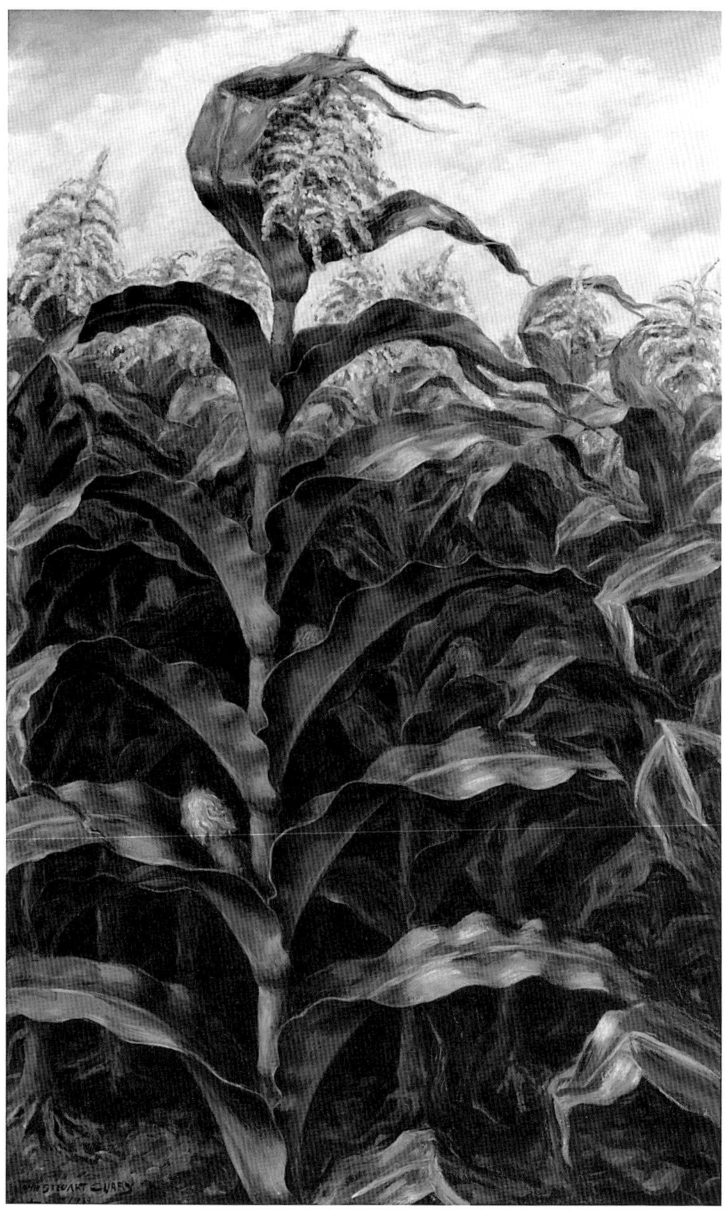

FIGURE 14

John Steuart Curry
Kansas Cornfield, 1933
Oil on canvas
60 × 38¼ in.
The Roland P. Murdock Collection, Wichita Art Museum, Wichita, Kansas. Photograph ©1997: Wichita Art Museum.

By that standard, *Kansas Cornfield* of 1933 (color plate 28, fig. 14) is a somewhat unusual work, emphasizing the crop clearly ready for the harvest. The painting was acquired by the Wichita Art Museum in 1939, the first purchase by that new institution. The artist explained the genesis of the image in a letter to the museum's agent: "I have tried to put into this painting the drama that I feel in the presence of a luxurient [*sic*] cornfield beneath our wind-blown Kansas skies."[64]

Curry was certainly not the first to be struck by the spectacle of a midwestern cornfield ripe in the summer sun. James Price, an Englishman who spent several years on a Kansas farm in the late nineteenth century, wrote of his crop with equivalent fascination:

> **On the evening of July 10th, I took a walk up my corn field, reached the other end, and looked across toward the setting sun. The sight was one of simple grandeur. The stalks were now about five feet high, covered with massive dark green foliage. The perfect stillness—not a leaf seemed to be moving—the heated atmosphere made a strange feeling of awe steal over me.[65]**

When the crop was good, as it often was in Curry's childhood, it was a source of comfort and prosperity for all. William Allen White, writing several years before the artist was born, found "something royal" in the bounty of "King Corn," which called for "reverential homage." At such moments, "the entire community is included in the promise of the coming kingdom. The days of pinching and running behind and putting up a poor mouth are done."[66]

In these times of plentiful harvests, farm communities celebrated with special festivities. The most spectacular of these was the triennial Corn Carnival in Atchison, which drew thousands of visitors to the town (which was not far from Curry's home) and garnered press attention throughout the region and beyond. The Corn Carnival, one visiting journalist wrote, won fame for Atchison just as Passion Plays did for Oberammergau or the Mardi Gras did for New Orleans.[67] Elsewhere in Kansas during the 1910s and 1920s, the corn grew as "high as an elephant's eye," yielding harvests that overflowed silos, the piled crop dotting the landscape with "corn dunes." Kansas artists celebrated this fecundity with images of bounty and beneficence, none more so than Topeka's Henry Worrall. His *Drouthy Kansas* (1878, fig. 15) is a whimsical harvest scene that shows melons and potatoes as big as boulders, cobs the size of logs, and bushels upon bushels of grain; the image sought to dispel easterners' lingering skepticism about local conditions of climate and agriculture, and it was much reproduced in the late

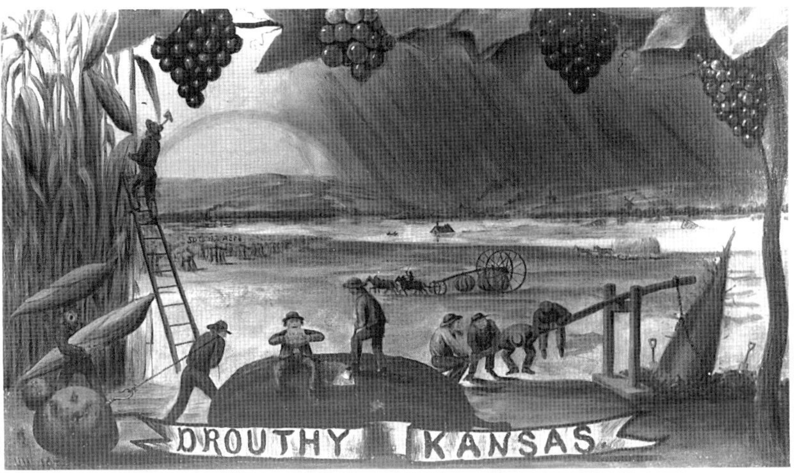

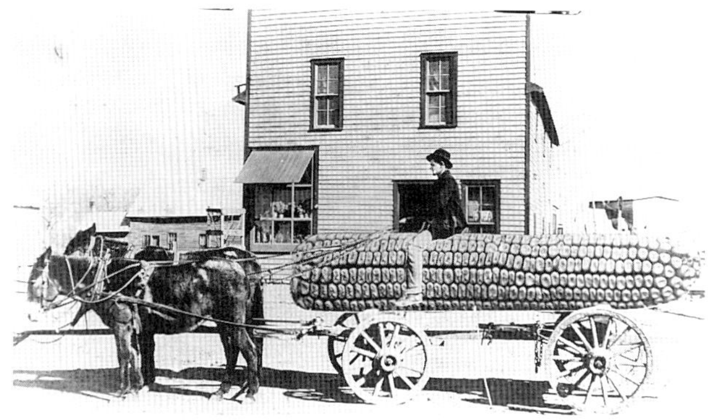

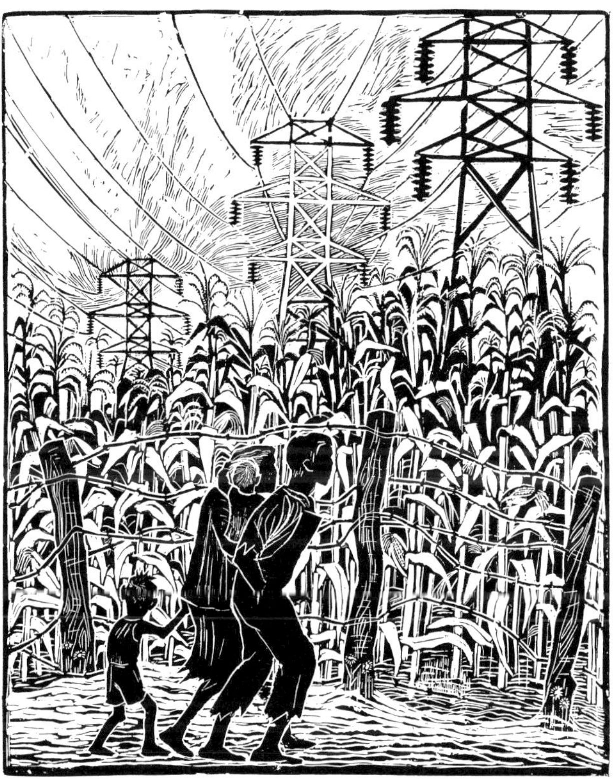

FIGURE 15 *(above)*

Henry Worrall (American, 1825–1902)
Drouthy Kansas, 1878
Oil on canvas
14 × 24 in.
Courtesy Kansas State Historical Society, Topeka.

FIGURE 16 *(above right)*

Postcard of "corn wagon," ca. 1900–1910. Courtesy Kansas State Historical Society, Topeka.

FIGURE 17 *(right)*

Lucienne Bloch (American, b. 1909)
Land of Plenty, n.d.
Woodcut
10⅝ × 8¾ in.
As reproduced in *America Today: A Book of 100 Prints* (New York: American Artists' Congress, 1936).

nineteenth century. The midwestern fascination with agricultural gigantism persisted into the twentieth century, producing fanciful postcards of oversized produce (fig. 16) and public murals that similarly immortalized the harvest.

Farm wealth was symbolized in the weight, bulk, and quantity of prize specimens, a gauge in which corn figured prominently. In Lucienne Bloch's woodcut *Land of Plenty* (fig. 17), a memorable achievement in social realist printmaking, tall corn and towering electric power lines, the symbols of national prosperity, are ironically juxtaposed with a destitute family, cruelly held apart from such promise by a barbed-wire fence. In *Kansas Cornfield,* Curry and his viewer do not stand apart from the ranks of healthy corn but rather seem surrounded by them, recalling the artist's childhood experiences on the Winchester farm. However, during the summer of 1933, when he visited his parents in Kansas, the life he recalled was under pressure of change. The bountiful corn harvests of prior years were diminishing, both locally and nationwide. In Kansas, the acreage devoted to corn was reduced slightly from 1931 and 1932, but the yield per acre and the state's overall production fell dramatically from the immediately preceding years.[68] And with that precipitous decline vanished much of the prosperity and optimism of the recent past.

The drop in farmers' fortunes was due to various factors, especially a prolonged drought, which destroyed the land. Moreover, the passage of the Agricultural Adjustment Act (AAA) in the spring of 1933, one of the major legislative thrusts of Franklin D. Roosevelt's first one hundred days, insured that

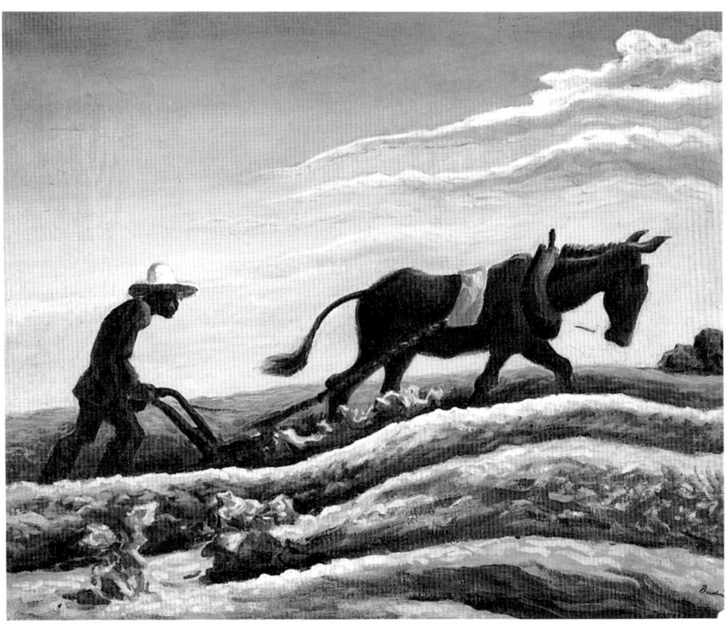

FIGURE 18 *(above)*

Thomas Hart Benton (American, 1889–1975)
Plowing It Under, 1929/34
Oil on canvas
20⅛ × 24 in.
Courtesy Lyman Field and the United Missouri Bank of Kansas City, Missouri. Photograph ©1997: T. H. Benton and R. P. Benton Testamentary Trusts/Licensed by VAGA, New York, N.Y.

FIGURE 19 *(right)*

Frederic Remington (American, 1861–1909)
Agriculture in Kansas, ca. 1883
Ink on paper
Location unknown
Photograph courtesy Kansas State Historical Society, Topeka.

acreage formerly dedicated to cultivation would be plowed under—in theory reducing overproduction and raising farm prices. The program proved controversial, even among midwesterners who might have been thought to benefit from it. In 1934 Thomas Hart Benton, Curry's Missouri colleague, reworked a farm scene he had painted five years earlier, retitling it *Plowing It Under* (fig. 18); he also produced a lithograph from the image, thereby broadening many times over the audience for his pictorial gibe at the AAA subsidy program. The corn that Curry painted in such ripe abundance on the farm in 1933—which, like Benton's image, served as the basis for a lithograph—may also convey a barbed message about the program. At the very least, it suggests that Smith Curry chose not to plow under his corn acreage, the proud stand of corn providing an implicit rebuke of the wasteful policy.

Although Kansas is known familiarly as the Sunflower State (a crop whose commercial possibilities were only belatedly recognized), and although it is the nation's prime producer of wheat, corn has long formed the basis for the agricultural economy in much of the state.[69] This is especially true in the northeastern quadrant of Kansas, in the valleys of the Kaw and Missouri Rivers, where the Curry family property lay. Geographers and cartographers refer to the counties there as part of the great corn belt of the central lowland. Even Frederic Remington recognized this; during his brief stint as a Kansas sheep rancher, he produced a sketch, *Agriculture in Kansas* (ca. 1883, fig. 19), depicting the seasonal cycle of corn planting, cultivation, and shucking. Curry's *Kansas Cornfield* might, then, be viewed as an image redolent of his home precinct, remote from the wild country of Barber County and from the wheat fields of western Kansas.

Beyond the context of Jefferson County, the vegetable also was proposed as symbol for the American nation, as early suggested in Elizabeth Remington's painting *Two Kings: Cotton and Corn* (ca. 1875, fig. 20). The cotton refers to the mainstay of the southern economy, providing an agricultural symbol for the former Confederacy. The corn, by contrast, symbolizes the Union cause in the North, suggesting its very different economy and society.[70] As a proud child of the Free State, Curry might also have found in corn a useful symbol for his social (as well as agricultural) sympathies.

In the 1890s, a campaign to establish corn as the national symbol gathered support from some artists and writers. One poet's rhyme represents the sentiments of many in that era:

The rose may bloom for England
The lily for France unfold;
Ireland may honor the shamrock;
Scotland her thistle bold;
But the shield of the Great Republic,
The glory of the West,
Shall bear a stalk of tasseled Corn
Of all our wealth the best![71]

The plant's beauties were extolled: "Is there anything in vegetable nature so delicately graduated as this long leaf?"[72] And artists were advised to employ its graceful form in painting and design: "[T]his beautiful plant will lend itself to artistic treatment in a greater variety of ways, and is . . . richer in aesthetic suggestiveness, than any other that has ever served as a national emblem."[73] Even former President Rutherford B. Hayes was enlisted in the campaign, proclaiming that "Corn is the destined emblem of America."[74]

Candace Wheeler, a leading designer of the day, used the occasion of the Chicago World's Columbian Exposition in 1893 to champion corn as "Columbia's emblem." She compiled a selection of prose and verse tributes to the crop that recommended itself for such purpose due to its ancient history in the New World: "Aztecs and Incas and the roving bands north and south of these central populations, had, from time immemorial, paid homage to it in rituals and songs and dances." Modern Americans should do no less, Wheeler wrote, for "no other plant is so typical of our greatness and prosperity as a nation; no other has such artistic meanings and possibilities; no other is so wholly and nobly and historically American."[75]

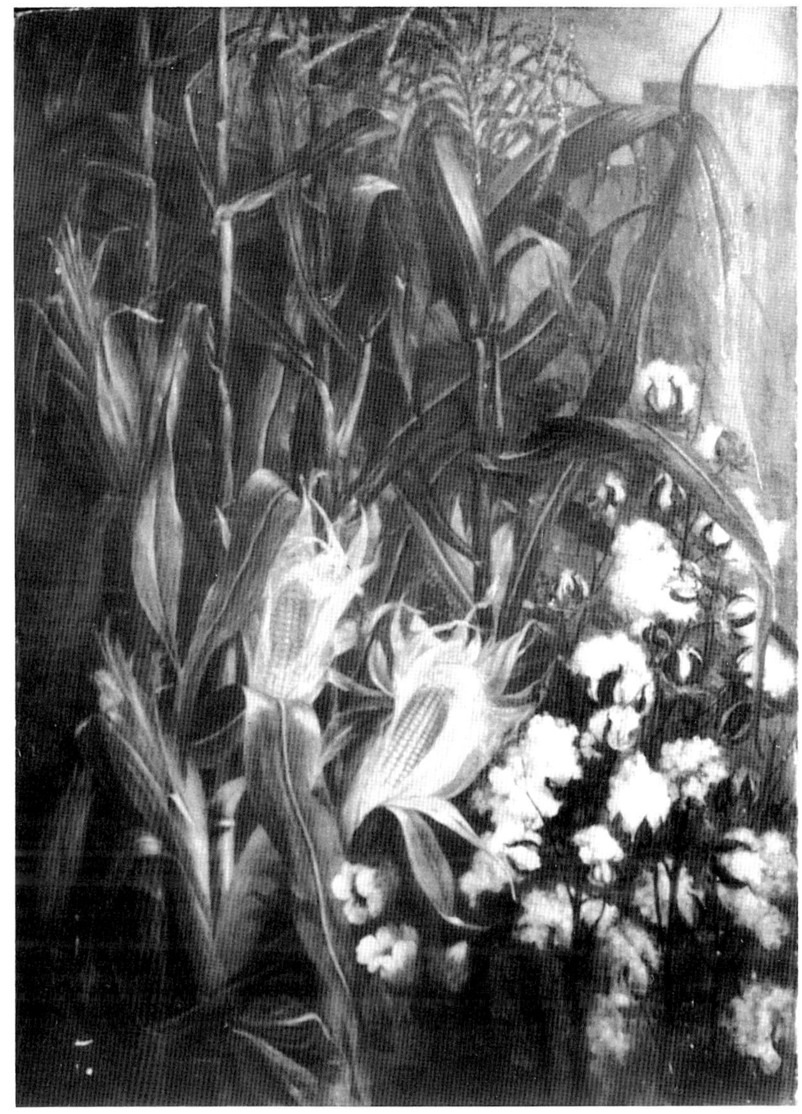

FIGURE 20

Elizabeth Remington (American, 1825–1917)
Two Kings: Cotton and Corn, ca. 1875
ca. 32 × 24 in.
Location unknown
Photograph courtesy Inventory of American Paintings, National Museum of American Art, Smithsonian Institution, Washington, D.C.

The corn that grew so widely, "From Superior's shore to Chili [*sic*],/ From the ocean of dawn to the west,"[76] served aptly as a hemispheric symbol as well. Appropriately, both the U.S. Capitol in Washington and the Canadian Parliament House in Ottawa have capitals adorned with corncob motifs, and maize recurs frequently in the art of Central and South America, both ancient and modern. A Mayan mural of corn stalks with cobs

FIGURE 21 *(right)*
Corn-husk costume from Atchison Corn Carnival program, 1905. Courtesy Kansas Collection, University of Kansas Libraries, Lawrence.

FIGURE 22 *(far right)*
John Steuart Curry
Costume design for the ballet *Pagan Poem: Grass,* 1941–42
Gouache on illustration board
20 × 15⅛ in.
Courtesy Spencer Museum of Art, University of Kansas, Lawrence. Gift of Daniel Bradley Schuster in memory of Ellen Curry Schuster.

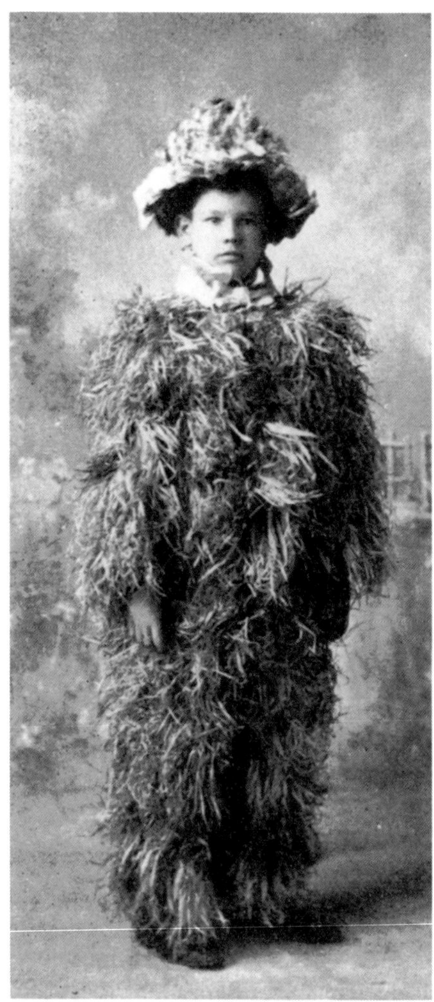

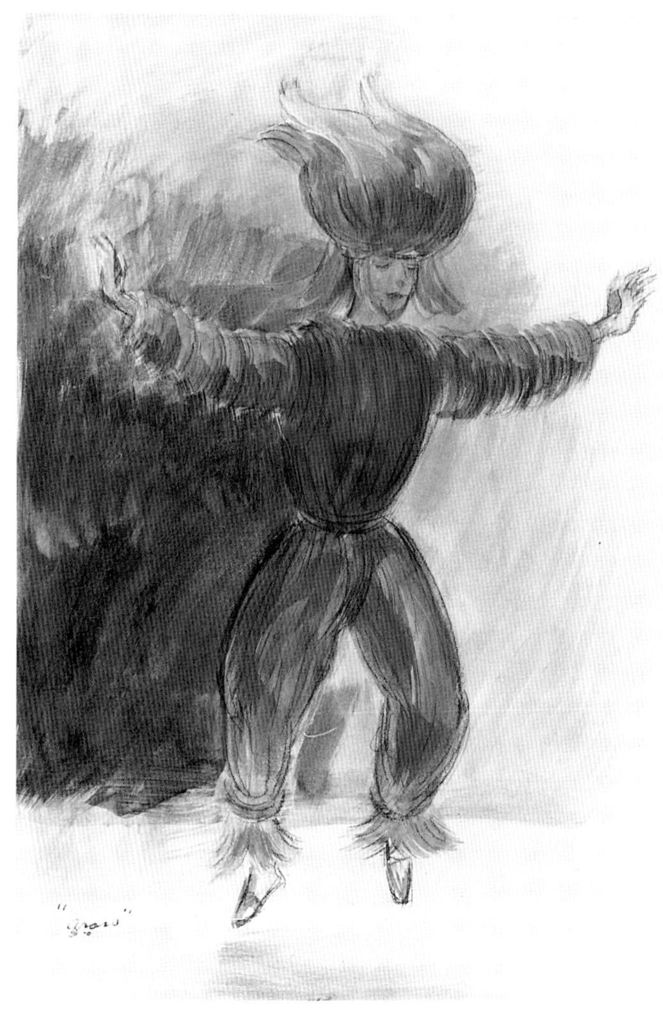

ripening into human heads suggests the long lineage of the crop in art and provides an antecedent for Curry's numerous sketches of the plant, its tumescent cobs bursting with power and fecundity.[77]

When *Kansas Cornfield* was shown in New York, critics were impressed with this life-sized "portrait" of the crop. The *New York Evening Post* reviewer Margaret Breuning remarked on the artist's nativism. "There is too little known of [his] exquisite paintings of native shrubs and flowers," she noted, praising the work's "dense mesh of lush vegetation and crisp leaves and flaunting tassels that seem to rustle and stir in the flashing pattern of light woven through them."[78] In his canvas, Curry had seemingly realized the hope of the plant's earlier advocates for its role in art.

Curry recalled that, as a child, the cornfields on his father's farm "held the same fascination for me as do the forests for those who live within them. I remember wandering through them and being overpowered by the fear of being lost in their great confines."[79] In his schoolboy history lessons he might have remembered tales of children who hid in cornfields to escape the murderous wrath of William C. Quantrill's Confederate raiders when, in August 1863, they sacked the abolitionist stronghold of Lawrence, in neighboring Douglas County. And he likely knew of the elaborate costumes made from corn and other crops in which harvest celebrants clad themselves (fig. 21). When Ralph Waldo Emerson wrote of an "occult relation between man and the vegetable,"[80] he probably was not thinking of the Atchison Corn Carnival, but Curry clearly was when he costumed figures of Grass or Wheat for the stage (fig. 22). He also might have had that in mind when he painted his stalks at human scale in *Kansas Cornfield.*

The prominent critic and champion of regionalism Thomas Craven was, like his friend Curry, a native Kansan, hailing from the farming community of Salina. In 1935 he wrote to the artist praising "the Corn picture," but admitting that "at first I did not get [it]."[81] What did Craven not get? Another friend, the painter Reginald Marsh, provided a clue. He once opined that Curry's *Ajax* (1936–37, color plate 37), the familiar image of a grandstanding bull, was really a self-portrait.[82] If Curry discovered self in livestock, might he not do likewise in the crops of the field? What Craven did not appreciate (and what Marsh perhaps only intuited) was that *Kansas Cornfield* might represent a self-portrait in regional, vegetal guise.

Other artists had humanized the corn stalk. For instance, the California sculptor Donal Hord's *Young Maize* (ca. 1931, fig. 23) personifies the ancient American plant, looming over germinating seeds. In an earlier generation, the southern poet Sidney Lanier, in a lengthy verse dedicated to corn, similarly posed a single superior stalk. The poet was enchanted by the promise of the corn harvest and, transfixed by "the stately corn-ranks rise," addressed the singular stalk, which, like Curry's plant, rises above its peers:

Look, out of line one tall corn-captain stands,
Advanced beyond the foremost of his bands,
And waves his blades upon the very edge. . . .

This "lustrous stalk" drew the poet's attention, for it "leads the vanguard of his timid time . . . sing[ing] up cowards with commanding rhyme." Standing tall in the field, rooted deep in the soil, Lanier's stalk by example instructs the poet, who

. . . fain, like thee, [would] grow
By double increment, above, below;
Soul homely, as thou art, yet rich in grace like thee,
Teaching the yeoman selfless chivalry. . . .

The poet praised the towering plant that

. . . lift'st more stature than a mortal man's,
Yet ever piercest downward in the mould
And keepest hold
Upon the reverend and steadfast earth
That gave thee birth. . . . [83]

Curry-as-"corn captain" strangely prefigures a 1967 painting by Thomas Hart Benton, *Wheat* (fig. 24), which similarly enlists a midwestern crop for personal purposes. Before a stand of ripened wheat reaching into the golden infinity, and behind two

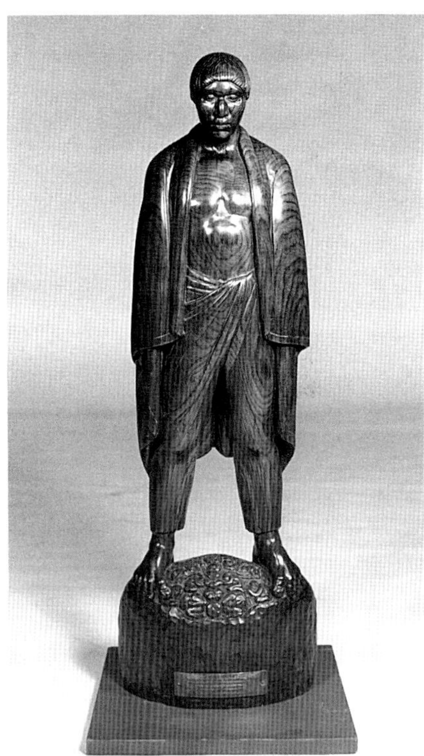

FIGURE 23 *(left)*
Donal Hord (American, 1902–1966)
Young Maize, ca. 1931
Rosewood
H: 29½ in.
Courtesy San Diego Museum of Art. Museum purchase through the General and Mrs. M. O. Terry Purchase Prize Fund.

FIGURE 24 *(below)*
Thomas Hart Benton (American, 1889–1975)
Wheat, 1967
Oil on wood
20 × 21 in.
Courtesy National Museum of American Art, Smithsonian Institution, Washington, D.C. Gift of Mr. and Mrs. James A. Mitchell and Museum Purchase.

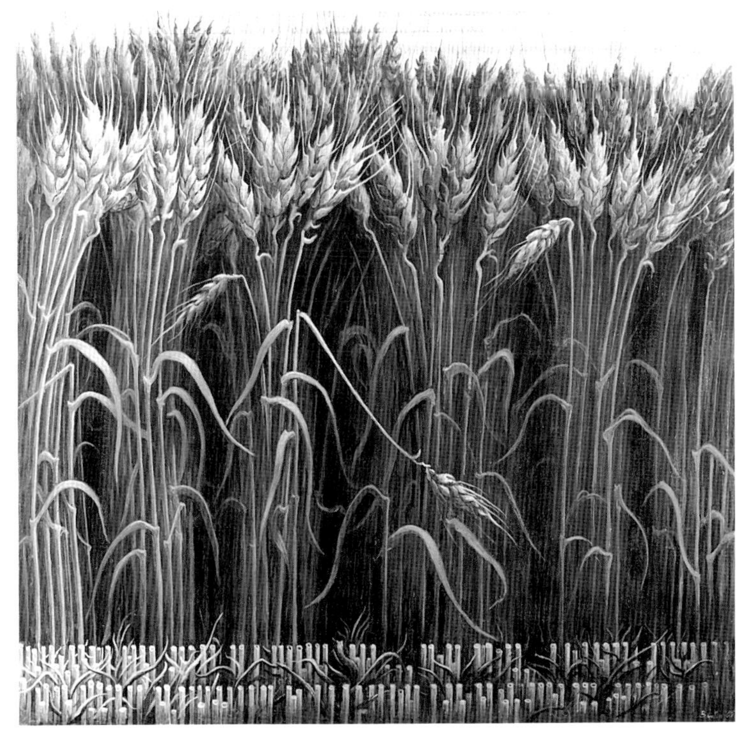

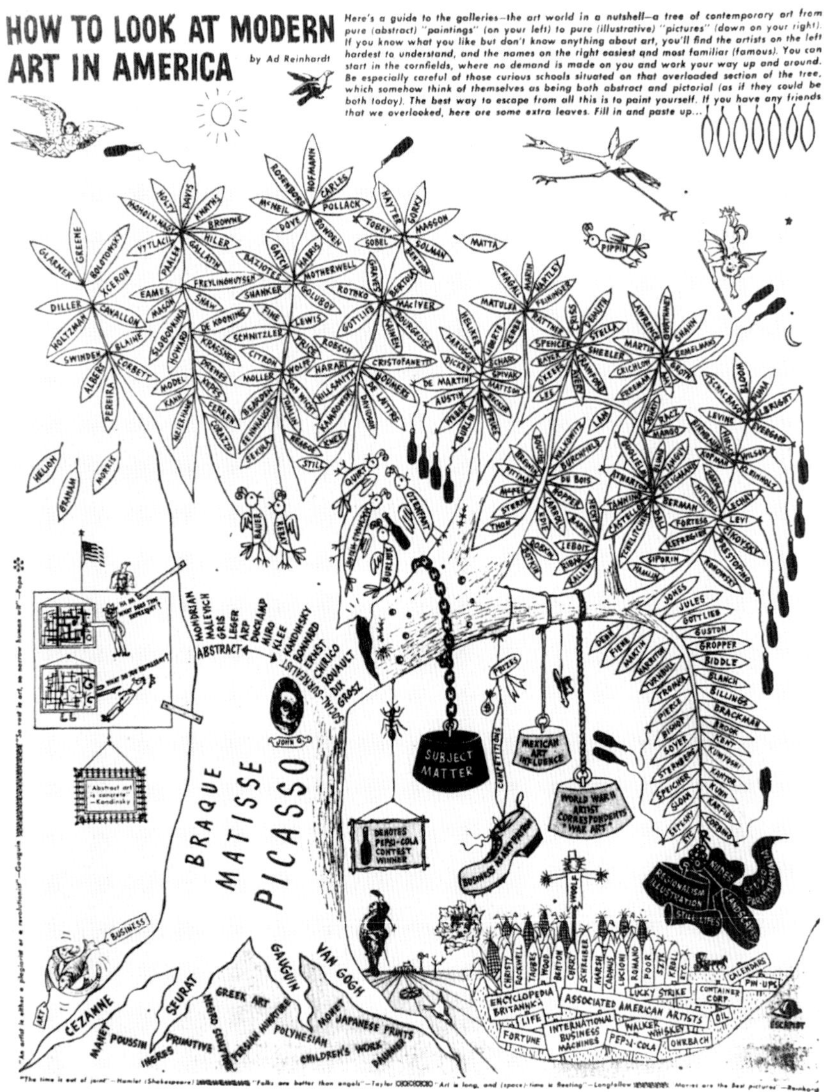

FIGURE 25

Ad Reinhardt (American, 1913–1967)
How to Look at Modern Art in America, 1946
Drawing published in *P.M.* (New York), 2 June 1946, section 1, page 16.
Photograph ©1997: Estate of Ad Reinhardt/Artists Rights Society (ARS), New York.

rows of already harvested stalks, a single blade bends sharply toward the ground. The painting was made late in Benton's life, after he had suffered several heart attacks and long after the premature deaths of his allies Curry and Grant Wood. In this simple design Benton transforms the motifs of his popular heyday into a meditation on life and death, transferred to and transformed by the agrarian setting. Curry likewise, in *Kansas Cornfield,* uses the plant symbolically; the painting presents a rumination on rootedness, a *memento terrae* from the prodigal who had left the land.

Lanier concluded by addressing the corn, describing a vision of another harvest in another era, when one with "bolder heart . . . manfully shall take thy part, / And tend thee, / And defend thee, / With antique sinew and with modern art."[84] In *Kansas Cornfield,* the poet's vision was realized. But even as Curry was discovering his place in the Kansas land and in modern art, other, younger painters were emerging, eventually to supplant him and his cohorts. In 1946—ironically, the year Curry died—Ad Reinhardt cartooned this new, hearty growth of Modern Art, sprouting from the trunk of Georges Braque, Henri Matisse, and Pablo Picasso (fig. 25). Beneath the splintered limb of Subject Matter and pendulous Regionalism, Reinhardt buried the realist painters, decorating the graves of Benton, Wood, and Curry with ears of corn.

NOTES

1. William Elsey Connelley, *James Henry Lane: The "Grim Chieftain" of Kansas* (Topeka, Kans.: Crane, 1899), 7.

2. Margo Jefferson, "The Many Moods (and Levels) of Langston Hughes," *New York Times*, 8 February 1995.

3. Hamlin Garland, Introduction, Palette and Cosmopolitan Art Clubs exhibition, exh. cat. (Chicago, 1895); quoted in William H. Gerdts, *American Impressionism* (Seattle: Henry Art Gallery, University of Washington, 1980), 104.

4. "John Steuart Curry: 'He puts farm life on canvas,'" transcript of a radio interview with the artist by Blanche Overlien on the program "Homemakers' Hour," broadcast on Wisconsin state stations WHA and WLBL, n.d. [transcript distributed 1937]. Curry Papers, Archives of American Art, Smithsonian Institution, Washington, D.C. (hereafter cited as Curry Papers/AAA), microfilm roll 165, frame 990. Although Curry was here living in and speaking of Wisconsin, his attitude toward the local was developed during his formative years in Kansas.

5. Henry G. Keller, Cleveland, Ohio, painter and teacher; quoted in Charles Burchfield, "Henry G. Keller," *American Magazine of Art* 29 (September 1936): 593.

6. Edward Alden Jewell, "Kansas Has Found Her Homer," *New York Times*, 7 December 1930.

7. H. E. Scudder, "Recent American Fiction," *Atlantic Monthly* 55 (January 1885): 125–26.

8. Edgar Watson Howe, *The Story of a Country Town*, ed. Sylvia E. Bowman (1883; repr. New York: Twayne, 1962), 100–101.

9. Kenneth Adams, interviewed by Sylvia Loomis, 23 April 1964; typescript, 12, Archives of American Art, Smithsonian Institution, Washington, D.C.

10. Isabel Doerr, "A Farmer's Son," in *Contemporary Kansas Poetry*, ed. Helen Rhoda Hoopes (Lawrence, Kans.: Franklin Watts, 1927), 49.

11. Laurence E. Schmeckebier, *John Steuart Curry's Pageant of America* (New York: American Artists Group, 1943), 10.

12. Quoted in John Alexander, "Death of Curry Ends Career in Art That Was Rooted in His Kansas Soil," *Kansas City Times*, 30 August 1946.

13. Quoted in "Hoover and the Flood: A Painting for *Life* by John Steuart Curry," *Life* 8 (6 May 1940): 61.

14. Quoted in Schmeckebier, *Pageant*, 11.

15. William B. McCormick, *New York American*, 2 February 1930; quoted in Schmeckebier, *Pageant*, 62.

16. "Curry Is Named 'Artist in Residence'; Wisconsin Acts to Aid 'Rural Culture,'" *New York Times*, 20 September 1936.

17. Curry, Chicago, to Margaret Steuart Curry, dated "Sabbath afternoon" [23 April 1917], Curry Papers/AAA, microfilm roll 2714, frame 560.

18. Curry, Chicago, to Margaret Steuart Curry, 21 June 1916, Curry Papers/AAA, microfilm roll 2714, frame 483.

19. Curry, Chicago, to T. Smith Curry, 12 November 1916, Curry Papers/AAA, microfilm roll 2714, frame 498.

20. Thomas Craven, "Curry of Kansas," *New York American*, 9 March 1935.

21. Anna Mynott Docking, "Artists of Topeka and Their Work," *Kansas City Star*, 27 April 1907.

22. Curry, Madison, Wis., to J. G. Butler, Director, Butler Art Institute, Youngstown, Ohio, 29 January 1942, Curry Papers/AAA, microfilm roll 164, frame 380.

23. Curry lecture notes; quoted in M. Sue Kendall, *Rethinking Regionalism: John Steuart Curry and the Kansas Mural Controversy* (Washington, D.C.: Smithsonian Institution Press, 1986), 95. According to Walter L. Strauss, Dürer's *The Prodigal Son* dates from 1496 (Walter L. Strauss, ed., *The Complete Engravings and Drypoints of Albrecht Dürer* [New York: Dover, 1972], cat. no. 11).

24. "Kansas Biographies: John Steuart Curry," *Kansas Library Bulletin* 2, no. 4 (December 1933): 8.

25. Schmeckebier, *Pageant*, 99–100.

26. "Kansas Heals Breach with a Native Son," *New York Herald Tribune*, 5 February 1935.

27. Margaret Hill McCarter, *The Price of the Prairie* (Chicago: McClurg, 1910), 292–93.

28. J. Edward Tufft, "Why Boys Leave the Farm," *The Earth* 14 (July 1917): 20.

29. Curry, Madison, Wis., to Pegeen Sullivan, Associated American Artists, New York City, 3 March 1943, Curry Papers/AAA, microfilm roll 165, no frame no.

30. "Kansas Heals Breach"; "Kansan at the Circus," *Time* 21, no. 15 (10 April 1933): 42.

31. "Kansas Heals Breach."

32. Schmeckebier, *Pageant*, 166.

33. Early in this century, the silo became a well-established rural landmark in eastern Kansas, indicative of modernity and prosperity, and by the 1910s it was being adopted in western Kansas as well. "The silo is winning its way in Kansas . . . against the conservatism of the old stockmen who have grown rich through the ranging of beef animals over the broad grass-covered prairies. . . . The silo is winning because it so quickly demonstrates its sterling worth by piling up extra profits." Cautioned this report: "it is ruinous to be without one" ("The Silo Is the Stockman's Mint," *The Earth* 11 [March 1914]: 11).

34. Margaret Hill McCarter, *The Cottonwood's Story*, 6th ed. (1903; Topeka, Kans.: Crane, 1914), 98.

35. "To Meet on Kansas Art," *Kansas City Times*, 20 July 1937.

36. William Allen White, *In Our Town* (New York: McClure, Phillips, 1906), 7.

37. "Up from a Kansas Farm," *Kansas City Times*, 8 August 1933.

38. John Ise, *Sod and Stubble* (New York: Wilson-Erickson, 1936), 302.

39. H. E. Wichers, "The Farm House," *Rural Life* 16 (March 1938): 8.

40. "Kansas Heals Breach," 17.

41. See, for instance, the sketches Curry made in the margin of his youthful essay "A Country Farm House on a Summer Afternoon," n.d. Curry Papers/AAA, microfilm roll 2747, no frame no.

42. Helen Rhoda Hoopes, "Winter Twilight on the Victory Highway," in Hoopes, *Kansas Poetry,* 67.

43. James P. Price, *Seven Years of Prairie Life* (Hereford, England: Jakeman and Carver, 1891; repr., Goff, Kans.: Great Plains Book Company, 1983), 21.

44. Reeves Lewenthal, "John Steuart Curry," in *John Steuart Curry: 20 Years of His Art,* exh. cat. (New York: Associated American Artists, 1947), unpaginated.

45. Schmeckebier, *Pageant,* 350.

46. Quoted in *American Art in the Newark Museum: Paintings, Drawings and Sculpture* (Newark, N.J.: Newark Museum, 1981), 305. Burchfield wrote that *Evening* additionally symbolized the end of the day, the end of the year, and the end of life for the three elderly people depicted.

47. Curry to Reeves Lewenthal, Director, Associated American Artists, New York City, 19 October 1945, Curry Papers/AAA, microfilm roll 165, frame 1212.

48. See photograph in Curry Papers/AAA, microfilm roll 168, frame 669. The inscription is not in the artist's hand. Reproductions of "The Old Folks" from *Survey* (July 1930), the *New York Times* (undated), and elsewhere (unidentified) are gathered in the artist's scrapbook, Curry Papers/AAA, microfilm roll 2748. For the caption, see Curry Papers/AAA, microfilm roll 2748, frame 624. Curry's first solo exhibition at the Whitney Studio Galleries, New York, included the painting as *The Old Folks.*

49. Among the most popular manifestations of this thrall were the antiquarian enthusiasms of New Englander Wallace Nutting, whose tinted photographs recreating domestic interiors peopled by Pilgrim families turned back the clock even beyond Ralph Earl's day. In addition to photographs for the popular market, Nutting was also a connoisseur of early American furniture, assembling one of the finest holdings of such materials from the seventeenth and early eighteenth centuries. Like Earl's portrait, much of Nutting's colonial collection wound up in the Wadsworth Atheneum, providing another possible source of inspiration to the Kansas artist in Connecticut.

50. Elizabeth Mankin Kornhauser, *Ralph Earl: The Face of the Young Republic* (New Haven: Yale University Press, 1991), 181.

51. The cause of death is generally attributed to a heart ailment or attack, although one report said it was caused by "a nervous breakdown" ("Kansan at the Circus").

52. Jane Comstock, entry on Curry's *Father and Mother,* in Novelene Ross, *Toward an American Identity: Selections from the Wichita Art Museum Collection of American Art,* exh. cat. (Wichita: Wichita Art Museum, 1997), 117.

53. Schmeckebier, *Pageant,* 125.

54. William Allen White, Emporia, Kans., to Curry, Westport, Conn., 11 July 1930, Curry Papers/AAA, microfilm roll 169, frame 40.

55. May Williams Ward, "Sky-Mountain," in Hoopes, *Contemporary Kansas Poetry,* 120.

56. Ian Frazier, *Great Plains* (New York: Farrar, Straus, Giroux, 1989), 15.

57. Willa Cather, *Death Comes for the Archbishop* (New York: Alfred A. Knopf, 1927), 235. Here, Cather was writing specifically of the arid Navajo country of the Southwest, but her words were equally applicable to the plains country of her Nebraska childhood or to Curry's neighboring Kansas.

58. Frazier, *Great Plains,* 182.

59. Schmeckebier, *Pageant,* 142.

60. Curry, Chicago, to Margaret Steuart Curry, n.d., Curry Papers/AAA, microfilm roll 2714, frame 482.

61. Kaj Klitgaard, *Through the American Landscape* (Chapel Hill: University of North Carolina Press, 1941), 262.

62. Quoted in *Kansas City Star,* 22 August 1937; clipping in "Kansas Artists" scrapbook, compiled by Lydia Sain, 1932–48, unpaginated; Kansas Collection, Spencer Research Library, University of Kansas, Lawrence (hereafter cited as SRL/KU).

63. Photograph of wheat threshing in Kansas, probably on Curry family farm (Curry Papers/AAA, microfilm roll 2748, frame 955). The picture appears to have been taken about 1920, while Curry was away from the farm pursuing work as an illustrator in New Jersey with financial support from his family.

64. Curry, Madison, Wis., to Elizabeth Navas, New York City, 30 June 1939, curatorial files, Wichita Art Museum, Wichita, Kansas.

65. Price, *Seven Years,* 31.

66. "A Kingdom Coming," *Daily Gazette* (Emporia, Kans.), 29 June 1895.

67. Alex Miller, *Des Moines Register and Leader;* quoted in Atchison Corn Carnival program, 13–14 September 1905, unpaginated. (Copy in Kansas Collection, SRL/KU.)

68. In 1931 Kansas farmers planted 6,573 acres in corn; in 1932, 7,362; and in 1933, 6,994. In 1931 they produced 115,028 bushels; in 1932, 136,197; in 1933 only 80,431. The yield per acre, 17.5 bushels in 1931 and 18.5 in 1932, fell drastically in 1933 to 11.5 bushels. (U.S. Department of Commerce, *Statistical Abstract of the United States* [Washington, D.C.: U.S. Government Printing Office, 1934], 609, table 594.]) In Jefferson County the pattern was repeated, as acreage planted in corn fell from 87,267 to 68,033 from 1929 to 1934. (U.S. Department of Commerce, *United States Census of Agriculture, 1935* [Washington, D.C.: U.S. Government Printing Service, 1936], 370–71, Agriculture-Kansas County Table 3.) The corn harvest also fell nationally, declining nearly twenty percent from 1932 to 1933, from 2,930,593 to 2,397,000 bushels (U.S. Department of Agriculture, *Agricultural Statistics 1967* [Washington, D.C.: U.S. Government Printing Office, 1967], 34, table 38).

69. In 1914 Kansas's Secretary of Agriculture had boasted that corn "has far most to do with making the large income from agriculture. In corn Kansas is a billionaire. . . . Corn is our monarch cereal and the

barometer of our prosperity. . . . The corn of the past twenty years has outvalued the tremendous wheat crops of the same period by $193,034,666. . . . Wheat has made Kansas famous, but it is the corn that makes her rich." (F. D. Coburn, "Kansas and Her Progress in Agriculture," *The Earth* 11 [March 1914]: 7)

70. The North was more commonly represented by wheat, which, according to Nancy Rash, held "a powerful meaning for the Union" (Nancy Rash, "A Note on Winslow Homer's *Veteran in a New Field* and Union Victory," *American Art* 9 no. 2 [summer 1995]: 89–90).

71. Edna Dean Proctor, "Columbia's Emblem," in *Columbia's Emblem, Indian Corn,* ed. Candace Wheeler (Boston: Houghton, Mifflin, 1895), 10.

72. Sarah Freeman Clark, "The Indian Corn as Our National Plant," *New England Magazine,* no. 4 (March 1891): 70.

73. John Fiske, "Importance of Maize in American History," in Wheeler, *Columbia's Emblem,* 31–32.

74. Quoted in Wheeler, *Columbia's Emblem,* 36.

75. Candace Wheeler, "Preface," in *Columbia's Emblem,* iii–iv.

76. Proctor, "Columbia's Emblem," in Wheeler, *Columbia's Emblem,* 9.

77. In this light, the visual connection between an undated Curry watercolor, *Corn Stalk and Cobs* (unlocated; a photograph is in the Curry Papers/AAA, microfilm roll 168, frame 838), and a Mayan mural painting, *Corn Stalk with Human Heads in Form of Tonsured Maize God* (ca. A.D. 700–900, East Temple Rojo, Cacaxla, Tlaxcala province, Mexico) is particularly interesting. (For mural, see Betty Fussell, *The Story of Corn* [New York: Knopf, 1992], frontispiece.)

78. Margaret Bruening, quoted in "Notes on 'Kansas Wheatfield,'" typescript, Curry Papers/AAA, microfilm roll 168, frame 950.

79. Curry, Madison, Wis., to Elizabeth Navas, New York City, 30 June 1939, curatorial files, Wichita Art Museum, Wichita, Kansas.

80. Ralph Waldo Emerson, "Nature" (1836), in *Selections from Ralph Waldo Emerson,* ed. Stephen E. Whicher (1957; repr., Boston: Houghton, Mifflin, 1960), 24.

81. Thomas Craven, Great Neck, N.Y., to Curry, 27 January 1935, Curry Papers/AAA, microfilm roll 166, frame 511.

82. "Curry of Kansas," *Newsweek* 22 (15 November 1943): 80.

83. "Corn" [1874], in *Poems of Sidney Lanier,* ed. by His Wife (Macon: Middle Georgia Historical Society, 1968), 53–59.

84. Ibid.

Space, Weather, Myth, and Abstraction in the Art of John Steuart Curry

HENRY ADAMS

"There is no such thing as good painting about nothing. We assert that the subject is crucial, and only that subject matter is valid which is tragic and timeless."

—Mark Rothko and Adolph Gottlieb[1]

In the 1930s the three major figures of the regionalist movement—Thomas Hart Benton, Grant Wood, and John Steuart Curry—enjoyed a degree of fame and media attention quite unprecedented for American artists (fig. 1). Christened "the Big Three," they were written up in *Time* and *Life* and treated as celebrities at nightclubs and hotels. For a decade, their artistic stature was not open to question.[2]

Then, in the early 1950s, as abstract expressionism came to dominate the art market and the gallery scene, all three were consigned to ridicule or oblivion. By 1954 a writer for *Time* magazine could declare: "Their paintings . . . are nostalgic reminders of a vanished era in recent U.S. history."[3] For forty years, the regionalists remained off limits for serious study. Although Benton, Wood, and Curry have all been the subject of book-length scholarly examinations during the last decade, they continue to generate intense hostility from such establishment art critics as Hilton Kramer and Robert Hughes.[4] Negative criticism, however, at least brings notoriety. While much of what has been written about their work is unflattering, Benton and Wood apparently have earned a permanent niche in the history of American art.

Benton, the most vociferous of the three, is routinely cited as the exemplar of bad art. When Robert Motherwell died in 1991, for example, Benton was singled out on the front page of the *New York Times* for embodying every provincial, wrongheaded thing that Motherwell had reacted against. Like the villain of a melodrama, Benton has become the artist we are trained to hiss when he steps upon the stage.[5]

Wood has attained a different kind of immortality. His *American Gothic* (1930; Art Institute of Chicago), a portrait of his sister and his dentist dressed up as farmers, has become the most frequently parodied painting in American art, a work regularly mimicked in advertisements and used to mock political figures. Why this whimsical piece captured the popular fancy is a puzzlement, but its appeal is undeniable, and as an icon of popular culture, it is perhaps the single most popular American painting.[6]

Of the Big Three, only John Steuart Curry remains in a critical limbo. Despite a fine 1986 study by M. Sue Kendall, his work has not experienced a significant revival. He has chiefly

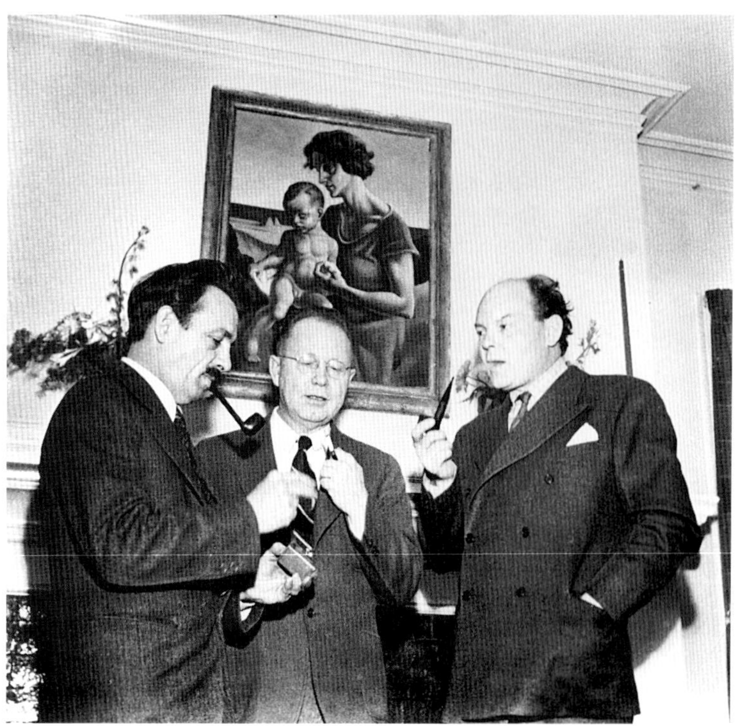

FIGURE 1

Benton, Wood, and Curry in Benton's home, Kansas City, Missouri, 1938. Photograph courtesy Curry Papers, Archives of American Art, Smithsonian Institution, Washington, D.C. Gift of Mrs. Stanley R. Fike.

earned attention in the press for embarrassing errors of realistic depiction, such as for representing a bull with its legs in the wrong position. ("Curry's Bull Gets off to a Bad Start," one headline noted.[7]) The critic John Canaday once reviewed his work so harshly that a reader fired back a letter declaring: "I'm tempted to draw a cartoon of you urinating on Curry's grave and call it *Baptism in Kansas II*."[8] For the most part, however, Curry has lacked even hostile attention. His paintings are generally omitted from surveys of American art, and when he is mentioned it is only because of his association with Benton and Wood. At best, Curry is considered an artifact of American popular culture, interesting chiefly for the subject matter of his work. Although in purely formal terms he was certainly the least conventional of the regionalist trio, the one whose pictorial arrangements stray the furthest from traditional norms, his role as an artist, as a creator of pictorial form, has not generated much interest or discussion.[9]

Curry's pictures are invariably disturbing not only because of their emotional subject matter—storms, deluges, and human conflicts—but also because of their technique. His outlines are generally fuzzy, and his drawing is ill-defined. Most significant, his compositions, which look at first like conventional illustrations, are extremely odd. Even Curry apologists have sensed this fact; their praise usually contains an unmistakable note of defensiveness.

He is nonetheless generally considered an illustrator of American life whose style and approach were fundamentally at odds with modern painting. When *Tornado* (1929) was first exhibited, the artist and writer Harry Wickey wrote that "this picture more than any other contemporary painting gave a knock-out blow to the School of Paris and all its American imitators."[10] In retrospect, Wickey's statement is humorous, given that French art was hardly decked by the force of Curry's contributions. But the notion that his work was unalterably opposed to French art, or to modernism of any sort, prevails in everything written about it.

A different view might be proposed. In fact, in his struggle to energize space and fill the pictorial field with dramatic tension, Curry broke the rules of traditional composition, creating highly original shape patterns. Like the abstract expressionists, he sought to expand the conventional language of painting to include forms that were archetypal and mythic in character. Thus, his finest paintings, such as *Line Storm* (1934), with its huge dark cloud looming over the composition, introduce a new conception of form into American art. To a surprising degree, his handling of form parallels the achievements of such abstract expressionist masters as Adolph Gottlieb, Barnett Newman, Ad Reinhardt, and Mark Rothko.

Curry's Technical Awkwardness

The first question we confront in Curry's work is whether his divergence from the norm was the result of ineptitude or of artistic originality. Any serious assessment must deal with certain technical deficiencies, noted even by his most ardent admirers. In a 1935 review in *Art News*, for example, Laurie Eglington remarked on Curry's "amazing unevenness," a point the critic Thomas Craven echoed in *Scribner's Magazine* three years later, when he observed that the artist's work was "disconcertingly uneven."[11] Thomas Hart Benton speculated that "John Curry may or may not be deficient in his craft."[12] And the painter Reginald Marsh noted: "Curry is not suave. . . . He fumbles; he is incomplete."[13] These defenders of his talent typically did not dwell on technical problems, which are obvious in the paintings and sketches.

Despite their powerful concepts, canvases such as *Parade to War* (1938, color plate 61) fail to stir us because of their manifest awkwardness. In that painting, Curry portrays marching soldiers; the head of the central figure is the skull of a dead man. We are asked to look beyond the pageantry of war to its essence: the senseless loss of young lives. But the work fails because of technical ineptitude—the doughlike figures lack structure and do not sit clearly in space. They are as flat and unconvincing as cardboard cutouts. Such weaknesses are even more embarrassing in his Wisconsin football paintings of 1937–38, whose figures seem to be made not of flesh and blood but of pneumatic tubes, like the Michelin man. While Curry was never a confident technician, the paintings of his later years tend to be particularly weak, perhaps because he was suffering from high blood pressure and memory lapses.

Even in his more successful works, such as the *Tragic Prelude* panel of the Kansas State Capitol murals in Topeka, there is a failure to meet routine challenges of rendering, such as giving convincing shape and texture to a sleeve (color plate 50). James Daugherty, whom Curry assisted with a mural project, complained that the Kansan was unable to deal with simple tasks such as drawing a flag.[14]

We might separate his grand conceptions from his execution and thus view these limitations as incidental. But Benton implicitly proposed another explanation—that Curry's confused rendering of form is intrinsically tied to the emotional turbulence of his work. As a friend, Benton no doubt muted his criticism, but an article he wrote in 1940 on *Wisconsin Landscape* (1937–39, color plate 56) contains surprisingly candid commentary. After observing that he first encountered the painting without forewarning, while serving as the judge of an eastern art show, Benton noted that he was initially revolted by the piece, for it seemed to possess "no readily graspable design"; it looked "like a big smear, like an oversize cover on a state automobile road map."[15] "The *Wisconsin Landscape* is a strange picture," he confessed. "It is at first sight slightly repellant [*sic*]. It is framed with an old hunk of gilded wood that John picked up somewhere. I wouldn't be surprised if he didn't paint the picture especially for that piece of busted down salvage. My first thought when the painting swung into view was John has gone nuts."[16] While for reasons of tact he did not state this directly, he implied that the landscape looked like junk in a flea market rather than a major work of art. As he studied the image, however, Benton warmed to it for reasons he could not entirely articulate: "It sticks in the memory as a grand sweeping exultant shout of 'yes' to the roll of the Earth."[17]

Beyond these brief phrases, Benton did not analyze his friend's handling of form nor explain why he shifted from regarding the piece as offensive, badly designed, and even a bit crazy to believing it was spiritually profound and emotionally gripping. He did, however, provide an interesting hint—one surprising in view of his supposed hostility to French painting. He compared the canvas to the work of Paul Cézanne, with its manifest spatial dislocations. "Looking back over the landscapes I have seen," Benton wrote, "I can think of nothing comparable to this Wisconsin landscape of John Curry's. It is likely to stand as a sort of unique performance in the history of American Art just as the Mt. St. Victoire series of [Cézanne] stands in French Art."[18]

At Curry's death, an anonymous reviewer for *Art Digest*—possibly influenced by Benton's essay—also compared the Kansan's work with that of Cézanne, noting that, like the Frenchman, Curry had difficulty "realizing" his ideas.[19] The comparison is apt in two respects. Like Cézanne's, Curry's paintings betray a peculiar confusion between design on a flat surface and design in depth. The checkerboard pattern of *Wisconsin Landscape,* for example, suggests a flat tablecloth. Yet Curry's agitated brushwork conflicts with any such simple pictorial solution. Also like Cézanne, his ambivalence about form possibly reflects a powerful emotional tension. Curry's stepdaughter, Ellen, testified to his stress when painting:

When he was working, his blood pressure would go up and the tension would build. He would never talk about what he was going to do, because he said if he talked about it too much he'd never do it. And he just seemed driven. Then when the painting was done he'd just collapse and he'd say, "I'll never paint again." The blood pressure would drop and he'd say, "No more ideas, I'm dry." That was the time when he was taciturn. He felt defeated and impotent.[20]

Curry's awkwardness, his ambivalence about space and the organization of design, may have signified more than a lack of skills. They may also, as his stepdaughter's recollection suggests, have been signs of deeply rooted psychological struggle.

Curry's Background as an Illustrator

Curry's experience and approach were fundamentally different from those of Benton and Wood. Although they are classified together as regionalists, during the period when they produced their key images, the three did not associate with each other and did not constitute an artistic group. The term *regionalism* did not come into vogue until after 1934, the year they were featured in *Time* magazine. Only then did they devise a common artistic creed. All three intended to produce strongly "American" and "midwestern" art, but each approached it from a separate starting point.

Of the three, Benton was the most practiced in modern art. He had worked in styles ranging from impressionism to synchromism and participated in 1916's *Forum Exhibition,* the first group show of modernist work by American artists. Also in 1916, he wrote a series of articles on abstract composition; later, he would be the teacher of Jackson Pollock, whose mature work is closely based on Benton's compositional principles. Ironically, the regionalist who today is most bitterly reviled as reactionary was the one best versed in the principles of abstract art.[21]

Grant Wood was considerably less adventurous, but his work, too, was forward-looking. Like Benton, he had visited Paris, and his early impressionistic landscape paintings seemed modern and progressive by early-twentieth-century Iowa standards. His later work also reveals a modernist influence: His cropping and unusual vantage points suggest an awareness of the photographs of László Moholy-Nagy and Alexander Rodchenko.[22]

On the other hand, Curry, whose background was that of an illustrator, had the most tenuous connection with modern art. Although he had once visited Paris, he did so to receive schooling in academic figure drawing at Basil Schoukhaieff's academy (color plate 3, fig. 2). Curry's chief training came from Harvey Dunn, an illustrator of western scenes who had studied with the dean of American illustrators, Howard Pyle.[23]

Dunn's importance to Curry's achievement can hardly be exaggerated, although this connection became something of an embarrassment because it suggested "illustration" rather than "art." Nonetheless, Curry remained loyal to Dunn, declaring that he was not merely an illustrator but an "artist," that he was "unmistakably American," and that he was "every inch a man."[24] These were qualities he admired and strove to emulate. When Curry was asked to list the artists he most admired, he included Dunn in the roster (albeit apologetically) along with such luminaries as George Bellows and Winslow Homer.

Dunn's art focused on three main themes, all of which relate closely to Curry's work: action paintings of cowboys, to illustrate the work of such novelists as Max Brand and Zane Grey; paintings of homesteaders on the plains, based on his childhood in South Dakota; and grisly scenes of the battlefields of World War I, based on his experience as a combat artist in France.[25]

Curry's most successful paintings conform to the general imagery of the prairie. He also created groupings of animals that are generically similar to the horses and cattle in Dunn's western illustrations. Less often, and less successfully, Curry created pacifistic paintings, such as *Parade to War* and *The Return of Private*

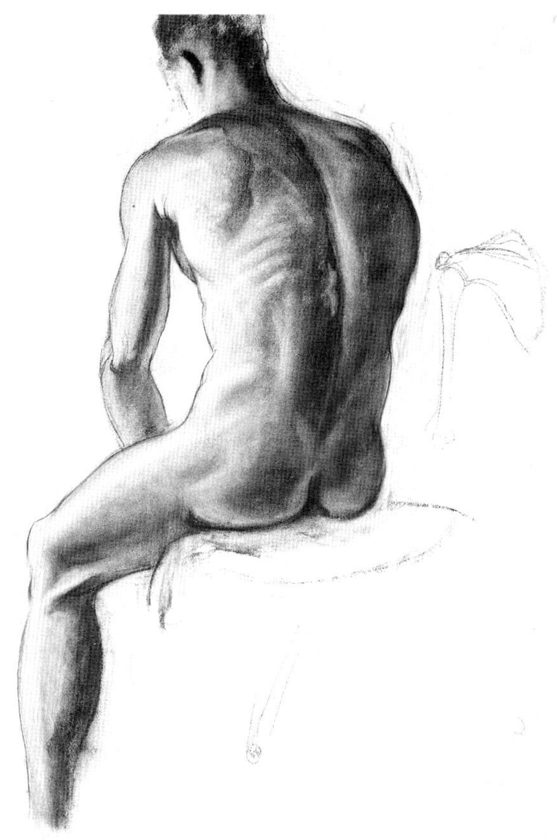

FIGURE 2
John Steuart Curry
Figure Study: Seated Male Nude, 1926–27
Charcoal on paper
25¼ × 19¼ in.
Estate of the artist. Courtesy Mongerson Wunderlich Gallery, Chicago.

Davis from the Argonne (1928–40), inspired by Dunn's renderings of wartime carnage. Dunn provided Curry with his essential subject matter, and he never strayed far from it, even though his pictorial treatment was distinct from that of his mentor.

The storm, which became Curry's favorite motif, was rare in academic painting (except for shipwreck scenes) but was a common theme of American magazine illustration. Frederic Remington introduced the prototype of cowboys and horses lost in a sweep of snow or sand, and Dunn followed suit with images of cowboys in snowstorms and fields of snow. One of Curry's early magazine illustrations, *The Mail to Lost Mine,* created for *Boy's Life* in 1923, shows a cowboy and his horse caught in a sandstorm, with the horse in a pose that echoes James Earle Fraser's *End of the Trail* (1898, National Cowboy Hall of Fame and Western Heritage Center, Oklahoma City).[26]

Farming in Kansas

Curry knew more about farm life than Benton or Wood, both city boys who did not grow up on farms. Agrarian routines were drilled into Curry at an early age: Rise early to feed the stock, and do half a day's work before riding into town to school. Yet his paintings do not inform us about work on a farm, only about the landscape.[27]

Benton and Wood, on the other hand, depicted the operations of farming with such accuracy that their paintings could illustrate a textbook on farm methods. They represented such basic activities as plowing and threshing, and they carefully diagrammed the machinery that performs this work. Wood's *Fall Ploughing* (1931, John Deere Collection, Moline, Illinois), for example, indicates how fields should be plowed and harvested and, in the foreground, contains a detailed rendering of an old John Deere sod-busting plow.[28] Similarly, Benton lovingly rendered the farm machinery of the 1930s—tractors, harrows, and threshers—recording their parts accurately enough so that one can identify the specific model. Even more intensely than Wood, he detailed how various crops—including grain, rice, and sugarcane—are grown and harvested.

When Curry portrayed farming, however, he did so in a curiously iconic fashion, as in *The Stockman* (1929, color plate 19), in which his father stands squarely in the center, surrounded by cows, pigs, and sheep. The actual tasks involved in caring for livestock—feeding, herding, castrating, shearing, and slaughtering—are not indicated. Apparently, Curry's sole representation of real farm work is in his mural panel *The Homestead* (1938, color plate 59), which shows fence posts being driven into the ground. Even here, however, he was less interested in recording how the chore is performed than in conveying the grandeur of the prairie setting.[29]

The Mythic Dimension

Because he painted stories that speak clearly to the viewer, we often forget that Curry's paintings are filled with things that are visually awkward and intrinsically improbable. For example, *Tragic Prelude* depicts figures at two different scales; some are about six feet tall, others, twelve feet tall. Yet while this scene is even less logical than the other sections of the mural, it has nonetheless always been the most popular and widely reproduced. The story is so vividly expressed that we ignore the strangeness of the visual language.

"Art is something beyond painting," Benton observed in describing Curry's work—thus obliquely defending his friend's deficiencies of technique.[30] Indeed, Curry's paintings have a mythic quality. They deal not simply with shapes but with shapes that are imbued with powerful meanings.

Curry once told Craven that his style was formed "on the King James version of the Bible" and on another occasion boasted that he was "raised on hard work and the Shorter Catechism."[31] Indeed, many of his paintings have biblical overtones—that is, they conflate Kansas happenings with Bible stories. *Hogs Killing a Snake* (1930, color plate 21) places a serpent in front of a tree in a fashion that recalls the snake of Eve's temptation and the Tree of the Knowledge of Good and Evil; *Baptism in Kansas* (1928, color plate 10) depicts its subject in the manner of a Renaissance altarpiece; *Tornado* (1929, color plate 20) contains a whirlwind like that described in the Book of Job; *Sanctuary* (1935, color plate 35) presents a range of animals, like those drowned in the Deluge, with a shape like that of Noah's Ark on the right; and *Tragic Prelude* portrays John Brown as a modern version of Michelangelo's Moses, bringing a new and tragic dispensation to the American land. Notably, each of these Bible stories is filled with terror and deals with God's inexplicable wrath.

For all their biblical connotations, Curry's paintings seem real because they grew directly from his own experience—from his visceral understanding both of his own body and of the Kansas landscape. Because of his interest in subjects such as boundlessness, emptiness, displacement, and annihilation, his paintings form a kind of bridge between the moralizing sentimentality of the nineteenth century and the existential anxiety of the twentieth.

Curry was a massive, fleshy, physically powerful man. Thomas Craven, with that almost homoerotic love of male strength that pervades the prose of the boosters of regionalism, once wrote that Curry had "the heft of a bull and the speed of a horse" and that he possessed "a large head and neck, powerful shoulders, and the tapering figure of a born football player."[32] Undoubtedly, Curry injected himself into his paintings, for he consistently favored figures of a similarly massive type; and in representing animals, he favored rotund and fleshy creatures, such as bulls and pigs. (His friend Reginald Marsh proposed that Curry's painting of Ajax the bull [1936–37, color plate 37] was a self-portrait.[33])

Yet despite this emphasis on mass and bulk, helplessness is a pervasive theme in Curry's paintings. Substantial figures, whether animal or human, are overwhelmed by some all-powerful natural force—a bolt of lightning, a flood, a thunderstorm, or a tornado. His compositions tend to be divided into two parts: a central unit, which is generally solid and densely packed; and a force that threatens this cohesiveness. Not simply active forces but space itself plays a role in making man insignificant. For in a way different from earlier American painters, Curry treats space as an infinite, endlessly unfolding expanse. Men and animals are reduced to tiny specks whose powers are laughable. Again and again in his work, mortal strength is rendered negligible in the face of the incomprehensible vastness of a cruel or uncaring universe.

The Kansas Prairie

Whereas biblical resonances contributed to the mythic quality of Curry's work, what made it distinctive was his sense of the Kansas landscape. He diverged from the other regionalists in his geographical roots as well as in his artistic training. His Midwest was distinctly different from that of Wood and Benton—a land bleaker in appearance, harsher in climate, and more precarious as a place for agriculture. The challenging qualities of Kansas as an environment are reflected in the challenging aspects of Curry's paintings.[34]

Located in the precise center of the continental United States, in the heart of the American heartland, Kansas is nonetheless an alien land to most Americans—treeless, formless, and frightening. It horrified most early visitors. The historian Francis Parkman described the Kansas plains as a "naked landscape . . . dreary and monotonous" and "a barren and trackless waste."[35] George Catlin, the renowned painter of American Indians, found the monotony of the prairie "painful" and "at length felt like giving up the journey, and throwing myself upon the ground in hopeless despair."[36] And the distinguished writer Washington Irving observed that "an inexperienced man may become bewildered and lose his way as readily as in the wastes of the ocean."[37] In an inspired metaphor, Clarinda Nichols, an early Kansas pioneer, wrote of a stretch of open prairie she had crossed: "I would not be willing to live so *far from land.*"[38]

On the prairie, every variation becomes symbolic. The painter John Noble wrote in 1924, near the end of his life:

You look on, on, on, out into space, out almost beyond time itself. You see nothing but the rise and swell of the land and

grass, and then more grass—the monotonous, endless prairie. A stranger travelling on the prairie would get his hopes up, expecting to see something different on making the next rise. To him the disappointment and monotony were terrible. "He's got loneliness," we would say of such a man.[39]

To others, however, the very monotony of the landscape had a unique grandeur. Walt Whitman, for one, wrote:

While I know the standard claim is that Yosemite, Niagara Falls, the upper Yellowstone and the like afford the greatest natural shows, I am not so sure but the prairies and plains, while less stunning at first sight, last longer, fill the aesthetic sense fuller, precede all the rest, and make North America's characteristic landscape.[40]

Writers began describing the prairie several decades before such imagery appeared in work of the the regionalist painters. Willa Cather, Hamlin Garland, Sinclair Lewis, and Ole E. Rolvaag produced much of their most notable work from 1890 to 1920, whereas the regionalist painters began depicting the Midwest almost a decade later. The most striking literary parallel for Curry's imagery is *The Wonderful Wizard of Oz,* written by L. Frank Baum in 1900.[41]

The Mixed-Grass and Short-Grass Prairie

Both Missouri and Iowa, the native states of Benton and Wood, respectively, belong to the tallgrass prairie, a region of naturally luxuriant growth, ideally suited for raising grain. Most of Kansas, on the other hand, lies in a drier and less fertile zone—that of the mixed-grass and short-grass prairie. The unreliable supply of water makes farming problematic in this area—possible when rainfall is sufficient but doomed to failure in drought. Curry was raised on a farm situated on the boundary of the region where agriculture is possible. Today, this land is used mainly to grow Russian wheat, which Mennonite immigrants from Russia introduced toward the end of the nineteenth century. Until early in this century, however, the main Kansas crop was corn, which required more water and was thus more susceptible to drought. Curry's father apparently supported himself primarily by raising pigs, sheep, and cattle, as suggested by the title *The Stockman,* a canvas in which he is portrayed. But he also tried to grow corn and hay, a shaky business on the dry Kansas prairie.

Kansas farmers had to cope with two potentially devastating cycles. One was the cycle of nature: Drought or locusts could wipe out a crop. The other cycle was that of prices: Falling prices, there as elsewhere, could sometimes make a year of good crops as difficult as a bad year. For instance, hundreds of Kansas farmers faced foreclosure in 1890, despite a record-breaking crop in 1889.[42]

In the late 1880s and early 1890s, the state was hit by disastrous droughts and plagues of locusts as well as by a series of economic panics culminating in the crash of 1893. Farmers marched on Washington, and fully half the population in the western part of the state, lured to the region by extravagant promotional claims and the promise of free land, pulled up stakes and headed for the East. As the historian Carl Becker wrote in a celebrated essay entitled "Kansas":

Until 1895, the whole history of the state was a series of disasters, and always something new, extreme, bizarre, until the name Kansas became a byword, a synonym, for the impossible and the ridiculous, inviting laughter, furnishing occasion for jest and hilarity. "In God we trusted, in Kansas we busted" became a favorite motto of immigrants, worn out with the struggle, returning to more hospitable climes; and for many years it expressed well enough the popular opinion of that fated land.[43]

The turn of the century brought improvement, due to new farming machinery, better knowledge of agricultural techniques, and several wet years. Curry was born in 1897, when the farm economy was rapidly getting better. Nonetheless, the Panic of 1893, the worst financial slump in the nation's history to that time, and the crop failures of earlier years were still a recent memory.

The good years did not last. In the 1920s, a period of prosperity for the country at large, farm prices took a drastic downturn, and farmers were hard-pressed. As prices dropped, they tried to compensate by raising larger crops, pushing themselves to the limit of endurance, and straining the capacity of their land. Thus, by late in the decade, farmers experienced the financial hardship that was to pervade the country a few years later. For this reason, paintings such as *Baptism in Kansas,* which portrays farm life of the 1920s, foreshadow the grim mood characteristic of the Depression era.

Conditions deteriorated even further after the stock-market crash of 1929. In addition to the Depression, the early 1930s were unusually hot and dry; the resulting crop failure and erosion transformed the drier areas of the midwestern states into a dust bowl. The worst years for Kansas farmers occurred just after Curry produced his first Kansas scenes. From 1931 to 1937 the region endured hot winds, exceptionally low rainfall, and the consequent eradication of crops. By 1938, when Thomas Craven wrote an essay on the artist for *Scribner's Magazine*, the farm owned by Curry's father had virtually collapsed. The livestock had been sold, the farm buildings stood unpainted, and the place was deeply in debt to the banks. The surrounding region had been economically devastated as well, and the town of Dunavant, where Curry had attended school, had virtually disappeared; the railroad tracks had been pulled up, the schoolhouse was gone, and all that remained of the bank was an iron safe, half-buried in a pile of bricks.[44]

Kansas Freaks

Such a hard life and landscape fostered somber people. Late in 1931, when a show of Curry's work opened at the Kansas City (Missouri) Art Institute, Mrs. Henry J. Allen, wife of a former governor, wrote a pained letter to a close friend of her husband, the Kansas newspaper editor William Allen White, complaining about the tone of Curry's work. "[W]hy paint outstanding friekish [*sic*] subjects and call them the 'spirit' of Kansas?" she asked.[45] Frequently cited in writings on Curry, her letter sums up the reaction of Kansans to his achievement. Alas, the answer to Mrs. Allen's question was simple: By now the state was notorious for its physical bleakness and as the home of freaks, ideologues, and religious fanatics.

In a celebrated essay of 1896, "What's the Matter with Kansas?," White himself had addressed the state's image. As he confessed: "Go east and hear them laugh at Kansas; go west and they sneer at her; go south and they 'cuss' her; go north and they have forgotten her. Go into any crowd of intelligent people gathered anywhere on the globe and you will find the Kansas man on the defensive."[46]

Although White ultimately took on the role of Kansas's chief booster, he was never able to erase this negative image. It was firmly in place by 1910, when Carl Becker noted that the state was associated with "freaks and ascetics."[47] By the 1920s, the bleakness was a national stereotype, frequently mined by muckrakers and critics. Charles B. Driscoll, a former newspaper editor in Wichita, wrote a scathing diatribe, "Why Men Leave Kansas," which H. L. Mencken published in his magazine *The American Mercury* in 1924.[48] Driscoll vividly described a gruesome roster of Kansas eccentrics: "I am aware, of course, that cranks and uplifters exist the world over. But in Kansas it is essential that these persons be listened to patiently and treated respectfully. They wield a great power. They take the paper. They have cousins who advertise."[49]

A few years after Curry began producing Kansas paintings, the psychologist Karl Menninger apologetically observed that the people of Kansas "have earned for themselves the name of being a humorless, puritanical people, incapable of joy and grudging in their attitude towards those happier than themselves."[50]

Undoubtedly the most vivid description of Kansas was provided by L. Frank Baum in *The Wonderful Wizard of Oz*. In simple sentences, he conveyed a stark image of a gray landscape and a gray, pleasureless people:

When Dorothy stood in the doorway and looked around, she could see nothing but the great gray prairie on every side. Not a tree nor a house broke the broad sweep of flat country that reached the edge of the sky in all directions. The sun had burned the plowed land into a gray mass, with little cracks running through it. Even the grass was not green, for the sun had burned the tips of the long blades until they were the same gray color to be seen everywhere. Once the house had been painted, but the sun blistered the paint and rains washed it away and even the house was as dull and gray as everything else.[51]

Tornados

In Kansas the weather becomes a substitute for scenery. As a child, Curry was constantly exposed to destruction by the elements: to corn shriveled to the ground by the southwest wind; to herds of cattle killed by the driving sleet of blizzards; to families forced to flee by tornados. As impressive as these disasters was the apprehension of weeks or months without rain, coupled with uncertainty over whether the crops would survive. "Among no other people," Craven wrote, "not even sailors on the high seas, is there so much talk about the weather, or such apprehensiveness of the destructive forces of nature. . . . From his first sentient moments, Curry heard men and women moaning about the weather."[52]

The most astonishing of these natural events was the tornado—the *Tyrannosaurus rex* of weather. The United States has more tornados than any other nation on earth, and the geography of Kansas is uniquely suited for their formation. Every spring, cold dry air coming down from Canada meets warm wet air from the Gulf of Mexico. The collision of these two fronts produces thunderclouds; roughly one in a thousand produces a tornado.

In the popular imagination, no state is so strongly associated with tornados as Kansas. The infamous desolateness of the state and reported erratic and intense nature of its people make it seem an appropriate setting for such violent acts of nature. Moreover, *The Wonderful Wizard of Oz* forever connected tornados with Kansas in the popular imagination. Curry's paintings of Kansas weather thus drew on popular stereotypes, although they had never before been expressed in visual form.

Curry's Masterworks

Although much of his work is too flawed technically to be considered major art, Curry did produce a few paintings that retain an enigmatic emotional power. His originality is captured in three masterworks: *Baptism in Kansas* (1928), *Tornado* (1929), and *Line Storm* (1934). He painted these Kansas outdoor scenes while living in Westport, Connecticut, before he returned to the Midwest and before he was recognized as part of the regionalist movement.

As the artist intuitively recognized, the oddness of the state, and the difficulties of basic survival there, had larger implications, somehow epitomizing the broader struggles of the nation, if not the general anguish of mankind in the twentieth century. Such local events as cattle-trough baptisms, tornados, and line storms touched on the question of man's place in the cosmos.

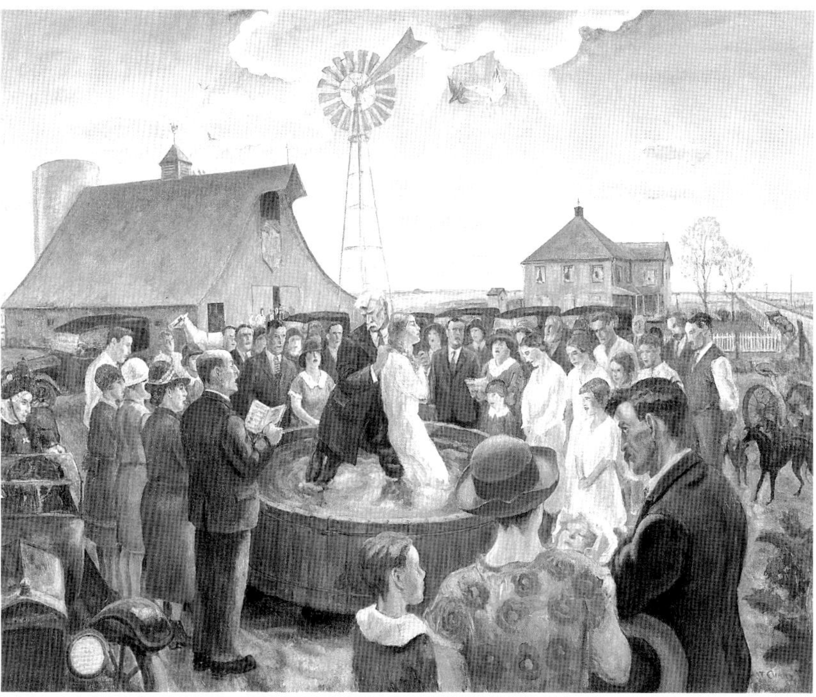

FIGURE 3
John Steuart Curry
Baptism in Kansas, 1928
Oil on canvas
40 × 50 in.
Collection of Whitney Museum of American Art, New York. Gift of Gertrude Vanderbilt Whitney.
Photograph © 1996: Whitney Museum of American Art

Baptism in Kansas

The ceremony portrayed in this canvas takes place around the cattle trough of a Kansas farm (color plate 10, fig. 3). Curry painted the piece in August 1928, a time when his illustrations were not selling, his wife was ill, his financial situation was growing desperate, and his future as an artist was in doubt. He risked all his cards on one big gamble, and the payoff must have exceeded his greatest expectations: This single work earned him widespread fame and preceded the first big successes of Grant Wood and Thomas Hart Benton by about two years.[53]

In retrospect, it is difficult to understand why so much excitement was aroused by what seems, at first glance, to be a rather straightforward illustration. Curry's painting combined two artistic stereotypes: the landscape with a farmhouse and red barn; and the religious scene in a triangular composition. These motifs rang with a new resonance, however, when placed in a Kansas setting.

With considerable skill, Curry pulls us gradually into the composition, as if we ourselves had just driven up in our Model T Ford and were about to join the congregation. In the foreground, he places elements that suggest arrival: a parked car and a couple who have arrived after the service has begun, with the woman checking her vanity mirror. These cropped features contribute to a sense of bustle and movement. The vantage point, above the woman's shoulder, places the viewer in a tense and ambiguous relationship to the ceremony, caught among the roles of participant, latecomer, and outsider.

At the center are two contrasting figures—the preacher in black and the woman being baptized in a white gown—who stand in the middle of the circular trough. They are ringed by the singing congregation and crowned by the circular form of the windmill, whose pinwheel functions as a kind of halo. The windmill and trough help specify the scene; since Kansas has little surface water, only the invention of the windmill and the availability of metal drills that could penetrate as far as three hundred feet belowground made the area fit for habitation and agriculture.[54] Barn, windmill, and farmhouse partially screen off Curry's baptism from the background, a flat section of prairie stretching in an unbroken line to the horizon.

While other artists (such as Harvey Dunn) had portrayed the prairie, none had endowed it with such a tense and uncomfortable quality. Curry essentially combined in one work the grotesque aspects of the Kansas experience—both the abnormality of the people, with their extreme religious practices, and the landscape itself, so dreary and bare. Both qualities challenged traditional concepts of home and place.

To East Coast viewers, *Baptism in Kansas* looked exotic. Kansas was strongly associated with peculiar devotional practices, as humorously described by Charles B. Driscoll in his *American Mercury* essay: "The rest of the country may have its doubts about, say, faith-healers, but such doubts have no effect upon the mind of Kansas. The towns and cities of the State hail and enrich whole droves of faith-healers of every known variety all the year round."[55] Thus, for the eastern snob, the image served as an intriguing anthropological report on what the critic Edward Alden Jewell described as the "religious fanaticism of the hinterlands."[56] The baptism by full immersion that the artist portrayed is uncommon in the northeast, and it looked particularly strange to easterners to have such a ritual performed not in a church but under the open sky.

Besides conveying the weird intensity of the baptizing Kansans, the work was startling for the spaciousness of the surroundings it depicted. Today, we are familiar with such landscapes, for *Baptism in Kansas* fostered countless magnificent renderings of this subject in the 1930s. But at the time Curry painted this picture, this imagery was unfamiliar, challenging, and more than a little fearsome.

The drama of the image lies in the fundamental tension between the traditional yet artificial arrangement of the figures and buildings in neat triangular units set against the prairie, which seems to drain the power from these pictorial conventions. Curry largely blocked the land from view with the foreground figures, the barn and house, the windmill, and a few scattered trees. Yet these flimsy screening elements make the land behind even more powerful and unsettling. At the far right, we can just make out a straight road leading, in an uninterrupted perspective wedge, toward the horizon. The sense of the unforgiving nature of the landscape, which makes human effort seem insignificant, perhaps even pointless, enhances the composition. Both in emotional effect and in design, Curry's conception is conflicted, even unresolved, because it draws us in two different directions—in toward the center and out toward the horizon—with equal force.

Among Curry's major Kansas paintings, *Baptism* comes closest to conforming to traditional ideas of composition. But at the same time, the overwhelming sensation of prairie space in the work has begun to disrupt the tidiness of such conventions. It represents a new departure, and it creates a new kind of emotional and pictorial tension.

Curry was acutely claustrophobic. His stepdaughter remembered that once, when his bedroom door became stuck, he panicked, pushed his way out a window, "and fell down the roof, and hurt his head."[57] The paradox of *Baptism in Kansas* is that it simultaneously expresses claustrophobia and agoraphobia: The crowd in the foreground makes us seem uncomfortably closed in; and the strange, nearly empty background makes us feel lost in topographical space.

More subtly than in *Tornado* or *Line Storm,* Curry here evokes the role of weather in determining human survival. A powerful underlying theme is the contrast between the baptismal cattle trough, filled with water pumped up from several hundred feet underground, and the blue, expansive sky, whose fluffy cumulus clouds offer no hope of rain on a scorching summer day. The work anticipates the later paintings of the Midwest that show a dry landscape where farming is no longer tenable.

Curry conceived *Baptism in Kansas* as one of a pair of paintings exploring the cycle from life to death in a small midwestern farming community. The other work, *The Return of Private Davis from the Argonne,* begun the same year, records the funeral of a young soldier in 1918 (color plate 12, fig. 4). Like *Baptism,* it was based on an event he had witnessed. This pendant painting, however, caused Curry such difficulty, both technical and emotional, that he did not complete it for twelve years. In its final form, *The Return of Private Davis* is a less-than-perfect match with *Baptism,* although sketches reveal that, originally, the compositions of the two works were nearly identical, with a similar semicircular arrangement of figures and related background elements.[58]

In *The Return of Private Davis,* the coffin in the center, surrounded by figures, directs our eye past the crowd, the gesturing preacher, and the line of cars that demarcates the foreground out to a stretch of empty prairie and white clouds on the horizon. In drawing our gaze toward a limitless distance, Curry reminds us that Davis died in a far-away place, for remote and mysterious reasons. As with *Baptism in Kansas,* what gives the painting poignancy is the sense of immense space.

Curry was not the first to attempt to capture a funeral on the midwestern plains, but his approach introduced a new level of

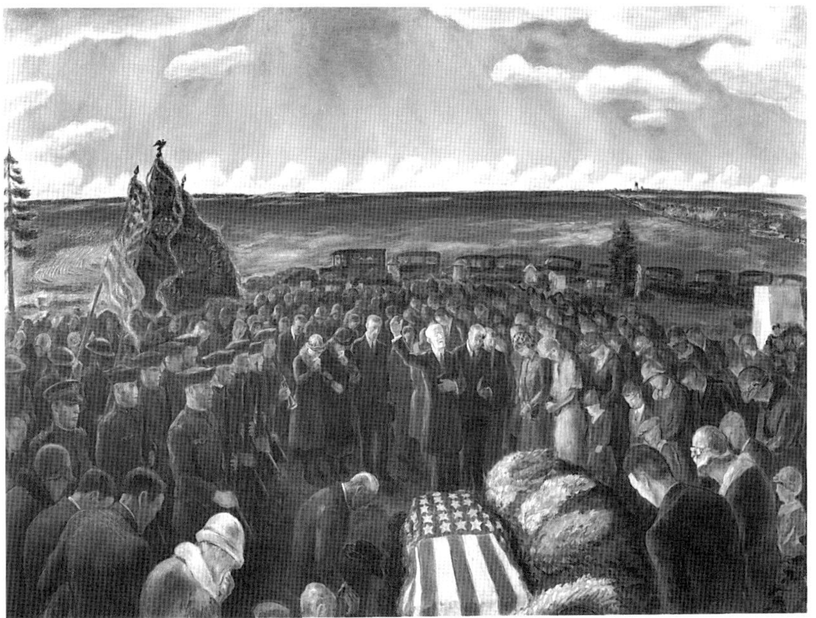

FIGURE 4
John Steuart Curry
The Return of Private Davis from the Argonne, 1928–40
Oil on canvas
38 × 52 in.
The Warner Collection of Gulf States Paper Corporation, Tuscaloosa, Alabama.

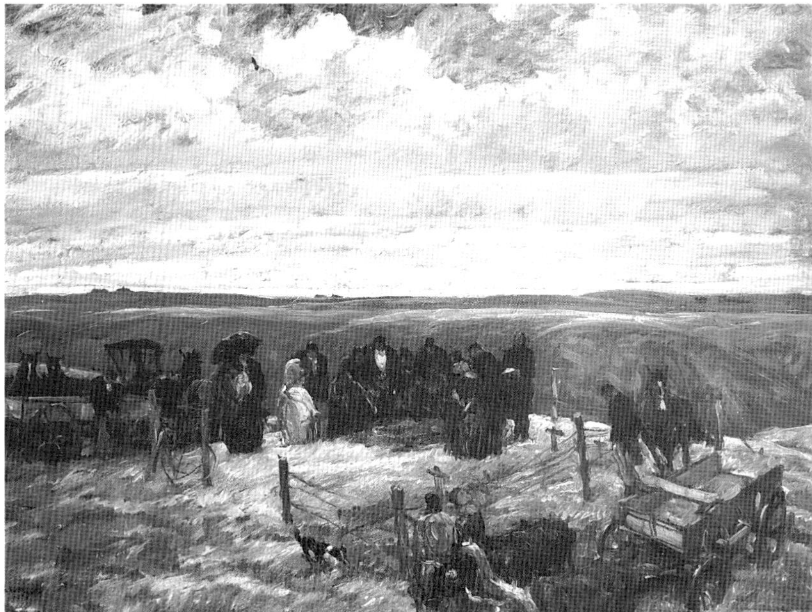

FIGURE 5
Harvey Dunn (American, 1884–1952)
I Am the Resurrection and the Life, probably 1926
Oil on canvas
26 × 36 in.
Courtesy South Dakota Art Museum, Brookings.

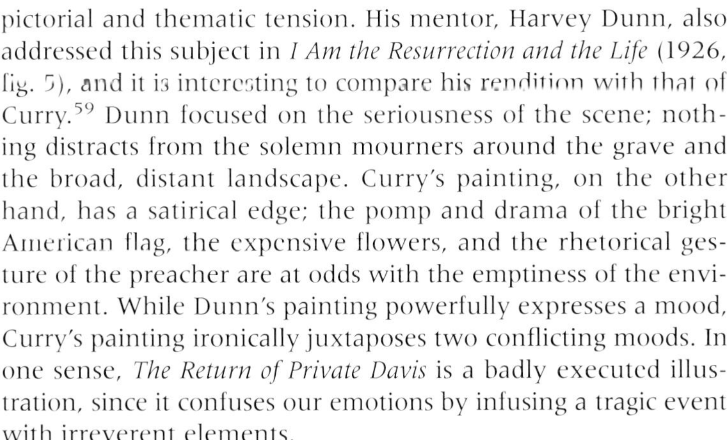

pictorial and thematic tension. His mentor, Harvey Dunn, also addressed this subject in *I Am the Resurrection and the Life* (1926, fig. 5), and it is interesting to compare his rendition with that of Curry.[59] Dunn focused on the seriousness of the scene; nothing distracts from the solemn mourners around the grave and the broad, distant landscape. Curry's painting, on the other hand, has a satirical edge; the pomp and drama of the bright American flag, the expensive flowers, and the rhetorical gesture of the preacher are at odds with the emptiness of the environment. While Dunn's painting powerfully expresses a mood, Curry's painting ironically juxtaposes two conflicting moods. In one sense, *The Return of Private Davis* is a badly executed illustration, since it confuses our emotions by infusing a tragic event with irreverent elements.

The difference between Curry's depiction of a funeral and Dunn's is subtle but, in the final analysis, significant. Curry's painting helps us reexamine its mate, *Baptism in Kansas,* and see what made it so remarkable. As later critics disparagingly pointed out, *Baptism* closely resembles a magazine illustration in its emphasis on narrative and anecdotal detail. But Curry broke the rules of how such an image should be organized. Both as a narrative and as a pictorial design, the effect is ironic and inherently subversive. This sense of irony—what Bertolt Brecht termed "the alienation effect"—transforms the image from a sentimental magazine illustration into a truly modern artistic statement.

When *Baptism in Kansas* was first exhibited, Edwin Alden Jewell considered it an ironic work, calling it "a gorgeous piece of satire."[60] The work has two essential ingredients of an American pictorial satire: a slightly caricatured treatment of homely figures and decrepit settings and a strong geometrical design. Both elements can probably be traced to the influence of Charles Burchfield, who had first exhibited in New York just a few years before Curry started *Baptism in Kansas.* Confirmation that Curry was swayed by Burchfield is the brooding "house with eyes" in the right distance of the painting—a quintessential Burchfield motif. Through Burchfield, Curry was able to distance himself from Dunn's example and create work that was tenser, more conflicted, and more ironic.[61]

Whereas the figures in Dunn's paintings invariably have a heroic, monumental quality, those in *Baptism in Kansas,* such as the bald man in the choir and the plump woman on the right with her gaping mouth and cloche hat, are middle-class caricatures. Curry emphasized their lack of heroic stature by placing the two doves in the sky and the windmill so as to give the work an artificial contrivance that consciously echoes a Renaissance altarpiece. He thus encourages us to compare this homely scene, with its crude water tank and faded barn, with classic interpretations of the Baptism of Christ by Piero della Francesca and Andrea del Verrocchio. The humble people Curry represented become all the more poignant because of the way they are implicitly contrasted with the heroic and spiritual images of the past.

Curry himself seems to have been only half-aware of what he was doing. In recounting the creation of *Baptism in Kansas,* he noted that he was "in a state of desperation, trying to get along at illustration, or anything I could do."[62] The statement is striking, not only for its reference to desperation (which hints, obliquely, at the power of the work) but also because it suggests that he did not clearly distinguish the piece from his earlier commercial endeavors.

Curry's satire is curiously ambivalent. At the same time he evidently wishes us to measure the distance between Kansans and the heroic figures of Renaissance religious painting, he apparently also wants us to recognize the similarities between the two. Perhaps, he suggests, if we could actually witness the rituals of the early Christians, they would not look so different from this cattle-trough immersion. Such an interpretation does not rid *Baptism in Kansas* of modernist irony but simply adds another layer. For if we are moved by the simple intensity of these Kansas freaks, we must be critical of the smugness of the cosseted, elite, urban audience for whom Curry made the painting—that is, ourselves.

Tornado

Curry followed *Baptism in Kansas* in 1929 with an even more potent conception, *Tornado* (color plate 20, fig. 6), which shows a farm family and their pets scurrying into a storm shelter while a terrifying twister bears down on them. Although a better painting than *Baptism in Kansas*—stranger, more forceful, more original—*Tornado* did not receive the same degree of effusive praise in the New York press, perhaps because the novelty of Kansas subjects was already wearing thin.

In 1933, however, *Tornado* won second prize at the Carnegie Institute's *Thirty-first Annual International Exhibition of Paintings* in Pittsburgh, an extraordinary honor for an emerging painter. The top award went to a rendering of weather of a very different sort, a beachscape by the French modernist André Dunoyer de Segonzac, *St. Tropez,* which capitalized on the new popularity of sunbathing. That sunny painting has long been forgotten. But Curry's cataclysmic composition was widely reproduced in surveys of American art for the rest of the 1930s and through the 1940s; its central image frightened generations of American children—this writer included.[63]

There were artistic precedents for Curry's motif, although no American painter had portrayed a tornado this way. Winslow Homer included a waterspout in his famous painting *The Gulf Stream* (1899; Metropolitan Museum of Art, New York), but it plays a secondary role to the other dangers he collects in that encyclopedia of fears and is far less frightening than the shark whose gaping jaws dominate the foreground.

More similar in effect to Curry's tornado are certain vortexes described in literature, such as the whirlpool in Edgar Allan Poe's story *Descent into the Maelstrom* or the suction created by the sinking whaler *Pequod* in Herman Melville's *Moby-Dick,* which pulls all the crew except Ishmael into the ocean depths. Curry's tornado is a kind of inverted whirlpool, more terrifying than the water kind because it defies every normal expectation. Rather than sucking down, it sucks things up, pulling buildings, people, and livestock into the open sky and performing strange prodigies of almost magical forcefulness, such as pushing straws through telephone poles or iron girders.

Curry was surely aware of the tornado in *The Wonderful Wizard of Oz,* which provides the most direct precedent for his painting, since the event takes place on a farmstead in Kansas. In Baum's novel, the tornado occurs offstage, as it were: Dorothy is resting on her bed when it lifts the farmhouse into Oz. She never sees the tornado but drifts gently off to sleep and is awakened only when the house drops down from the sky. In Curry's painting, however, the tornado swirls into the center of the drama.

Laurence Schmeckebier's 1943 book, *John Steuart Curry's Pageant of America,* the only biography of the artist, is confusing about the genesis of this painting. Schmeckebier describes at length a Kansas tornado whose devastation Curry witnessed and even quotes a long letter from the artist's mother describing the particulars of the storm. This cataclysm occurred 1 May 1930, when a tornado passed close to the Curry farm, killing two people, injuring twenty, and leaving a damage trail that extended for thirty-two miles. But since this occurred a year after Curry produced *Tornado,* it obviously did not inspire the painting.[64]

According to his widow, Curry never actually saw a tornado. But surely he had experienced the terror captured in the painting. When he was growing up, his family often fled to the cellar with their pets while terrible thunderstorms passed overhead. And he must often have heard reports of these devastating storms, since 263 documented tornados hit Kansas between

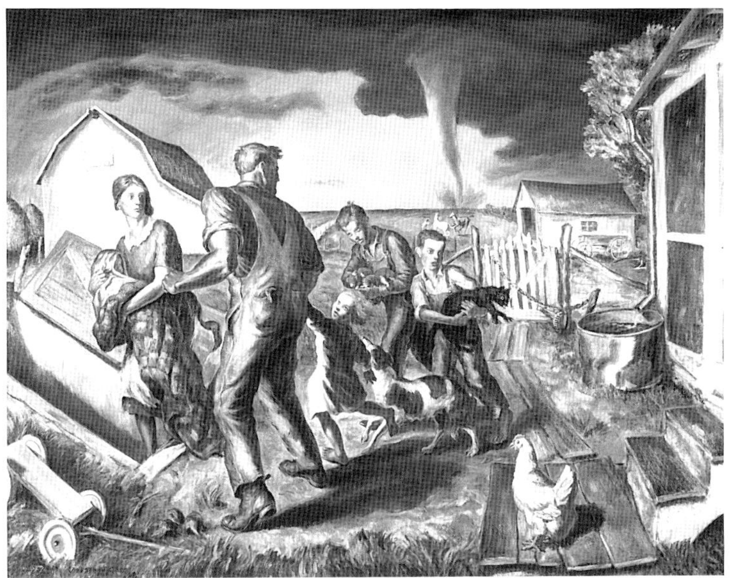

FIGURE 6

John Steuart Curry

Tornado, 1929

Oil on canvas

46¼ × 60½ in.

Muskegon Museum of Art, Muskegon, Michigan. Hackley Picture Fund purchase.

1897 (the year he was born) and 1929, when he made this painting.[65] Several of these tornados caused astonishing devastation, which must have been talked about for years afterward. For example, the Great Bend, Kansas, twister of 1915 destroyed 160 homes and killed two people and a thousand sheep. According to one contemporary report, "Hundreds of dead ducks fell from the sky."[66] Less destructive but equally amazing was the tornado that passed through Elmont, Kansas, 5 June 1917. The local schoolhouse vanished, leaving behind only the foundation. Teachers lay on the ground under the building as it was swept away; astonishingly, they suffered only bruises.[67]

Two particularly devastating tornados of the mid-1920s, when Curry was living in Westport, received national publicity and may have partially inspired his painting. The first was the so-called Tri-State tornado, the worst in American history, which ravaged Missouri, Illinois, and Indiana 18 March 1925. Actually several tornados, it created a path of destruction 219 miles long. It killed 689 people (234 in Murphysboro, Illinois, alone) and injured more than 2,000. Howard E. Rawlinson of Mount Vernon, Illinois, was a boy at the time and later wrote an account of the disaster for *American Heritage* magazine; he recalled seeing severed human and animal limbs scattered in the branches of trees and a Jersey cow that had been run through by a two-by-four.[68]

Even closer in time to Curry's painting was the St. Louis tornado of 29 September 1927, which swept through the city's downtown and tore apart 200 blocks; 72 people died, and 500 were injured. The storm moved east and caused seven more deaths in Illinois—six when a crucible of molten metal was overturned. The funnel finally dissipated over Granite City, Illinois.[69]

One striking aspect of *Tornado* is the accurate rendering of the twister's funnel. Curry may have learned of this columnar shape from a first-hand description. On 22 June 1928, Will Keller, a Kansas farmer, became the first man known to look up the funnel of a tornado, when one lifted the roof off his home:

I looked up and to my astonishment I saw right into the heart of the tornado. There was a circular opening in the center of the funnel, about fifty to one hundred feet in diameter and extending straight upward for a distance of at least half a mile, as best I could judge under the circumstances. The walls of this opening were rotating clouds and the whole was brilliantly lighted with constant flashes of lightning which zigzagged from side to side.[70]

While Keller's account may have helped Curry comprehend the tornado's form, it appears, to this writer, that the artist relied for visual guidance on the many photographs taken by Ira Blackstock of a tornado that passed through Hardtner, Kansas, 2 June 1929. These were among the first pictures of a tornado to be published and the first to document a tornado's shape clearly.[71] Visible from the south at a distance of thirty miles, the tornado moved slowly to the east and often stood nearly stationary, providing Blackstock with a perfect motif. His photographs record a funnel strikingly similar in shape to that on Curry's canvas. The storm cloud from which the twister descends has a jagged edge against clear sky that also resembles Curry's design.[72] One photograph—showing a barn on the left, a tree on the right, and the tornado in the center—seems to have provided the general compositional framework of the painting.

The foreground of *Tornado* has one of Curry's best-designed figure groups, reminiscent of the work of baroque artists such as Peter Paul Rubens, whom Curry studied and admired. (The backward-turning farmer, for example, recalls the figure of Adonis pulling away from Venus in paintings by Rubens and

Titian.) Buildings on either side act like the coulisse of a stage set, allowing a dramatic arrangement of figures between them. Were it not for their distress, the main figures in the painting might come from a Currier and Ives print of the ideal American farm; father, mother, two boys, a girl, and an infant are set against barn, farmhouse, and white picket fence. Such homely accessories as a tub to catch rainwater and a child's cart add vividness and poignancy to the scene.

Curry tellingly characterizes—or stereotypes—each principal figure. The farmer, in his bibbed overalls, is broad-shouldered and manly. His out-thrust arms seem ready to land a powerful punch, if only there were an object, and his head is blackly silhouetted against the light, to emphasize his Grecian profile and prominent jaw. The mother, pale, fearful, timid, and obedient, looks up to him helplessly, while clutching an infant in her arms. The two young boys have, despite the danger, managed to grab a favorite pet. Like her mother, the little girl seems helpless; she stretches her hand out to her father, who jerks her roughly toward the shelter.[73]

Each animal contributes something to the effect. Three running horses in the distance (a motif borrowed from French romantic painting), a terrified black cat, and an excited dog heighten the drama. The litter of piglets held by a boy injects a sentimental note. And the complacent white chicken in the foreground, apparently determined to stand stupidly in the path of the storm, seems comical.

Two motifs probably allude to reports of the destruction wrought by tornados. The running horses refer to reports of horses and cattle being lifted and blown into the air, such as in 1899, when a twister hit Kirksville, Missouri, and blew two women and a boy over a church, where they landed, unharmed, more than a thousand feet away. "As I was going through the air," one of the women recalled, "I saw a horse soaring and rotating about with me. . . . I prayed God that the horse might not come in contact with me, and it did not."[74] The chicken also recalls various reports of chickens having been completely defeathered after being hit by tornados.[75]

In formal terms, the painting was a logical sequel to *Baptism in Kansas,* but, as suggested, it is visually and psychologically stronger. *Baptism* is both claustrophobic and agoraphobic, and Curry pursued a similar idea in *Tornado.* More dramatically, he presents us with an unsettling experience of conflicting pictorial pulls. The drama is focused on the figural group in the foreground, which forms a neat triangular unit. Yet we feel sucked into the distance by the tornado on the horizon, which has just descended from the cloud, raising billows of dust.

The fundamental shape patterns of the two works are similar: If we invert the cattle trough and windmill in the first painting, the result suggests the spiraling form of the tornado in the second. In *Tornado* Curry informs this mushroom shape with a new significance; it represents not a static concept but a whirling, destructive vortex. As it bears down upon us, it threatens to sweep everything in the painting out into space and oblivion.

Curry's recurring motif is a mushroom shape, which serves as a template into which he squeezes different objects—a tree, a growing corn plant, a tornado, or a figure with outstretched arms. When this shape appears in his pictures, it almost always expresses a powerful tension—simultaneously sheltering and ruinous. This duality is perhaps clearest in some of his early paintings, in which a central tree is contrasted with something horrific—such as the serpent in *Hogs Killing a Snake* or the bolt of lightning that cuts the composition in two in *Lightning.* In his later works, the mushroom motif becomes more ominous, as in *Tornado,* where it is purely destructive, and *Tragic Prelude,* in which John Brown, with his outstretched arms, is equated with the tornado that whirls across the prairie in the distance.[76]

At its deepest level, *Tornado* clearly has psychological meanings that go beyond the dangers facing a specific Kansas farm. Schmeckebier notes that the painting was created at a time when Curry's first marriage was in turmoil. (In the spring of 1932 he would abandon his wife to follow the Ringling Brothers and Barnum & Bailey Circus; she died that July.) Thus, besides its overt symbolism, the painting reflects the artist's personal tensions.

Despite the seemingly conventional technique of *Tornado,* its major idea is the possibility of explosion and dismemberment. With its distended figures and exploding buildings, the work appears to threaten to transform itself into a synthetic cubist composition. Traditional composition has here been pushed to an expressive limit, has come to the verge of becoming something completely different.

Symbolically as well as visually, the painting portrays a world that is in danger of flying apart. Indeed, it is hard to tell whether the canvas is a celebration of traditional American ideals—the nuclear family, hard work, the farm, the manly man, and the feminine female—or a kind of dismemberment of these ideals to create a new system of order. (As the French revolutionary Saint-Juste once commented, "The disorder of the present is the order of the future.")

Tornado is perhaps Curry's most potent expression of a theme—weather—that dominated his art. He used the theme to create an image of fear that pervades the entire pictorial space. Even empty areas of the composition are symbolically activated. Even the invisible becomes expressive.

Line Storm

Remarkable as it is, *Tornado* still might be disparaged as an illustration; as one critic commented scathingly, "[E]verything's there but the egg under the chicken."[77] Curry adopted a very different approach to create *Line Storm* (color plate 33, fig. 7), which Thomas Craven described as "the finest of all his western landscapes."[78] Perhaps no other American landscape conveys a more powerful sense of space. Its first owner, the playwright Sidney Howard, boasted that owning the canvas allowed him to possess "as large a slice of the U.S.A. as it is possible to get into a cramped New York apartment."[79]

Yet for all the praise it received, *Line Storm* is among the oddest paintings in American art, a piece that violates nearly every rule of traditional composition. Throughout the canvas, Curry seems to have been torn between producing a conventional landscape painting, filled with hackneyed motifs, and making something more mysterious and abstract. The result is a highly ambivalent but truly fascinating work. Some sort of passion and energy overpowers the painting's technical shortcomings. In traditional terms, the handling of form is clumsy and flat, but curiously, the ultimate effect is the evocation of a feeling of almost infinite depth. The painting is at once disorienting and profoundly, ineffably, tragic.

We might think of *Line Storm* as a somewhat awkward conjunction of two parts: a picturesque farm scene, with house, barn, and hay wagon; and the dark, ominous cloud that looms over them. The great wedge of cloud shape had its origins in the 1932 painting *Elephants* (color plate 24, fig. 8), a work that, Curry noted, was intended to create a sensation of fear. Here the huge mass of the storm cloud is similarly frightening and, in its inexorable movement, not unlike an animal stampede.[80] At its simplest level, the painting portrays the drama of the hay wagon, pulled by two mules, racing to escape the approaching storm. To a 1930s viewer familiar with farming, the significance of this race was plain to see: Hay left out in the rain will spoil. Not only that, but paradoxically, the rainwater can create a spontaneous combustion, the hay beginning to smoke and, eventually, bursting into flames.

Viewers of the time also would have recognized that the painting portrays a distinctly American form of apocalypse. For line storms of this type, which occur only rarely in Europe, are common in the Midwest.

Indeed, the cloud of *Line Storm* is very much like the one portrayed in *Tornado* but seen from a different angle. In *Tornado* we look down the edge of such a storm system, which is shown receding toward the horizon, with the left part of the sky clear and the right side darkened. The cloud in *Line Storm*, on the

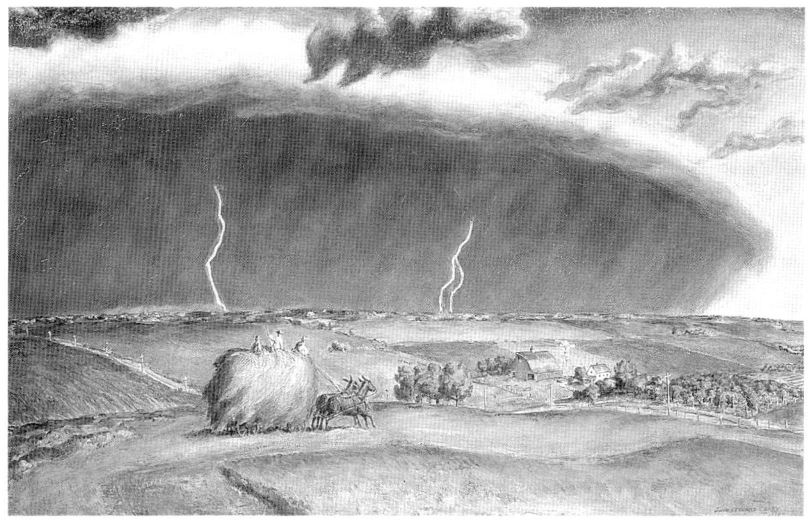

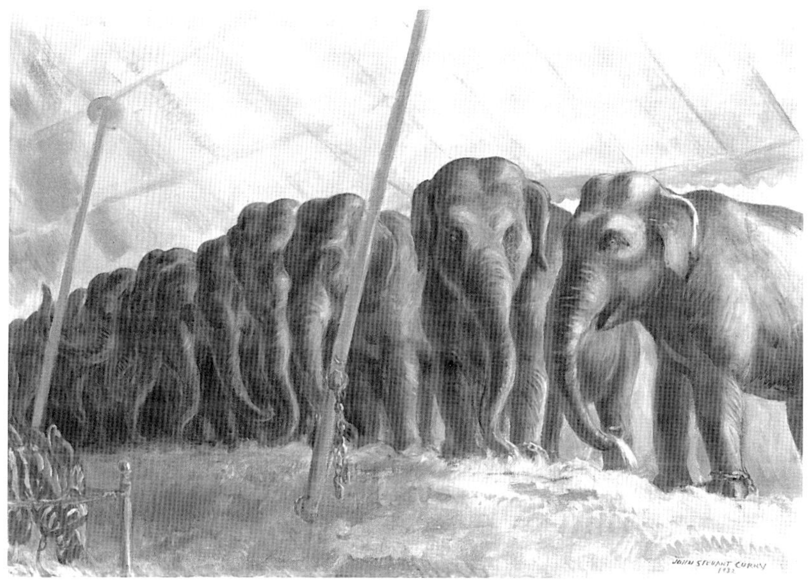

FIGURE 7 *(top)*

John Steuart Curry
Line Storm, 1934
Oil and tempera on panel
36 × 48 in.
Babcock Galleries, New York.

FIGURE 8 *(above)*

John Steuart Curry
Elephants (Circus Elephants), 1932
Oil on canvas
25¼ × 36 in.
National Gallery of Art, Washington, D.C. Gift of Admiral Neill Phillips in memory of Grace Hendrick Phillips. Photograph © 1997: Board of Trustees, National Gallery of Art.

other hand, rushes toward us like an ocean wave about to crest. Although no tornado is visible, such clouds sometimes do hold tornados, which funnel down unpredictably. They can also unleash winds, rains, and hail that are fierce enough to destroy a crop and that can, in the case of hail, prove life threatening to both man and beast.[81]

Destruction. Fire. Ice. Blinding Light. Impenetrable Darkness. The cloud is, potentially, a death cloud.

Curry situated the painting in a real place, the Heart Ranch in Barber County in western Kansas, near the Oklahoma border. In 1931 he had painted the site more accurately in *Spring Shower* (color plate 23, fig. 9), which contains the germs of the later idea but is more conventional.[82] In its general approach, *Spring Shower* evokes John Constable's English landscapes, which show similar rolling, treeless terrain and a like pattern of rain showers and passing storms. Yet both technically and emotionally, Curry's painting is quite different in its final impact.

Curry's struggle to find compositional rhythms to unify the design, like those used by Constable and others, is very evident. A pond on the left and a red barn and white farmhouse on the right create accents to draw the eye into the design. A winding road leading through the center toward a distant hill connects these elements. Billowing clouds and a funnel of rain create movement and drama.

But when compared to works by artists such as Constable, Curry's design seems diffuse and wobbly. Because of their ill-defined brushwork, the pond, the barn, and the winding road do not sit securely in space. Moreover, the compositional elements do not quite harmonize, since the landscape is too large for them to dominate the design. As a consequence, peripheral elements become distracting. Our eye is not guided along a well-defined path but wanders off in confusion to the edge of the painting as well as into the far distance.

In *Line Storm,* Curry takes this process one step further, moving the genre another step away from the controlled, picturesque formula of traditional landscape painting while, curiously, lifting elements even more directly from well-known works of the past than in *Spring Shower.* The painting thus exhibits a violent tension between familiar landscape motifs and the startling eccentricity with which they are organized.

With its hay wagon, hay fields, red barn, and white farmhouse, *Line Storm* contains stock motifs of calendar art and prints by Currier and Ives. Near the center we even find three trees, which echo those in Rembrandt's hallowed landscape print *The Three Trees* (1643). Yet unlike a well-trained commercial artist, Curry does not direct the eye inward toward those motifs to form a climax. Instead, as in *Baptism in Kansas* and

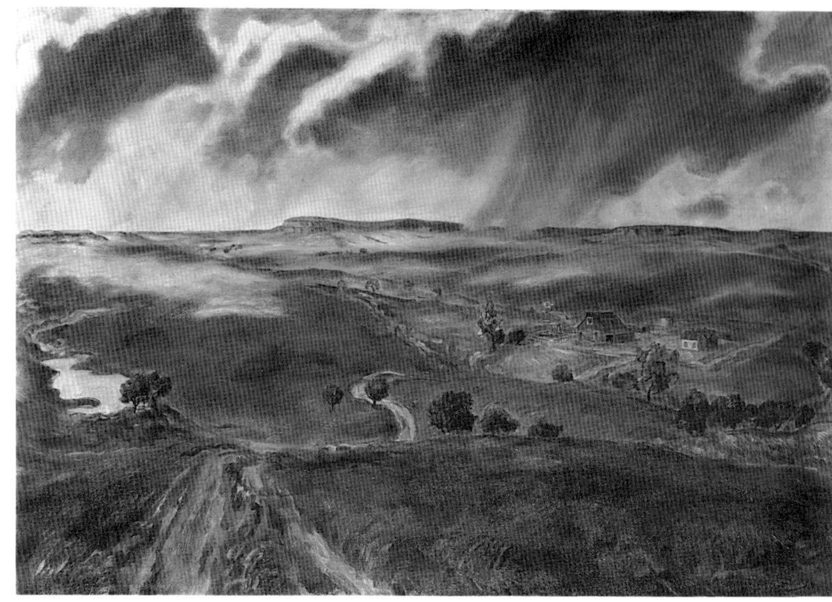

FIGURE 9

John Steuart Curry
Spring Shower, 1931
Oil on canvas
29⅞ × 43⅞ in.
The Metropolitan Museum of Art, New York. Arthur Hoppock Hearn Fund, 1932.
Photograph © 1995: The Metropolitan Museum of Art

Tornado—but even more forcefully than in those works—he inscribes the design with conflicting lines of visual movement.

While the hay wagon rushes diagonally, from left to right, two roadways appear to push in the opposite direction, and two flashes of lightning create an inverted pyramid that thrusts toward the upper edges of the image. Thus we feel conflicting pressures that push our eye out to either side of the far horizon and up to the far reaches of the sky. Even the way the field is painted sparks tension, for—as if painted by Cézanne—it seems caught between receding into depth and tipping up and becoming flat.

Then there is the dark cloud, which dominates the composition. Such vast storm clouds move from east to west, in a line running parallel to the western horizon. Thus we must imagine this cloud moving in our direction like a breaking wave. In addition, it seems to form a dark wedge, moving from left to right, that is about to obscure the sky completely. Perhaps most disturbingly, we are conscious that as the cloud moves toward us, the earth rolls toward it in a countermovement that almost makes us queasy. Thus the painting provides no fixed, stable point where we can rest; everything is slipping and sliding.

Curry's "awkward" technique plays a part in this effect, since *none* of the forms seems able to decide where it should rest. The sky moves; the hay wagon moves; roads and lightning flashes shoot off in different directions; the fields tip and turn; and the earth itself seems about to slip away from beneath our legs.

Judged by traditional standards, the composition of *Line Storm* fails in three respects. First, it is divided in two instead of being a unified whole. Second, it is unbalanced. The storm cloud is darker and heavier than the landscape, and the strong triangle, created by the lightning flashes is inverted and unstable. The customary triangular design has been turned upside down, with less weight at the bottom than at the top. Third, the composition lacks a main focus. Curry promises a center of interest with elements such as the wagon and the barn. But rather than aiming the design in toward these elements, he pushes our view out toward the periphery.

In customary terms, the painting is a clear-cut failure. Yet while its composition is not satisfactorily regular, few paintings are as gripping in their expression of anxiety as *Line Storm.* Its anxious design perfectly expresses its anxious subject. Interestingly, the dominant dark cloud is essentially an abstract expressionist form, not unlike those found in paintings by artists such as Mark Rothko and Clyfford Still. It is a shape that seems at once abstract and spiritually alive. Thus, bizarrely, the painting presages the very artistic trend that would eclipse the regionalist movement. Curry might have said, as Rothko once did: "I think of my pictures as dramas; the shapes in the pictures are the performers."[83]

Conclusion

Regionalism is usually presented in surveys of American art as a realistic style—the antithesis of abstraction. The case of Curry's work suggests that such a polarity is fundamentally misleading. Although he achieved prominence in the regionalist movement, he was never a very skillful painter from a technical standpoint, and the impulses at the core of his art drew him away both from competent academic rendering and from traditional composition. Yet his movement away from these pictorial norms, especially in paintings such as *Baptism in Kansas, Tornado,* and *Line Storm,* was hailed by critics as a step forward, because it increased the strength and tension of his work.

Thus regionalism, as Curry practiced it, was not realism in a conventional sense. It might better be termed "mythic realism," since its aim was to articulate a mythic consciousness of human beings and their place in the American land. In his best paintings Curry created a new visual language, in which man's relation to space, weather, and the land serve to express basic existential anxieties and fears. The very lack of conventional technical competence or logical coherence in Curry's handling of form and composition helped push his art toward a mythic "beyond" and gave it greater force of expression.

The exact nature of the "myth" that Curry sought to express is intriguing to contemplate. What were the essence and origin of the fear that seems to permeate his work? Certainly it is plausible to see these paintings as reflections of emotional crises in the artist's personal life, connected with his uncertainties as an artist and the collapse of his first marriage. It is also tempting to search for an analogue to his storms and tornados in political events of the time. *Tornado,* for example, was completed around the time of the stock market crash (although it seems to have been conceived shortly before). *Line Storm* was painted soon after Hitler had seized power in Germany (although before his armies had swept Europe and posed a threat to the United States). In retrospect, these works seem to capture the desperation of the historical moments during which they were created.

Without question, Curry's paintings were a response to the desperate plight of the American farmer—threatened by financial forces beyond his control as well as by drought, dust storms, hailstorms, and floods. Because of his Kansas background, Curry recognized that weather can constantly threaten a man's livelihood and his very existence. Moreover, as a metaphor, weather was particularly effective because it is enveloping, all-pervasive. It suggests any danger that surrounds us and that permeates even the invisible.

The terrible state of farmers at this time is powerfully expressed in a letter written by Curry's father, Smith Curry, in July 1934, around the time the artist painted *Line Storm.* In it, a father's pride in his son's accomplishments is mixed with fear that a lifetime's struggles have been for naught, and that a whole way of life may be wiped out:

Architects office decorative dpt:

I owe the Wichita fedral farm loan Bank of Wichita Kans. a loan which I canot pay. Am about to loose [*sic*] our homestead on which we have lived for forty years and reared our family. I have a son an Artist John Stewart Curry. Could you let him work it out on [fresco] or mural work on some public building? This will be a novel request to you but we farmers trade work whenever we can since money disappeared from us. He is instructor in Art in the New York Students Art league and Cooper memorial Art association. Several of his works have been purchased by the Metropalitan museum and Whitney gal-

leries. Mrs. Whitney also [has] some of his works in her private collections. He also won second in the Caragie international Art exhibit in Pittsborg last fall. A Frenchman took first and he second. Cravens *Mus. of Art* last edition gives him a good rating.[84] Investigate him and if you give him some redecorating or murals I am sure he will do that much to hold the old boyhood homestead.[85]

Curry's best paintings, in short, grew out of a sense of loss and destruction that was rooted in his own experience.

After *Line Storm,* Curry's artistic progress grew more erratic. Between 1928 and 1934, he essentially defined the qualities of his style. To a large degree, his later work reformulates the same stylistic issues and themes. In addition, with a few exceptions, the later work is less successful. A few of these paintings, however, move even further than *Line Storm* from normal ideas about how a painting should behave. *Wisconsin Landscape,* for example, is bewildering in its undulating shapelessness and is even less focused than *Line Storm.*

Still more remarkable is a panel in Curry's Kansas State Capitol murals depicting the prairie at night. Despite the fame of the murals, this panel, the most magnificent of the group, has never been successfully photographed, for it is too dark an image to capture. To understand the painting, one must stand in front of it and fall into it as into a pool of water. A vast prairie seascape of rough brushwork and deep indigo hues, the work has no recognizable forms except for a few crudely rendered waving grasses and a line of baby skunks cutting across the foreground. (Curry was fond of skunks; a family of them lived under his Westport studio.)

In paintings such as these, every square inch of pictorial surface is tense and conflicted, in a manner reminiscent of Cézanne. Nothing falls comfortably into a defined section of space. Everything is restless and unresolved. In such works, Curry came to the verge of a Rothko-like abstraction and created compositions as diffuse, as extended, as mystical, and as mysterious as those of the abstract expressionists. Though doubtless too personal and enigmatic to be understood by most people, let alone to be considered a "masterpiece" by most critics, the prairie at night panel in a real sense represents the culmination of Curry's artistic journey.

Traditionally, the abstract expressionists are supposed to have spurned every aspect of regionalism. A closer study of their origins, however, reveals that they were often closely linked with their artistic forebears—notably, for example, in the close relationship, both personal and artistic, between Jackson Pollock and Thomas Hart Benton.[86] Curry's major paintings provide an intriguing instance of a concern with myth and abstraction that was implicit in the regionalist approach and that presages subsequent developments. I do not propose that John Steuart Curry was necessarily significant as a direct influence on the work of abstract expressionist painters. However, I do suggest that his best paintings reflect a move in the same direction—marking a step in the progression from realism, to mythic realism, and finally to mythic abstraction.

NOTES

For all its faults, I would like to dedicate this essay to the memory of my father, Thomas Boylston Adams (1910–1997), who died while I was completing it.

1. The statement originally appeared in *New York Times*, 13 June 1943; quoted in Diane Waldman, *Mark Rothko: A Retrospective*, exh. cat. (New York: Solomon R. Guggenheim Museum, 1978), 39.

2. The regionalists clinched their national notoriety when they were featured in a cover story by Thomas Craven, "U.S. Scene," *Time* 24, no. 6 (24 December 1934): 24–27. Curry was later profiled in *Life*, "John Curry: He Paints at Wisconsin as Artist-in-Residence," *Life* 7, no. 26 (25 December 1939): 34–37. The term *Big Three* came into vogue in 1935. Apparently, it was first used by Edward Alden Jewell, "Beware the Pendulum," *New York Times*, 17 November 1935. Reminiscing about his own fame, Benton recalled: "For ten years I lived in a generally continuous glare of spotlights. Like movie stars, baseball players and loquacious senators, I was soon a figure recognizable in Pullman cars, hotel lobbies and night clubs. I became a regular public character" (Thomas Hart Benton, *An Artist in America*, 4th rev. ed. [Columbia: University of Missouri Press, 1983], 278).

3. "As They Saw It: Three from the 30s," *Time* 63 (1 March 1954), 72.

4. Hughes has likened Benton to a corpse: "If ever an American artist had seemed dead and buried a decade ago, along with the movement he had led, that man was surely Thomas Hart Benton." Robert Hughes, *Nothing If Not Critical: Selected Essays on Art and Artists* (New York: Alfred A. Knopf, 1990).

5. "Motherwell Dies at Age 76," *New York Times*, 18 July 1991.

6. Wanda Corn, "*American Gothic:* The Making of a National Icon," in *Grant Wood: The Regionalist Vision* (New Haven: Yale University Press, 1983), 129–207.

7. The essential book on Curry is M. Sue Kendall, *Rethinking Regionalism: John Steuart Curry and the Kansas Mural Controversy* (Washington, D.C.: Smithsonian Institution Press, 1986). For the bull with its legs in the wrong position, see the unidentified newspaper clipping, ca. 1937, reproduced in Kendall, *Rethinking Regionalism*, 126–27. Laurence Schmeckebier's biography, *John Steuart Curry's Pageant of America* (New York: American Artists Group, 1943), contains many additional illustrations of Curry's work.

8. "Art Critic Panned for Curry Review," *Kansas City Star*, 6 December 1970. According to Polly Burroughs, Benton wrote this letter. Polly Burroughs, *Thomas Hart Benton: A Portrait* (Garden City, N.Y.: Doubleday, 1981), 188.

9. While seemingly more vulnerable as an artist, Curry has never been attacked as intensely as Benton and Wood. He was not even mentioned by H. W. Janson in the first major assault on the regionalist painters, "Benton and Wood: Champions of Regionalism," *Magazine of Art* 39 (5 May 1946): 184–86, 198–200.

10. Quoted in Schmeckebier, *Pageant*, 346.

11. L. E. [Laurie Eglington], "Exhibiting in New York: John Steuart Curry, Ferargil Galleries," *Art News* 33, no. 16 (26 January 1935): 6; Thomas Craven, "John Steuart Curry," *Scribner's Magazine* 103, no. 1 (January 1938): 41.

12. Thomas Hart Benton, "Wisconsin Landscape," *Demcourier* 11, no. 2 (April 1941): 14. This issue was devoted to Curry's work.

13. Quoted in Schmeckebier, *Pageant*, 349. Other similar comments might also be cited. Thus, for example, Edward Alden Jewell once described Curry's work as "labored" and "unconvincing" (Edward Alden Jewell, "John S. Curry Art Is Put on Display, Solo Exhibition at Walker Gallery," *New York Times*, 17 January 1938). A reviewer for *Time* once noted that a New York exhibition of Curry's work "encouraged head-shaking by detractors" ("Professor Curry," *Time* 31, no. 4 [24 January 1938]: 32–33).

14. Quoted in Schmeckebier, *Pageant*, 35. According to an unidentified acquaintance: "Curry was truly modest—and as Churchill said about Attlee, he had much to be modest about. I recall with sadness how he agonized and fumbled over his paintings, the smallest of them. . . . He as much as confessed to me that he considered himself an amateur" ("Art Critic Panned").

15. Benton, "Wisconsin Landscape": 13.

16. Ibid.

17. Ibid.: 14.

18. Ibid.

19. "Curry Dies," *Art Digest* 20 (15 September 1946): 9.

20. Bret Waller, "An Interview with Mrs. Daniel Schuster," *Kansas Quarterly* 2, no. 4 (fall 1970): 14.

21. Henry Adams, *Thomas Hart Benton: An American Original* (New York: Alfred A. Knopf, 1989), 110–33. Benton's articles on "The Mechanics of Form Organization in Painting" appeared in *Arts* 10 (November 1926): 285–89; *Arts* 10 (December 1926): 340–42; *Arts* 11 (January 1927): 43–44; *Arts* 11 (February 1927): 95–96; and *Arts* 11 (March 1927): 145–48.

22. For example, Benton's cover illustration for *O'Chatauqua*, reproduced in Corn, "*American Gothic*," 49, presents an aerial view that recalls the photographs of Moholy-Nagy and Rodchenko. See Selim O. Khan-Magomedov, *Rodchenko: The Complete Work* (Cambridge, Mass.: MIT Press, 1987), 266, 267; and Andreas Haus, *Moholy-Nagy: Photographs and Photograms* (New York: Pantheon, 1980).

23. For Dunn, see Robert F. Karolevitz, *Where Your Heart Is: The Story of Harvey Dunn, Artist* (Aberdeen, S.D.: North Plains Press, 1970). Almost with embarrassment, Thomas Craven noted that "Curry, alone among American artists of distinction, has developed in a straight line" (Craven, "John Steuart Curry": 38). For Pyle, see Charles D. Abbott, *Howard Pyle: A Chronicle* (New York: Harper and Brothers, 1925); and Henry Clarence Pitz, *The Brandywine Tradition* (Boston: Houghton, Mifflin, 1969).

24. Craven, "John Steuart Curry": 39.

25. Karolevitz, *The Story of Harvey Dunn*, 120.

26. Curry also did another early storm scene, *Mounties Seeking Shelter from a Snowstorm*, for *Boy's Life* in 1921. See Schmeckebier, *Pageant*, 27, 32. Dunn likewise produced such winter scenes, two of which are reproduced in Karolevitz, *The Story of Harvey Dunn*, 141.

27. Craven, "John Steuart Curry": 37.

28. Joni L. Kinsey, *Plain Pictures: Images of the American Prairie* (Washington, D.C.: Smithsonian Institution Press, 1969), 127. This book is the indispensable study of the literature and imagery of the Great Plains.

29. Schmeckebier, *Pageant,* 176–77, 309.

30. Benton, "Wisconsin Landscape": 14.

31. Craven, "John Steuart Curry": 37; quoted in Schmeckebier, *Pageant,* 8.

32. Craven, "John Steuart Curry"; 38.

33. Quoted in Schmeckebier, *Pageant,* 180.

34. Kinsey, *Plain Pictures.*

35. Quoted in Kinsey, *Plain Pictures,* xiii. The phrases come from Parkman's *Oregon Trail,* first published in 1849.

36. George Catlin, *Letters and Notes on the Manners, Customs and Conditions of the North American Indians,* 2 vols. (1841; repr., New York: Dover, 1973), 1, 59.

37. Washington Irving, *A Tour on the Prairies,* vol. 3 of *Works of Washington Irving* (Boston: Dana Estes, 1900), 111–12.

38. Joseph G. Gambone, "The Forgotten Feminist of Kansas: The Papers of Clarinda I. H. Nichols, 1854–1885," *Kansas Historical Quarterly* 39, pt. 2 (summer 1973); quoted in Kinsey, *Plain Pictures,* 104.

39. John Noble, *American Magazine* (August 1924): 44; quoted in Walter Prescott Webb, *The Great Plains* (Boston: Ginn, 1931), 1.

40. Walt Whitman, *Specimen Days* (1882; repr., Boston: David Godine, 1971), 94.

41. One frequently finds writers who played a role in defining the work of the regionalists, as Sherwood Anderson did for Burchfield, as Sinclair Lewis did for Grant Wood, as Mark Twain did for Benton. When Curry illustrated books for the Limited Editions Club in the early 1940s, he hinted at the kind of writers who had shaped his vision, such as James Fenimore Cooper in *The Prairie.*

42. A character in John Ise's 1936 novel *Sod and Stubble* declares: "When you have cattle and hogs you have to worry your head off about feed for them, or sell them for next to nothing; and as soon as you sell them you get good crops again, and have to worry about buying them back, at twice as much as you got. That's the way with farming out here. Whenever you raise anything, there's too much, and you have to give it away; and then when you don't raise anything, there isn't enough, and you have to buy feed, and pay three prices for it. You never can get anything for anything except when you haven't anything. It looks as if there was something wrong with the way the whole business is ordered" (John Ise, *Sod and Stubble* [New York: Wilson-Erickson, 1936; repr., Lawrence: University of Kansas Press, 1996], 216).

43. Carl Becker, "Kansas," in *Essays in American History Dedicated to Frederick Jackson Turner* (New York: Henry Holt, 1910; repr., in *Heritage of Kansas: Selected Commentaries on Past Times,* ed. Everett Rich, Lawrence: University of Kansas Press, 1960), 90–91.

44. Craven, "John Steuart Curry": 37.

45. Mrs. Henry J. Allen to William Allen White, 16 December 1931. Curry Papers. Archives of American Art, Smithsonian Institution, Washington, D.C. (hereafter cited as Curry Papers/AAA), microfilm roll 2743, frame 46.

46. William Allen White, "Editorial: What's the Matter with Kansas?" *Emporia Gazette,* 11 August 1896. As reprinted in *American Heritage* 30, no. 6 (October–November 1979): 85.

47. Becker, "Kansas."

48. Charles B. Driscoll, "Why Men Leave Kansas," *American Mercury* 3, no. 10 (October 1924): 175–78.

49. Driscoll, "Why Men Leave Kansas": 177.

50. Karl A. Menninger, "Bleeding Kansas," *Kansas Magazine* [1] (1939): 3–6.

51. L. Frank Baum, *The Wonderful Wizard of Oz,* illus. William Wallace Denslow (Chicago: George M. Hill, 1900; repr., New York: William Morrow, 1987), 12. For more on Baum, see David Manix, "The Father of the Wizard of Oz," *American Heritage* 16, no. 1 (December 1964): 36–51, 108–9.

52. Craven, "John Steuart Curry": 38.

53. In October 1928, about a month after Curry completed *Baptism in Kansas,* the canvas was included in the Corcoran Gallery of Art's *Eleventh Biennial Exhibition of Contemporary American Oil Paintings.* Edward Alden Jewell, writing in the *New York Times,* praised it above all other pictures in the show. Shortly afterward, Gertrude Vanderbilt Whitney awarded Curry a stipend that, with a later extension, freed him from economic distress for one year. Her high regard for *Baptism in Kansas* is suggested by the fact that when the Whitney Museum of American Art opened in November 1931, she posed beside the canvas—which she had purchased for the museum's permanent collection—for a photograph published in the *New York Times.* Apparently more than any other painting, it epitomized her goals for the new American art. In January 1930 Whitney Galleries had organized a show of Curry's work, which was enthusiastically praised. Margaret Breuning of the *New York Post* compared Curry to "young Lochinvar out of the West," and later that same year Jewell declared in the *New York Times* that "Kansas Has Found Her Homer" (7 December 1930). See Kendall, *Rethinking Regionalism,* 27; Adams, *Benton,* 216.

54. Leo Huberman, *We, the People: The Drama of America,* illus. Thomas Hart Benton, rev. ed. (New York: Harper and Brothers, 1947), 143. Windmills became an iconic element in many paintings of the later 1930s and early 1940s, playing a central role in such works as Benton's *Nebraska Evening* (1941), Alexander Hogue's *Drouth Stricken Area* (1936), and Joe Jones's *American Farm* (1936).

55. Driscoll continues: "I have read on the first page of a Kansas newspaper, as a sober recital of fact, a circumstantial story of a miracle performed by a female faith-healer who drove a storm away before proceeding to heal the multitude with applications of olive oil and prayer. The wonder woman mispronounced a very larger percentage of the commonest English words, but she measured her Kansas winnings by the bucketful at a season when the doctors of medicine were obliged to put off the rent collectors until there should be a better crop of corn." Driscoll, "Why Men Leave Kansas": 178.

56. Edward Alden Jewell, "Corcoran Gallery's 11th Exhibition," *New York Times,* 4 November 1928; quoted in Kendall, *Rethinking Regionalism,* 22.

57. She recalled another incident as well: "When he went to the Mayo clinic one time, they asked him to wait in some room. The door snapped to, and he went over to the door and found it was locked (for some reason their waiting rooms were like that). He was terrified, as I remember it now, completely scared" (Waller, "Interview with Mrs. Daniel Schuster": 16).

58. Schmeckebier, *Pageant,* 59–60. It is worth noting that Curry completed *The Return of Private Davis* in 1940, at a time when it appeared as though the United States would be drawn into another world war.

59. Karolevitz, *The Story of Harvey Dunn,* 123. The date of the painting has been the subject of confusion. See Kendall essay in this volume, note 24. Records of the South Dakota Art Museum have traditionally given the date as 1926. Recently, however, a date of 1943 was added to the museum's object record for reasons that are unknown. Like Kendall, I believe that the painting dates from 1926, which seems to fit best with Dunn's stylistic development and with the period of his major activity as an illustrator. Of course, Dunn may have worked on it at a later time, and may well have repainted some part of it as late as 1943.

60. Jewell, "Corcoran Gallery's 11th Exhibition"; as quoted in Kendall, *Rethinking Regionalism,* 22. Among the few to have commented on Curry's inclusion of the doves was John Canaday, art critic for the *New York Times;* he nonetheless misconstrued their ironic significance: "Curry gave himself away as an artist of impossible loyalties to the past and specious loyalties to the present when he introduced the pair of doves circling by fortuitous coincidence in the rays of Kansas light, like the dove of the Holy Spirit generating divine radiance in Italian Renaissance paintings of the Baptism of Christ" ("John Steuart Curry: Burial in Kansas," *New York Times,* 1 November 1970).

61. Burchfield first exhibited his work in New York in 1924. His depictions of the unpainted buildings of run-down farms and small towns quickly caught other painters' eyes. For example, he seems to have been a major inspiration for Benton's sketching trips around the United States. As Thomas Craven noted: "It is not too much to say that without Burchfield's pioneering discoveries Benton would never have found himself" (Thomas Craven, "Our Art Becomes American," *Harper's Monthly Magazine* 171 [September 1935]: 430–41).

62. Curry to Margit Varga, 28 February 1942, Curry Papers/AAA, microfilm roll 166; quoted in Kendall, *Rethinking Regionalism,* 22.

63. Bret Waller, "Curry and the Critics," *Kansas Quarterly* 2, no. 4 (fall 1970): 44; Craven, "John Steuart Curry": 40; Schmeckebier, *Pageant,* 108–9. *Tornado* was reproduced in color in a popular survey of American art, Peyton Boswell, Jr., *Modern American Painting* (New York: Dodd, Mead, 1939), 71.

64. Schmeckebier, *Pageant,* 108–11; Thomas P. Grazulis, *Significant Tornados, 1680–1991* (St. Johnsbury, Vt.: Environmental Films, 1993), 304.

65. Grazulis, *Significant Tornados,* 301–4; Bret Waller, "An Interview with Mrs. John Steuart Curry," *Kansas Quarterly* 2, no. 4 (fall 1970): 8.

66. Grazulis, *Significant Tornados,* 744; Keay Davidson, *Twister: The Science of Tornados and the Making of an Adventure Movie* (New York: Pocket Books, 1996), 61.

67. Grazulis, *Significant Tornados,* 755. For a concise history of destructive tornados, see C. W. Guswelle, "The Winds of Ruin," *American Heritage* 29, no. 4 (June–July 1978): 90–97.

68. Ibid., 795–96 (with an aerial photograph showing the damage to Murphysboro).

69. Grazulis, *Significant Tornados,* 814.

70. Quoted in Davidson, *Twister,* 90.

71. A few photographs of tornados had earlier appeared in the press. The first, recording a tornado funnel that had hit Waynoka, Oklahoma, ran in the *Alva (Okla.) Pioneer* 17 May 1898. That image, however, appears to have been a composite, produced by combining a photograph of the funnel itself with one of a more dramatic cloud base. The photograph was later reused and incorrectly described as a record of a tornado that passed through Kirksville, Missouri, 27 April 1899. In 1912 more accurate photographs were published of a tornado that struck Ponca City, Oklahoma, 25 April 1912. See Grazulis, *Significant Tornados,* 683, 733. Curry apparently slightly changed the shape of the tornado in his painting after he first exhibited the picture, making the base of the funnel narrower.

72. See Grazulis, *Significant Tornados,* 828, where two of Blackstock's photographs are reproduced. Curry's painting is particularly similar to figure 60; see Schmeckebier, *Pageant,* 113.

73. The distorted pose of the girl closely resembles the running figures of Pablo Picasso. Specifically, it recalls the figure in *The Race* (1922), reproduced in Alfred H. Barr, Jr., *Picasso: Fifty Years of His Art,* exh. cat. (New York: Museum of Modern Art, 1946), 126.

74. Quoted in Davidson, *Twister,* 122. The horses in the painting also allude to the fact that, well into the twentieth century, on the smaller and less prosperous Kansas farms, horses rather than engines were used to pull machinery. Draft horses reached a record number in Kansas in 1919, when there were 1,300,000 such animals. After that date, machinery became more common, and, by 1936, the number of draft animals had dropped to 545,000.

75. Fascinated by these reports, the late chemist Bernard Vonnegut, brother of the novelist Kurt Vonnegut, Jr., conducted a series of experiments to determine the wind speed necessary to defeather a chicken. The degree of this defeathering might provide a means, he reasoned, to determine the wind speeds of tornados. Unfortunately, Vonnegut's wind-tunnel experiments demonstrated that the feathers came off in an inconsistent manner. See Davidson, *Twister,* 43, 92.

76. Of Curry's major paintings, perhaps only *Line Storm* makes use of a differently configured central motif. In that canvas the destructive cloud becomes more formless, like the creature in the famous 1958 horror movie *The Blob.* Even in this instance, however, it may not be stretching things too far to see the cloud as a deformation of the same archetypal pattern. For Curry, the form seems to have symbolized his fear of the unknown.

77. Waller, "Interview with Mrs. John Steuart Curry": 9. Similarly, Edward Alden Jewell wrote of the painting: "It may be adversely criti-

cized if you like, because of its insistence on story-telling; the picture may be called primarily an 'illustration'" (Edward Alden Jewell, "In the Realm of Art: Carnegie International Opens," *New York Times,* 22 October 1933).

78. Craven, "John Steuart Curry": 40.

79. Sidney Howard to Curry, 3 March 1936, Curry Papers/AAA, microfilm roll 164; quoted in Kendall, *Rethinking Regionalism,* 34.

80. Schmeckebier, *Pageant,* 235. The jump from elephants to storm clouds may have been prompted, in part, by the fact that tornados are similar in form to an elephant's trunk. One 1896 twister in Texas was described at the time as looking like "an elephant's trunk in search of food." See Davidson, *Twister,* 148.

81. Deaths caused by hail are rare in the United States. In 1930 hail killed a farmer near Lubbock, Texas, and hailstones have been known to kill hundreds of sheep and tens of thousands of birds at one time. A massive hailstorm in the Dakotas in 1883 forced a number of settlers from the area.

82. Kinsey, *Plain Pictures,* 141–42; Schmeckebier, *Pageant,* 135–36.

83. Waldman, *Mark Rothko,* 22.

84. This appears to be a reference to Thomas Craven, *Men of Art* (New York: Scribner's, 1930).

85. Smith Curry to "Architects office decorative dpt," 17 July 1934, Records of the Works Progress Administration, National Archives and Records Administration, College Park, Md., Selections from Record Group 69, R DC5, F O384.

86. See Stephen Polcari, "Jackson Pollock and Thomas Hart Benton," *Arts* Magazine 53 (March 1979): 120–24; idem, *Abstract Expressionism and the Modern Experience* (Cambridge: Cambridge University Press, 1991).

The Use of Religious Motifs in Curry's Art

ROBERT L. GAMBONE

In 1927 John Steuart Curry, fresh from studying at the Paris atelier of Basil Schoukhaieff, produced the important lithograph *The Three Wisemen* (fig. 1). Its iconography provides an early demonstration of how Curry crafted personal images suggested by his Kansas upbringing, wrestling with these themes to reinterpret his past and provoke hard questions about the meaning and use of religion.[1]

Curry's depiction of the Magi following the Star of Bethlehem resembles Gustave Doré's lithograph *The Star in the East* (1866, fig. 2), a work familiar to Curry from childhood and one he studied at Geneva College.[2] While Doré employs the conventional iconography of the Magi riding camels, Curry pictures his wise men riding black horses and clothed in flowing, shroud-like garments that conceal their faces; they swoop down upon the earth in a depiction more appropriate for the Apocalypse than the birth of Christ. Such dire imagery was familiar to Curry from his instruction with the illustrator Harvey Dunn and later study with Charles Locke at the Art Students League in New York City. Locke introduced his students to Renaissance artists such as Albrecht Dürer, whose print *The Four Horsemen of the Apocalypse* (1498) had made the image of horsemen carrying disease and destruction famous. Apocalyptic evocations would have been even more familiar from the preaching Curry heard as a boy reared in the premillennial Scots Covenanter tradition.[3] According to that tradition, Scripture was the Word of God, which must be accepted literally. In practice, this meant that the pestilence, famine, and earthquakes described in the Revelation of St. John the Divine were to be taken as matters of fact. And since that book interpreted those events as heralding the Day of the Lord, modern-day believers were encouraged to see such calamities taking place during their own time as signs of the imminence of that day. This indoctrination remained with Curry long after the 1920s, by which time he had abandoned his childhood faith.

Letters he wrote to his parents while he was studying at the School of the Art Institute of Chicago demonstrate that Curry maintained the religious world view of his youth, abstaining from smoking and drinking and continuing the family pattern of attending two Sunday services at Presbyterian churches.[4] One might think of these letters as reassurances to anxious parents, but a close reading reveals an earnest, questioning attitude rather than an effort to placate. Curry discloses that he is torn between a desire to go sketching on Sunday and his obligation to attend church and keep the Sabbath. "I wouldn't go out in the morning," he wrote. "I'll go to church. I can't feel terrible about it. I don't like to stay around my room."[5] He also describes attending the Fourth Presbyterian Church and Sunday School, noting that "the lesson was the third chapter of John on the new birth" and marveling that the minister allowed the distribution of communion to everyone.[6] To resolve discrepancies between his Covenanter upbringing and the more liberal worship he encountered in Chicago, the eighteen-year-old Curry read theology and made friends with students of the Moody Bible Institute.

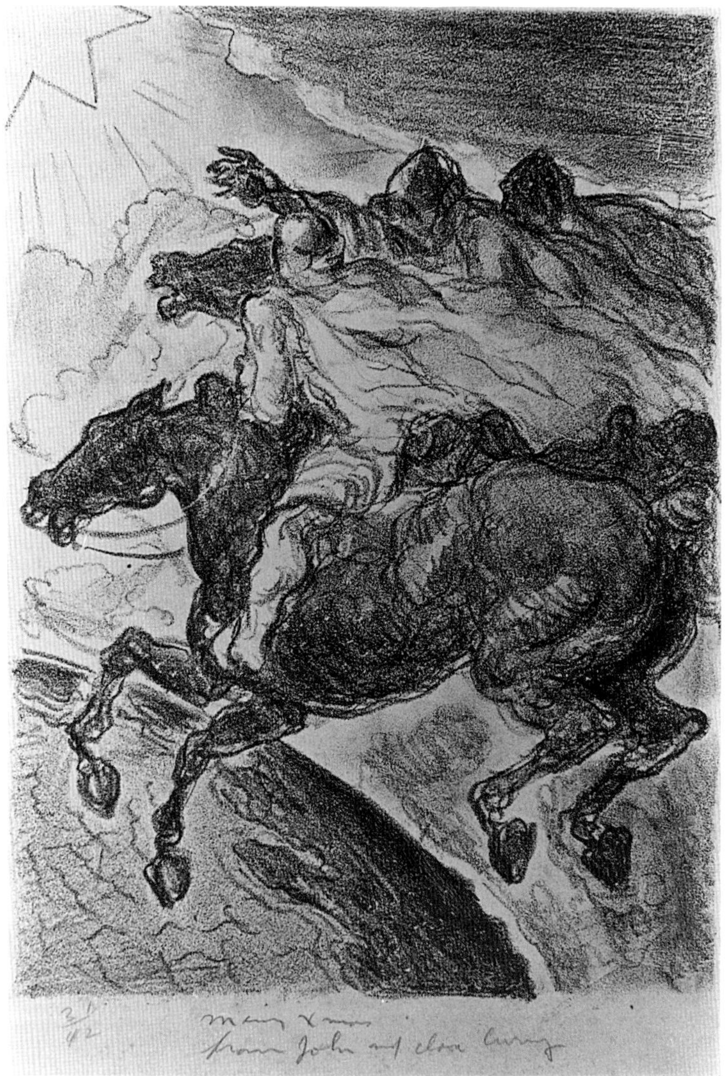

FIGURE 1

John Steuart Curry,
The Three Wisemen, 1927
Lithograph
8¾ × 5¼ in.
Courtesy Syracuse University Art Collection, Syracuse, New York.

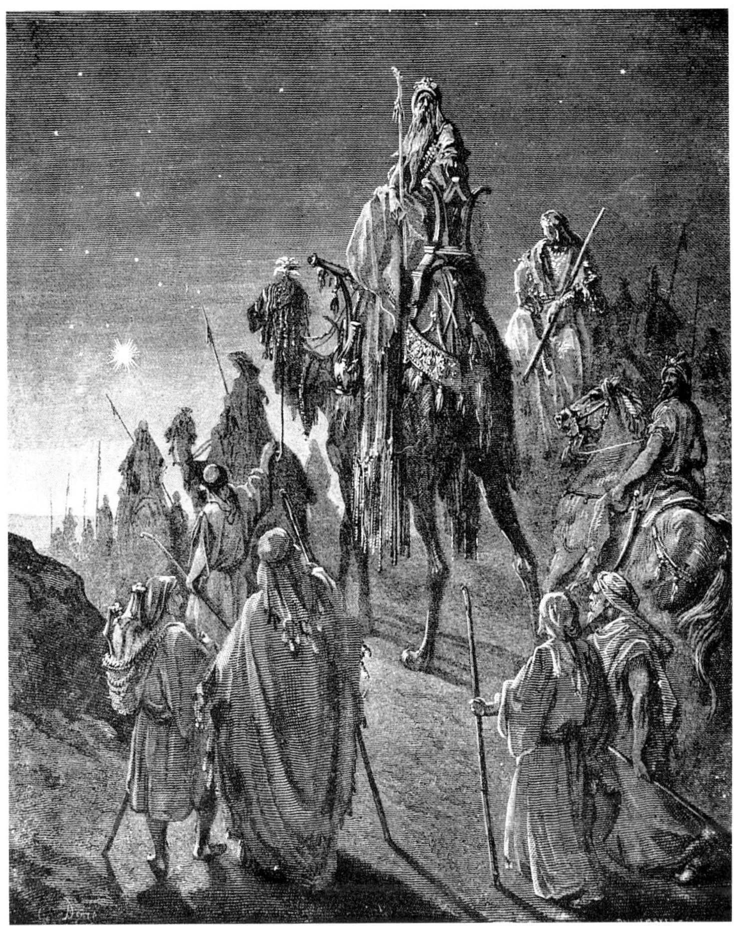

FIGURE 2

Gustave Doré (French, 1832–83)
The Star in the East, 1866
Lithograph
9½ × 7¹¹⁄₁₆ in.
As reproduced in *The Bible, with Illustrations by Gustave Doré* (London: Cassell, Petter and Galpin, 1880), unpaginated.

Dwight L. Moody founded the institute in 1886 for the purpose of training evangelists. A premillennialist missionary, he also believed in the imminent return of Christ, which would usher in a thousand-year period of grace. Students at the institute debated other conservative Protestants who held a *post*-millennialist view, wherein Christ's triumphant reappearance would transpire only *after* a thousand-year period of grace. Moody Institute instructors hosted national conferences at their Chicago center at which they encouraged Moody students gathered from around the country to scrutinize contemporary events for signs of the approaching apocalypse. The largest of these conferences was held in February 1914, two and a half years before Curry moved to Chicago.

Curry may have felt impelled to establish a connection with the Moody Institute because of letters from his mother in which she recalled how the Reverend David H. Coulter, pastor of their Covenanter church, had prophesied the coming of World War I.[7] (Around this time, Curry even ventured a premillennial prophecy of his own.[8]) The emotional atmosphere engendered by the war, Curry's soul-searching, his mother's admonitions about the coming millennium, and his friendships with Moody students all led him to write home saying that he was considering enlisting, with Moody Institute students, in a U.S. Army company of churchgoing young men.[9] This letter suggests that by 1917 he had pondered premillennialism and felt comfortable enough with its implications to consider casting his lot with Moodyites while risking his life in the war effort.

Curry's beliefs found reenforcement at Geneva College, a Presbyterian-affiliated school in Beaver Falls, Pennsylvania, which he attended from September 1918 through December 1919.[10] While there, he must have wrestled with his memory of the dual tragedies of losing both his brother Paul and a high-school buddy, William Davis, to the war. Curry's mother wrote that Paul had had "a glorious death," meaning that he had died saved in a religious sense. To Curry, however, there was no glory in this, just a tragic waste of life.[11]

Despite these broodings, Curry remained attached to his beliefs when he moved on to study with Dunn early in 1920. Dunn urged Curry to read his Bible and adhere to his Christian faith.[12] That the man responsible for launching Curry's career as an illustrator possessed such convictions no doubt further influenced him to explore connections between religion and art.

Seven years later, Curry was something of a different man. In June 1927, having spent nine months studying in Paris, he returned to the States; soon thereafter, he drew *The Three Wisemen.* He had found Parisian cabaret life and his visits to the Louvre to be heady, powerfully broadening experiences.[13] These, plus his continuing reflections on the carnage of World War I, led him to question and ultimately abandon his religious rearing. His letters after 1927 contain no references to religion. While premillennialist themes continued to provide Curry with raw material for his art—and appealed because he believed they would be readily understood by the general public—he now viewed premillennialism, and organized religion, from the viewpoint of an outsider. *The Three Wisemen* represents his first working out of this changed attitude. Thus, as noted, the Magi do not bring word of Christ's birth but rather herald the end of the world; fusing Christian hope with premillennial fear became

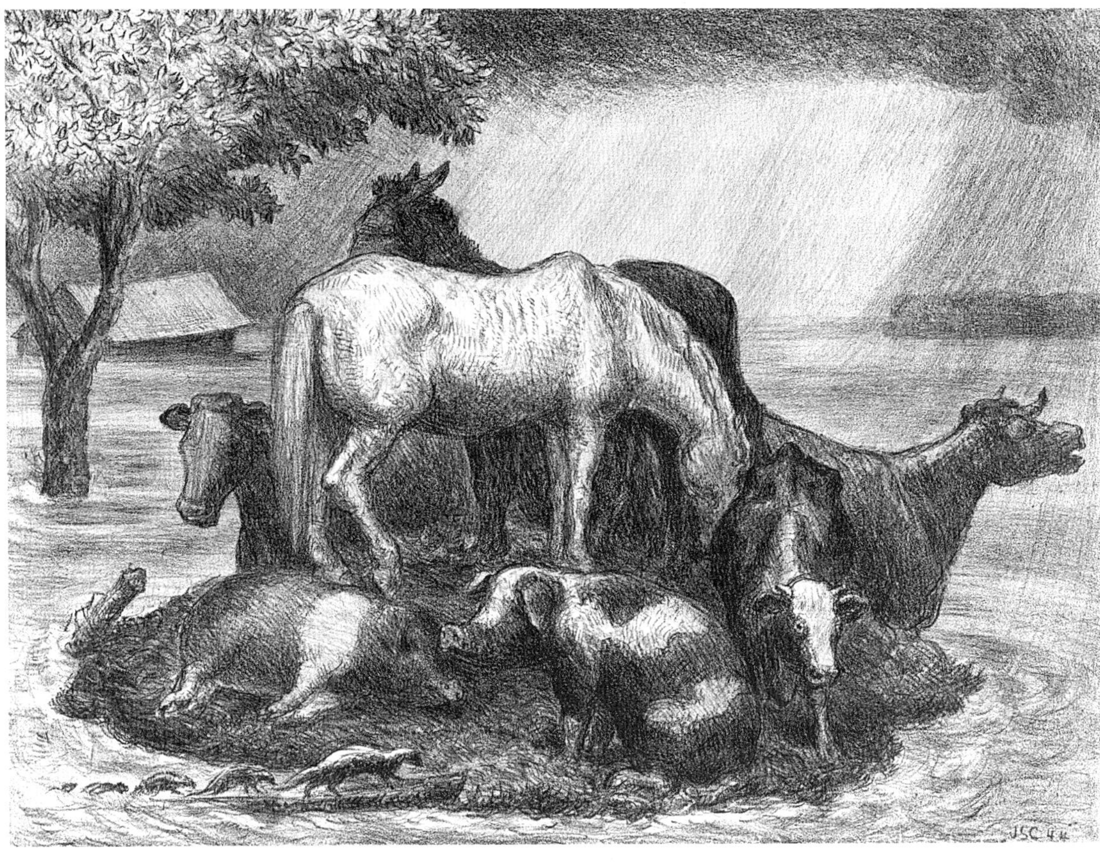

FIGURE 4

John Steuart Curry
Sanctuary, 1944
Lithograph
11¾ × 15¾ in.
Courtesy Columbus Museum of Art, Columbus, Ohio. Gift of Mr. and Mrs. Seward D. Schooler.

the principal means by which Curry expressed his newfound skepticism, and it forms a leitmotif in all of his religiously oriented works.[14]

Curry demonstrated a preoccupation with premillennialism in his art all through the 1920s and 1930s. Three lithographs in particular, each of which later became a painting—*Flight into Egypt* (fig. 3), *Sanctuary* (fig. 4), and *Mississippi Noah* (fig. 5)—carry a broadly accessible religious significance inflected with premillennialist overtones. First drawn in 1928, *Flight into Egypt* was reworked in 1929, the composition reversed, and the title changed to *The Family Migrates.* That year Curry also did an oil painting based on this lithograph, calling it *The Ne'er Do Well* (see p. 153).[15] The relationship between the artist's Kansas past and his use of nature as a metaphor expressive of the sublime has long been noted.[16] But analysis of the sequence of events involved in producing these two lithographs and the oil painting clarifies how Curry established direct parallels between events in the Middle West and those depicted in the Bible.

Although by 1928 Curry considered himself a professional artist, he was not yet earning a living as one; he borrowed money from his brother and sister-in-law, required his wife to work, and was accepting commercial projects.[17] Doubts about his abilities

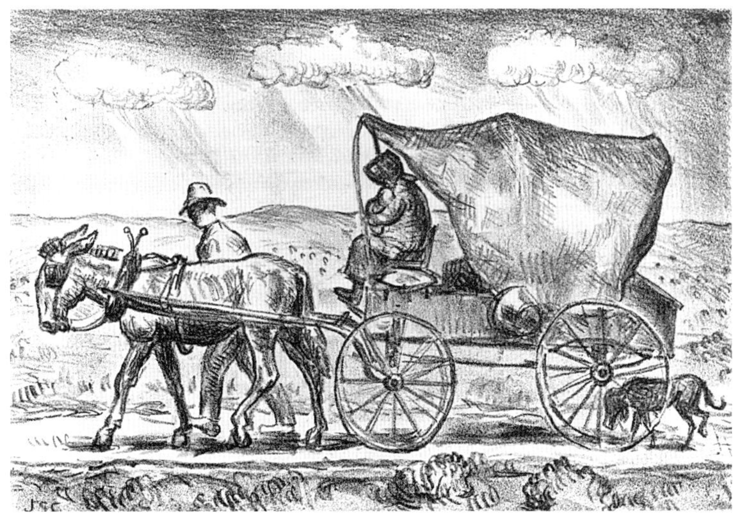

FIGURE 3

John Steuart Curry
Flight into Egypt, 1928
Lithograph
4½ × 6⅝ in.
Collection of Davenport Museum of Art, Davenport Iowa.

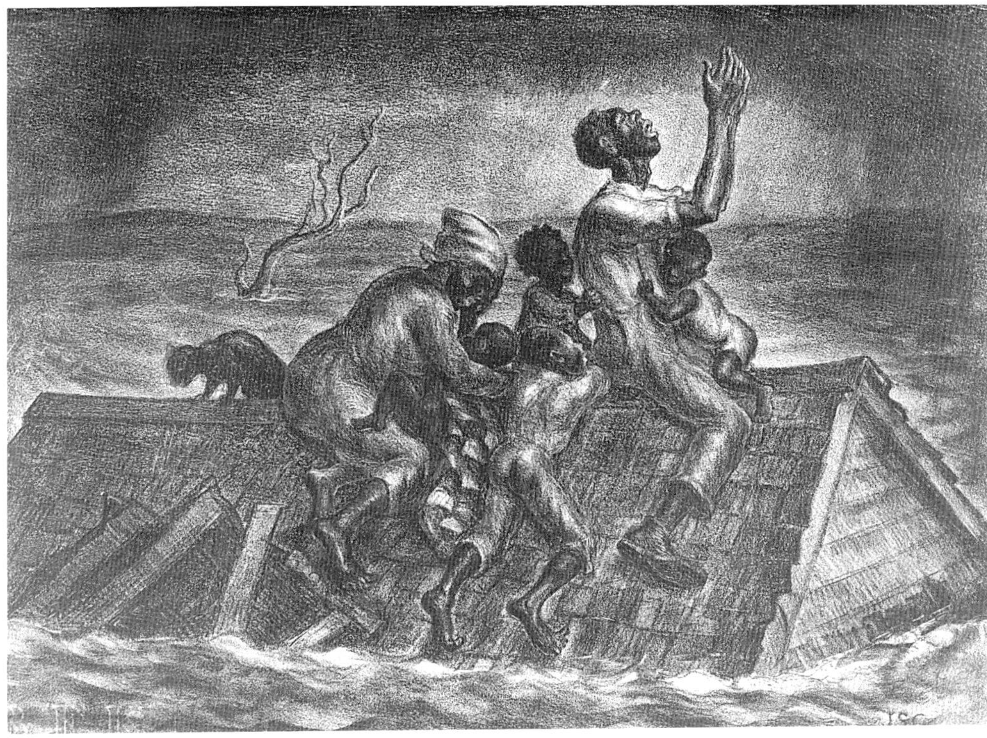

FIGURE 5
John Steuart Curry
Mississippi Noah, 1932
Lithograph
9¾ × 13⅝ in.
Collection of Davenport Museum of Art, Davenport, Iowa.

resurfaced. A decade had elapsed since Curry had decided he would rather be an artist than a farmer.[18] His precarious financial state must have raised the specter of admitting failure as an artist, which ultimately meant he might have to return to farming. No doubt the depressed conditions of agriculture during the late 1920s made this prospect seem bleak, if not apocalyptic.[19]

In the summer of 1929, Curry returned home for six weeks to a Kansas greatly changed from the one he had known in his youth. From the front porch of his parents' farmhouse, he sketched the seemingly endless stream of impoverished farm folk, migrating west from drought-stricken Oklahoma and Arkansas. He also drew scenes of destruction wrought by that year's flooding of the Kaw River in eastern Kansas.[20] The new title Curry assigned his lithograph in 1929, *The Family Migrates,* and the title he gave the painted version, *The Ne'er Do Well,* implying failure, destitution, and aimless drifting, reveal the anxious state in which he worked that summer as well as the despair of midwestern farmers.

Curry's original title, *Flight into Egypt,* refers to Matthew 2:13–18, in which Joseph and Mary, fearing for their child's life after Herod has ordered that newly born male children be put to death, escape from Bethlehem with Jesus to seek haven in a foreign land. Having recently returned from Paris, Curry had vivid memories of Renaissance paintings in the Louvre of biblical scenes in which the figures wore contemporary attire. (Later, as an art instructor, he lectured on this very aspect of Renaissance art.[21]) Curry dressed his Holy Family in quintessentially American garb but not that of 1920s Kansas. Rather, the woman's ankle-length dress and sunbonnet and the Conestoga wagon hint of the mid–nineteenth century, when the Curry family arrived in Kansas as hopeful frontier settlers. From the perspective of the 1920s droughts and the 1929 Kaw River flood, that hope of long ago seemed false.

Recalling the premillennialist belief that a period of tribulation would precede the Day of the Lord, it struck Curry as apt, just as it had in *The Three Wisemen,* to depict an event from Christ's infancy in an ominous light. Curry used *Flight into Egypt* as a Christmas card around 1929–30; by retitling it *The Family Migrates,* he made clear the connections among Depression-era midwestern farmers, the emigration of nineteenth-century Kansas pioneers, the wandering of the Holy Family, and the hoped-for Day of the Lord.[22]

As noted, during that fateful summer Curry also made sketches stemming from the Kaw River flood, later developing them into the lithographs *Mississippi Noah* and *Sanctuary.*[23] (In 1935 these works took new form as the oil paintings *The Mississippi* [color plate 34] and *Sanctuary* [color plate 35]). Early European explorers had named both Kansas and the Kaw River after the native inhabitants, variously referred to as Kansa or Kanza.[24] The flooded river depicted in *Sanctuary* and *Mississippi Noah* is symbolic of the state. Curry's initial sketch, made near Lawrence, shows a cluster of figures anxiously watching the rising water. Their diminutive size and the props of general store, car, dog, and road signs pointing to Topeka, Atchison, and St. Joseph give this sketch a specific geographic focus.[25] But as Curry reworked his sketches into lithographs, he eliminated local referents in favor of a generic conception, enhancing the works' spiritual power and meaning.

In *Sanctuary,* animals huddle on an isolated patch of high ground beneath a leaden sky, hoping to secure refuge from the rampaging river. A submerged farm building and the upper limbs of a tree indicate that this site was once fertile, productive land. Mules, pigs, and cows collapse in exhaustion on the waterlogged hill or stand forlorn. One lowing cow makes a desperate cry; in the lower-right corner, a sodden troop of skunks floats in upon a log.

Why did Curry radically alter his on-the-scene sketches of the Kaw, eliminating overt references to Kansas? A lithograph by Gustave Doré, *The Deluge* (ca. 1866, fig. 6), provides a clue. Doré, who, as noted, was an artist Curry admired, depicts a hilltop protruding from an ocean of water; a mother tiger and her cubs huddle peacefully there with four human infants whose parents sink into the turbulent waves. Among the most dramatic episodes in Genesis, the Flood represents God's decision to destroy the earth and sinful humanity, sparing only Noah's family. Noah is instructed to save a male and female representative of every animal species so that a righteous earth can be reestablished after the deluge. The narrative pattern of destruction preceding salvation appealed to Curry as he viewed the Kaw flooding and sought visual metaphors for it.

Also implicit in Doré's conception, and explicit in the American folk art of Edward Hicks (fig. 7) and William Hallowell (fig. 8), with which Curry was also quite familiar, is the theme of the Peaceable Kingdom, which stems from Isaiah 11:6–9. This biblical passage contains the prophecy that the coming Day of the Lord will end world strife and usher in a new age of peaceful coexistence.

Doré's depiction of a tigress protecting her cubs while standing harmlessly next to four children and Isaiah's concluding verses, comparing the Day of the Lord to swelling waters, offered Curry images that were useful as he sought to interpret events he witnessed in the Kansas of 1929. In *Sanctuary,* Isaiah's imagined kingdom and Doré's mountaintop become a bit of upland pasture to which mules, cows, pigs, and skunks cling for life. The threat of drowning parallels the mood of *The Deluge,* but the title equates these animals to fugitives imploring God's protection. Curry suggests that the oasis where they huddle will not be breached. Like animals from Noah's ark, they will be spared, and, like animals of the Peaceable Kingdom, they will coexist. Once again, the threatened day of destruction holds out a promise of messianic grace and salvation.

The theme of maintaining faith despite seemingly insurmountable odds also underlies *Mississippi Noah.* It was first drawn in 1932, as Curry was developing ideas for *Sanctuary.* The immediate source for the work lies in the disastrous Kaw flood, but the title reveals that Curry envisioned this flood as related to the one that had plagued the Mississippi Valley in the spring of 1927, causing monumental destruction all the way from Minnesota to the Delta.[26] The magnitude of that disaster galvanized the federal government into action. Secretary of Commerce Herbert Hoover personally took charge of relief, overseeing rescue operations and planning refugee rehabilitation. Directing Red Cross workers, National Guardsmen, and countless volunteers via radio and telegraph, he endeared himself to many Americans and ensured his election as president in 1928. But the Wall Street crash of October 1929 and its aftermath were to erase Hoover's prestige. In 1932, Franklin D. Roosevelt swept to victory largely because many blamed the nation's economic collapse on the Republican president. The ironic twist of events linking the Mississippi floods with the rise and fall of Herbert Hoover probably interested Curry because of the parallels he saw between his own and Hoover's keen awareness of the plight of American blacks.

Hoover won attention during the Mississippi flood relief for his efforts to increase the number of black citizens on Red Cross relief staffs: He recommended that a Negro Advisory Commission be formed to oversee relief and resettlement operations and proposed giving rural blacks surplus disaster funds to buy land and escape sharecropping—a proposal that was not enacted into law.[27] Among his other notable initiatives with respect to blacks were his orders to desegregate the U.S. Department of Commerce in 1928 and his unsuccessful attempt to get Republicans to add a plank promoting federal antilynching legislation to their 1928 party platform.[28]

Like Hoover, Curry sympathized with blacks. Beginning with *The Fugitive* (1934–36, color plate 31, fig. 9), in which a young black hides amid tree limbs as a white mob searches for him in the distance, he imbued his figures of black people with a religious symbolism. The figure's outstretched arms and body

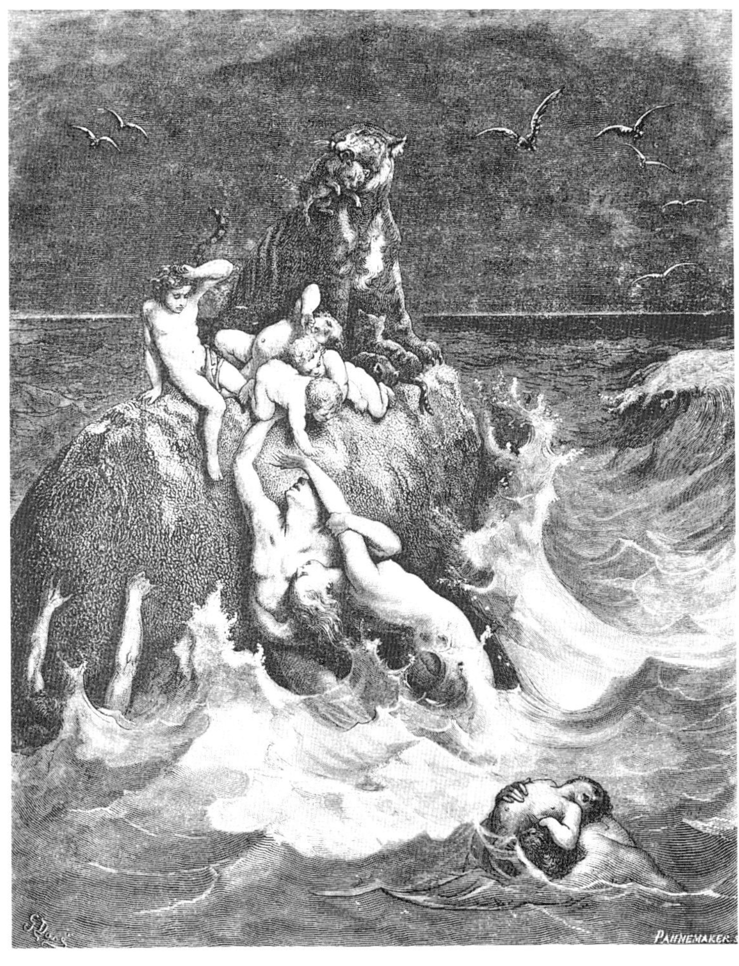

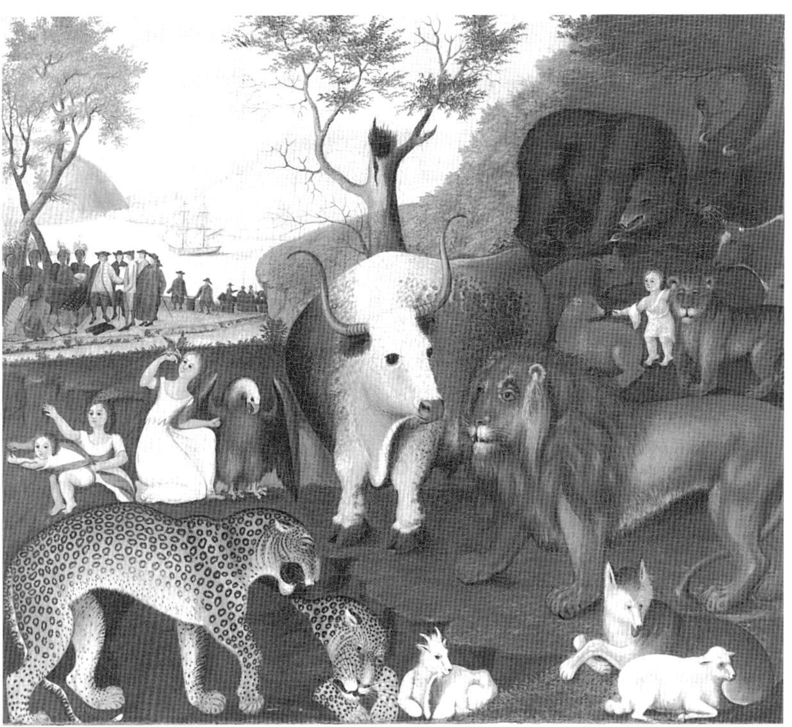

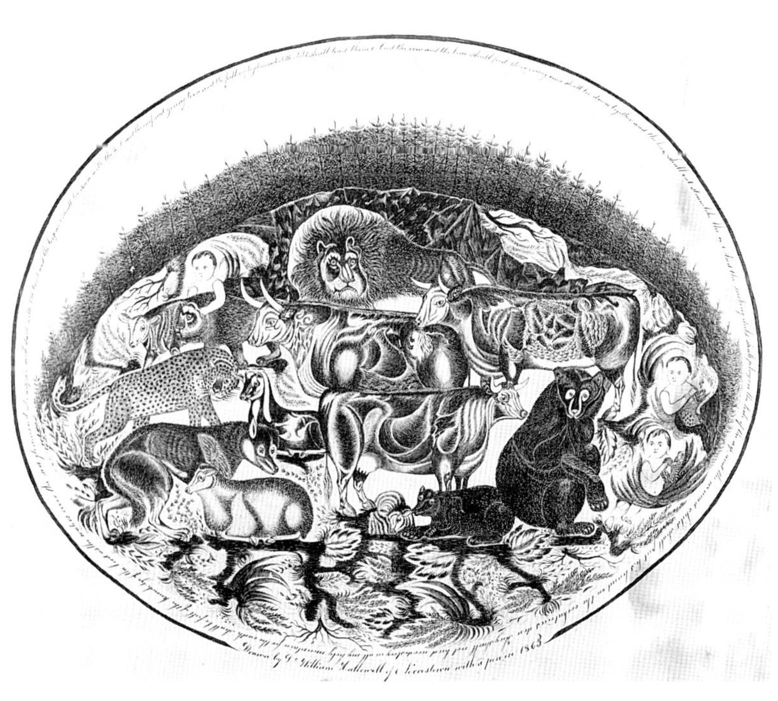

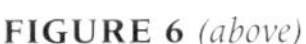

FIGURE 6 *(above)*

Gustave Doré (French, 1832–83)

The Deluge, ca. 1866

Lithograph

9¹¹⁄₁₆ × 7¾ in.

As reproduced in *The Bible, with Illustrations by Gustave Doré* (London: Cassell, Petter and Galpin, 1880), unpaginated.

FIGURE 7 *(above right)*

Edward Hicks (American, 1780–1849)

Peaceable Kingdom, 1846

Oil on canvas

25 × 28½ in.

Fine Arts Museums of San Francisco. Gift of Mr. and Mrs. John D. Rockefeller, 3rd.

FIGURE 8 *(right)*

William Hallowell (American, 1801–1890)

Peaceable Kingdom, 1865

Ink on paper

16¾ × 19¾ in.

Courtesy New York State Historical Association, Cooperstown.

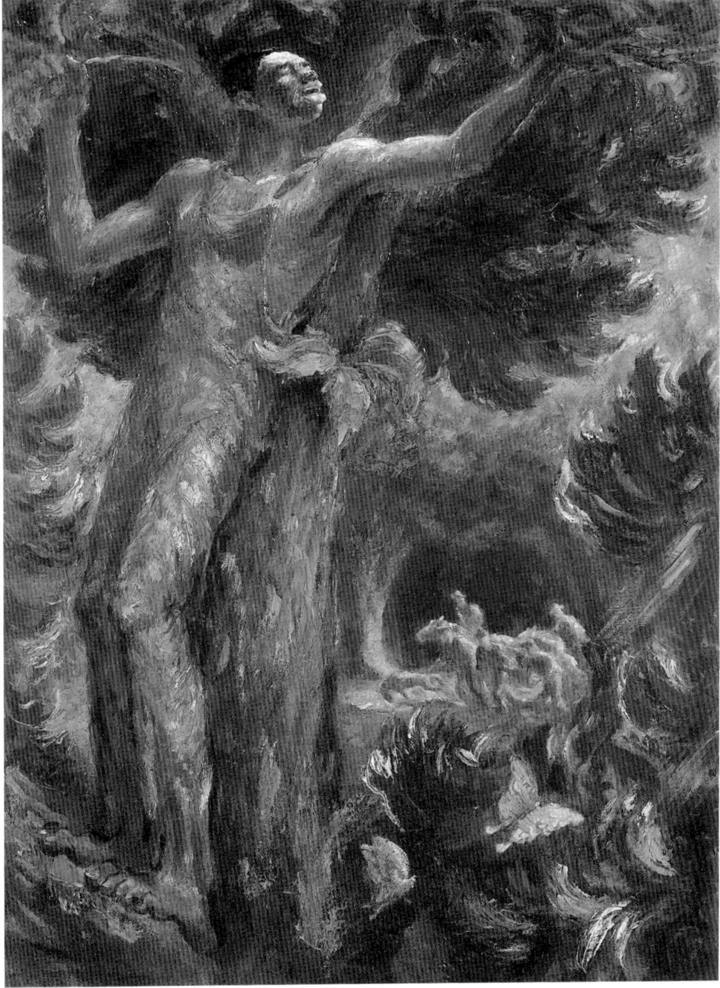

FIGURE 9

John Steuart Curry
The Fugitive, 1934–36
Oil on canvas
38 × 36 in.
Private collection.
Photograph courtesy Kennedy Galleries, Inc., New York

pressed against the tree trunk recall the posture of the crucified Christ.[29] In *Freeing of the Slaves* (color plate 43, fig. 10), his rejected 1936 design for the U.S. Department of Justice building in Washington, D.C., Curry repeated the gesture of supplication in *The Fugitive* (also prominent in *Mississippi Noah),* expressing the idea of ultimate deliverance from suffering through divine intervention. The flood victims in *Mississippi Noah* are blacks. The parallel with the Noah story provided a particularly apt metaphor for the title. But the impetus to depict a *black* Noah reflected Curry's association of the flood with the situation of black people in America.

The various factors that moved Curry to produce his Mississippi-flood lithograph and painting lingered with him through the 1930s. He linked the disparate themes of apocalyptic destruction and deliverance, Negro spirituals, the social condition of blacks, the role of Herbert Hoover, and the Mississippi flood in his ambitious history painting *Hoover and the Flood* (1940, fig. 11). Curry stresses Hoover's humanitarianism by showing him surveying the raging waters, accompanied by National Guardsmen, Red Cross relief workers, refugees, farm animals, praying blacks, and even a Mississippi riverboat in the distance. The braying animals at left are lifted literally from *Sanctuary;* the center of the composition, occupied by an elderly black man with uplifted arms, echoes the supplicating figure in *Mississippi Noah.* Curry also borrowed imagery from popular culture in this canvas. The old man's costume mimics that of the preacher in the 1936 film *The Green Pastures,* based on Marc Connelly's dramatic and immensely successful 1929 recasting with black actors of the Noah story for the Broadway stage. And the distant Mississippi riverboat recalls the opening scene from Jerome Kern and Oscar Hammerstein II's hit 1927 musical, *Show Boat.*

Curry's flood-related images were not the first ones to display his interest in water as symbolic of cataclysmic change and redemption: He had addressed the theme in the 1928 painting *Baptism in Kansas* (color plate 10, fig. 12), which depicts a Disciples of Christ (or Campbellite) immersion rite being performed on a prairie farm. Standing knee-deep in a round cattle trough, a young woman clad in white, braided hair draped across her shoulder, closes her eyes and clasps her hands to her breast in anticipation of the dunking she is about to receive at the hands of a mustachioed minister. Off to the right, six white-robed figures, standing in two files, await their own baptismal plunge. Congregants holding hymnals gather around to witness and accompany the rite with appropriate songs. Behind them, a line of Model Ts forms a mechanical backdrop, while rays of sunlight beam from a cloud-flecked sky and two doves swoop down.

Curry flattens out the barn and farmhouse along the horizon, establishing a boundary for the action. He enhances this effect by placing a Kansas farm family in the lower-right corner, shown from the waist up and positioned with their backs toward us. The lower parts of their bodies remain cropped; by implication, they extend into the viewer's space. This arrangement reinforces the sensation that we, too, are witnesses to the baptism. Curry draws attention to the centrality of this immersion rite by echoing the circular form of the trough in the curved row of spectators standing around and beyond it. The minister and the neophyte are centrally aligned along a vertical axis that Curry emphasizes by extending an imaginary line

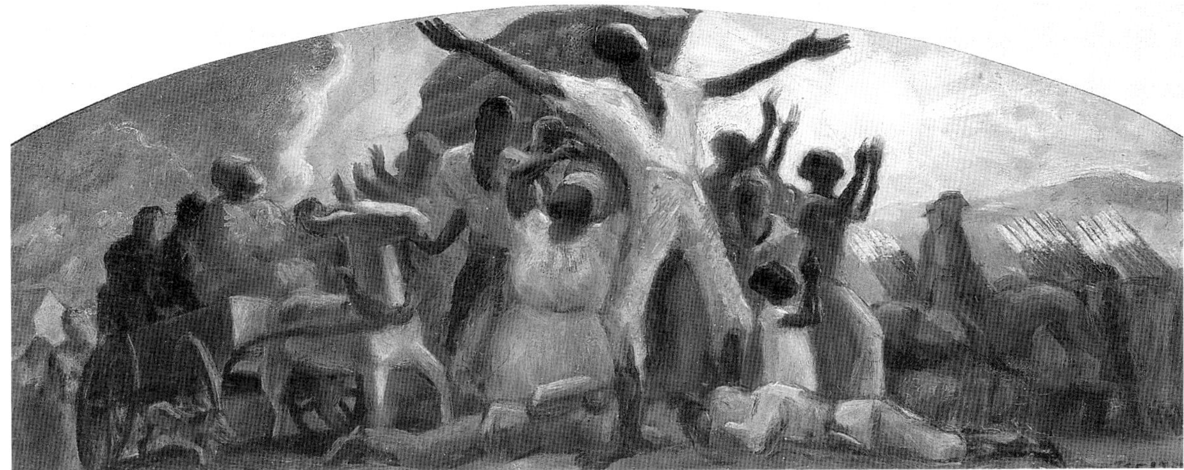

FIGURE 10

John Steuart Curry
Freeing of the Slaves, 1936
Mural study, U.S. Department of Justice building, Washington, D.C.
Oil on paperboard (now mounted on board)
14½ × 33¼ in.
Greendyke Fine Art, Pittsford, New York.

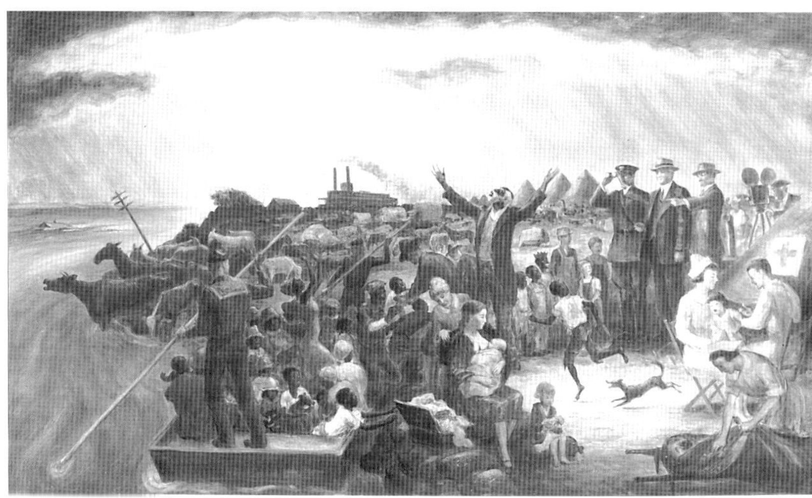

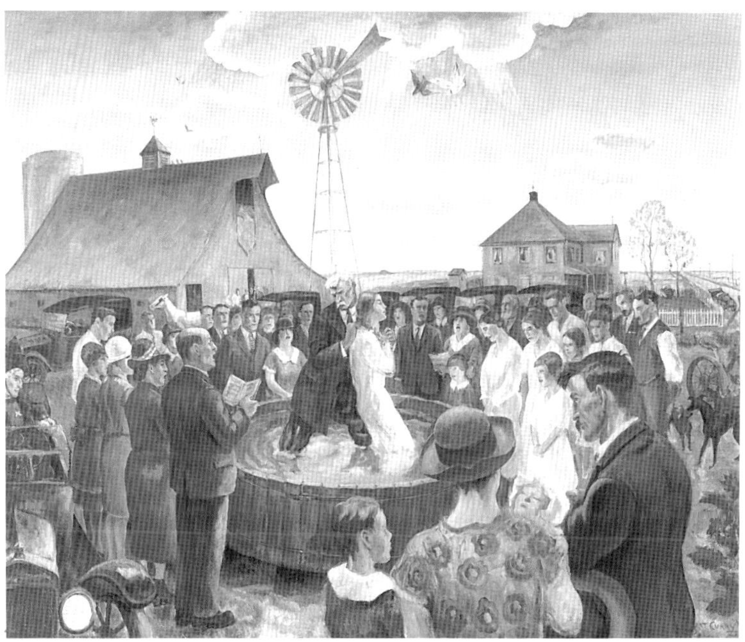

upward through the carefully positioned windmill and downward through the figure of the young boy standing next to his mother in the foreground. Curry stressed the veracity of this scene when explaining it to the reporter Margit Varga of *Life* magazine:

This baptism was on the farm of our neighbor, Will McBride. It was under the auspices of the Christian Church, or Campbellites, as we called them. We were Presbyterians and were sprinkled only, but were interested spectators at all immersion baptisms. . . . It was not considered a strange procedure. . . . My presentation of the scene is fairly accurate, even to the doves descending in the ray of light from heaven. I consider this presentation as near as anything that has been done, in recent times, to the original "Baptism in Jordan." . . . [Y]ears later I put down what my poor abilities permitted me.[30]

FIGURE 11 *(above left)*

John Steuart Curry
Hoover and the Flood, 1940
Oil on panel
37½ × 63 in.
Morris Museum of Art, Augusta, Georgia.
Photograph courtesy Sotheby's, New York.

FIGURE 12 *(above)*

John Steuart Curry
Baptism in Kansas, 1928
Oil on canvas
40 × 50 in.
Collection of Whitney Museum of American Art, New York. Gift of Gertrude Vanderbilt Whitney.
Photograph © 1996: Whitney Museum of American Art

The judicious assembling of all elements in *Baptism in Kansas* indicates that the artist took great pains to maximize the dramatic impact. It is unlikely, then, that the scene is a literal rendering. Why did Curry depict a Campbellite immersion instead of the sprinkling baptism traditionally practiced by the Scots Covenanters? Indeed, his mother complained about this very point.[31] In contending that *Baptism in Kansas* is as close as one could come in modern times "to the original 'Baptism in Jordan,'" Curry revealed that he wanted the painting to be experienced as a religious work. In Western tradition, religious art is intended to stimulate contemplation of the event depicted. Is this true for *Baptism in Kansas*?

The canvas reveals a dichotomy. Curry points up the Campbellites' selective adherence to Scripture in the context of the modern world. While basically hewing to a conservative, literal interpretation of the Holy Word, and while also clinging to such traditional practices as immersion baptism, Campbellites also adopted contemporary fashion (as reflected in the short dresses and cloche hats worn by the younger women in the painting) and relied on up-to-date technology (as evidenced by the Model Ts and electric power lines). In sharp contrast to the relative modernism exhibited by the congregation, the minister's handlebar moustache and knee-length morning jacket, as well as the braided hair of the woman he baptizes, seem like nineteenth-century features on this twentieth-century farm, strangely out of place. Vertically aligned with the windmill—an increasingly archaic feature on newly electrified farms—the minister and his neophyte are more tightly linked to a vanishing past. The appearance of *two* birds overhead strikes another ambiguous note, since they cannot be equated with the solitary white dove mentioned in the Scriptures of Jesus' Baptism and standard in all depictions of the "Baptism in Jordan."[32]

A witness to Campbellite baptisms as a boy, Curry knew of the sect's origins within the Scots Presbyterian (that is, Covenanter) Church. This tie to Covenanter tradition provided a link in his mind between the two now-distinct denominations, allowing him to substitute the Campbellite dunking rite—which was pictorially more interesting—for the staid, undramatic sprinkling practiced by the Covenanters. Curry's decision to paint Campbellites not only had personal significance for him but also constituted a timely topic that coincidentally reinforced his ambivalent feelings about religion.

The Disciples of Christ were founded in 1832 by Alexander Campbell, the son of a Presbyterian minister from what is now West Virginia, who preached there and in Indiana, Ohio, Kentucky, and Tennessee, gathering disaffected Baptist congregations into a new church organization. Adherents followed a strict mandate "to disciple all people, immersing all Christians in the name of the Trinity."[33] They believed that this mandate summed up the requirements of the early Christian community, a thesis Campbell fully articulated in his book *The Christian System* (1835). He and the Disciples of Christ envisioned all churches pursuing this mandate, thereby eliminating contentious dogma and reuniting Christians into one church. To attain this end, Disciples increasingly stressed unity above other considerations. By 1896 the influential Aetna Street Church in Cleveland proposed open membership, whereby everyone who professed belief in Christ, even the non-immersed, would be fully accepted into fellowship.[34]

In opposition, conservatives within the sect loudly disclaimed belief in a socially conditioned Bible and attacked the practice of accepting non-immersed members. The growing rift among Disciples dominated business at annual church conventions. At the 1920 gathering in St. Louis, conservatives criticized the acceptance of non-immersed members into mission congregations, and the convention adopted a resolution forbidding the practice.[35] Conservatives foisted this same policy upon local churches; what applied to missionaries sent across the country to preach obviously applied as well to those who sent them. Under pressure from liberals of the Campbell Institute, located at the University of Chicago Divinity School, the Disciples officially reversed this policy in 1921, prompting conservative churches within the fold to withhold funds from the national organization until the church reaffirmed immersion baptism. Alarm over this rift led the delegates to the Disciples' 1922 national convention to adopt a statement of creed that upheld the traditional rite. At the following year's convention, however, conservatives failed to sustain their efforts, and delegates again adopted a noncommittal doctrinal program. The immersion debate culminated in 1925, when national-convention delegates voted to revoke the open-membership policy. After that, liberals and conservatives convened separately, produced their own publications, and managed independent educational, missionary, and administrative organizations.

During this same period, as pointed out, Curry was rethinking premillennialism and renouncing the farm to become an artist. He was no doubt keenly aware of the anomaly of Campbellites, committed to Christian unity yet divided over baptism and scriptural interpretation. In *Baptism in Kansas,* Curry not only recalled immersion rites he had witnessed but also developed a lively, even spectacular picture that exposed tensions between religious faith and the modern world.

In this regard, it is worth comparing *Baptism* with another work from 1928, *Bathers* (color plate 11, fig. 13), which depicts immersion of another kind yet also affords insight into Curry's increasingly skeptical religious views. The works bear several

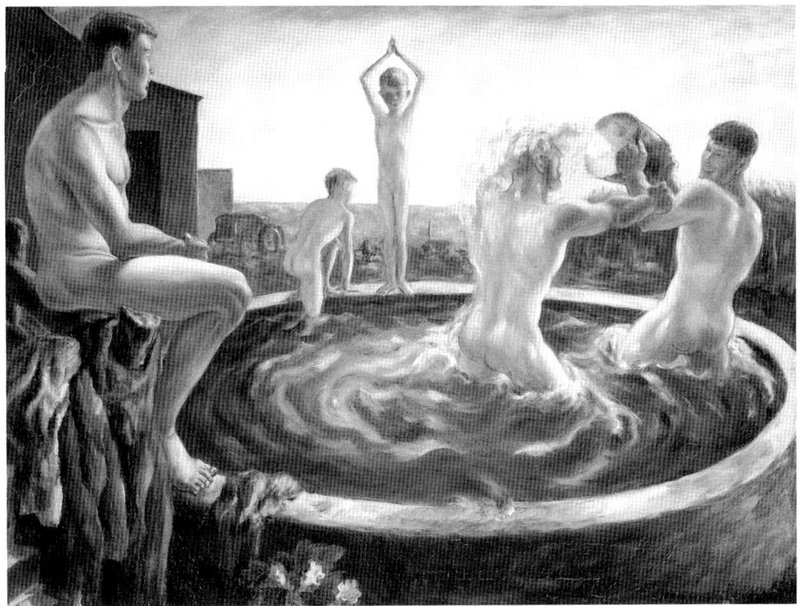

FIGURE 13
John Steuart Curry
Bathers, 1928
Oil on canvas
40 × 50 in.
John Steuart Curry Foundation.

similarities. Both are set in a farmyard around a centrally placed watering tank whose curvilinear form dominates the composition. Two principal figures, semi-immersed in the water and forming the central motif, are reinforced by groups of onlookers. The close-in viewpoints and tilted perspectives in both paintings invite our participation. The nude boy standing at the far rim of the tank in *Bathers*, arms raised overhead, creates a strong vertical focus, functioning like the windmill in *Baptism in Kansas*. The farm buildings and low-lying horizon are similarly positioned in both works. These formal parallels underscore obvious differences between the images. *Bathers* revolves around a subject that is rare in American art—the male nude. Its main figures are unselfconscious about their rugged masculine bodies, which are positioned thigh-deep in the water. Their exposed buttocks reveal that their genitalia must be exposed, too, yet the men revel without embarrassment. They play about like schoolmates, an analogy underscored by the two preadolescent boys in the background, one of whom, in climbing out of the tank, mimics the posture of the centrally positioned man. This innocent yet sexually charged camaraderie, like the unselfconsciousness of a naked Adam before the Fall, contrasts with the fully clothed minister and the woman neophyte in *Baptism in Kansas*. Their nineteenth-century appearance, bowed heads, and clasped hands connote a self-conscious modesty bordering on prudery.

Significantly, the most prominent figure in *Bathers* is the heroically proportioned male nude seated at left. He is a composite of many *ignudi* that Michelangelo painted in the margins of the Sistine Chapel ceiling to unite various episodes of Genesis, from Creation to the Flood.[36] By emphasizing his all-American male *ignudo* in *Bathers*, Curry invites comparison between the relaxed attitude of acceptance and lack of shame that this seated nude represents with the *ignudi* of Michelangelo, who call attention to depraved human nature in the scenes of the Fall and Flood that they bracket. Those scenes of impending doom and imminent salvation are the very ones that interested Curry and that he reinterpreted in midwestern settings in light of premillennial Covenanter theology. Curry suggests an ambiguous relationship to, and alienation from, the world of premillennialism by highlighting the disjunctive elements in *Baptism in Kansas* while affirming as more authentic the innocent state of *Bathers*. By emphasizing these dissociative messages in both works, Curry signals his alienation from rigid codes of premillennialism and his acceptance of a more liberal humanistic outlook.[37]

Curry also expresses spiritual ambivalence in two paintings from 1929, *Gospel Train* (color plate 15, fig. 14) and *Prayer for Grace* (color plate 18, fig. 15). Like *Baptism in Kansas*, each of these works relies for effect on an emotionally charged religious rite. In *Prayer for Grace*, overheated preaching causes a group of revivalists to fall to their knees, raise their hands, and confess their sins. Abandoning the pulpit, the minister solicitously attends to a distraught woman kneeling in the aisle. *Gospel Train*, on the other hand, portrays Pentecostal worship. The title derives from a popular nineteenth-century hymn that speaks of the blessed, secure in their salvation, riding a train bound for glory. Curry wryly alludes to this hymn by picturing a large cartoon locomotive and several Pullman cars labeled "the gospel train" tacked to the sanctuary wall behind the musicians. In both paintings, intense beams of light shine down upon the congregation, highlighting the worshipers' waving arms. While suggesting the brilliance of God's presence, these beams also may be a reference to the artificially illuminated storefront settings where revival meetings often occurred. The parallel with *Baptism in Kansas*, in which windmill, sunlight, and pigeons form similarly ambiguous allusions, is deliberate.

As in *Baptism*, Curry thrusts us into an intimate view of the action. The worm's-eye perspective in *Gospel Train* tilts the floor upward as it recedes into space, enhancing the feeling that the action is wheeling about us. Figures, cropped at the left and right margins in both paintings, and off the bottom in *Gospel Train*, indicate our proximity and confirm our involvement, not

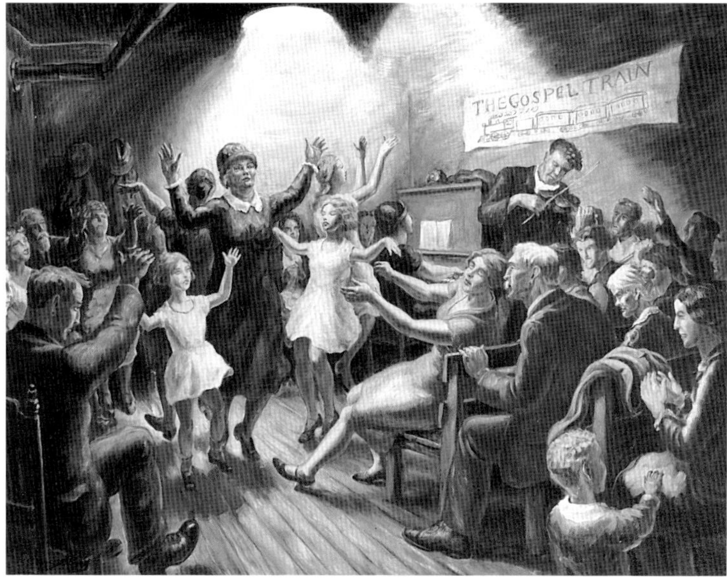

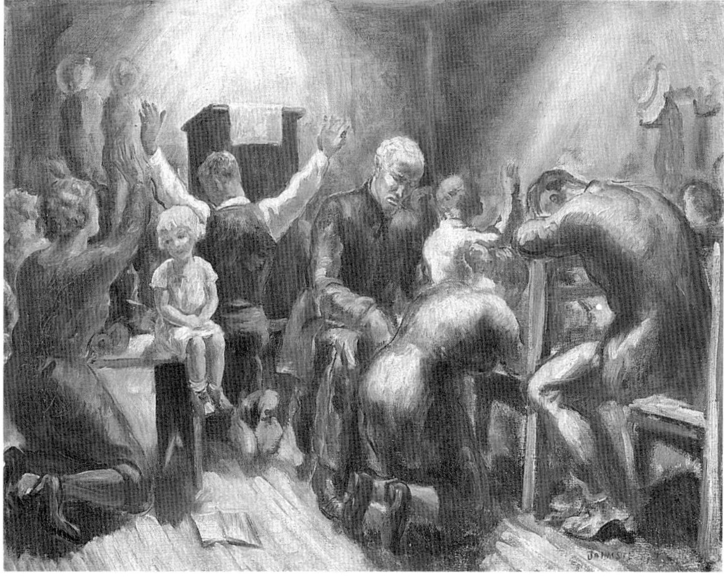

FIGURE 14 *(top)*

John Steuart Curry
Gospel Train, 1929
Oil on canvas
40 × 52 in.
Courtesy Syracuse University Art Collection, Syracuse, New York.

FIGURE 15 *(above)*

John Steuart Curry
Prayer for Grace, 1929
Oil on canvas
20 × 26 in.
Jean Chapman Born

as discrete observers but as participating Pentecostals. Curry saw several parallels between Pentecostals and Covenanters, making the former a logical choice for his art. These parallels are found in the doctrines of Justification, Adoption, and Sanctification as defined in the Shorter Catechism, which Curry memorized as a boy. Covenanters and Pentecostals alike believed that a sinful—and, therefore, damned—humanity had to be made righteous (Justification) and acceptable to God (Adoption). This could only be accomplished through God's freely sovereign act, manifested in an outpouring of grace (Sanctification) upon humanity. What distinguished Pentecostals from Covenanters was the intensely personal way in which Pentecostals experienced Sanctification—through speaking in tongues and accompanying emotional states; these were regarded as proof that God's chosen people had received his grace.

This tripartite doctrine—Justification, Adoption, and Sanctification—became the focal point around which Pentecostal groups rallied. And important centers where their rallies were held were Topeka, Kansas, and St. Joseph, Missouri, cities Curry visited in 1929 and where he developed themes he would use in these paintings.[38] Given his interest in religion and his scrupulous concern for "doing the right thing" mentioned in letters prior to 1928, Curry would have recognized that Covenanter theology, however different in practice from Pentecostalism, had much in common with it. Searching in 1928 and 1929 for an artistic vocabulary to express his changing attitude toward religion, Curry saw in Pentecostalism dramatic visual opportunities that were lacking in staid Covenanter worship yet linked theologically with the religion of his youth.

The figures of the little girls in *Gospel Train* and *Prayer for Grace* reveal Curry's attitude. When he attended Pentecostal gatherings, he frequently took along his young adopted daughter, Ellen, who later recalled that she grew up believing such settings were perfectly natural.[39] Her naïveté and childlike acceptance could not have escaped Curry, preoccupied as he was in questioning his relationship to his Covenanter roots and busily formulating an artistic means to express his thoughts. In *Gospel Train,* beneath the brilliant light shining down on the whirling figures, two girls, a blonde and a redhead, are the focus of attention. Clothed, respectively, in vivid yellow and lime green dresses, they glow as if casting light on those around them. In *Prayer for Grace,* Curry contrasts the kneeling, weeping adults with the lone figure of a cherubic little girl, who sits calmly with folded hands, head inclined, silently watching the proceedings. The children in both works create a contrast with the somberly clad adults who surround them. Echoing Jesus' admonition, "[U]nless you change and become like little children you will never enter the kingdom of heaven,"[40] their appearance seems to distinguish them from the world and action of Pentecostal adults. It also raises a question: What is to be taken more seriously, the innocent world of childhood or the peripatetic world of religious enthusiasts, whether Pentecostal or Covenanter?

As the United States moved from isolationism toward engagement in World War II, Curry's religious pictures shifted from revealing personal attitudes toward a concern with America's response to this international crisis. *The Return of Private Davis from the Argonne* (1928–40, color plate 12) and *Our Good Earth* (1940–41, color plate 63, fig. 16) reflect this shift.[41]

The Return of Private Davis was inspired by an event in 1918 that, as suggested earlier, deeply affected Curry—the death in combat of his high-school friend William Davis. Among the first Kansans killed in the Argonne, Davis received full military honors after his body was returned home for burial. Curry made several sketches of the grave site immediately after the funeral, tucking them away until 1926, when, moved by his visit to American soldiers' cemeteries northeast of Paris, at Aisne-Marne, Oise-Aisne, Meuse-Argonne, and Saint-Mihiel, he began the painting.[42] A watercolor sketch shows a few mourners clustered about a bare coffin; in the distance, a solitary tree and the silhouette of a chapel indicate that the scene takes place on the open prairie. In the finished painting, a crowd of mourners includes a division of uniformed soldiers, regimental flags and rifles in hand for a final salute. Beyond the crowd, parked cars separate the circularly clustered mourners from the seemingly boundless prairie. Draped with the American flag, the coffin is banked with floral tributes. Heads of mourners barely visible in the foreground indicate a continuously encircling crowd abutting our space. At center, a black-clad minister offers a final benediction.

The circular arrangement of enframing automobiles, cropped figures, and centrally positioned minister repeats the composition of *Baptism in Kansas,* which also deals with a rite of passage. Although the funeral might allude to the Christian belief in resurrection, Curry makes no reference to this concept. Instead, he borrows the device of the open grave underscoring the finality of death from *Burial at Ornans* (1849–50) by the French realist Gustave Courbet, a painting he studied in the Louvre the same year he visited the American cemeteries. Curry took twelve years to complete this canvas, by which time America was inching toward involvement in another war. Perhaps he wanted the work to convey a warning of the ultimate consequences of war; that message rings clearly in *Parade to War* (1938, color plate 61), which shows ranks of eagerly marching soldiers sporting death-mask faces.

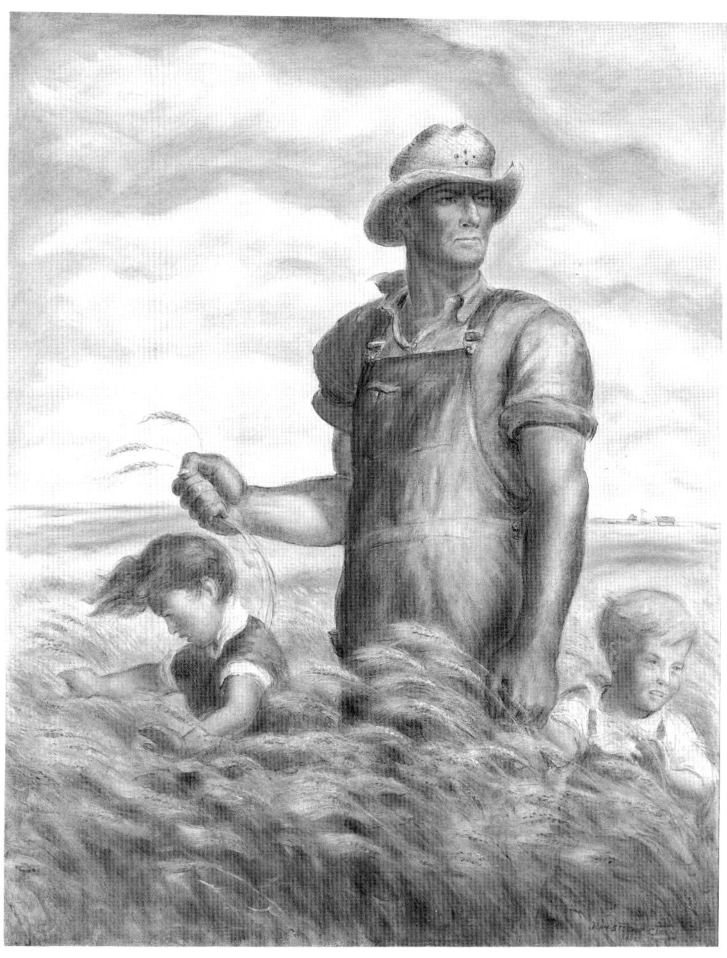

FIGURE 16
John Steuart Curry
Our Good Earth, 1940–41
Oil and tempera on canvas
52 × 40 in.
College of Agricultural and Life Sciences, University of Wisconsin–Madison

Once America entered the war, Curry attempted to rally to the cause, reworking a 1938 lithograph into a painting entitled *Our Good Earth* for a U.S. Department of the Treasury propaganda poster. In it, a muscular young farmer stands in a wheat field, two children playing at his side. This stalwart figure symbolizes the power of American agriculture, geared up to feed millions of GIs fighting to defend the earth for future generations, as represented by the innocent children. The farmer's noble form recalls idealized images of Renaissance humanism and, by implication, the optimistic understanding of human nature implicit in Renaissance art. Specifically, the figure recalls

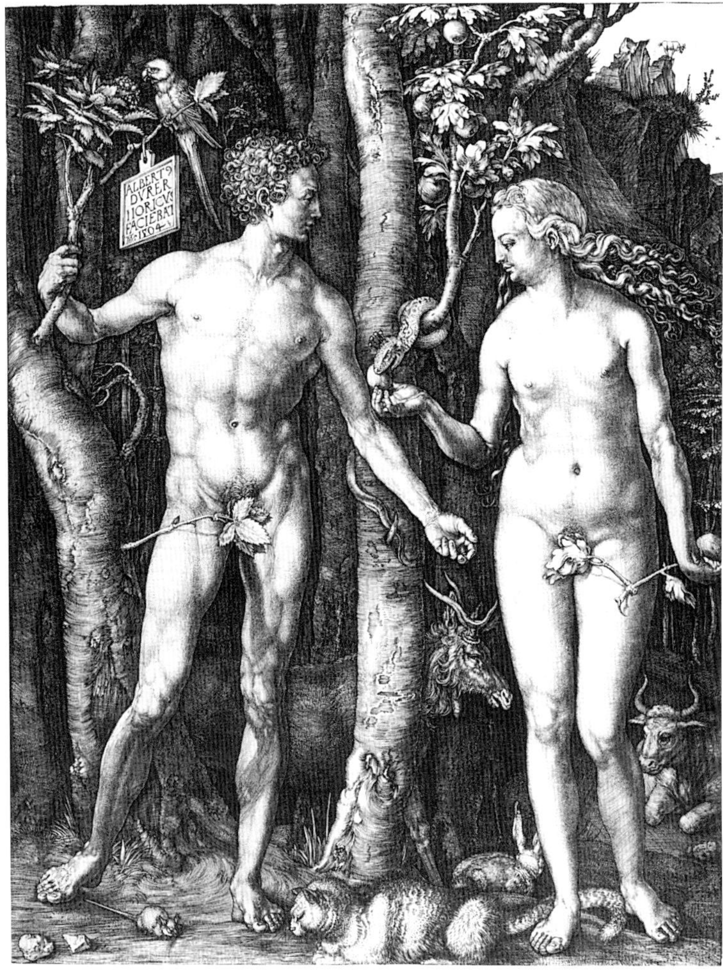

FIGURE 17

Albrecht Dürer (German, 1471–1528)

Adam and Eve, 1504

Wood engraving
9⅞ × 7⅝ in.
Courtesy Trustees of the British Museum, London.
Photograph © British Museum.

Adam in Albrecht Dürer's engraving *Adam and Eve* (1504, fig. 17). Although Curry reverses the pose and places the left arm closer to the body, the turn of the farmer's head, his flexed right arm holding agricultural produce, and his massive upper body all stem from Dürer.

Curry's source in Dürer is significant. The Adam legend represented the quintessential Christian symbol for the human condition: Created innocent and living harmoniously with all things, Adam, the master of Eden, sinned after eating the forbidden fruit. Because of this disobedience, conflict, suffering, and death became the human condition. Yet artists and theologians of the Renaissance believed that humanity, despite its fallen state, retained an inherent dignity, even nobility, made possible by God's forgiving act of grace through Jesus Christ. Covenanters filtered the Adam story through the lens of strict Calvinism, adding the doctrine of predestination—the idea that one is either among the elect or forever damned—and making it mandatory to pray and await a sign of election offering assurance of salvation. Curry scrupulously observed this dogma in his youth, sought answers to his growing questions about it with the Moodyites as a young man, and then rejected it—and organized religion in general—by the end of the 1920s, affected by both World War I and his experiences in Paris. Despite this rejection, Curry continued using religious imagery in a wide body of work. Despondent at the outbreak of World War II, yet called upon to use his talents for the war effort, he resorted to familiar imagery to make his point. *Our Good Earth* portrays a virile farmer, the American Adam, holding out the promise of an abundant harvest. Yet this same farmer is also representative of fallen humanity, raising this crop to feed GIs who will, after all, fight and kill in the war. The inherent irony in the image was made emphatic when the Department of the Treasury reproduced his lithograph with the caption "Our Good Earth—Keep It Ours" to underscore the wartime struggle.

Curry's abiding sense of despair over the potential human toll in the war contributed to his weakening health. During the war years, high blood pressure aggravated his depression and forced him to undergo an operation in 1945. Resting with Thomas Hart Benton on Martha's Vineyard in the autumn of that year, he brooded over his failure as an artist.[43] Curry died ten months later. By that time, regionalism was no longer a dominant art style. But Curry's extensive use of religious imagery and his grounding in premillennial theology and the culture of Kansas Protestantism mark his work as an enduring testimony to the transformation of religious thought in American culture during a complex and turbulent time.

NOTES

1. For an earlier study of the relationship between Curry and his religious background viewed within the wider context of regionalism and religious fundamentalism, see Robert L. Gambone, "That Old Time Religion: Painting, Drawing and the Culture of Revivalism in America, 1915–1940," Ph.D. diss., University of Minnesota, 1985. See also idem, *Art and Popular Religion in Evangelical America, 1915–1940* (Knoxville: University of Tennessee Press, 1989).

2. Although Curry's parents were strict Scots Covenanters, they were atypical Kansas farm folk in that they had traveled to Europe for their honeymoon, returning with several color reproductions of works by Giovanni Bellini and Peter Paul Rubens as well as a reproduction volume of Gustave Doré engravings. As a boy, Curry studied these and recalled them years later when, as a student at Geneva College, he decided to dedicate himself to a career in commercial art. Writing to his mother in January 1919, he asked that she save the Doré volume: "I really am beginning to appreciate a few things we had but did not know of till now." Curry to Margaret Curry, 20 January 1919, Curry Papers, Archives of American Art, Smithsonian Institution, Washington, D.C. (hereafter cited as Curry Papers/AAA), microfilm roll 2714. Doré's Bible illustrations vividly depicted events from the life of Jesus as recounted in the Gospels and about which Curry heard ministers expound. Well before he received formal training in art, he would have understood that religious art, or thematic art whose underlying context was inspired by religious stories, constituted an important source of creativity for artists working in the Western tradition.

3. So named because of their allegiance to the Solemn League and Covenant of 1557 pledged by all members, Scots Covenanters professed belief in the Calvinist doctrines of predestination, election, and divine retribution for sin. See, for example, "The Shorter Catechism," in *The Constitution of the United Presbyterian Church in the United States of America* (unpaginated, n.d.) Later in life Curry noted, "I was raised on hard work and the Shorter Catechism," adding that his artistic style "was formed on the King James version of the Bible." See Thomas Craven, "John Steuart Curry," *Scribner's Magazine* 103, no. 1 (January 1938): 37, 41. Curry's premillennialist family attended two church services every Sunday, participated as deacons in church functions, taught in the church Sabbath school, and served as missionaries on the church's gospel team. See Curry Papers/AAA, "Excerpts from J. S. Curry letters to Mildred Curry Fike, October 1972," typescript, box 1 of 1, acq. 11/75, folder 19, "Letters 1917 John Steuart Curry to Family." See also Delber H. Elliot, ed., *Semi-Centennial of the Reformed Presbyterian Church of Winchester, Kansas* (unpaginated, 1918). Asked what her husband most remembered about this religious upbringing, Kathleen Curry noted, "If you don't stand firm and do the right thing you're going to be damned. That was always there." See Bret Waller, "An Interview with Mrs. John Steuart Curry," *Kansas Quarterly* 2, no. 4 (fall 1970): 6–12.

4. See letters dated 3 January, 3 February, 12 February, and 23 April 1917, Curry Papers/AAA, microfilm roll 2714, Gift of Mrs. Stanley R. Fike.

5. Curry to Margaret Curry, 12 November 1916, Curry Papers/AAA, microfilm roll 2714.

6. Curry to Margaret Curry, 3 February 1917, Curry Papers/AAA, microfilm roll 2714.

7. In a letter to Mary Wickerham 23 July 1945, Curry recalled his mother discussing the Reverend Coulter's prophecy. Curry Papers/AAA, microfilm roll 164.

8. Late in 1917, Curry wrote to his parents: "Read my Propetsy [*sic*]. To keep up with the times I have been reading the prophets. In Revelations the plage [*sic*] will be the storms of the earth of about a talents weight. Sounds like shrapnel. Daniel in the 12th chapter and the last says there will be much running to and fro. And after the word has been scattered over the world the end will be. The last three verses: After the daily sacrifice and the abomination which is set up it will be 1335 days till the new heaven and the new earth. Could the daily sacrifice mean the lives lost each day and the abomination which maketh desolate is surely understood [?] Europe looks pretty bad and [illegible]. After that it shall be 1335 days. That is the way I translate the scriptures. The 4th [verse] ends '[M]any shall run to and fro and knowledge shall be increased.' The word is certainly translated and knowledge is certainly manifest. But Daniel is told to visit his lot in that day. Perhaps this is the great trouble that the world is doomed to go through." Curry to his parents, 10 December 1917, Curry Papers/AAA, microfilm roll 2714.

9. "The 4th. Presbyterian Church is raising a Co. They have an army officer drilling them; and last night the head recruiting Capt. spoke. . . . I really will join something. The Co. at the Church with the Moody Institute fellows will be a fine place to get in." Curry to his parents, 12 March 1917, Curry Papers/AAA, microfilm roll 2714. There is no evidence that Curry eventually either joined the army with his Moodyite friends or enlisted on his own.

10. Curry's letters home from Geneva College are filled with references to attending numerous church services, receiving communion, sermon topics that interested him, and visits to, and Sunday dinners with, various ministers. See, for example, letters to his parents jointly, 15 May and 1 June 1919; and to Margaret Curry, 22 September, 20 October, and 26 December 1919. Curry served as an artist for the college yearbook; the illustrations are preserved in Curry Papers/AAA, microfilm roll 2803.

11. Bret Waller, "An Interview with Mrs. Daniel Schuster," *Kansas Quarterly* 2, no. 4 (fall 1970): 15.

12. Writing to his mother on 2 February 1920, Curry noted: "Mr. Dunn told me in his discourse on truth, and that is what he talked about, truth, to read my Bible. You know artists aren't supposed to be Christians. I never heard a more honest and real sermon than yesterday's." Curry Papers/AAA, microfilm roll 2714.

13. The secular urban pleasures to which Curry was drawn in Paris are evident in his various drawings and watercolors from this period, many of which are reproduced in Laurence E. Schmeckebier, *John Steuart Curry's Pageant of America* (New York: American Artists Group, 1943), 43–44. Reproduced there are *Montmartre, Paris Cafe, The Belle of the Dome,* and *Streetwalker.*

14. Most writers who have addressed religious aspects of Curry's art regard his pictures as reflections of a vengeful or majestic God-in-nature theme, which they broadly attribute to the influence of his

Scots Covenanter rearing. See, for example, Irma B. Jaffe, "Religious Content in the Painting of John Steuart Curry," *Winterthur Portfolio* 22, no. 1 (spring 1987): 23–45. Such commentary, however, does not take sufficiently into account the theologically complex and nuanced ways in which Curry presented, critiqued, and continually reassessed his own theological tradition, especially with respect to premillennialist ideas.

15. Sylvan Cole, Jr., ed., *The Lithographs of John Steuart Curry: A Catalogue Raisonné* (New York: Associated American Artists, 1976), pl. 6, gives the title of the lithograph as *Flight into Egypt* and ascribes a date of "ca. 1928," noting that the series consists of a numbered edition of 100 lithographs. Ann C. Madonia, *Prairie Visions and Circus Wonders: The Complete Lithographic Suite of John Steuart Curry,* exh. cat. (Davenport, Iowa: Davenport Art Gallery, 1980), 17, agrees with this date and title. Joseph S. Czestochowski, *John Steuart Curry and Grant Wood: A Portrait of Rural America* (Columbia: University of Missouri Press with the Cedar Rapids Art Association, 1981), 77, gives the title as *Family Migrates* and assigns a date of 1929. Schmeckebier, *Pageant,* 125–26, reproduces both the oil painting and the initial sketch for it with the title *The Ne'er Do Well,* dated to 1929. Czestochowski relies on Schmeckebier for his date but notes that the title *Family Migrates* is a contemporary one recorded in *Handbook of the American Artists Group,* vol. 2, no. 1555 (New York: American Artists Group, 1936), 23.

16. See, for example, Schmeckebier, *Pageant,* 106–203; Craven, "John Steuart Curry," 36–44, 96, 98; Czestochowski, *Portrait of Rural America,* 14–15; and Lawrence Alloway, "The Recovery of Regionalism: John Steuart Curry," *Art in America* 64, no. 4 (July–August 1976): 70–73.

17. Schmeckebier, *Pageant,* 40.

18. As Curry wrote to his father on 12 November 1916: "Mighty glad to get your letter telling me about the farm. But I believe I would rather draw a picture of myself shoveling manure than do it." Curry Papers/AAA, microfilm roll 2714, frame 498. In a 1970 interview, Curry's wife revealed that "John left the farm as quickly as he could. He didn't want to be a farmer, though he loved to go back, naturally. But then, after he'd been there a little time, he'd leave again. The drama and poetry of his youth would come back to him, but he wasn't prepared to stay. . . . I don't think he would have wanted to go back and live on the farm again." Waller, "Interview with Mrs. John Steuart Curry," 8.

19. For an excellent review of the state of agriculture in the 1920s and 1930s, see Wayne D. Rasmussen, ed., *Agriculture in the United States* (New York: Random House, 1975).

20. Schmeckebier, *Pageant,* 61; Czestochowski, *Portrait of Rural America,* 121.

21. Notes from Curry's slide lectures on the techniques of the Renaissance reveal that he well understood the conflation of biblical event and present historical time that many artists used to make their works resonate with their contemporaries. Lecturing on Benozzo Gozzoli's fresco *The Shame of Noah,* for example, Curry states: "Notice that he puts his biblical characters into a setting which is logical and in keeping not with the characters of the Bible but with the artist himself. The artist, in other words, has used a biblical story in such a way as to make it very real and meaningful to his public. Both the artist and his public are acquainted with these farm activities, then into this Florentine scene the artist puts these people from the Bible, and as a result these people . . . and the story which they portray become as real as anything else in the contemporary life of the artist." "Lecture notes on 48 slides for use in public lectures, slide 16," typescript Curry Papers/AAA, microfilm roll 168.

22. Curry's Christmas card bearing an image with the title *The Family Migrates* is preserved in the Harry Wickey Papers, Archives of American Art, Smithsonian Institution, Washington, D.C., microfilm roll 3683. There is no date on the card, which falls in a sequence of papers that indicate it was made at some time between 1928 and 1931.

23. *Sanctuary* was first done as an oil painting in 1935. In 1944 Curry reversed the composition and issued a large-format (11¾ × 15¾ in.) lithograph of this work. That same year, he produced a second, smaller version (9 × 11⅞ in.), which followed the same compositional alignment as the painting. *Mississippi Noah* was first produced as a lithograph in 1932, followed three years later by a revised lithographic version and an oil on canvas. The oil is entitled simply *The Mississippi.* All three works have the same composition, although the 1932 stone (9¾ × 13⅝ in.) is softer and lighter in effect than the 1935 stone (9⅞ × 13¾ in.), which exhibits slight alterations in the tree floating in the river and the debris clinging to the base of the roof. Both Cole, *Lithographs,* 24, and Madonia, *Prairie Visions,* 20, give 1935 as the date for the second stone. Czestochowski, *Portrait of Rural America,* 123, dates the second stone "ca. 1934."

24. Floyd Benjamin Streeter, *The Kaw: The Heart of a Nation* (New York: Farrar and Rinehart, 1941), 4–5.

25. Schmeckebier, *Pageant,* 118, 120, reproduces only this one sketch but writes that "Curry made several sketches similar to this one of a flood in the Kaw River valley near Lawrence, Kansas, while home in 1929."

26. Caused by heavy winter snows and almost continuous rainfall during the spring of 1927, the flood is estimated to have destroyed hundreds of thousands of homes, wiped out crops throughout the Mississippi River basin, killed countless numbers of livestock, and left six hundred thousand people homeless. See David Burner, *Herbert Hoover: The Public Life* (New York: Alfred A. Knopf, 1979), 193–94.

27. Ibid., 195.

28. Ibid., 196.

29. Schmeckebier, *Pageant,* 267, equates the gesture of supplication with both prayer and terror. Matthew Baigell, "The Relevancy of Curry's Paintings of Black Freedom," *Kansas Quarterly* 2, no. 4 (fall 1970): 21, suggests a crucifixion.

30. Curry to Margit Varga, 28 February 1942, Curry Papers/AAA, microfilm roll 166.

31. In an undated letter, Margaret Curry wrote: "Why don't you paint a Covenanter Communion, John, you know how it is—the pulpit with its flowers, the long table in white—the quiet solemnity over all as we gather for the memorial service. I'm sure it is something Benton and Wood couldn't possibly do." Curry Papers/AAA, microfilm roll 166.

32. The fact that one of these birds sports grayish black feathers rather than pure white plumes calls to mind the portion of the Noah episode in the Book of Genesis when the rain has stopped falling. Noah first

sends out a raven, which is unable to find a resting spot; later he dispatches a white dove, which eventually returns with an olive branch in its beak, signifying that it has found land. In Christian exegesis, these two birds are often seen to represent the contest between sin (the raven) and peace and grace (the dove). Curry may have intended this analogy in his painting, which after all depicts a Christian rite during which the "stain of original sin" is wiped away so that the life of grace can commence. Given Curry's intense interest in the Flood theme, the link between the two doves in *Baptism in Kansas* and the Noah story reinforces the relationship of Curry's religious paintings with his lithographs of 1928–35.

33. Stewart G. Cole, *The History of Fundamentalism* (New York: R. R. Smith, 1931), 132; Winthrop Hudson, *Religion in America* (New York: Scribner's Sons, 1965), 122–44; Robert G. Torbet, *A History of the Baptists* (Philadelphia: Judson Press, 1950), 287–92.

34. Cole, *Fundamentalism,* 133.

35. Ibid., 137.

36. Schmeckebier, *Pageant,* 59, was the first to note the connection between the pose and form of the figure in Curry's painting and the work of Michelangelo.

37. Curry relied on compositional and visual parallels to link a 1932 lithograph, *Baptism in Big Stranger Creek,* with *Baptism in Kansas* and, by implication, with the ambiguous religious message conveyed in that painting.

38. Schmeckebier, *Pageant,* 100, records that *Gospel Train* was one of the first works the artist produced during his trip back to Kansas in 1929. Curry traveled the short distance to St. Joseph, Missouri, to sketch a Pentecostal meeting.

39. Waller, "Interview with Mrs. Daniel Schuster": 18.

40. Matthew 18:3.

41. Curry also painted an important commission for the December 1941 issue of *Esquire* magazine, entitled *The Light of the World,* that uses a religious theme and betrays his anxiety. The work is discussed in Gambone, *Art and Popular Religion,* 213–19.

42. Schmeckebier, *Pageant,* 59, reproduces one watercolor sketch, noting that there were several other preliminary studies. He adds on page 254 that related sketches were made at the time of Curry's 1926 cemetery visits.

43. Benton quotes Curry as saying: "Maybe I'd have done better to stay on the farm. No one seems interested in my pictures. . . . I lived at the wrong time." See Thomas Hart Benton, *An Artist in America,* 4th rev. ed. (Columbia: University of Missouri Press, 1983), 321.

John Steuart Curry and the Pathos of Modern Life

PAINTINGS OF THE OUTCAST AND THE DISPOSSESSED

PATRICIA JUNKER

All men are from the ground,
and Adam was created of the dust.
In the fulness of his knowledge the Lord distinguished them and
appointed their different ways;
some of them he blessed and exalted,
And some of them he made holy and brought near to himself;
but some of them he cursed and brought low,
and he turned them out of their place.
As clay in the hand of the potter—for all his ways are as he
pleases—so men are in the hand of him who made them, to give
them as he decides.

SIRACH 33: 10–13

"For the past few years I have felt the need to enliven my imagination by new contacts with American life."[1] So John Steuart Curry told members of the Art Association of Madison, Wisconsin, in January 1937, just after he had arrived in that city to assume the post of artist-in-residence at the University of Wisconsin. In part, Curry's quest involved uprooting himself, sometimes relocating only briefly but sometimes for extended periods. He was, he admitted to his Madison audience, a restless artist. He required the periodic change of environment, the experience of the little known or the completely unfamiliar.

In his art and in his life, Curry was, as he put it, driven "past the ballyhooers of the status quo . . . to the attractions at the other end of the fair ground" (fig. 1).[2] Even from his vantage point in the east coast artists' colony of Westport, Connecticut, where he spent the first half of his career, Curry saw that the most revealing aspects of the American social landscape were to be found not on his immediate horizon but well beyond—in the Midwest—and on the fringe. The restive, even dispossessed farm families he encountered for the first time on his 1929 trip home to Kansas were one kind of marginal group. The circus troupers with whom the artist traveled in 1932 were another. These types inspired a group of genre paintings whose subjects may easily be regarded as the American scene's sideshow elements. Migrant road menders, uprooted farmers, and circus itinerants all ran counter to traditional views of family and community. Their often pathetic lives and heroic survival served Curry once again as living parables of faith tested—as emphatic reminders that God works in strange ways.

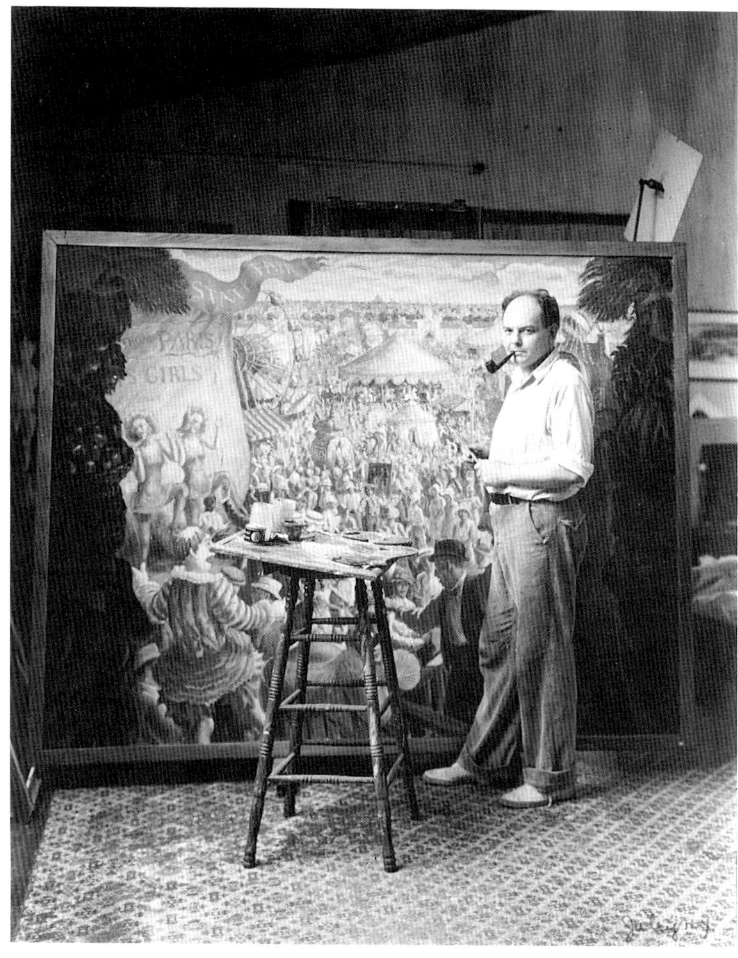

FIGURE 1
Curry at work on *State Fair* in his Westport, Connecticut, studio, 1928. Photograph courtesy Mrs. John Steuart Curry.

The Midwest in 1929

For an artist who was from the outset of his career inextricably connected with rural Kansas, Curry had been in his formative years fairly peripatetic. In the course of a decade, his art studies had taken him from Kansas City to Chicago to Beaver Falls, Pennsylvania, to Leonia, New Jersey, to New York City, and, finally, to Paris. By the late fall of 1928, when his *Baptism in Kansas* (color plate 10) brought him national attention as *the* painter of the Midwest scene, the artist had not seen his childhood home in years.

But in the summer of 1929 Curry went home to Kansas, and he went home *to paint.* He went in faith and with the hope that the experience would bring forth new, potent subjects—paintings of a freshness, directness, immediacy, and intensity to surpass even the acclaimed *Baptism.* The east coast critics eagerly awaited his next brilliantly illuminating stories of life "out there," and his new patron, Gertrude Vanderbilt Whitney, lent financial support.[3] A subsidy from Mrs. Whitney through Juliana Force, director of the Whitney Studio Galleries, had made the trip possible. Curry must have known that work resulting from his travels home would be much anticipated, the basis, it was undoubtedly understood, for a solo exhibition at the Whitney Studio Galleries—a highly visible showcase for new talent. He was, he knew, poised for success. He was ready to embrace the Midwest experience.

Curry's snapshots, drawings, and watercolor studies show that the summer of 1929 offered high drama indeed. He saw the devastation left by a tornado that had passed through Winchester, Kansas, very near his family's farm; the ravages of floods in the Kaw River valley; and the dust storms in Oklahoma. The effects of these events on those who endured them became the focus of his art over the next year.

When Curry saw and sketched the dust storms that turned the Oklahoma skies a dull yellow, he must have recognized in them a powerful destructive force, but it was one that could not easily be summarized pictorially. They were not like the tornado or raging floodwaters, singularly dramatic meteorological events. But Curry knew what the dust storms meant in the lives of farmers, even if in 1929 he could not have understood the magnitude of the social and economic calamity that they would eventually wreak on the Middle West. They represented a malignancy that was only slowly revealed through the lives of those who suffered by them.

Typically, Curry saw this natural disaster in human terms, creating one oil, *The Ne'er Do Well* (fig. 2), that suggests economic upheaval. In this canvas Curry produced, in fact, one of American art's first images of the homeless taking to the roadways of Kansas and Oklahoma—an image that would within but a few years become emblematic of the Great Depression in America.

The artist told his biographer, Laurence Schmeckebier, that *The Ne'er Do Well* represented migrants, the homeless people he saw on the roads around his father's farm in Dunavant.[4] Curry knew that these were farmers forced off their land by drought—by circumstances beyond their control—and forced into the kind of hopeless wandering westward that John Steinbeck would describe so movingly a decade later in *The Grapes of Wrath.* Not surprisingly, he recognized in such scenes a story that

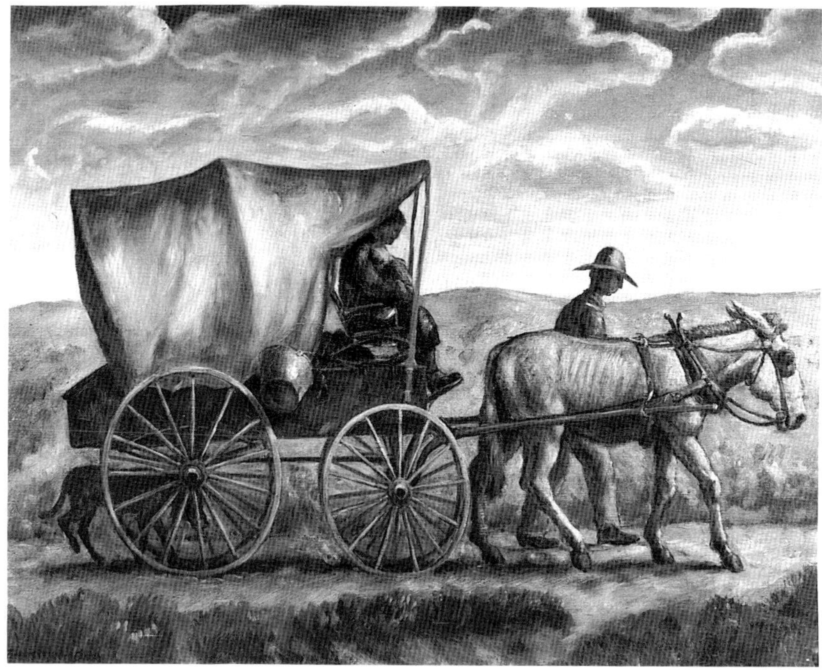

FIGURE 2

John Steuart Curry
The Ne'er Do Well, 1929
Oil on canvas
20 × 26 in.
Courtesy Whitney Museum of American Art, New York. Gift of Gertrude Vanderbilt Whitney.

was as old and emotionally charged as Scripture, from the Old Testament trials of Job or the Exodus of the Israelites to the New Testament flight into Egypt of the Holy Family. He distilled from this distinctly modern and midwestern scene a timeless image of the dispossessed.

The linking here of the moral tale of the profligate and the plight of the uprooted farmer is an especially potent conjunction, one that points up the conceptual breadth, the compelling ambiguity that is a hallmark of all of Curry's best, most expressive work. By his title, *The Ne'er Do Well,* Curry presents a story that is far from simple, predictable, or straightforward, one that is as complicated as life itself. Here is pure pathos without the benefit of explanation. We are not told where blame for this sorry state of affairs lies—whether the subjects' situation is the result of inner weakness or external forces. There is no moralizing or overt propagandizing here. Action is focused solely on the human condition. The poignant scene—a man, woman, and child exiled from their homeland—challenges belief in the Protestant work ethic. Indeed, the image calls into question the foundations of Americans' faith. This is a painting that resonates with conflicting emotions. It is an image capable of eliciting, simultaneously, pain, pity, scorn, and shame.

In the same year, Curry painted *Road-workers' Camp* (fig. 3) and addressed the subject of the uprooted on a larger scale and with more narrative detail. The scene is a curious one—an encampment in a farmer's pasture. There, among the grazing horses and mules eating grain from a trough, some squatters have parked their tin lizzie and rickety homemade trailers and pitched a tent. All seem quite at home in these strange surroundings. In the center-foreground a young man reclines in a leisurely way upon a broken and ragged chaise, smoking and listening to the declarations of the stern young woman who sits beside him, a baby in her arm. At left, a woman tends to a small boy and another woman washes dishes or laundry; both of them wear kitchen aprons. At right, a group of men are absorbed in a game of cards. Children and dogs run playfully through the campsite. It is late in the day. Everyone has eaten, as discarded tin cans attest, and they are at ease.

Who are these people? Curry himself may have wondered when he encountered such a group on his drive through Oklahoma. They are *road-workers,* his title tells us, a term that is itself ambiguous. This varied group—infants, toddlers, mothers, young men, and even an elderly couple—represented in 1929 a new kind of nomad born of the automobile. Road menders traversed the Midwest throughout the summer months, repairing the rudimentary dirt roads that made up the growing network of auto ways. By 1929, road menders, and autocampers, too, were an increasingly common sight on western roadways, squatting in barnyards or orchards or pitching their tents in managed campgrounds.[5]

The circumstances by which these folk have taken to "working the road" cannot be discerned. Depending upon the viewer's experience, they might be either vagrants or gypsies, arousing curiosity, amusement, or indignation. Or, to one who knew farm life, as Curry did, this image might well have spurred a different, sobering thought. Here was a sign: a scene auguring national social upheaval. "A half million people moving over the country; a million more restive, ready to move; ten million more feeling the first nervousness," as John Steinbeck would later describe it.[6]

Yet at first glance, the image is not a bleak one. Indeed, the painting is far more evocative for its quaint and charming vignettes. It offers an unsettling twist on the eighteenth-century fête galante, a delightful picnic piece, a rustic party, a lively and detailed study of human interaction. Curry has a richly layered story to tell here, an approach he favored over one-sided social satire or propaganda.[7] The realities of his subject were, in fact, many-faceted, as complex as the individual lives represented in

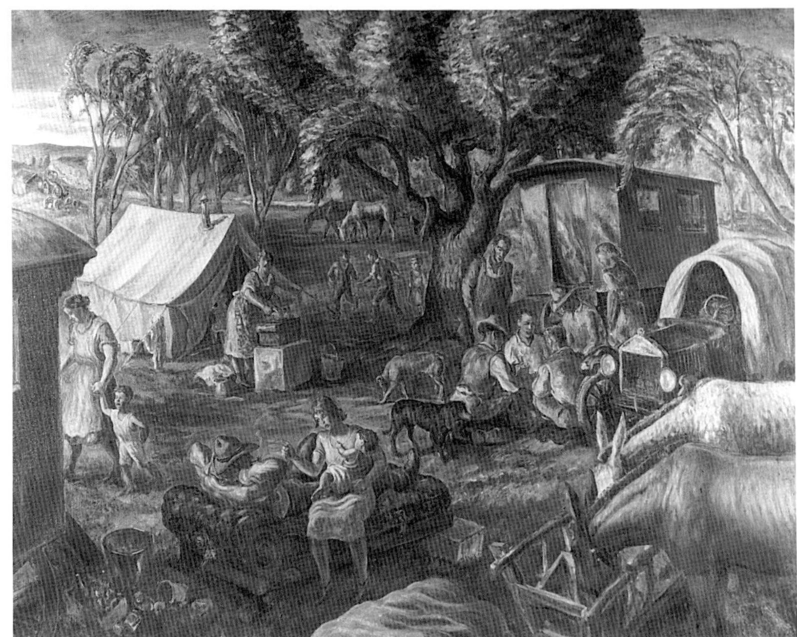

FIGURE 3

John Steuart Curry
Road-workers' Camp, 1929
Oil on canvas
40¼ × 52¼ in.
Courtesy Sheldon Memorial Art Gallery, University of Nebraska, Lincoln. F. M. Hall Collection.

this scene. Each figure is subtly delineated, drawn with attention to nuances of pose and movement that reveal character: A stalwart mother seems dutifully to take a reluctant young boy to wash up; a self-righteous young wife appears to chastise her amused husband. These are not the miserable and the wretched; there is spirit in the figures. Whatever their travails, these nomads have managed to transfer into their unconventional life on the road all the conventions of family and community. Men enjoy camaraderie. Women maintain discipline and cleanliness. If there is redemption in the lives of the uprooted, it lies, Curry suggests here, in the basic human instinct to preserve order to the last. And if there is hope in this scene, it rests in Americans' innate belief in the promise of the open road.

The social implications of *Road-workers' Camp* went unnoticed by New York critics. Curry's Kansas and Oklahoma pictures were praised for their "witty presentation" and "their picturesqueness" when they were exhibited at the Whitney Studio Galleries in January 1930, in the artist's first solo show.[8] Florence Kellog, writing about *Road-workers' Camp* in *Survey,* saw it as an updated version of Currier and Ives: "There is the road gang—men, women, children, pets and household equipment jumbled together in an arcadian community—so reminiscent of those prints of the sixties of the pioneer camps."[9] Life "out there," as

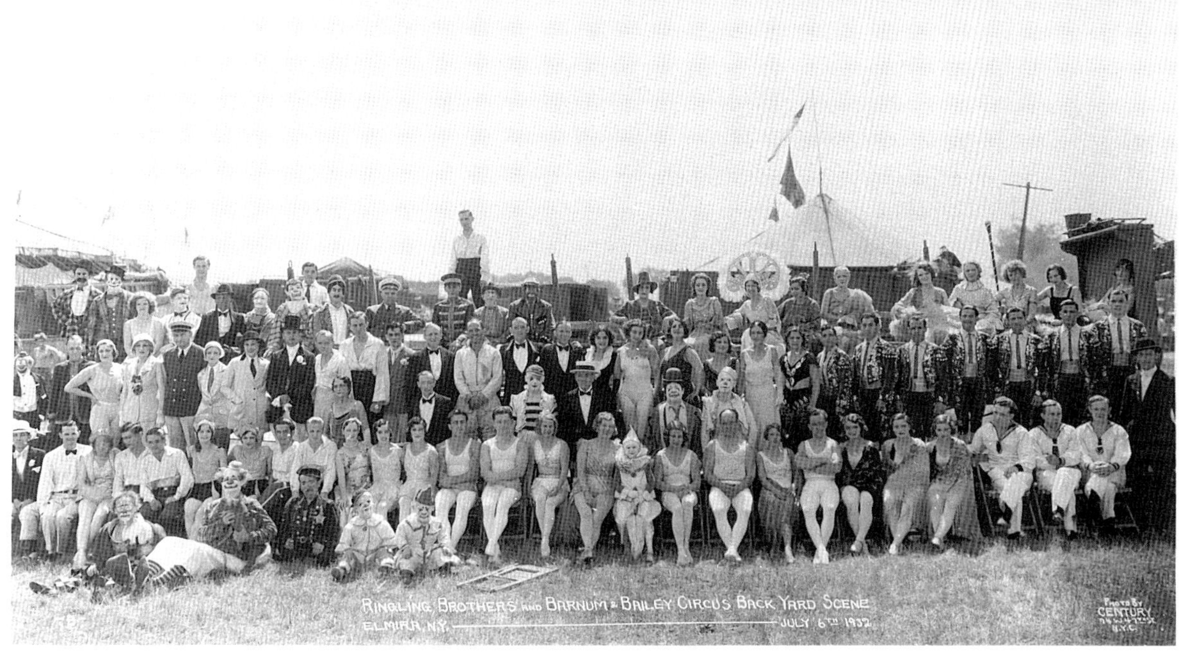

FIGURE 4

Ringling Brothers and Barnum & Bailey Circus backyard scene, Elmira, New York, 6 July 1932. Photograph by Century Flashlight, Edward J. Kelty, President. Courtesy Robert L. Parkinson Library and Research Center, Circus World Museum, Baraboo, Wisconsin. Tom M. Scaperlanda Circus Collection.

Kellog titled her article, was far enough removed from the common experience of his audience that it seemed the stuff of a delightful romance. Few knew these road workers. "They appear in early evening and depart at the first streak of dawn, and none knows whence or whither," observed one Minnesota writer of such itinerants in 1924; "We only know that they have been."[10] And few had given them pictorial form. "One must give Curry credit for setting out boldly to paint things for which other artists have not yet abandoned their apples," wrote a Chicago critic of Curry's Kansas paintings in January 1931.[11] In choosing this subject, the artist was ahead of his time. Yet, in retrospect, his pictorial language—the language of romance, of the picturesque—softens its impact. In part, Curry's presentation reflects his time—its ambivalence toward social change, its limited view of what were then unknowable fates. It would take several years of nationwide instability, and the realism of photographers such as Walker Evans and Dorothea Lange, to make the sad truth of the Dust Bowl clear.

The Circus

Last week I saw [Curry's] exhibit in Kansas City and feel just as I did when I saw the pictures in Topeka last year. . . . I feel Mr. Curry has a great force in delineating the subjects he has chosen, but to say he portrays the "spirit" of Kansas is entirely wrong, I think. To be sure, we have cyclones, gospel trains, the medicine man. And the man hunt. . . . But why paint outstanding friekish [sic] **subjects and call them the "spirit" of Kansas? . . . I wonder if this sort of work that Mr. Curry is doing is not just a phase through which he will pass, and will soon come to see something beautiful in life and particularly life in Kansas.**[12]

By early 1932 Curry was, as he put it, struggling to get "on my feet."[13] The Depression was taking its toll. Maynard Walker, his agent at Ferargil Galleries in New York, had sought to help by launching a campaign to encourage patronage in the Middle West, sending the artist's Kansas paintings on tour to Chicago, St. Louis, Topeka, Kansas City, and several smaller cities in Kansas through 1931. But the effort had failed miserably, producing no sales and forcing Curry to endure the criticism of his fellow Kansans, people such as Mrs. Henry J. Allen of Wichita, the art-collecting wife of a former governor, quoted above—the kind of patron on whom Curry and Walker had pinned their hopes. Kansans, it seemed, had endured enough of their state's darker side to disincline them from embracing it in their pictures.

Economic troubles were no doubt hastening the breakup of Curry's already troubled marriage. Separated from his wife, Clara, who was by then incapacitated by depression, Curry was living in New York trying to paint, searching for inspiration.[14] He had little money for a return to Kansas, but he was desperate for "a new viewpoint of life."[15] In April 1932 he joined up with the Ringling Brothers and Barnum & Bailey Circus as the troupe embarked from Manhattan on its spring tour, traveling with it during the next two months from Washington, D.C., through Pennsylvania and New Jersey, and departing in mid-June after it finished its swing through southern Connecticut (fig. 4).[16]

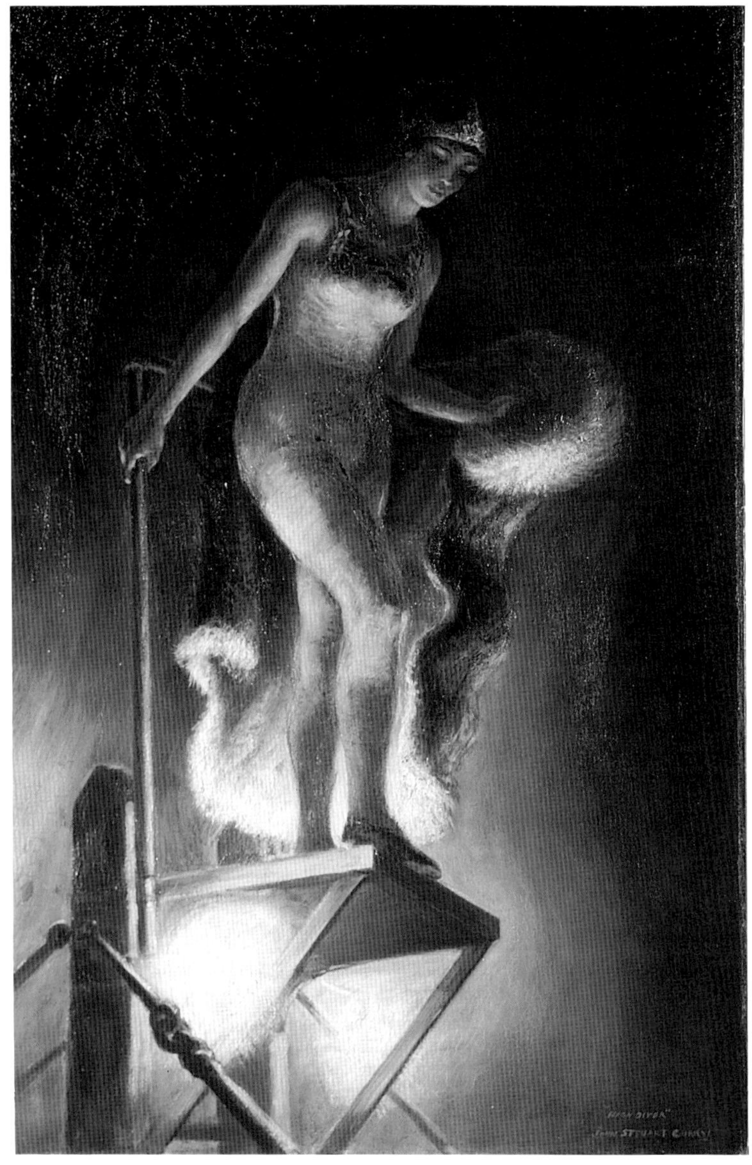

FIGURE 5

John Steuart Curry
Female Acrobat (High Diver), 1929–37
Oil on canvas
45¼ × 30 in.
Mrs. John Steuart Curry.

The subject of the circus had proven to be a rich one for artists as separate in time and as divergent in style as Honoré Daumier, Henri de Toulouse-Lautrec, Henri Matisse, Pablo Picasso, and Curry's American contemporary, Walt Kuhn. Curry would have been drawn to the color and action of the circus for their own sake—as he was to the *State Fair* (color plate 13), painted in 1928 from his vivid memories of that grand event as he had known it in childhood. The circus—and circus aerialists especially—had intrigued Curry for years. In 1931 he was still at work on a large oil entitled *Female Acrobat* (1929–37, fig. 5), which he had included in the celebrated group show of circus paintings that marked his debut with the Whitney Studio Galleries in April 1929. *The Circus in Paint,* organized by Juliana Force, was a clever exhibition, set in a make-believe circus tent, complete with a sawdust floor and circus props. Edward Alden Jewell in the *New York Times* had declared the show "Mrs. Force's crowning achievement of the season," while William E. McCormick, writing in the *New York American,* called the exhibition:

the merriest and most original picture show—in its setting—that I can recall. Between Mrs. Force's original idea for the exhibition and its execution by Louis Bouche, the transformation of these galleries . . . is done with real wit and with such high good humor that the "W. S. G. World Famous Circus" is the artistic tour de force of the season of 1928–1929.

Henry McBride of the *New York Sun* saw in *The Circus in Paint* the promise of commercial success for all involved: "[A]ll the pictures in this exhibition look attractive," he wrote, "and any one of them seems to insinuate that that spectator is an idiot who does not start in immediately to collecting circus pictures."[17] Curry's *Female Acrobat,* though it went unsold, nevertheless helped secure his relationship with Mrs. Force and Mrs. Whitney.[18] In August 1931, obviously looking to refine *Female Acrobat,* Curry inquired of *Billboard* magazine where and how he might observe high-diving acts that featured a "dive through flames" at night performances. He may well have followed the magazine editor's advice to take in the acclaimed high-diving act featured in Billy Ritchie's Water Circus when it appeared that month at Olympic Park in Irvington, New Jersey.[19]

Precisely why Curry chose to follow the circus is not clear, though his irrepressible desire for renewing experiences was most certainly at the heart of this move in the spring of 1932. Curry's own statements suggest that he saw the circus as a kind of vital studio in which to observe and sketch humans and animals in action. "The circus is one of the most colorful phases of the American scene," he told a reporter in 1933. "I am immensely drawn by the excitement and movement."[20] In reviewing Curry's circus work in April 1933, *Time* magazine suggested

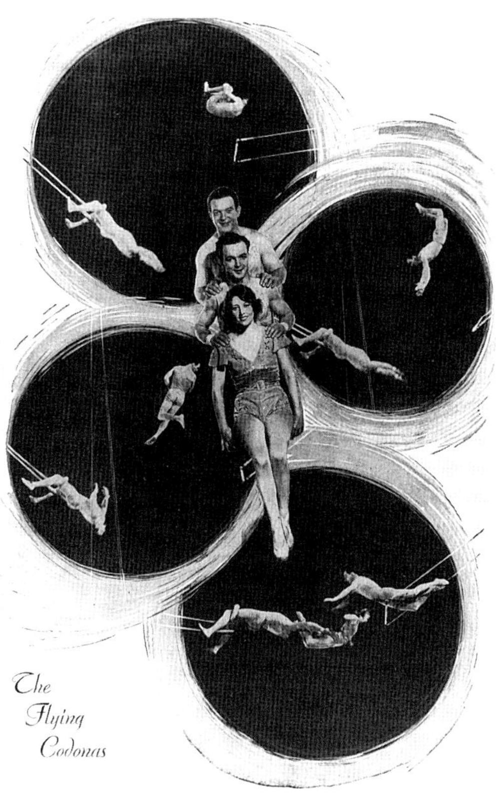

FIGURE 6

The Flying Codonas, from the *Magazine and Daily Review,* Ringling Brothers and Barnum & Bailey Circus, 1932. Photo courtesy Robert L. Parkinson Library and Research Center, Circus World Museum, Baraboo, Wisconsin.

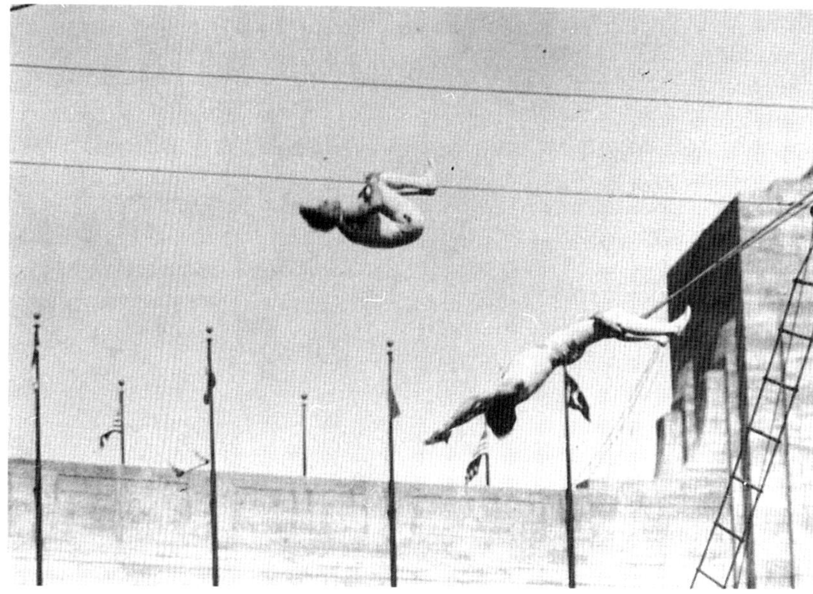

FIGURE 7

Alfredo and Lalo Codona practicing the aerial triple somersault, Los Angeles Memorial Coliseum, n.d. Photograph by M. F. Weaver, Los Angeles. Courtesy Robert L. Parkinson Library and Research Center, Circus World Museum, Baraboo, Wisconsin.

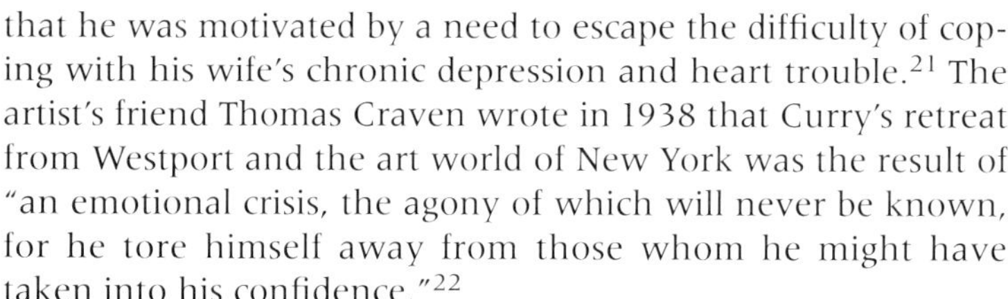

that he was motivated by a need to escape the difficulty of coping with his wife's chronic depression and heart trouble.[21] The artist's friend Thomas Craven wrote in 1938 that Curry's retreat from Westport and the art world of New York was the result of "an emotional crisis, the agony of which will never be known, for he tore himself away from those whom he might have taken into his confidence."[22]

Alfredo Codona, the famous trapeze artist, told *Esquire* magazine in 1937 that it was he who had made the necessary arrangements for Curry to join the Ringling Brothers and Barnum & Bailey troupe for the 1932 tour.[23] How the two men had become acquainted is not known, but, as noted, Curry had long been fascinated with aerialists as a subject for dynamic pictures, and he may have sought out the celebrated flyer. It is conceivable that he realized the singular marketing potential in a series of circus pictures. The wide popularity of the circus may well have suggested that paintings of its headliners—especially of its famous aerialists—held the promise of sure sales. For Codona, the prospect of being painted by a celebrated American artist must have seemed a great honor.

Codona would have seen the advantage in having an artist of Curry's renown make paintings and lithographs of the aerial act for which he and his brother, Lalo, and their partner, Vera Bruce, were known the world over (fig. 6). In 1932 Codona was the only man alive who could perform a triple somersault off the trapeze, to be caught by Lalo as he swung by his knees—truly a death-defying feat (fig. 7). "The history of the triple somersault is a history of death," Codona had told a reporter in 1930. "As long as there have been circuses, there have been men and women whose sole ambition was to accomplish three full turns in the air.... The triple somersault has killed more persons than all other dangerous circus acts combined."[24] Alfredo and Vera—who would become his third wife in September 1932—were celebrated, too, for the aerial trick known as the "double pass" or the "passing leap," a spectacular display of the team's perfect coordination. Swinging some sixty feet above the arena, Vera would catapult from Lalo's hands to Alfredo's trapeze just as Alfredo was soaring over her into his brother's hands.[25] The length of their swing was reportedly some eighteen to twenty-four inches longer

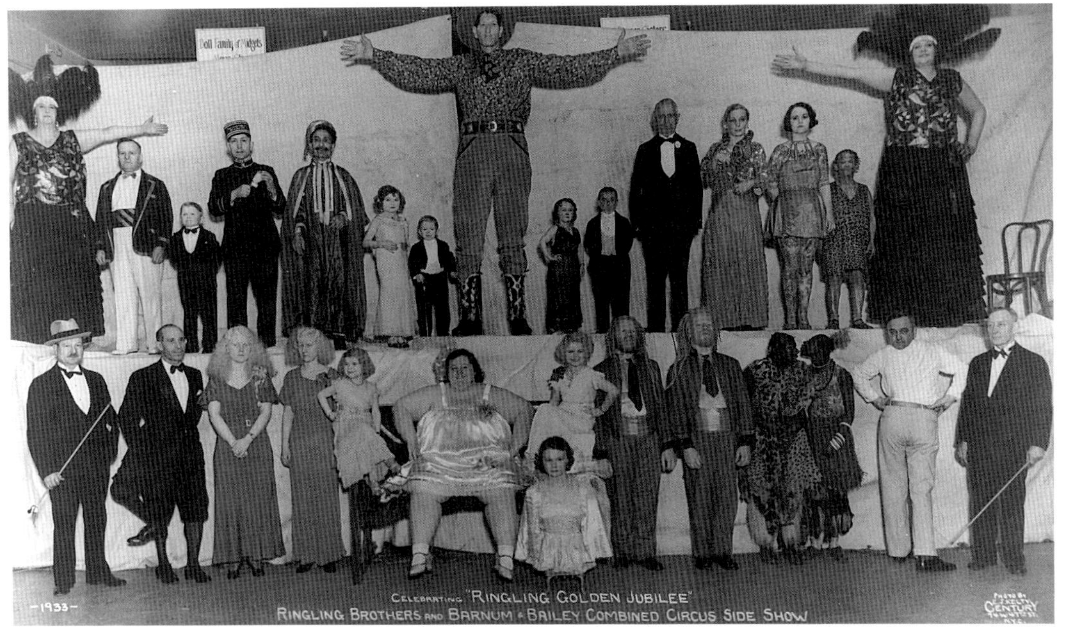

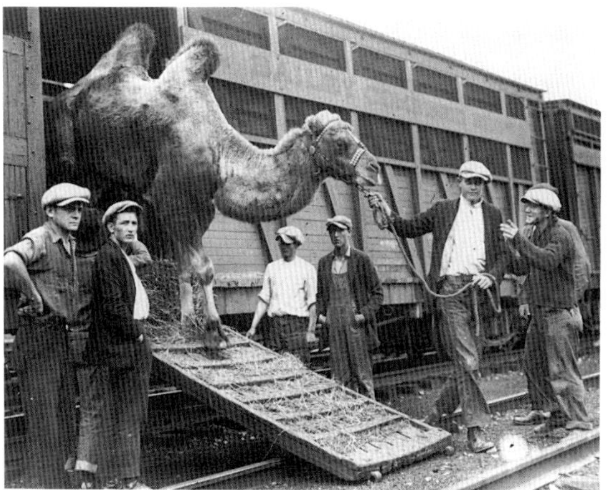

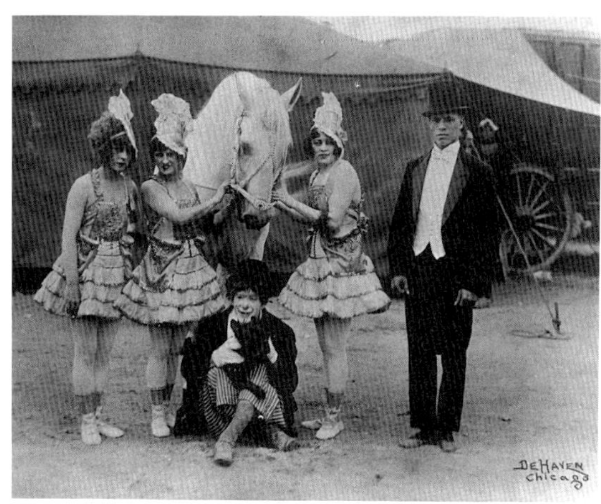

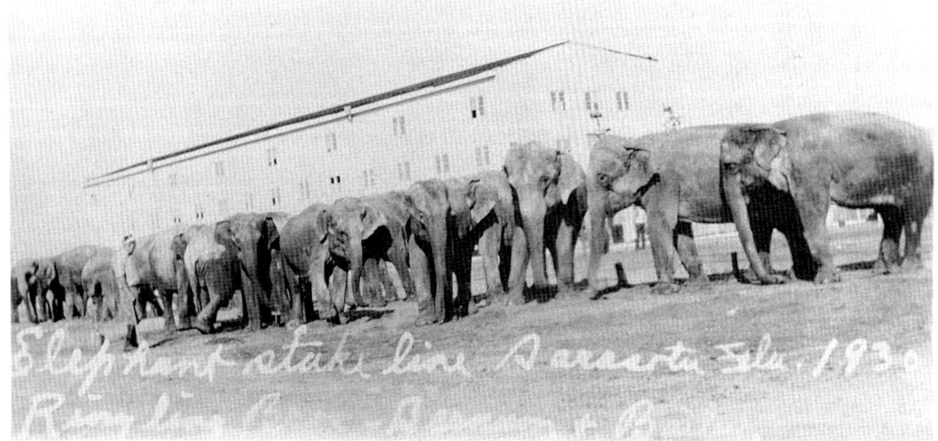

FIGURE 8 *(top)*

Ringling Brothers and Barnum & Bailey combined circus sideshow, 1933. Photograph by Edward J. Kelty, Century Flashlight. Courtesy Robert L. Parkinson Library and Research Center, Circus World Museum, Baraboo, Wisconsin.

FIGURE 9 *(middle left)*

Unloading the circus train, 1930. Photograph courtesy Robert L. Parkinson Library and Research Center, Circus World Museum, Baraboo, Wisconsin.

FIGURE 11 *(middle right)*

Orrin Davenport Troupe. Photograph by DeHaven Studios, Chicago. Courtesy Robert L. Parkinson Library and Research Center, Circus World Museum, Baraboo, Wisconsin.

FIGURE 10 *(bottom)*

Elephant stake line, Ringling Brothers and Barnum & Bailey Circus, Sarasota, Florida, 1930. Photograph by Eddie Jackson, Macon, Georgia. Courtesy Robert L. Parkinson Library and Research Center, Circus World Museum, Baraboo, Wisconsin.

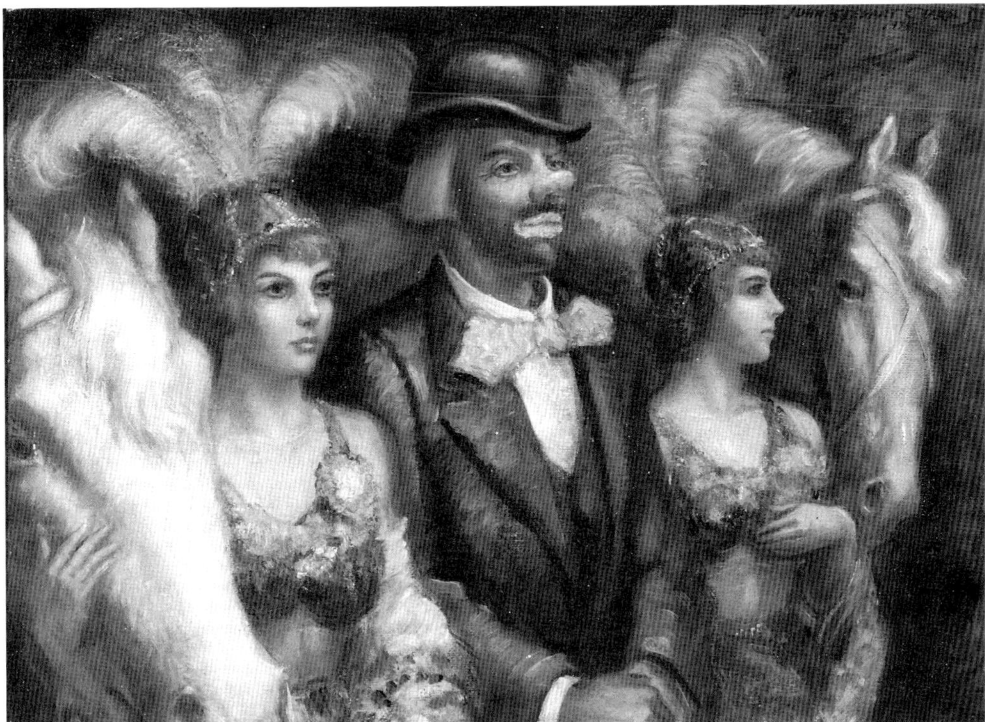

FIGURE 12

John Steuart Curry
Clown and Equestrians, 1935
Oil on fiber board
18 × 25 in.
Photograph courtesy Sotheby's.

than that of any other act, a fact that "may have accentuated the impression of a longer and more birdlike flight than is noticeable in other acts," one fan recounted.[26] The Codonas had been featured in several Hollywood films, and Alfredo and Vera had been stand-ins for Johnny Weissmuller and Maureen O'Sullivan in *Tarzan, the Ape Man* (1932). The Codonas were superstars.

It seems reasonable to assume that Curry's personal troubles at this time might have led him to focus on the poignant human stories that were revealed to him in the wings under the big top and on the back lots. A few of the circus paintings reflect an effort to probe the psyches of circus performers. *The Runway* (1932, color plate 26) offers a rare insider's close-up view of the performers offstage. He produced studies, too, of circus "freaks," such as the 800-pound Baby Ruth Pontico and the eight-foot-tall Von Droyson sisters—people whose peculiar physical attributes, sadly, provided their source of livelihood and hence stood, in some respects, as a measure of their self-worth (fig. 8).[27] Certainly the pick-up crews that the circus troupe relied on in each town offered subjects rich in pathos, but Curry did not paint them. Typically, those who filled out such crews were children of the Depression, the sad-faced, starving youths who look out from photographs (fig. 9), hardly wide-eyed romantics fantasizing about living the circus star's glamorous life. Only rarely, as in *At the Circus* (1936, color plate 38), did Curry look out at the common folks who made up the big-top audience, to remind viewers that the circus was Everyman's entertainment.

He also created a few lively studies of big-top animals, the finest being the oil *Elephants* (1932, color plate 24) and the drawings related to it. For Curry the circus was filled with forms, both human and animal, to be studied and drawn (fig. 10).

Most of Curry's circus paintings, however, feature the great athletes, the headliners, the center-ring acts—the high-wire Wallendas, the amazing acrobatic equestrians of the Orrin Davenport Troupe (figs. 11 and 12), the wild-cat trainer Clyde Beatty, and of course the aerialists, including Tamara and the Codonas. And Curry focused much of his attention and energy on the Codonas.

The attraction of the Codonas is easily understandable. Their trapeze act, the climax of each evening's program, provided a rich sensory experience and an emotional wringing that was not soon forgotten, as one writer's vivid recollection attests:

It is suffocatingly hot in the big top. For hours the sun has been beating down on the canvas roof. A vast heat is rising from the thousands of persons in the circus audience. The huge tent has been darkened and a dozen high-powered beams are playing fierce light and more heat on the two performers waiting their cue. This is a three-ring circus . . . but for the aerial trapeze work of the internationally famous Codonas . . . all rings have been cleared. Even the blasé candy-butchers and the clowns

are silent: watch it, everybody, this is something! A swift look passes between the two up high in the rigging, two lithe bodies in tights. Ready? With his eyes, Alfredo Codona, the *Flieger,* or flyer, shoots the question across the thirty-odd feet to his brother Lalo, the *Fanger,* or catcher. The silent answer is: Ready.

The house is hushed. The circus band swings into rhythmic brass music—Alfredo and Lalo poise a moment on their trapezes, which hang perpendicularly now. Suddenly, both start swinging. Alfredo . . . hangs from the bar of his trapeze by his hands. But Lalo . . . is suspended from the bar of his trapeze by his knees—so that his hands will be free to catch his brother. Both performers synchronize their swings for so much depends here on split-second timing, but the swings are not of the same length. Long years of practice have taught the brothers to sense the moment when the swings are shooting through the air in precisely the relation necessary for the successful completion of the act. Alfredo is at the top of his swing, high near the roof of the tent—when he lets go the trapeze.

He hurtles up—turns a somersault in the air—shoots up still higher and turns a second somersault—

Here Lalo, swinging by his knees, has reached the top of his swing, and is beginning to drop. But the act is not over. Alfredo, still fifty feet from the ground, tosses his body over for a *third* somersault and falls doubled up but with his arms straightening out, toward the strong hands of Lalo, tensed to receive him! A breath-taking moment and Lalo's hands have closed over Alfredo's wrists. Applause breaks out from an astounded and delighted audience.[28]

It was the breathtaking flying of the Codonas and not their offstage lives that captivated Curry. Not that their personal stories did not offer the material of high drama and art. Any portraitist of Curry's intelligence could have seen that Alfredo Codona embodied the "show must go on" spirit of the circus. In April 1932, when Curry befriended the great flyer, Alfredo was still grieving for his second wife, the famous circus aerialist Lillian Leitzel, who a few months earlier had fallen to her death during a performance on her signature apparatus, the high rings, in Copenhagen. Alfredo also suffered, in the weeks that Curry observed him, from intense physical pain, having torn a muscle in his right arm one night at Madison Square Garden, at the outset of the tour.[29]

Nonetheless, Alfredo persevered. "The recuperative powers of circus people form one of the cheering things of life," he once said.[30] He had been raised in the circus, trained by his acrobat father from the time he could walk to perform at the highest level of endurance. He was able to overcome physical limitations, distraction, and fear to execute successfully, night after night, a feat that was unsurpassed by any athlete: hurtling himself through the air at the astonishing speed of sixty-two miles per hour, managing to make three rotations before connecting with the outstretched hands of his brother as Lalo flew on the other trapeze. To hear Alfredo describe it, the triple somersault was as much an act of sheer will as it was one of physical strength. "At a propulsion of more than sixty miles an hour," he once explained, "the body is traveling so fast that by the time the second revolution is reached, the space gauges of the brain have ceased to function properly." He continued:

The body is going faster than it can be controlled, and for a split instant one loses all knowledge of time, space, distance or surroundings. Then, in another split instant, as the body begins to fall and slows slightly with the third somersault, that ability to gauge must be regained, so that when the performer breaks out of the third revolution and toward the hands of the catcher, his brain must be clear again. It is a lack of clarity here which causes death.[31]

Alfredo freely admitted that he nightly fought the "invisible demon" of the circus tent—what the performers called "casting," the psychological transgressions that threatened an athlete's life. "It has to do with that part of an instant when the mind seems to let go, to refuse longer to hold to the terrific burden of concentration which has been placed upon it," he told an interviewer. "It is like a sharp knife struck suddenly against a set of tightly drawn strings. . . . Why it happens, or how it happens, a performer rarely knows."[32]

Clearly, Codona was a fascinating character and an intriguing portrait subject. Yet Curry must have seen that straightforward portraiture was too limited a vehicle to encompass the full dimensions of this amazing man.

"My particular interest was in the Codona flying trapeze act," Curry told a reporter for the *Bridgeport Sunday Post.* "To capture and understand the swift and intricate rhythm of that act took long and close observation. In Philadelphia I saw twelve straight performances of that act. After each movement I would make a quick sketch and later develop it from my knowledge and memory. Alfredo Codona greatly assisted me by showing me the different catches and explaining the difficult movements."[33] Curry also had the benefit of numerous publicity photographs that caught the critical moment of each of the Codonas' aerial feats.

The Codonas' look and style were distinctive, and their fans knew it. One observer claimed:

I consider that in the main their superiority in each instance should be attributed to that wonderful and quite exceptional "lift" which they possessed owing to the remarkable power

and development of their arms and back. This "lift" enabled them to rise materially higher than the ordinary performer when they released their hold of the swinging trapeze, thus affording them a greater space of time, after executing their somersaults, in which to finish the remainder of their particular feat.... Furthermore, Alfredo possessed—quite apart from his skill as a showman—the great advantage of a most attractive appearance, a lithe and perfect figure and a beautifully developed body.[34]

Curry's close study of the Codonas reflects his great respect for accuracy. The transcendent quality of their act lay, for Curry, embedded in the athletes' particular forms and specific movements, which he mined assiduously for insight into the human spirit.

His fascination with the Codonas also demonstrates Curry's complete absorption in the pictorial challenges presented him by the circus generally and by the aerialists specifically. "It took a week of observation before I could sort the confusion of the show into pictorial form," he said. "I was faced with the problem, as in the Codona act, of giving motion and rhythm to flying figures without the aid of a ground plane, as seen through a maze of ropes, poles, and bright lights."[35] The Codonas offered the artist, quite literally, a new perspective—a means of throwing off the conventions of picture-making—horizon, linear perspective, local color—and of working toward a fresh, dynamic design: Curry watched not from the floor of the arena but from the aerialists' platform. He was afforded a proximity to the flyers that no other observer had known, and he saw them removed from any familiar frame of reference—in an ambiguous space, enveloped in an otherworldly aura of light. Studying them, Curry was himself ungrounded, forced to consider the Codonas' physical and spiritual remove from the real world, their reliance solely upon their own internal mechanisms—timing, speed, strength, concentration, will, and faith. He was forced to consider them in the abstract.

Curry's weeks of study culminated in a brilliantly colored, richly painted canvas, a spare, vertiginous composition that captures perfectly the aerialists' topsy-turvy world (color plate 25, fig. 13). The thick body of Lalo, the catcher, swings into the composition, upside down, at lower right. The compact Alfredo, in a tight tuck, almost indistinguishable as a human form, spins at upper left, rising up as he hurtles away from his bar, which drops away. At the center of the composition is the all-important void, the space that Alfredo must traverse. It is that space that represents the Codonas' synchrony and speed and daring; it represents, too, the moment of greatest fear for the spectators. All other space is undefined as the viewer looks up and into the blinding lights.

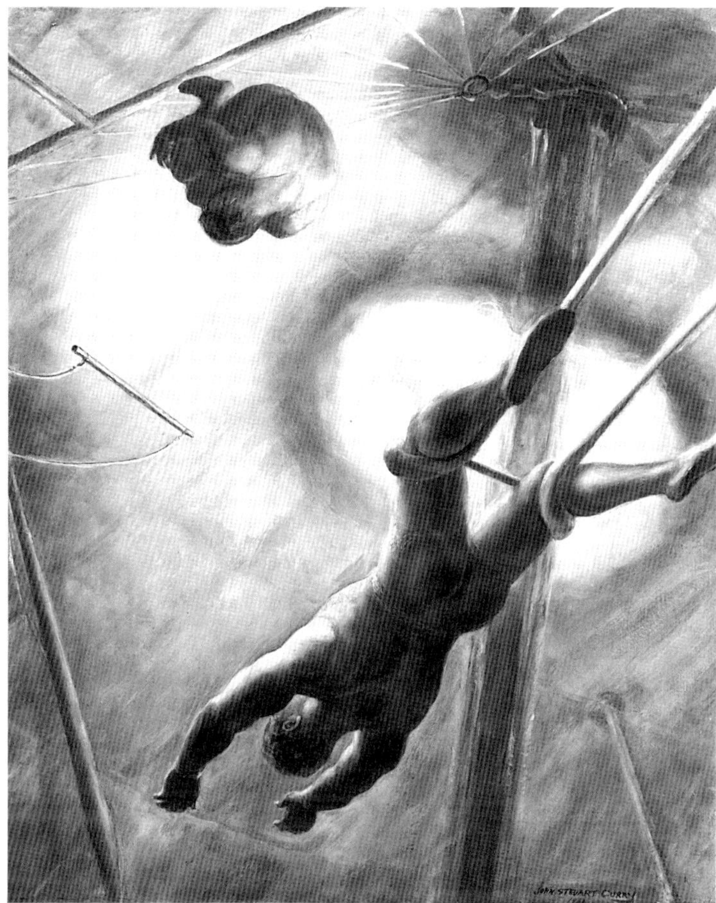

FIGURE 13

John Steuart Curry

The Flying Codonas, 1932

Tempera and oil on composition board

36 × 30 in.

Collection of Whitney Museum of American Art, New York. Purchase. Photograph © 1997: Whitney Museum of American Art

With *The Flying Codonas,* Curry found the pictorial means to elevate the particular to the universal. Although the image depicts his friends Lalo and Alfredo, it is not a portrait but a study in human form. There are few details of setting, time, or place. There are no narrative devices to communicate the background or outcome of the action. All is suspended, leaving the viewer to contemplate the meaning of the forms in space, the relationship of the figure at upper left to the one at lower right. It is an abstract design, yet it is true to the observed event.

At work on *The Flying Codonas* in the summer of 1932, Curry felt he had achieved a breakthrough. Such was his absorption in the painting that, even as he mourned wife Clara's death—she died of a weak heart in late July—and struggled with his own sense of guilt, Curry could not contain his excitement at this work-in-progress. "I wish you could come out some weekend and see what I have started," he wrote to Maynard Walker. "I have the possibilities of the greatest work I have ever done and these next two months will tell the story."[36] He submitted the canvas to the much anticipated *First Biennial Exhibition of Contemporary American Painting* at the newly opened Whitney Museum of American Art that November. The artist's enthusiasm for the work was immediately validated: Juliana Force—that great fan of the circus in paint—purchased *The Flying Codonas* for the museum's permanent collection.

Demonstrating his marketing flair, Walker opened a show of Curry's circus paintings at Ferargil Galleries on April 3, only days ahead of the arrival of the Ringling Brothers and Barnum & Bailey Circus at Madison Square Garden and the start of its 1933 season. His promotion was ingenious: The circus performers themselves were the first guests invited to preview the exhibition. The Codonas attended, along with the Reiffenach sisters equestrian team, Baby Ruth Pontico, and Hugo Zachini, the human cannonball, who was himself a painter.[37] The event brought Curry's show press attention that extended even beyond the art pages and the advantage of endorsement from the performers. "The Codonas like the exact muscular timing of their *Passing Leap," Time* magazine reported. "Baby Ruth likes the baby blue of her eyes against her light pink dress."[38] The ironic contrast between the circus people's praise and the biting comments of Curry's fellow Kansans at the unveiling of his Kansas pictures in 1931 was not lost on critics. "Unlike Kansans, [the circus stars] like Curry, call his pictures 'wonderful' despite a few technical mistakes," *Time* pointed out.[39]

Although Ferargil's much publicized preview of Curry's circus pictures may be viewed as a marketing ploy and a clever way for the artist to get even publicly with Kansans who had snubbed him, the artist's effort to cultivate interest and support among the circus subjects suggests something fundamental about his motivation. He cared deeply that the performers should find him a worthy recorder of their talents, just as he cared that Kansans should embrace him as their chronicler. He was himself very much the performer seeking validation and appreciation, not among the elite but among those who lived the trying or colorful lives that attracted him. His art was an appeal to the common man. "John's vision of Art was unusual. It was very much bound up with spectator response," as Thomas Hart Benton characterized it:

He saw his work instrumentally. His Art must move others. It must live by and through what others felt about it, by the sympathetic responses of those who faced it. The key to his character lies in this submergence of his personal ego in a concept of social function. The artist is nothing in himself. He becomes something only as the world finds meaning in his creations. That is, of course, profoundly true of all artists, though few make the humble obeisance to the fact that John Curry did. Few also search so persistently as he searched for simplicity of symbols which would carry meaning to common men—few at least in our day.[40]

For all their marketing efforts, and despite the circus performers' warm endorsement, Curry and Walker could not have been satisfied by the results of the circus exhibition. Critics were mixed in their appraisals of the work, but all seemed to see the circus series as a further step in the evolution of the artist rather than as a clear watershed. "While he has drawn on the incredibly pictorial subject matter afforded by the circus," Margaret Breuning wrote in the *New York Post,* "he has strengthened his technical achievement. His drawing evokes mass and rhythmic movement of realistic forms, his palette is richer, and his control of his means of expression, as well as of his material, far greater than in previous work."[41] Writing in the *New York Times,* the usually supportive Edward Alden Jewell was unimpressed by what he saw as labored pictures and uninspired themes. Holding them up against Curry's Kansas paintings, Jewell found the new canvases severely wanting:

To speak the unhappy truth straight out, there seems far less evocative sawdust in John Steuart Curry's "Circus" cycle... than there was *genius*... in his memorable 'Kansas' saga a few years ago. The present canvases are, to my mind, disappointing. Whatever their good points, they somehow saliently miss the clear, intense flame of creative expression that made the earlier work so inescapably vital and true.... Were it not for the Kansas pictures... one would not feel disposed to such severity. This indispensable artist will find himself again, let there be no misgivings about that.[42]

With the notable exception of *The Flying Codonas,* few of the circus pictures sold.[43] In unveiling these works, Curry's own timing was off. The deepening Depression worked against picture sales—any picture sales. And following upon the highly acclaimed and still memorable Kansas paintings, the circus subjects seemed to many critics an odd diversion for an artist whose reputation was already bound up with the idea of the Midwest.

Drawing such a distinction between the Kansas and circus pictures must have struck Curry as unfair. For to him, the circus experience, at its most fundamental level, offered only variations on those basic themes that he had encountered all his life in the Midwest and that formed the core of his art. Here, too, one encountered the poignant stories that raised questions about widely held social values while also reinforcing a sense of faith in humanity. Like the dispossessed farmers he had observed, the circus itinerants were outsiders—immigrants, for the most part—denied a place within any traditional community. They comprised their own distinct, international community that had its own social order. They endured extraordinary trials in their daily existence—worries about paychecks, salary cuts, and unemployment at season's end as well as fears of injury and the agony of chronic pain. Yet by the strength of their discipline, these athletes and entertainers surmounted human frailties and managed at times to achieve a level of physical perfection and a kind of spiritual transcendence. When Alfredo Codona put all worldly concerns and self-consciousness aside and entrusted his life to the sure timing sense and powerful hands of his brother, Lalo, he gave himself up to faith as surely as did Curry's young, exultant young woman baptized by submersion in a barnyard in Kansas. At such moments of greatest testing, circus performers—those whom ordinary people came to laugh, sneer, or marvel at—were exemplars of selflessness and faith, embodying the highest ideal of spirituality as Curry had been taught it from childhood.

What, in retrospect, did Curry's travels with the circus contribute to his art? This period of intense focus sharpened his technique, as his drawing and use of color clearly show. The brilliant hues and light effects of subsequent paintings, such as *Line Storm* (1934, color plate 33) and *Wisconsin Landscape* (1937–39, color plate 56), owe much to the color and light Curry saw under the big top. The circus also helped to spur his imagination over time, his drawings providing a source of inspiration for paintings to the very end of his life. But most important, this interlude brought forth what is arguably his most original painting, *The Flying Codonas.* It was not original in terms of subject—the circus and such spectacles had attracted artists since the seventeenth century. Curry's Kansas subjects were surely more novel. Its originality lay in its brilliant synthesis of form and idea. The ever-moving, kaleidoscopic world of the circus gave Curry the pictorial means to tell a story in a dynamic nonlinear way, free from narrative conventions—from the conventions of genre or history painting. *The Flying Codonas* cannot be termed a regionalist picture, a depiction of the American scene; it transcends specific associations with time and place. Yet it remains wholly human centered. It is a celebration of the human spirit—and a thoroughly modern painting.

NOTES

1. John Steuart Curry, "An Address before the Art Association of Madison," typescript, 6, 19 January 1937, Curry Papers, Archives of American Art, Smithsonian Institution, Washington, D.C. (hereafter cited as Curry Papers/AAA), microfilm roll 165, no frame no.

2. Ibid., 5.

3. See Florence Kellog, "Out There: Paintings by John Steuart Curry," *Survey* 64 (July 1930): 311–13. On 28 September 1929, Curry wrote to Juliana Force: "I have made no plans for showing any of the pictures I am sending you, other than the 'Baptism,' as they represent my work which you made possible during this past year." Whitney Museum of American Art Papers, Archives of American Art, Smithsonian Institution, Washington, D.C. (hereafter cited as Whitney Papers/AAA), microfilm roll N592, frame 117.

4. Laurence E. Schmeckebier, *John Steuart Curry's Pageant of America* (New York: American Artists Group, 1943), 125.

5. For a detailed study of autocampers in this period, see Warren James Belasco, *Americans on the Road: From Autocamp to Motel, 1910–1945* (Cambridge, Mass., and London: MIT Press, 1979).

6. John Steinbeck, *The Grapes of Wrath* (New York: Viking Press, 1939), 207.

7. In an article in *Art Digest* in 1935, Curry denigrated propagandists who reduce their human subjects to two-dimensional caricatures. He used the example of a sweatshop worker, who, upon seeing an exhibition of socially conscious art, voiced the unanimous disapproval of his fellow laborers, declaring: "[I]f this in reality is what the workers are, miserable beasts, then we are poor material out of which to build a new social order. . . . Cartoonists, illustrators, fashionable portrait painters are all loaded down with stock mannerisms and symbols, but none so much as the radical artist. A little intelligent observation and a more powerful art expression would arise." See Curry, "Curry's View," *Art Digest* 9, no. 20 (1 September 1935): 29.

8. Writing in the *New York Evening Post* 1 February 1930, Margaret Breuning noted that "[Curry's] stockman or roadworkers or his glimpses of prairie expanses and artesian wells do not occur on our immediate horizon but they have a convincing air of veracity both in their witty presentation and in their individuality of technical expression" (hereafter cited as Breuning, *Post*). Henry McBride, writing the same day in the *New York Sun,* described *Road-workers' Camp* as "a subject in which picturesqueness triumphantly overrides our modern mechanics." Compare these comments with those of a Topeka journalist, writing four years later: "Perhaps another reason some of us do not enjoy such pictures is because that of which they treat is too near to us. The ugliness of pioneer life on the prairies is something we want to forget until a longer vista of time has softened and mellowed the memories." See Carl P. Bolmar, "Gleanings from the Field of Art," *Topeka State Journal,* 7 January 1933.

9. Kellog, "Out There": 311.

10. Clifford C. Leck, "Tourist Camps," *Minnesota Municipalities,* October 1924; as quoted in Belasco, *Americans on the Road,* 75.

11. Tom Vickerman, "Of Pigs, Tornadoes, and Tawny Yellow Paintings," *Chicago Post,* 4 January 1931.

12. Mrs. Henry J. Allen, Wichita, Kansas, to William Allen White, 16 December 1931, Curry Papers/AAA, microfilm roll 2743, frame 46.

13. Curry to Maynard Walker, 1 August 1932, Maynard Walker Gallery Papers, Archives of American Art, Smithsonian Institution, Washington, D.C. (hereafter cited as Walker Papers/AAA), microfilm roll 2023, frames 24–25.

14. Clara Derrick Curry's nervous breakdown and the emotional crisis that it brought forth in Curry have been widely cited as the principal reasons why he joined the circus that spring. See "Kansan at the Circus," *Time* 21, no. 15 (10 April 1933): 42.

15. Curry, "Address": 6.

16. The 1932 itinerary is preserved in the Ringling Brothers and Barnum & Bailey Circus route book, Robert L. Parkinson Library and Research Center, Circus World Museum, Baraboo, Wisconsin. I am grateful to Fred Dahlinger, the center's director, for sharing his great knowledge of the Ringling circus and for bringing source material to my attention.

17. Edward Alden Jewell, "Art and the Circus," *New York Times,* 7 April 1929; William E. McCormick, "'Circus in Paint,' in Whitney Galleries," *New York American,* undated clipping in Whitney Papers/AAA, microfilm roll N591, frame 754; and Henry McBride, "Whitney Studio Club Arranges a 'Circus,' *New York Sun,* undated clipping in Whitney Papers/AAA, microfilm roll N591, frame 752. The clever exhibition received notice in newspapers around the country.

18. See *The Circus in Paint,* exh. cat., New York: Whitney Studio Galleries, 1929 (Introduction by Lloyd Goodrich). Also see Juliana Force's installation shots and photo files on the show, Whitney Papers/AAA, microfilm roll N591, frames 713 et seq. *Female Acrobat* (later called *High Diver)* is seen in the file photograph, frame 730. The exhibition price list shows that Curry's painting was, at $75, the least expensive oil by far (Whitney Papers/AAA, microfilm roll N591, frame 712). However, gallery records show that it went unsold. See Whitney Studio Galleries ledger, Whitney Papers/AAA, microfilm roll NWh4, frame 624.

19. Leonard Traube, Eastern Outdoor Editor, *Billboard,* to Curry, 10 August 1931, Curry Papers/AAA, microfilm roll 1666, no frame no.

20. Quoted in "Artist's Brush Brings Circus on Canvas," a notice about the 1933 Ferargil Galleries show, unidentified, undated newspaper clipping in Curry scrapbook, Curry Papers/AAA, microfilm roll 2748, no frame no.

21. "Kansan at the Circus": 42.

22. Thomas Craven, "John Steuart Curry," *Scribner's* 103, no. 1 (January 1938): 40.

23. See Louis Zara, "The Flying Codonas," *Esquire* 8, no. 1 (July 1937): 154. "It was he who secured permission for John Steuart Curry to travel with the Ringling circus and paint," Zara wrote. "Curry's oil *The Flying Codonas* may in time become as famous as the subjects who posed for it."

24. Alfredo Codona, as told to Courtney Ryley Cooper, "Split Seconds," *Saturday Evening Post* 203, no. 23 (6 December 1930): 75. For profiles of the Codonas, see Zara, "Codonas": 94, 153–54, 156; and Cosmopolite, "Alfredo Codona and the Art of the Aerial Acrobat," *The White Tops,* undated clipping, 21, 24, in Codona vertical file, Robert L. Parkinson Library and Research Center, Circus World Museum, Baraboo, Wisconsin. This extensive file includes photographs and other newspaper and magazine clippings.

25. The Codonas' flying leap is described by Zara, "Codonas": 153.

26. Cosmopolite, "Alfredo Codona": 24.

27. Curry's *Von Droyson Sisters* was included in his circus-series show at Ferargil Galleries. See Ferargil Galleries, *Announcement!: An Exhibition of Paintings of the Circus by John Steuart Curry,* 3–16 April 1933, printed broadside. The painting's location is unknown. Curry's *Baby Ruth* was sold at Sotheby Parke Bernet, 23 May 1974, lot 75; its location is unknown.

28. Zara, "Codonas": 94. The order of the circus's 1932 program appears in *The White Tops* 6, no. 1 (May 1932): 1. The Codonas were the next-to-last act, followed by Hugo Zachini, the human cannonball.

29. See Cosmopolite, "Alfredo Codona": 21.

30. Codona, "Split Seconds": 75.

31. Ibid.: 76.

32. Ibid.

33. *Bridgeport (Conn.) Sunday Post,* 11 June 1933, unsigned, untitled clipping in Curry scrapbook, Curry Papers/AAA, microfilm roll 2748, no frame no.

34. Cosmopolite, "Alfredo Codona": 21.

35. Ibid.

36. Curry to Maynard Walker, 1 August 1932, Walker Papers/AAA, microfilm roll 2023, frame 25.

37. See "Circus Troupe to View Art of Sawdust Ring," *New York Herald Tribune,* 29 March 1933. The exhibition preview was even reported in the circus fans' periodical *The White Tops* 6–7, no. 12–1 (April–May 1933): 10.

38. "Kansan at the Circus": 41.

39. Ibid.

40. Thomas H. Benton, "John Curry," *University of Kansas City Review* (winter 1946): 88. This essay is reprinted in the present volume.

41. Breuning, *Post.*

42. Edward Alden Jewell, "Allied Artists of America," *New York Times,* 3 April 1933.

43. Of the eleven works on the 1933 checklist that can be identified as oils, eight were still with Curry in 1943, when Schmeckebier published his biography and reproduced them, along with many of the watercolors and drawings. Sometime after 1934 and before Curry left Ferargil in 1935, Frederick Newlin Price, the gallery's director, purchased *The Runway* and donated it to his alma mater, Swarthmore College.

Alien Corn

AN ARTIST ON THE MIDDLE BORDER

M. SUE KENDALL

En route to Hollywood in the mid-1930s to adapt Sinclair Lewis's novel *It Can't Happen Here* for the screen, the playwright Sidney Howard wrote a letter to the New York art dealer Maynard Walker, the agent then representing John Steuart Curry: "The more I see of this country from my train window, the more I feel I must own Curry's *Line Storm*"[1] (1934, color plate 33, fig. 1). Howard bought the painting, explaining that it satisfied his desire to get "as large a slice of the U.S.A. as it is possible to get into a cramped New York apartment."[2] In March 1936 he wrote to the artist himself: "The picture is now hanging on the wall of my dining room," Howard informed him. "When one lives on a New York side street with nothing to look at through the front window but the brownstones across the way and only the rear end of an apartment house to look at in back, that much of Kansas on the wall is a great help."[3]

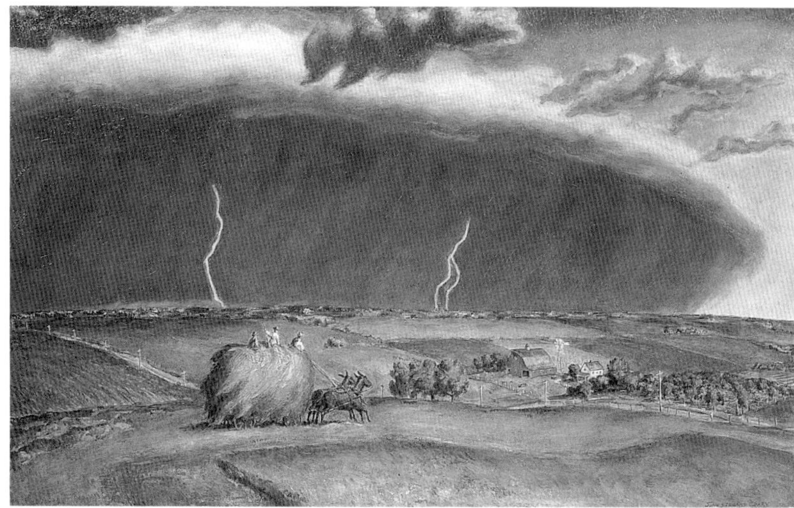

FIGURE 1
John Steuart Curry
Line Storm, 1934
Oil and tempera on panel
36 × 48 in.
Babcock Galleries, New York.

For Sidney Howard, it was the sight of a loaded hay wagon racing across the Kansas plains to beat the approaching storm that was appealing. For another, it was Curry's threatening tornado that summoned a kind of atavistic recognition and remembrance of things past. In 1931 a Connecticut real estate broker wrote to Curry, offering to buy *Tornado* (1929, color plate 20), which he had just seen illustrated in an arts magazine: "I think I find in the photograph a certain native quality which interests me because I was born and brought up in Michigan and while I never have seen a tornado of just this kind I can well remember school being let out and running for dear life for home, with the branches torn off the trees, windows broken and roofs coming off around me, but at any rate the whole picture seems to strike a sort of home chord in me."[4]

By the late 1920s, there was a growing interest in images such as these, capable of striking "a sort of home chord," pictures with the power to anchor an experience and bind emotion to memory. It was just this "certain native quality" in Curry's pictures that sparked the interest of New York gallerygoers who had never even been to Kansas. Curry's stock with that audience soared in the fall of 1928 following the debut of *Baptism in Kansas* (1928, color plate 10) in the *Eleventh Biennial Exhibition of Contemporary American Oil Paintings* at the Corcoran Gallery of Art in Washington, D.C. Immediately after the exhibition closed, Curry was invited to join the roster of artists represented by the new Whitney Studio Club of New York and was given a stipend by Mrs. Gertrude Vanderbilt Whitney to subsidize his career for the next year.[5] He held a one-man show at the Whitney Studio Club Galleries early in 1930.[6] His exhibition at the Ferargil Galleries in New York in the fall of that year led the *New York Times* to proclaim, "Kansas Has Found Her Homer."[7] Also in 1930, Mrs. Whitney purchased *Baptism in Kansas* for the Whitney Museum of American Art, which ceremoniously opened its doors to the public 18 November 1931.[8] The photograph in the *Times* featuring Mrs. Whitney as "the patron and founder of a new museum" showed her posing proudly beside *Baptism in Kansas,* standard-bearer for the new American art.[9]

Later recalling the events that led up to *Baptism in Kansas,* Curry wrote that it "was painted in August, 1928. I was in a state of desperation trying to get along at illustration, or anything I could do. I took a month off and painted this picture. It was painted without notes or sketches from memory of a baptism that took place in 1915."[10]

The fact that a full-immersion baptism in a cattle trough did take place in Kansas in 1915, a year when the creek beds were running dry, is documented by historical photographs (fig. 2). Less easily documented are the artist's reasons for choosing such unprecedented subject matter for his first serious attempt at oil painting. But though contemporary critics hailed *Baptism in Kansas* as a novelty, it of course did not fall from the sky like the heavenly doves. In many ways, it was a natural outgrowth of a number of intersecting influences, both cultural and personal. The painting should be viewed in the context of similar cultural expressions on the part of other midwestern expatriates who, like Curry, spent time in Paris during the 1920s.[11]

Baptism in Kansas appeared at a time when many artists were responding enthusiastically to the general call for an indigenous

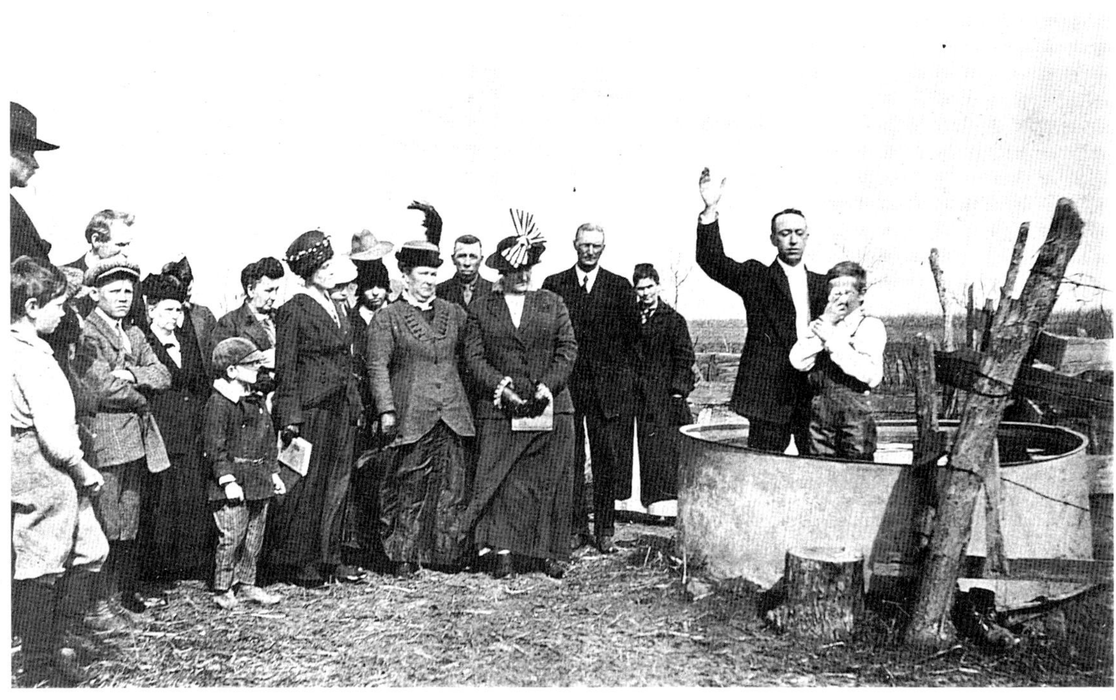

FIGURE 2
Vern Sizemore baptizing the Kaiser boy near Linn, Washington County, Kansas, ca. 1915. Photograph courtesy Kansas State Historical Society, Topeka.

American art that sounded in the wake of World War I. At the close of that unprecedentedly savage and devastating conflict, a longing for security, order, and simple virtues took hold both in America and in Europe.[12] One result of this new cultural atmosphere was a retreat from the radical artistic experimentation of the prewar decade that had given rise to such movements as cubism, orphism, and suprematism. The abstraction emphasized in those modernist directions was now hotly rejected as symptomatic of the climate that had led to the war. In the United States, stress was now placed on producing straightforward, widely accessible writing and art in which plain folk, everyday life, and quintessentially American scenes were portrayed. Seeking inspiration for such work, artists increasingly turned to the sources where the nation's core character was seen to be most vividly evident: the land and people of rural America, especially the South and Midwest. The general term that came to be applied to this emerging trend was regionalism. In the late 1920s, before *Baptism in Kansas* thrust Curry so dramatically into the regionalist ranks, critics were finding themes of the new movement most effectively expressed in work by such artists as Charles Burchfield and Edward Hopper.[13]

Along with broad cultural trends, events in Curry's own life may help explain the origins of *Baptism in Kansas.* Curry's younger brother, Paul, "a brilliant student who was taken ill while at Harvard Law School in 1926," had died at the Mayo Clinic in Rochester, Minnesota, in November 1927.[14] The tragedy may have spurred Curry to recall a powerful religious experience from his youth and to explore that memory in paint. *Baptism* was to be one of a number of Curry images, such as *State Fair* (1928, color plate 13) and *Tornado,* that drew upon distant childhood memories. In this, he was in company with Thomas Hart Benton; scholars have pointed to the death of the latter artist's father as a compelling factor in the emergence of his regionalist expression.[15]

A combined artistic and personal factor influencing the emergence of Curry's Kansas-based imagery—not to mention his turn from commercial illustration to oil painting—may well have been his studies in the early 1920s with the South Dakota–born illustrator Harvey Dunn. Surveys of American art often cite images such as *Baptism in Kansas* as revolutionary because they seem to be radical departures from prevailing modes of painterly expression. A more likely scenario, however, is the occurrence of a sort of "paradigm shift," in which influences from the world of illustrators spill over to the sphere of artists who paint "museum pictures"; a mode of expression in one discipline, cross-pollinated to a new context via an individual with a foot in each world, can appear to represent a radical change, when all that really took place was a change of context.[16] Indeed, Benton once characterized Curry as a "Middle Western farm boy who began on Fredric [*sic*] Remington and Harvey Dunn and who has never repudiated these interests but even spent his life sublimating them."[17]

Harvey Dunn was known primarily for his advertisements and story illustrations in *Collier's, American Magazine, Cosmopolitan, McCall's,* and the *Saturday Evening Post.*[18] But, as his biographer, Robert Karolevitz, reveals, there was also a secret body of work on which Dunn labored for his own enjoyment, paintings that Curry would have seen in his teacher's studio.[19] According to Karolevitz, "[B]ack in his Tenafly, New Jersey, studio (to which he moved in 1919), Dunn dedicated himself to portraying the life of prairie pioneers, working on the pictures intermittently over a period of more than a quarter of a century"[20] (fig. 3). There were, apparently, two Harvey Dunns—the successful commercial illustrator, heir to the legacy of Howard Pyle, and the private painter of life on the South Dakota plains:

These were HIS pictures as differentiated from those for which he accepted payment. . . . When he finished a Dakota picture, he usually stored it away in what he called his "morgue." They tended to be prairie pictures for prairie folks, and Harvey never foisted his homey art on anyone he thought might not be able to appreciate the depth of feeling involved. Several times he dusted off a few canvases and took them across the Hudson to the annual meeting of the South Dakota Society of New York City. There he found men and women who recognized and appreciated what he was doing, not as art dilettantes but as Dakota natives like himself who had seen and experienced the earthy existence his pictures portrayed. . . . For all his commercial success, Harvey Dunn was most at home when his brushes were depicting the rigors and the romance of homesteading. Breaking plows, box wagons, stone boats and sod houses had far more interest and meaning to him than the products of manufacturers or the specific needs of magazine editors. He readily admitted his preference for painting the Dakota scenes above all others.[21]

Dunn took a liking to Curry. He must have seen himself in the young Kansan, recalling the "raw-boned farmer from South Dakota" who had arrived at the Art Institute of Chicago in 1902 looking "somewhat Ichabod Crane-ish in his store-bought suit."[22]

Several of Curry's early regionalist paintings bear a strong resemblance to some of Dunn's private prairie pictures that were lying around his studio in various stages of completion. For example, Curry's *Kansas Wheat Ranch* (1930) is strikingly similar to Dunn's *The Deserted House,* painted the same year.[23] And, unusual as the subject matter may be, it is but a short distance from Dunn's 1926 rendering of a prairie funeral, *I Am the Resurrection and the Life* (see p. 121) to Curry's own painting of

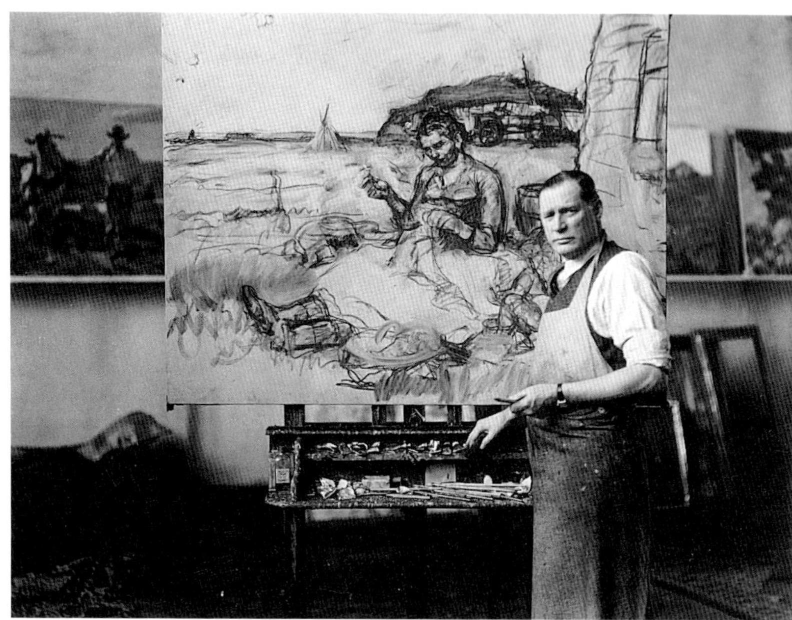

FIGURE 3

Harvey Dunn working on a prairie picture in his Tenafly, New Jersey, studio. Photograph courtesy South Dakota Art Museum, Brookings.

that subject, *The Return of Private Davis from the Argonne* (1928–40, color plate 12).[24]

A final development leading up to *Baptism in Kansas* was the training Curry received under Basil Schoukhaieff at his drawing academy in Paris. Increasingly dissatisfied with the work he had been doing as an illustrator, Curry went there in October 1926, with money advanced by the banker and art patron Seward Prosser.[25] In the heady atmosphere of the French capital, where he stayed for eight months, Curry refreshed his senses, saw that classical artists such as Peter Paul Rubens were closer kin than modernists such as Henri Matisse and Pablo Picasso, and kept company with some of the many midwestern artists and writers who were then living and working in the city.

Produced the year after he came back from Paris, *Baptism in Kansas* also shares a certain "Return from Bohemia" quality with the early regionalist work of Grant Wood, who likewise had received art training abroad. Eager now to explore his roots, Curry gravitated for subject matter to the Kansas of his youth.[26] But unlike Wood, Curry did not go back to the Midwest. His return was to a bohemia of another sort, the thriving artists' colony of Westport, Connecticut, which he had called home for several years.

The fact that Curry no longer lived in the Midwest was not lost on native Kansans, who would be asked, three years after the debut of *Baptism in Kansas,* to show the kind of appreciation for his work that New Yorkers were giving it. In 1931 his one-man exhibition of paintings that had appeared at Ferargil Galleries the previous fall was invited to be shown at the Art Institute of Chicago and then at the City Art Museum in St. Louis. Curry's agent, Maynard Walker, immediately began trying to find an institution in Kansas that would also take the show. He was finally able to persuade the Mulvane Museum in Topeka to accept it.[27] Before the exhibition opened there, Walker mounted an extensive letter-writing campaign to generate enthusiasm for his client's art: "I have been writing to everybody in Topeka about the work of John Steuart Curry. It's really great stuff," he confided.[28] He also sent out copies of the good reviews Curry had been receiving in New York, and he tried (unsuccessfully) to convince a local citizen to purchase a Curry painting for a Kansas museum.[29]

Walker's attempt to promote Curry in Topeka in 1931 was, in the agent's words, "a flop."[30] One Topekan wrote to inform Walker that "the public resented the so-called crude angle toward Kansas" that they sensed in paintings such as *Tornado* and *Manhunt* (1931, color plate 22) and in lithographs such as *Holy Rollers* (1930).[31] It did not seem to matter "how important Curry is in Eastern art circles"—most Kansans resented having the state's miserable weather, its religious fanaticism, and its lynch mobs captured in paint and paraded before high-minded New York gallery-goers.[32] In the words of one Wichita native, "[B]eing Kansas born I cannot agree with the enthusiasm of the art critics of the *New York Times*."[33]

Sidney Howard's popular play of 1933, *Alien Corn*, presents a variation on the familiar theme of the artist as an outsider in the Middle West; it centers on a talented young Viennese pianist, Elsa Brandt, who is unhappy in her teaching position at the Conway College for Women "a few hours west of Chicago" and homesick for the cultural life of her native city. In the final act she decides to forsake the culturally barren college and pursue a career as a concert pianist back in Vienna.[34] "Alien corn" is a commonly used agricultural term that refers to any nonindigenous species introduced to a given region. Certain adaptation difficulties are to be expected, and sometimes the species does not adapt at all.

By leaving Kansas at an early age and earning fame in New York, Curry had, in the eyes of many in his native state, become just another sneering outsider; by 1931 he was alien corn. His paintings seemed to ridicule Kansas eccentricities in the same way that condescending New Yorkers had been doing for years. The fact that Curry had been praised by New York art critics and had caught Mrs. Whitney's eye not only failed to impress most Kansans—it actually worked against him. Despite Maynard Walker's vigorous efforts, there would be no sales of Curry's art in Kansas in 1931.

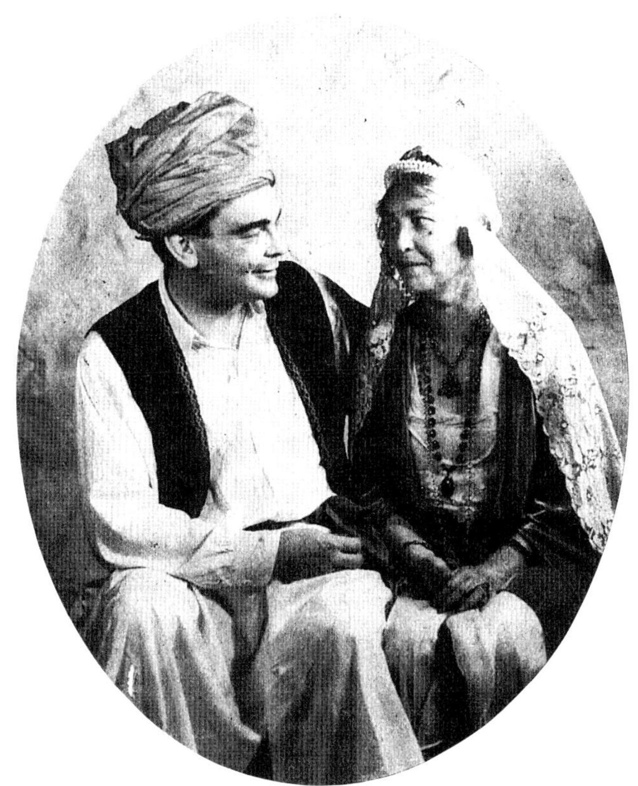

FIGURE 4

Curry and Mattie Farnham in "Arabian" costume at the Westport Country Club Artists' Masque Ball, 1931. Clipping from the *New York Times*, 27 September 1931. Photograph courtesy Curry Papers, Archives of American Art, Smithsonian Institution, Washington, D.C.

Without a doubt, Curry was on more congenial ground back in Westport. He continued to develop his regionalist expression at a safe distance, far removed from Kansas itself. He had moved to Westport from Greenwich Village with his bride, Clara, in 1924. He bought a studio on Otter Pond Road that served as his home base until 1936, when he became artist-in-residence at the University of Wisconsin. By all accounts, Curry loved life in Westport. Even months after moving to Madison, he still referred to his "state of worry over our removal from the East."[35]

The artist's daylight hours in Westport may well have been spent painting the tornados, revival meetings, and prairie landscapes of Kansas. But evenings might find him in full "Arabian" costume at the Westport Country Club's Artists' Masque Ball (fig. 4), or presiding as witty auctioneer at the Silvermine Artist Guild's annual "Fakir Show and Dance Grotesque." Dancing and "a collation" followed this event and others like it.[36]

Apparently, it was easy to come by "a collation" in Westport during the 1920s. Two decades later, the artist Guy Pène duBois recalled that "in the prohibition period the summers at Westport . . . exceeded the riotousness of New York. There gin and orange juice ruled the days and nights. . . . Work was an effort made between parties."[37] More recently, the writer Barbara Probst Solomon, who spent childhood summers at her parents' cottage there, vividly recaptured 1920s and 1930s Westport—and traced the town's origins—in an essay for the *New Yorker,* "Westport Wildlife." The essay is a personal odyssey "of literary discovery about the Westport of bootleggers and summer places inhabited by the Fitzgeralds, whom my parents never knew."[38] Located on the bay where the Saugatuck River empties into Long Island Sound, Westport was a small, inconsequential place during the nineteenth century; the surrounding land was dominated by onion fields. Early in the twentieth century, however, the area was settled by a set of talented, energetic people who were drawn to its rural beauty, affordable cost of living, and proximity to New York City.

Among the first writers to spend time there was F. Scott Fitzgerald. In 1920, flush with the success of his first novel, *This Side of Paradise,* he and his bride, Zelda, rented a cottage on South Compo Road. Solomon recalls Zelda's "moonlight swims and wild beach parties . . . at the Hendrick's Point beach," just a few minutes away from her parents' place.[39] Curry must have been aware of the mythic presence of Scott and Zelda in Westport. His good friend and fellow artist Reginald Marsh featured Zelda frolicking in the fountains at Union Square and near the Plaza Hotel on a curtain he painted for the Greenwich Village Follies.[40]

Curry's years in Westport comprised a crucial and formative period in his career. While there, he moved away from illustration to pursue painting. A Westport neighbor, James Daugherty, suggested that he study in Paris; and, as noted, it was the financial support of another Westporter, Seward Prosser, that enabled him to do so. Finally, it was on Curry's return to Westport that he began to produce the body of Kansas-inspired work that would earn him fame as a midwestern regionalist. Yet so much has been made of the down-home, "Curry-of-Kansas" persona that was presented in the mass media, that it has been easy to lose sight of the actual milieu of the artist in Westport:[41]

Nineteen-twenty, the year the Fitzgeralds came to Westport, was a dynamite year. Jazz, the "new woman," bobbed hair, the automobile, and the idea of country life as a summer playground belonging to the middle as well as the upper class had permeated America. Expatriates living in Europe were making stylish the idea of place as an essential piece of aesthetic baggage. Provincetown was old-fashioned bohemia, Hollywood was in its infancy, and a good part of the Hamptons was still potato fields. Westport was small and rural enough, and unstructured enough socially, to attract a new class of bourgeois outsider-insiders, who did not observe the previously defined boundaries of class. . . . Westport culture had a shiny professional edge to it: the new styles of art and commerce seemed as smoothly intermingled as Henry Luce's budding magazine empire, Busby Berkeley musicals, and the department-store dream palaces of the time.[42]

Many artists were drawn to Westport during this period, among them Karl Anderson (brother of the novelist Sherwood Anderson), Edward Boyd, Arthur Dove, James Earle Fraser, Charles Prendergast, and Everett Shinn.[43] But the town was more than a watering hole for painters, sculptors, and illustrators. Among Curry's literary friends there was Van Wyck Brooks (fig. 5).[44] That critic's call in 1918 for the creation of a "usable past" had been at the very heart of the urge to rediscover America that evolved into regionalism.[45]

Westport hosted a multifarious contingent of cultural movers and shakers:

The town was a kind of laboratory version of what would soon be considered modern New York culture. Not far from Fitzgerald . . . John Held, Jr., a boyhood friend of Harold Ross, who founded *The New Yorker* in 1925, was creating "the Held girl"—the flapper who appeared on the covers of *Smart Set* and became the image of the Jazz Age. [T]he popular historian Hendrik Willem Van Loon . . . Ford Madox Ford's brother, Oliver Hueffer, who was also a writer, and the illustrator Howard Munce all lived in Westport, and in the twenties a young, unknown Southern writer, Thomas Wolfe, spent considerable time with the editor Maxwell Perkins, who had a home in nearby New Canaan. Over the years, the dance-and-music world flocked there, too: Ruth St. Denis, Ted Shawn, George Balanchine, and Oscar Levant settled in Westport. It became a town full of the inventors of culture, both highbrow and popular. . . . Joanna Foster's "Recollections" and Dorothy and John Tarrant's "A Community of Artists" list, among others, the creators of the Gerber baby, Little Orphan Annie, Popeye, Superman, the Kewpie doll, Blondie, and Joe Palooka."[46]

Curry's frescoes in the auditorium of Bedford Junior High School in Westport illuminating the themes of *Comedy* and *Tragedy* (color plates 29 and 30) are a virtual paean to the "inventors of culture, both highbrow and popular," who were populating the vibrant new art colony.[47] Popeye is there, with Olive Oyl. Sherwood Anderson is featured. So is Westporter Rose O'Neill, holding her famous invention, the Kewpie doll.

(Curry's studio was only a few hundred yards from O'Neill's home; she had done a special drawing of the Kewpie doll for him.[48]) Westporter James Earle Fraser, sculptor of the Buffalo nickel, is in an upper box near Eugene O'Neill. Flanking the stage in the *Tragedy* panel, watching Lady Macbeth in the background and John Barrymore as Hamlet in the foreground, are Curry's closest Westport friends, Moffit and Winifred Johnston, themselves popular Shakespearean actors who lived on Narrow Rocks Road.[49] They appear here as surrogate spectators, *repoussoir* figures directing our attention inward toward the other characters in the mural. Curry and his new wife, Kathleen, serve a parallel function in the *Comedy* fresco.

Painted in 1934, these frescoes were a gift from the artist to the town he loved; Curry asked only to be reimbursed for the cost of his materials and to be supplied with an assistant who could help with the tedious daily task of mixing plaster.[50]

Curry presents the ancient Greek themes in a modern theatrical setting, using figures from the American entertainment scene of the 1920s and 1930s to create an "almost wildly contemporary iconography of movies and Broadway stage."[51] Ziegfeld chorus-line dancers and Will Rogers rub elbows with Mutt and Jeff and Mickey Mouse; circus clowns and cartoonists are juxtaposed with Dreiser and Shakespeare. These frescoes, a boisterous conglomerate of popular culture, are a virtual microcosm of the lively art colony of Westport itself, where painters are neighbors of playwrights and ideas mingle over shared "collations."

Curry's first wife, Clara, had died in July 1932, soon after he finished touring with the Ringling Brothers and Barnum & Bailey Circus; that event may well have been on his mind when he composed the *Tragedy* fresco.[52] The falling aerialist spotlighted there derives from sketches Curry had made during his time with the circus. The strong diagonal composition that drops from the wings of the angel in the fresco, down and across the bed linens of Harriet Beecher Stowe's tragic character Little Eva, to the weeping clown at the foot of her bed, uses a dramatic vertical drop that subliminally echoes the sinking feeling in one's stomach during a fall or when news of a personal tragedy hits.

By contrast, the feeling conveyed in the *Comedy* fresco is one of uplift. This is symbolized, quite literally, in the uplifted arms of the group of chorus dancers who emerge from backstage; of the famous ballroom dancers Irene and Vernon Castle; of Amos 'n' Andy; and of the central figure, Charlie Chaplin. Curry's spotlighting of Chaplin here is meaningful. As the cultural historian Lawrence Levine, among others, has observed, Chaplin was both a champion of popular culture and an astute social commentator:

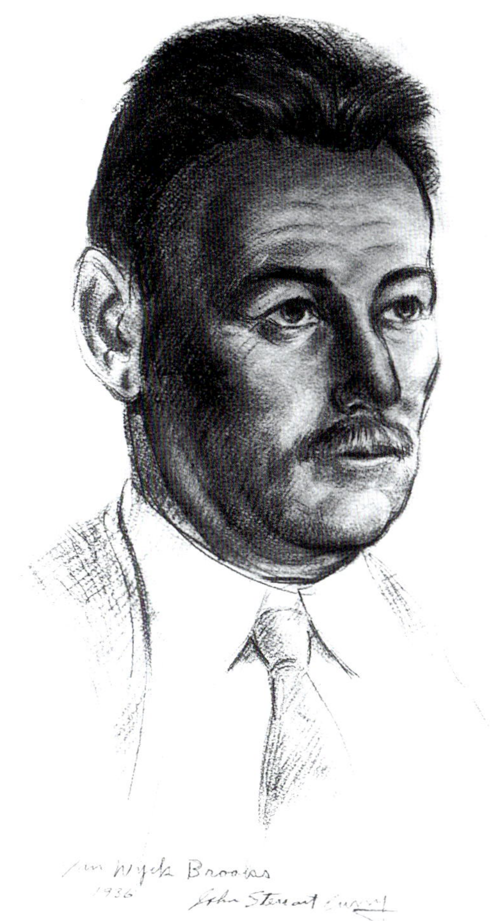

FIGURE 5

John Steuart Curry
Van Wyck Brooks, 1936
Pastel on paper
Location unknown
Photograph courtesy Curry Papers, Archives of American Art, Smithsonian Institution, Washington, D.C.

Charlie Chaplin . . . and a legion of other popular comedians . . . created a rapport with their audiences that generated a sense of complicity in their common stand against the pretensions of high culture. Thus when Chaplin, clad in his rags and twirling a cane, mocked cultured gentility as he selected, with meticulous deliberation, a butt from his sardine-tin cigarette case and lit it while strictly observing all the proper forms, he was speaking for the audience as well as for himself.[53]

Indeed, Curry's Chaplin, mocker of the pretensions of high culture, makes a fitting poster boy for the kind of artistic expression that Thomas Hart Benton and his fellow midwestern regionalists seemed to be promoting. As Benton put it:

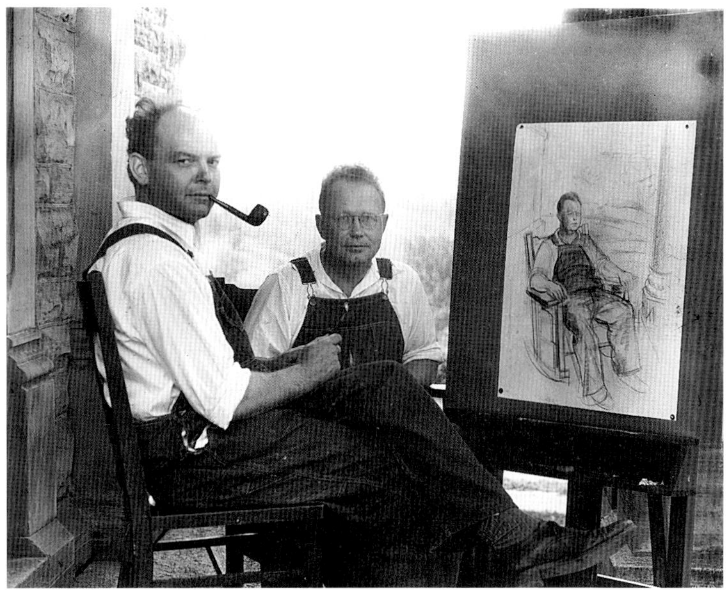

FIGURE 6
Curry sketching Grant Wood during his visit to the Stone City Colony and Art School, Stone City, Iowa, July 1933. Photograph by John W. Barry, Cedar Rapids, Iowa. Courtesy John W. Barry, Jr.

We came in the popular mind to represent a home-grown, grass-roots artistry which damned "furrin" influence and which knew nothing about and cared nothing for the traditions of art as cultivated city snobs, dudes, and *ass*thetes knew them. A play was written and a stage erected for us. Grant Wood became the typical Iowa small towner, John Curry the typical Kansas farmer, and I just an Ozark hillbilly. We accepted our roles.[54]

Benton was featured on the cover of *Time* magazine in December 1934 as the leader of those "earthy Midwesterners" of the new regionalist movement.[55] The accompanying story featured a photo of Curry and Grant Wood, their sleeves rolled up, wearing matching farmers' bibbed overalls. The irony of this homespun image of Paris-trained artists seemingly plucked from the plains was lost on most readers of *Time.* Curry, still living in Westport, had traveled to Iowa in July 1933 for a first-time meeting with Wood. On his arrival at Wood's Stone City Colony and Art School, the two donned matching overalls and posed for publicity pictures taken by a courier from the *Cedar Rapids Gazette* (fig. 6).[56] It was one of those shots that made its way to the pages of *Time* the following year. By 1934, those who represented Curry were taking a new approach in their attempts to get the artist accepted in Kansas and to build a market for his pictures there. This time around, little mention was made of his success in East Coast art centers; he was now presented to his fellow Kansans as "a simple man who paints in overalls instead of a smock."[57]

By the time the photo of Curry in overalls appeared in *Time,* he was back in Westport, enjoying his friends' and neighbors' favorable response to the *Comedy* and *Tragedy* frescoes. After just one panel had been completed, a headline in the *Westporter-Herald* announced that "Curry's Frescoes Receive Enthusiastic Comment among Westport Artists."[58] The formal unveiling of the finished works in November 1934 featured an address by the artist, a musical program by the junior-high-school band, and a cash award to the winner of an essay contest about the murals. According to the local press, the panels "Won [the] Admiration of Local Art Lovers."[59] Unfortunately, Curry's good fortune with mural art would not last long.

There was a hint of the trouble that lay ahead in local newspaper coverage of Curry's next mural assignment, a pair of panels for the high school in nearby Norwalk. A reporter for the *Bridgeport Post* wondered whether there was "a joker" in one of the panels:

The panel, 6½ by 13 feet [*sic*] depicts the ancient industries of Norwalk, as weaving, sowing grain, harvesting, old modes of travel, raising tobacco, forging iron, hauling with oxen and shipbuilding, all indigenous to the town and city. . . . But the wheels of the stage coach are painted at standstill with every spoke visible, while the double span of white horses hitched to the coach are painted galloping across the valley at top speed. Is the conflict between the wheels at standstill and the galloping horses one of Mr. Curry's jokes, or was it unpremeditated? . . . Is he playing a . . . little joke on Norwalk, with the standstill wheels?[60]

Apparently, this questioning of the artist's intentions went no further. Today the "standstill wheels" still stand still while the horses run full speed in the Norwalk High School murals. Next time around, the artist would not have the final say.

The Norwalk murals had been funded by the Public Works of Art Project, a New Deal work-relief program for artists in need set up in 1933.[61] On 16 October 1934, the Section of Painting and Sculpture was organized under the aegis of the U.S. Department of the Treasury in order to "secure the best quality art to embellish public buildings."[62] The U.S. Department of Justice and Post Office buildings, then under construction on Federal Triangle, would showcase the new experiment in government patronage, featuring art selected on the basis of "quality" rather than on the basis of artists' economic need. In the spring of 1935, an advisory committee for the Section invited eleven famous painters, including Curry, to accept mural commissions for the buildings without having to submit to a jury; another ten slots (seven in the Post Office and three in the Department of Justice) would be awarded based on a closed, juried competition among 244 other artists who were invited to participate.[63]

Curry's first assignment was to paint two lunettes for the Department of Justice building. Karal Ann Marling has ably placed one of these paintings (color plate 46) in the broader context of "the awful realities of enforced migration during the Great Depression" and the migrant-family photographs of Dorothea Lange:

Lange found a family of four walking toward somewhere else *On U.S. 66 near Weatherford, Western Oklahoma* in 1938. . . . The lonesome whistle that called this Okie family to come away, go somewhere else, and start afresh echoed through a Mural America obsessed with the migrations of the frontier era. . . . John Steuart Curry's *Movement of the Population Westward [Westward Movement]* on the fifth floor of the Justice Building is the Depression's classical paean to American restlessness and hope: "[We] see," caroled the Section press release, "families of pioneers with their covered wagons and cattle facing the hardships of the trail and the dangers of the unknown." There is, in fact, only one family marching westward across Curry's lunette—the heroic American family of all time and of 1937. Father takes the lead. With his young son clinging to his side, he squints into the setting sun, looking confidently beyond the prairie and his time in history. Mother solemnly cradles her baby and bows her head, a lithe pioneer madonna in homespun. Their steady gait, measured off in human terms by three left legs striding forward in sinuous unison, sets a processional cadence. The mass of rearing horses, covered wagons, and ox teams presses on behind them and at their pace. The energy and determination of the family control and guide the inexorable movement of a nation bound for somewhere else.[64]

The year before painting the lunette, Curry had explored the restlessness inherent in the American spirit for an article in *Fortune* magazine, "The Great American Roadside."[65] It was clearly with an eye to the present that he now painted his historical mural: "It is significant that a part of the civilization that went into the Indian territory fifty years ago on wheels is now leaving still on wheels," he remarked.[66] The fact that Curry personally identified with the American need to be on the move is directly reflected in *Westward Movement:* On the far right, next to the anthropomorphic corn stalk, the round-faced figure with the corncob pipe is the artist himself.[67]

Although Curry was required to submit a number of preliminary studies before receiving final approval for *Westward Movement* (color plates 44 and 45), he was eventually able to complete the panel to the advisory committee's satisfaction.[68] The companion lunette, however, would prove to be another story. The subject matter assigned was the "Freedom of the Slaves and Welcoming of the Immigrants from Europe."[69] Curry's first sketches (color plates 40–43) were rejected by the Section and returned to him for reworking with the advice that he delete the immigrants and concentrate the design on the central group of Negroes.[70] Curry developed some further designs, but these, too, were rejected, not only by the Section but also by the architect and by a Justice Department official; the central figure was a freed slave, his arms uplifted in what detractors termed a "hallelujah" pose.[71] Eager to appease the committee, Curry worked to vary this pose: "Think the Negroes will be something different," he wrote, "and I can make the gesture more one of rejoicing."[72] But even after he had made numerous revisions, the Commission of Fine Arts feared that the "praise de Lawd" gesture would generate the kind of controversy the Section tried hard to avoid.[73] Charles Moore, chairman of the Commission of Fine Arts in charge of the mural program, reported that the "Emancipation sketches seem questionable as being violent expressions of emotions now undergoing the scrutiny of historical students" and called for the artist to render "a less vociferous expression of the event."[74]

The ecstatic religiosity in the "hallelujah" pose of Curry's freed slave signaled trouble to those Washington officials who had begun to hear the rumblings of protest among black leaders who resented the stereotypes of blacks being popularized by Hollywood movies. The rumblings grew louder as the 1930s wore on.

Sentiments had been different just a few years earlier. In 1928 even the organ of the National Association for the Advancement of Colored People (NAACP), the *Crisis,* had praised King Vidor's *Hallelujah!,* especially citing the director's expressive use of his actors' hands to capture the mood of black religion. *Crisis* editor W. E. B. Du Bois lauded "the scenes of religious ecstasy [that] rise to magnificent drama, unexcelled in my experience and singularly true to life."[75] In 1930 black and white audiences alike had lauded Marc Connelly's Pulitzer Prize–winning Broadway play *The Green Pastures,* which presented reverent though humorous versions of Old Testament stories as told by an aged black preacher to his congregation, as a sensitive treatment of southern black folk religion.[76] (Curry was certainly aware of the play; in a 1933 letter to the artist, one of his friends wrote, "I've been press agenting *The Green Pastures* for the past 8 weeks.")[77]

By 1934, however, increasing numbers of black critics were seeing such depictions, not to mention the idle and thickheaded characters played by Stepin Fetchit or the mammies and maids of Louise Beavers and Hattie McDaniel, as demeaning and offensive. *Crisis* announced that it was "high time the American Negro took up arms on the Hollywood front."[78] By the time *The Green Pastures* was filmed in 1936, there were plenty of blacks who would agree with this more recent characterization of it:

"Gangway! Gangway! For de Lawd God Jehovah!" cried the black archangel Gabriel, and the screen was bombarded with the liveliest collection of agreeable toms, uncle remuses, aunt jemimas, and corn-patch pickaninnies ever assembled in one motion picture.[79]

The release of *Jezebel* (1938) and *Gone with the Wind* (1939) marked the peak of the Hollywood plantation genre:

But even as this zenith was being reached, a process of ideological revision of the slavery motif had begun. During the production of *Gone with the Wind,* blacks stirred in protest against its depiction of slaves and slavery, and the NAACP was able to pressure David O. Selznick into cutting some of its more offensive scenes (drawn from the novel). And after its long anticipated premiere, pressure was kept up against the film, with limited results, by the National Negro Congress, various black newspapers, and sympathetic left groups including the Communist party.[80]

By 1936 it was difficult to look at the outstretched arms of the freed-slave figure in Curry's mural sketches without seeing Al Jolson, his face smeared with burnt cork like a minstrel singer, belting out "Mammy" in *The Jazz Singer* (fig. 7). ("Jolson's ever-crooning-swooning darky jester was a classic example of the minstrel tradition at its sentimentalized, corrupt best."[81]) Curry's drawings were judged against the backdrop of the plantation-genre movies that were just then "undergoing the scrutiny of historical students."[82]

When thinking about the *Freeing of the Slaves* sketches and their relationship to the movies, it is also important to recognize that nearly all of Curry's history paintings were made with a nod to Hollywood stereotypes. This was in part because he was an avid moviegoer. His thorough enjoyment of this pastime was among his stepdaughter's fondest memories of him:

He and Lloyd Garrison [dean of the University of Wisconsin Law School] used to go to the movies together, and they'd sit down in front and they'd laugh, you know, at the comedies; and we children wouldn't sit with them, because it was such a humiliation for us because they made such a ruckus. One time the manager came, and he was going to put them out of the theater. He thought they were children, and here were these two respectable citizens.[83]

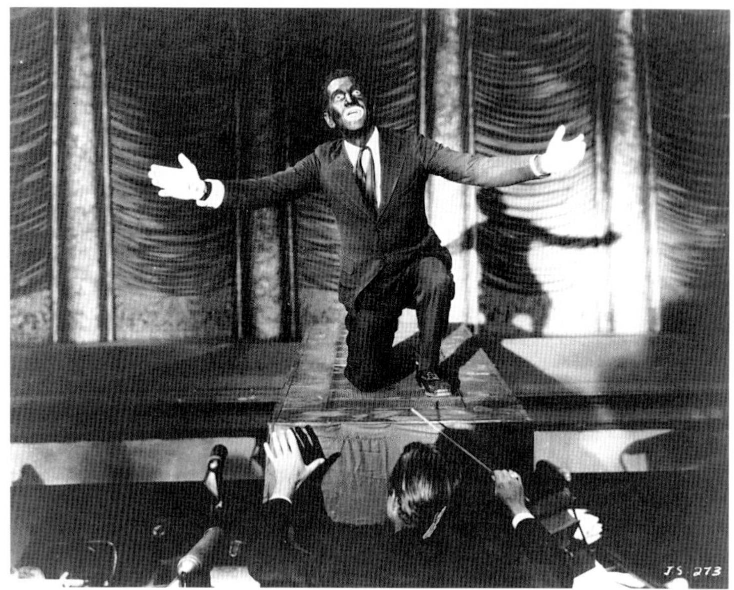

FIGURE 7
Al Jolson in *The Jazz Singer,* Warner Bros., 1927. Photograph courtesy Wisconsin Center for Film and Theater Research, Madison.

Indeed, the national appeal of the Benton-Curry-Wood brand of regionalism derived in part from those artists' knowledge of and attention to operable stereotypes in the mass media.[84] For example, when Curry was asked to draw illustrations for Mary O'Hara's popular novel *My Friend Flicka* (1941), which had been turned into a successful film in 1943, he immediately wired the publisher asking for movie stills: "Since this book has been pictorialized to millions through the movie I feel I must have a little similar data."[85] Curry had put a like request to a Union Pacific Railroad official in Omaha in 1939, when doing preparatory sketches for the Kansas history murals in the State Capitol: "I have seen the moving picture 'Union Pacific,' and it has given me some ideas on several points."[86] One of the panels shows the sixteenth-century Spanish conquistador Francisco Vásquez de Coronado, an early explorer of Kansas, astride a golden Palomino—then the latest champion of the silver screen[87] (fig. 8). To produce this image, Curry had first ordered conquistador attire from United Costumers, Inc., in Hollywood.[88] He then had several University of Wisconsin students don the costume and pose in his Madison studio (fig. 9).

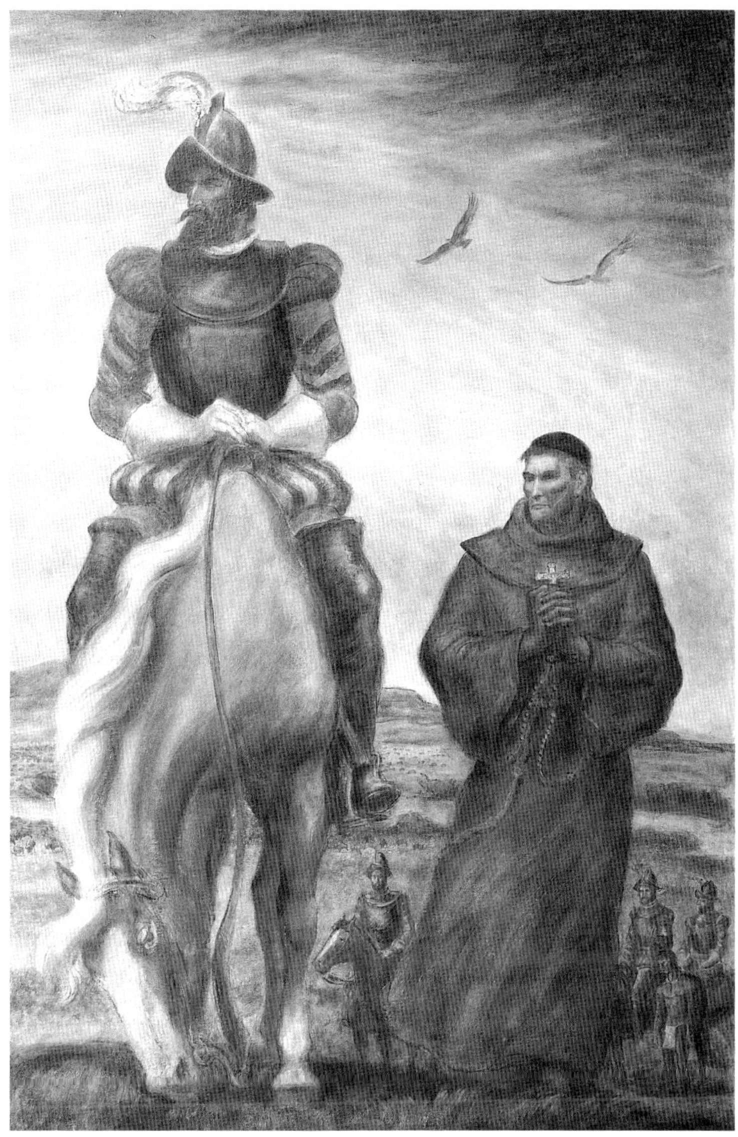

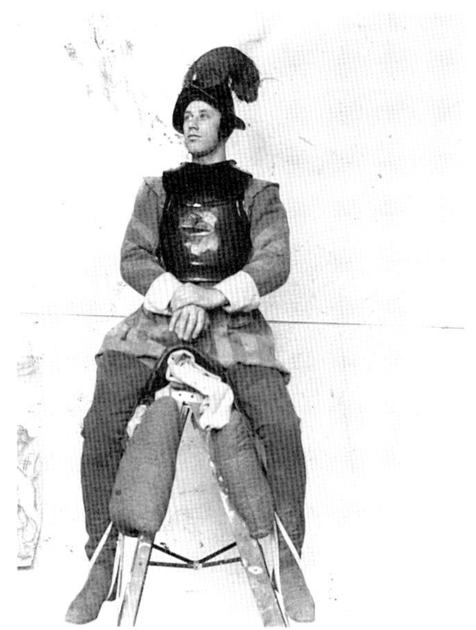

FIGURE 8 *(left)*

John Steuart Curry

Tragic Prelude, from the Kansas State Capitol murals, 1937–42.
Coronado is at left.
Photograph courtesy Kansas State Capitol, Topeka, and David C. Mathias.

FIGURE 9 *(above)*

Model for figure of Coronado, wearing Hollywood costume and astride a sawhorse in Curry's Madison studio, 1940. Photograph courtesy Curry Papers, Archives of American Art, Smithsonian Institution, Washington, D.C.

The artist followed the same procedure in depicting other historical figures in the State Capitol panels. As a result, these characters appeared far more familiar to a modern American audience than if they had been derived from old photographs or drawings in dusty history books. This is history wearing a 1930s costume, transregional in approach, presented in a visual language that was, thanks to Hollywood, recognizable to all participants in this new mass culture.

But some movie stereotypes were more palatable than others, and Curry's freed slave, while instantly familiar, was too controversial to be featured in murals funded by the federal government. After turning out numerous revisions, Curry felt he could not make the slave's expression any "less vociferous" without compromising the original design beyond recognition, so he abandoned the theme altogether.[89] The panel that was finally executed, *Law versus Mob Rule* (1937, color plate 48), shows, in the words of a federal guidebook, "the fugitive, taking refuge from the anarchy of a lawless mob in the protection of constituted authority."[90]

In fairness to Curry, his use of the "hallelujah" gesture was not strictly a racial stereotype. He had employed similar gestures for white celebrants at revival meetings in paintings such as *Gospel Train* (color plate 15) and *Prayer for Grace* (color plate 18), both from 1929. The gesture is also seen in his quasi-religious 1931 painting of a carnival faith healer, *The Medicine Man (Aqua Vita)*.[91]

Furthermore, Curry had shown himself to be quite capable of producing sensitive and individualistic portrayals of blacks.

An artist could not live in the New York City of the 1920s, as Curry had, without being touched by the vitality of the Harlem Renaissance and the various developments in the visual arts related to depictions of blacks. In 1925, for instance, the magazine *The Survey* ran a special issue featuring a large series of "drawings and portraits of black people, famous and unknown, by the German-born artist and designer Winold Reiss." These images were used to illustrate the influential anthology *The New Negro: An Interpretation,* edited by Alain Locke, that was published the same year.[92] Curry's studies of black youths from the 1920s should be seen in the context of this new presentation of "Harlem types."

During the same period, many black American artists, struggling against prejudice and the lack of opportunities for study, exhibition, and patronage, went to Paris, "where they found a freedom and acceptance unavailable to them at home."[93] There, modernists were probing the mysteries of African art as an alternative to the classical academic tradition.[94] Curry produced several portrait studies of young Africans while at Basil Schoukhaieff's academy in Paris.[95] He did several similar studies in 1927, following his return to Westport (color plate 8). These came from sketching visits he made to the New Jersey State Home for Boys, which was headed by his father-in-law, Calvin Derrick, a pioneer in the field of social work.[96]

Curry also put his art to work for the cause of social justice for blacks. His interest in weaving such content into his painting grew steadily during the 1930s. In 1931 he shocked and embarrassed Kansans by depicting a Kansas lynch mob in the painting *Manhunt* (color plate 22). In 1933 he participated in the John Reed Club's exhibition *The Social Viewpoint in Art,* and he lingered around the etching presses of the cartoonist for the Communist newspaper, the *Daily Worker.* During the next two years he made several more works on the theme of lynching that would be displayed in the controversial exhibition *An Art Commentary on Lynching.*[97]

Organized by NAACP Secretary Walter White in cooperation with the College Art Association, the exhibition was originally scheduled to open at the Jacques Seligmann Galleries in New York on February 15, 1935. This was to coincide with the day that hearings on antilynching legislation before the U.S. Congress were to begin. However, an "outburst of opposition" caused the Seligmann Galleries to withdraw four days before the opening. The show was moved to the Arthur U. Newton Galleries on East 57th Street, opened on the set date with author Pearl S. Buck as featured speaker, and ran for two weeks. More than three dozen artists, including Peggy Bacon, Thomas Hart Benton, George Biddle, Paul Cadmus, Reginald Marsh, Isamu Noguchi, and José Orozco, contributed works to the show. Included, too, was a lithograph by the late George Bellows, *The Law Is Too Slow* (1923, fig. 10), which had been used as the frontispiece for Walter White's influential 1929 book, *Rope and Faggot: A Biography of Judge Lynch.*[98] Sherwood Anderson and Erskine Caldwell wrote brief forewords for the exhibition catalogue. The cover featured Curry's lithograph *The Fugitive,* one of three works he contributed.[99]

While a number of artists and writers were asked to make work for the antilynching exhibition, there were, according to Walter White, only three whose existing work on the theme "caused the idea to come into being": Reginald Marsh, Julius Bloch, and John Steuart Curry.[100] At the time of the exhibition, *Manhunt* was already in the collection of Arthur B. Springarn, vice-president of the NAACP.[101] *The Fugitive* existed both as a lithograph and as a painting (color plate 31). Another *Manhunt* lithograph had been published in 1934 by the Contemporary Print Group in New York in a portfolio entitled *The American Scene, Series 2.*[102]

The resurgence of the Ku Klux Klan in the 1920s and the Scottsboro affair of 1931 had brought the problem of lynching and white-mob violence to the attention of socially conscious Americans. "The social, political, and economic disturbances of the times," Curry wrote early in 1937, "have brought forth those artists who, taking their themes from these issues, have produced telling and effective works for the cause of social and political justice."[103] Curry numbered himself among such artists. In July of that year, he was invited to paint murals for the State Capitol in Topeka.[104]

The next month, the *Kansas City Star* ran a "human interest" story under the headline, "The Ku Klux Klan Goes 'Ko-ed.'" "The long dormant Ku Klux Klan," the story noted, "arises to renewed activity, its membership stimulated as ladies take their places beside knights in the hooded ranks."[105] Chatty figure captions accompanied photos taken "behind locked doors in a secret hideaway" of hooded Klanswomen caught off guard, rouging their lips or trying to struggle out of their robes at meeting's end without mussing their hair. The Klan was rearing its ugly head in Kansas again in 1937 (fig. 12)—just as Curry was deciding on subject matter for his Topeka murals—but the atmosphere in some quarters, as the tone of the newspaper article suggests, was less one of alarm than of benign curiosity.[106]

Given a social climate in which elements such as the Klan could find acceptance, it is no wonder that Curry's attempt to paint murals for Kansas would result in a controversy so intense that the project would never see completion.[107] His John Brown in *The Tragic Prelude* would be no kin to the baby-kissing grandpa in Thomas Hovenden's 1884 depiction (fig. 13).[108] Taking his cue from "the disturbances of the times," Curry

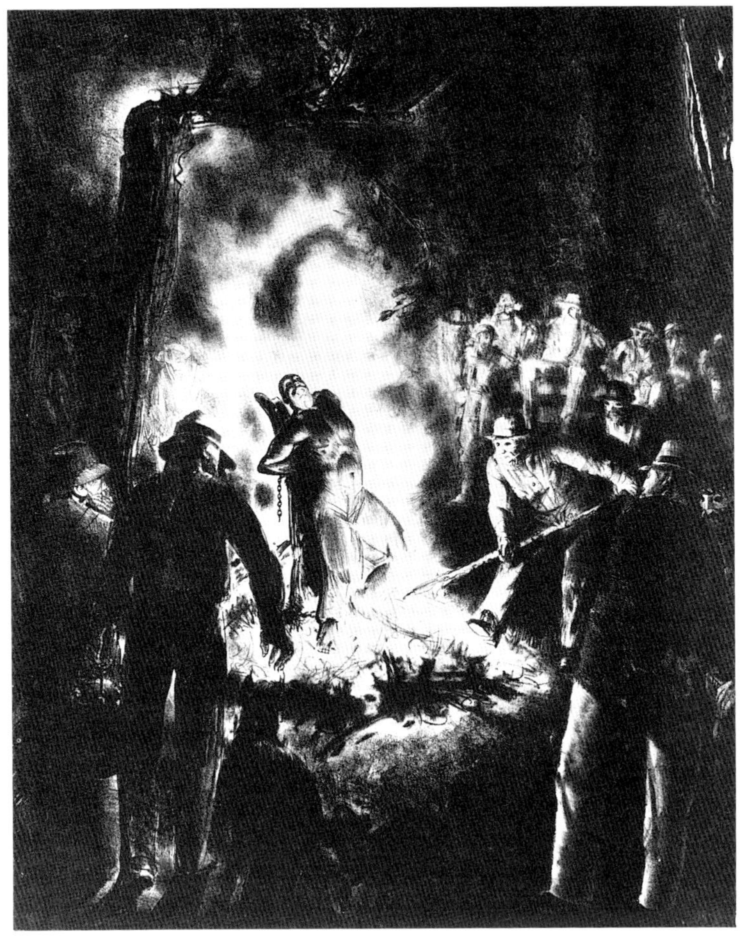

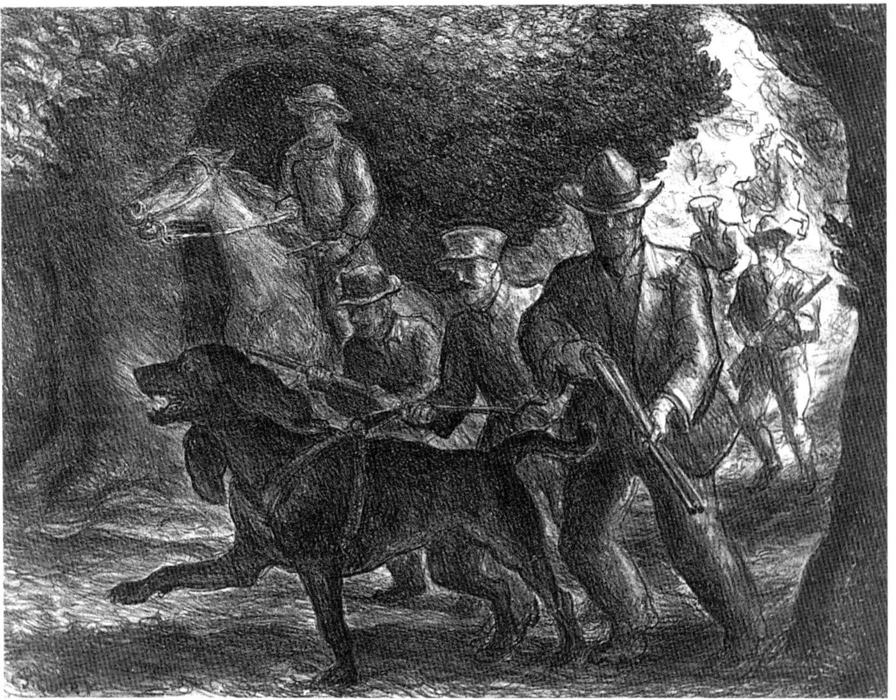

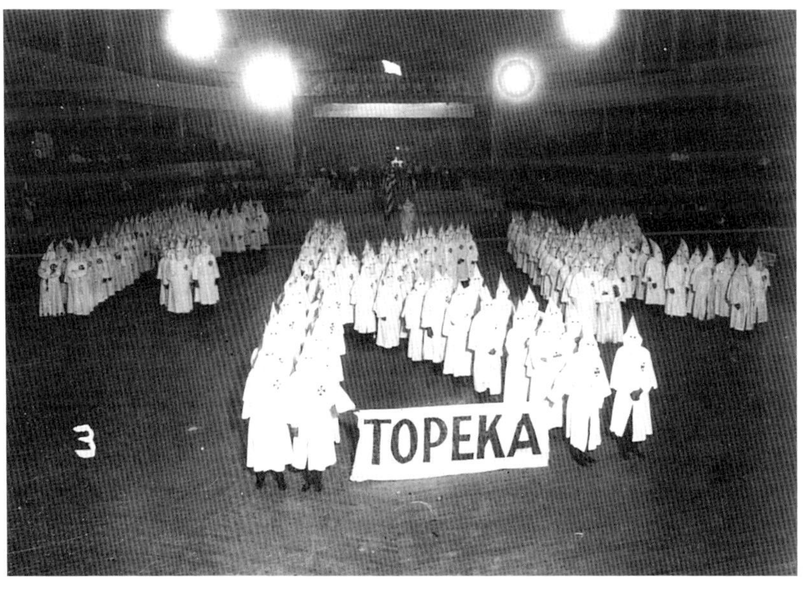

FIGURE 10 *(above)*

George Bellows (American, 1882–1925)
The Law Is Too Slow, 1923
Lithograph
12¹⁵⁄₁₆ × 14½ in.
Photograph courtesy Amon Carter Museum, Fort Worth, Texas.

FIGURE 11 *(above right)*

John Steuart Curry
Manhunt, 1934
Lithograph
9¾ × 12⅞ in.
Photograph courtesy Davenport Museum of Art, Davenport, Iowa.

FIGURE 12 *(right)*

Ku Klux Klan members spelling out "KKK" in auditorium in Topeka, Kansas, 15 September 1923. Photograph courtesy Kansas Collection, University of Kansas Libraries, Lawrence.

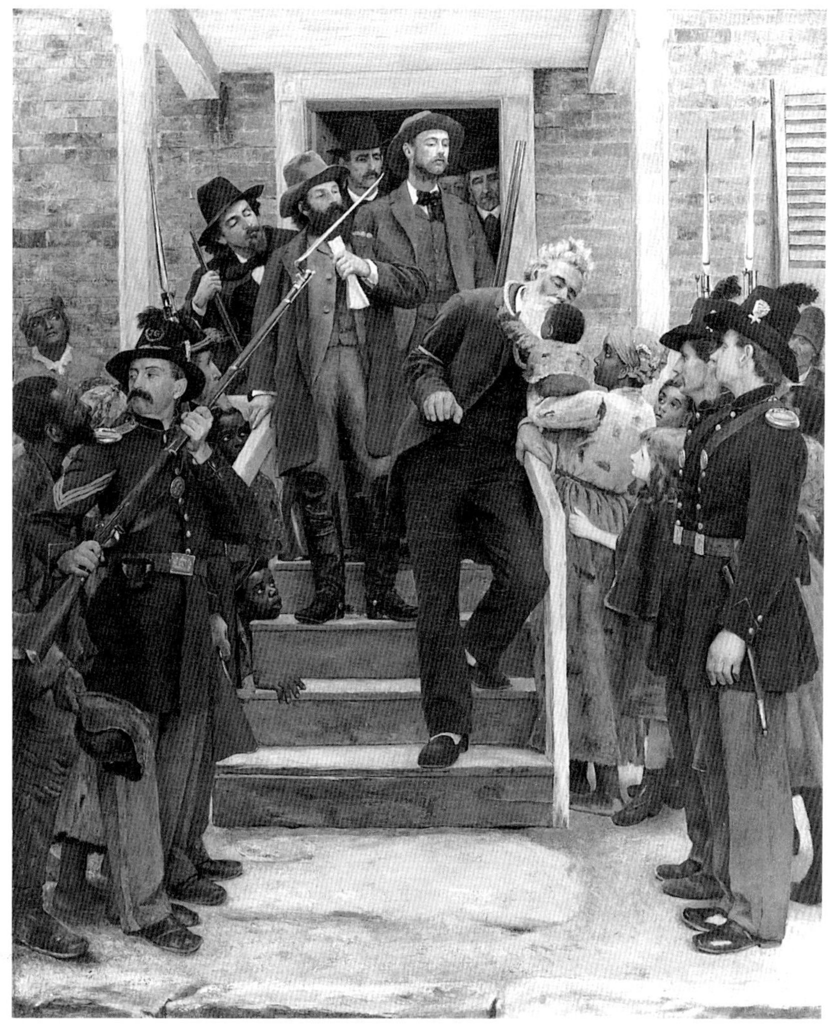

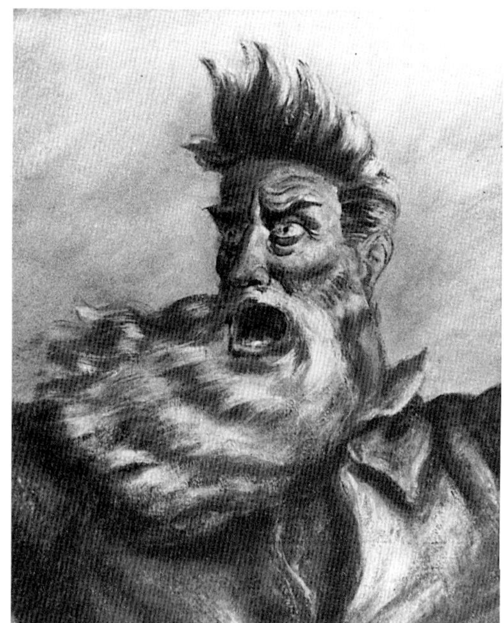

FIGURE 13 *(left)*

Thomas Hovenden (American, 1840–1895)
The Last Moments of John Brown, 1884
Oil on canvas
46 × 38 in.
Fine Arts Museums of San Francisco. Gift of Mr. and Mrs. John D. Rockefeller 3rd.

FIGURE 14 *(above)*

John Steuart Curry
John Brown, **from the Kansas State Capitol mural** ***Tragic Prelude,***
1937–42.
Photograph courtesy Kansas State Historical Society, Topeka.

painted the fiery abolitionist as "God's Angry Man."[109] Striding straight into the Kansas of the 1930s, this John Brown is mad as hell and is not going to take it anymore (fig. 14). As the State Capitol mural sketches began taking shape, Kansans girded their loins against Old John Brown and young John Curry . . . those meddling outsiders . . . that alien corn.

NOTES

1. Quoted in "In Curry, Kansas 'Found Its Homer,'" *Kansas City Star,* 2 September 1946. Howard also wrote screenplays based on the Lewis novels *Arrowsmith* (1931) and *Dodsworth* (1936). His last screenplay was for *Gone with the Wind* (1939); see Richard Harwell, *GWTW: The Screenplay by Sidney Howard* (New York: Collier, 1980), 14.

2. Quoted in "In Curry, Kansas 'Found Its Homer.'"

3. Sidney Howard to Curry, 3 March 1936, Curry Papers, Archives of American Art, Smithsonian Institution, Washington, D.C. (hereafter cited as Curry Papers/AAA), microfilm roll 164, frame 230.

4. H. Tracy Kneeland, Hart, Kneeland & Poindexter, Real Estate Brokers, Hartford, Conn., to Curry, 18 November 1931, Curry Papers/AAA, microfilm roll 166, frames 763–64.

5. For an insightful discussion of the context of Curry's early patronage, see Avis Berman, *Rebels on Eighth Street: Juliana Force and the Whitney Museum of American Art* (New York: Atheneum, 1990), 266–72.

6. See *The Whitney Studio Club and American Art, 1900–1932,* exh. cat. (New York: Whitney Museum of American Art, 1975), 20.

7. Edward Alden Jewell, "Kansas Has Found Her Homer," *New York Times,* 7 December 1930, late city edition, sec. 9, 11.

8. *Whitney Studio Club,* 7, 20. Juliana Force, on behalf of Mrs. Whitney, purchased several of Curry's works from his first one-man show at the Studio Club. See Berman, *Rebels on Eighth Street,* 272.

9. The photograph appeared in the Rotogravure section of the *New York Times,* 22 November 1931.

10. Curry to Margit Varga, Curry Papers/AAA, 28 February 1942, microfilm roll 166.

11. On the overwhelming proportion of midwesterners among American literary expatriates in Paris in the 1920s, see Frederick J. Hoffman, *The Twenties: American Writing in the Postwar Decade,* rev. ed. (New York: Free Press, 1965), 49–52.

12. See, for example, Alfred Haworth Jones, "The Search for a Usable American Past in the New Deal Era," *American Quarterly* 23 (December 1971): 710–24; and Karal Ann Marling, "A Note on the New Deal Iconography: Futurology and the Historical Myth," in *Prospects: An Annual of American Cultural Studies,* vol. 4, ed. Jack Salzman (New York: Burt Franklin, 1981), 421–40.

13. On the rhetoric surrounding Burchfield's early work, see M. Sue Kendall, "Serendipity at the Sunwise Turn: Mary Mowbray-Clarke and the Early Patronage of Charles Burchfield," in Nannette V. Maciejunes, Michael D. Hall, et al, *The Paintings of Charles Burchfield: North by Midwest,* exh. cat. (New York: Harry N. Abrams in association with the Columbus Museum of Art, 1997), 89–99. For an excellent presentation of the critical discourse about Hopper, see Andrew Hemingway, "To 'Personalize the Rainpipe': The Critical Mythology of Edward Hopper," in *Prospects: An Annual of American Cultural Studies,* vol. 17, ed. Jack Salzman (New York and Cambridge: Cambridge University Press, 1992), 379–404.

14. R. Eugene Curry, Armonk, N.Y., to Dorothy Francis, Marshalltown, Iowa, 13 June 1975. I am very grateful to the late Eugene Curry for sending me a copy of this letter as well as for the many clippings, photographs, and remembrances related to his brother John that he shared with me over the years.

15. See, for example, Karal Ann Marling, "Thomas Hart Benton's *Boomtown:* Regionalism Redefined," in *Prospects: An Annual of American Cultural Studies,* vol. 6, ed. Jack Salzman (New York: Burt Franklin, 1981), 89; and Erika Doss, *Benton, Pollock, and the Politics of Modernism: From Regionalism to Abstract Expressionism* (Chicago: University of Chicago Press, 1991), 31, 57. Benton himself made this link in his autobiography: "[W]hile I watched my father die and listened to the voices of his friends . . . I was moved by a great desire to know more of the America which I had glimpsed in the suggestive words of his old cronies." Thomas Hart Benton, *An Artist in America,* 3rd rev. ed. (Columbia: University of Missouri Press, 1968), 76–77.

16. The phenomenon of a "paradigm shift" in the cross-pollination of ideas between scholarly disciplines was first noted in Thomas S. Kuhn, *The Structure of Scientific Revolutions,* 2nd ed. (Chicago: University of Chicago Press, 1970). For an illuminating account of the spheres of art and commerce in this period, see Michele H. Bogart, *Artists, Advertising, and the Borders of Art* (Chicago and London: University of Chicago Press, 1995).

17. Thomas Hart Benton, "Review of Laurence E. Schmeckebier's *John Steuart Curry's Pageant of America," Wisconsin Magazine of History* 27, no. 3 (March 1944): 348.

18. Robert F. Karolevitz, *The Prairie Is My Garden: The Story of Harvey Dunn, Artist* (Aberdeen, S.D.: North Plains Press, 1969), 66.

19. Robert F. Karolevitz, *Where Your Heart Is: The Story of Harvey Dunn, Artist* (Aberdeen, S.D.: North Plains Press, 1970), 101. At times Dunn sounds like the consummate regionalist: "I prefer painting pictures of early South Dakota life to any other kind . . . my search for other horizons has led me around to my first." Quoted in Karolevitz, *The Prairie Is My Garden,* 61.

20. Karolevitz, *The Prairie Is My Garden,* 44.

21. Karolevitz, *Where Your Heart Is,* 101.

22. Karolevitz, *The Prairie Is My Garden,* 19.

23. The present location of *Kansas Wheat Ranch* is unknown. *The Deserted House* is illustrated in Karolevitz, *The Prairie Is My Garden,* 52, 81. The date of the painting was supplied by Francine Marcel, curator of the South Dakota Art Museum, Brookings.

24. The date of the painting has been the subject of confusion. Records of the South Dakota Art Museum have traditionally given the date as 1926, although recently a date of 1943 was added to the museum's object record for reasons that are unknown. In a telephone interview with the author 21 May 1982, Sheila Agee, assistant director of the South Dakota Art Museum, Brookings, dated *I Am the Resurrection and the Life* to 1926. The museum's present curator, Francine Marcel, confirmed that date in a telephone conversation with the author on 8 January 1997, citing correspondence in museum files as of 1977 that gave the date of the painting as 1926. It is also interesting to note that beginning in January of 1928, Dunn's work began to appear regularly on the covers of the *American Legion Monthly.* Dunn had served in World War I as one of the eight official artists of the American Expeditionary Force (Karolevitz, *Where Your Heart Is,* 35–43, 71).

25. Laurence E. Schmeckebier, *John Steuart Curry's Pageant of America* (New York: American Artists Group, 1943), 35–36.

26. *Return from Bohemia* is the title of a 1935 pastel drawing by Wood (IBM Collection, New York) in which he dramatizes his return to Iowa after art study abroad. See Wanda M. Corn, *Grant Wood: The Regionalist Vision* (New Haven: Yale University Press, 1983), 112. The term *region of memory* was used by the Southern Agrarians; see James M. Dennis, *Grant Wood: A Study in American Art and Culture* (New York: Viking Press, 1975), 152. Wood's relation to the Midwest is also admirably addressed in Anedith Nash, "*Death on the Ridge Road:* Grant Wood and Modernization in the Midwest," in *Prospects: An Annual of American Cultural Studies,* vol. 8, ed. Jack Salzman (New York: Burt Franklin, 1983), 281–301.

27. Maynard Walker, quoted in "In Curry Kansas 'Found Its Homer.'" Maynard Walker, Ferargil Galleries, New York, to Curry, Westport, Conn., 27 February 1931, Curry Papers/AAA, microfilm roll 166, frame 722.

28. Maynard Walker to Marco Morrow, Capper Publications, Topeka, Kans., 14 March 1931, Curry Papers/AAA, microfilm roll 166, frame 723. In the same letter, Walker wrote: "It might interest you to know that we first got interested in Curry through the recommendation of Karl Anderson, Sherwood's brother, who feels like I do about Curry."

29. Maynard Walker to Senator Arthur Capper, Capper Publications, Topeka, Kans., 14 March 1931; Capper, U.S. Senate, Washington, D.C., to Walker, 24 March 1931, Curry Papers/AAA, microfilm roll 166, frames 720–21.

30. Maynard Walker to William Allen White, Emporia, Kans., 25 November 1931, Curry Papers/AAA, microfilm roll 166, frames 767–68.

31. L. T. Hull, Washburn College, Topeka, Kans., to Ferargil Galleries, New York, 16 May 1931, Curry Papers/AAA, microfilm roll 166, frame 736.

32. The quote is from a letter from Maynard Walker to R. A. Holland, Kansas City Art Institute, 25 November 1931, Curry Papers/AAA, microfilm roll 166, frame 765. This topic is handled in greater depth in the first chapter of M. Sue Kendall, *Rethinking Regionalism: John Steuart Curry and the Kansas Mural Controversy* [New Directions in American Art, vol. 2] (Washington, D.C.: Smithsonian Institution Press, 1986).

33. Mrs. Henry J. Allen, Wichita, Kansas, to William Allen White, Emporia, Kansas, 16 December 1931, Curry Papers/AAA, microfilm roll 166, frames 771–72.

34. Sidney Howard, *Alien Corn: A Drama in Three Acts,* in *The Best Plays of 1932–33,* ed. Burns Mantle (New York: Dodd, Mead, 1933), 205–37. Howard's keen awareness of the gap between country folk and big-city art dealers is evident in his other popular play of those years, *The Late Christopher Bean.* It is included in the same volume, 238–70.

35. The quote is from Curry's "Address at the Agricultural College, 24 February 1937," typescript, Curry Papers/AAA, microfilm roll 165.

36. "Artists Pocket Change with Pride at Party," *Bridgeport (Conn.) Post,* 11 July 1931; "Fakir Show of Silver Mine Guild," *New Canaan (Conn.) Advertiser,* 16 July 1931. Sold in the auction were paintings and sculptures parodying the styles of local artists. Curry was described as a "relentless but side-splitting auctioneer." Silvermine was an art colony about four miles from Norwalk.

37. Quoted in Barbara Probst Solomon, "Westport Wildlife," *New Yorker* 72, no. 26 (9 September 1996): 82. DuBois's memoir, *Artists Say the Silliest Things* (New York: American Artists Group, 1941), gives a lively account of Westport in the 1920s.

38. Solomon, "Westport Wildlife": 78–85.

39. Ibid., 83.

40. Zelda's well-publicized pranks and Marsh's painting are discussed in Jeffrey Meyers, *Scott Fitzgerald: A Biography* (New York: HarperCollins, 1994), 68–69. Curry's close friendship with Reginald Marsh, evident from the tone of their correspondence, is also mentioned in Schmeckebier, *Pageant,* 53, 180–81.

41. On the "Curry-of-Kansas" moniker see, for example, "Curry of Kansas," *Life* 1, no. 1 (23 November 1936): 28–31. See also virtually any survey history of American art published since the 1930s.

42. Solomon, "Westport Wildlife": 81.

43. This list is suggestive but incomplete. For more on the subject, see William Slaughter, *Westport Artists of the Past: A Bicentennial Exhibition, 1976,* exh. cat. (Westport, Conn.: Westport Bicentennial Arts Committee, 1976). I am grateful to the late R. Eugene Curry for sending me a copy of this publication.

44. Curry's friendship with Brooks is mentioned in James Hoopes, *Van Wyck Brooks: In Search of American Culture* (Amherst: University of Massachusetts Press, 1977), 143.

45. Van Wyck Brooks, "On Creating a Usable Past," *Dial* 64 (11 April 1918): 339, 341. See, for example: Warren I. Susman, "History and the American Intellectual: Uses of a Usable Past," *American Quarterly* 16, no. 2, pt. 2 (summer 1964): 243–63; Jones, "The Search for a Usable American Past"; and Marling, "A Note on New Deal Iconography."

46. Solomon, "Westport Wildlife": 82.

47. The facility is today the Kings Highway School. See Joanna Foster, "John Curry's Murals," *Westport (Conn.) News,* 18 February 1987, 12ff. The murals underwent a substantial restoration in 1996; see Thane Grauel, "Expert Restores Curry's Kings Highway $1 Million Frescos," *Westport (Conn.) Minuteman,* 11 July 1996, 3, 10.

48. Foster, "The Way Westport Was": 12. O'Neill would "come and sit with" Curry's wife, Kathleen, "while John was painting" the frescoes; letter from Mollie Donovan, Westport, Conn., to the author, 18 January 1997.

49. Foster, "The Way Westport Was": 12. Curry's friendship with the Johnstons is attested in the letter cited in note 48.

50. Donald Munson, "Westport Artist, John Stuart [*sic*] Curry, Wins New Acclaim," unidentified newspaper clipping (1934), Curry files, Westport Public Library. Further information on the commissioning of these murals is found in Vivien Testa, "The Curry Frescoes," 1971, typescript, Curry files, Westport Public Library. Testa's account, based on interviews with several people who were involved in the process, relies most heavily on the recollections of Henrietta Sturgis Cholmeley-Jones, former member of the Westport Art Committee and a local WPA art supervisor from 1934 to 1938. According to her, Curry approached the four-person committee with the request to do a fresco, "if the School Board would supply the necessary materials with a boy to put the wet plaster on the wall." Testa adds that "the money was raised by contribution from the townspeople. . . . Curry used local people for his models. The school custodian, Charles Langenberg, posed for the gravedigger in the tragedy mural." For more on Cholmeley-Jones, see John Kazzi, "Westport Seeks to Preserve WPA Art," *The Hour* (Norwalk, Conn.), 2 October 1982.

51. Constance S. Silver, quoted in Mollie Donovan, Westport, Connecticut, press release (July 1996), "Restoration of John Steuart Curry Frescos to Start." The author wishes to thank Patricia Powell of the Elvehjem Museum of Art for this typescript.

52. Curry's travels with the Ringling Brothers and Barnum & Bailey Circus are treated in an essay by Patricia Junker in this volume, pp. 151–64. See also *Aerialist's Fall,* in Schmeckebier, *Pageant,* figs. 219–20, 228. In 1931 the famous aerialist Lillian Leitzel fell twenty-five feet to the ground while on tour with the circus in Copenhagen, dying two days later. Schmeckebier claims that the falling-aerialist sketches were not connected with that event, but Leitzel was quite popular in America, and her death would have been widely publicized. Curry also developed these sketches into a lithograph, the first of ten of his prints to be published by Associated American Artists; see *The Missed Leap* (1934), in *The Lithographs of John Steuart Curry: A Catalogue Raisonné,* ed. Sylvan Cole, Jr. (New York: Associated American Artists, 1976), pl. 23.

53. Lawrence W. Levine, *Highbrow/Lowbrow: The Emergence of Cultural Hierarchy in America* (Cambridge: Harvard University Press, 1988), 235. Apropos of the Shakespearean theme in Curry's *Tragedy* panel, see the superb chapter "William Shakespeare in America," 13–81.

54. From "American Regionalism: A Personal History of the Movement," in Thomas Hart Benton, *An American in Art: A Professional and Technical Autobiography* (Lawrence: University Press of Kansas, 1969), 151.

55. Thomas Craven, "U.S. Scene," *Time* 24, no. 6 (24 December 1934): 24–27.

56. Author telephone interview with photographer John Barry, Jr., Cedar Rapids, Iowa, 20 June 1982. Other photos from the session appeared in Adeline Taylor, "One Famous Artist Sketches Another," *Cedar Rapids Gazette,* 16 July 1933, 4.

57. The quote is from Jennie Small Owen, "Kansas Folks Worth Knowing: John Steuart Curry," *Kansas Teacher* 46, no. 5 (March 1938): 33–35. For a fuller description of this second attempt to win support for Curry in Kansas, see Kendall, *Rethinking Regionalism,* 34–39. By 1942, at least according to the curator Gordon Washburn, it had become clear that the aim of developing a market for regional art in its various home territories had not developed as artists (and their New York agents) had hoped: "[T]hough many of our artists are painting their fathers' pastures it is only our city dwellers who buy the results." Gordon Washburn, "An Artists' Society Sponsors a Regional Show," in *Great Lakes Exhibition: Paintings by Artists of the Great Lakes Region,* exh. cat. (Buffalo, N.Y.: Albright Art Gallery for The Patterson Society, 1942), unpaginated.

58. "Curry's Frescoes Receive Enthusiastic Comment among Westport Artists," *Westporter-Herald,* 31 August 1934. Typescript supplied by Mollie Donovan, Westport, Connecticut.

59. "November First Set as Tentative Date for Formal Unveiling of Curry Murals at Bedford Jr. High," *Westporter-Herald,* 9 October 1934. Typescript supplied by Mollie Donovan, Westport, Connecticut.

60. "Is Artist John Curry Having a Little Fun in His Norwalk Mural?" *Bridgeport (Conn.) Post,* undated [late 1935?], Curry files, Westport Public Library.

61. For an excellent study of the Department of the Treasury's New Deal art projects, see Karal Ann Marling, *Wall-to-Wall America: A Cultural History of Post-Office Murals in the Great Depression* (Minneapolis: University of Minnesota Press, 1982). The PWAP is discussed on pp. 42–48.

62. Treasury Department order, quoted in Belisario R. Contreras, "The New Deal Treasury Department Art Programs and the American Artist: 1933 to 1943," Ph.D. diss., American University, Washington, D.C., 1967, 96.

63. Marling, *Wall-to-Wall America,* 56.

64. Ibid., 133–36.

65. "The Great American Roadside," *Fortune* 10, no. 3 (September 1934): 53–63, 172, 174, 177. Eleven Curry illustrations appeared with the article.

66. Though Curry refers here to his 1938 mural *The Oklahoma Land Rush* (color plate 60) in the U.S. Department of the Interior building in Washington, D.C., the sentiment still applies. John Steuart Curry, typescript of mural description, Curry Papers/ AAA, microfilm roll 165, frame 1059.

67. That the figure is a self-portrait is confirmed in Schmeckebier, *Pageant,* 300.

68. Several of these preliminary studies are reproduced in Schmeckebier, *Pageant,* figs. 299–307.

69. Contreras, "New Deal Treasury Department Art Programs," 144.

70. Photographs of several of the rejected studies are published in Matthew Baigell, "The Relevancy of Curry"s Paintings of Black Freedom," in *John Steuart Curry: A Retrospective Exhibition of His Work Held in the Kansas State Capitol, Topeka, October 3–November 3, 1970,* exh. cat. (Lawrence: University of Kansas Museum of Art, 1970), 19–29.

71. Edward Rowan, superintendent, Section of Painting and Sculpture, Treasury Department, Washington, D.C., to Curry, 22 March 1935; and Rowan to Curry, 13 February 1936, National Archives and Records Service, Record Group 121, Entry 133, box (121) 408, file: "John S. Curry—Dept. of Justice Bldg., Wash., D.C."

72. Curry to Edward Rowan, superintendent, Section of Painting and Sculpture, Treasury Department, Washington, D.C., 16 March 1936, National Archives and Records Service, Record Group 121, Entry 133, box (121) 408, file: "John S. Curry—Dept. of Justice Bldg., Wash., D.C."

73. The Section's steering of a careful course to avoid controversy, not only with Curry but also with other artists, is discussed throughout Marling, *Wall-to-Wall America.*

74. Charles Moore, Commission of Fine Arts, Washington, D.C., to Edward Rowan, superintendent, Section of Painting and Sculpture, Treasury Department, Washington, D.C., 30 March 1936, National Archives and Records Service, Record Group 121, Entry 133, box (121) 408, file: "John S. Curry—Dept. of Justice Bldg., Wash., D.C."

75. Quoted in Thomas Cripps, *Slow Fade to Black: The Negro in American Film, 1900–1942* (New York: Oxford University Press, 1977), 252.

76. Marc Connelly, *The Green Pastures,* ed. with intro. by Thomas Cripps (Madison: University of Wisconsin Press, 1979), 22–23. See also Cripps, *Slow Fade to Black,* 258–61; and David Levering Lewis, *When Harlem Was in Vogue* (New York: Alfred A. Knopf, 1981), 245.

77. Beverly Kelley, Delaware, Ohio, to Curry, 3 January 1933, Curry Papers/AAA, microfilm roll 167. The two had apparently met during Curry's tour with the Ringling Brothers and Barnum & Bailey circus.

78. The quote is from Loren Miller, "Uncle Tom in Hollywood," *Crisis* 41, no. 11 (November 1934): 329, 336. For other stirrings of discontent among blacks at that time, see Victor Daly, "Green Pastures and Black Washington," *Crisis* 40, no. 5 (May 1933): 106.

79. Donald Bogle, *Toms, Coons, Mulattoes, Mammies, and Bucks: An Interpretive History of Blacks in American Films,* rev. ed. (New York: Continuum, 1990), 67.

80. Ed Guerrero, *Framing Blackness: The African American Image in Film* (Philadelphia: Temple University Press, 1993), 26. Guerrero also analyzes the ways in which the rise of fascism helped put an end to the plantation genre, as "Hollywood dropped the inscription of slavery and the plantation myth for themes more likely to turn a profit for the duration of the war" (27).

81. The quote is from Bogle, *Toms, Coons, Mulattoes, Mammies, and Bucks,* 26.

82. The quote is taken from the previously cited letter from Charles Moore about the Curry mural sketches; see note 74.

83. Bret Waller, "An Interview With Mrs. Daniel Schuster," in *John Steuart Curry: A Retrospective,* 17.

84. An eloquent analysis of the stereotypes present in Benton's first regionalist painting is given in Marling, "Thomas Hart Benton's *Boomtown,*" 73–137.

85. Reeves Lewenthal to Curry, 5 October 1943; Curry to Harry Abrams, 15 October 1943, Curry Papers/AAA, microfilm roll 166, frames 159, 162.

86. W. S. Basinger, Union Pacific Railroad, Omaha, Neb., to Curry, 5 May 1939; Curry to Basinger, 10 May 1939, Curry Papers/AAA, microfilm roll 165.

87. For a more detailed discussion, see Kendall, *Rethinking Regionalism,* 63–65.

88. Invoice 4349, United Costumers, Inc., Hollywood, Calif., to Curry, 15 January 1940, Curry Papers/AAA, microfilm roll 164, frame 223.

89. Curry would later be given the opportunity to complete this theme for the Law School library at the University of Wisconsin (color plate 68) by the school's dean, his friend Lloyd K. Garrison, great-grandson of the famed abolitionist William Lloyd Garrison; see Kendall, *Rethinking Regionalim,* 76–77.

90. *Art Guides: Justice Building* (Washington, D.C.: Art in Federal Buildings, Inc., n.d.), 17, from the Justice Department Library files. The mural mirrors a widespread concern in the 1930s with mob violence and "legal lynchings"; see, for example, Marlene Park, "Lynching and Antilynching: Art and Politics in the 1930s," in *Prospects: An Annual of American Cultural Studies,* vol. 18, ed. Jack Salzman (New York and Cambridge: Cambridge University Press, 1993), 315ff. For the presentation of this theme in the movies, see "The Mob and the Search for Authority, 1933–1937," in Andrew Bergman, *We're in the Money: Depression America and Its Films* (New York: Harper and Row, 1971), 110–22.

91. An illustration of this painting is in Schmeckebier, *Pageant,* fig. 184. Its present location is unknown.

92. Eleven of the "Harlem Types: Portraits by Winold Reiss" are reproduced in Robert Sklar, ed., *The Plastic Age (1917–1930)* (New York: Braziller, 1970), 199–206; information on the Locke anthology is on p. 181.

93. See Wayne Craven, *American Art: History and Culture* (New York: Harry N. Abrams, 1994), 544.

94. Ibid.

95. "House Is Museum for Curry Pictures," *Newburyport (Mass.) Daily News,* 5 June 1952.

96. Several of these watercolor sketches are in the collection of Mrs. John Steuart Curry. The youths are dressed in institutional brown clothing.

97. John Kwiat, "John Reed Club Art Exhibition," *New Masses* (February 1933): 23–24; Gertrude Benton, "Art and Social Theories," *Creative Arts* 12, no. 3 (March 1933): 216–18. The cartoonist was Jacob Burck; Curry's interest in him is described in an essay by Edward Laning in *East Side, West Side, All around the Town* (Tucson: University of Arizona Museum of Art, 1969). The artist praised Burck's work in John Steuart Curry, "Curry's View," *Art Digest* 9, no. 20 (September 1935): 29.

98. Walter White, *Rope and Faggot: A Biography of Judge Lynch* (New York: Knopf, 1929); Bellows's lithograph appeared in an advertisement for the book in *Crisis* 36, no. 3 (March 1929): 103. For contemporaneous coverage of the exhibition, see: "Mysterious Protests Bar 'Lynching Show,'" *Art Digest* 9, no. 10 (February 1935): 14; "Protests Bar Show of Art on Lynching," *New York Times,* 12 February 1935; "To Show Lynching Art," *New York Times,* 13 February 1935; "Art Commentary on Lynching," *Art News* 33, no. 21 (23 February 1935): 13; "Art: Lynching Show Opens in Spite of Opposition 'Outburst,'" *Newsweek* 5, no. 8 (23 February 1935): 19, with illustrations; "An Art Exhibit against Lynching," *Crisis* 42, no. 4 (April 1935): 106; and "Art as a Cure for Lynching," *Christian Century* 52, no. 16 (17 April 1935): 516–17. The exhibition is discussed in greater depth—and many of the artworks are illustrated—in Park, "Lynching and Antilynching," 311–65. For more on Curry's involvement in the exhibition, see Kendall, *Rethinking Regionalism,* 79–82.

99. A copy of the exhibition catalogue is in the "Lynching" folder, Schomburg Collection, New York Public Library.

100. Quoted in Park, "Lynching and Antilynching," 326.

101. The exhibition catalogue listed the painting as being in his collection.

102. See Cole, *The Lithographs of John Steuart Curry,* plate 22.

103. Curry, "Speech before the Art Association of Madison, January 19, 1937," typescript 6, Curry Papers/AAA, microfilm roll 165, no frame nos.

104. The murals are the subject of Kendall, *Rethinking Regionalism.*

105. "The Ku Klux Klan Goes 'Ko-ed'," *Kansas City Star,* 15 August 1937.

106. I thank Charles C. Eldredge for calling this photograph to my attention. For more on the activities of the Klan in Kansas, and for the role of the newspaperman William Allen White (who helped sponsor Curry's murals) in fighting it, see Lila Lee Jones, "The Ku Klux Klan in Eastern Kansas during the 1920's," *Emporia State Research Studies* 23, no. 3 (winter 1975): 5–41. See also "Why Kansas Bans the Klan," *Literary Digest* 75, no. 6 (11 November 1922): 13; "William Allen White's War on the Klan," *Literary Digest* 83, no. 2 (11 October 1924): 16; Genevieve Yost, "History of Lynchings in Kansas," *Kansas Historical Quarterly* 2, no. 2 (May 1933): 182–219; and F. W. Schruben, *Kansas in Turmoil: 1930–1936* (Columbia: University of Missouri Press, 1969), 180–89.

107. For a fuller account, see Kendall, *Rethinking Regionalism.*

108. The legend that the Hovenden painting depicts, that John Brown stooped to kiss a baby on his way to the gallows, was well known in Kansas while Curry was painting his murals; see James C. Malin, "The John Brown Legend in Pictures: Kissing the Negro Baby," *Kansas Historical Quarterly* 8, no. 4 (November 1939), facing 340.

109. The phrase is taken from a 1932 novel about John Brown; see Leonard Ehrlich, *God's Angry Man* (New York: Simon and Schuster, 1932). Curry's *Tragic Prelude* is the cover illustration for Bruce Olds, *Raising Holy Hell: A Novel of John Brown* (New York: Penguin, 1997).

A Stranger to the Ivory Tower

JOHN STEUART CURRY AND THE UNIVERSITY OF WISCONSIN

LUCY J. MATHIAK

Although he is best known as a regionalist artist, John Steuart Curry also made significant contributions to rural life and to higher education through his unique role as artist-in-residence at the University of Wisconsin from 1936 to 1946 (fig. 1). Curry came to Wisconsin as part of an educational experiment that linked a famous artist with rural citizens who wanted to create art. Although the story of that experiment is one of people, place, and time, there is an institutional dimension as well, for the project produced a vibrant rural art program that continued after Curry's death and served as a model for similar programs elsewhere. This essay discusses the presence and impact of the artist and the art program within the tradition of educational innovation at the university as well as the socioeconomic and cultural context of rural Wisconsin life during the decade Curry lived there.[1]

Curry's appointment as artist-in-residence was in keeping with the concept of the "service university" that had distinguished Wisconsin's public higher-education structure since the beginning of the century. Represented by what had come to be known as "the Wisconsin Idea"—a broad initiative to foster the economic, social, intellectual, and moral development of the people of the state—the principal tenets of this vision included the notion that "the boundaries of the campus are the boundaries of the state." Asserting the benefits of "the democratization of knowledge," Wisconsin's concept of a comprehensive educational institution went beyond scholarship to promote an unprecedented triad at the core of the campus mission: teaching, research, and public service.[2]

Given "a long rope and a wide field" by university President Glenn Frank, Curry needed only to reside in Madison and use the studio specially built for him on the campus to earn his $4,000 annual salary.[3] Had he used the guaranteed income to hide away, immersed in his own work, the experiment would have failed. But as an editorial written at the time of his death noted:

He was not content in the artist's attic. He was a stranger to the ivory tower. He knew what art means in its deeper significance and he toiled to show it to others, to inspire an appreciation and an active interest in it for thousands of people to whom it had been something a million miles away from their own lives.... His Wisconsin rural artists, farmers and village housewives, were his pride and his joy. A youngster he could help with a brush or an idea was a thrill to him beyond his biggest mural.[4]

When Curry accepted the appointment at Wisconsin in 1936, there was no model for an artist-in-residence to inspire such

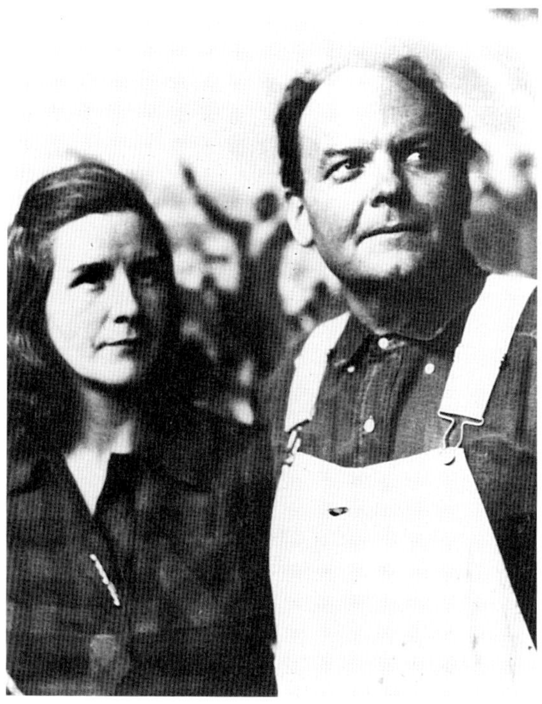

FIGURE 1
John and Kathleen Curry, Madison, Wisconsin, 1944. Photograph courtesy Curry Papers, Archives of American Art, Smithsonian Institution, Washington, D.C. Gift of Mrs. Stanley R. Fike.

artistic production among rural populations. The organizers' plans were based on theory during the first few years; they had yet to identify their clientele. As the rural sociologist and program cofounder John Barton wrote in 1962, "We little knew when we started out combing the countryside in 1939 that a movement of such significant extent and value would result."[5] Nonetheless, the university's rural art program had become an integral link to the people of the state within two decades of its inception. By the mid-1950s the program had grown from an idea into a statewide organization drawn from regional and local associations and related regional exhibitions, classes, and workshops.

The university that named John Steuart Curry artist-in-residence was a complex world of groundbreaking discovery, dynamic personalities, and state politics. College of Agriculture scientists were engaged in some of the major vitamin discoveries of the early twentieth century; John R. Commons was revolutionizing the understanding of labor relations; and the history department was about to hire Merle Curti, the young scholar who in 1944 would be awarded the Pulitzer Prize.

Glenn Frank, who was essential to the approval and financing of Curry's appointment, was just months away from the January 1937 Board of Regents vote that ended his controversial tenure as university president. Tending toward the iconoclastic, Frank sought to reshape the university in ways that presaged late-twentieth-century educational debate and yet brought him into conflict with the state's progressive political leaders. He believed the university should develop well-rounded decision makers; he argued that education had become overly specialized and that progress could only be achieved by reorienting higher education to train students as generalists rather than as narrowly defined scholars.[6]

Frank championed the Experimental College and other radical educational initiatives, despite Progressive Governor Philip La Follette's denunciation of such programs as unwarranted investments with questionable returns.[7] Indeed, Frank often found himself at odds with the governor and other powerful state economic and political leaders.[8]

Thomas Brittingham, the philanthropist and head of the prominent Wisconsin lumber family whose trust underwrote the artist-in-residence position, came into conflict with Frank several times during the early 1930s. Their main clash occurred when Brittingham led the trust's efforts to keep biochemistry Professor Karl Paul Link from relocating to California. Working with Harry Russell, dean of the College of Agriculture, the Brittingham Trust had proposed to underwrite a generous five-year professorship so that Link would remain at the university. The terms of the gift specified that Link continue his research program and teach advanced students. The regents rejected the gift as having "too many strings attached." Frank, who had initially worked with Brittingham on the proposal, reversed his position because of objections by the Board of Regents. Upset by the public controversy over its attempted philanthropy and Frank's support of the regents, the Brittingham family decided in 1931 not to fund more projects for the university. They reversed this decision in 1936, when trustees voted to support the artist-in-residence position.[9]

Even with the trust now resuming its support, Brittingham carefully pointed out that the university, not he, had selected Curry and had set the terms of the appointment. Writing in 1938, he attributed his caution to the Link experience:

Several years ago the university and this trust got into a great argument as to whether the Trust could make gifts to the University with "strings attached." We did nothing for a long time and only recently the Regents gave us a mild apology and I would not want to say or do anything which would upset the cheap politics which were back of the whole thing.[10]

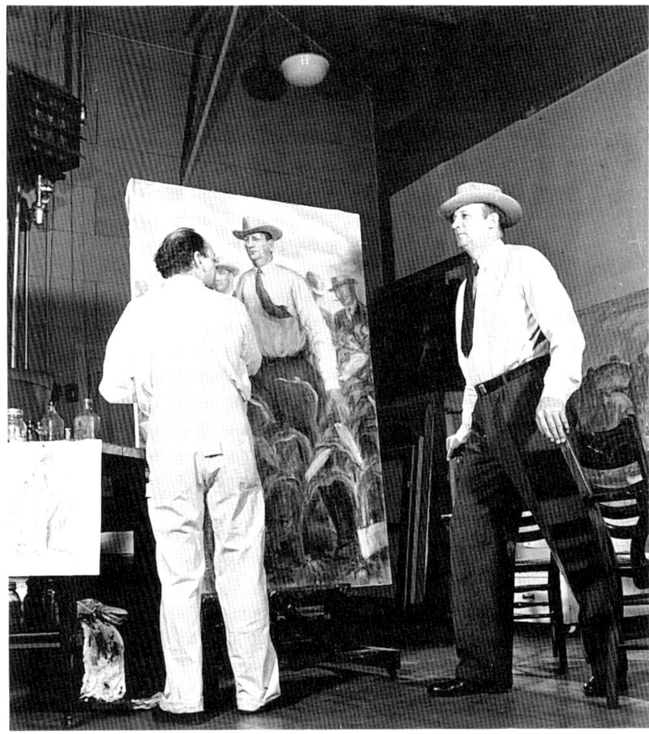

FIGURE 2

Curry painting Dean Chris L. Christensen, Madison, Wisconsin, 1941. Photograph by Eric Schall. Courtesy Curry Papers, Archives of American Art, Smithsonian Institution, Washington, D.C.

The choice of the artist-in-residence position as the first project under resumed Brittingham funding was a move toward better university and patron relations. Happy "to be connected in a small way with having Curry at Madison," the philanthropist was proud of the program's accomplishments. "The fact that John Curry has stirred up so much interest in art at the University and throughout the State is the answer to whether his new position is a success or a failure," he wrote. "I know that it has surpassed the optimistic view I had when the matter was first brought to me."[11]

Despite conflicts with the Board of Regents and the state's elected officials, President Frank had made several innovative appointments, including that of Chris L. Christensen as dean of the College of Agriculture in 1931 (fig. 2). Adding Christensen to the staff advanced Frank's goal of creating resources on the economic and social sides of farming that would balance the campus's traditional contributions to agricultural science and technology.

Like Frank, Christensen had been hired from outside the university community, with credentials quite different from those of the faculty he was to lead.[12] The two men promoted their shared ideals of voluntary economic reform, social change through an educated citizenry, and radical reconstruction of higher education in order to meet social needs. The warm, outgoing, and well-liked dean became a key advocate for Frank's vision, both on and off campus.

Because he shared Frank's view that a revitalized rural culture was essential to future American prosperity, the new dean reshaped the university's annual Farm Short Course. Within a few years, the short-course program's offerings on machinery, livestock, and crop production had been expanded, based on the curriculum of the people's college that Christensen had observed during his studies in Denmark in the early 1920s. The revitalized program operated in the classrooms and, after hours, in the dormitories. Its new curriculum offered drama, literature, music, the visual arts, debate, citizenship, and current events to the Wisconsin farmers who enrolled. In 1934 Christensen added John Barton to the faculty. Barton applied his six years of experience in the Danish folk-school movement to reshape research carried out by rural-sociology faculty and expand the duties of the county extension agents who worked with the state's rural populations.[13] Barton and Christensen formulated the proposal for the rural art program and the artist-in-residence position. Their endeavors drew strong support from Frank, who proclaimed that "[T]here is poetry as well as production on a farm. Art can help us to preserve the poetry while we are battling with the economics of farming."[14]

Although Curry came to Wisconsin to encourage the production of art by rural citizens, he also served as a bridge between campus and community, between prominent art patrons and the rural art program, and between the national art world and the state. His position as artist-in-residence established him as a prominent figure on campus and in the larger local community, but he was not always comfortable in his public role. Robert Hodgell, a student who worked closely with Curry, later described the social gatherings of deans, college presidents, writers, musicians, and others at the Currys' Madison home as "[m]anaged graciously by [his wife,] Kathleen, who spoke of making John a 'spearhead of culture,' and borne with a somewhat alcoholic impatience by John who, in spite of his bright-eyed cherubic look, always seemed ill at ease behind the inevitable bow tie."[15]

Curry met with powerful, famous, and average citizens alike during the last ten years of his life. His guests included Grant Wood and farmwives, Helen Hayes and college students, Frank Lloyd Wright and dairy farmers, Wisconsin business leaders and high-school students. The artist, his wife, and stepdaughter, Ellen, made many friends in the local community. Still, as the *Wisconsin State Journal* publisher Don Anderson recalled years after the artist's death:

It was not easy to become friends with John Curry. A gentle and soft-spoken man, he would not seek favor or acceptance in dishonest agreement of opinion, even little polite white lies. Easy conversation was not his forte, and even friendly talks with him tended to become two-sided monologues rather than dialogue. But once contact was established there was no more delightful man to be with.[16]

Such memories were reflected in Ellen Curry Schuster's recollection of visits to the family's Seminole Highway farm by Curry's friend Dr. Theodore Erickson, the first neurosurgeon on the University of Wisconsin Medical School faculty. The two reclusive men would sit side by side without talking. After a few hours of silent companionship, one or the other would finally proclaim the night to be a "wonderful visit," upon which the doctor would return to his home in Madison.[17]

During his university decade, Curry participated in hunting parties in Jefferson County, fishing trips to the Great Lakes, and packing trips in the American West. As a result, there exists a rich collection of artistic mementos and "buddy stories" that add to the lore of his years in Madison: Curry as the embarrassed hunter who shot a hole in a tire of the Fort Atkinson, Wisconsin, businessman Edward Jones's car; Curry the balding, rotund painter being mistaken for Winston Churchill on a camping trip out West during World War II; and Curry approaching a trip down the Wisconsin River in June 1941 with the Sauk City, Wisconsin, writer August Derleth as if it were a dangerous voyage on uncharted Amazonian waters.[18]

Curry was well connected in southeastern Wisconsin society; among his friends were those who helped produce added support for the university's rural art experiment and the people associated with it.[19] For example, when the artist died, the Madison business leader Adolph C. Bolz and his wife, Eugenie, longtime art patrons, headed the memorial fund that was named in Curry's honor and was used to establish purchase awards for the annual rural art shows.

From 1936 to 1939, Barton, Christensen, and Curry led the program's work with rural artists with support from Wisconsin's extensive network of county agents. They followed up stories of rural people who produced art in their spare time, traveling to meet rural artists in their homes and arranging for them to visit Curry in his Madison studio. In addition, he gave lectures to the Farm Short Course students and civic groups.

As the artist sketched the football team, livestock, and other elements of university life, he became a part of the campus and the community (fig. 3). A sports fan, Curry regularly attended Wisconsin football practices, where his quest to get a better sketching position often placed him in the middle of scrim-

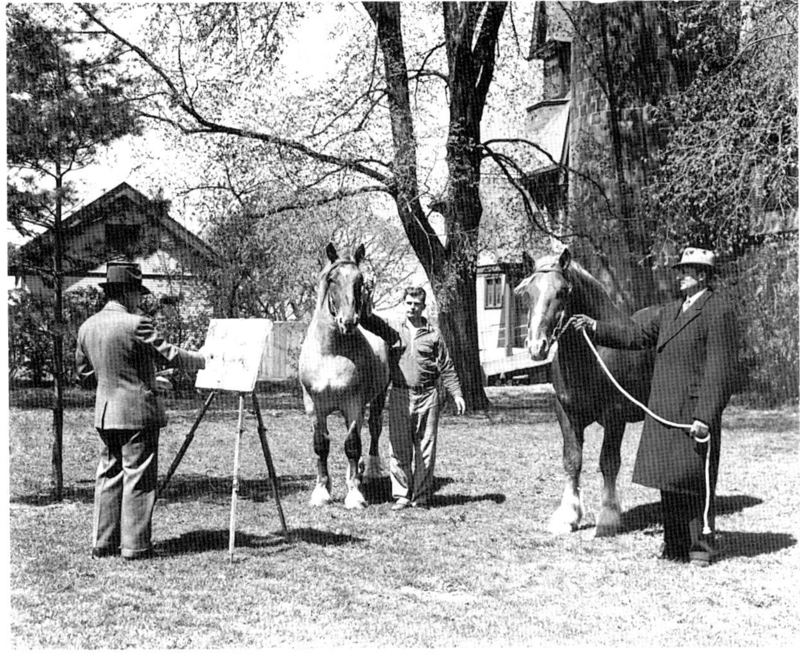

FIGURE 3

Curry sketching prize stallions on the University of Wisconsin campus, with Dean Chris L. Christensen at right, ca. 1936. Photograph courtesy State Historical Society of Wisconsin.

mages. When the artist and his pencils went flying, he would "get up and go back to work, apologizing for interrupting the play."[20]

Paradoxically, John Steuart Curry was both an ideal and an unlikely choice to serve as a bridge between the university and the citizenry: A very shy, private man, he had accepted a position that inherently required a great deal of visibility and public activity. He had attained national visibility as a painter, printmaker, and muralist even before arriving in Wisconsin. The first issue of *Life* magazine in November 1936 featured "Curry of Kansas" and his work, and other articles on Curry, the rural art program, and the artist's family appeared in subsequent issues of *Life* as well as in *Time, Redbook,* and other popular periodicals. His themes—particularly his sympathetic depiction of Kansas farm life—spoke to the daily experiences of ordinary people who, like Curry's proposed clientele, made their living from the land. Yet this humble, soft-spoken man was not a social leader. Described in an editorial written the day after he died as "a tender man, with a voice of velvet and a manner gentle and retiring,"[21] the artist found that the more formal aspects of the position held the least appeal for him. "He doesn't like to make speeches to formal groups," the *Christian Science Monitor* reported in 1941. But Curry found great pleasure in other aspects of his position and was "in his glory when he takes a day off and travels through some distant counties, pushing his car up some rutted side road to a far-off farmhouse, to go into a man's home to see what he has painted."[22]

The lack of a clearly defined program for the artist-in-residence made interactions between Curry and rural people an important factor in the success or failure of this educational experiment. He promptly answered citizens' letters asking for help or advice, except during the prolonged periods of illness that marked the last five years of his life. Even then, he asked friends to help unpack and display work by rural artists, as a secretary transcribed his critiques and words of encouragement. And, while he may have exercised his wry wit in some letters, his tone generally was kind, gentle, and respectful, even when there was no easy way to meet the correspondent's needs.

While Curry was in Madison, the rural art program came to represent a safe means by which artists could display their work and develop their craft. It was not always easy for the artists, most of whom worked with significant disadvantages in resources, education, and social acceptance, to come forward. In order to understand the hardships that rural artists faced, it is important to recognize the social and economic context within which they labored during the 1930s and 1940s.

A large number of the program's artists lacked electricity on their farms and in small rural communities. The hardship created by such conditions is captured in the following passage describing the advent of electrical power:

> **Incandescent lighting ended the use of lanterns and brightened the interior of the home. . . . Shadowy corners and dimly-lit hallways became a thing of the past. Leisure time was increased; [The Tennessee Valley Authority] reported that electric lights added two to four waking hours per day; another study showed that ninety-one "8-hour days" per year were added to the waking hours of farm families. New lighting also encouraged reading and stimulated children's interest in schoolwork. The American Society of Electrical Engineers stated that incandescent lights reduced by 50 percent the amount of time required to perform chores with a lantern.**[23]

Curry arrived in Wisconsin at the same time that the Rural Electrification Administration (REA) and public and private utilities began their drive to bring electricity to people on and off the farm. Nonetheless, progress was slow and uneven. In the early 1930s, only sixteen percent of Wisconsin's farm homes received electricity delivered by power lines; another ten percent had generating engines to provide power. By 1940 just over half of all Wisconsin farms received electricity from power stations. However, although more than seventy percent of farms in some counties had electricity in 1944, the percentage was closer to thirty-five in others.[24]

Thus, while some two hundred uses for electricity in farm life had been developed by 1930, those conveniences were beyond the reach of a significant segment of the state's farm population. Farmers carried out milking and other chores by hand and under poor lighting conditions; homemakers spent about twenty more days per year washing clothes than did their city counterparts who owned electric washers. Even after electrical power could be had, changes in the basic labor processes were slow for rural families who lacked the means to rewire their houses and outbuildings or buy the appliances that would bring greater leisure.[25]

Electrification also brought the direct power necessary to install and use indoor plumbing. In 1930 only sixteen percent of Wisconsin's rural homes had water piped directly into the house. Although some improvements may have decreased the amount of time needed to get water for cooking, bathing, cleaning, and laundering, families without electrical pumps spent ten or more hours each week pumping and carrying water from the source to the house. Rural families also devoted more time to food storage and safety than did their urban counterparts; without electric refrigerators, greater attention needed to be paid to the health risks associated with poor storage and handling.[26]

Other aspects of farm production added to the rural artists' difficulties in finding time for their art. On many farms, fieldwork was still carried out with teams of horses and work crews rather than with gasoline-powered tractors and modern implements. The demands of crop production and the labor required to feed hungry families and farmhands created a tension between artistic drive and the long hours and material resources necessary for economic survival. The challenges facing such artists are illustrated by a letter sent by the Lancaster, Wisconsin, artist Anna Staver to Curry (fig. 4):

I am a very busy farmer's wife. Not only busy keeping house but under the circumstances I must help out of doors much of the time. . . . I love to paint better than anything in the world. I work with watercolors and some oils. In case there should be a way for instruction would it be very costly? As funds are meager now I must consider cost.[27]

Financial circumstance and basic access to supplies posed additional challenges, forcing many rural artists to be resourceful in their choice of materials and their methods. A modest range of art supplies was available through the Sears, Roebuck and Montgomery Ward catalogues, but, before the 1950s, art-

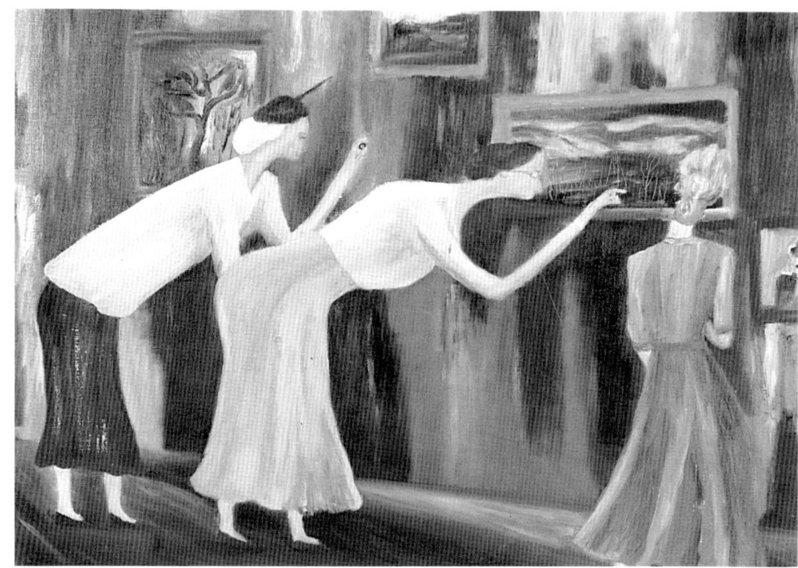

FIGURE 4

Anna Staver (American, b. 1898)
The Three Critics, n.d.
Oil on canvas
28 × 36 in.
Private collection.

supply stores generally were not found outside urban centers. As one farmer wrote, "I did not have no artist paint, but [I] took difference [*sic*] color 10 cent cans of enamel which I had and painted these landscapes on canvas."[28] Moreover, many farms simply did not generate enough income to permit spending on such extras. Under these conditions, artists used such unorthodox surfaces as cardboard, glass, and linoleum, covering them with house and barn paints, kitchen enamels, watercolors, crayon, or pencil. They applied these media, individually or in combination, producing images that did not fall into a single category of subject or style.

The rural citizens who overcame these obstacles in order to make art did so largely without the benefit of formal art instruction. As late as the 1937–38 school year, 79.5 percent of Wisconsin's widespread 7,777 school districts consisted of one-room schools; only three percent of the state's schools employed three or more teachers.[29] Even when rural school districts offered the full complement of kindergarten through high school grade levels, art education rarely went beyond the rudimentary, if it was offered at all. Individual teachers encouraged students who showed particular talent or interest in art, but few teachers were trained in art education. Consequently, many rural artists had no access to art instruction until they were adults and could take courses outside the primary or secondary educational setting. A number of these artists obtained instruction from community members who had arts backgrounds, from area normal or technical schools or, in a few cases, on short-term scholarships to midwest art institutes.

University education was equally removed from the expectations and realities of Wisconsin's farmers and townspeople. The university was part of people's lives to the extent that its faculty and extension agents were directly involved in improving agricultural and homemaking practices. But the campus and its liberal-arts components represented an alien world in which the rural artists' welcome was not obvious or assured. By appointing Curry within the College of Agriculture, using the network of county extension agents and the annual Farm and Home Week program, and arranging visits to the homes of rural artists, program organizers created an inclusive structure that served as an important bridge between the campus and remote areas of the state.[30]

The university's success at working with rural artists of the 1930s and 1940s developed from strong respect for the cultures and experiences of the artists themselves rather than the imposition of the values and assumptions of Curry or his colleagues. When he arrived in December 1936, Curry declared that he had "no ambition to 'wreak' good on the state."[31] Rather, he proposed to do a year's hard work in his campus studio, which would be open to the people of the state if they were interested and wanted his advice. He set the same nonhierarchical tone in his approach to his formal university appointment. More bemused than impressed by his new position, he most visibly used the honorary title "professor" when he painted "Professor Curry" on his studio trash cans.[32]

Art is an expression of self for those who create it, and consequently the products of these rural artists were as varied as their lives, personalities, and interests. The people who struggled to produce art despite the limitations of time and material resources did so because they could not imagine life without artistic expression. When asked what art meant in his life, the Tomahawk, Wisconsin, farmer Herman Krause answered, "My art is like a smoldering fire on which I draw when inspiration dictates and when the day's work is done I can sit down and enjoy the humble efforts of a humble artist." The response of the Fort Atkinson farmwife Millie Rose Lalk (fig. 5) to the same query was simpler but no less powerful—"Everything."[33] Curry's comments and observations at the time reflected the same needs and themes. Once asked whether he could foresee a time when he would quit painting, Curry responded, "How can I? That's all I know."[34]

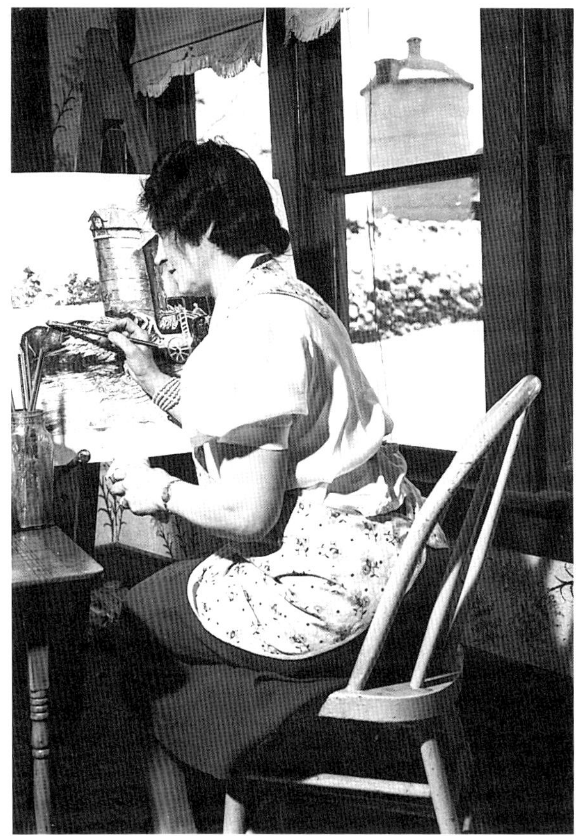

FIGURE 5
Millie Rose Lalk of Fort Atkinson, Wisconsin, at work at her easel. Photograph courtesy State Historical Society of Wisconsin.

Whereas Curry created images to tell the stories of his life and to depict what his biographer, Laurence Schmeckebier, characterized as "the pageant of America," rural artists used their work to capture the large and small events of country life. They frequently chose to portray village street scenes, the drama of survival in winter storms and other severe weather, the heroic actions of family members, and such fundamentals of daily life as laundry, fieldwork, and even making a pie (fig. 6). As the rural art program assumed institutional form, the artists' thematic repertoires expanded to include images of contented artists surrounded by their paintings or members of the local art club making critiques of art on display. Like Curry, rural artists used their work to document historic events or worlds that had passed or were about to pass into history. The itinerant farm laborer Walter Thorp used colored pencils and crayon to create a complex composition in which passenger pigeons, though then already extinct, inhabit the sky (fig. 7). Similarly, Ambrose Ammel, a Fond du Lac taxidermist, used oil paints to

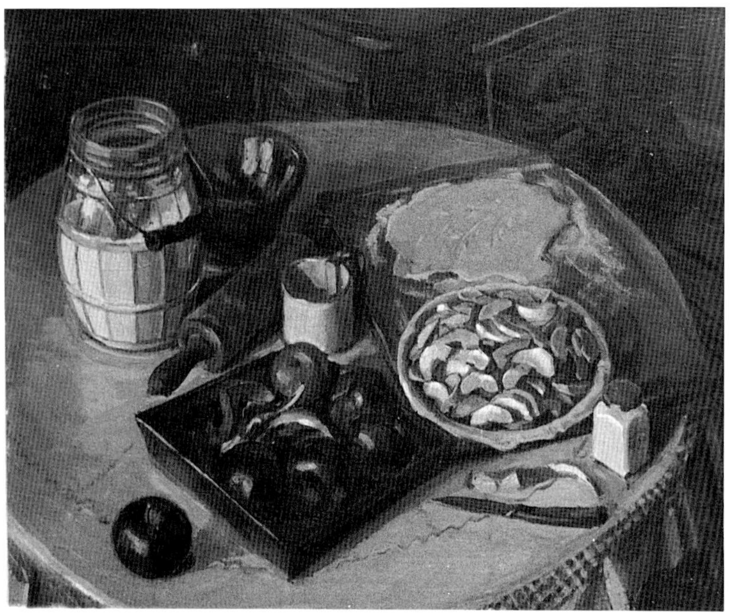

FIGURE 6

Christian Olson (American, b. 1905)
Apple Pie, n.d.
Oil on Masonite
30 × 35 in.
Courtesy Oshkosh Public Museum, Oshkosh, Wisconsin.

produce a complex series documenting the use of horses in threshing and other farm work.

Curry's activities with nonprofessional artists were loosely structured to meet the diverse needs he encountered. His relationships with these individuals could not be measured easily; nor did they fall into neat categories, often extending far beyond the advice offered in letters, studio visits, and gallery tours. Some artists were in their teens or early twenties when they entered the program, and thus they encountered Curry during a transition to formal art training and professional or semiprofessional status.

Kansas native Robert Hodgell met Curry sometime around 1940, when he was painting the Topeka Statehouse murals. He enrolled at the University of Wisconsin but worked primarily with the artist in a quasi-apprenticeship that included assisting on the biochemistry department and Wisconsin State Fair murals and similar projects in 1943 and 1946, respectively. Lois Ireland was a Waunakee schoolgirl too young to drive to Madison when she first visited Curry's studio (fig. 8). She also ended up at the university, where she studied art and worked under the guidance of the agricultural journalist Byron Jorns.[35]

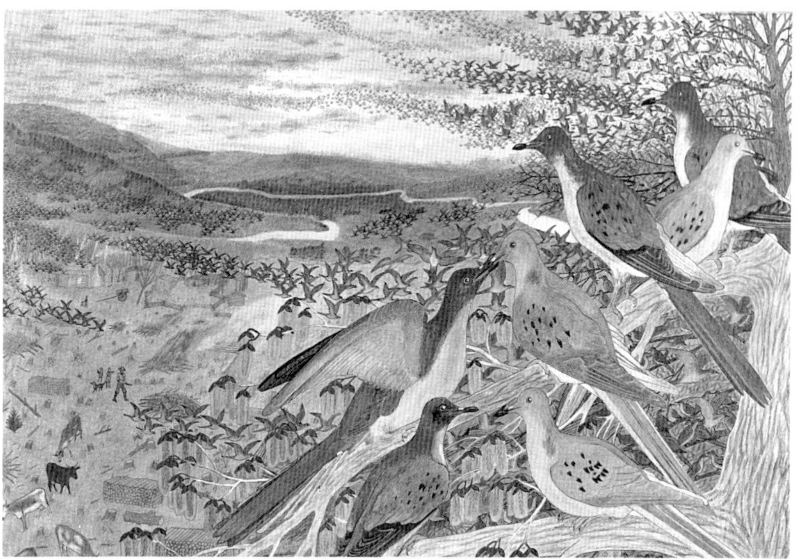

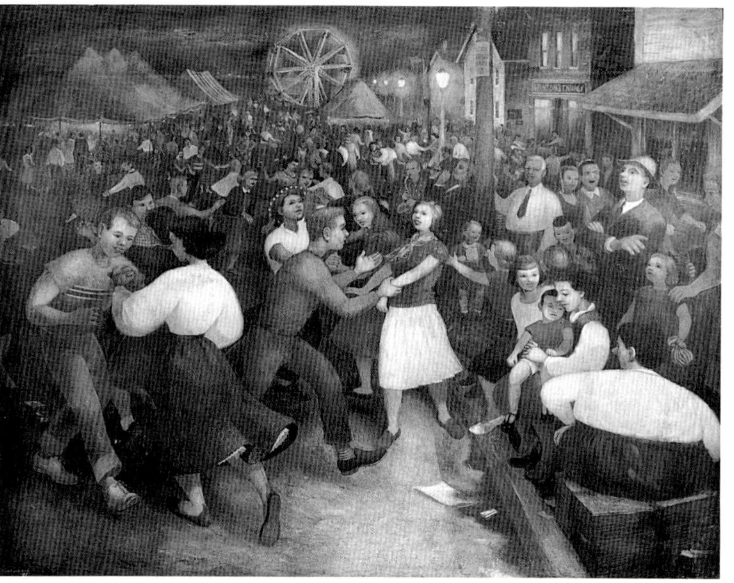

FIGURE 7 *(top)*

Walter Thorp (American, 1887–?)
The Passenger Pigeons, n.d.
Pencil and crayon
31½ × 43 in.
Courtesy permanent collection of Rural Art, University of Wisconsin.

FIGURE 8 *(above)*

Lois Ireland (American, b. 1928)
Street Dance, 1951
Oil on canvas
31 × 47 in.
Private collection.

Curry gave critiques of young artists' work, encouraged them to get formal training, used his influence to help them gain admission to art institutes and other educational venues, and promoted the utility of formal anatomy courses in enhancing an artist's knowledge of the human form.[36] He had no generic answers, nor did he advocate a uniform course of study. He considered each student's skills, interests, resources, and needs when dispensing educational and career advice along with his support.

Not all artists wanted formal training; indeed, many were in stages of their adult lives that precluded such training even when they desired it. Far more participants were adults with families, farms, and jobs than were school- or college-age youth with prospects for formal study. Such adult participants were the primary targets of the rural art program; they also brought to it a much broader range of needs, interests, and abilities. Curry, Barton, and their associates met, with varying degrees of success, needs that came up as the program took shape. In some cases, the program's organizers worked with local art clubs and the University Extension to develop adult-education classes in remote areas of the state.[37]

In one case, Curry and Barton became involved in elaborate efforts to obtain an art scholarship for the Black River Falls laborer Clarence Monegar, a widower with five children who specialized in wildlife watercolors. Curry was so impressed with the quality of Monegar's work that he attempted to arrange for representation through Reeves Lewenthal of Associated American Artists and offered to underwrite the costs of proofs for a lithograph produced by the artist.[38] To his ultimate exasperation, Curry also lent Monegar, who had a penchant for long, unexplained disappearances, his tools. He later lamented his generosity in a letter to Barton: "The lithographs are here, but I have not given Clarence any. In fact, I have not seen him. In fact, I would like to see him and get my lithograph tools back."[39]

Monegar was not the only artist to receive materials—on loan or otherwise—from Curry. He passed supplies along to artists who were going through hard times or who could benefit from the use of a particular color or medium. These practices required delicate diplomacy on Curry's part, however, since such generosity could offend the intended recipient, who might choose to do without rather than admit need.

Studio tours and less formal visits also were important elements of the rural art program. The "open door" was the rule, and Curry arranged gallery tours to meet his visitors' schedules—such as a time for high-school students so that they need not miss classes. When circumstances warranted, Curry would draw promising artists into deeper associations. This happened when he invited Vachel Davis, an Illinois coal miner, to "come up some day. Maybe I can show you some tricks." Although Curry's invitations were sincerely offered, many artists were intimidated. "Here was I, a poor no-account coal miner, painting at the same easel on which the great John Steuart Curry painted the head of John Brown," Davis recalled. "When my knees started to shake a little, Mr. Curry would ask me, 'What's the matter, didn't you eat any breakfast?'"[40]

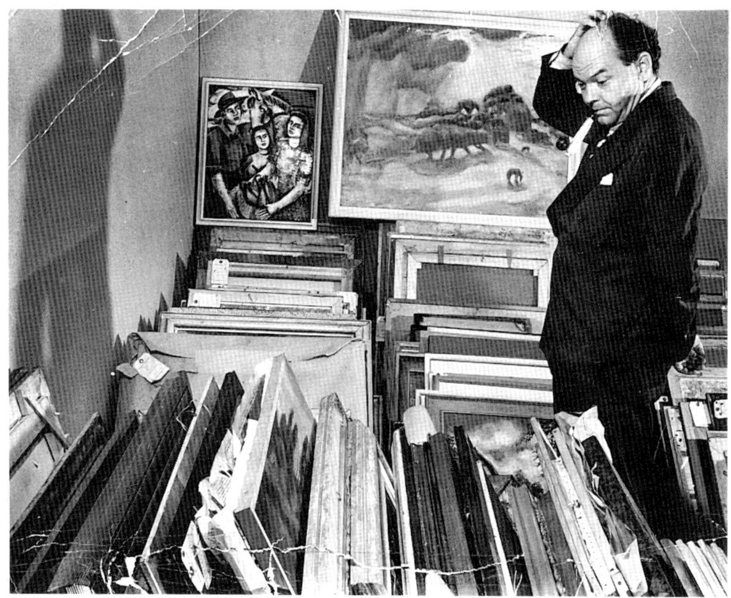

FIGURE 9
Curry judging rural art exhibition entries, 1940. Photograph by the *Milwaukee Journal.* Courtesy Mrs. John Steuart Curry.

In 1939 Christensen, Barton, and the rural sociologist John Kolb were delegates to an American Country Life Association conference. Viewing an exhibition there on rural subject matter prompted Wisconsin's delegates to plan an experimental exhibition by rural artists in Madison to be held during the 1940 Farm and Home Week. With only three months to organize the show, Barton, Curry, and Christensen searched for both artists and art. Using personal contacts, the local media, and county agents, they assembled work by thirty artists from seventeen counties at Memorial Union on the campus. The first rural art show generated such keen interest from amateur artists throughout the state that it became an annual event; the number of participants grew from thirty in 1940 to 105 in 1947 (fig. 9). Years later, remembering "Mr. Curry's patience," one participant described the impact of the first exhibition:

After that 1940 luncheon I came home all enthusiastic. The next week . . . I went to our county agent to ask him if we could have a rural art show with our Dairy Show. Our first show was hung up in the northwest corner of the balcony. Our pictures mingled with the smell of disinfectant, mooing cows, squealing pigs, seed samples, polished apples, and tobacco smoke. . . . This year we are hanging the exhibit in the Avalon Hotel lobby. We have been exhibiting seventeen years.[41]

The highlight of the annual show was Curry's tour of the gallery, when he discussed the merits of each piece and offered suggestions on technique and medium. For many participants the honor of being chosen to exhibit was matched by the anxiety of displaying their work in public and waiting for Curry's comments. The importance of his encouraging tone is illustrated by the negative experience of Lloyd Scarseth, a Galesville farmer who had saved the six-dollar fee to enter an art show near his hometown. When the big day arrived, Scarseth stood next to his pictures, waiting for the judges to review and discuss his work. The judges made their way around the exhibition but passed by Scarseth, refusing to acknowledge either the work or the artist; the farmer reported "feeling like my head was kicked in."[42]

Like Scarseth, many people who were drawn to the rural art program had tried unsuccessfully to exhibit their work, find art classes, or receive approval from their families and communities. As a result, recognition from Curry and his successor, the painter Aaron Bohrod, provided tangible encouragement. The annual shows also included luncheons, which provided opportunities for artists from around the state to develop a sense of community. These meals were regularly attended by the artists, the artist-in-residence, Barton, university extension art professor James Schwalbach, local art patrons, and other interested citizens of Wisconsin. Curry's writer friend August Derleth was a frequent visitor to the exhibitions and thereby formed friendships with many artists. Derleth encouraged many of the participants also to explore creative writing and ultimately helped initiate the Wisconsin Regional Writers Program, which was modeled after the rural art program.[43]

Some artists were occasional participants in the rural art shows; others exhibited faithfully. In general, the shows gave participants important chances to share the frustrations and rewards of their work, to learn new techniques, and to catch up on each other's lives. Participants formed lasting friendships with each other, with the program organizers, and with the artists-in-residence. John Barton became a trusted confidant who was called upon during times of trouble and celebration alike. John Curry became a mentor and friend who took pride in the artists' accomplishments and with whom artists shared inspirations and doubts. The value of this aspect of the program is best articulated in a 1943 letter to Curry from Walter Thorp: "Most men chase the $ from dawn until dark & die with their work half done and their dreams unaccomplished. I dream of drawing a good picture for the rural art display next year."[44] Within a decade of the first exhibition, the program began building a permanent collection of work through purchase awards made by the *Wisconsin Agriculturist* or through the Curry memorial fund established after the artist's death.

Curry maintained the demanding pace of his dual roles as artist and artist-in-residence despite trips to the Mayo Clinic, surgeries at University Hospital, and the ill health that, as noted, plagued him during the last five years of his life. His death from a heart attack came as a blow to the artists who had experienced their first significant encouragement and recognition through the rural art program. An editorial eulogizing the artist stated the feelings expressed in many private notes to his family:

John Steuart Curry was one of the good and great things of this world. His goodness is plain in his canvases, the reflections of his own mind and heart. And it shines as well in the devotion and adoration of the friends this shy and softly-speaking man attracted in his life in Madison.[45]

NOTES

1. This essay is dedicated to the memory of Dr. Daniel Schuster and Ellen Curry Schuster, whose friendship, encouragement, and assistance were invaluable to my research on John Steuart Curry. I also would like to acknowledge the support of Emeritus Dean Leo Walsh, College of Agricultural and Life Sciences (formerly the College of Agriculture), University of Wisconsin, Madison, who made the original research possible. Finally, I thank the many people who, between 1983 and 1985, shared with me their stories about Curry.

2. E. David Cronon and John W. Jenkins, *Politics, Depression, and War,* vol. 3 of *The University of Wisconsin: A History, 1925–1945* (Madison: University of Wisconsin Press, 1994), 10–12. See also Robert C. Nesbit, *Wisconsin: A History* (Madison: University of Wisconsin Press, 1989), 26–427.

3. "Introducing State's 'Artist in Residence,'" *Milwaukee Journal,* 10 January 1937.

4. "John Steuart Curry," *Wisconsin State Journal,* 30 August 1946.

5. John Rector Barton, Santa Barbara, Calif., to James Schwalbach, Madison, Wis., 28 May 1962. John Rector Barton Papers, MSS, State Historical Society of Wisconsin (hereafter cited as Barton Papers/SHSW).

6. John W. Jenkins, *A Centennial History: A History of the College of Agricultural and Life Sciences at the University of Wisconsin–Madison* (Madison, Wis.: College of Agricultural and Life Sciences, 1991), 92–94, 114–18.

7. The Experimental College was organized within the College of Letters and Science and was headed by Professor Alexander Mieklejohn. The college represented Frank's efforts to make his mark in curricular and pedagogical reform by establishing a "learning community" to serve as an educational laboratory within the liberal arts college. It began operation in 1927, with 119 male freshman students. The experiment ended in 1932. Cronon and Jenkins, *Politics,* 143–211.

8. Cronon and Jenkins, *Politics,* 215–35.

9. Ibid., 236–43.

10. Thomas E. Brittingham, Jr., Wilmington, Del., to Edna H. Brinkley, Madison, Wis., 28 February 1938. Norman Bassett Papers, MSS, State Historical Society of Wisconsin (hereafter cited as Bassett Papers/SHSW).

11. Ibid.

12. Jenkins, *Centennial History,* 88–120.

13. Ibid., 108–18.

14. Quoted in Marjorie Patten, *The Arts Workshop of Rural America* (New York: Columbia University Press, 1937), 4.

15. Quoted in *John Steuart Curry, 1897–1946,* exh. cat. (Madison, Wis.: Madison Art Center, 1979), unpaginated.

16. Quoted in *Curry, 1897–1946.*

17. Author interview with Ellen Curry Schuster, Rush, N.Y., 23 May 1986.

18. Adolph Bolz, Madison, Wis., to John Barton, Madison, Wis., 6 May 1947, Barton Papers/SHSW; Eugenie Mayer Bolz, Madison, Wis., to John Barton, "Saturday, the 5th," Barton Papers/SHSW; author interviews with Dr. Theodore Erickson, Madison, Wis., 6 June 1984, Ellen Curry Schuster, Rush, N.Y., 23 May 1986, and Mrs. Edward Jones, Sr., Fort Atkinson, Wis., 18 June 1984; *Curry, 1897–1946.*

19. Author interviews with Ellen Curry Schuster, Rush, N.Y., 23 May 1986, and Mrs. Edward Jones, Sr., Fort Atkinson, Wis., 18 June 1984; *Curry, 1897–1946.*

20. Joseph Caposella, "Regular Guy Who Couldn't Quit," *Wisconsin State Journal,* 30 August 1946.

21. "John Steuart Curry," *Wisconsin State Journal,* 30 August 1946.

22. "Yes, Art and Farming Mix; Wisconsin 'Resident' Proves It," *Christian Science Monitor,* 6 November 1941.

23. D. Clayton Brown, *Electricity for Rural America: The Fight for the REA* (Westport, Conn.: Greenwood Press, 1980), 116.

24. Lemont K. Richardson, *Wisconsin REA: The Struggle to Extend Electricity to Rural Wisconsin, 1935–1955* (Madison, Wis.: Agricultural Experiment Station, 1961), 5, 78–79.

25. Brown, *Electricity,* x–xi, 115–18; author interviews with Mrs. Carl Ubbelohde, Plymouth, Wis., 31 August 1984, Lloyd Scarseth, Galesville, Wis., 4 September 1984, and Elizabeth Faulkner Nolan, New Berlin, Wis., 29 August 1984.

26. Brown, *Electricity,* xiii; Nesbit, *Wisconsin: A History,* 479–80.

27. Anna Staver, Lancaster, Wis., to Curry, Madison, Wis., 24 October 1941, Curry Papers, Archives of American Art, Smithsonian Institution, Washington, D.C. (hereafter cited as Curry Papers/AAA), microfilm roll 167, frame 020.

28. Paul Stitzer, Mount Hope, Wis., to George Dehnert, County Agent, Lancaster, Wis., 11 February 1946, Barton Papers/SHSW.

29. Nesbit, *Wisconsin: A History,* 528–29.

30. Bruce Cartter, County Agent, Marinette, Wis., to John Barton, Madison, Wis., 9 January 1942; John Barton, Madison, Wis., to Bruce Cartter, Marinette, Wis., 16 January 1942; J. N. Kavanaugh, County Agent, Green Bay, Wis., to John Barton, Madison, Wis., 29 January 1942; John Barton, Madison, Wis., to J. N. Kavanaugh, Green Bay, Wis., 19 February 1942; Paul Stitzer, Mount Hope, Wis., to George Dehnert, County Agent, Lancaster, Wis., 11 February 1946, Barton Papers/SHSW.

31. "Introducing State's 'Artist in Residence,'" *Milwaukee Journal,* 10 January 1937.

32. Thomas Craven, "John Steuart Curry," *Scribner's Magazine* 103, no. 1 (January 1938): 98; "Introducing State's 'Artist in Residence,'" *Milwaukee Journal,* 10 January 1937; "Professor Curry," *Time* 31, no. 4 (24 January 1938): 32–33.

33. Survey research of John Black and Millie Rose Lalk, n.d., Curry Papers/AAA, microfilm roll 167, frame 025; author interviews with Mrs. Carl Ubbelohde, Plymouth, Wis., 31 August 1984, Lloyd Scarseth, Galesville, Wis., 4 September 1984, and Elizabeth Faulkner Nolan, New Berlin, Wis., 29 August 1984.

34. Caposella, "Regular Guy."

35. Author interview with Lois Ireland Zwettler, Oconomowoc, Wis., 26 November 1984.

36. Curry, Madison, Wis., to Iris Furman, Omro, Wis., n.d., Curry Papers/AAA, microfilm roll 165, frame 013.

37. Mrs. Carl Ubbelohde, Waldo, Wis., to Curry, Madison, Wis., 25 September 1939, Curry Papers/AAA, microfilm roll 165, frame 065; Mrs. Lela Smith, Lancaster, Wis., to Curry, Madison, Wis., 19 September 1941, Curry Papers/AAA, microfilm roll 167, frame 019; Curry, Madison, Wis., to Lela Smith, Lancaster, Wis., n.d., Curry Papers/AAA, microfilm roll 167, frame 019; Anna Staver, Lancaster, Wis., to Curry, Madison, Wis., 24 October 1941, Curry Papers/AAA, microfilm roll 167, frame 020; Curry, Madison, Wis., to Anna Staver, Lancaster, Wis., 30 October 1944, Curry Papers/AAA, microfilm roll 167, frame 020.

38. Willard Beatty, Office of Indian Affairs, U.S. Department of the Interior, to John Rector Barton, Madison, Wis., 10 June 1942, Curry Papers/AAA, microfilm roll 167, frame 021; Curry, Madison, Wis., to John Rector Barton, 25 June 1942, Curry Papers/AAA, microfilm roll 167, frame 023; Curry, Madison, Wis., to Reeves Lewenthal, Associated American Artists, New York, 6 March 1942, 30 March 1942, 16 April 1942, and 2 May 1942, Curry Papers/AAA, microfilm roll 167, frames 010, 014, 018; author interview with Bryant Kearl, Madison, Wis., 15 June 1984.

39. Curry, Madison, Wis., to John Rector Barton, 25 June 1942, Curry Papers/AAA, microfilm roll 167, frame 023.

40. Caposella, "Regular Guy."

41. Elizabeth Faulkner Nolan to John Rector Barton, Madison, Wis., 12 February 1958, Barton Papers/SHSW.

42. Author interview with Lloyd Scarseth, Galesville, Wis., 4 September 1984.

43. Author interview with Elizabeth Faulkner Nolan, New Berlin, Wis., 29 August 1984.

44. Walter Thorp to Curry, Madison, Wis., 3 January 1943, Curry Papers/AAA, microfilm roll 167, frame 026.

45. "John Steuart Curry," *Wisconsin State Journal,* 30 August 1946.

Twilight of Americanism's Golden Age

CURRY'S WISCONSIN YEARS, 1936–46

PATRICIA JUNKER

The start of this World War the Second ended an era of our times. We will look back on it as an age of comfort and plenty. With all our values changed we will find in remembering it as a "golden age" that the art born of that time takes on an added glory as a symbol of the peace and culture and the American awakening that we knew.

—John Steuart Curry, draft of a memorial tribute to Grant Wood, 28 October 1942[1]

John Steuart Curry died too soon. Like his friend Grant Wood, he was denied the benefit of hindsight perspective on regionalism's boom years. From 1938 onward Curry endured years of frustration in his art without knowing, as Thomas Hart Benton came to understand, that the pitfalls he suffered in his painting in these years were unavoidable because the populism he embraced—the engagement of Everyman in American economic development, politics, and culture—exacted its toll on the individual creative spirit. Curry remained committed to populism to the end. He believed that from the years of the Great Depression to the onset of World War II he had seen and participated in the rise of a golden age—an age when Americans saw that their most important act of self-reliance was cultivation of the land and when American art ascended to new heights by serving and celebrating that agrarian culture. It was not in his makeup to question the value of any effort to further that cultural ideal. "John Curry," Benton wrote admiringly in 1941, "has the drive of those who love the world better than Art and who will risk innovation for the sake of that love."[2]

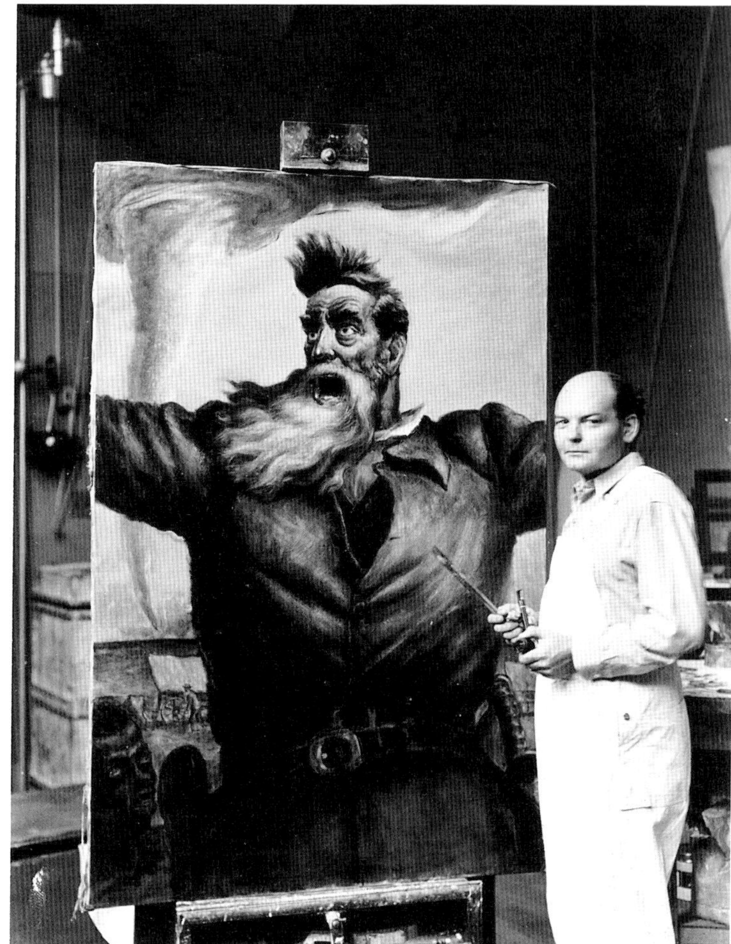

FIGURE 1
Curry with the canvas *John Brown* in his Madison studio, ca. 1939. Photograph by Arthur M. Vinje, Madison, Wisconsin. Courtesy Mrs. John Steuart Curry.

In the latter half of his career, Curry found innovation enough in the grand social experiment that was the University of Wisconsin's artist-in-residence program in the College of Agriculture, the first such program to be established at an American university. In September 1936 he became the first artist appointed to that post. He threw himself into the position with a kind of missionary zeal, and from his barnlike studio on the Madison campus he enthusiastically played his part "as gracious host to art lovers and future farmers of Wisconsin," even as he struggled to find satisfaction in his painting.[3] The experience did not suggest any new direction for Curry's art. Rather, his work there—cultivating the creative spirits of the people of rural Wisconsin and painting for a midwestern audience—validated what he had created up to that point, and amply so. His appointment at Wisconsin enabled him to put into practice what he had long advocated in theory: that art should be made relevant to the daily lives of rural men and women. It is for this reason that Curry's Wisconsin years are singularly important. For his art, these were years of reflection rather than innovation. They were also years of discouragement, as the painter struggled with public scrutiny. Ironically, the Wisconsin period shook Curry's faith in populism. He produced during this time the crowning achievements of his career: his great historical mural cycle for the Kansas Statehouse in Topeka, with its unforgettable *John Brown* (fig. 1), and his glorious celebration of Middle America, the monumental *Wisconsin Landscape.* But he did so without wide public acceptance—without the enthusiastic support of "his people" for which he had always hoped. Though in 1936 he had earned official recognition as a painter of and for rural people, Curry died only a decade later, disappointed and misunderstood. His disappointments point up the difficulties inherent in subordinating art to social function.

A Year of Anticipation, 1937

In April 1937, as he approached his fortieth birthday, Curry sized himself up in a revealing self-portrait, and obviously he was pleased with what he saw (color plate 49, fig. 2). In Madison only five months, he must have envisioned the painting as an appropriate means of introducing himself to the people of his adoptive home state.

Curry depicts himself here as a painter grounded in the great traditions. He has employed conventions of Roman or Renaissance portraiture to celebrate himself as Wisconsin's new painter laureate. The emblems of his authority are clearly visible in the space behind him. At left is a heraldic bird—the mythical jayhawk, perhaps, the symbol of the Kansan, a tribute to the artist's homeland and inspiration and a sign, as well, of his spiritual connection to the Middle West. At right is a signature work, one of his well-known circus paintings, this a study of an equestrienne, a work that testifies to Curry's reputation as both a skilled painter of the human figure in action and an accomplished *animalier.* Because the artist's circus paintings derived from an extended period of travel with the Ringling Brothers and Barnum & Bailey troupe in 1932, such a work speaks as well of his extraordinary dedication to living among the subjects of his paintings in order to achieve in his art an air of reality that comes from direct observation. He holds his brushes—his favorite large, round-bristled brush for his characteristic loose and broad strokes, and smaller sable brushes for linear accents.[4] The brushes are conspicuously crossed in front of him in a manner akin to the gesture of the Egyptian god Osiris, who, in pictorial representations, traditionally holds in one hand a three-part flail, symbol of threshing, and, in the other hand, a crook, emblem of the shepherd, thus personifying agriculture and the self-renewing vitality of nature.[5]

This big, barrel-chested, round-domed, pipe-smoking artist of the rural people puts on no airs but presents himself casually, in his corduroy barn jacket. He appears every bit the farm boy-turned-artist. "I am glad to be associated with the College of Agriculture," Curry had told an assembly of Madison's artists that January. "While in my youth I fled from the arms of agriculture to the more seductive charms of art, now I return."[6] At this juncture, Curry's life was inextricably bound to the farmer's life.

Curry approached his new life in Wisconsin with the self-confidence of an artist at the top of his profession. The celebrated painter of rural baptisms and revival meetings, of Kansas cyclones, and of the circus, he had enjoyed, by 1937, a succession of critically acclaimed shows at the Ferargil and Walker galleries in New York and had been recognized for his entries in important exhibitions of contemporary art—the Corcoran Gallery of Art and Pennsylvania Academy of the Fine Arts annuals, the Carnegie International Exhibition of Paintings, and the Whitney Biennial, among others. He had seen his best work purchased by major institutions, including the Whitney Museum of American Art and the Metropolitan Museum of Art in New York as well as by the University of Nebraska, the City Art Museum in St. Louis, and the Hackley Art Museum in

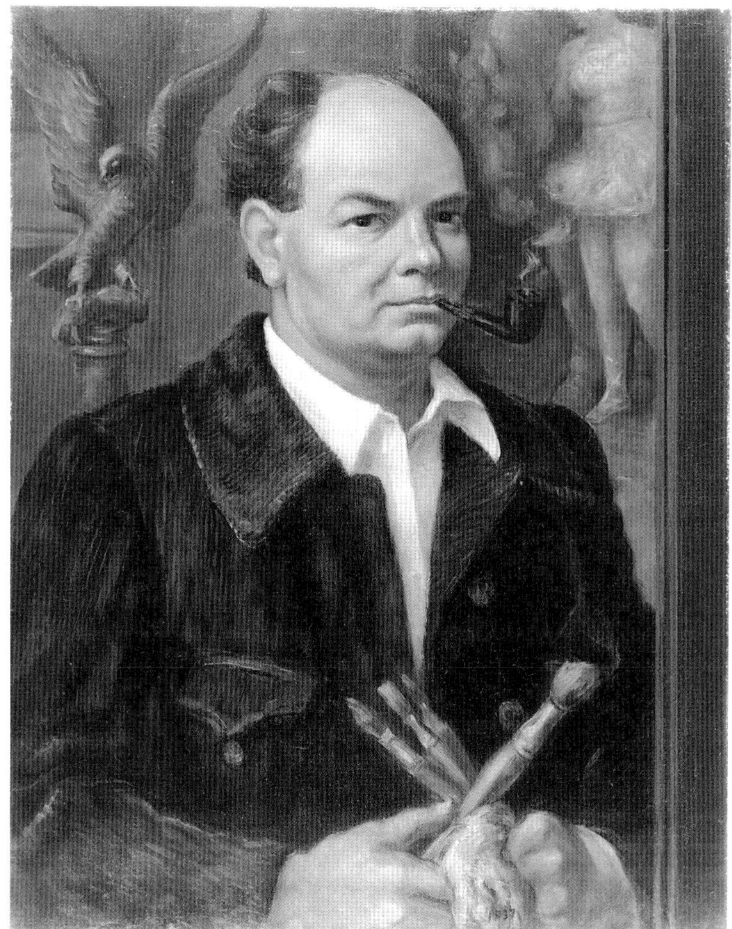

FIGURE 2

John Steuart Curry

Self-Portrait, 1937

Oil and tempera on canvas

30×24 in.

Fine Arts Museums of San Francisco. Gift of Mr. and Mrs. J. Burgess Jamieson.

Muskegon, Michigan, all in the Midwest. He had just been selected by a national jury to paint murals for the new U.S. Department of Justice building in Washington, D.C. He was known in households throughout the country, having been honored with a profile in the very first issue of *Life* magazine, in November 1936.[7] And now he had secured an enviable job within a leading American university—a position that represented an unprecedented acknowledgment of the role of art in American life and an unparalleled opportunity for a living artist to effect social change, to say nothing of the financial security that it also afforded. He was and would remain in the public eye. He had the respect of fellow artists, of critics, of museum directors and curators, of the progressive educators at the University of Wisconsin, and of art students from all walks of life.

In 1937 Curry was also at the height of his artistic powers, as the self-portrait attests. There is a palpable spirit here in Curry's rendering of his face and figure. He has succeeded beautifully in recreating human vitality on canvas. He has almost sculpted his massive figure and smooth round head in paint, building up form from layer upon layer of color—oil and oil glazes with touches of tempera and selectively applied varnishes. The image is solidly but broadly painted, every sure stroke of Curry's broad bristle brush revealed. The texture of his corduroy jacket stands up off the canvas. Wisps of hair and the laugh lines around his eyes have been carved out of the paint with the handle of his brush. There is pure joy revealed in such painting. But Curry had worked hard to achieve that facility and sense of freedom. He had been a diligent student of his craft, working, for instance, to master human anatomy and locomotion, as in his circus studies, or, later, laboring to learn the newfound Maroger formula for recreating the subtle glazes of Old Master paintings.[8] A decade after he began to work seriously as an artist, Curry must have felt that his journeyman days were over. "A skilled acrobat goes into training at the age of three and reaches his best at about 24," he had told members of the Art Association of Madison in January. "So in this art of painting you can allow yourself at least ten years of work before you can in your own mind feel the freedom and satisfaction of a controlled craft."[9] The 1937 self-portrait suggested great things to come.

In his address to the Art Association, Curry revealed his hopes for his art in the years ahead as he worked as artist-in-residence at the university. He looked forward to new opportunities for creating public murals, seeing such projects as a most emphatic way of bringing art into the lives of all Americans. He celebrated the return to realism that populism had inspired—a realism both in stylistic terms and in the depiction of the unadorned aspects of modern life. He saw this as a distinctly American artistic quality, a characteristic shared by the best of our native painters, a key link to the country's past: "The artists of today have the opportunity to use the alive and vital issues as subject matter, and they are doing it," Curry declared.

This eagerness to seize on all aspects of American life has given rise to a school classified as the painters of the American scene. This classification has been applied to many of us who have been painting only recently, but in truth there have been American artists since the primitive days painting the life and spirit of their time. We owe a great debt to such forerunners as Nast, Eakins, Ryder, Pyle, Homer, and of our present day, Bellows and Sloan.[10]

He stated his belief that the experiences of world war, of economic depression, and of a melting-pot society produced by the waves of immigration in the late 1800s and early 1900s had prepared artists of his generation to fight social and political injustice through their work, and he eagerly anticipated their productions. Curry was unequivocal in his assertion that Wisconsin's unique artist-in-residence program was perfectly suited to his populist ideology. He looked forward to bringing art to the state's farm families, to painting themes relevant to their lives and times, and to reinvigorating his own art through his contacts with the rural environment and rural people. He was inspired, he said, and Wisconsin, he assured his fellow artists, offered material for spirited painting: "I approached the life of the circus looking for dramatic action, color and lively personalities. I found them," he explained, adding, "I came to Madison looking for dramatic action, color, and lively personalities. I have found them."[11]

Curry had every reason to be stimulated by his new environment. Madison in 1937 was anything but an intellectual and cultural backwater. The University of Wisconsin, inextricably linked with the state's exceptional record of progressivism, was perhaps the finest and most public-oriented state university in the country, having earned a reputation for excellence in many fields and for service to the populace as a whole. "The university is the fourth department of the state, along with the judicial, executive and legislative branches," economics professor Richard T. Ely had declared at the beginning of the century, early in the administration of the famous Progressive Party governor, Robert La Follette.[12] In life sciences, earth sciences, medicine, and engineering, the university's research programs and facilities were made available to all Wisconsin residents. Geologists helped rural communities to find their road-surfacing materials locally; biochemists tested milk samples and developed the Steenbock method for irradiating milk and other food products with the essential vitamin D; epidemiologists tested the state's water samples; hydraulic engineers worked to keep its rivers and streams free of industrial waste and thus helped to preserve natural resources; and the College of Agriculture was helping to solve the problem of soil erosion, something that would understandably interest Curry, who had witnessed firsthand the effects of the prairie dust storms of the late 1920s.[13]

Madison was home to liberal and creative thinkers. Curry's close friends included not only Chris Christensen, dean of the College of Agriculture, but also the great civil-rights activist Lloyd Garrison, who was dean of the law school, and the art historian Oskar Hagen, author of one of the first textbook histories of American art. He knew the La Follettes, Philip and Robert, Jr., who as governor and U.S. Senator, respectively, revitalized their late father's anti–laissez faire economic and social ideas; Curry would record in paint the scene at Philip La Follette's rousing speech at the first rally of the National Progressive Party, held in Madison on 28 April 1938 (color plate 58). Curry had also met the architect Frank Lloyd Wright, whose home and school, Taliesen, were in nearby Spring Green. Indeed, Madison offered stimulating local color and material aplenty for a socially engaged art.

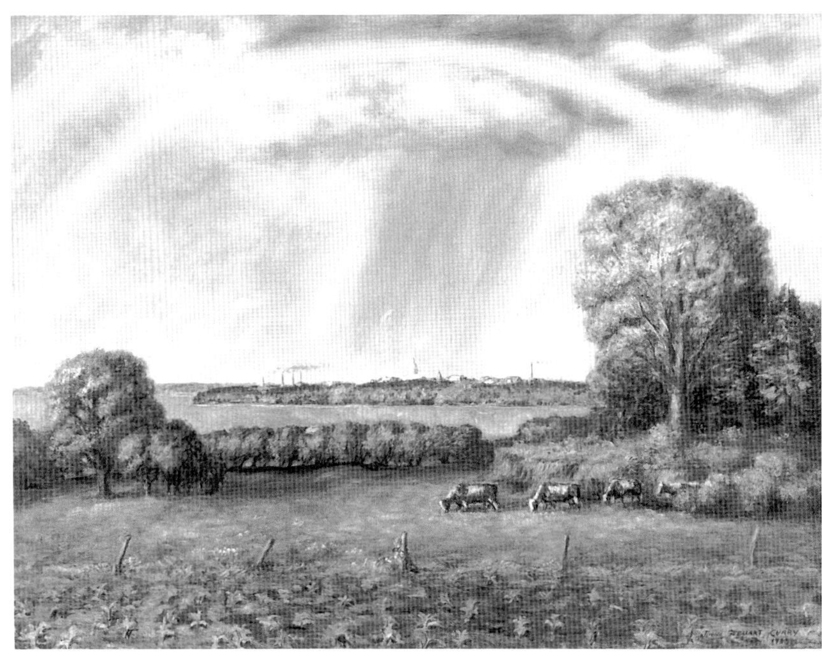

FIGURE 3

John Steuart Curry

View of Madison with Rainbow, 1937

Oil on canvas

36½ × 48 in.

Estate of the artist. Courtesy Mongerson Wunderlich Gallery, Chicago.

A Year in Art: Curry's Wisconsin Paintings, 1937

In January 1938, Maynard Walker opened a show of Curry's latest work at his New York gallery—a much anticipated event.[14] More than just a review of Curry's newest paintings, the exhibition was a report on his year as artist-in-residence. It offered a means of assessing his embrace of the opportunities afforded him at the university. In reporting on Curry's full year of various activities, *Time* magazine asked the crucial question that had been on the minds of critics and fellow artists for months:

He gave a show at the College Union, lectured on art to farm boys in agriculture courses, went on field trips with Dean Chris Christensen of the College. His face-cracking cherubic grin and piping voice made him popular with Wisconsin students. Question?: How did this affect the painting of a Kansan who six years ago put Kansas on the U.S. artistic map?[15]

Judging by the paintings in the Walker Galleries show, all measured against the standard of his emotionally charged Kansas paintings, Curry had not yet connected with rural Wisconsin. The paintings suggest that his university activities engaged him more than the farm landscape or those farm experiences that he had so movingly portrayed in his Kansas images. These new paintings were grounded not on the farm but on and around the campus, and for the most part they evoked earlier models. The one Wisconsin landscape—a springtime view of Madison as seen across Lake Mendota from Picnic Point (1937, fig. 3)—looked back to nineteenth-century American art, especially to the landscapes of George Inness. University life was represented by two canvases, both of which are reminiscent of Curry's earlier circus pictures: *The Stallion* (1937, fig. 4), the artist's first Madison oil, derived from sketches he had made of the agriculture school's prize Percheron stallion at the Wisconsin stock show in January 1937; and an animated football subject, *Goal Line Play,* with one airborne figure—a variation of sorts on *The Flying Codonas* (1932, color plate 25). There was also an uncharacteristic tabletop still life, the impressionistic *Spring Flowers.* The only farm landscape in the exhibition was the repainted *Kansas Sunrise,* which Curry had begun two years earlier in Westport, Connecticut, working from sketches made on his 1929 and 1930 trips home.[16] Among the works on view, the 1937 self-portrait surely stood out as the sole original response to the artist's time and place. This group of paintings

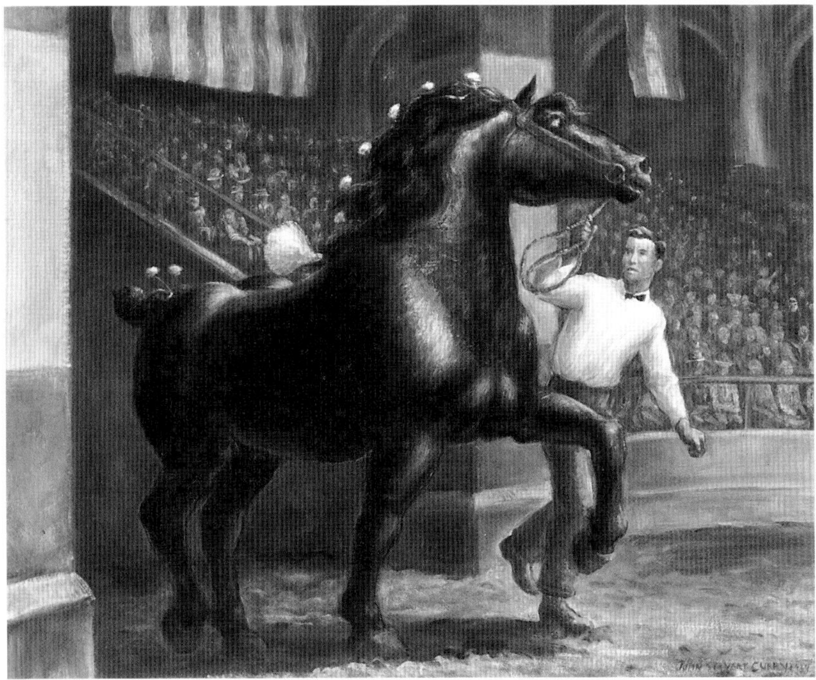

FIGURE 4

John Steuart Curry
The Stallion, 1937
Oil on canvas, mounted on board
24½ × 30½ in.
Courtesy New Britain Museum of American Art, New Britain, Connecticut. Gift of Stevan Dohanos.

must have seemed surprising productions indeed from a painter who had expressed his deep desire to "take the same things from Wisconsin that he took from Kansas scenes" and who had spoken so poetically of seeing art "in the shine of brown earth as it rolls from the plowshare, in the swing of the fork as the hired man scatters hay-cocks after an untimely rain, and in the healthy gusto with which threshers eat their food."[17]

Critics were divided in their assessments of the achievement represented by this group of paintings, but all saw them as distinctly different from Curry's earlier Kansas works. "Curry retains, if he does not greatly augment, the esteem in which he is held as one of our most purposeful and intelligent painters," Howard Devree wrote with some degree of enthusiasm in the *Magazine of Art*.[18] The writer for the *New York Sun* welcomed Curry's departure from the dark palette and unsettling subjects of the Kansas paintings:

He has got away from those tawny, dust-swept Kansas prairies, the tornadoes and the rest with which his name was formerly most tellingly associated, and is now concerned with things that embody a more cheerful view of existence. His palette has been freshened up greatly, as most pleasingly revealed in his lush "Spring Flowers" and his "View of Madison." . . . Both of these canvases are full of nice coloration and alive with the freshness and joy of living. So why bother with anything else?[19]

Margaret Breuning, in *Parnassus*, also lauded Curry's colorism but lamented a lack of the freshness and spirit that she thought had characterized his previous work: "Some of the paintings have been worked over until they seem to have lost most of their vitality," she wrote. "And vitality has been one of Curry's chief assets."[20] *Time*, however, was simply confounded by a perceived lack of imagination in many of the paintings, seeing "an unaccustomed air of old-fashioned dewiness" in the *View of Madison with Rainbow* and "an even stranger touch of Renoir" in the still life, while contending that *Goal Line Play* "looked like a monument to a lost opportunity."[21] And Edward Alden Jewell in the *New York Times* bluntly declared that the paintings offered little insight into the potential value of the Wisconsin artist-in-residence effort: "Although the experiment seems admirable and full of promise, this reviewer cannot but feel that it is not so much in the new work now shown but in future achievements on the artist's part that we must look. . . . Each of the 1937 canvases seems in some degree disappointing."[22]

There were no sales from the 1938 show. And there would never again be another solo exhibition of new work for Curry. In his frustration, Curry blamed Walker and, in 1941, decided to leave him for Reeves Lewenthal's Associated American Artists. Walker's response to his longtime client's decision, while defensive, is also telling of the forces at work upon Curry's art during these years—forces that mitigated against the steady production of saleable easel pictures:

I have certainly not been happy about the few sales. In defense of our own efforts, I need not point out that you have been occupied in the five years the Walker Galleries have been in existence, in many other works which were profitable to you but on which we received nothing. Among these are the Government murals, the illustrations for the Limited Editions Club, lithographs for the AAA [Associated American Artists], and your work at the University. In these five years you have given us material for only one show of paintings, with not many saleable pictures in it. . . . All these things may have some bearing on our poor sales results of the last few years. Many times I have felt that you were neglecting to supply us with workable material, but I know you were engaged on other important things and I didn't want to interrupt.[23]

Walker had a point. After 1937, Curry grew less dependent on private patronage and on the traditional commercial-gallery system of promoting and distributing work and became increasingly involved with mural commissions and illustration in addition to his work for the university.

Curry was a beneficiary of New Deal government programs to support artists through commissions for public works, and much of his effort by 1937 was focused on murals. In April 1935 he was selected to design murals for the U.S. Department of Justice building in Washington under support from the U.S. Department of the Treasury's newly established Section on Painting and Sculpture (color plates 44–48); he was completing this work when he arrived in Madison. By June 1937 Curry was engaged in a project that would consume him for the next four years: a commission from the Kansas state legislature to create murals for the Statehouse in Topeka (color plates 50–55). In 1938 he would begin murals for the U.S. Department of the Interior building (color plates 59 and 60). In 1941 he painted landscape murals for the First National Bank, Madison. He created murals for the university as well, completing *Freeing of the Slaves* in the Law School library in 1942 (color plate 68) and finishing *The Social Benefits of Biochemical Research* for the biochemistry building, after three years of work, in 1943 (color plates 64–66).

By 1937 Curry had also returned to book and magazine illustration. His reembrace of this enterprise was motivated not by financial need but by his desire to address social themes and his goal of bringing high-quality original art to the masses. In December 1937 he was chosen, along with Benton, Wood, and Henry Varnum Poor, as the first artists commissioned to illustrate important works of American literature for beautiful new editions published by George Macy's Limited Editions Club. Over the next ten years Curry would illustrate three volumes for Macy—James Fenimore Cooper's novel *The Prairie*, *The Literary Works of Abraham Lincoln*, and Stephen Vincent Benét's epic Civil War poem *John Brown's Body*. He did illustrations for other publishing houses, too. These included a volume on *The Wisconsin*, with the Sauk City writer August Derleth, for Farrar and Rinehart's The Rivers of America series; Walt Whitman's *Leaves of Grass* for Peter Pauper Press; and Mary O'Hara's popular novels *My Friend Flicka* and *Thunderhead* for J. B. Lippincott. His monumental *Hoover and the Flood*, depicting Herbert Hoover's formidable relief efforts during the Mississippi River floods of 1927, was produced for *Life* magazine in 1940, and his heroic *The Light of the World*, an allegory on world war, was painted for the Christmas 1941 issue of *Esquire*. He made propaganda paintings for the war effort as well, including *Our Good Earth* (1940–41, color plate 63), which were reproduced as posters.

Although Curry's university appointment carried no teaching requirement or specific assignments, the artist himself had laid out an ambitious five-year plan when he accepted the post in September 1936. He intended, *Literary Digest* reported, to paint murals and paintings of current agricultural topics, "particularly soil erosion, which is a pet project of Dean Christensen's." He added that he planned to participate in art-appreciation classes, to offer instruction and encouragement to anyone who wished to learn to paint, and to work especially closely with the Farm Short Course students so as to appreciate better their agricultural problems as he helped them to understand art. He wanted, moreover, to furnish "a living museum for the University at large" by mounting exhibitions of his work as often as possible. "As he finishes a mural or canvas, he will exhibit it first in Madison," *Literary Digest* announced.[24]

At that early point in his tenure, Curry did not foresee the intense interest that his appointment would engender among art enthusiasts beyond the campus. He could not have anticipated the demands that would be placed on his time by people from across Wisconsin. An extant calendar of his appointments from September through November 1943 indicates the very full schedule that Curry kept: It shows studio visits from the university's art-education classes and from a group of high-school teachers and students as well; service on a regional art show jury in Green Bay; a slide lecture to a community gathering in Monroe; and individual meetings with several art students, including an eleven-year-old girl and a soldier based at nearby Truax Field.[25] But both Curry and Christensen came to measure the value of the artist's appointment by his accessibility: "His greatest work, Christensen and Curry agree, is with the individual farmer or agriculture student who may visit in his studio," reported the *Milwaukee Journal* in announcing the renewal of Curry's university contract in October 1941. His studio, the paper explained, was always open: "Curry has no telephone there, but neither has he any lock on the door when he's at home. He's the type of man who can stand an onlooker or two, even when he's creating. . . . He's perfectly willing to spend half a day with some student and his attempts at art when he could be working himself."[26]

When Curry laid out his ambitious five-year plan, he could not have known that much of his time and energy in these years would be devoted to a project that had nothing to do with rural Wisconsin: his commission to paint murals on Kansas themes for the Statehouse in Topeka. In June 1937, Kansas Governor Walter A. Huxman announced a campaign to raise funds for the murals and presented Curry with what must have seemed, for this Kansas-born painter, the opportunity of a lifetime. It would be the project that defined the second half of his career. All of his creative efforts from late 1937 onward—and much of his frustration as well—must be understood in relation to his consuming work, from 1937 through 1941, on the Kansas murals.[27]

Even in Wisconsin, it was Kansas that continued to stir Curry's imagination. His first sketch for *John Brown,* the central figure in his Kansas mural cycle, was included in the 1938 Walker Galleries show and was singled out by critics, along with the sturdy 1937 *Self-Portrait,* as a herald of great things to come from Curry. Ironically, that exhibition of Curry's latest efforts did not include another work-in-progress, the monumental *Wisconsin Landscape.* Yet it was that canvas, and not the Kansas murals, that would in the end, after years of struggle and disappointment, find a responsive national audience and bring Curry the wide public acclaim that otherwise eluded him through his last decade.

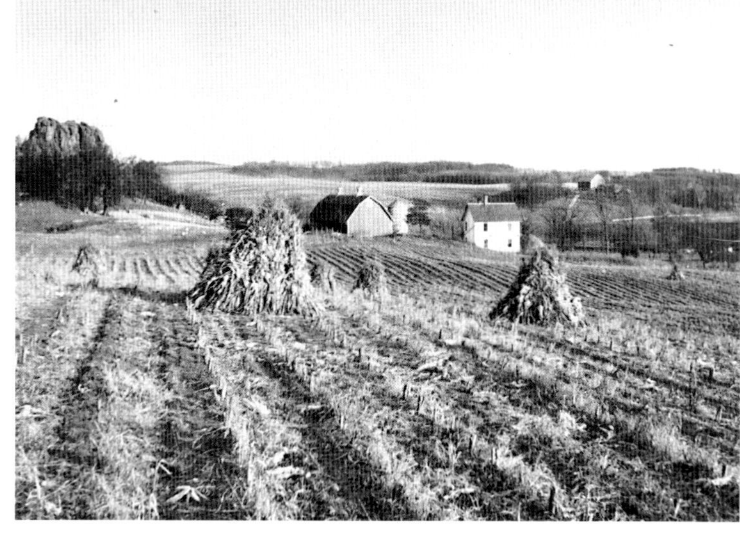

FIGURE 5
Photograph of a southern Wisconsin farmstead, possibly taken near Belleville, in Montrose Township, Dane County, in August 1937. Photograph courtesy Curry Papers, Archives of American Art, Smithsonian Institution, Washington, D.C. Gift of Kathleen Curry.

Wisconsin Landscape, 1937–39

In mid-August 1937, Curry received a commission from the Farm Foundation of Chicago to paint a memorial to its founder, Alexander Legge, who had died in 1933. Legge was born on a farm in Dane County, Wisconsin, outside Madison. He spent his career in the farm-implement business, in Nebraska, Iowa, and Chicago, rising to the presidency of International Harvester Company in 1922. Along the way, he acquired a vast store of information about agricultural science and economics. He was an advisor to U.S. presidents and served as chairman of the Federal Farm Board. He had established the Farm Foundation in 1933 for the improvement of farm life and the "well-being of people on the land."[28] The Farm Foundation has continued to support programs in such areas as land tenure, rural education, the rural church, farm management, and water-resource management. The Legge Memorial Committee believed that a southern Wisconsin scene would be an especially appropriate tribute to Legge, whose affection for what he called "the most beautiful farm landscape in the world" grew from more than a simple, sentimental attachment to his place of birth.[29] Dane County's distinctive patchwork fields of grain, pasture, and woodland were the result of modern, scientific soil management, and in the early 1930s they represented the most enlightened attitudes toward soil conservation, crop rotation, and cultivation to be found anywhere in the nation. The Wisconsin landscape was beautiful in both a visual and an ethical sense.

Curry's attraction to this particular commission may have stemmed initially from a sense of kinship with Legge. Like Curry, Legge was the son of devout Scotch Presbyterian immigrant farmers, strong stock, who in the 1870s had suffered the devastation of their wheat crop in Wisconsin and were forced to begin anew, penniless and deeply in debt, in Nebraska. Curry knew that Legge understood the vicissitudes of nature and that he had devoted his life to developing practical solutions to the problems inherent in working the soil. He must have admired Legge as he did Agriculture College Dean Chris Christensen, whose pet project was soil conservation through contour farming.

The memorial committee, its members all closely connected to agriculture, had a clear idea of the kind of painting that would best honor Legge and expressed their concept to Curry in granting him the commission. This would not be a romantic look back at the Legge farm in the nineteenth century. Rather, it would celebrate what that farmscape had become through scientific advancement and the dissemination of scientific research to farmers through cooperative extension services such as those offered by the University of Wisconsin. This was to be a work symbolizing twentieth-century farming and modern soil science and the visions of men, like Legge, who helped farmers to put agricultural theory into practice.

That summer, committee members had toured the farmland around Legge's birthplace in Montrose Township, in the southwestern corner of Dane County, amid rolling hills, apparently

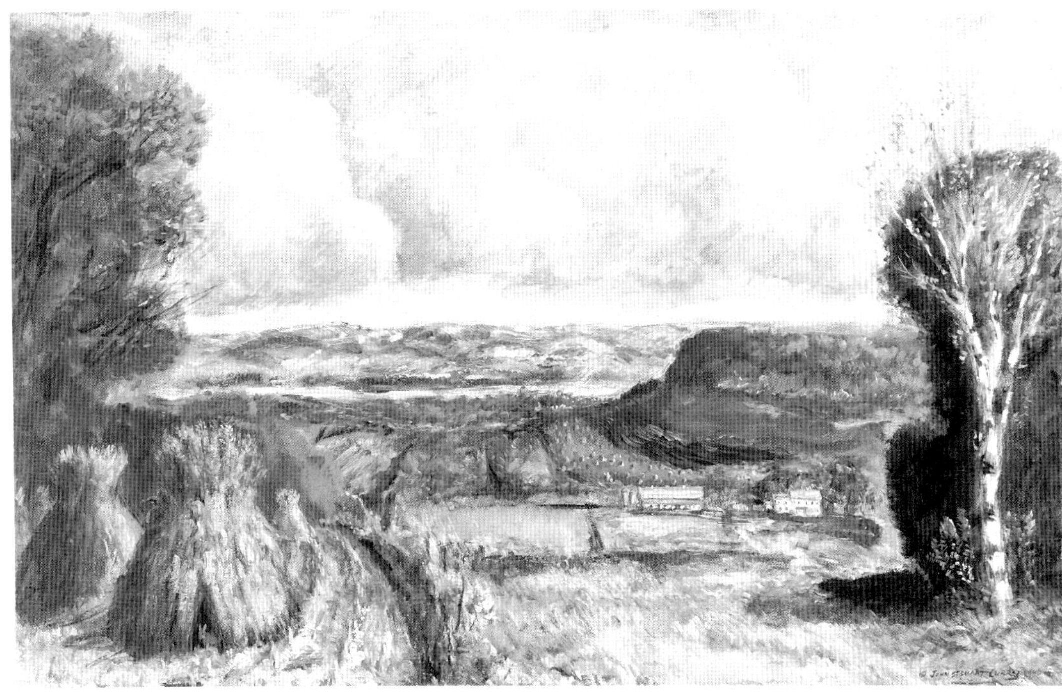

FIGURE 6

John Steuart Curry

Preliminary study for *Wisconsin Landscape*, 1937

Oil on canvas

38 × 59½ in.

Estate of the artist.

Photograph courtesy Mongerson Wunderlich Gallery, Chicago.

exulting in the aesthetics of scientific land cultivation. Curry may have accompanied them.[30] William Elliott, a vice president of International Harvester, was keen that the painting should show modern land management through crop rotation: "If we could get the yellow stubble fields and possibly some small grain in the shock, in contrast to the meadows and the green corn fields, that would be interesting." Henry C. Taylor, director of the Farm Foundation, wrote to Curry of Elliott's ideas; he added that Elliott "also indicated his interest in the possibility of having the scene come later in autumn when there would be more color in the foliage of the trees and when some of the corn might be in the shock. Of course, much of the corn goes into silos in that area, which would not be so good." To show southern Wisconsin's rural landscape in all its interconnected intricacy required a great expanse of canvas: "I had in mind a painting from 7 to 7½ feet in length," Taylor told Curry.[31]

Looking to absorb all the details of the distinctive farm landscape of southern Wisconsin's dairy land, Curry seems to have relied on a series of photographs that he himself may have taken near Legge's birthplace, outside Belleville (fig. 5). These snapshots were possibly made that August, just after Curry was given the commission, when the woodlands surrounding the golden fields of corn and grain were still green. The photographs—and Curry's subsequent painting—show how well he understood the salient features of the local dairy farmstead, with its typically vast acreage, its large, long, two-story, gambrel-roofed stock barn (the second floor of which was used to store grain), a tall silo typically attached to one end, and its cluster of smaller buildings—granaries, corncribs, and machine sheds. With their expansive fields of corn and grain for food stores, Wisconsin's dairy farms were large enterprises. The extraordinarily tall corn silo represented the region's particular innovation in dairying; with silage, farmers could keep larger herds of dairy cows than they might otherwise during the winter and at a cost significantly lower than with dry feed. From the time they pioneered the use of these storage structures in the late nineteenth century, Wisconsin farmers built silos that reportedly stood as the largest in the world, some reaching holding capacities of up to two hundred acres of corn.[32] The stubble fields were a hallmark of this region, lending a distinctive linear patterning to the landscape, as Curry's photograph shows. In the modern Wisconsin farmscape, shaped by scientifically informed crop rotation, these brown, stubbly, fallow fields lay alongside lush green fields under cultivation, the whole assuming a magnificent formal structure, an abstraction in line, color, and shape that represented in fact a human ideal—respect for and harmony with nature.

The painting that is likely Curry's initial large-scale oil study—for it is closer to the photographs than is the final version—shows how clearly he understood the details of the area's farm landscape (fig. 6). Though loosely painted, the composition has been carefully laid out to show the alternating patches of cultivated and stubble fields. One prominent element is the hillock at right showing the practice of contour cropping, an

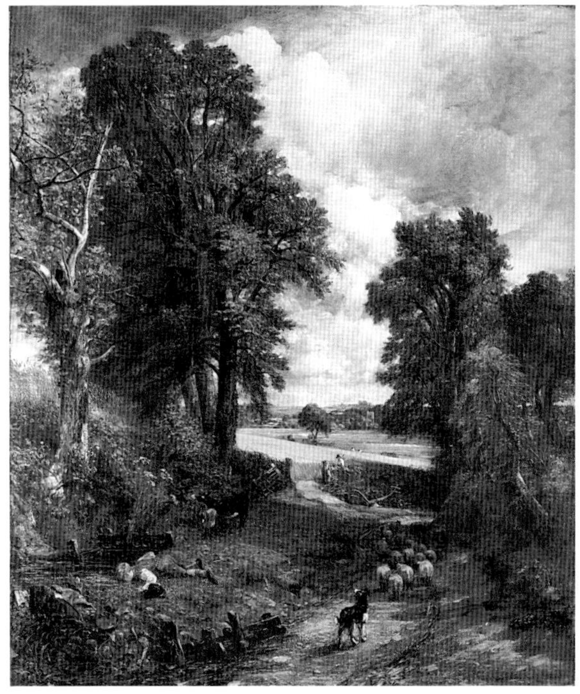

FIGURE 7

John Constable (English, 1776–1837)
The Cornfield, 1826
Oil on canvas
56¼ × 48½ in.
Courtesy National Gallery, London.

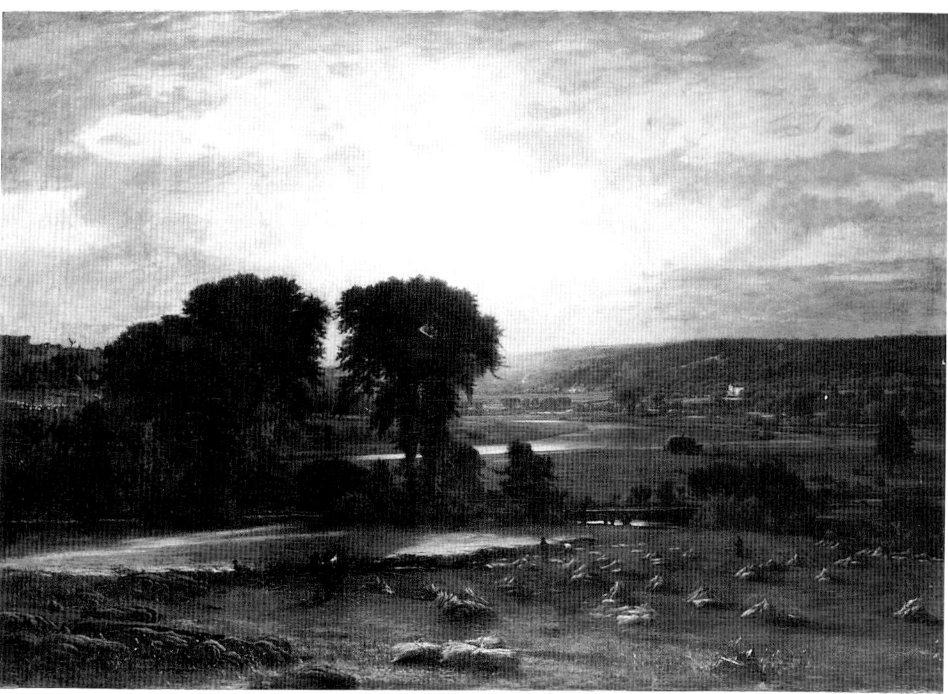

FIGURE 8

George Inness (American, 1825–1894)
Peace and Plenty, 1865
Oil on canvas
77⅝ × 112¾ in.
Courtesy The Metropolitan Museum of Art, New York. Gift of George A. Hearn, 1894.

important means of soil conservation then being developed in southern Wisconsin under the guidance of the College of Agriculture. Although this feature does not appear in the completed *Wisconsin Landscape,* its appearance in this version suggests how closely Curry studied scientific land management.[33]

In October 1937, while still at work on the Farm Foundation commission, Curry traveled to Manhattan, Kansas, to address the annual meeting of the American Country Life Association. He presented a slide lecture on artistic interpretations of rural life as seen through the ages; in it he revealed what clearly were some of his sources for *Wisconsin Landscape.* He declared his great admiration for the naturalism of John Constable's sweeping panoramas of the farmlands of the Stour Valley, paintings that to Curry were keenly true to nature, to farm life, and to atmospheric effects. Possibly referring to Constable's *The Cornfield* (1826, fig. 7), he reveled in its agricultural details and in the idyllic whole: "We see the shocks of corn, the country people active in that field of corn," he said, "the beautiful trees silhouetted against the horizon, the trees practically enfolding the farm house, and in the background the great expanse of open sky."[34] Curry also praised the nineteenth-century painter George Inness as one who "opened the way for the modern American artist who portrays his native land," and he showed his audience the monumental *Peace and Plenty* of 1865 (fig. 8).[35] Inness's glorious, expansive celebration of the harvest offers an elaborate horizontal and linear pattern of fields and meandering stream. By its long, nearly uninterrupted horizon, which divides the canvas almost exactly in half, the composition draws the viewer into vast space and directs his gaze outward, beyond the edges of the painting. This sweeping view of an American harvest suggests an abundance in the real world that could only be conveyed on a canvas nine feet wide.

Constable's naturalism and Inness's nationalism and optimism were on Curry's mind as he created *Wisconsin Landscape* in 1937 (color plate 56, fig. 9). Although he would rework the painting over the next several years, continuing to develop light effects, the composition itself probably never varied significantly from its dramatic overall horizontal pattern, bold ribbons of

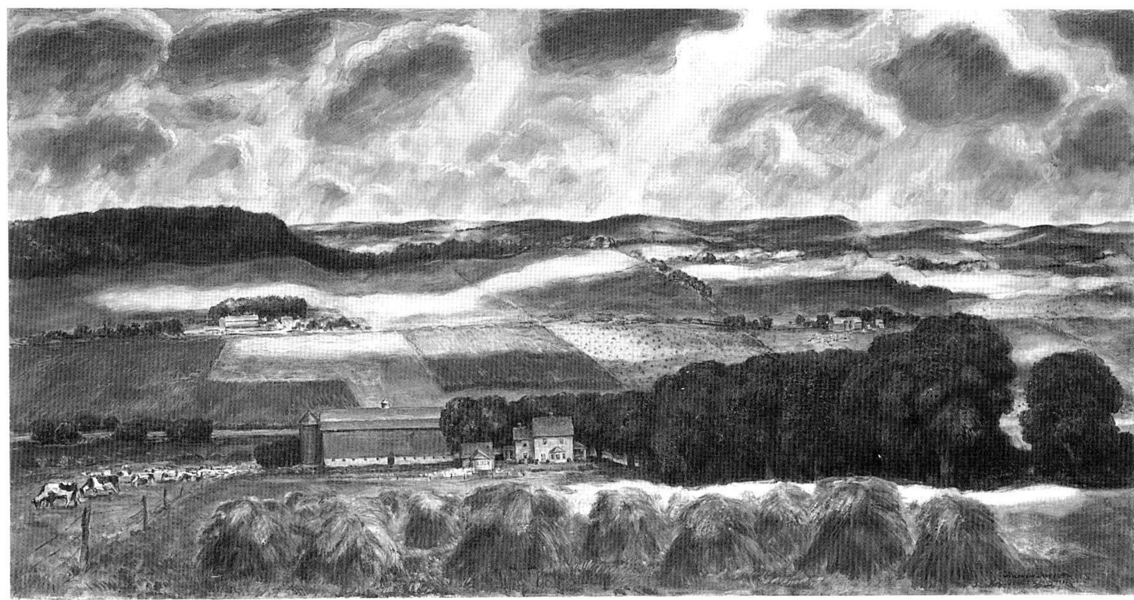

FIGURE 9

John Steuart Curry
Wisconsin Landscape, 1937–39
Oil on canvas
42 × 84 in.
Courtesy The Metropolitan Museum of Art, New York. George A. Hearn Fund, 1942.
Photograph © 1981: The Metropolitan Museum of Art.

color in earth and sky that were, for Curry, true to his subject.[36] He must have seen the Wisconsin landscape as the living embodiment of Inness's blessed and boundless land of plenty, and hence the compositional devices he chose to delineate it—sweeping horizon, broad sky, limitless space, and its overall golden, seemingly divine, light—were appropriately borrowed from the nineteenth-century visionary.

It is surprising that Curry's painting, which so carefully and honestly depicts the features of the Wisconsin landscape as the Legge Memorial Committee outlined them, which celebrates an agrarian ideal long associated with America's greatness, and which exalts modern agriculture, did not find a home in the Chicago headquarters of the Farm Foundation.[37] Why the foundation never acquired the canvas remains a mystery. Although Henry C. Taylor had assured Curry that International Harvester would raise the requisite $2,500 to pay for the painting when he told the artist to proceed, the foundation in the end refused to purchase the painting. Perhaps Curry felt that the work somehow fell short of the Memorial Committee's expectations, for something happened that seemingly shook his confidence in his initial effort.

Curry kept *Wisconsin Landscape* in his studio until late in 1938, when he showed it publicly for the first time at Walker Galleries. He did not include it in his retrospective exhibition at Lakeside Press Galleries in Chicago in March and April 1939. And when Curry did exhibit it again at Walker Galleries in November 1939, the canvas was, Carlyle Burrows reported in the *New York Herald Tribune,* significantly repainted.[38]

For all his early disappointment with it, *Wisconsin Landscape* eventually won critical acclaim, restoring Curry's faith in the painting as one of his finest works and no doubt raising Maynard Walker's hopes for it. As the first new Curry work seen in New York in some time, *Wisconsin Landscape* understandably attracted attention when it was shown at Walker Galleries in 1939. "With the first flush of the American Scene movement already passed," noted *Art Digest,* "a good many people are wondering what direction the art of the famous Midwest triumvirate, Benton, Curry, and Wood, will take. For this reason, a new canvas by Curry... takes on added interest."[39] But the painting generated more than just passing notice. There is, in fact, a sense of awe in the comments of some critics who found themselves writing at length about it. Burrows, for one, declared that:

None of the paintings in the fourth anniversary show of work by American artists at the Walker Galleries is quite so impressive as John Steuart Curry's large panorama of farms and barns called "Wisconsin Landscape."... Curry has put all of his intense ardor for landscape into the picture.... [He] has dramatized the theme in the variable light of a typically strong Mid Western sky, which admits flashes of clear sunlight into the sweeping blanket of cultivated fields, and the work is at

the same time a kind of dramatic poem on the opulence of the Wisconsin country.[40]

Art Digest described it as an uncharacteristically bold, if still unresolved work,

a daring attempt to orchestrate with rich brilliant colors over a wide field of tones. From a foreground streak of intense yellow, put on with Ryderesque arbitrariness, Curry's new work weaves through the color and value scale to a deep purple in the horizon. It is thick with pigment and alive with light, but somewhat on the raw side in its total effect. Obviously Curry is working hard on a new tack himself, as he continues as artist-in-residence at Wisconsin University.[41]

When *Life* magazine asked for his thoughts on the painting in May 1940, Curry replied: "I worked two years at it, off and on. I feel it is my greatest landscape."[42] By November 1940, when *Wisconsin Landscape* was shown in the Art Institute of Chicago's annual exhibition of American paintings and sculpture, Walker had put a $6,000 price tag on it. The following January, still unsold, the canvas won the Jennie Sesnan Medal for the best landscape in the annual juried show at the Pennsylvania Academy of the Fine Arts. In April 1941, Benton wrote movingly of the painting in a tribute to his friend Curry:

It is immensely big and powerful. As you look at it it becomes beautiful. It sticks in the memory as a grand sweeping exultant shout of 'yes' to the roll of the Earth. It is not a picture for the children of the Fogg museum. It will not fit in with the lisping puerilities of aesthetic minded professors or those sad people who take up art criticism as a profession. It is something for men and women who live in a living world. . . . Looking back over the landscapes I have seen I can think of nothing comparable to this Wisconsin landscape of John Curry's. It is likely to stand as a sort of unique performance in the history of American Art just as the Mt. St. Victoire series of [Cézanne's] stands in French Art.[43]

What happened between 1937 and 1939 to change Curry's feelings of dissatisfaction toward his *Wisconsin Landscape,* enabling him to find effective means to create a painting of such expressive power? The answer to this question may lie not in the artist's physical environment—his feeling toward the Wisconsin landscape itself—but in the dramatically shifting political temper of that time. As war loomed over Europe, Curry's fears were increasingly played out on canvas. The theme of war and peace lay at the heart of his Kansas mural program, conceived in 1937. In 1938 he painted *Parade to War* (color plate 61), a shocking scene in which trooping soldiers sport the faces of death. And by 1940 he had turned again to *The Return of Private Davis from the Argonne* (color plate 12), one of his earliest canvases and a poignant statement on the human loss that war represents. He sold the completed painting to the American Legion Post in Milwaukee. He feared what America's entry into war would mean to rural life—the strain on farm families as young men went off to war and the increasing shift of human resources toward industry and away from agriculture; this was the subject of other works, notably *The Farm Is a Battleground, Too; Leaving the Farm for Army Training Camp;* and the stirring *Our Good Earth.*[44] War would, he feared, mean the end of a way of life that had represented for Curry an ideal world of humankind and nature. And it also meant, for him, the tragic end of an art rooted in this ideal. "After the [First] World War there began a splendid resurgence in art in America," Curry told the *Cincinnati Times* in 1939. "And we are in the midst of this movement now, but war will kill it. War and beauty do not go together. In the madness and hysteria of war, artists are kept busy grinding out horrible atrocity pictures."[45]

In this dour frame of mind, Curry painted and repainted *Wisconsin Landscape,* working on the alternating bands of sunlight and shadow that animate the scene. It is likely that he was thinking of that light allegorically, since the clouds that hover over this idyllic scene carry with them the suggestion of impending doom. As he thought further about the great precedent offered by Inness's *Peace and Plenty,* created as a celebration of the end of America's Civil War, Curry also must have considered the historical importance of his view of Wisconsin prosperity—and, by extension, the country's prosperity—as war threatened.[46]

In early December 1942, Curry submitted *Wisconsin Landscape* to the *Artists for Victory* exhibition at the Metropolitan Museum of Art. The show was organized by artists representing the twenty-three leading art societies that together had formed an emergency wartime agency they called Artists for Victory, Inc. Curry's submission was not exactly a move calculated to make a political statement. Having no new easel paintings of significance to offer to such a highly visible exhibition, he simply chose among the best of his still-unsold canvases. He advised Reeves Lewenthal at Associated American Artists to send either *Wisconsin Landscape* or the oil *John Brown* (1939, color plate 62) as his entry—both paintings begun five years earlier—hoping that he could sell one of them, even at $3,500, the top price to be paid for the show's first purchase prize.[47]

On December 4, Curry received the news that *Wisconsin Landscape*—among 532 paintings in the exhibition—had been awarded the highest honor. Having secured first prize, the canvas would be bought for the museum's permanent collection. In a time of war and fear, this painting had resonated with jurors. It had embodied the very spirit of the *Artists for Victory* show. For the artists of Curry's generation, *Wisconsin Landscape* had become, perhaps, their *Peace and Plenty,* that symbol of a time, or, in Curry's words, "of the peace and culture and the American awakening that we knew."[48]

Although the war energized Curry's art and lent a new poignancy to his earlier subjects, he never again produced a canvas that carried the expressive power of *Wisconsin Landscape.* He died, dispirited, in August 1946—dispirited both by the cultural changes wrought by world war and by what he must have seen as the ultimate failure of his populist goals. For what Benton saw as Curry's singular "inner cry for sympathy which made him great" also had the power to destroy him.[49] When his fellow Kansans denigrated his Topeka murals and drove him away in disgust, his mural cycle never completed, Curry did not recover from the hurt. His widow described the Kansas commission as "absolutely shattering. I think it really contributed toward his death."[50] But in another way, his laudable commitment to painting for a wide audience also worked against his art. It led him, on occasion, into odd mass-market endeavors—commercial illustrating and advertising projects, such as his promotional paintings for the American Tobacco Company, done in 1944, and the campaign for National City Bank that he was working on at his death. "Straining to envelop the feelings of his customers," as Benton put it, Curry left himself vulnerable to the vagaries of popular taste.

Still, Curry was by nature inclined to put the perceived needs of his audience first. This he did even in his work as the University of Wisconsin's artist-in-residence. He could easily have used the position to paint unencumbered by any consideration of the public at large. Instead, he gave freely of his time to Wisconsin's art enthusiasts, often to the detriment of his own productivity. In the end, it seems, he realized this truth and saw that in his great populist experiment he had not been free to accomplish what he had wished.

Writing to the artist Clare Leighton a year before his death, Curry reflected on his Wisconsin experience in a way that seems redolent of deep personal disappointment. "The main thing is to get something done as an artist," he told her, as she pondered taking a similar artist-in-residence position herself. He went on:

It has been my experience and observation that what really counts is your own work. You can lecture to cheering mobs and go around making wonderful impressions on this and that group, but the only thing that counts and the only thing that is remembered is what you have accomplished as an artist. You could spend a beautiful lifetime lecturing to women's clubs and it would be lovely until somebody came along with the latest thing. I do not want to appear too cynical because I find the great majority of people are anxious to learn but also there are a great many people filling in time and will do it at your expense.[51]

If Curry's humanity was his weakness, however, it was also his greatest strength. It is the force that animates *John Brown* and informs the broad, humanistic vision of *Wisconsin Landscape.* Benton understood this and in considering Curry's career paid the late artist this generous tribute:

Perhaps he could not have found so much that was real in America without also finding that which was false. All considered, however, John Curry comes off well. He never deliberately sold himself out. His failures were failures of time and place and his successes will outweigh them in the end. . . . I will risk this—whatever may be said of Grant Wood and me, it will surely be said of John Curry that he was the most simply human artist of his day.[52]

NOTES

1. Curry, "[Memorial tribute to Grant Wood]," 28 October 1942, typescript, Curry Papers, Archives of American Art, Smithsonian Institution, Washington, D.C. (hereafter cited as Curry Papers/AAA), microfilm roll 168, no frame no.

2. Thomas Hart Benton, "Wisconsin Landscape," *Demcourier* 11, no. 2 (April 1941): 14.

3. Chris L. Christensen, "Artist in Residence," *Demcourier* 11, no. 2 (April 1941): 15.

4. Curry's studio assistant in Madison, the painter William Ashby McCloy, describes the artist's distinctive brushes in "A Personal Reminiscence," in *John Steuart Curry: A Retrospective Exhibition of His Work Held in the Kansas State Capitol, Topeka, October 3–November 3, 1970. Kansas Quarterly* (repr., Lawrence: University of Kansas Museum of Art, 1970), 4.

5. I am grateful to my colleague Steven A. Nash, Associate Director and Chief Curator, Fine Arts Museums of San Francisco, for suggesting this allusion.

6. Curry, "Address before the Art Association of Madison, Tuesday, 19 January 1937," typescript, 7, Curry Papers/AAA, microfilm roll 165, no frame nos.

7. "Curry of Kansas," *Life* 1, no. 1 (23 November 1936): 28–29.

8. M. Jacques Maroger had worked at the Louvre and claimed to have discovered the oil technique of Jan van Eyck and Peter Paul Rubens. Having emigrated to the United States, he taught at the School of Fine and Applied Art in New York and had a tremendous influence on early-twentieth-century painters, especially Reginald Marsh, who gave Curry advice about Maroger's formula. See Marsh, "Curry," *Demcourier* 11, no. 2 (April 1941): 7. He also acquired notes from a class in Maroger's technique given at the School of the Art Institute of Chicago in April 1941. See Curry Papers/AAA, microfilm roll 166, frame 23.

9. Curry, "Address," 10.

10. Ibid., 5.

11. Ibid., 7.

12. Quoted in H. Russell Austin, *The Wisconsin Story: The Building of a Vanguard State* (Milwaukee, Wis.: Milwaukee Journal, 1948), 246.

13. Among Curry's personal papers is a copy of an illustrated pamphlet, "A Few Public Services Carried On by the University of Wisconsin," which outlines these services and emphasizes the message that "The University of Wisconsin Serves ALL Citizens of the State." See Curry Papers/AAA, microfilm roll 167, frame 321.

14. New York, Walker Galleries, *John Steuart Curry: New Work—1936–7*, 10–19 January 1938, unpaginated.

15. "Professor Curry," *Time* 31, no. 4 (24 January 1938): 32.

16. *Goal Line Play* (1938, oil and tempera on canvas) is reproduced in Laurence E. Schmeckebier, *John Steuart Curry's Pageant of America* (New York: American Artists Group, 1943), fig. 268, but the artist had destroyed the much-maligned canvas before 1943. *Spring Flowers* (1937, oil and tempera on panel) is reproduced in Schmeckebier, *Pageant*, fig. 104; it was acquired by a private collector in Chicago before 1943. *Kansas Sunrise* (1935–37, oil and tempera on panel) is in the collection of the Marion Kistler Beach Art Museum, Kansas State University, Manhattan, Kansas.

17. Curry is indirectly quoted in "Resident Artist: John Steuart Curry Takes Unique Post to Encourage Rural Painting," *Literary Digest* 122, no. 16 (17 October 1936): 22; Curry, quoted in "John Steuart Curry: He Puts Farm Life on Canvas" [radio interview by Blanche Overlein on the program "Homemakers' Hour," broadcast on Wisconsin's state stations WHA and WLBL], Curry Papers/AAA, microfilm roll 165, frame 990. The transcript was bound and distributed by the University of Wisconsin Extension Services in 1937.

18. Howard Devree, "Curry Has Show," *Magazine of Art* 31, no. 1 (January 1938): 36.

19. Untitled clipping in Curry scrapbook, *New York Sun*, 15 January 1938, Maynard Walker Papers, Archives of American Art, Smithsonian Institution, Washington, D.C. (hereafter cited as Walker Papers/AAA), microfilm roll 2160, no frame no.

20. Margaret Breuning, "Art in New York," *Parnassus* 10, no. 2 (2 February 1938): 26.

21. "Professor Curry," 33.

22. Edward Alden Jewell, "John S. Curry Art Is Put on Display," *New York Times*, 17 January 1938. In his introduction to the catalogue accompanying the exhibition, the University of Wisconsin art historian Laurence Schmeckebier wrote: "With no claim to pretensions, this exhibition is the record of the first year's accomplishment. . . . The result can be seen in the works themselves. An older painting such as the *Kansas Sunrise* with which he had long been dissatisfied he is at liberty to rework to a higher degree of technical and artistic perfection. The exhilarating freshness of Wisconsin hills and lakes is incorporated in the panorama *View of Madison* at Easter time. And with the autumn season Curry's known love for colorful and dramatic action finds renewed expression in the driving *Line Play* of collegiate America's most popular sport." Schmeckebier, "Curry at Wisconsin," in Walker Galleries, *Curry: New Work*, unpaginated.

23. Maynard Walker, New York City, to Curry, Madison, Wis., 31 January 1941, Walker Papers/AAA, microfilm roll 2023, frame 55.

24. Curry's plans are outlined in detail in "Resident Artist": 23.

25. "John Steuart Curry—Schedule," September to 18 November 1943, Curry Papers/AAA, microfilm roll 165, no frame no.

26. "U.W. Experiment Has Shown That Art, Agriculture Do Mix," *Milwaukee Journal*, 26 October 1941.

27. The story of Curry's ill-fated Kansas murals is fully and brilliantly told in M. Sue Kendall, *Rethinking Regionalism: John Steuart Curry and the Kansas Mural Controversy* (Washington, D.C.: Smithsonian Institution Press, 1986).

28. So Legge is quoted in *The Farm Foundation Story: The First Twenty Years* (Chicago: Farm Foundation, 1953), 3. The memorial committee also commissioned a biography of its founder, which has served as my principal source of information about Legge's life and career. See Forrest Crissey, *Alexander Legge, 1866–1933* (Chicago: Alexander Legge Memorial Committee, 1936).

29. So Legge's description was related to Laurence Schmeckebier, perhaps by Curry himself. See Schmeckebier, *Pageant,* 133.

30. It is clear from Taylor's letter to Curry that the two men had discussed the possible commission prior to Taylor's granting approval for the artist to proceed. See Henry C. Taylor, Director, Farm Foundation, Chicago, to Curry, Madison, Wis., Curry Papers/AAA, 19 August 1937, microfilm roll 165, no frame number. Taylor writes: "I have just received a letter from Mr. Wm. S. Elliott of the International Harvester Co., stating that the Harvester people are ready to take the full responsibility for raising the $2,500 to pay for the painting of the landscape so dear to the heart of Alexander Legge, and which was shown to us by Mr. Leo E. Lunenschloss a few weeks ago." His words suggest that Curry would have known exactly the landscape to which Taylor was referring, possibly from having toured with him.

31. Ibid.

32. I have relied on the useful thumbnail sketch of the distinctive southern Wisconsin landscape in Ingolf Vogeler et al., *Wisconsin: A Geography* (Boulder, Colo.: Westview Press, 1986), 131–34.

33. M. Sue Kendall has discussed Curry's abiding interest in soil conservation, and I am indebted to her for my own reading of the Wisconsin farm landscape. See Kendall, *Rethinking Regionalism,* 121–25.

34. Curry, "Excerpts from an address by John Steuart Curry, Artist in Residence, College of Agriculture, University of Wisconsin, before American Country Life Association, Manhattan, Kansas, Friday, October 15, 1937," typescript, unpaginated, text accompanying slide no. 28, Curry Papers/AAA, microfilm roll 168, no frame no.

35. Ibid., text accompanying slide no. 38.

36. The horizontality of the scene is the essential quality of what may well have been an early preliminary watercolor study, now in the artist's estate. The watercolor is discussed and reproduced in Charles C. Eldredge's essay in the exhibition brochure *John Steuart Curry's America* (Kansas City, Mo.: Exhibits U.S.A., 1992), unpaginated.

37. The Farm Foundation, now located in Oak Brook, Illinois, was unable to produce correspondence that might shed light on the history of the picture. I am grateful to Sandy Young of the foundation staff for her attempts to find documents on the Curry commission.

38. Carlyle Burrows, "Notes and Comment on Events in Art," *New York Herald Tribune,* 3 December 1939.

39. "New Curry Picture," *Art Digest* 14, no. 3 (November 1939): 18.

40. Burrows, "Notes and Comment."

41. "New Curry Picture": 18.

42. Quoted in "Cranbrook-Life Exhibition: Great Detroit Art Center Holds a Democratic Show of 60 Paintings by Living Americans," *Life* 8, no. 22 (27 May 1940): 65.

43. Benton, "Wisconsin Landscape."

44. *The Farm Is a Battle Ground, Too* (1942, oil on canvas) is in the collection of the Davenport Museum of Art, Davenport, Iowa. *Leaving the Farm for Army Training Camp* (1941, tempera on panel) is in the collection of the New Britain Museum of American Art, New Britain, Connecticut.

45. Quoted in "Great Renaissance of Art Seen If United States Escapes War," *Cincinnati Times,* undated clipping, 1939, Curry Papers/AAA, microfilm roll 165, no frame no.

46. For discussion of Inness's *Peace and Plenty,* see LeRoy Ireland, *The Works of George Inness: An Illustrated Catalogue Raisonné* (Austin: University of Texas Press, 1965), 78, no. 311; and Nicolai Cikovsky, Jr., *George Inness* (New York: Praeger, 1971), 35–38, fig. 30.

47. See Curry, Madison, Wis., to Reeves Lewenthal, New York City, 9 September 1942, Curry Papers/AAA, microfilm roll 165, no frame no.

48. Curry, "Grant Wood."

49. Thomas H. Benton, "John Curry," *University of Kansas City Review* (winter 1946): 89.

50. Kathleen Curry, quoted in Bret Waller, "An Interview with Mrs. John Steuart Curry," in *John Steuart Curry: A Retrospective Exhibition,* 10.

51. Curry, Madison, Wis., to Clare Leighton, Durham, N.C., 19 May 1945, letter in collection of Mrs. John Steuart Curry.

52. Benton, "John Curry," 90.

The Life and Career of John Steuart Curry

AN ANNOTATED CHRONOLOGY

PATRICIA JUNKER

"And if I can't be an artist I'll be nothing": Years of Study

1897

14 November John Steuart Curry born at the family farm near Dunavant, Jefferson County, in the northeastern corner of Kansas. He is the first child of Margaret and Thomas Smith Curry.

ca. 1903–16

Attends Hickory Point (Kansas) public elementary school. Attends Winchester (Kansas) High School, where he is a track and football star. Does not graduate, leaving at the end of his junior year to study art.

"When I was a boy on a farm near Dunavant," he said, "the prevailing idea was that any artist was either a wastrel or a lazybones, or both. I will admit that I got tired of pitching wheat bundles and that tossing a paint brush is more to my taste as a sheer matter of labor. The highest calling, the most honored in the community, was that of a foreign missionary, the next in line was a preacher, and then came a farmer.

"In spite of the high esteem of farmers and preachers, and the low esteem of painters, except good house painters, I found myself during the dinner hour on the farm backing one of the draft horses up against the barn, tethering it, and drawing it. I can't say why. My family had no leanings in that direction, certainly my immediate family had none. My father was a farmer, a fattener of livestock.... The only thing that he took any artistic pride in was the construction of concrete water tanks which didn't hold water. But he was a remarkable man. Of the eighty-five acres he farmed, he made enough to take my mother to Europe on their honeymoon—an unheard-of thing forty years ago when the elite of Kansas hardly came to New York even....

"My mother," Mr. Curry continued, restoking his pipe, "was also a remarkable woman. She brought home from that trip good reproductions of the best art of Europe. Instead of grain and feed calendars in our house as the only art we had Rubens, Bellini and Millet. That was unusual and had a great deal to do with forming my future."

([Royal Cortissoz,] "Kansas Heals Breach with a Native Son," New York Herald Tribune, *5 February 1935)*

1916

Summer Works as a section hand on the Missouri Pacific Railroad. In late summer, studies for one month at the Kansas City Art Institute.

That month at the Kansas City Art Institute's summer school in 1916 taught the boy from Kansas a great deal, even if it didn't transform him into a full-fledged painter. After being laughed at, he was ignored, and one of the most disconcerting chapters in the history of the school is the fact that not one teacher or student ever has been found who recalls him. Charles Wilimovsky, now of Chicago, was teaching painting at the Institute then and he told Curry later he recalled him, but Curry says he doesn't believe him. At all events, he says Wilimovsky kept him on the right track, drawing everything in sight—chairs, tables, houses, animals and human beings.

("Up from a Kansas Farm" [interview with Curry], Kansas City Times, *8 August 1933)*

1 October Supported by his family, arrives in Chicago to study at the School of the Art Institute. Enrolls in classes with painter Edward J. Finley Timmons.

Mighty glad to get your letter telling me about the farm. But I believe I would rather draw a picture of myself shoveling manure than do it... I'm mighty thankful to you for sending me. I don't know when I can make art pay.

(Curry to his father, 12 November 1916. Curry Papers, Archives of American Art, Smithsonian Institution, Washington, D.C. [hereafter cited as Curry Papers/AAA], microfilm roll 2714, frame 498.)

1917

January Begins second term at the School of the Art Institute of Chicago, taking classes in drawing from antique casts and in still-life painting.

I have been promoted to the advanced still life painting class.... It may take me all year to get into life [drawing], but cast drawing will not hurt me.... My roommate got into [Fred de Forest] Schook's illustration class, the highest in the school and it is great. They have models posing every afternoon for two weeks. And you should see some of their work. It is fine. I wish I was in that class; I will some day.

(Curry to his father [3 January 1917]. Curry Papers/AAA, microfilm roll 2714, frames 514–15.)

I have started painting in the advanced class and I like it fine.... [Timmons] says my work is coming fine, so I feel fairly well. He gave me a big blow in his gallery lecture this morning. There is a picture of a moonlit scene by Carlson that I liked fine and I pulled Timmie over by his coat sleeve and showed it to him. So this morning he gave a big blow about my judgment and that all great men come from the farm.

. . . He calls me Jack Kansas as that is what I have on my smock.

(Curry to his parents, Sabbath [11 January 1917]. Curry Papers/AAA, microfilm roll 2714, frame 518.)

And if I can't be an artist I'll be nothing. I'm not a scholar and I hate to haul manure.

(Curry to his mother, 21 June 1916 [sic, *but actually 1917]. Curry Papers/AAA, microfilm roll 2714, frame 484.)*

February From early in his stay in Chicago, the subject of religion occupies considerable space in Curry's letters home. Struggling with theological issues and feeling the need to reconcile his stern Scots Presbyterian (Covenanter) upbringing with the more liberal views he encounters in the city, he gravitates to the Moody Bible Institute and associates with students there. But no experience is to prove as affecting as his discussion with the Reverend Thomas McKnight of Chicago's Reformed Presbyterian Church.

I had a talk with Mr. McKnight. I never had any one talk to me in such a free manner. . . . I felt as if I had seen a new light, when he talked to me. He explained the life of Christ in a new way and Christ's way of personal work. He believes that Christ lived among and influenced his disciples by his life and when his call came the disciples were ready to go and that they were not called so miraculously as we suppose. He talked to me in the most friendly way, of leading a Christian life everyday. And to be saved by faith and a good life. He left out all the "hallelluiah, I know I'm saved" stuff and talked to me like I think a Christian ought to talk. . . . Ma, I can't tell you how I felt to be able to talk to a man on Christianity and my own welfare, and without feeling afraid, self conscious, or with slobbery praying to save my soul. We did pray, but it was honest, straight stuff. I can't explain to you the difference between prayers, but there is a mighty big one. . . . I may forget my good intentions but I can't forget my talk with him.

(Curry to his mother, Sabbath [12 February 1917]. Curry Papers/AAA, microfilm roll 2714, frames 535–37.)

March Writes home that he is contemplating enlisting in the army. In a series of letters to his parents through the year, discusses his urge to join the fight in Europe, his various service options, and his studies.

The world moves. I am tempted to join the army. The 4th. Presbyterian Church is raising a Co. . . . My work may suffer now but it will be helped too. . . . The Co. at the church with the Moody Institute fellows will be a fine place to get in. Also I should like to join a Kansas reg. The artillery is the place to be in this war. They are not in the trenches and that means everything. . . . I expect to study for 5 years without making money. I can't do lettering or commercial stuff. I don't think I can. It is too much like algebra. I try to paint values, color, and draw well. These are the main things.

(Curry to his parents, Sabbath, [12 (?) March 1917]. Curry Papers/AAA, microfilm roll 2714, frames 543–44 and 547–48.)

April Writes home of his decision to study illustration at the School of the Art Institute of Chicago and to make a career in that field.

Well now don't think I am doing any extraordinary school work. I have only found what I should work on. I draw life every morning. I'm sure you are right when you say that color will come when I get looser. Sketching helps me to paint more than anything else. . . . O, I wish I was in the country. I sometimes feel like coming home and hauling manure. . . . I want to get in Mr. Schook's class of illustration next Christmas. I'm sure he can help me. I can learn more from a single teacher than from several. I must study with H. [Harvey] Dunn when I become more proficient.

(Curry to his mother, Sabbath [23 April 1917]. Curry Papers/ AAA, microfilm roll 2714, frames 559–60.)

I am with Schook again. I believe he is an old fool for sure. In many ways anyhow. He thinks a picture is a design first, middle, and all the time. He paints on a picture upside down anyway to get "in-tricket" shapes as he says. Feeling comes last with him. Floor designs is his real field if only he knew it. I must study with Harvey Dunn. He is making the illustrators of today.

(Curry to his parents, Sabbath, 19 November 1917. Curry Papers/AAA, microfilm roll 2714, frames 576–77.)

December Turns down parents' offer to send him east to study with Harvey Dunn, electing to stay in Chicago another term.

Dad and you are certainly good to offer me the chance to go east and study. But I don't believe I'll go this winter. I am settled here and there is much I can learn. . . . I need drawing and study in light and shade, which I can get this winter. My study in the east with Dunn would be all right if he would take a personal interest in my work, but I'm afraid he has many other students who would be farther advanced and Dunn is a specialist.

(Curry to his mother, Sabbath [10 December 1917]. Curry Papers/AAA, microfilm roll 2714, frames 580–82.)

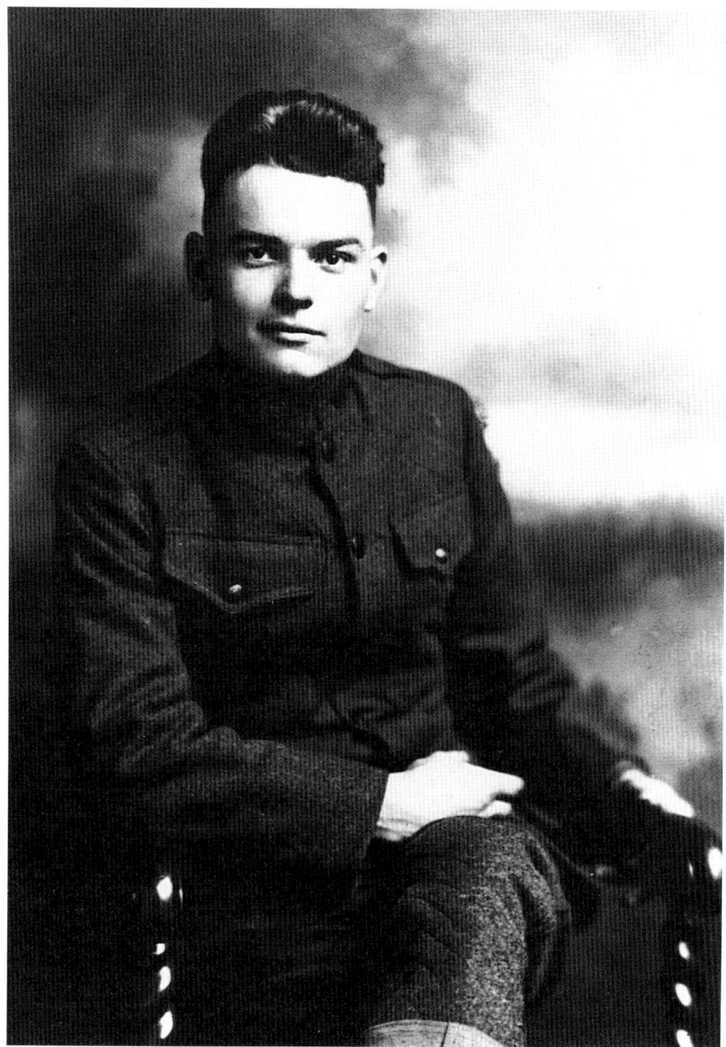

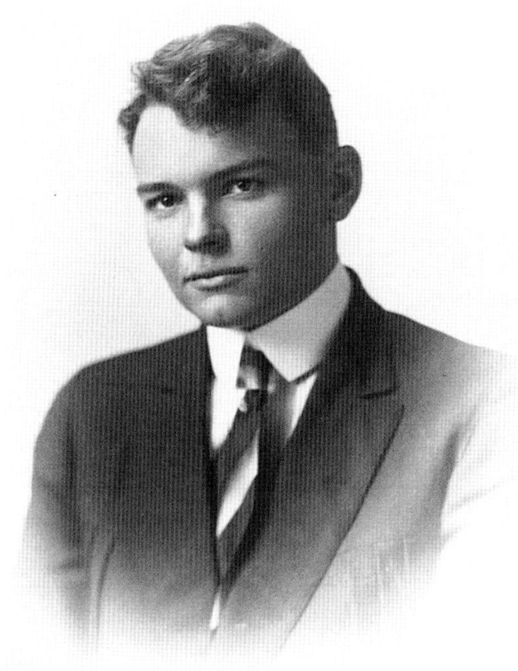

FIGURE 1 *(left)*
Curry as a volunteer for the Student Army Training Corps, Geneva College, September 1918. Photograph courtesy Curry Papers, Archives of American Art, Smithsonian Institution, Washington, D.C. Gift of Mrs. Stanley R. Fike.

FIGURE 2 *(above)*
Curry at Geneva College, 1918. Photograph courtesy Curry Papers, Archives of American Art, Smithsonian Institution, Washington, D.C., gift of Mrs. Stanley R. Fike.

1918

23 March Finishes term at the School of the Art Institute of Chicago.

September Enrolls as a special student at Geneva College, Beaver Falls, Pennsylvania, an institution affiliated with the Scots Presbyterian (Covenanter) Church. Studies art, joins Student Army Training Corps, and plays football for two seasons. Stays through December 1919 (figs. 1 and 2).

1920

February Introduces himself to Harvey Dunn at the illustrator's home and studio in Tenafly, New Jersey; settles in nearby Leonia.

Well the luck of everything is with me so far.... Yesterday I called Mr. Dunn expecting to see him today. He invited me out right then.... He took me to lunch and I met his wife and two little children. Mother, he has a wonderful place. Just what I am going to have some day.

I walked into his studio. Another man was just leaving.... The gentleman was the Art Editor of the *Sat. Evening Post.* Dunn introduced me to him.

Mr. Dunn is a large fair-haired man with a wonderful personality. We talked about art and I listened to his philosophy of life. He looked at my work and pronounced it good in spirit and rotten in drawing and technical ability.

He asked me everything, about you and Dad and my previous life. I talked to him straight out. I told him how I had pursued him for years. How I placed my faith in him. Ma, I told him about everything.

Well he isn't taking students now. But he told me to settle in Leonia among his former students and he would direct my efforts. He assured me that in three years I would be able to afford a second hand car.

I asked him about the art game. He told me that the magazines were searching for good illustrators. I asked him how his former students were doing: "Well," he said, "they're riding around in cars with their families, building studios and making from $2000 to $15,000 a year."

Mr. Dunn told me that he liked me personally. That I seemed honest and sincere and possessed of an artistic mind. He told me he liked the way I had feared him and the fact that I was not awed by his personality.

Ma, if I work I can make good. I can't get returns right away but give me two years. Mr. Dunn said that in a year I might be able to do some real work, but that to attempt the editors before I was ready would be folly.

I have his backing now. When I get settled he told me he would come down and fix me up and start me out in my study. I can't wish anything better. . . .

I can't tell you how I feel about the whole thing. I think that I have my opportunity. I haven't worked. Dunn told me that. But I must work and I can. . . .

Mr. Dunn told me in his discourse on truth, and that is what he talked about, truth, to read my Bible. You know artists aren't supposed to be Christians. I never heard a more earnest and real sermon than yesterday's.

(Curry to his mother, 2 February 1920. Curry Papers/AAA, microfilm roll 2714, frames 617–22.)

I'm settled temporarily at 175 Broad Avenue. I'm having a studio fixed up. It will cost 25$ or 30$ a month. Studios are hard to get anywhere. . . . I have gone ahead with my plans counting on your helping me for awhile. At least a year or two. It would be much better for me if I would spend that time in study. Dunn advised me to if it was possible.

I like Leonia. It is like a country town. Lots of churches and good schools. The people are very nice. There are many artists. . . . They are real artists, none of this Washington Square, Greenwich Village, Bohemians. . . . These men take their work seriously. They believe in divine inspiration. That is what Dunn preaches. . . . Dunn was influenced by Howard Pyle and the spirit and work of Pyle still lives.

(Curry to his mother, 5 February 1920. Curry Papers/AAA, microfilm roll 2714, frames 624–27.)

Dunn looked over my stuff Thursday evening. Showed me how rotten it was and assured me I was learning. Friday night he took me to the illustrators show at the Waldorf.

I sat among the great and just looked. I saw [Charles Dana] Gibson, [James Montgomery] Flagg, [Norman] Rockwell, all the great and mighty. I'm to be with them in a few years.

(Curry to his mother, Sabbath [3 (?) March 1920]. Curry Papers/AAA, microfilm roll 2714, frames 643–44.)

1921

Begins publishing illustrations. During the next four years his work accompanies stories in such popular youth magazines as *Boy's Life, St. Nicholas, Country Gentleman,* the *Saturday Evening Post,* and other Curtis magazines.

1923

23 January In New York, marries Clara Derrick, of Jamesburg, New Jersey. The couple met through Curry's brother Eugene, who worked for Clara's father, Calvin Derrick, head of the New Jersey State Home for Boys.

Well, I am married, happy and glad of it. We had a dandy little wedding. . . .

I was awfully afraid you would think I had eloped with a model or some female of the Greenwich Village type. My new wife has lots of sense and affection and as well she makes a dandy appearance. . . .

Clara and I want to get out home next spring or in the summer some time. As it is we'll confine our honeymoon to New York for the present. If business picks up we can travel next summer.

I haven't much else to say except that I'm surely well taken care of. You'll like Clara fine. Everybody does and that fortunately applies to me.

(Curry to his parents, 25 January 1923. Curry Papers/AAA, microfilm roll 2714, frames 677–78.)

1924

Settles in Westport, Connecticut, buying a studio at Otter Ponds.

Summer Visits Cooperstown, New York, and makes series of watercolors of picturesque views around Otsego Lake.

15 November–7 December Oil *The Fence Builders* included in *Winter Exhibition,* National Academy of Design, New York (cat. no. 317), but attracts no notice in the press.

1925

Assists James Daugherty on a mural for the Cook Travel Agency booth at the Sesquicentennial Exposition in Philadelphia. Daugherty urges Curry to pursue further study abroad, suggesting either the Slade School in London or Basil Schoukhaieff's drawing academy in Paris.

1926

October With money advanced by banker and art patron Seward Prosser, leaves with Clara for Paris to study under Schoukhaieff. Settles in the studio of sculptor Hunt Dietrich. In addition to producing impressive figure and portrait studies in charcoal, paints watercolors of the colorful street characters of Montmartre.

Came to New York to be an illustrator. Was not a brilliant success. Went to Paris and learned something from M. Schoukhaieff of the Russian Academy. Learned something, also, from the Louvre and have been trying since to carry out my ideas of how an American should paint.

(Curry to Frederic Newlin Price, 17 November 1930. Maynard Walker Papers, Archives of American Art, Smithsonian Institution, Washington, D.C. [hereafter cited as Walker Papers/AAA], microfilm roll 2023, frame 9.)

Dissatisfied with his work, he went to Paris and studied under Schoukhaieff. "Finally," he said, after looking at Matisse and Picasso, "at whose feet the whole art world was worshiping," he decided that "they were good but not good for me. Now, at the age of twenty-nine years, I grew up. I discovered my tradition. I discovered Rubens."

("Circus Limner Terms P.W.A. Best Art Spur," New York Herald Tribune, *29 April 1934)*

1927

May Drawings by Schoukhaieff's students, many of whom are American, are exhibited at Drouant Galleries on the rue de Rennes. In a review, Curry's drawings are singled out (color plates 4 and 5, figs. 3 and 4).

June After a final week abroad, in London, returns home to Westport. Receives commissions for decorative wall maps for James Borning's travel agency in New York and for Seward Prosser's home in Woods Hole, Massachusetts.

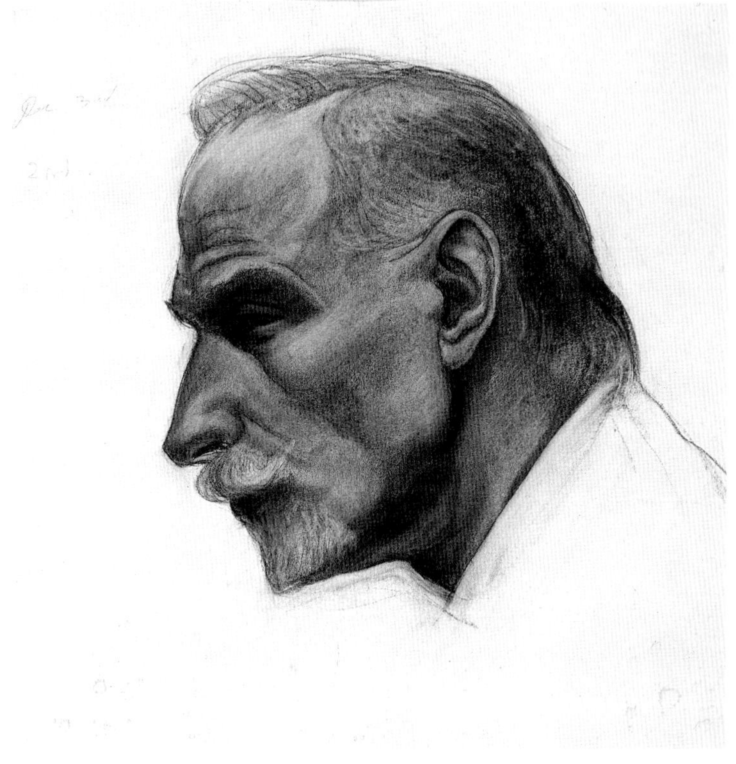

FIGURE 3 *(above)*

John Steuart Curry
Study of a Head: Man, 1926–27
Charcoal on paper
24 × 17 in.
Estate of the artist. Photograph courtesy Mongerson Wunderlich Gallery, Chicago.

FIGURE 4 *(facing page)*

John Steuart Curry
Study of a Head: Man with Glasses, 1926–27
Charcoal on paper
25½ × 19¼ in.
Estate of the artist. Photograph courtesy Mongerson Wunderlich Gallery, Chicago.

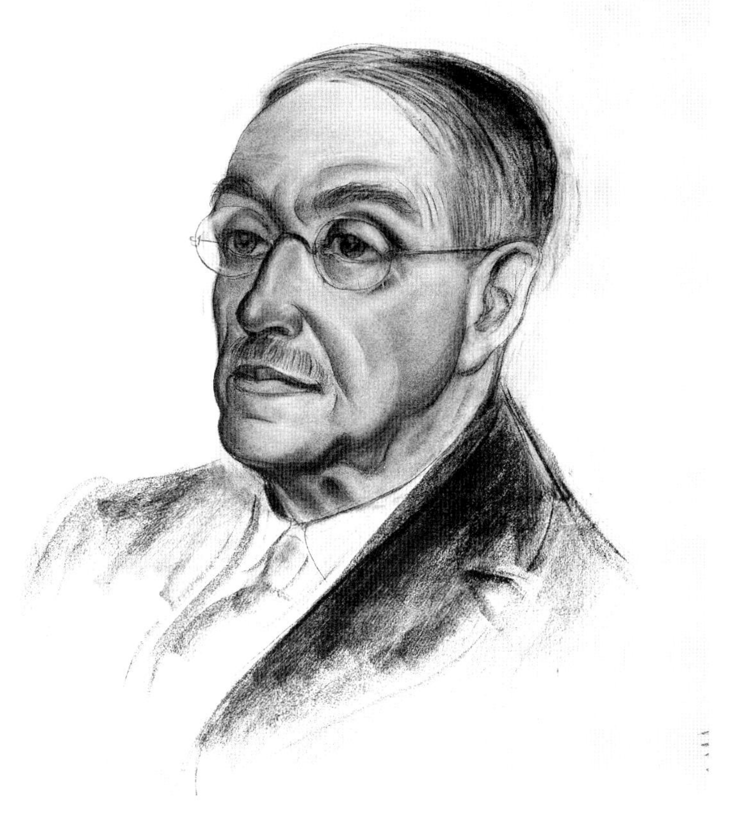

Fame on the Ascendancy: "Jack Kansas" Makes His Mark

1928

29 April–26 May Oil *Steeplechaser, Auteuil* included in *Thirteenth Annual Exhibition of Paintings by the Members of the Club,* Whitney Studio Club, New York (cat. no. 39).

28 October–9 December Oil *Baptism in Kansas* (color plate 10) included in *Eleventh Biennial Exhibition of Contemporary American Oil Paintings,* Corcoran Gallery of Art, Washington, D.C. (cat. no. 122), garnering high praise—Curry's first serious attention from the New York press.

In quite [a] different mood [from storytelling pictures], John Steuart Curry has succeeded more brilliantly. His "Baptism in Kansas" is a gorgeous piece of satire and . . . admirably composed. Religious fanaticism of the hinterland saturates the scene, only inanimate nature looking on as with a smile of cynical coolness. Yonder are some big barns and an impartial windmill. In the center foreground is one of those circular watering troughs, consecrated now to the ceremonies attached to immersion. Knee-deep stand the parson and his trembling neophyte, a woman with rather wild eyes, who knows full well that the mystical waters will soon cover her. A stirred company surrounds this impending climax, its more musically inclined members singing a hymn. Overhead clouds seem stricken with ontological portent, and two otherwise quite ordinary farmyard doves swoop like symbols straight from the Apocalypse. Finally, on all sides spread the flat Kansas prairies, stretching to a horizon that fences from the outer worlds this shut-in frenzy of the human soul.

(Edward Alden Jewell, "Corcoran Gallery's 11th Exhibition," New York Times, *4 November 1928)*

7 December Gertrude Vanderbilt Whitney, soon to become Curry's patron, announces the establishment of the Whitney Studio Galleries, replacing the Whitney Studio Club as a showcase for contemporary art. The exhibition space will occupy the main floor of her studio residence at 8 West Eighth Street, New York, and will be managed by Juliana Force.

1929

27 January–17 March Oils *Baptism in Kansas* and *Storm Breaking over Lake Otsego* (color plate 14) shown in *124th Annual Exhibition of Paintings and Sculpture,* Pennsylvania Academy of the Fine Arts, Philadelphia (cat. nos. 89, 102).

April Oil *Female Acrobat* (later entitled *The High Diver)* included in the exhibition *The Circus in Paint,* Whitney Studio Galleries (no cat. no.).

Summer Visits family in Kansas for six weeks. Makes a series of sketches of Kaw River valley floods, of devastation left by a tornado that had passed through Winchester (near the Curry farm), and of dust storms in Oklahoma.

24 October–8 December *Baptism in Kansas* included in *42nd Annual Exhibition of American Paintings and Sculpture,* Art Institute of Chicago (cat. no. 49).

2 November Juliana Force, on behalf of Whitney Studio Galleries, grants Curry subsidy of $200 per month through 1 March 1930.

1930

26 January–16 March Oil *State Fair* (color plate 13, fig. 5) included in *125th Annual Exhibition of Paintings and Sculpture,* Pennsylvania Academy of the Fine Arts (cat. no. 488).

28 January–8 February First solo show, *Exhibitions by John Steuart Curry, James D'Agostino, Loutchansky,* Whitney Studio Galleries (catalogue).

John Steuart Curry, at the Whitney Studio Gallery, appears like young Lochinvar to come out of the West. At least the themes of his lively canvases are not familiar ones in this region. His stock-

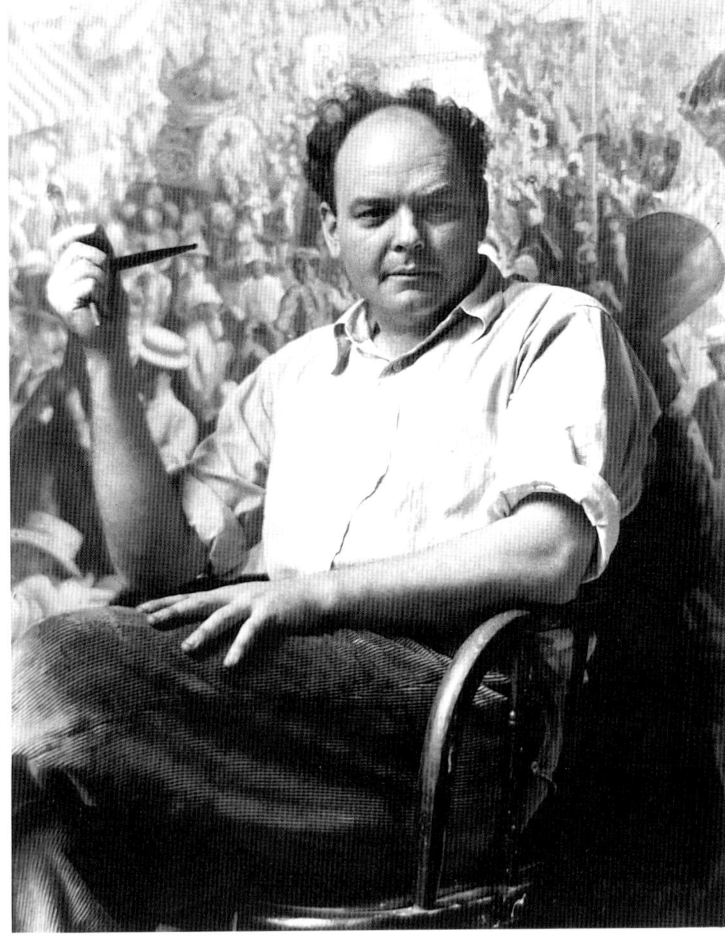

FIGURE 5
Curry in his Westport, Connecticut, studio at work on the oil *State Fair,* 1928. Photograph courtesy Mrs. John Steuart Curry.

man or roadworkers or his glimpses of prairie expanses and artesian wells do not occur on our immediate horizon but they have a convincing air of veracity both in their witty presentation and in their individuality of technical expression. They give us the American scene with an admixture of realism and sentiment that distinguish our native expression.

(Margaret Breuning, New York Evening Post, *1 February 1930)*

Mr. Curry as a painter is commendably 100 per cent. He finds his subjects in this land and in no other. He is not a finished workman as yet and drifts occasionally into unnecessary confusion of manner, but there is no doubt that he is on the trail of interesting material.

(Henry McBride, New York Sun, *1 February 1930)*

Pictures of life in the Middle West furnish John Steuart Curry a New York introduction in the Whitney Studio galleries. He has concerned himself with the humdrum of the life in which he was reared, dealing wholly with humans, recording their labors, their exaltations and their perils, weaving a story that goes beyond illustration and touches the realm of emotion. . . . The pictures say, as if in words, that everyday human material has furnished this brush with its fill of inspiration, apart from the externals of scenery, or the promptings of inner vision.

(Frederick W. Eddy, "Paintings Tell Human Interest Story," New York World, *2 February 1930)*

March Oil *Russian Giant* included in *Spring Exhibition,* Whitney Studio Galleries (no cat. no.).

24 March Juliana Force extends Curry's monthly subsidy of $200 through 1 November.

May Visits Kansas again. Paints in the Gyp Hills, southwest of the town of Medicine Lodge, Barber County, on the Kansas-Oklahoma border. Also makes sketches of Heart Ranch and of the devastation left by a tornado in Jefferson County, near the Curry family farm.

10 September Attracts attention from Frederic Newlin Price, director of Ferargil Galleries, New York, who proposes that Curry have an exhibition there.

30 October–14 December Oil *Tornado* (color plate 20) shown in *43rd Annual Exhibition of American Paintings and Sculpture,* Art Institute of Chicago (cat. no. 43).

29 November–12 December Solo exhibition, *John Steuart Curry,* Ferargil Galleries (no catalogue).

[Curry] is an artist who lives in, knows and paints the American scene. But, best of all, he does it with a highly developed personal idiom. His work is vivid and compelling, yet he depicts nothing more thrilling than Kansas scenes, although he does allow himself occasionally the luxury of cyclones and their attendant thrills and horrors. He translates the facts of this world which environs him with such perception and sympathy that his penetrating record registers vividly. He has grown in his power of concentrated design and of selective vision. He depends less and less upon the subject matter of his canvases and leans more and more heavily upon his ability to gather up all his elements of design in formal relations of beauty and power.

He hesitates at nothing. I am sure he would step in where angels not only fear to tread but would urge him not to. Yet in most cases he emerges victorious, fusing esthetic emotion and warm human sympathy in one striking impression of dramatic vigor.

(Margaret Breuning, "Ferargil Gallery," New York Post, *6 December 1930)*

Kansas is Mr. Curry's State, and these pictures could only have been painted by a native son.

Kansas wheat fields, farm houses and cyclones have furnished playwrights and poets with material, but it would hardly seem to offer the painter in search of local color imagination-stirring material. But Mr. Curry is steeped in his subject and has seen it, pictorially, with the result that his pictures have the convincing vitality which is concomitant with a genuine emotional reaction. Seen in a group, they are vivid records of the life of a small-town Middle West community. Dramatic tornadoes, portentous thunderstorms, peaceful, interminable wheat fields are only part of the panorama. Other aspects deal with human events, revivalist meetings and anecdotes of family and farm life on a Kansas wheat ranch. Accurate, convincing portrayal of a locality is, however, only one side of the picture, as it were; it is his ability to invest the familiar and everyday with emotion, to transform the particular to the universal, that gives his work its special quality of interest.

(Brooklyn Eagle, *7 December 1930)*

Every now and again we have a view of a new artist who is trying to express the true meaning of American life, who draws inspiration from the very soil he treads, whether it be the sidewalks of New York or the prairies of Kansas. Such an artist is John Steuart Curry, of Kansas, who is exhibiting his paintings at the Ferargil Gallery. Mr. Curry passed some time in the art schools of both this country and Paris, but he did not succumb to the temptation to adopt a style that is merely fashionable. Thinking for himself, he turned to the subject he knew best, the Western American scene, and in painting it has produced some authentic impressions of its character.

(Carlyle Burrows, "News and Comments on Current Art Events," New York Herald Tribune, *7 December 1930)*

It is a very great satisfaction to observe the steady rise into prominence of John Steuart Curry, whose painting has, for years, been recommending itself as qualified to fill an important role in the drama of contemporary American art.... It is to be hoped that all who possibly can will get in to see this exhibition which, although many of Mr. Curry's best canvases are unavoidably absent, is a stimulating affair, containing work that is often as rich in present accomplishments as it is with arrows pointing forward.

(Edward Alden Jewell, "Kansas Has Found Her Homer," New York Times, *7 December 1930)*

23 December–18 January 1931 Featured in a special exhibition organized by Ferargil Galleries at the Art Institute of Chicago, *John Steuart Curry, Louis Ritman, and Harold Weston* (no catalogue). Oils, watercolors, and lithographs are included. Maynard Walker, of Ferargil Galleries, arranges for the exhibition to travel to the City Art Museum, St. Louis (1–15 March 1931) and the Mulvane Museum, Topeka, Kansas (late March–late April 1931).

Many persons in Winchester and Dunavant have had the privilege of visiting the Mulvane Art Museum and viewing the oil paintings and drawings by John Steuart Curry on exhibition there. John now has a national reputation as an artist and his work is largely connected with Kansas scenes—a tornado, farm and prairie, cattle and other subjects.... John Curry may well be called the true Kansas artist, if not also the foremost artist of Middle West scenery. Winchester and Kansas may well be proud of his genius.

*(*Winchester [Kansas] Star, *17 April 1931)*

1931

March Solo exhibition, *Work of John Steuart Curry,* Ferargil Galleries (no catalogue).

12–25 October Solo exhibition, *John Steuart Curry: Recent Paintings,* Ferargil Galleries (no catalogue). There follows a vigorous campaign by Maynard Walker to place the exhibition in American museums and to encourage museum acquisitions of Curry's work. Having put forth this effort, Walker asks Curry for a commitment to exclusive representation by Ferargil:

Everyone who has been in—critics, public and what-not—says emphatically this is the best show you have ever had. I know it is too. There are even some promising prospects of sales.... Certainly you should have every reason to be encouraged and inspired....

I should like to know at once about making a permanent arrangement for handling your pictures. I have already made some efforts to get exhibitions of the new things in other cities: Wichita, Kansas City, Detroit, etc., but if you are not going to give us control of your work, I do not see how we can afford to promote it to this extent, in view of the fact that it involves a great deal of expense and time. I think we have demonstrated our belief in you and are entitled to consideration.

(Maynard Walker to Curry, 16 October 1931. Curry Papers/AAA, microfilm roll 166, no frame no.)

And speaking of the native quality, there are few American painters who have it in a more undiluted form than John Steuart Curry, who is holding a one-man show at the Ferargil Galleries. His pictures are graphic records of the life he knows and has been a part of. The tornadoes, the fields, episodes in small towns, prayer meetings, the quack doctor, herds of cattle are among his subjects and form a panorama of the American scene.

It is because painting is for him a medium for expressing his reaction to the life that he knows best that accounts in a large measure for the vitality and individuality of his work.

Mr. Curry is living in the East now. But his reaction to an environment which he necessarily knows less intimately has not brought about any cessation of the emotional directness which characterized his early work.

("John Steuart Curry," Brooklyn Daily Eagle, *18 October 1931)*

12 November William Allen White, influential publisher of the *Emporia (Kansas) Gazette,* helps mount a campaign to bring Curry's art to Kansas. The following letter, to Wichita newspaperman Henry Ware Allen, is representative of White's efforts:

I met, in New York the other day, John Curry, a young Kansas artist who seems to be making his way pretty rapidly in the Eastern art circles. I saw his exhibit at the Ferargil Galleries, and talked with men who know about art and they say Curry is a comer.

I have been wondering why Kansas cannot make some show of recognition of Curry. We ought to have some shows for him in Wichita, Emporia, Lawrence, Topeka, Salina, and Hutchinson.... I believe if I would urge it, Curry would come out and talk to various Kansas groups and I am sure we could make a place for him out here.

Our politicians and our freaks get so much advertising that when a man from Kansas lifts his head to the higher realm of artistic creation, it seems to me the state should do something to recognize and reward him.

(William Allen White to Henry Ware Allen, 12 November 1931. Walker Papers/AAA, microfilm roll 2023, frame 17.)

18 November Whitney Museum of American Art opens in New York. Notice in the *New York Times* carries a photograph of Mrs. Whitney standing before *Baptism in Kansas,* acquired for the new museum's permanent collection.

The Whitney Museum, devoted exclusively to the work of Americans and of artists identified with the American cultural movement, may well be looked upon as a symbol in that it draws sharply to focus the fact of an art's coming into its own. The road has been long and the path of accomplishment stretches off ahead into a future no man can confidently foretell. Here, at any rate, is a milestone, a testimonial of recognition and of faith.

And yet the victory of Paris has entailed its price. A new American generation has meanwhile been growing to maturity, with other notions in its head. We perceive that the modern French creed of individualism has been slowly assimilated. On a constantly increasing scale American artists manifest a determination to be themselves in their own fashion. And "their own fashion" turns out to be something much closer to what can only be called the American idiom than any esthetic speech of the past.

Triumphantly did painters like George Bellows, Robert Henri and Arthur B. Davies emerge from the wave of alien influences whose undertow might well have carried less individual spirits out of all contact with the native scene. As opposed to Max Weber, who has been said by even his heartiest admirers to epitomize the whole European art spectacle, we may summon up abstractionists like John Marin, Georgia O'Keeffe and Arthur Dove, or more literal interpreters like James Chapin, Edward Hopper and John Steuart Curry, whose work is deeply and unmistakably American.

(Edward Alden Jewell, "American Art Comes of Age: The Opening of a New Epoch," New York Times Magazine, *22 November 1931)*

25 November–21 December *Tornado* included in *Winter Exhibition,* National Academy of Design (cat. no. 65).

In each [Academy] exhibition one comes upon work that, while indubitably "there," does not seem to belong in these hallowed chambers.... Sometimes a man like John Steuart Curry slips into the fold, and (as when finding the "Tornado") we gaze in mute amazement, wondering how it happened.

(Edward Alden Jewell, New York Times, *29 November 1931)*

Maynard Walker writes to William Allen White to encourage him in his efforts to find patrons in Kansas:

Mr. Curry is deeply appreciative as we are of your fine help in furthering his work. It is great for him to have such a friend at court and certainly if any section of the country should respond to his fine art, it is Kansas....

Curry's unique contribution and importance in American art is rapidly being noised abroad here. The Whitney Museum opened the other day and his painting was honored by being reproduced twice in the *New York Times* Rotogravure Section. Another painting was reproduced in the Rotogravure Section of the *Herald Tribune* and also in the *New York American.* You understand these paintings were singled out from some 500 paintings shown at the Whitney Museum. Curry was mentioned among the first Americans in critical articles by Edward Alden Jewell, appearing in last Sunday's *Times* and in a story in the *Times* Magazine Section, which I am sending you herewith. His large painting "The Tornado," which you saw in the exhibition, was accepted by the National Academy of Design and seriously considered for the Second Altman Prize.

I mention all this to assure you that his fame is on the ascendancy and if Kansas is to do anything about it, she had better get busy.

(Maynard Walker to William Allen White, 25 November 1931. Curry Papers/AAA, microfilm roll 166, no frame no.)

6 December Largely due to Walker's and White's efforts, an exhibition of fourteen Curry paintings, arranged by Ferargil Galleries, opens at the Kansas City Art Institute. It subsequently travels to the Spooner-Thayer Gallery, the University of Kansas; the Kansas State Agricultural College, Manhattan; the City Club, Emporia; and the Wichita Art Association.

Curry, one of the most stirring painters exhibiting in eastern galleries, is not only a thorough-going Kansan, who features the "Great Russian" sunflower in all his exhibitions, but there are qualities in his pictures, as there are in the portrait he has painted of himself, that personify Kansas.

Painters and others who like pictures will know on sight that he is honest—that he is making a picture a certain way because that is the way the picture takes form in his mind, and not because it will sell better painted that way than some other. This honesty is enough to commend him because it is as rare as the artist's knowledge of the truth.

(Minna K. Powell, "Spirit of Kansas in Oil," Kansas City Star, *6 December 1931)*

16 December Mrs. Henry J. Allen, wife of a former Kansas governor, writes to William Allen White expressing her resentment over the negative impressions of the state that many of Curry's canvases appear to convey:

Last week I saw the exhibit in Kansas City and feel just as I did when I saw the pictures in Topeka last year. . . . I feel Mr. Curry has a great force in delineating the subjects he has chosen, but to say he portrays the "spirit" of Kansas is entirely wrong, I think. To be sure, we have cyclones, gospel trains, the medicine man. And the man hunt, and we have had an automobile tip over a bank and kill a man, as he portrayed in his canvas "The Death of Ray Godard." But why paint outstanding friekish [*sic*] subjects and call them the "spirit" of Kansas?

The strongest canvas in his show, I think, is his own self portrait, and that countenance alone reveals the man; one whose boyhood has only seen the most sordid conditions of life, and one who has not yet been able to see any of the glories of his home state, or the beauties of the simple life of the farmer, or broad, far-reaching landscapes, to say nothing of such scenes as the Flint Hills. Pictures, to be great art, do not mean to my mind pretty ones, but there must be some uplift in them.

In his Topeka exhibit, he had a number of studies of Kansas hogs—I thought strong, realistic and typical; also a small canvas of rolling pasture and on the side hill in the distance two bulls fighting. It was dusk and all the glamour of the plains was depicted. This to my mind was typical. The only canvas in the Kansas City exhibit that had a bit of that feeling was the one of the lone bull well to the front of the pasture, sniffing the ground and ready to paw. In this, I find suppressed emotion and in that suppressed action I feel great strength. I also like his treatment of the sunflower and I especially like the tobacco plant.

I wonder if this sort of work that Mr. Curry is doing is not just a phase through which he will pass, and will soon come to see something beautiful in life and particularly life in Kansas.

I was glad when I noted that Mrs. Whitney had bought four of his canvases. For a year and a half I have had letters from interested friends, beseeching that somebody buy his pictures in order that he might continue his work. I wonder if Mrs. Whitney did not recognize in him a strong young artist, but principally bought because she thought in building up her purely American museum of art that she was acquiring something particularly typical of Kansas soil and the middle west.

All this because Mr. Curry is said to paint the very spirit of Kansas and not because I wish to criticise him as an artist, but just his theme. I do not wish to broadcast my feeling about this matter, and I probably am all wrong, but being Kansas born I cannot agree with the enthusiasm of the art critics of the *New York Times* and the *Kansas City Star.*

(Mrs. Henry J. Allen to William Allen White, 16 December 1931. Curry Papers/AAA, microfilm roll 2743, frame 46.)

1932

14 February George Washington Centennial Exposition, Washington, D.C., opens, and Curry's mural there, *Labor's Cooperation in the Revolution,* is unveiled. (The work has since been destroyed.)

27 March–17 April Oil *Spring Shower* (color plate 23) included in *107th Annual Exhibition,* National Academy of Design (cat. no. 303).

June Metropolitan Museum of Art, New York, purchases *Spring Shower.*

25 July Clara Curry dies at her family's Jamesburg, New Jersey, home. Curry writes Maynard Walker to let him know:

Clara died last Monday night and was buried beside her mother Wednesday. I was twenty minutes too late to see her alive. I feel very terribly and have been searching my mind and memory for the answer of our life together and her death. I saw her before I went on the Circus trip and told her just as soon as I got on my feet I would come back and do everything I could for her and I did come back the morning I heard the Metropolitan had taken the picture *[Spring Shower]*. She was sick then unto death but no one knew it but her. The doctor thought she was getting better but she simply worried and fretted herself from one state to another.

She did everything for me and everything to me too it seems. I tried to put her here with a nurse and I was to carry on my work in New York and come out weekends but she got worse and her father took her home.

It is dreadful to feel that she has been unkind but I was desperate to free my mind to carry on the work but in her weakened state she was unreasonable and I would have held her hand more often if I had known of this end.

I wish you could come out some weekend and see what I have started. I have the possibilities of the greatest work I have ever done and these next two months will tell the story. I would like to see you soon, as I feel very badly.

(Curry to Maynard Walker, 1 August 1932. Walker Papers/AAA, microfilm roll 2023, frames 24–25.)

15 September Begins teaching in the night school at the Cooper Union, New York; continues through June 1935, when his position is eliminated.

1 October Begins teaching at Art Students League, New York; continues through 1 December 1936.

22 November–5 January 1933 Oil *The Flying Codonas* (color plate 25) included in *First Biennial Exhibition of Contemporary American Painting,* Whitney Museum of American Art (cat. no. 62). Following exhibition guidelines, Curry has submitted the painting as an example of his best recent work.

"A brush capable of speaking American without an accent": A Celebrated Regionalist

1933

15 January Whitney Museum of American Art announces acquisition of *The Flying Codonas.*

29 January–19 March Oil *Hogs Killing a Snake* (color plate 21) included in *128th Annual Exhibition of Paintings and Sculpture,* Pennsylvania Academy of the Fine Arts (cat. no. 308).

3–16 April Solo show, *An Exhibition of Paintings of the Circus by John Steuart Curry,* Ferargil Galleries (printed checklist).

The coming of the circus next week to Madison Square Garden will find a plumpish, youngish but baldish American artist more excited than any small boy in New York. The circus coming to town will mean a reunion with old friends to John Steuart Curry, who was "on the show" with them last year, trouping with them through New England and, incidentally, painting them.

He will greet Alfredo Cadona [*sic*], greatest of aerialists; Clyde Beatty, who makes the lion cry the minute he enters the cage; the Wallendas, who do shoulder pyramids on a tight wire with no net underneath; and Zacchini, the human projectile, who was an artist himself before he found the good life in living dangerously with the circus. Then Mr. Curry will invite his friends and erstwhile subjects to view themselves as he has seen them at an exhibition of his circus pictures at the Ferargil Galleries. . . . It is the first exhibition of its kind in this country. . . .

As Mr. Curry arranged his exhibits yesterday at the galleries he admitted that he felt a nostalgic urge when he heard this week the vernal pipings of Dexter Fellows, advance agent for the circus. He recalled the hard driving weeks under canvas and in circus trains; the dozens of performances he saw while trying to catch just the angle at which Cadona came out of his triple somersault to grab the hands of his brother as the latter flashed by on a trapeze; the humors of the mess tent with Sky High, the human Alp, coddling a weak stomach while envying the robust appetites of the little folk. "Not that anything very exciting happened," he said. "No elephants broke loose from picket pins or anything like that. I didn't save anybody's life, and mine was never in danger, except from pneumonia. That is the threat to every one who travels with a circus. The hard work, the draughty dressing rooms, the inadequate sleep causes every one to be subject to colds. A tremendous number die of pneumonia."

("Circus Troupe to View Art of Sawdust Ring," New York Herald Tribune, *29 March 1933)*

The flowers that bloom in the spring are not, as we all know, the real harbingers of an urban springtide. It is, rather, the sawdust and tanbark and the feral scents of the circus which mark the arrival of the vernal equinox for the city dweller. There is, therefore, an appropriate juxtaposition of events in the simultaneous arrival of spring, the circus, and John Steuart Curry's paintings of the circus, at the Ferargil Galleries. The glitter and flow of the circus have always fascinated painters, particularly in contemporary life, when real pageantry has practically disappeared from the world. Mr. Curry, who traveled with the circus several months to study it at first hand, has fallen under the spell of this glamour but he has also penetrated the character of its dazzling performers and limns them with sympathy and understanding; he is a realist who seems able to penetrate reality and discover in it the final illusion. The surface, brilliance of color, and flashing movement of all the picturesque personnel of the circus are faithfully recorded, but the artist has not been beguiled by the wealth of this material, but has subordinated it to his flair for design. While he has drawn on the incredibly pictorial subject matter afforded by the circus he has strengthened his technical achievement. His drawing evokes mass and rhythmic movement of realistic forms, his palette is richer, and his control of his means of expression, as well as of his material, far greater than in previous work, with no loss of the spontaneous freshness of personal reaction which has always delighted the admirers of his work (and who would wish to be omitted from this list?). "June Evening," "Clowns Making Up," and the "Riding Clown" reveal a rich humanity, a fine perception of character under unfamiliar guises, which affirms a fact already suspected that the circus is a microcosm of ordinary life, in which the disposition of emotional values may be shifted from that of ordinary experience as the bits of colored glass make a different pattern with each turn of the kaleidoscope, but the essential qualities of life and living remain the same. It is obvious that it is not so much the circus that has triumphed as the artist who has depicted it in his own vigorous yet sensitized idiom.

(Margaret Breuning, "John Steuart Curry," New York Post, *9 April 1933)*

1 June–1 November *Baptism in Kansas* shown in *A Century of Progress Exhibition of Painting and Sculpture,* Art Institute of Chicago (cat. no. 536).

Early July Visits Grant Wood at Stone City Colony and Art School, Stone City, Iowa, established by Wood. Teaches there for a week, then visits his family in Kansas.

8 August Spends a few days in Kansas City in conjunction with an exhibition of his works arranged by Ferargil Galleries at Lucy Drage's shop on Country Club Plaza.

22 August Works included in the exhibition *American Painting since Whistler,* organized by Maynard Walker for the Kansas City Art Institute. The exhibition gives Walker an opportunity to promote midwestern artists, including Thomas Hart Benton and Grant Wood.

Mr. Walker, who, previous to reversing Horace Greeley's advice and going east, conducted the art department of the *Kansas City Journal-Post,* was asked to act as critic of the column for one issue apropos of the current exhibition. Writing from the background of his years on 57th Street, he gave the Mid-West this to digest:

"One of the most significant things in the art world today is the increasing importance of real American art. I mean an art which really springs from American soil and seeks to interpret American life. Not only are American artists foregoing Europe to stay at home and produce works that demand worldwide attention, but American collectors and art patrons are staying home to buy them.

"And very noticeably much of the most vital modern art in America is coming out of our long backward Middle West. Largely through the creative output of a few sincere and vital painters, the East is learning that there is an America west of the Alleghenies and that it is worth being put on canvas.

"In Chicago, perhaps the most stirring thing I found in the whole World's Fair were the murals which Thomas Benton, Missouri born, has made for the Indiana State building. I understand that Indianans are enraged because a Missourian instead of a native son was selected to paint the murals, but they will all be pointing with mighty pride before long. In my opinion they are not only Benton's greatest achievement but are the finest murals in America. Why should the Mexican Rivera make a laughing stock of us when we have men like Benton?

"Another high spot in the Chicago show is the painting 'Baptism in Kansas,' by John Steuart Curry, a native of Kansas. This painting is probably more famous in Europe than it is in America and Curry, still in his early thirties, is generally spoken of in the East as one of the leaders in American art. . . . Curry's themes have been mainly of the Middle Western scene, and in such subjects as 'Kansas Tornado,' 'Hogs Killing a Rattlesnake' and 'Kansas Pastures' he has created immortal epics from homely scenes hitherto wholly neglected.

"Grant Wood is another Middle Westerner who has made this world sit up and take notice by his thoroughly American paintings. He became famous overnight through his painting 'American Gothic.'

"The sad part of it is that the West has been so slow in recognizing and fostering these famous sons of hers. Too often, when they have done a masterpiece as Benton has done for Indiana, all they get is anger and boos. If we could have more institutions like the Whitney Museum of American Art, which has done so much good in supporting the real American artists like Curry and Benton and Wood and others like them, it would not be long before America would have an indigenous art expression."

("Mid-West Is Producing an Indigenous Art," Art Digest *7, no. 20 [1 September 1933]: 10)*

19 October–10 December *Tornado* included in *Thirty-first Annual International Exhibition of Paintings,* Carnegie Institute, Pittsburgh; awarded second prize ($1,000).

In John Steuart Curry's "Tornado" we have no such subtleties, a 'rattling good story' told with emphasis and detail. The twister in the skies is descending with dramatic speed upon a country dooryard, sending the family scurrying to the open cellar. The mother carries a baby; the father pulls one of the younger children along by the arm, older boys carry, one a litter of puppies, the other a squalling cat, a rooster stands on the doorstep debating, horses whirl in the distance at the mercy of the wind. Every *I* is dotted. And the huddle spells an exciting experience that is fairly close to coming true on the canvas. "Good theatre!" Mr. Shakespeare might say.

(Elisabeth L. Cary, "Carnegie International 'Subject' Pictures," New York Times, *29 October 1933)*

1934

Early months Begins *Comedy* and *Tragedy* frescoes (color plates 29 and 30) for the auditorium of Bedford Junior High School (now Kings Highway School), Westport, Connecticut.

28 April Lectures at the Art Students League, New York, on the New Deal's Public Works of Art Project.

The Administration's recognition of artists as a part of the Public Works project "will do more than any educational program or private subsidy to bring about an art consciousness in this country," John Steuart Curry, young Kansan artist known as a painter of the circus and of Kansan life, said in a lecture yesterday.... "[T]here is nothing the matter with the American artist except a lack of opportunity to produce for a definite end.

"In Mexico," he said, "the social revolution cut loose a stored-up energy in painting and gave the latent ability present a chance to grow.

"In Russia the violent patriotism is making use of the artist. The same conditions holding here would raise up a host of brilliant and competent artists. The more opportunity to work, the more the artist will grow in grace and power. The present government has recognized artists as a part of the Public Works project [fig. 6]. This is revolution for this country.... "

Mr. Curry cited Grant Wood of Cedar Rapids, Iowa, as an example of an artist who had won success in painting scenes of the daily life that surrounded him....

"These people," he said, "are painting their own life. The people of the state are interested in this production. They buy the art of Iowa painters.

"There may be no great art produced, but what is produced will be real. The subject will be indigenous to the life of the people, and that is the beginning of a healthy art."

("Circus Limner Terms P.W.A. Best Art Spur," New York Herald Tribune, *29 April 1934)*

29 May Sheldon Memorial Art Gallery, University of Nebraska, Lincoln, purchases *Road-workers' Camp.*

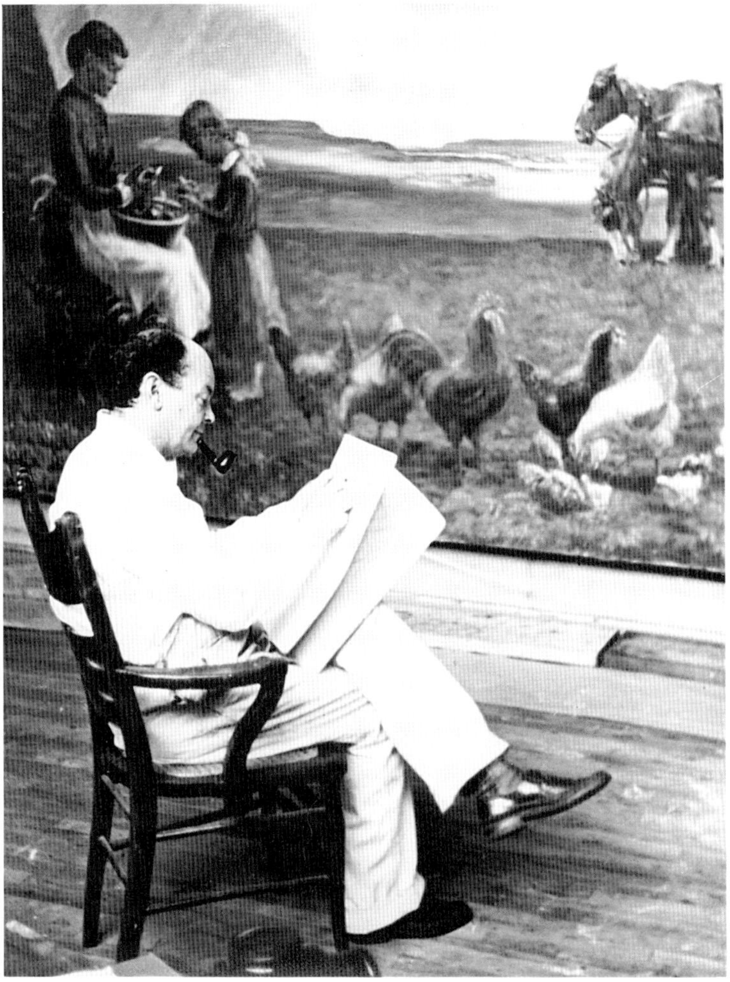

FIGURE 6

Curry at work on *The Homestead,* a mural design for the U.S. Department of the Interior building, Washington, D.C., 1938. Photograph courtesy Mrs. John Steuart Curry.

The career of the young American artist John Steuart Curry would seem to indicate that the old adage about the prophet in his own country still holds. Critics acknowledge that Curry is today one of Kansas's most distinguished artist sons, yet none of his paintings has found a home in the public collections of that state. The purchase of his "Roadmenders' Camp" by the University of Nebraska brings to mind the sparse recognition he has received in his native Midwest. The painting, acquired as part of the F. M. Hall Collection, through the Ferargil Galleries, is termed the first noteworthy canvas by Curry to be placed in any public collection in a section which he has made famous to the contemporary art world. Nebraska has stolen a march on her neighbor to the south.

("Curry Recognized," Art Digest *8, no. 20 [1 September 1934]: 7)*

1 June–1 November Four oils—*Road-workers' Camp, Tornado, Gospel Train* (color plate 15), and *The Flying Codonas*—included in *A Century of Progress Exhibition of Paintings and Sculpture,* Art Institute of Chicago (cat. nos. 565–68).

2 June Marries Kathleen Gould Shepherd, a friend from Westport.

Summer Travels through the Midwest on commission from *Fortune* magazine, sketching material for illustrations to accompany an article, "The Great American Roadside," examining the American auto-tourism craze and industry (published September 1934).

Fall Completes frescoes for Bedford Junior High School, Westport.

27 November–10 January 1935 Oil *The Fugitive* (color plate 31) included in *Second Biennial Exhibition of Contemporary American Painting,* Whitney Museum of American Art (cat. no. 188).

24 December *Time* magazine cover story on the "U.S. Art Scene" highlights the "earthy Midwesterners," whose art, presumably liberated from the influence of European modernism, signals the rise of a native school of representational, regionally based art that pursues rural themes—an art "destined to turn the tide of artistic taste in the U.S." Written by New York critic Thomas Craven (himself a Kansan), the article identifies Thomas Hart Benton, Charles Burchfield, Reginald Marsh, Grant Wood, and Curry as the leading exemplars of the regionalist school.

1935

21 January–4 February Solo exhibition, *Recent Work by John Steuart Curry,* Ferargil Galleries (printed checklist).

John Steuart Curry has returned to his native heath; gone back, for theme material, to the Kansas prairies, whence he emerged some six or seven years ago to convince a great many of us that here was a brush capable of speaking American without an accent. . . . Curry, in these more recent paintings, comes before us once more without disguise: a Kansan with tales to tell that can be told by nobody else. . . . There is a freer play of brush now, a surer and certainly more daring use of color. Some of these skies may leave us amazed and unconvinced; but it is pretty safe to assume that a son of the Middle Western prairies knows what he is talking about—especially one with so genuine a gift for expression.

(Edward Alden Jewell, "Curry Presents Kansas Pictures," New York Times, *23 January 1935)*

Henry Mencken—the late Henry Mencken, they call him in Kansas—was pretty rough on Kansas as never turning out any artists or sprouting any ideas, and all that. . . . [B]ut here today is a Kansas artist crashing New York with a lot of Kansas pictures and making them like it. He is John Steuart Curry, former Kansas farm boy. . . .

He painted Kansas—always Kansas—and he proved that an American prairie or buffalo wallow may yield more inspiration than the aperitifs or the velvet jackets that feature the "Boul Mich" or the Rue Edgar Quinet. He did some marvelous circus pictures, but it was his Kansas landscapes that brought him his now unquestioned success.

A bit of anti-climax appears in the fact that a garage keeper at Medicine Lodge is the only Kansan who ever bought one of his pictures—a score for Mr. Mencken, perhaps. But Mr. Curry says they don't need to because they have Kansas.

(Lemuel F. Parton, "Who's News Today: A Kansas Artist Who Might Confound Mencken," New York Sun, *24 January 1935)*

I saw your exhibition yesterday, and you have covered yourself with glory. Really, I was not prepared for such magnificent work. I knew that you had it in you, but I had no idea that you were moving forward so rapidly. The exhibition so far surpasses your Circus pictures that there is no comparison, surpasses it in every way, in the richness of its content, in conception, poetry, drawing, and composition. . . .

My main purpose in writing this is to congratulate you, and to tell you that you should count yourself one of the most fortunate of men in these hard times. You are young; you are one of the few living artists who have done anything worth preserving; and you are not repeating your first successes but advancing daily in artistic power.

(Thomas Craven to Curry, 27 January 1935. Curry Papers/AAA, microfilm roll 2746, no frame no.)

There is so much more to painting than the picture it makes! In addition to its pictorial charm, there are the beauties of drawing, its coloring, its design, and all those manifold aspects of order, rhythm, emotion, intuition and expression which must be manifested with grace and force. Any of these aspects nobly rendered is enough to win something of acclaim for the artist producing it. Yet a great painting is more than the sum of these elements. A great painting also manifests the artist's spirit and, in so doing, reveals the spirit of his race and generation. . . .

No doubt America, in these years of change, evidences a spirit particular to our times, a spirit the historian of the future will be able to define. Some of us—those of us who see several hundred contemporary American pictures every week—think we perceive already the character of this spirit. We find it appearing in certain recent paintings by Eugene Speicher, Alexander Brook, Edward Hopper, Charles Burchfield, Reginald Marsh, Thomas Benton, Henry Schnackenberg, Charles Sheeler, Grant Wood, and John Steuart Curry, to mention but a few. Finding it emergent, we wait impatiently to have it brought full-fledged before our eyes.

It was with considerable hope, accordingly, that I hurried to see the latest paintings by one of this "group." John Steuart Curry is the man; his exhibition has just opened at the Ferargil Galleries; and I am happy to record that towards his goal of rediscovering America for us, he strides distinctly forward.

Practically all the works on view attest his admirable aim.... One, however, combines in a single canvas the several elements of a great painting. Entitled *The Line Storm,* it depicts with skill in the craft and with uncommon vigor in the thought, a tremendous storm of black cloud and yellow lightning in the moment before its awful force strikes the grace of a mid-Western countryside.

Yet there is more to the painting than the picture it makes. In it the spirit of the artist and perhaps his generation stands disclosed, a powerful spirit born of America, inspired by America and dedicated to American ideas and ideals. To my mind, the canvas is an historical work of art, historical in that it mirrors our contemporary will to believe in ourselves, to believe in our own resources and in our native beauty. Should Curry go on painting as memorably as this he might create, single-handed, a renaissance in American art.... Speed the coming day!

(Malcolm Vaughn, New York American, *26 January 1935)*

Mr. Curry returned last summer to his native Kansas for inspiration. Like Antaeus, this contact with mother earth has given him strength; his draftsmanship is surer and his power of coherent, incisive design much greater. This artist like many American painters is a romantic and a realist. In such imaginative conceptions as "The Fugitive" he is veraciously explicit in his detail of setting; or, in "Line Storm," a Brobdingnagian drama of thunderclouds racing over the prairies with forks of lightning piercing their sinister gloom, he gives the theatrical scene a soberly realistic touch in the hay wagon and the figures hurriedly finishing its loading.

Moreover, in these paintings of Kansas there is a spontaneity, an unforced note which was sometimes lacking in his circus subjects, where occasionally one felt the artist working over his notes, ably, to be sure, but without the "first, fine careless rapture" that the real experience afforded him. Here is first hand knowledge; the strange colors of sunsets, the closeness of the sky stretching over the flat infinity of land, the unusual effects of light, that all are unfamiliar to the effete Easterners, seem credible in Mr. Curry's rendering.

(Margaret Breuning, New York Post, *26 January 1935)*

27 January–3 March Oil *The Return of Private Davis from the Argonne* (color plate 12) included in *130th Annual Exhibition of Paintings and Sculpture,* Pennsylvania Academy of the Fine Arts (cat. no. 177).

February Responding to Thomas Craven's December 1934 *Time* magazine article celebrating painters of the U.S. scene, painter Stuart Davis, editor of *Art Front,* the Marxist-leaning publication of the American Artists' Union, delivers a blistering attack on each of Craven's stars. Davis sees their subjects as representing a conservative idealism that borders on fascism.

These artists are reported to have in common, first—a passion for local Americana, and second—a contempt for the foreign artist and his influence. They have the "my country right or wrong" attitude and are suspicious of strangers....

They offer us, says *Time,* "direct representation in place of introspective abstractions." Is the well-fed farm-hand under the New Deal, as painted by Grant Wood, a direct representation or is it an introspective abstraction?...

The U.S. scene in art and direct representation, as opposed to introspective abstraction—this is the program of these artists, a program so general and undefined as to be valueless. In the absence of theory we must judge them solely by their works.

By John Steuart Curry we have a series of rural subjects, cheaply dramatic and executed without the slightest regard for the valuable, practical and technical contributions to painting which have been carried on in the last fifty years. How can a man who paints as though no laboratory work had ever been done in painting, who willfully or through ignorance ignores the discoveries of Monet, Seurat, Cezanne and Picasso and proceeds as though painting were a jolly lark for amateurs, to be exhibited in county fairs, how can a man with this mental attitude be considered an asset to the development of American painting? The people of Kansas, who are glorified in Curry's pictures do not buy his paintings, *Time* reports.... Apparently the people of Kansas have some discrimination as to what kind of "direct representation" they want. Apparently they resent the insult to their intelligence implied in these works, which always present the obvious and stop.

(Stuart Davis, "The New York American Scene in Art," Art Front *1, no. 3 [February 1935]: 6)*

5 February Kansas State Agricultural College, Manhattan, announces it will pursue acquisition of the oil *Sun Dogs,* by public subscription, making it the first public institution in Kansas to purchase a Curry work.

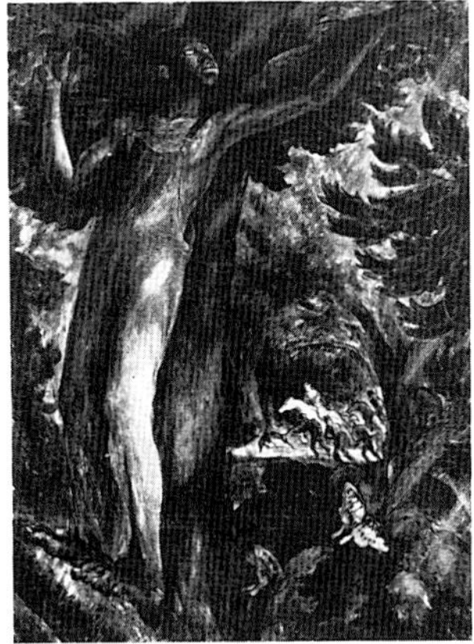

FIGURE 7

Cover of the exhibition catalogue *An Art Commentary on Lynching,* featuring Curry's lithograph *The Fugitive* (1934–36). Photograph courtesy Archives of the University of Iowa Library, Ames.

15 February–2 March *The Fugitive,* its related lithograph, and the oil *Manhunt* are exhibited in *An Art Commentary on Lynching,* a controversial exhibition at the Arthur U. Newton Galleries, New York. Organized by the National Association for the Advancement of Colored People, the show is intended to bring to public attention the need for federal antilynching legislation. Curry's lithograph, *The Fugitive,* is reproduced on the cover of the catalogue, which includes brief commentaries by Sherwood Anderson and Erskine Caldwell (fig. 7). The exhibition attracts the patronage of artists, writers, and intellectual and cultural leaders, including Alfred Barr, Jr., Stephen Vincent Benét, Pearl S. Buck, Lloyd Goodrich, Sidney Howard, Dorothy Parker, Arthur Schomburg, Carl Van Doren, and Thomas J. Watson.

13 March–9 April Oil *Oak Tree: Summer* included in *110th Annual Exhibition,* National Academy of Design (cat. no. 156).

1 April U.S. Department of the Treasury's Section of Painting and Sculpture announces commissions for murals in the new U.S. Department of Justice building, Washington, D.C. Curry is one of eleven painters and two sculptors selected by a national advisory committee. Among the suggested topics for murals encompassing the broad theme of "What Law Has Done for Man" is "Freeing the Slaves," which Curry addresses in his initial design. That design is rejected, and Curry submits *Law versus Mob Rule* and *Westward Migration,* depicting the haphazard meting-out of justice in still unformed communities, as designs for lunettes on the building's fifth floor.

5 June Hackley Art Museum, Muskegon, Michigan, announces purchase of *Tornado.*

Provincial museums can never hope to compete in the world's art marts for the sort of paintings that Mellons & Morgans like. But they can play another and more exciting game by buying modern pictures which some day might rise to the rank and worth of Old Masters. Such a picture is John Steuart Curry's famed *Tornado.*

("Muskegon's Tornado," Time *25, no. 24 [17 June 1935]: 30)*

29 September Maynard Walker tells Curry in confidence that he will soon leave Ferargil to start his own gallery and wants to take Benton, Wood, and Curry with him. Asks Curry to enter into contractual agreement with him, which the artist eventually agrees to do.

1 October Ferargil Galleries announces traveling exhibition of works by Benton and Curry.

12–28 November Oils *The Mississippi* (color plate 34) and *Hogs Killing a Rattlesnake* shown in *Opening Exhibition: Paintings by Six Americans,* Walker Galleries, New York (cat. nos. 8 and 9). The other artists represented are Benton, Wood, Thomas Eakins, Winslow Homer, and Albert Pinkham Ryder.

Artist-in-Residence: Return to the Midwest

1936

14 January–13 February Watercolor *The Butte, Barber County* included in *Second Biennial Exhibition—Part I: Sculpture, Drawings and Prints,* Whitney Museum of American Art (cat. no. 74).

16–30 March Oil *Gospel Train* exhibited at the Town Hall Club, New York (printed brochure).

30 April Maynard Walker begins a campaign to get Curry a teaching position in the Midwest. Dr. Mark Nesbit of Madison suggests to him that there might be an opportunity at the University of Wisconsin, and Walker inquires:

I have been interested for some time, along with Grant Wood, Thomas Craven and Thomas Benton, in locating some institution in the West which might be interested in giving John Steuart Curry a place on its staff whereby he might carry on either a mural project in connection with teaching, as Grant Wood does at Iowa City, or simply conduct painting classes.

In conversation yesterday with Dr. Nesbit of Madison, it occurred to me that there might be a possibility of effecting this at the Wisconsin Union. Curry is the type of progressive artist who would be very valuable to your people and I think the environment there would be a happy one for him. The whole point is that Curry's friends feel that he should be located in the West somewhere instead of here in this too effete East. He feels that he would like to return West but the difficulty is of making a living. Curry is a very fine person and a very great artist. All who know him believe in him thoroughly and I think if any project out there could be placed in his hands, it could not be effected without a great deal of ground work and thoughtful planning.

(Maynard Walker to Porter Butts, Director, Wisconsin Union, University of Wisconsin, 30 April 1936. Walker Papers/AAA, microfilm roll 2023, frame 35.)

19 September University of Wisconsin president Glenn Frank announces that Curry is to become artist-in-residence there, a position then unique in American universities.

For at least five years Mr. Curry will live in a simple one-room studio which the university is erecting on the campus for him and there have contact with all phases of university life, but most especially with the farm youth attending the College of Agriculture.

"Mr. Curry, along with Grant Wood and Thomas Hart Benton, is distinctive in the degree to which his art draws its strength from the very soil of America," said President Frank today. "In beginning this venture we are undertaking to give added impetus to regional art as a force for rural as well as urban culture in this Middle West area." . . .

Dr. Frank . . . pointed out that several universities have had "poets in residence," notably the University of Michigan, but never an "artist-in-residence." . . .

Mr. Curry will teach no formal classes. He will, instead, mingle with the students, discuss art and its relation to society with them at round table meetings, and will drop in at regular classes for special comments.

Every opportunity will be granted him, Dr. Frank said, to become acquainted with the rich farmlands of Wisconsin so that he "may come to think in terms of the roots and soil of Wisconsin just as he has of his native Kansas."

Mr. Curry will receive $4000 a year, the funds to come from the trust estate of the late Thomas Brittingham, whose bequests at one time financed Alexander Mieklejohn in his establishment of the University of Wisconsin's Experimental College. A $4,000 grant from the state Emergency board will finance construction of the studio.

("Curry Is Named 'Artist in Residence'; Wisconsin Acts to Aid Rural Culture," New York Times, *20 September 1936)*

Curry, who with Grant Wood and Thomas Benton, has stuck to his native heath—the Midwest—as the subject for his paintings, has more than proved that even Kansas can produce art. All three of them agree that regional painting needs stimulation to bring American painting to the place it rightfully should hold.

Wood, a crusader in their campaign for regionalism, decided that the Midwest needed a stronghold, that Curry was the man to command it, and that Madison, Wisconsin, seat of the University, was the ideal location. Wood approached Glenn Frank, President of the University, and Dean Christian L. Christensen of the Agricultural School, with his idea.

Farmer Interest—Both were enthusiastic. Christensen for many years had longed for some means of arousing the interest of farmers in art. As a student in his youth at the Agricultural School of the University of Denmark, he had seen the wide-spread and consuming pleasure that Danish tillers of the soil derived from paintings. That experience had taught him that they must be approached by subjects they understood. In Wood's proposal, he saw the germ of such an appeal for this country's crop growers.

Last summer, Curry left his Connecticut home in Westport, an art colony on Long Island Sound, to visit Madison. He was not only completely charmed by the geographical location of the University, whose simple, handsome buildings fringe the uneven shore of Lake Mendota, but equally well he liked President Frank, Professor Christensen, and the proposition they offered him. He accepted.

Curry's Plans—As America's first "artist in residence," Curry will pursue the following elastic plans, worked out by him and subject to change entirely at his own discretion.

1. He will do murals and paintings of current agricultural topics, particularly soil erosion, which is a pet subject of Dean Christensen's. In this Mr. Curry has chosen pure art as his goal: He is not out to paint propaganda either for or against the Administration. Instead, he will attempt to cull the drama, destruction and spirit from the subject, and represent it pictorially in his own style.

2. He will attend art-appreciation classes in the Liberal Arts courses and informally discuss the painters whose works have a particular interest and significance for him. . . .

3. He will give instruction or encouragement—but not in scheduled classes—to those who want to paint. . . .

4. He will attempt to establish and develop a feeling for art among the agricultural students by discussing with them agricultural as well as art problems. He wants to eliminate the inhibitions with which non-urban residents look upon painting.

5. Curry will furnish a living museum for the University at large; for while he is there, his works will be shown extensively. As he finishes a mural or canvas, he will exhibit it first in Madison.

6. Aside from these specific duties, he will individually discuss and help any student interested in art from any other approach.

Potent Art—Despite this intensive program, Curry has no fears that he will be robbed of time to do his own creative work. Nor does the idea of spending five years in Wisconsin appall him, as it might other successful artists. The thirty-nine-year-old painter wants to take the same things from Wisconsin that he took from Kansas scenes, and show that there are potent subjects in places most artists would scoff at. For people who say, "Fine, but is it art?" Curry bluntly says, "To hell with them." . . .

From the work on his five-year plan, plus the paintings of Benton and Wood, Curry hopes a strong regionalism will grow. That, he believes, would be the best thing for American art.

("Resident Artist: John Steuart Curry Takes Unique Post to Encourage Rural Painting," Literary Digest *122, no. 16 [17 October 1936]: 22–24)*

10 November–10 December Oil *The Rainbow* included in *Third Biennial Exhibition of Contemporary American Painting,* Whitney Museum of American Art (cat. no. 68).

4 December Curry arrives in Madison to take up post as artist-in-residence in the University of Wisconsin College of Agriculture.

"I don't think Kansas offered me the opportunity which is here at the University of Wisconsin. I have tried for recognition from Kansas, but have had little success. This indicates, some say, the wisdom of the Kansans, while others, undoubtedly more short-sighted, think I should have had some expression of sorts from my native state.

"Even the people who think I'm a bum artist believe it is a great step Dean Christensen is taking in having the university recognize art in this way."

("Curry, U. W. 'Artist In Residence,' Here; Believes Plan Great Step Forward," [Madison, Wis.] Capital Times, *4 December 1936)*

Above all else, Curry is coming to Wisconsin to paint. "Any influence I may exert will be because of my work itself, not because of anything I may say, or write," he says.

("Curry Takes New Post on U. W. Campus," Milwaukee Sentinel, *5 December 1936)*

John Steuart Curry has left his native state, its religion and its work, from which came the inspiration for "Baptism in Kansas," "Line Storm," "Tornado in Kansas," and "The Road Menders," the pictures which swept him to his place as a top ranking United States artist six or seven years ago.

Here on the campus he will become an artistic hub for the state and play an even more important part in the trend which he and Thomas Hart Benton and Grant Wood started when they stripped American art of affected European trappings and began the regional art movement which has shifted the creative center of the nation. . . .

Now Curry will use the two-story studio on the agricultural campus, with huge windows facing the north and a 16-foot wall on which he can hang massive canvases for murals. . . .

Until he came to the university Curry was in Washington doing murals for the department of justice and the unfinished work has been shipped here. His first job, he said, is to complete that work. He will exhibit the murals first in Madison, a procedure which he will follow with most of his work.

"I'd be very pleased to do murals here," he said, "and it might be that I could use student help on them. That is the best kind of teaching."

("Prairie Artist Finds New Soil," Milwaukee Journal, *6 December 1936)*

1937

January Solo exhibition, *A Selected Group of Work by John Steuart Curry,* organized by Walker Galleries and sponsored by the College Art Association, begins a national tour, opening at the Delgado Museum, New Orleans (catalogue).

19 January In his first public lecture since arriving at the University of Wisconsin, addresses the Art Association of Madison:

Grant Wood, under the banner of regional art, has tried to make people realize that painting is something that can be enjoyed here and now by you and you. That you might have artists alive and producing in your own neighborhood, that you might even be proud of their works, that you might even be artists, that art need not be something that is sent from Chicago, New York, or Paris for your edification. . . .

The social, political, and economic disturbances of the times have brought forth those artists who, taking their themes from these issues, have produced telling and effective works for the cause of social and political justice. I need not enumerate the other and various phases of our painting Renaissance. Just give us time. Give us ten years, and if we can escape the paralyzing hand of war we will accomplish something even in that short time. . . .

For the past few years I have felt the need to enliven my imagination by new contacts with American life.... While in my youth I fled from the arms of agriculture to the more seductive charms of art, now I return....

However, the people of Wisconsin can be assured of this—I do not come to wreak good on them. To the interested citizens, I will appreciate your interest in my work, and to the artists, I will give my most sincere advice if it is wanted and very gladly....

I approached the life of the circus looking for dramatic action, color, and lively personalities. I found them. I came to Madison looking for dramatic action, color, and lively personalities. I have found them. Thomas Benton after returning to Missouri said to me that he believed that in the next ten years the economic and political power of the nation would shift to the middle west. I believe this will happen, and I expect to see Wisconsin in the center of one of the most colorful periods of American history.

(Curry "Address before the Art Association of Madison, Tuesday, 19 January 1937." Curry Papers/AAA, microfilm roll 165, no frame nos., typescript pp. 5–7.)

24 January–28 February Oil *Osage Oranges* included in *132nd Annual Exhibition of Paintings and Sculpture,* Pennsylvania Academy of the Fine Arts (cat. no. 220).

15 February City Art Museum, St. Louis, announces purchase of *The Mississippi.*

11 March Elected an associate of the National Academy of Design.

13 March–13 April Oil *The Fugitive* included in *112th Annual Exhibition,* National Academy of Design (cat. no. 124).

April Makes a two-day field trip through the soil-erosion areas of Wisconsin with Dean Chris L. Christensen. Installs mural panels in U.S. Department of Justice building, Washington, D.C.

By June Is at work on *Ancient Industry* and *Modern Hat Industry* murals for Norwalk (Connecticut) High School.

19 June Kansas Governor Walter A. Huxman announces campaign to raise funds for a mural project for the statehouse in Topeka, adding that discussions with Curry are under way. By mid-July Huxman has appointed a committee of powerful Kansas newspaper publishers to review Curry's designs and advance the fund-raising effort.

August Receives commission from the Farm Foundation, Chicago, for a painting of the Wisconsin landscape as a memorial to the late Alexander Legge, founder of the Farm Foundation and president of International Harvester Corporation. The painting is never acquired by the foundation.

24 September–17 October Has first show in Madison, *An Exhibition of Work by John Steuart Curry,* at the Wisconsin Union (catalogue).

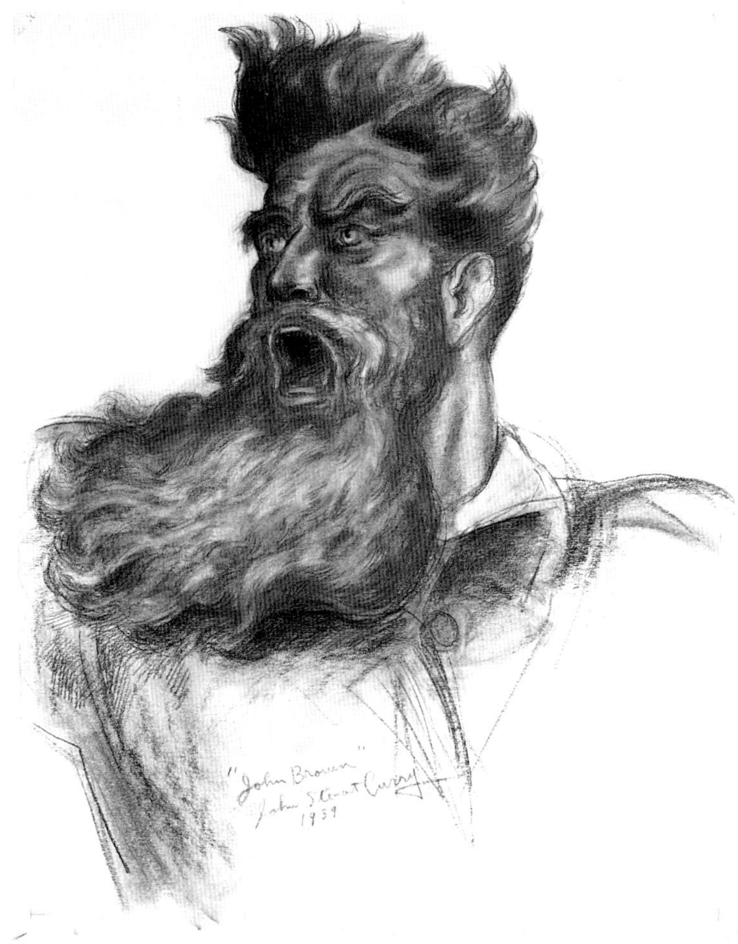

FIGURE 8
Curry's study for *John Brown,* for his mural design for the Kansas statehouse, Topeka, 1939. Photograph courtesy State Historical Society of Wisconsin.

10 November–12 December Oil *The Stallion* shown in *Annual Exhibition of Contemporary American Painting,* Whitney Museum of American Art (cat. no. 59).

12 November Kansas Murals Commission approves Curry's designs for the statehouse (fig. 8).

Since undertaking the project of murals for the State Capitol I have received many suggestions relating to subject matter and the mode of approach. In such a situation the court of last appeal must be the artist himself.

The theme I have chosen is historical in more than one sense. In great measure it is the historical struggle of man with nature.

This struggle has been a determining factor in my art expression. It is my family's tradition and the tradition of a great majority of Kansas people. And though I fully realize the importance of Kansans in the field of politics and the various phases of education and human welfare, these phases are removed from my vital experience and that experience is necessary for me to make a forceful art expression.

Back of the historical allegory is the great back drop of the phenomena of nature and to those who live and depend upon the soil for life and sustenance in these phenomena is God.

TRAGIC PRELUDE (color plates 51 and 52)

In the words of William Allen White, the period depicted in these two panels was "a tragic prelude to the tragic years to come."

At the left . . . Coronado and Padre Padilla, the Franciscan missionary, look out across the Kingdom of Quivera, above which float the omnipresent buzzards.

To the right . . . stands the figure of the plainsman and buffalo hunter. . . .

Centered on the north wall is the gigantic figure of John Brown. In his outstretched left hand the word of God and in the right a Beecher's bible. Beside him facing each other are the contending free soil and pro-slavery forces. At their feet, two figures symbolic of the million and a half dead of the North and South.

In this group is expressed the fratricidal fury that first flamed on the plains of Kansas, the tragic prelude to the last bloody feud of the English-speaking people. Back of this group are the pioneers and their wagons on the endless trek to the West, and back of all the tornado and the raging prairie fire, fitting symbols of the destruction of the coming Civil War.

THE EIGHT PANELS IN THE ROTUNDA

These panels being groups in separate pairs offer a problem in design. . . . These designs as submitted are not yet completed and must be understood from that point of view. . . .

THE PLAGUES

(1) Like ancient Egypt, Kansas is at times beset by plagues. In this panel is depicted drought and grasshoppers.

(2) Soil Erosion and Dust. . . .

This panel is designed as a significant warning and voices the concern of government and educational forces interested in preserving the nation's resources.

CORN AND WHEAT

In these two panels are two basic products of our fruitful land. . . .

Two panels are at the left of the West Corridor Entrance:

(1) Commemorating the sacrifice of life of those who forged westward on the old Santa Fe trail. This depicts the burial of a child. . . .

(2) The Great Cattle Drives. This panel depicts the great herds that for thirty years were driven from Texas to the roaring rail points of central and western Kansas. . . .

KANSAS PASTORAL (color plates 53–55)

In this comparatively quiet corridor is portrayed Kansas in the time of fruitful harvest. . . .

I have been accused of seeing only the dark and seamy side of my native state. In these panels I shall show the beauty of real things under the hand of a beneficent Nature—and we can suppose in these panels that the farm depicted is unmortgaged—that grain and cattle prices are rising on the Kansas City and Chicago markets—so that we as farmers, patrons, and artists can shout happily together, "Ad Astra Per Aspera."

(Curry, "Description of Murals for Kansas State Capitol," undated typescript [November 1937]. Curry Papers/AAA, microfilm roll 165, no frame no., typescript pp. 1–4.)

18 November–16 January 1938 *The Fugitive* included in *48th Annual Exhibition of American Paintings and Sculpture,* Art Institute of Chicago (cat. no. 57).

10 December At a gala dinner at the Waldorf-Astoria hotel, New York, the Limited Editions Club, New York, announces awards of $2,000 each to four artists—Curry, Benton, Wood, and Henry Varnum Poor—to illustrate classic works of American literature.

1938

10–19 January Solo exhibition, *John Steuart Curry: New Work,* Walker Galleries (catalogue).

John Steuart Curry, who first won public recognition painting Kansas regional life, including baptisms and tornadoes, is steadily enlarging his pictorial horizons. His current show at the Walker Gallery—the first he has had in several years—is largely a Wisconsin affair. As newly appointed painter-in-residence at the University of Wisconsin, he has completed at least one excellent landscape—a view of the City of Madison, and a football picture showing Wisconsin battling Marquette, during the last year. "Kansas Sunrise," which was begun several years ago, also was completed there, and there is a sturdy self-portrait on display. All these things will repay the compliment Madison has paid him by making him her painter-laureate. There is nothing lifeless or perfunctory about Curry's latest work, and for a realist who is steadily deepening and enriching his expression these six canvases and several watercolors and drawings are an imposing year's work.

(Carlyle Burrows, "Curry at Wisconsin," New York Herald Tribune, *16 January 1938)*

John Steuart Curry is holding his first exhibition at the Walker Galleries since his appointment a year ago as Artist-in-Residence at the University of Wisconsin. Whatever demands have been made upon him by this collegiate assignment, they have not interfered with his prodigious capacity for work, for he presents here six canvases and a group of water colors and drawings all completed in this twelve-month period. The robust realism which marked his previous work—he has depicted the cataclysmic forces of nature, floods, tornadoes, forked lightning—has not become enfeebled; he looks unblinkingly on the rising sun in one canvas and in another casually throws a rainbow across the scene.... There is, however, a lack of verve in much of this recent work; some of the paintings have been worked over until they seem to have lost most of their vitality—and vitality has been one of Curry's chief assets. The football canvas, although not happy in color, would be commendable, if it possessed the movement of the sketch made for it. The drawings, in fact, reveal the artist's qualities, particularly in draftsmanship, better than many of the canvases.

(Margaret Breuning, "Art in New York," Parnassus *10, no. 2 [2 February 1938]: 26)*

Last week at Manhattan's Walker Galleries six new paintings and half-a-dozen drawings by Curry encouraged head-shaking by detractors. The healthy springiness and sweep of the artist's well-known Kansas pictures appeared only in an oil-and-tempera panel of a prancing Percheron stallion painted at the Wisconsin stock show a year ago. A landscape *View of Madison* painted last spring had an unaccustomed air of old-fashioned dewiness. A still life, *Spring Flowers,* had an even stranger touch of Renoir. For action subjects the artist had apparently confined himself to football games in Wisconsin's Camp Randall stadium producing a series of sketches and one big canvas, *Goal Line Play,* which looked like a monument to a lost opportunity.

But to most gallery-goers Curry's new *Self Portrait*... was not only an honest and successful job but the likeness of a more mature if not a more professorial artist. And the possibility that Curry critics might soon have to shake their heads up & down instead of from side to side was evident in a few rough sketches for the murals he has been commissioned to paint for the Kansas State Capitol at Topeka.

("Professor Curry," Time *31, no. 4 [24 January 1938]: 32–33)*

30 January–6 March Oil *The Old Folks (Mother and Father)* (color plate 17) included in *133rd Annual Exhibition of Paintings and Sculpture,* Pennsylvania Academy of the Fine Arts (cat. no. 306).

9 March Solo exhibition, Fond du Lac, Wisconsin (typed checklist).

16 March–13 April Oil *Kansas Sunrise* shown in *113th Annual Exhibition,* National Academy of Design (cat. no. 198).

28 April–30 May Watercolor *The Prodigal Son* included in *17th Annual Exhibition of Watercolors by American Artists,* Art Institute of Chicago (cat. no. 209).

Probably May Exhibition of three oils, *John Steuart Curry: Artist of Rural Life,* University of Wisconsin College of Agriculture, Madison (catalogue).

June With letters of introduction from Wisconsin Governor Philip F. La Follette and U.S. Secretary of State Cordell Hull, embarks on a summer tour of Europe.

20 October–4 December Oil *Self-Portrait* (1937, color plate 49) included in *49th Annual Exhibition of American Paintings and Sculpture,* Art Institute of Chicago (cat. no. 55).

1939

1 March–28 April Retrospective, *A Loan Exhibition of Drawings and Paintings by John Steuart Curry,* Lakeside Press Galleries, R. R. Donnelly and Sons Company, Chicago (catalogue).

April Preliminary sketches for Kansas murals are unveiled, causing a furor among some Kansas residents (fig. 9).

The proverbial Kansas tornado—a favorite subject of John Steuart Curry—seems about to break loose over the sketches offered by that artist as a basis for the murals he has contracted to paint on the walls of the Kansas statehouse corridors.

As expected, it appears to be the content rather than the execution of the pictures which has drawn violent protest from some of the observers of the sketches thus far. There is, for example, one panel with a tornado cloud in it—a sore subject with Kansas, which long has smarted under the injustice of a designation as the "tornado state" which applies at least as much to other states in the Midwest. There is also a mounting duststorm in another panel, and a corn field, stripped by grasshoppers.

All these things harass the spirits of the sensitive souls. Why not paint the beautiful, the inspirational, the good? Well, Curry is going to do that, too. Stark old John Brown will be in one mural, typifying the state's struggle for freedom. There is a spirited sketch of the epic trail drives. Peaceful scenes in prosperous towns and in pretty towns are other subjects.

After all, wouldn't it be an unbalanced viewpoint which presented only the favorable aspects of a state? Kansas does not have the motto *ad astra per aspera* for nothing. The tornadoes,

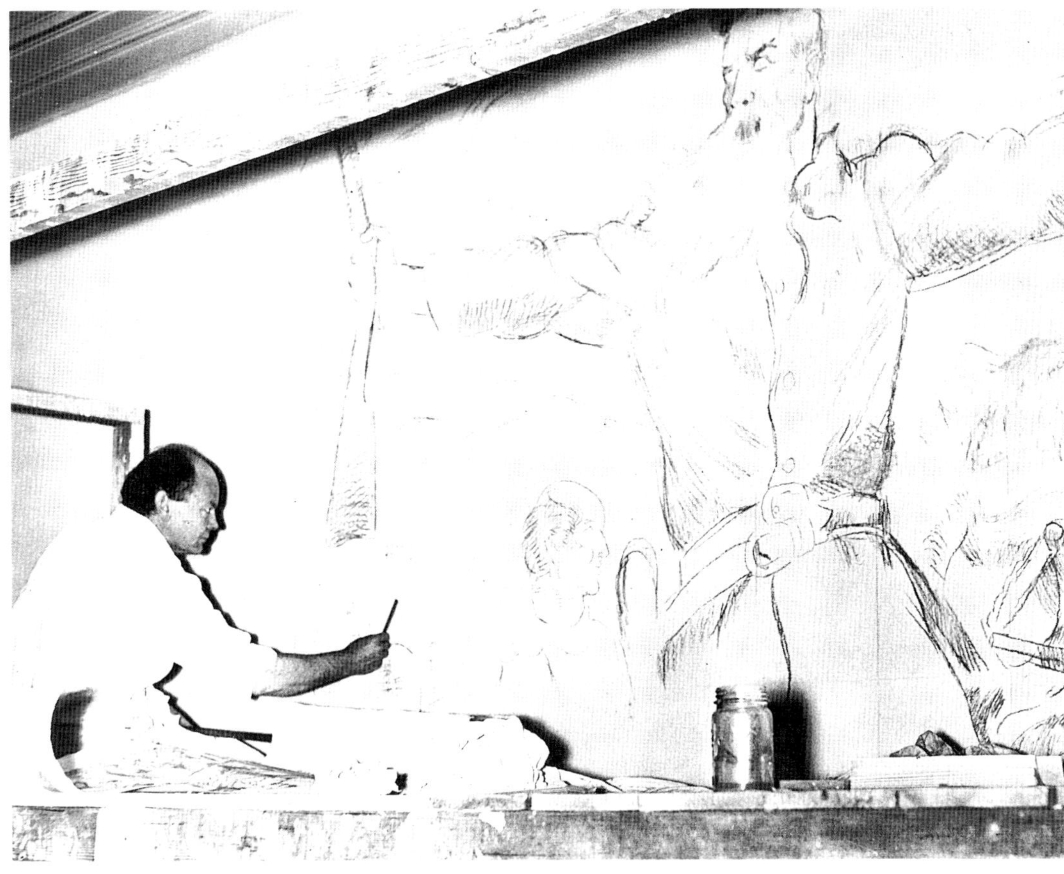

FIGURE 9

Curry on scaffold, at work on the *Tragic Prelude* segment of the murals for the Kansas statehouse, Topeka. Photograph courtesy Curry Papers, Archives of American Art, Smithsonian Institution, Washington, D.C.

duststorms, grasshoppers and other great vicissitudes are a part of the state's heritage—the part which gives Kansas the grim strength, the whalebone resilience which are notable in its history. The bad is as much a part of the whole drama of the state as the good.

Yet we expect the Kansas art tornado to rage, logic or no logic. Over nothing, it seems, can people become so worked up as over a mural.

*(*Kansas City Star, *14 April 1939, as quoted in Calder M. Pickett, "John Steuart Curry and the Topeka Murals Controversy,"* Register of the Museum of Art, the University of Kansas *2 [December 1959]: 37)*

[TO] MR. CURRY, MURALIST AT STATE HOUSE.

HEAVEN'S SAKES!

GO GET A PICTURE OF A BUFFALO, AND STUDY IT, THEN RUSH IT, THEN ERASE THAT BLOTCHED PIG OF A THING YOU NOW HAVE ON THE WALL AND PUT THE BUFFALO THERE.

That no more resembles a buffalo than you do an artist. A pig or a frog not a BUFFALO.

(Unidentified Kansan, telegram to Curry, undated [probably April 1939]. Curry Papers/AAA, microfilm roll 165, no frame no.)

November Oil *Wisconsin Landscape* (color plate 56) is placed on view at Walker Galleries.

With the first flush of the American Scene movement already passed, a good many people are wondering what direction the art of the famous Midwest triumvirate Benton, Curry, and Wood, will take. Benton has already shown where he is headed and his Persephone and the landscape and still lifes in his show last season broke definitely with his former style. The other two have not been heard from recently. For this reason, a new canvas by Curry on view at the Walker Galleries takes on added interest.

Entitled simply *Wisconsin Landscape,* the huge rolling landscape panorama is a daring attempt to orchestrate with rich brilliant colors over a wide field of tones. From a foreground streak of intense yellow, put on with Ryderesque arbitrariness, Curry's new work weaves through the color and value scale to a deep purple in the horizon. It is thick with pigment and alive with light, but somewhat on the raw side in its total effect. Obviously Curry is working hard on a new tack himself, as he continues as artist-in-residence at Wisconsin University.

("New Curry Picture," Art Digest *14, no. 3 [1 November 1939]: 18–19)*

22 November Begins installing completed murals, *The Homestead* and *The Oklahoma Land Rush* (color plates 59 and 60), in the new U.S. Department of Interior building, Washington, D.C.

December *Wisconsin Landscape* is on view at Walker Galleries as part of *Fourth Anniversary Exhibition by Walker Group Artists* (no catalogue).

1940

Begins a group of murals, *The Social Benefits of Biochemical Research* (color plates 64–66), for the University of Wisconsin's biochemistry building.

10 January–18 February Oil *John Brown* (color plate 62) included in *Annual Exhibition of Contemporary American Art*, Whitney Museum of American Art (cat. no. 24).

28 January–3 March Oil *Belgian Stallions, No. 2* shown in *135th Annual Exhibition of Paintings and Sculpture*, Pennsylvania Academy of the Fine Arts (cat. no. 250).

14 March–11 April *Wisconsin Landscape* included in *114th Annual Exhibition*, National Academy of Design (cat. no. 41).

19 March Geneva College, Beaver Falls, Pennsylvania, notifies Curry that it will confer upon him an honorary Doctorate of Arts.

May Begins painting murals in Kansas statehouse, Topeka.

6 May Oil *Hoover and the Flood* reproduced in *Life* magazine; the illustration depicts Herbert Hoover's large-scale relief efforts, as U.S. Secretary of Commerce, during the Mississippi River valley floods of 1927.

30 May Alonzo Cudworth American Legion Post No. 23, Milwaukee, unveils *The Return of Private Davis from the Argonne*, acquired as a gift of thirty local donors.

11 November–5 January 1941 *Wisconsin Landscape* included in *51st Annual Exhibition of American Paintings and Sculpture*, Art Institute of Chicago (cat. no. 45).

18 November Agrees to illustrate *The Wisconsin*, by Sauk City, Wisconsin, poet and writer August Derleth, part of The Rivers of America book series published by Farrar and Rinehart, New York.

27 November–8 January 1941 Oil *Wisconsin Still Life* shown in *Annual Exhibition of Contemporary American Painting*, Whitney Museum of American Art (cat. no. 36).

December Special edition of James Fenimore Cooper's novel *The Prairie*, with Curry's illustrations, is published by the Limited Editions Club. Walker Galleries exhibits the illustrations, 2–25 December.

12 December Accepts commission to paint landscape murals in the First National Bank, Madison.

1941

7 January Contacts Reeves Lewenthal, director of Associated American Artists gallery, New York, saying he wishes to leave Walker Galleries and sign with Lewenthal.

15 January–19 February Drawing *John Brown* included in *Annual Exhibition of Sculpture, Watercolors, Drawings, and Prints*, Whitney Museum of American Art (cat. no. 85).

16 January Notifies Maynard Walker that he will be joining Associated American Artists, thus ending his ten-year association with Walker:

> During the past two years I have become very unhappy and discouraged about the sale of my paintings. I have come to the conclusion that I have done about everything that I can for you, and that you have done about everything you can do for me.
>
> I have written to Lewenthal of the Associated American Artists to see if they would like to take me on, and they have agreed to do this. I feel that the painting that I am doing now cannot be sold in the market in which you are selling. I appreciate to the fullest the time and effort that you have put in pushing my work, but I feel that the situation has come to an impasse. In a way, I am certain you will feel relieved, because I know you have not gotten rich on my production.
>
> *(Curry to Maynard Walker, 16 January 1941. Walker Papers/AAA, microfilm roll 2023, frame 49.)*

Walker responds:

> Maybe I am just plain dumb, but I am still at a complete loss to understand your action and the general method of procedure. After ten years of hard trying and real faith in you it seems pretty strange not to have had at lest some preliminary discussion of your discontent. . . .
>
> I have always felt you should paint as you felt—that your best work would only result this way. And I've not complained to you about size and subject nearly as much as clients have complained to me. I have believed in your work even though it might not be easy to sell. I have believed you should go on painting the things you were impelled to paint; I have been sure they would be appreciated some day.
>
> All these things may have some bearing on our poor sales results of the last few years. Many times I have felt that you were neglecting to supply us with workable material, but I know you were engaged on other important things and didn't want to interrupt. . . .
>
> I feel that we are entitled to some small commission on the final total payment (if and when you receive it) for the Kansas mural. I fully realize that I did not arrange the final contract but my work in your behalf in that direction goes back many years and

some part of the final consummation is certainly the results of my long campaign which I started in 1931 with the showing of your work at the Museum there.

(Maynard Walker to Curry, 31 January 1941. Walker Papers/AAA, microfilm roll 2023, frame 55.)

26 January–2 March *Wisconsin Landscape* featured in *136th Annual Exhibition of Paintings and Sculpture,* Pennsylvania Academy of the Fine Arts (cat. no. 329). Awarded the Jennie Sesnan Medal as the exhibition's best landscape.

March Objection to Kansas statehouse murals becomes so strong that Mural Commission member Paul Jones Lyons proposes moving them from Topeka to the Wichita Art Gallery. Curry writes to his dealer Reeves Lewenthal about the situation:

The Mural Commission are my friends and have done everything to back me up. My enemies consist of the Executive Council in the State Capitol which is composed of the Governor and various elected state officials such as the Treasurer, Mr. J. Parker, who is my chief antagonist. Also, another great enemy is the *Kansas Star*'s representative, Mr. Cecil Howe. Their great objection was to removing some slabs of marble in the rotunda which would have allowed me more space for my painting. No one has been able to swerve them from their opposition to removing the marble and just recently the only Negro delegate in the house voiced objection to the John Brown panel, saying that it was untrue to state history and the house has passed a resolution approving the Executive Council's position on the marble. One other thing that seems to bother more than any other is that I have portrayed John Brown as a roaring fanatic and I also painted his hands blood red. There are a great many things that have entered into such a situation, such as local artists who thought they should have had the commission, etc.

I have written to Senator Allen giving approval to the idea of moving the decorations to Wichita if they can find a suitable place. I think if they can this would be a good idea because Wichita is the liveliest metropolitan center in Kansas. I also suggested that if they cannot find a good space for them, just to leave them where they are and have it out as it stands. I have given up any idea of doing the rotunda.

(Curry to Reeves Lewenthal, 14 March 1941. Curry Papers/AAA, microfilm roll 165, no frame no.)

April April issue of *Demcourier* magazine, published by Demco Library Supplies of Madison, is dedicated to Curry. It includes articles by Benton, Wood, Reginald Marsh, and Curry.

John Curry has the power to stir people. He has what it takes to be a living person rather than just a person. You may not like his painting, but in the end, if you are intelligent, you come to like his Art. . . .

John Curry, under that bald pate of his, has the creator's mind. He has the drive of those who love the world better than Art and who will risk innovation for the sake of that love. When they stick John's critics in the ground they'll just stick them there and forget them.

That won't be the case with John Curry.

(Thomas Hart Benton, "Wisconsin Landscape," Demcourier *11, no. 2 [April 1941]: 14)*

My prediction is that the artist of the new day that is upon us will fulfill a double purpose. First that of propagandist for the coming social upheavals and second, strangely enough, he will be asked to give pattern to the new concepts of decoration and design. His field will increasingly embrace every phase of modern life. His imagination and talents will beautify everything: the kitchen sink, the family car, the office desk, as well as the painting that hangs on the wall or the statuary in a public building. The artist of this new day will be, perhaps, more completely a servant of the people than he has ever been in preceding generations.

(Curry, "The Artist Has the Last Word," Demcourier *11, no. 2 [April 1941]: 24)*

2 April Kansas Secretary of State Clarence W. Miller sends Curry a copy of Senate Resolution 20, which affirms that marble will not be removed from the statehouse rotunda to make way for Curry's last mural panels. The resolution makes it impossible for the artist to finish the project. He refuses to sign the murals that are already in place.

The work in the east and west wings stands as disjointed and un-united fragments. Because this project is uncompleted and does not represent my true idea, I am not signing these works, I sincerely believe that in the fragments, particularly in the panel of John Brown, I have accomplished the greatest panels I have yet done, and that they will stand as historical monuments. To the Mural Commission and to the children who donate their pennies, as well as to all others who have believed in me, I wish to express my appreciation and to assure you that I have done the best I could with the space at my command.

(Curry quoted in "Curry Will Not Sign Kansas Murals," Topeka Capital, *24 May 1942)*

6 April Kansas legislature reluctantly votes a final appropriation for the statehouse murals.

To Kansas senators art is a serious problem at 2:30 in the morning. At that hour yesterday morning the senators growled lustily at the murals painted by John Steuart Curry on the walls of the statehouse corridors and then unanimously voted $2,000 to finish the job of paying for them.

The item was included in the miscellaneous appropriations bill, passed by the house early this morning. It got to the senate and the clerk was droning away on the items when Senator Skovgard of Washington heard an item about murals.

"What's this," he demanded, "about an appropriation for murals?...

"Are we proposing to pay for those grotesque paintings?" demanded Skovgard heatedly. "Why those figures are not human beings."

"Maybe they are pre-historic monsters like they find in the chalk beds," said Senator Van de Mark of Cloud, arch critic of the John Brown mural.

Senator Skovgard moved that the item be stricken from the bill....

Senator Stanley chipped in with, "I want to hurry and vote against it before some of us get to looking like those figures."...

"Some of these murals show objects that are supposed to be human beings, and they haven't any eyes," said Senator Van de Mark. "I am going to vote for this appropriation because I want to see those pictures finished even if it does cost $2000."...

Senator Hotchkiss of Osage came to the defense of the murals. He said he liked them, as did Senator Cole of Jackson.

"I'd be glad to vote for this appropriation if it meant white paint to cover them up," remarked a senator.

Curry has some work yet to do on the pictures and in his summer vacation from his work as artist in residence at Wisconsin university is to come to Topeka to finish the job.

("Kansas Legislature: Vote Cash for Murals," Kansas City Star, *7 April 1941)*

June Embarks on Wisconsin River trip with August Derleth, in preparation for a book in The Rivers of America series.

6 September Completes murals for the First National Bank, Madison.

In these murals for the First National Bank I have tried to present the Wisconsin scene in as beautiful and simple manner as possible.

In the large square is represented a scene of forest farm land and distant lake. In the panel over the door a view of Madison and Lake Mendota seen from a hypothetical hill.

The two smaller decorations are fitting to the decorative scheme as well as being typical of this countryside.

(Curry, "Statement by the Artist," 8 September 1941. Curry Papers/AAA, microfilm roll 165, no frame no.)

26 October Brittingham Trust announces it will grant $20,000 to fund Curry's artist-in-residence position at the University of Wisconsin for another five years.

The artist in residence example here has set a pattern for elsewhere in the country and the Carnegie Foundation has endowed several similar positions in other institutions. Distinctive about them all is the fact that the artist has to do no teaching.

("U. W. Experiment Has Shown That Art, Agriculture Do Mix," Milwaukee Journal, *26 October 1941)*

1942

Elected to membership in the National Institute of Arts and Letters.

Encouraged by Lloyd K. Garrison, dean of the University of Wisconsin Law School, and with funds from a private donor (Milwaukee brewer Robert Uihlein), begins work on a mural, *Freeing of the Slaves* (color plate 68, fig. 10), for the Law School library. The design is based on his 1936 sketch for the U.S. Department of Justice building mural, rejected by the U.S. Department of the Treasury's Section on Painting and Sculpture.

The Literary Works of Abraham Lincoln, with illustrations by Curry, is printed by the Collegiate Press, Menasha, Wisconsin, and published by the Limited Editions Club.

25 January–1 March Oil *Flowers* included in *137th Annual Exhibition of Paintings and Sculpture,* Pennsylvania Academy of the Fine Arts (cat. no. 358).

6 February Reeves Lewenthal writes that he has received U.S. government approval to organize a program to commission paintings from leading artists. The paintings will be reproduced and distributed by government public-relations departments in order to encourage popular support for America's war effort. Curry's contribution is the oil *Our Good Earth* (color plate 63), done under the sponsorship of Abbott Laboratories.

The first artist to get going on this project must be none other than you—John! Here is what you must paint—and paint like you have never painted in your career: your choice of any subject just so long as it is connected with our great emergency and production or military effort. I visualize you doing a symbolic subject as forceful, as heroic, as breathtaking as your "John Brown"! A painting that will be so thunderous that it will stop people cold—cause them to think—or admire and respect those participants in the various branches of our services. Perhaps you can

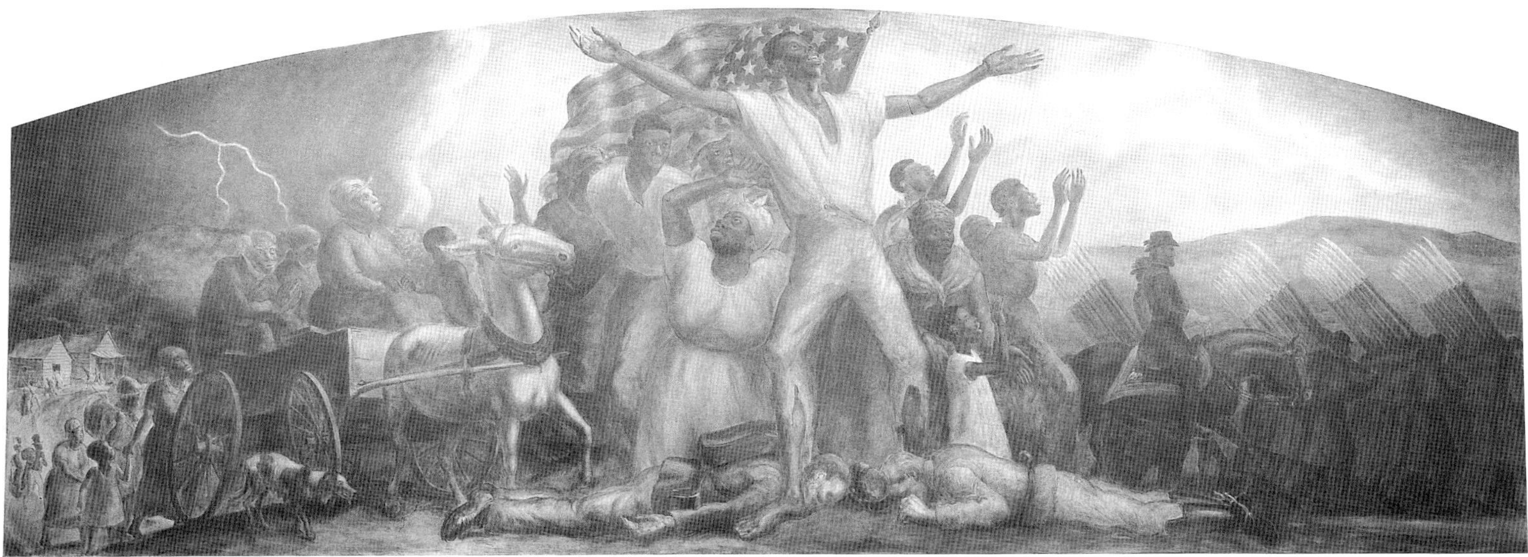

FIGURE 10

John Steuart Curry
Freeing of the Slaves, 1942
Mural, Law School library, University of Wisconsin, Madison
Oil and tempera on canvas
14 × 37 ft.
Photograph courtesy University of Wisconsin, Madison.

do a heroic figure of a soldier guarding over or fighting for the preservation of all those benefits and advantages we enjoy in our democracy; or perhaps, could be fighting for the preservation of our peaceful, fertile farmlands, can be effectively portrayed in the background; or, perhaps, shadows of our former hero soldiers can drift off into the distance behind this forceful foreground figure. This all sounds trite in words, but of course your interpretation would not make it so. Then again, you might do a nurse—or a flyer—or a marine—or a sailor—in some symbolic composition.

These are merely suggestions—you undoubtedly have many ideas of your own—the important thing, John, is to do a picture that excites you tremendously, one which will become an important standard bearer of the Second World War! Think about it—dream about it—and send me sketches or describe ideas and let us get started.

(Reeves Lewenthal to Curry, 6 February 1942. Curry Papers/ AAA, microfilm roll 165, no frame no.)

Farmers are exerting all-out effort and working 70 and 80 hours a week. There is no problem as we see it out here in getting farmers to work as hard as they can, for they are now doing exactly this.

Another point that to me seems important is that with patriotic and courageous Americans it seems very doubtful whether it is strategic or desirable to use fear as the motive in picturing to them the needs of the war program. Our people are patriotic. Thousands of our young men are volunteering before they are drafted. Bond sales are at a high level. Our people expect to win the war and are prepared to pay any price that may be necessary. They do not need to be threatened by some fear complex in order to do their best. They are responding to incentives that are on a much higher plane and more effective than fear.

Can't your Writers' War Board develop a theme more positive? I will try to think of an idea and will send it on to you just as soon as possible.

(Curry to Reeves Lewenthal, 7 October 1942. Curry Papers/AAA, microfilm roll 165, no frame no.)

July Completes *Freeing of the Slaves* mural, Law School library, University of Wisconsin.

September Elected to membership in the Wisconsin Academy of Sciences, Arts, and Letters.

28 October Grant Wood dies, and Curry issues a tribute:

In the years ahead of us Grant Wood's paintings will stand like quiet monuments in their interpretation of that life.

No other contemporary artist's work had the unique appeal that Grant's work had. Pope Pius XI wrote Grant asking to see more of his reproductions. The Parisian critics were enthusiastic over "Daughters of Revolution" and the common man saw in these paintings something that he reacted to.

We who are here can only add our word of thanks and appreciation expressing our debt to the artist and to his works.

(Curry, 28 October 1942. Curry Papers/AAA, microfilm roll 165, no frame no.)

29 October–10 December Oil *Oak Tree* shown in *53rd Annual Exhibition of American Paintings and Sculpture,* Art Institute of Chicago (cat. no. 88).

4 December Francis Henry Taylor, director of the Metropolitan Museum of Art, announces that the purchase prize for the exhibition *Artists for Victory* has been awarded to *Wisconsin Landscape;* the oil is then acquired for the museum's permanent collection. The exhibition's Jury of Award includes Alfred H. Barr, Jr., Juliana Force, Henri Marceau, A. Hyatt Mayor, Daniel Catton Rich, Charles H. Sawyer, and Henry B. Wehle.

7 December *Artists for Victory: An Exhibition of Contemporary American Art* opens at the Metropolitan Museum of Art (catalogue).

1943

24 January–28 February Oil *Belgian Stallions* (color plate 57) shown in *138th Annual Exhibition of Paintings and Sculpture,* Pennsylvania Academy of the Fine Arts (cat. no. 133).

17 February–9 March Portrait *Chris Christensen* (color plate 67) included in *117th Annual Exhibition,* National Academy of Design (cat. no. 246).

28 April Elected an Academician of the National Academy of Design. In September Curry presents *Belgian Stallions* to the academy to fulfill a requirement for Academician status.

23 July Mrs. Althea Miner, Chris Christensen's secretary, writes to Reeves Lewenthal about the intention of University of Wisconsin faculty members and some Madison residents to raise funds to acquire Curry's portrait of Christensen for the College of Agriculture.

September Completes *The Social Benefits of Biochemical Research* murals in the hall and seminar room of the university's biochemistry building, a three-year project sponsored by the Brittingham Trust.

By October Special edition of Walt Whitman's *Leaves of Grass* published by Peter Pauper Press, Mount Vernon, New York, with illustrations by Curry. Finishes illustrations for Mary O'Hara's novels *My Friend Flicka* and *Thunderhead,* published by J. B. Lippincott, Philadelphia.

20 October–21 November Oils *Stallion and Jack Fighting* (color plate 27), *The Fugitive,* and *Line Storm* (color plate 33) included in the exhibition *Ten Americans,* Institute of Modern Art, Boston (cat. nos. 7–9). The other artists represented are Benton, Wood, Alexander Brook, Edward Hopper, Dan James, Jack Levine, Reginald Marsh, Charles Sheeler, and Franklin Watkins.

November First biography and critical study of Curry's work, *John Steuart Curry's Pageant of America,* by Laurence E. Schmeckebier, published by American Artists Group, New York.

23 November–4 January 1944 Drawing *Nude* shown in *Annual Exhibition of Contemporary American Art,* Whitney Museum of American Art (cat. no. 22).

1944

Special edition of Stephen Crane's *The Red Badge of Courage,* with illustrations by Curry, is published by the Limited Editions Club.

20 January Commissioned by the War Department to create a series of field studies of Medical Department activities. Curry is assigned to Camp Barkeley, Texas.

1945

3 January–8 February Drawing *Male Figure Study* included in *Annual Exhibition of Contemporary American Sculpture, Watercolors, and Drawings,* Whitney Museum of American Art (cat. no. 172).

19 January–25 February Oil *The Passing Leap* shown in *Annual Exhibition of Paintings and Sculpture,* Pennsylvania Academy of the Fine Arts, Philadelphia (cat. no. 126).

23 August IBM Corporation purchases *The Old Folks (Mother and Father)* as part of an effort to acquire paintings representative of each of the United States. Curry's canvas is to represent Kansas.

25 October–1 January 1946 Oil *Death of Beauty* featured in *56th Annual Exhibition of American Paintings and Sculpture,* Art Institute of Chicago (cat. no. 33).

19 November Reeves Lewenthal proposes a commission for a nationwide advertising campaign for National City Bank—a series on the major industries of Central and South America that would take Curry to Cuba, Uruguay, and Panama.

27 November–10 January 1946 Oil *Tree* included in *Annual Exhibition of Contemporary American Painting,* Whitney Museum of American Art (cat. no. 30).

1946

Works on illustrations for *John Brown's Body: A Poem,* by Stephen Vincent Benét, published by Limited Editions Club in 1948.

By 19 August Completes mural for Wisconsin State Fair, *Youth Helps Rebuild a World.*

29 August Dies of a heart attack in Madison.

31 August Memorial service is conducted at Grace Episcopal Church, Madison.

1 September Buried in Winchester, Kansas. Services are held in the Reformed Presbyterian Church, which Curry's grandfather had helped found in 1868.

In the golden sunlight of a Sunday afternoon, one of Kansas' greatest artists, John Steuart Curry, member of a famed triumvirate that included Thomas Hart Benton and Grant Wood, who spread scenes of the Midwest across canvases of the world, came home to be buried in the churchyard of the Reformed Presbyterian Church here.

While some 500 of his fellow Kansans looked on to pay him tribute, the noted artist was lowered into a simple grave, marked only by a granite boulder, that over-looked the windmills, barns, and farm homes which he portrayed so often. . . .

A great Kansas artist, who had painted boldly, in vivid and often controversial fashion, was home to stay.

(Ray Morgan, "John Steuart Curry Buried at Winchester in Community Typical of Kansas He Loved," Topeka Daily Capital, *2 September 1946)*

America has lost one of the great creative personalities of our time. For the strength and reality of his paintings, history must record John Steuart Curry as one of the true artists of American life.

He was a product of the Middle West—born and raised among Kansas farm people—and he understood the men and women of this great Mississippi region. He knew their fine qualities of leadership, their ambitions, their struggles toward a better standard of living, and their determination to preserve and breathe life into the ideals of democracy. These basic cultural qualities he sought to capture on his canvases.

Artist Curry did much to dignify the culture and society of rural America. He saw the important place of good painting and good literature and good music in everyday life. By his feeling for reality and life and movement, he helped bring these fine things more sharply into our consciousness.

His work displays a wide range of subjects. But everything he did reflects the faith, hope, and striving of the American mind and soul.

America has lost much in John Steuart Curry's passing. I personally have lost a great and loyal friend.

(Chris L. Christensen, former dean of the University of Wisconsin College of Agriculture [Undated typescript. Curry Papers/AAA, microfilm roll 2747, no frame no.])

5 September–15 October Retrospective exhibition, *The Art of John Steuart Curry,* on view at Milwaukee Art Institute (catalogue).

SELECTED BIBLIOGRAPHY

Archival Sources

Don Anderson Papers, Archives of American Art, Smithsonian Institution, Washington, D.C. Gift of Don Anderson.

Associated American Artists Gallery Papers, Archives of American Art, Smithsonian Institution, Washington, D.C. Gift of Sylvan Cole, Jr.

John Steuart Curry Papers, Archives of American Art, Smithsonian Institution, Washington, D.C. Gift of Kathleen Curry; Gift of Mrs. Stanley R. Fike.

R. Eugene Curry Papers, Archives of American Art, Smithsonian Institution, Washington, D.C. Gift of R. Eugene Curry.

Ringling Brothers and Barnum & Bailey Circus Archival Collections, Robert L. Parkinson Library and Research Center, Circus World Museum, Baraboo, Wisconsin.

Maynard Walker Gallery Photographs, Archives of American Art, Smithsonian Institution, Washington, D.C. Gift of the Frick Art Reference Library on behalf of Maynard Walker.

Maynard Walker Papers, Archives of American Art, Smithsonian Institution, Washington, D.C. Gift of Maynard Walker.

Whitney Museum of American Art Papers, Archives of American Art, Smithsonian Institution, Washington, D.C. Lent by the Whitney Museum of American Art.

Books and Exhibition Catalogues

Adams, Henry. *Thomas Hart Benton: An American Original.* New York: Alfred A. Knopf, 1989.

An Art Commentary on Lynching. New York: Arthur U. Newton Galleries, 1935.

The Art of John Steuart Curry. Milwaukee, Wis.: Milwaukee Art Institute, 1946.

Benton, Thomas Hart. *An American in Art: A Professional and Technical Autobiography.* Lawrence: University Press of Kansas, 1969.

_____. *An Artist in America.* 4th rev. ed. Columbia: University of Missouri Press, 1983.

Boswell, Peyton, Jr. *Modern American Painting.* New York: Dodd, Mead, and Company, 1939.

Catalogue of a Loan Exhibition of Drawings and Paintings by John Steuart Curry. Chicago: Lakeside Press Galleries, 1939.

The Circus in Paint. New York: Whitney Studio Galleries, 1929.

Cole, Sylvan, Jr., ed. *The Lithographs of John Steuart Curry: A Catalogue Raisonné.* New York: Associated American Artists, 1976.

Craven, Thomas. *Modern Art.* New York: Simon and Schuster, 1934.

_____. *A Treasury of American Prints.* New York: Simon and Schuster, 1939.

Czestochowski, Joseph S. *John Steuart Curry and Grant Wood: A Portrait of Rural America.* Columbia: University of Missouri Press with the Cedar Rapids Art Association, 1981.

Dennis, James M. *Grant Wood: A Study in American Art and Culture.* New York: Viking Press, 1975.

Doss, Erika. *Benton, Pollock, and the Politics of Modernism: From Regionalism to Abstract Expressionism.* Chicago: University of Chicago Press, 1991.

Exhibition by John Steuart Curry, James D'Agostino, Loutchansky. New York: Whitney Studio Galleries, 1930.

An Exhibition of Work by John Steuart Curry. Madison: Wisconsin Union, 1937.

Gambone, Robert L. *Art and Popular Religion in Evangelical America, 1915–1940.* Knoxville: University of Tennessee Press, 1989.

Guedon, Mary Scholz. *Regionalist Art: Thomas Hart Benton, John Steuart Curry, and Grant Wood: A Guide to the Literature.* Metuchen, N.J.: Scarecrow Press, 1982.

John Steuart Curry. New York: American Artists Group, 1945.

John Steuart Curry. Milwaukee, Wis.: Milwaukee Art Institute, 1946.

John Steuart Curry: A Regionalist Reconsidered. Davenport, Iowa: Davenport Museum of Art, 1992.

John Steuart Curry: A Retrospective Exhibition of His Work Held in the Kansas State Capitol, Topeka, October 3–November 3, 1970. Kansas Quarterly. Reprint. Lawrence: University Press of Kansas, 1970.

John Steuart Curry: Artist of Rural Life. Madison: College of Agriculture, University of Wisconsin, 1938.

John Steuart Curry, 1897–1946. Lawrence: University of Kansas Museum of Art, 1957.

John Steuart Curry (1897–1946): Rural America. Chicago: Mongerson Wunderlich Gallery, 1990.

John Steuart Curry: Everyday Life in Art. Dayton, Tenn.: Bryan College, 1984.

John Steuart Curry: New Work, 1936–7. New York: Walker Galleries, 1938.

John Steuart Curry Reexamined. New London, Conn.: Lyman Allyn Museum, 1954.

John Steuart Curry: Themes and Variations. Washington, D.C.: National Collection of Fine Arts, Smithsonian Institution, 1972.

John Steuart Curry: 20 Years of His Art. New York: Associated American Artists, 1947.

John Steuart Curry's America. Kansas City, Mo.: Exhibits U.S.A., 1992.

Kendall, M. Sue. "John Steuart Curry's Kansas Pastoral: The Modern American Family on the Middle Border." In *John Steuart Curry and Grant Wood: A Portrait of Rural America.* Edited by Joseph S. Czestochowski. Columbia: University of Missouri Press, 1981, pp. 36–41.

_____. *Rethinking Regionalism: John Steuart Curry and the Kansas Mural Controversy.* Washington, D.C.: Smithsonian Institution Press, 1986.

Leaders in Wisconsin Art, 1936–1981: John Steuart Curry, Aaron Bohrod, John Wilde. Milwaukee, Wis.: Milwaukee Art Museum, 1982.

Madonia, Ann C. *Prairie Visions and Circus Wonders: The Complete Lithographic Suite by John Steuart Curry.* Davenport, Iowa: Davenport Art Gallery, 1980.

Overlien, Blanche. *John Steuart Curry: He Puts Farm Life on Canvas.* Madison: University of Wisconsin Extension Service, 1937.

Paintings by Six Americans. New York: Walker Galleries, 1935.

Park, Marlene. "Lynching and Antilynching: Art and Politics in the 1930s." In *Prospects: An Annual of American Cultural Studies.* Edited by Jack Salzman. Vol. 18. New York: Cambridge University Press, 1993.

Recent Work by John Steuart Curry. New York: Ferargil Gallery, 1935.

A Retrospective Exhibition of Work by John Steuart Curry. Syracuse, N.Y.: Joe and Emily Lowe Art Gallery, Syracuse University, 1956.

Schmeckebier, Laurence E. *John Steuart Curry's Pageant of America.* New York: American Artists Group, 1943.

A Selected Group of Work by John Steuart Curry. New York: College Art Association, 1937.

Spring Exhibition. New York: Whitney Studio Galleries, 1930.

Ten Americans. Boston: Institute of Modern Art, 1943.

The Whitney Studio Club and American Art, 1900–1937. New York: Whitney Museum of American Art, 1975.

Serials

Alloway, Lawrence. "The Recovery of Regionalism: John Steuart Curry." *Art in America* 64 (July–August 1976): 70–73.

"As They Saw It: Three from the 30s." *Time* 61 (1 March 1954): 72–73.

Baigell, Matthew. "The Relevancy of Curry's Paintings of Black Freedom." *Kansas Quarterly* 2 (fall 1970): 19–29.

Benton, Thomas Hart. "Wisconsin Landscape." *Demcourier* 11 (April 1941): 13–14.

_____. "Review of Lawrence E. Schmeckebier's *John Steuart Curry's Pageant of America.*" *Wisconsin Magazine of History* 27 (March 1944): 348–51.

_____. "John Curry." *University of Kansas City Review* (winter 1946): 87–90.

_____. "What's Holding Back American Art." *Saturday Review of Literature* 34 (15 December 1951): 9–11.

Breuning, Margaret. "In the Studio of John Steuart Curry." *London Studio* 12 (June 1937): 326–30.

Christensen, Chris L. "Artist in Residence." *Demcourier* 11 (April 1941): 4–5.

Craven, Thomas. "Art and Propaganda." *Scribner's Magazine* 95 (March 1934): 189–94.

_____. "U.S. Scene." *Time* 24 (24 December 1934): 24–27.

_____. "Our Art Becomes American." *Harper's Monthly Magazine* 171 (September 1935): 430–41.

_____. "Home-Grown Art." *Country Gentleman* 105 (November 1935): 18–19, 70–73.

_____. "Kansas Refuses Curry." *Kansas Magazine* (1937): 85–87.

_____. "John Steuart Curry." *Scribner's Magazine* 103 (January 1938): 37–41, 96, 98.

Curry, John Steuart. "Letter." *Art Front* 1 (April 1935): 1.

_____. "Curry's View." *Art Digest* 9 (1 September 1935): 29.

_____. "The Artist Has the Last Word." *Demcourier* 11 (April 1941): 24.

"Curry, American." *Newsweek* 29 (7 April 1947): 90.

"Curry and Circus Romanticism." *Art Digest* 7 (15 April 1933): 16.

"Curry, a Pioneer in Art." *Art Digest* 9 (15 February 1935): 16.

"Curry Dies." *Art Digest* 20 (15 September 1946): 9.

"Curry in Wisconsin." *Art Digest* 12 (15 January 1938): 8.

"Curry of Kansas." *Life* 1 (23 November 1936): 28–31.

"Curry of Kansas." *Newsweek* 22 (15 November 1943): 80.

"Curry of Kansas Is Reviewed by Chicago." *Art Digest* 13 (April 1939): 21.

"Curry Recognized." *Art Digest* 8 (1 September 1934): 7.

"Curry's Rebus Murals." *Art Digest* 9 (15 November 1934): 7.

Czestochowski, Joseph. "John Steuart Curry's Lithographs: A Portrait of Rural America." *American Art Journal* 9 (November 1977): 68–82.

Davis, Stuart. "The New American Scene in Art." *Art Front* 1 (February 1935): 6.

Devree, Howard. "Curry Has Show." *Magazine of Art* 31 (January 1938): 36.

L.E. [Laurie Eglington]. "Exhibiting in New York: John Steuart Curry, Ferargil Galleries." *Art News* 33 (26 January 1935): 6.

"Football Sketches." *School Arts* 42 (September 1942): 22–23.

Heller, Nancy, and Julia Williams. "John Steuart Curry: The American Farmlands." *American Artist* 40 (January 1976): 46–51, 96.

"He Painted Kansas." *Newsweek* 28 (9 September 1946): 72, 74.

"Hoover and the Flood: A Painting for Life by John Steuart Curry." *Life* 8 (6 May 1940): 61.

Jaffe, Irma B. "Religious Content in the Painting of John Steuart Curry." *Winterthur Portfolio* 22 (spring 1987): 23–45.

"John Steuart Curry—Comes Out of the West." *Art Digest* 9 (1 February 1935): 19.

"John Steuart Curry, 1897–1946." *Bulletin from Associated American Artists* (September 1946): 1–2.

"John Steuart Curry: He Paints at Wisconsin as Artist-in-Residence." *Life* 7 (25 December 1939): 34–37.

"Kansan at the Circus." *Time* 21 (10 April 1933): 41–42.

"Kansas Biographies: John Steuart Curry." *Kansas Library Bulletin* 2 (December 1933): 5–8.

"Kansas Finds 'Her Homer' in J. S. Curry." *Art Digest* 5 (15 December 1930): 16.

"Kansas Pastures." *Arts and Decoration* 42 (December 1934): 31.

[Kellogg, Florence]. "Out There: Paintings by John Steuart Curry." *Survey* 64 (July 1930): 311–13.

Kittredge, William A. "An Appreciation." *Demcourier* 11 (April 1941): 19–22.

"Land Office Business." *Time* 34 (28 August 1939): 36, 38.

Lansford, Alonzo. "Honor Paid Career of John Steuart Curry." *Art Digest* (1 April 1947): 15.

"'The Light of the World': An Interpretation of the State of Our Time, Created Especially for This Issue of *Esquire* by 'The Most Moving of Living Painters,' John Steuart Curry." *Esquire* 16 (December 1941): 100 and foldout.

"Manhattan, Kan., Takes 'Plunge' on Curry's Painting." *Newsweek* 5 (16 February 1935): 24–25.

Marsh, Reginald. "Curry." *Demcourier* 11 (April 1941): 6–7.

"The Midwest."*Art Digest* 9 (15 February 1935): 21.

"Mid-West Is Producing an Indigenous Art." *Art Digest* 7 (1 September 1933): 10.

"Murals, with Curry Sauce." *Time* 40 (13 July 1942): 49–50.

"Must Be Sane." *Art Digest* 11 (1 August 1937): 13.

Owen, Jennie Small. "Kansas Folks Worth Knowing: John Steuart Curry." *Kansas Teacher* 46 (March 1938): 33–35.

Pearson, Ralph M. "Artist's Point of View: John Steuart Curry and the American School of Painting." *Forum* 97 (February 1937): 113.

Pickett, Calder M. "John Steuart Curry and the Topeka Murals Controversy." *Register of the Museum of Art, the University of Kansas, Lawrence, Kansas* 2 (December 1959): 2–12.

Pousette-Dart, Nathaniel. "John Steuart Curry: A Kansas Painter Who's Typically American." *Art of Today* 6 (February 1935): 7–8.

"Professor Curry." *Time* 31 (24 January 1938): 32–33.

"Resident Artist: John Steuart Curry Takes Unique Post to Encourage Rural Painting." *Literary Digest* 122 (17 October 1936): 22–23.

Salpeter, Harry. "Education of a Regionalist." *Esquire* 17 (March 1942): 84–85, 177–79.

Schmeckebier, Laurence. "John Steuart Curry, 1897–1946." *College Art Journal* 6 (1946): 59–60.

_____. "John Steuart Curry." *College Art Journal* 17 (1957): 55–58.

"Sons of Sunflower Strife: Curry's Murals of John Brown Create Storm in Kansas." *Newsweek* 18 (7 July 1941): 58.

"Speaking of Pictures . . . These Tell the Story of John Steuart Curry of Kansas." *Life* 15 (29 November 1943): 18–20.

"Tragedy, Comedy: Frescoes." *Survey Graphic* 24 (February 1935): 58–59.

Walker, Maynard. "John Steuart Curry, 1897–1946." *Kansas Magazine* (1947): 72–73.

Waller, Bret. "Curry and the Critics." *Kansas Quarterly* 2 (fall 1970): 42–55.

_____. "Editor's Introduction." *Kansas Quarterly* 2 (fall 1970): 1–2.

_____. "An Interview with Mrs. Daniel Schuster." *Kansas Quarterly* 2 (fall 1970): 13–18.

_____. "An Interview with Mrs. John Steuart Curry." *Kansas Quarterly* 2 (fall 1970): 6–12.

Wear, Ted. "John Steuart Curry and His Kansas Murals." *American Artist* 4 (October 1940): 5–8.

Wood, Grant. "John Steuart Curry and the Midwest." *Demcourier* 11 (April 1941): 2–4.

Newspapers

Alexander, John. "Death of Curry Ends Career in Art That Was Rooted in His Kansas Soil." *Kansas City Times,* 30 August 1946.

"A Native Son of Kansas Painted His Love for Her Prairies and Citizens." *Kansas City Star,* 8 August 1933.

"Artist Curry Paints Kansas Life with a Homesick Brush." (*Westport, Conn.) Westporter Herald,* 4 July 1930.

"Artist Trio Make Debut at Whitney's." *New York American,* 16 February 1930.

"Art News." *Kansas City Journal-Post,* 9 August 1931.

Austin, Whitley. "Curry's Struggle from Farm to Fame Reflected in His Vitality." *Hutchinson (Kans.) News-Herald,* 6 February 1938.

Bolmar, Carl P. "Gleanings from the Field of Art." *Topeka (Kans.) Daily State Journal,* 28 March 1931.

Borland, Hal. "Curry's America: Strong, Bold, Lush." *New York Times Magazine,* 23 March 1949.

Breuning, Margaret. "Ferargil Gallery." *New York Evening Post,* 6 December 1930.

_____. "Ferargil Galleries." *New York Evening Post,* 17 October 1931.

_____. "John Steuart Curry." *New York Evening Post,* 8 April 1933.

Burrows, Carlyle. "News and Comment on Current Art Events." *New York Herald Tribune,* 7 December 1930.

_____. "Curry at Wisconsin." *New York Herald Tribune,* 16 January 1938.

Caposella, Joseph. "Regular Guy Who Couldn't Quit." *Wisconsin State Journal,* 30 August 1946.

"Circus Limner Terms P.W.A. Best Art Spur." *New York Herald Tribune,* 29 April 1934.

"Circus Troupe to View Art of Sawdust Ring." *New York Herald Tribune,* 29 March 1933.

Craven, Thomas. "Curry of Kansas." *New York American,* 9 March 1935.

"Curry Is Named 'Artist in Residence'; Wisconsin Acts to Aid Rural Culture." *New York Times,* 20 September 1936, late city edition, sec. 2, 2.

"Curry Takes New Post on U.W. Campus." *Milwaukee Sentinel,* 5 December 1936.

"First Madison Exhibit of Curry Paintings." *Wisconsin State Journal,* 26 September 1937.

Foster, Joanna. "The Way Westport Was: John Curry's Murals." *Westport (Conn.) News,* 18 February 1987.

"In Curry, Kansas 'Found Its Homer,'" *Kansas City Star,* 2 September 1946.

"Introducing State's 'Artist-in-Residence.'" *Milwaukee Journal,* 10 January 1937.

Jewell, Edward Alden. "Kansas Has Found Her Homer." *New York Times,* 7 December 1930, late city edition, sec. 9, 11.

_____. "Curry Presents Kansas Pictures." *New York Times,* 23 January 1935, late city edition, sec. 1, 15.

"John S. Curry Dies; Mural Painter, 48." *New York Times,* 30 August 1946, late city edition, sec. 1, 17.

"John Steuart Curry." *Brooklyn Daily Eagle,* 18 October 1931.

"John Steuart Curry" (editorial). *New York Times,* 31 August 1946, late city edition, sec. 1, 14.

"John Steuart Curry Dwells on Kansas Scene." *New York Sun,* 17 October 1931.

"John Steuart Curry's Fine Exhibit Opens in N.Y.C. Dec. 12." (*Westport, Conn.) Wesporter-Herald,* 28 November 1930.

"Kansas Heals Breach with a Native Son." *New York Herald Tribune,* 5 February 1935.

McCormick, W. B. "A Ferargil Show." *New York Journal,* 1 August 1931.

Mechlin, Leila. "New Mural Painting by Curry Given Permanent Placement in Justice Building, Washington, D.C." *(Washington, D.C.) Evening Star,* 17 April 1937.

"New U.W. Artist Arrives." *Madison (Wis.) Capital Times,* 4 December 1936.

"Nine American Paintings." *New York Herald Tribune,* 19 June 1932.

Parton, Lemuel F. "Who's News Today: A Kansas Artist Who Might Confound Mencken." *New York Sun,* 24 January 1935.

Powell, Minna K., and H. C. H. "Kansas Produces Gifted Creative Painters, Sculptors, and Print-Makers." *Kansas City Star,* 15 March 1933.

"Prairie Artist Finds New Soil." *Milwaukee Journal,* 6 December 1936.

Read, Helen Appleton. "The Whitney Bi-ennial." *Brooklyn Daily Eagle,* 27 November 1932.

Rubin, Morris H. "Impatient to Feel Spring and the State's Soil, Curry Comes to Campus." *Wisconsin State Journal,* 4 December 1936.

"Service for John Steuart Curry." *New York Times,* 1 September 1946, late city edition, sec. 1, 36.

"To Meet on Kansas Art." *Kansas City Times,* 20 July 1937.

"Up from a Kansas Farm." *Kansas City Times,* 8 August 1933.

"U.W. Experiment Has Shown That Art, Agriculture Do Mix." *Milwaukee Journal,* 26 October 1941.

Vaughan, Malcolm. "Pioneer Curry." *New York American,* 26 January 1935.

Vickerman, Tom. "Of Pigs, Tornadoes, and Tawny Yellow Paintings." *Chicago Post,* 4 January 1931.

"Yes, Art and Farming Mix; Wisconsin 'Resident' Proves It." *Christian Science Monitor,* 6 November 1941.

Theses and Dissertations

Contreras, Belisario R. "The New Deal Treasury Art Programs and the American Artist: 1933 to 1943." Ph.D. diss., American University, Washington, D.C., 1967.

Gokey, Edward Alan. "John Steuart Curry's *The Gospel Train.*" M.A. thesis, Syracuse University, 1993.

Keesee, Vincent A. "Regionalism: The Book Illustrations of Benton, Curry, and Wood." Ph.D. diss., University of Georgia, Athens, 1972.

LENDERS TO THE EXHIBITION

Art Institute of Chicago

Babcock Galleries, New York

Jean Chapman Born

Collection of Beth and John Cartland

College of Agricultural and Life Sciences, University of Wisconsin–Madison

Cummer Museum of Art and Gardens, Jacksonville, Florida

Mrs. John Steuart Curry

John Steuart Curry Foundation

Curtis Galleries, Inc., Minneapolis

Elvehjem Museum of Art, University of Wisconsin–Madison

Fine Arts Museums of San Francisco

The FORBES Magazine Collection, New York

Greendyke Fine Art, Pittsford, New York

Joslyn Art Museum, Omaha, Nebraska

Madison Art Center, Madison, Wisconsin

Memphis Brooks Museum of Art, Memphis, Tennessee

Metropolitan Museum of Art, New York

Minnesota Museum of American Art, St. Paul

Mongerson Wunderlich Gallery, Chicago

Museum of American Art of the Pennsylvania Academy of the Fine Arts, Philadelphia

Museum of Fine Arts, Boston

Muskegon Museum of Art, Muskegon, Michigan

National Academy of Design, New York

National Gallery of Art, Washington, D.C.

Saint Louis Art Museum, St. Louis, Missouri

Virginia Steele Scott Collection, Huntington Library, Art Collections, and Botanical Gardens, San Marino, California

Spencer Museum of Art, University of Kansas, Lawrence

Swarthmore College Art Collection, Swarthmore, Pennsylvania

Syracuse University Art Collection, Syracuse, New York

The Warner Collection of the Gulf States Paper Corporation, Tuscaloosa, Alabama

Whitney Museum of American Art, New York

D. Wigmore Fine Art, Inc., New York

One anonymous lender

ABOUT THE AUTHORS

Henry Adams is curator of American art at the Cleveland Museum of Art and professor of American art at Case Western Reserve University. Formerly the Samuel Sosland Curator of American Art at the Nelson-Atkins Museum of Art, he has published on many aspects of nineteenth- and twentieth-century American art. His books include *John La Farge* (1987), *Thomas Hart Benton: An American Original* (1989), and *Albert Bloch: The American Blue Rider* (1997).

Charles C. Eldredge is Hall Distinguished Professor of American Art, The University of Kansas. Formerly director of the National Museum of American Art, Smithsonian Institution, Washington, D.C., he has published on a wide range of topics, with particular emphasis on American modernism. His books and exhibition catalogues include *Georgia O'Keeffe: American and Modern* (1993) and *Art in New Mexico, 1900–1945: Paths to Taos and Santa Fe* (1986). He has contributed essays to such volumes as *The Spiritual in Art: Abstract Painting, 1890–1985* (1987) and *Life Cycles: The Charles E. Burchfield Collection* (1995).

Robert L. Gambone was formerly deputy director of the Rose Art Museum, Brandeis University, and before that, he served as director of the Brauer Museum of Art, Valparaiso University, Valparaiso, Indiana. He is the author of *Art and Popular Religion in Evangelical America, 1915–1940* (1989).

Patricia Junker is associate curator of American Art at the Fine Arts Museums of San Francisco. She is a coauthor of collection catalogues for the Fine Arts Museums and the Smith College Museum of Art, Northampton, Massachusetts. Her 1990 exhibition catalogue, *Winslow Homer in the 1890s: Prout's Neck Observed* was awarded the 1991 Henry Allen Moe prize for scholarship by the New York State Historical Association.

M. Sue Kendall is an independent scholar whose research has focused on American regionalist painters. She is the author of *Rethinking Regionalism: John Steuart Curry and the Kansas Mural Controversy* (1986) and is a contributor to the exhibition catalogue *Charles Burchfield: North by Midwest* (1997).

Lucy J. Mathiak is an independent scholar based in Madison, Wisconsin.

Theodore F. Wolff was an art critic for the *Christian Science Monitor* from 1977 to 1990. His recent books include *Enrico Donati: Surrealism and Beyond* (1996), *Art Criticism and Education,* and *Joyce Treiman* (both 1997).

INDEX

Page numbers in *italics* refer to illustrations.

Photograph Credits

Noel Allum, New York: page 90
E. Irving Blomstrann, New Britain, Connecticut: page 200
Joe McDonald, San Francisco: pages 139, upper right; 178, left; 197